CULTURAL HERITAGE LAW AND POLICY

Series Editors

PROFESSOR FRANCESCO FRANCIONI

Professor Emeritus of International Law, European University Institute, Florence, and Professor of International Cultural Heritage Law, LUISS University, Rome

PROFESSOR ANA VRDOLJAK

Professor of Law and UNESCO Chair in International Law and Cultural Heritage, University of Technology, Sydney

Intersections in International Cultural Heritage Law

CULTURAL HERITAGE LAW AND POLICY

The aim of this series is to publish significant and original research on and scholarly analysis of all aspects of cultural heritage law through the lens of international law, private international law, and comparative law. The series is wide in scope, traversing disciplines, regions, and viewpoints. Topics given particular prominence are those which, while of interest to academic lawyers, have significant bearing on policymaking and current public discourse on the interaction between art, heritage, and the law.

Intersections in International Cultural Heritage Law

Edited by

ANNE-MARIE CARSTENS
ELIZABETH VARNER

OXFORD
UNIVERSITY PRESS

OXFORD
UNIVERSITY PRESS

Great Clarendon Street, Oxford, OX2 6DP,
United Kingdom

Oxford University Press is a department of the University of Oxford.
It furthers the University's objective of excellence in research, scholarship,
and education by publishing worldwide. Oxford is a registered trade mark of
Oxford University Press in the UK and in certain other countries

First Edition published in 2020

Published in the United States of America by Oxford University Press
198 Madison Avenue, New York, NY 10016, United States of America

British Library Cataloguing in Publication Data
Data available

Library of Congress Control Number: 2019955610

ISBN 978–0–19–884629–1

Series Editor's Preface

Often, and increasingly, for many, the field of international cultural heritage law is encapsulated by the specialist culture conventions adopted under the auspices of the UN Educational, Scientific and Cultural Organization (UNESCO). These treaties remain the core of the international community's efforts to protect and safeguard cultural heritage. But there was and continues to be a long and rich stream of international, regional and state practice which preceded and continues to inform the interpretation and implementation of these instruments, and international efforts in the field of international cultural heritage law.

Any understanding of international cultural heritage law would be incomplete, and ineffective in practice, without appreciating its place within public international law, and its various specialist fields. Or as the title of this volume indicates at its 'intersections'.

These 'intersections' may take many forms. They may involve the application of substantive norms of cultural heritage law to other areas of public international law, such as international economic law and international criminal law, or, vice versa, the application of other specialized branches of international law, such as human rights law, or international humanitarian law, in cultural heritage adjudication. Outside of these hypotheses, the growing body of international cultural heritage law increasingly provides criteria of interpretation for other norms of international law that constitute the applicable law by courts and tribunals in international adjudication and arbitration.

Prepared at a time of elevated public awareness of ever-increasing dangers to cultural heritage, in its many forms, this collection edited by Carstens and Varner provides us with the latest developments in specialist areas of general public international law. It serves as a reminder of the ongoing, diverse challenges faced by the international community in the field and evolving responses to them. The diversity of responses and competing interests also speak to a particular challenge to this field, namely the perils of fragmentation and entailing problems arising from competing principles and norms.

This is the challenge the editors of this book have taken up by bringing to the fore the numerous strands of international law that have recently engaged in the protection and safeguarding of cultural heritage. It is a significant, and perhaps endless, task, as long as the threats to the destruction and damage to cultural heritage worldwide remain.

Francesco Francioni and Ana Filipa Vrdoljak
March 2020

Contents

V. INTERSECTIONS OF INTERNATIONAL, NATIONAL, AND COMMUNITY INTERESTS IN CULTURAL HERITAGE

Table of Cases

INTERNATIONAL COURT OF JUSTICE (AND PERMANENT COURT OF INTERNATIONAL JUSTICE)

INTERNATIONAL CRIMINAL COURT

NUREMBERG TRIBUNAL

UN HUMAN RIGHTS COMMITTEE

WORLD TRADE ORGANIZATION

NATIONAL JURISDICTIONS

Australia

HIGH COURT OF AUSTRALIA

Austria

REGIONAL COURT OF VIENNA FOR CIVIL MATTERS

Belgium

Canada

France

The Netherlands

United Kingdom

United States of America

Table of Instruments

I. INTERNATIONAL INSTRUMENTS

II. EUROPEAN AND REGIONAL INSTRUMENTS

III. DOMESTIC INSTRUMENTS AND LEGISLATION

Australia

Canada

Germany

Poland

Switzerland

The Netherlands

United Kingdom

United States

List of Contributors

Janet Blake is Associate Professor of Law at the University of Shahid Beheshti (Tehran), where she teaches International, Environmental, and Human Rights Law and is a member of the UNESCO Chair for Human Rights, Peace and Democracy and the Centre for Excellence in Education for Sustainable Development, both based at the university. She is also a member of the Cultural Heritage Law Committee of the International Law Association and has acted as an international consultant to UNESCO since 1999, mostly in the field of safeguarding intangible cultural heritage. She has published several books and articles (in English and Persian) on cultural heritage law, cultural rights/diversity, wildlife protection law, environmental protection law and justice, and sustainable development.

Guido Carducci is a law professor in Paris, attorney-at-law in Rome, and International Tenant and Arbitrator in London with 4-5 Gray's Inn Square. He is a Chartered Arbitrator and acts as arbitrator, expert, and counsel in commercial, art, and investment matters. He is the former Chief of the International Standards Section at UNESCO (HQ Paris) and was in charge of international standard-setting in cultural property law, treaty-making, implementation of treaty obligations, and State responsibility for UNESCO and its Member States. He acted also as UNESCO Mediator between the UK and Greek Governments concerning the Parthenon Marbles in the British Museum. He has published forty articles and two monographs. He holds two PhDs. from the Universities of Rome I and Paris II and the Diploma from The Hague Academy of International Law.

Anne-Marie Carstens is Visiting Assistant Professor of Law at the University of Maryland Carey School of Law. For the duration of this project, she served as Visiting Professor of Law and Researcher at Georgetown University Law Center. She has authored the forthcoming book *Safeguarding Cultural Property During Armed Conflict* and numerous other publications on public international law, cultural heritage law, and intellectual property law. She previously practiced litigation and international arbitration law for a large multinational firm in Washington and in London, served in the federal government as an expert consultant on cultural property issues in foreign policy, served on a working group that established a new national museum, and chaired the Cultural Heritage and the Arts interest group of the American Society of International Law. She holds a DPhil in Law from Oxford Universityand a JD degree from Georgetown University.

Sarah Dromgoole is Professor of Maritime Law at the University of Nottingham (UK). Her research focuses primarily on the legal protection of the underwater cultural heritage, as well as the law relating to shipwrecks more generally. She has published extensively in this field, on domestic, comparative, and international law aspects. Of particular note are her edited collections of national perspectives on the underwater cultural heritage and her monograph on *Underwater Cultural Heritage and International Law*. She is a member of the Joint Nautical Archaeology Policy Committee, which brings together governmental and non-governmental bodies with a role in the management of UK underwater cultural heritage. Her work with this committee over many years has enabled her to have direct engagement with the process of law and policy reform at national and international levels. She received her PhD from the University of Southampton. [Dr Dromgoole retired from the University of Nottingham and her membership of the Joint Nautical Archaeology Committee in 2018.]

Gabriele Gagliani is Contract Professor at Bocconi University in Milan (Italy) and Adjunct Professor at Case Western Reserve University School of Law in Cleveland (Ohio, U.S.A.). He is also Professeur Invité at the Université Senghor de la Francophonie (Organisation Internationale de la Francophonie) and serves as external consultant on international law matters to intergovernmental organizations, sovereigns, and individuals. He has been Visiting Research Fellow at the British Institute of International and Comparative Law (BIICL) in London (UK), Intern in the Permanent Mission of Italy to the United Nations, World Trade Organization section, in Geneva (Switzerland). He holds a PhD from the École Normale Supérieure/Université Paris Saclay in Paris (France) and from the University of Palermo (Italy), an LLM in international economic law (IELPO LLM, with distinction) from the University of Barcelona and a Bachelor and Master of Laws (summa cum laude) from the University of Milan. He works in English, French, Italian, and Spanish.

Patty Gerstenblith is Distinguished Research Professor of Law at DePaul University and Director of its Center for Art, Museum & Cultural Heritage Law. She was founding president of the Lawyers Committee for Cultural Heritage Preservation (2005–11), a director of the US Committee of the Blue Shield, and senior advisor to the American Bar Association's Art and Cultural Heritage Law Committee. In 2011, she was appointed by President Obama to serve as the chair of the President's Cultural Property Advisory Committee in the US Department of State, on which she had previously served as a public representative in the Clinton administration. From 1995 to 2002, she was editor-in-chief of the *International Journal of Cultural Property*. Her publications include the casebook, *Art, Cultural Heritage and the Law*, and numerous articles on cultural heritage issues. She holds a PhD in Art History and Anthropology from Harvard University and a JD from Northwestern University.

Kristin Hausler is the Dorset Senior Fellow and Director of the Centre for International Law at the British Institute of International and Comparative Law (London). She studied law in Switzerland and Canada, as well as art history at Christie's (NYC). Before joining the Institute, she worked at the Museum of Anthropology (Vancouver) on a repatriation project with Indigenous communities. She has also contributed to the work of Geneva Call on engaging non-State actors in the protection of cultural heritage. Kristin regularly provided training on international law and cultural heritage law. She is a member of the ILA Committee on Global Cultural Heritage Governance.

Andrzej Jakubowski is an assistant professor at the Institute of Legal Studies, University of Opole, Poland, and the Chair of the ILA Committee on Participation in Global Cultural Heritage Governance. He also serves as the Deputy-Editor-in-Chief of the *Santander Art and Culture Law Review.* Dr Jakubowski authored the book *State Succession in Cultural Property* and edited the volume *Cultural Rights as Collective Rights: An International Law Perspective* and co-edited two other volumes: *Fragmentation vs. the Constitutionalisation* *of International Law: A Practical Inquiry* and *Cultural Heritage in the European Union: A Critical Inquiry into Law and Policy*.

Lucas Lixinski is Associate Professor at the Faculty of Law, UNSW Sydney. He researches primarily in the areas of international cultural heritage law and international human rights law. He is also Rapporteur of the International Law Association Committee on Participation in Global Cultural Heritage Governance, and Vice President of the Association of Critical Heritage Studies. His monograph on international heritage law's exclusionary effects vis-à-vis communities was published by Oxford University Press in 2019.

Robert Peters Senior Government Official at the bureau of the Federal Government Commissioner for Culture and the Media, Germany. Currently, he works at the German Federal Foreign Office in the Division of Multilateral Cultural Policy. He is a member of the International Council of Museums (ICOM) Ethics Committee and a member of the International Law Association (ILA). Starting in 2009, he worked for the Federal Government Commissioner for Culture and the Media, Germany, in the Division of National and International Protection of Movable Cultural Property as well as in the Division of Cooperation in International Cultural Affairs. He previously worked as Assistant Legal Officer in the Office of International Standards and Legal Affairs at UNESCO Headquarters in Paris. He studied International and European Law in Berlin, Bologna, Hamburg, and Florence and obtained his PhD at the European University Institute in Florence, Italy, in the field of International Cultural Heritage Law with a specific focus on restitution disputes.

Ottavio Quirico is Associate Professor in the School of Law at the University of New England (UNE) in Australia, Honorary Lecturer at the Centre for European Studies of the Australian National University, and Alumnus of the European University Institute. He holds a PhD from the University of Social Sciences of Toulouse (France) and was, inter alia, a Marie Curie Fellow at Université Panthéon-Assas (Paris, France). His research covers the legal and political implications of international relations. He has lectured in universities worldwide, practiced in Europe, and acted as a consultant to the United Nations.

Sabine von Schorlemer holds the Chair of International Law, Law of the EU and International Relations and the UNESCO Chair in International Relations, both at Technische Universität Dresden. She is an elected member of the German Commission for UNESCO, a member of the Advisory Committee for the funding initiative 'Patrimonies' of the Gerda Henkel Foundation, and of the International Law Association (ILA) Committee on Participation in Global Cultural Heritage Governance. Professor von Schorlemer inter alia served as State Minister of for Higher Education, Research and the Arts, as an Advisor of the German Foreign Ministry on UN Politics, and as an Independent Expert for the UNESCO Director-General and the UN High Commissioner for Human Rights, respectively. Among others, she is, together with P T Stoll, the editor of a commentary on the UNESCO Convention on the Protection and Promotion of the Diversity of Cultural Expressions (2005) and has published several books and more than a hundred articles related to UN topics.

Vanessa Tünsmeyer is a researcher at the Maastricht Centre for Human Rights, where her research focuses on the repatriation of indigenous cultural heritage. She has worked as a researcher in the area of European law at Freiburg University (Germany), and was a guest researcher at UBC in Vancouver (Canada). Her research interests comprise public European and international law, international human rights law and cultural heritage law. She has published (joint) contributions on EU administrative law, indigenous rights, and the return of indigenous heritage in Australia and Canada. She holds an LLB in European law and an LLM in international law, both from Maastricht University.

Vassilis P Tzevelekos is Senior Lecturer in Law at the University of Liverpool, School of Law and Social Justice (UK). He researches primarily in the areas of general public international law (theory) and (European) Human Rights Law. He has published in various areas, including extraterritoriality and state responsibility.

Elizabeth Varner is Museum Director of a national museum; an Adjunct Professor at Indiana University Robert H. McKinney School of Law where she teaches Art, Museum and Cultural Heritage Law as well as Entertainment Law; and an arbitrator and mediator. She is on the American Alliance of Museum's Leadership and Management Network Executive Committee and Chair of the Curatorial Ethics Subcommittee; the US Committee, International Council of Museums board; and the American Bar Association's Art and Cultural Heritage Committee, Steering Committee. She was formerly Executive Director of two museums and has previously worked for government agencies assisting with guiding the management and use of over 200 million cultural and scientific objects;working with international and public-private partnership issues; developing policies; addressing legal issues; protecting cultural property; and investigating, prosecuting, and repatriating cultural property. She is the former President of the Lawyers' Committee for Cultural Heritage Preservation. Varner has an MA from the Smithsonian-Corcoran College of Art + Design and a JD from Tulane University School of Law.

Karolina Wierczyńska is an Associate Professor at the Institute of Law Studies of the Polish Academy of Sciences in Warsaw (Poland) and managing editor of *Polish Yearbook of International Law*. Her research interests focus on international criminal law and jurisprudence, comprising the issues of cultural heritage crimes. In her two monographs (published in Polish in 2010 and 2016) she explored the notion of genocide in the context of the jurisdiction of ad hoc international criminal tribunals, and admissibility before the ICC. She recently co-edited two volumes: *Fragmentation vs. the Constitutionalisation of International Law: A Practical Inquiry* and *The Case of Crimea's Annexation under International Law*.

Nout van Woudenberg is currently Strategic Policy Adviser Kingdom Affairs of the Ministry of Foreign Affairs of the Kingdom of the Netherlands. Before working with the Caribbean countries of the Kingdom of the Netherlands, he worked for fourteen years as Legal Counsel at the International Law Division of the same Ministry. In that capacity, he acted as Vice-Chair and Chair of the UNESCO Committee for the Protection of Cultural Property in the Event of Armed Conflict. Also, he was a member of the Dutch delegation in regard to the return of cultural objects displaced during the Second World War, and held negotiations with Ukraine, the Russian Federation, and Germany. He wrote several articles on repatriation, restitution, and recovery of cultural objects, the protection of cultural objects during armed conflict, underwater heritage, the process of lending and borrowing cultural State property and immunity from seizure for cultural objects on loan. He was member of the OMC Working Group on Mobility of Collections during the years 2008–12. He has a doctorate in international law and wrote his dissertation on state immunity for cultural objects on loan.

List of Abbreviations

AFISMA	African-led International Support Mission in Mali
AJIL	American Journal of International Law
AKTC	Aga Khan Trust for Culture
ANSAs	armed non-State actors
AQIM	Al-Qaida in the Islamic Maghreb
ARSIWA	Articles on the Responsibility of States for Internationally Wrongful Acts
AWHF	African World Heritage Fund
CAHDI	Committee of Legal Advisers on Public International Law of the Council of Europe
CESCR	United Nations Committee on Economic, Social and Cultural Rights
CETS	Council of Europe Treaty Series
Ch	chapter
CILJSA	Comparative and International Law Journal of Southern Africa
CITES	1973 Convention on the International Trade in Endangered Species of Fauna and Flora
CMI	International Maritime Committee
CPA	Coalition Provisional Authority (Iraq)
CRAterre	Centre de recherche et d'application en terre
Crim	Criminal
CUP	Cambridge University Press
Doc(s)	Document(s)
DOD	(US) Department of Defense
EC	European Commission
ECCC	Extraordinary Chambers in the Courts of Cambodia
ECHR	European Convention on Human Rights
ECOSOC	United Nations Economic and Social Council
ECOWAS	Economic Community of West African States
ECtHR	European Court of Human Rights
EIA	environmental impact assessment
EJIL	European Journal of International Law
EPA	École du Patrimoine Africain
ERR	Einsatzstab Reichsleiter Rosenberg
EU	European Union
FBI	Federal Bureau of Investigation
FO	Foreign Office files, National Archives (UK)
FSIA	Foreign Sovereign Immunities Act
GHG	greenhouse gases
GPO	Government Printing Office (US)
HMSO	His/Her Majesty's Stationery Office (UK)

HRCBiH	Human Rights Chamber for Bosnia and Herzegovina
IAC	international armed conflict
IAComHR	Inter-American Commission on Human Rights
IACtHR	Inter-American Court of Human Rights
IAL	Institute of Art and Law
ICC	International Criminal Court
ICCROM	International Centre for the Study of Preservation and Restoration of Cultural Property
ICCPR	International Covenant on Civil and Political Rights
ICESCR	International Covenant on Economic, Social and Cultural Rights
ICH	intangible cultural heritage
ICJ	International Court of Justice
ICLQ	International & Comparative Law Quarterly
ICOM	International Council of Museums
ICOMOS	International Council on Monuments and Sites
ICPRCP	Intergovernmental Committee for Promoting the Return of Cultural Property to its Countries of Origin or its Restitution in Case of Illicit Appropriation
ICRC	International Committee of the Red Cross
ICRW	International Convention for the Regulation of Whaling
ICTR	International Criminal Tribunal for Rwanda
ICTY	International Criminal Tribunal for the Former Yugoslavia
IFAR	International Foundation for Art Research
IFLA	International Federation of Library Associations and Institutions
IJCP	International Journal of Cultural Property
ILA	International Law Association
ILC	International Law Commission
ILM	International Legal Materials
INTERPOL	International Criminal Police Organization
Intl	International
IPCC	Intergovernmental Panel on Climate Change
ISIL	Islamic State of Iraq and the Levant (also ISIS or Daesh)
IWIGA	International Work Group on Indigenous Affairs
J	Journal
LNOJ	League of Nations Official Journal
LNTS	League of Nations Treaty Series
LOAC	law of armed conflict
MENA	Middle East and North Africa
MINUSMA	United Nations Multidimensional Integrated Stabilization Mission in Mali
MLA	mutual legal assistance
MNLA	Mouvement national de libération de l'Azawad/National Movement for the Liberation of Azawad
MUJAO	Movement for Unity and Jihad in West Africa
NAGPRA	Native American Graves Protection and Repatriation Act
NATO	North Atlantic Treaty Organization

NGO	non-governmental organization
NIAC	non-international armed conflict
n(n)	note(s)
No(s)	number(s)
OUP	Oxford University Press
OUV	Outstanding Universal Value
P	Press
PCIJ	Permanent Court of International Justice
Res	Resolution
SACC	Strategy for Action on Climate Change (UNESCO)
U	University
UCH	Underwater Cultural Heritage
UCS	Union of Concerned Scientists
UDHR	Universal Declaration of Human Rights
UK LOAC Manual	UK Ministry of Defence, Joint Service Manual of the Law of Armed Conflict
UN	United Nations
UNCLOS	United Nations Convention on the Law of the Sea
UNESCO	United Nations Educational, Scientific and Cultural Organization
UNESCO Military Manual	UNESCO, Protection of Cultural Property Military Manual
UNFCCC	United Nations Framework Convention on Climate Change
UNGA	United Nations General Assembly
UNHRC	United Nations Human Rights Council
UNIDROIT	International Institute for the Unification of Private Law
UNODC	United Nations Office on Drugs and Crime
UNSC	United Nations Security Council
UNTS	United Nations Treaty Service
USC	United States Code
US LOW Manual	US Department of Defense, Law of War Manual
vol	volume
WCO	World Customs Organization
WTO	World Trade Organization
YB	Yearbook

Intersections in Public International Law for Protecting Cultural Heritage Law

Past, Present, and Future

Anne-Marie Carstens and Elizabeth Varner

The recent spate of threats to cultural heritage, including in Syria, Iraq, Mali, Nepal, and Yemen, has led to increased focus on the sources of international cultural heritage law. International law governing the protection and preservation of cultural heritage, both tangible and intangible, has grown rapidly over the past several decades with the introduction of new treaties and other instruments, the development and elucidation of customary rules, the increasing involvement of a variety of international bodies and other international actors, and the creation of a rich body of jurisprudence from international tribunals. The very recognition of international cultural heritage law as an emerging and identifiable field within public international law itself testifies to this expansive development.[1]

This volume on *Intersections in International Cultural Heritage Law* highlights and reflects that international cultural heritage law is not a discrete and contained body of law, but rather a diverse body of law whose component parts are drawn from—and often developed and contained within—principal fields of public international law. In fact, the content of international legal rules designed to protect and to foster the preservation of cultural heritage has emerged almost exclusively within other fields of international law. These 'intersections' have formed in two ways: when public international law has been used as a vehicle for providing greater protection for cultural heritage, and when concern for cultural heritage protection or codification of rules within cultural heritage-centric instruments have helped fuel developments within other areas of public international law.[2]

[1] The growing collection of international legal instruments dedicated to protecting, preserving, or otherwise governing the treatment of cultural property themselves attest to the development of this field. Several leading international law publishers, too, have added series in the last two decades that are dedicated to cultural heritage law or cultural heritage policy, including the series from Oxford University Press in which this volume appears.

[2] Several of these themes were explored at an international conference on 'Intersections in International Cultural Heritage Law' held at Georgetown University Law Center in March 2016. Several contributors presented papers that evolved into the chapters presented here. The editors therefore thank the Georgetown University Law Center, which served as host and sponsor, as well as the Cultural Heritage and the Arts Interest Group of the American Society of International Law and the Georgetown

Anne-Marie Carstens and Elizabeth Varner, Intersections in Public International Law for Protecting Cultural Heritage Law
In: *Intersections in International Cultural Heritage Law*. Edited by Anne-Marie Carstens and Elizabeth Varner. © Oxford University Press 2020. The several contributors DOI: 10.1093/oso/9780198846291.003.0001

International cultural heritage law has matured from rules and initiatives that sometimes have resided in other areas of international law for generations. Perhaps the longest-standing such rules are the conventional and customary rules barring the unnecessary destruction of certain cultural institutions and of historic monuments during times of armed conflict, which emerged in the codified laws and customs of war more than a century ago alongside corollary rules that protect hospitals and schools, for example, or that prohibit pillage and bombardment of undefended towns.[3]

International cultural heritage law thus represents a field pieced together from constituent parts—the international rules, principles, and norms that combine to protect cultural property—formed at various intersections of public international law. One traversing the trail of international cultural heritage law to gain an understanding of its content and its scope would cross multiple intersections. This journey would include collecting rules not just from the law of armed conflict, but also from international criminal law, international human rights, the law of the sea, international intellectual property law, and other areas of international law. At these intersections, one would also encounter the many actors and institutions that create international law or facilitate its development. For these reasons, these intersections serve as the principal activity centers where international law protecting cultural heritage first emerged and continues to develop.

This volume is devoted to exploring primary points of intersection in international cultural heritage law and public international law. The chapters are authored both by contributors from within the cultural heritage field and by contributors who concentrate largely on specific areas of public international law where intersections with cultural heritage protection arise. Together their contributions establish how strains of international cultural heritage law and the associated areas of public international law are often mutually reinforcing, and increasingly so. They also sometimes reveal the limitations that public international law sometimes imposes on the progressive development of cultural heritage protections or present approaches for drawing more effectively on cultural heritage law or public international law to resolve continuing challenges in the international protection of cultural heritage.

Art Law Association. They also express gratitude to the three participants whose featured contributions fostered thoughtful discussion on these topics: Professor Patty Gerstenblith, Professor Sir Frank Berman, and Professor Roger O'Keefe.

[3] See eg Convention (II) with Respect to the Laws and Customs of War on Land and its Annex: Regulations concerning the Laws and Customs of War on Land (adopted 29 July 1899, entered into force 4 September 1900) 187 CTS 429, arts 25, 27, 28, 47, 56 (1899 Hague Convention); Convention (IV) Respecting the Laws and Customs of War on Land and its Annex: Regulations concerning the Laws and Customs of War on Land (open for signature 18 October 1907, entered into force 26 January 1910) 187 CTS 227, arts 25, 27, 28, 47, 56 (1907 Hague Convention).

I. The Development of Intersections for International Cultural Heritage Law and Public International Law

The 'intersections' of international cultural heritage law and public international law have formed in two ways: when public international law has been used as a vehicle for providing greater protection for cultural heritage, and when concern for cultural heritage protection or codification of rules within cultural heritage-centric instruments helped fuel developments within other areas of public international law. Drawing again from the example of the law of armed conflict, the drafters of the 1954 Hague Convention for the Protection of Cultural Property in the Event of Armed Conflict (1954 Hague Convention)[4] sometimes relied on the earlier 1949 Geneva Conventions, particularly the convention dedicated to civilian protection,[5] as a model instrument rather than cutting all of its provisions from whole cloth. Both instruments, for example, provide in nearly verbatim language for 'Protecting Powers' that are responsible for safeguarding the interests of the Parties to the conflict.[6] Yet the 1954 Hague Convention also went further than the 1949 Geneva Conventions in certain respects. It provided that the rules governing the conduct of hostilities applied also in conflicts 'not of an international character',[7] a principle that occasioned little objection in the context of cultural property protection despite having been the subject of vociferous dissent during the adoption of the 1949 Geneva Conventions only four years earlier, in the context of civilian protection.[8]

The easy adoption of this principle in the 1954 Hague Convention subsequently smoothed the path leading to the 1977 adoption of Additional Protocol II to the 1949 Geneva Conventions, a treaty devoted exclusively to codifying customary rules governing non-international armed conflict.[9] The 1977 Additional Protocols then served the same function in return, with Additional Protocol I codifying rules of distinction and proportionality as part of new conventional rules for taking precautions against the effects of hostilities and precautions in attack,[10] which were

[4] Convention for the Protection of Cultural Property in the Event of Armed Conflict (adopted 14 May 1954, entered into force 7 August 1956) 249 UNTS 240 (1954 Hague Convention).

[5] Convention Relative to the Protection of Civilian Persons in Time of War (adopted 12 August 1949, entered into force 21 October 1950) 75 UNTS 287 (1949 Fourth Geneva Convention).

[6] 1949 Fourth Geneva Convention, art 9; 1954 Hague Convention, art 21.

[7] 1954 Hague Convention, art 19.

[8] See *Final Record of the Diplomatic Conference of Geneva of 1949* (4 vols, Federal Political Department (Switzerland) 1949–51) esp vol 2 *passim*.

[9] Protocol Additional to the Geneva Conventions of 12 August 1949, and Relating to the Protection of Victims of Non-International Armed Conflicts (adopted 8 June 1977, opened for signature 12 December 1977, entered into force 7 December 1978) 1125 UNTS 609 (1977 Additional Protocol II).

[10] Protocol Additional to the Geneva Conventions of 12 August 1949, and Relating to the Protection of Victims of International Armed Conflicts (adopted 8 June 1977, opened for signature 12 December 1977, entered into force 7 December 1978) 1125 UNTS 609, arts 57–58 (1977 Additional Protocol I).

later incorporated in a new protocol specific to cultural property protection, the Second Protocol to the 1954 Hague Convention.[11]

In addition, whereas the protection of cultural property once resided in provisions in larger treaties that codified the laws and customs of war, and were also often encompassed by generalized rules governing the protection of civilian property, the interest in preserving cultural heritage ultimately fostered the creation of entire treaty regimes dedicated to protecting cultural heritage. This process started principally with the 1954 Hague Convention. At the same time, specific rules for protecting cultural property and the more general rules governing civilian and State property became mutually reinforcing and resulted in tiered levels of protection that depended on distinctions between various categories of property.

The law of armed conflict was not sufficient, though, as the exclusive regime for protecting cultural heritage in international law. It was ill-equipped for managing other repercussions of armed conflict, such as demands for returning or restituting property, or punishing the most serious violations of the law of armed conflict. Historically, postwar negotiations and armistice agreements served as de facto enforcement mechanisms for resolving such issues, but they consistently resulted in lopsided enforcement that favored victors. When the First World War followed closely on the heels of the first binding international treaties on the laws and customs of war—the 1899 and 1907 Hague Conventions governing land warfare[12]—the subsequent negotiations and peace treaties called for restitution of a variety of cultural artifacts, but they also attempted to establish the first international criminal tribunal.[13] While unsuccessful, these efforts nonetheless laid the groundwork for a new international criminal regime that would respond to the lack of norms for enforcing the law of armed conflict and that could prosecute and punish the high-level perpetrators of the most serious violations.

The very limitation of this principal regime to circumstances of armed conflict and occupation further meant that it provided no financial support for preserving cultural heritage, for example, and few mechanisms to stem the illicit trade in cultural artifacts. Nor did it foster international cooperation in protecting 'the cultural heritage of mankind' from threats that included not only the hazards of warfare, but also illicit looting, natural disasters, deterioration, climate change, and other threats that could endanger cultural heritage irrespective of war. Following largely unsuccessful efforts initiated within the framework of the League of Nations,[14]

[11] Second Protocol to the Hague Convention of 1954 for the Protection of Cultural Property in the Event of Armed Conflict (adopted 26 March 1999, opened for signature 17 May 1999, entered into force 9 March 2004) 253 UNTS 172, arts 7–8 (1999 Second Protocol).

[12] See also Convention (IX) on Bombardment by Naval Forces in Time of War (open for signature 18 October 1907, entered into force 26 January 1910) 205 CTS 345.

[13] Commission on the Responsibilities of the Authors of the War and on Enforcement of Penalties, *Report Presented to the Preliminary Peace Conference* (29 March 1919), in (1920) 14 AJIL 95 (Report of the Commission on Responsibilities).

[14] See eg Draft Convention on the Protection of Historic Buildings and Works of Art in Times of War, 19 LNOJ 937 (1938) Annex; Draft International Convention for the Protection of National Historic or

the United Nations Educational, Scientific and Cultural Organization (UNESCO) was created after the Second World War inter alia to promote international efforts to protect cultural property, yet several decades would pass before new treaty regimes on these diverse fronts firmly took root. The 1970 UNESCO Convention on the Means of Prohibiting and Preventing the Illicit Import, Export and Transfer of Ownership of Cultural Property (1970 UNESCO Convention)[15] and the 1972 Convention concerning the Protection of the World Cultural and Natural Heritage (1972 World Heritage Convention)[16] focused on curbing the illicit trafficking in cultural objects and artifacts and on establishing a system of international cooperation for protecting universally recognized cultural sites, respectively. The 1970 UNESCO Convention aimed to regulate downstream markets for stolen and illicitly excavated cultural objects through import and export restrictions; it also established diplomatic avenues for seeking return and restitution, though these combined measures have proved insufficient for addressing significant losses of movable cultural heritage that stem from armed conflict.[17] The 1972 World Heritage Convention, on the other hand, quickly grew to become one of the most popular international treaties, establishing a monetary fund for preservation and its well-known World Heritage List on which cultural sites possessing 'outstanding universal value' can be inscribed.[18]

Still, foundational principles of international law played an important role in the development of these regimes. The underlying premise of efforts to regulate the international trade in stolen and illicitly excavating objects rests on principles of cultural nationalism, for example, sometimes at odds with the principles of cultural internationalism that pervade the obligations set out in the law of armed conflict and the 1972 World Heritage Convention.[19] The World Heritage Convention's

Artistic Treasures, League of Nations Doc CL 34.1936.XII (1936) Annex and Corr 2; Recommendations Adopted by the International Committee on Intellectual Co-operation (League of Nations) League of Nations Doc CL 176.1932.XII (23 July 1932) 2.

[15] Convention on the Means of Prohibiting and Preventing the Illicit Import, Export and Transfer of Ownership of Cultural Property (adopted 14 November 1970, entered into force 24 April 1972) 823 UNTS 231 (1970 UNESCO Convention).

[16] Convention concerning the Protection of the World Cultural and Natural Heritage (open for signature 16 November 1972, entered into force 15 December 1975) 1037 UNTS 151 (1972 World Heritage Convention).

[17] 1970 UNESCO Convention, arts 5–14. See Patty Gerstenblith, 'The Disposition of Movable Cultural Property' in Anne-Marie Carstens and Elizabeth Varner (eds), *Intersections in International Cultural Heritage Law* (OUP 2020) (Ch 1).

[18] 1972 World Heritage Convention, arts 11–16.

[19] See eg 1970 UNESCO Convention, art 4 (defining the cultural property that 'forms part of the cultural heritage of each State'); 1972 World Heritage Convention, art 6 (subject to principles of sovereignty, recognizing that 'it is the duty of the international community as a whole to co-operate' in protecting world heritage). These concepts of 'cultural nationalism' and 'cultural internationalism' were first posited by John Henry Merryman and have been subjected to substantial examination and critique since that time. See eg John Henry Merryman, 'Two Ways of Thinking About Cultural Property' (1986) 80 AJIL 831; Robert Peters, 'Nationalism versus Internationalism: New Perspectives Beyond State Sovereignty and Territoriality in the Protection of Cultural Heritage' in Anne-Marie Carstens and Elizabeth Varner (eds), *Intersections in International Cultural Heritage Law* (OUP 2020) (Ch 15).

regime of international cooperation to protect endangered cultural sites, in turn, was constrained by the operation of fundamental principles of sovereignty and territoriality, forcing the drafters to place the principal responsibility for nominating and protecting sites in the hands of the national authorities in whose territory a qualifying site sits. This approach sometimes frustrated protection at the international level for endangered sites, especially transboundary sites.[20]

During this same period, a blending and merging also occurred of the traditional 'Hague Law'—prescriptive rules that governed the conduct of hostilities and occupation, with its formulation based on military objectives—and the more recent 'Geneva Law'—the body of law premised on humanitarian ideals and focused principally on protecting victims and reducing human suffering during armed conflict. Both remained complementary but distinct through the immediate postwar period, with the former still represented primarily by the 1899 and 1907 Hague Conventions, and the latter represented most prominently by the four Geneva Conventions adopted in 1949 to govern the treatment of victims, especially civilians. The adoption of the 1977 Additional Protocols I and II to the 1949 Geneva Conventions was widely heralded as the merging of these two regimes under the umbrella of international humanitarian law, with the formally separate 'law of war' or 'law of armed conflict' either subsumed within international humanitarian law or constituting one of its two main branches.[21] Though the treaty names indicate that they are dedicated to the protection of victims, the 1977 Additional Protocols codified and clarified the foundational rules from the Hague and Geneva regimes, placing the protection of cultural property directly alongside the protection of civilians and civilian property, and affording corollary protections and applying the same principles to both.[22] In addition, Additional Protocol II incorporated the most well-entrenched rules from both regimes—those rules achieving the greatest consensus that they had passed into customary international law—to establish a regime specifically applicable to non-international armed conflicts (NIACs).[23]

Indeed, after the First World War and especially since the Second World War, the international community had grown increasingly aware and sensitive to the

[20] See 1972 World Heritage Convention, arts 6, 11; Lucas Lixinski and Vassilis P Tzevelekos, 'The World Heritage Convention and the Law of State Responsibility: Promises and Pitfalls' in Anne-Marie Carstens and Elizabeth Varner (eds), *Intersections in International Cultural Heritage Law* (OUP 2020) (Ch 10).

[21] See eg Elvina Pothelet, 'Grave Breaches' in Dražan Djukić and Niccolò Pons (eds), *The Companion to International Humanitarian Law* (Brill 2018) 357; Daniel Thürer, 'International Humanitarian Law: Theory, Practice, Context' (2011) 338 *Recueil des Cours de l'Académie de la Haye* 50–51; Theodor Meron, 'The Humanization of the Law of War' (2003) 301 *Recueil des Cours de l'Académie de la Haye* 25–26; François Bugnion, 'Law of Geneva and Law of the Hague' (2001) 83 Intl Rev Red Cross 905.

[22] 1977 Additional Protocol I, arts 50–58.

[23] For discussion of how these obligations have been incorporated into recent military manuals, see Elizabeth Varner, 'Comparing Interpretations of States' and Non-State Actors' Obligations Toward Cultural Heritage in Armed Conflict and Occupation: Military Manuals and the Law of War' in Anne-Marie Carstens and Elizabeth Varner (eds), *Intersections in International Cultural Heritage Law* (OUP 2020) (Ch 2).

orchestrated destruction and seizure of cultural heritage as one facet of the persecution of minority groups, directly linking civilian protection with cultural property protection. So many of the existing regimes, with their focus on State sovereignty and respect for territorial integrity, though, failed to provide avenues for cultural groups to seek the protection and preservation associated with their collective identity, in and out of armed conflict. They were often also an imperfect fit for fostering the preservation of, and preventing the exploitation of, intangible cultural heritage, including traditional knowledge, customs, and folklore. These realities led to a push to connect the preservation of cultural heritage, both tangible and intangible, to other international regimes, such as major treaties on international intellectual property law or emerging international human rights law.[24]

The shortcomings of these regimes stimulated developments in both, but they also supported the development of a regime focused exclusively on protecting intangible cultural heritage. This expansion occurred first through a series of soft law instruments and ultimately through the adoption in the first years of this century of the 2003 Convention for the Safeguarding of the Intangible Cultural Heritage (2003 Intangible Cultural Heritage Convention or ICH Convention).[25]

Another cultural property-specific regime was adopted in the early years of the new millennium that was dedicated to the protection of underwater cultural heritage. Advances in technology had increased discoveries of historic shipwrecks and other underwater cultural heritage that had rested on the ocean floor sometimes for centuries, and the historic character of the contents created financial incentives for Parties to recover artifacts relying on the law of finds and law of salvage long established in maritime law. The comprehensive 1982 UN Convention on the Law of the Sea (Law of the Sea Convention or UNCLOS)[26] includes, among its hundreds of provisions, a provision expressly establishing a duty to protect archaeological and historical objects found at sea, beyond territorial waters.[27] Yet marine archaeologists, former maritime powers, and others stakeholders agitated for a more comprehensive treaty regime that would favor in situ protection that was realized in the 2001 Convention on the Protection of the Underwater Cultural Heritage.[28]

[24] See eg Agreement on Trade-Related Aspects of Intellectual Property Rights (adopted 15 April 1994, entered into force 1 January 1995) 1869 UNTS 299, Annex 1C to the Marrakesh Agreement Establishing the World Trade Organization (TRIPS Agreement); International Covenant on Economic, Social and Cultural Rights (adopted 16 December 1966, entered into force 3 January 1976) 999 UNTS 3 (ICESCR). For a discussion of cultural rights, in particular, see Vanessa Tünsmeyer, 'Bridging the Gap Between International Human Rights and International Cultural Heritage Law Instruments: A Functions Approach' in Anne-Marie Carstens and Elizabeth Varner (eds), *Intersections in International Cultural Heritage Law* (OUP 2020) (Ch 13).

[25] Convention for the Safeguarding of the Intangible Cultural Heritage (adopted 17 October 2003 entered into force 20 April 2006) 2368 UNTS 3 (2003 Intangible Cultural Heritage Convention or ICH Convention).

[26] United Nations Convention on the Law of the Sea (adopted 10 December 1982, entered into force 16 November 1994) 1833 UNTS 397 (Law of the Sea Convention or UNCLOS).

[27] ibid, art 303.

[28] Convention on the Protection of the Underwater Cultural Heritage (adopted 2 November 2001, entered into force 2 January 2009) 2562 UNTS 3 (2001 Underwater Cultural Heritage Convention or

The Rome Statute for the International Criminal Court (Rome Statute)[29] also entered into force, creating a permanent international criminal tribunal for the first time following several ad hoc tribunals, including the International Military Tribunal (Nuremberg Tribunal) and International Criminal Tribunal for the Former Yugoslavia (ICTY).[30] The Rome Statute expressly provides that intentionally directing attacks against buildings dedicated to religion or historical monuments qualifies as a 'war crime'.[31] Prosecutions before the International Criminal Court (ICC) reinforced the connection of cultural heritage destruction to targeted cultural groups, and the ICC even issued orders for reparations.[32] The international community also placed additional focus on the losses of cultural heritage due to another kind of criminality, namely transnational organized crime. The 2000 United Nations Convention against Transnational Organized Crime (2000 Palermo Convention) expanded the enforcement regime by facilitating international cooperation to curb looting and the illicit sale of antiquities as part of a broader framework to crack down on organized criminal networks and illicit trafficking.[33]

Contemporary international cultural heritage law also represents the culmination of efforts of a full panoply of international actors, whose concern for protecting cultural heritage has grown more widespread and prevalent. Cultural heritage protection was long relegated primarily to the cultural heritage arm within the United Nations, UNESCO, which continues to employ multiple strategies to respond to threats, as recently shown in Mali.[34] Now, though, more international

UCH Convention). For discussion of the application of this treaty to certain shipwrecks, see Sarah Dromgoole, 'The 2001 UNESCO Convention on the Protection of the Underwater Cultural Heritage and Its Principles Relating to the Recovery and Disposition of Material from Shipwrecks' in Anne-Marie Carstens and Elizabeth Varner (eds), *Intersections in International Cultural Heritage Law* (OUP 2020) (Ch 12).

[29] Rome Statute of the International Criminal Court (adopted 17 July 1998, entered into force 1 July 2002) 2187 UNTS 3 (Rome Statute).

[30] Statute of the International Criminal Tribunal for the Former Yugoslavia (adopted 25 May 1993 in UNSC Res 827, as amended).

[31] Rome Statute, art 8(2)(e)(iv). For discussion of the evolution of cultural heritage crimes up through the Rome Statute, see Anne-Marie Carstens, 'The Swinging Pendulum of Cultural Heritage Crimes in International Criminal Law' in Anne-Marie Carstens and Elizabeth Varner (eds), *Intersections in International Cultural Heritage Law* (OUP 2020) (Ch 4).

[32] See eg Karolina Wierczyńska and Andrzej Jakubowski, 'The *Al Mahdi* Case: From Punishing Perpetrators to Repairing Cultural Heritage Harm' in Anne-Marie Carstens and Elizabeth Varner (eds), *Intersections in International Cultural Heritage Law* (OUP 2020) (Ch 5).

[33] United Nations Convention Against Transnational Organized Crime (adopted 15 November 2000 UNGA Res 55/25, entered into force 29 September 2003) 2225 UNTS 209 (2000 Palermo Convention). See Janet Blake, 'Trafficking in Cultural Property: Where Cultural Heritage Law and the International Fight against Transnational Organized Crime Coincide' in Anne-Marie Carstens and Elizabeth Varner (eds), *Intersections in International Cultural Heritage Law* (OUP 2020) (Ch 6).

[34] See Guido Carducci, 'The Role of UNESCO in the Elaboration and Implementation of International Art, Cultural Property, and Heritage Law' in Anne-Marie Carstens and Elizabeth Varner (eds), *Intersections in International Cultural Heritage Law* (OUP 2020) (Ch 7) (discussing comprehensive role of UNESCO in this field); Sabine von Schorlemer, 'Military Intervention, the UN Security Council, and the Role of UNESCO: The Case of Mali' in Anne-Marie Carstens and Elizabeth Varner

bodies and agencies, such as the UN Human Rights Council (UNHRC) and the UN Security Council (UNSC),[35] and a growing number of non-governmental organizations, including the International Committee of the Red Cross (ICRC), consider cultural heritage within their mandate. International tribunals, including the International Court of Justice (ICJ), also reached cultural heritage issues that arose independent of international criminal prosecutions.[36]

International protection of cultural property also emerged from other sources. Several states adopted new domestic regimes that bolstered immunity from seizure for cultural objects that crossed borders in international art loans.[37] New instruments aimed at combatting global threats generally, as in the case of climate change and other environmental threats, also prove adaptable to the specific threats facing cultural heritage.[38] Taken together, this shift indicates a mainstreaming of cultural heritage protection within the international legal system.

II. The Contemporary Intersections of International Cultural Heritage Law and Public International Law and Their Future Trajectory

The chapters in this volume address several issues occurring at principal intersections where international cultural heritage law and public international law converge. These broadly defined intersections include:

(1) the law of armed conflict and the protection of cultural heritage;
(2) cultural heritage-based offenses in international criminal law and in the legal regime for combatting transnational organized crime;
(3) the United Nations system and the protection of cultural heritage;
(4) special legal regimes for world cultural heritage and underwater cultural heritage; and
(5) international, national, and community interests in cultural heritage.

(eds), *Intersections in International Cultural Heritage Law* (OUP 2020) (Ch 3) (discussing role of UNESCO and others in responding to threats and damage at World Heritage site of Timbuktu).

[35] Kristin Hausler, 'The UN Security Council, the Human Rights Council, and the Protection of Cultural Heritage: A Matter of Peace and Security, Human Rights, or Both?' in Anne-Marie Carstens and Elizabeth Varner (eds), *Intersections in International Cultural Heritage Law* (OUP 2020) (Ch 8).

[36] Gabriele Gagliani, 'The International Court of Justice and Cultural Heritage: International Cultural Heritage Law Through the Lenses of the World Court Jurisprudence?' in Anne-Marie Carstens and Elizabeth Varner (eds), *Intersections in International Cultural Heritage Law* (OUP 2020) (Ch 9).

[37] Nout van Woudenberg, 'Developments Concerning Immunity from Seizure for Cultural State Property on Loan' in Anne-Marie Carstens and Elizabeth Varner (eds), *Intersections in International Cultural Heritage Law* (OUP 2020) (Ch 14).

[38] See eg Ottavio Quirico, 'Nested Boxes: Tangible Cultural Heritage and Environmental Protection in Light of Climate Change' in Anne-Marie Carstens and Elizabeth Varner (eds), *Intersections in International Cultural Heritage Law* (OUP 2020) (Ch 11).

The coverage of intersections in this volume nonetheless is by no means exhaustive, either within the identified intersections or within public international law. Significant developments in cultural heritage protection have emerged at several additional intersections beyond the scope of this volume, such as in international economic law or in international intellectual property law, for example.

Moreover, the developments in protection occurring at the identified intersections have not occurred in isolation but instead often overlap with developments that are occurring (or have occurred) at other intersections. For example, international criminal law developed from the law of armed conflict, such that the two regimes contain overlapping language and concepts, though this volume devotes a separate section to each regime. As a further illustration, the volume devotes a section to the role of the United Nations, even though the instrumental role performed at several intersections by its agencies or bodies—such as UNESCO, the UN Security Council, the UN Human Rights Committee, and the ICJ—are featured throughout the volume. Even within just one arm of the United Nations, UNESCO has been a chief actor in promoting, facilitating, and implementing many of the treaties discussed in this volume, including the 1954 Hague Convention, the 1970 Convention, and the 1972 World Heritage Convention, as well as newer treaties, such as the 2001 Underwater Cultural Heritage Convention.

Of course, core principles such as sovereignty and territoriality and arguments over cultural nationalism versus cultural internationalism run throughout. These overlapping areas reinforce rules for protecting cultural heritage and other legal regimes in public international law.

This volume nonetheless represents merely a starting point for a thematic analysis of ways in which cultural heritage protection and public international law intersect. The origins and placement of rules protecting cultural heritage within different segments of public international law continue to shape the development of international cultural heritage law, as well as to inform our understanding of it. The reverse can also be true. Some principles or developments appeared early in cultural heritage law, thus paving the way for the increased recognition of the same principle or thematic development in other areas of international law.

O'Keefe has observed that without an understanding of the situation and tools available, reaction from the point of view of international law to the destruction and looting of the cultural heritage of Iraq, Syria, and elsewhere risks doing more harm than good.[39] However, despite the occasional ill-informed commentary and institutional misstep, he maintains that legal responses at the international and national levels to the recent cultural cataclysms have been impressively sensible. He also argues that it is the practicalities of enforcing the laws that are the barriers to protecting cultural heritage, in response to those who argue that the

[39] Roger O'Keefe, 'Cultural Heritage and the Laws of Armed Conflict: Ecce Homo' (conference on Intersections in International Cultural Heritage Law, Washington, DC, 29 March 2016).

current legal tools themselves are insufficient. Nonetheless, several contributors participating in this book have expressed dissatisfaction with specific aspects of international regimes for cultural heritage protection, while sometimes acknowledging the practical limitations of the current cultural heritage laws or the public international regimes in which they reside. They also have advanced arguments to utilize various sections of public international law or to expand cultural heritage laws to strengthen cultural heritage protections. It is likely that given the barriers to enforcement of existing cultural heritage laws (such as State sovereignty, limited resources, complications of non-State actors, and the vagaries of applicability of laws), which show no sign of waning, efforts to expand or improve the existing legal regimes will continue.

As the world changes, laws will continue to evolve to accommodate international developments and dissatisfaction with the damage, destruction, and theft of cultural heritage. As a consequence, it is likely that these intersections and multi-directional influences will also continue in the future. This likely trajectory reflects the view that it can be easier either to use a proven body of law (with existing State obligations) or to develop additional cultural heritage laws based on existing public international law than to reinvent the wheel.

Developments in international cultural heritage law at some intersections are nonetheless at a more advanced or more emergent stage by comparison with others, which also will shape the future trajectory of international regimes for protecting cultural heritage. Of the intersections covered in this volume, dynamic developments are anticipated in several emerging areas, including the protection of intangible cultural heritage, efforts to combat cultural heritage trafficking as an important aspect of transnational organized crime, and the recourse to international human rights. Developments in intangible cultural heritage and cultural heritage trafficking as a transnational organized crime, in particular, will likely remain active as they are relatively new areas governed by more recent treaties,[40] and thus are currently underdeveloped areas where State practice and interpretations continue to evolve. Future developments will probably also occur in the context of international human rights law because the law of armed conflict and international criminal law have not adequately embraced, nor left 'space' for, several important values in cultural heritage protection that reflect how losses of cultural heritage can adversely impact a community's identity and distinctive characteristics. The international human rights regime therefore presents an alternate avenue for new rules or developments that directly link the protection of human rights with the protection of symbolic objects and practices, particularly for minority communities.

The expansion of international actors that address or attempt to combat threats to cultural heritage also likely will continue. Within the UN system, both the UN

[40] 2001 Underwater Cultural Heritage Convention; 2000 Palermo Convention.

Human Rights Council and the UN Security Council (and, to a lesser extent, the ICJ) have grown increasingly active in the new millennium and will probably continue this activity, particularly given the continuing NIACs. These actors have expanded the conception of cultural heritage destruction by characterizing it as a threat to international peace and security and as an affront to human or community rights. This characterization likely will serve as further impetus for more public and private actors to become active in protecting cultural heritage or redressing its loss.

Fewer concrete developments are likely to take place at other intersections, which instead will experience more nuanced shifts. At some intersections, such as the law of armed conflict and international criminal law, new instruments or treaties are unlikely because the intersections already have a rich body of existing instruments and a long history of development paired with relatively recent clarifications of several existing obligations. The area thus is relatively stabilized by existing treaty and customary practice, though changes in interpretations of obligations are likely as State practice evolves and conflicts with non-State actors continue. The primary area of expansion likely will continue in the direction of greater application of the law of armed conflict to NIACs. The adoption of the Rome Statute establishing and governing a permanent international criminal tribunal, on the other hand, largely put an end to ad hoc international criminal codes that incorporated offenses based on attacks on cultural heritage to varying degrees. Recent and future prosecutions of cultural heritage-based offenses nonetheless will clarify how effective international criminal law will be in enforcing violations of the law of armed conflict and in deterring future violations.

Few major developments are expected similarly in some more specific areas, such as for the protection of underwater cultural heritage or the immunity from seizure for cultural objects in transboundary art loans. Minimal anticipated movement for underwater cultural heritage protection is attributable to the adoption of a UNESCO-based treaty, to which few current leading maritime States have shown themselves likely to join, and the continuing prominence of applicable rules from the UN Law of the Sea Convention. Continuing issues with State sovereignty and enforcement in the high seas also likely will contribute to a period of relative doctrinal stagnation. For international art loans, significant strides have taken place in the past two decades, with a flurry of States adopting rules that immunize international art loans from seizure or other adverse action, with important exceptions; still, at this juncture, the most-affected States have already taken recent domestic action on this front, while the adoption of an international treaty that would codify the core tenets of this protection remains elusive.[41] Developments therefore will continue on a smaller front with respect to the number of countries still adopting

[41] United Nations Convention on States and Their Property (2001) (adopted as Annex to UNGA Res 59/38 (2 December 2004) (2004 UN Convention)).

or clarifying such rules and with further expected clarifications for the somewhat-varying exceptions to such immunity. UNESCO also is certainly likely to continue its robust activity in promoting cultural heritage protection across several intersections, though the organization is not likely to see significant accretions to its mandate.

Principles of international law will continue to shape the development of international cultural heritage law in important ways. Principles of sovereignty in particular likely will continue to wield significant influence, just as this volume demonstrates that they have done so to date. While the expansion of the law of armed conflict and international criminal law to NIACs reflects a whittling away of sovereignty principles, as historically understood, such principles continue to have outsized influence on the international regime governing illicit trafficking in cultural objects and the protection of world cultural heritage. No significant regimes have advanced in nearly a quarter-century to address the continuing problem of illegal looting and trafficking of artifacts. Efforts to address illicit trafficking as an international law enforcement problem or a threat to international peace and security represent attempts at partial fixes, but none appreciably stems the tide of illicitly trafficked cultural goods from zones of conflict and occupation or from elsewhere. Discontent also is likely to continue with the condition of World Heritage sites, particularly in States that are unable or disinclined to care for them, where sovereignty and territoriality principles will probably continue to restrict external care for these sites to some extent. Incremental changes may occur with respect to mitigating certain threats to cultural heritage, though, such as environmental threats that increasingly endanger the integrity of World Heritage sites on several continents.

Over the next century, the intersections of international cultural heritage law and public international law themselves will likely multiply to address both existing and future challenges. These new intersections will present new avenues for protection, some perhaps not yet envisioned, while other developments will intersect with those already well mapped.

PART I

THE LAW OF ARMED CONFLICT AND THE PROTECTION OF CULTURAL HERITAGE

This part focuses on the intersection of the law of armed conflict and the protection of cultural heritage. The law of armed conflict (often referred to alternatively as international humanitarian law) arguably includes the most comprehensive regime for protecting cultural property, with a range of rules that include the negative duties to refrain from unnecessary destruction and seizure, affirmative obligations of States Parties to protect and preserve cultural property in certain circumstances, and obligations to protect cultural property by applying the principles of proportionality and distinction. At the same time, other principles of international law have influenced the development of those obligations, such as principles of sovereignty and territoriality, and the evolution of these principles themselves have shaped increasing obligations to protect cultural property during non-international armed conflicts and by non-State actors. These developments have led to rules for protecting cultural property that better reflect changes in the nature of contemporary armed conflicts.

Patty Gerstenblith begins the part by addressing shortcomings in the law of armed conflict both for stemming losses of movable cultural heritage during armed conflict and for returning cultural objects at the close of conflict.[1] She points to the bifurcation between international legal regimes applicable to armed conflict and those designed to curb the illicit trafficking in cultural objects, primarily during peacetime, as the principal obstruction to a cohesive regime for stemming losses of cultural objects from zones of conflict or occupation. She additionally observes that the law of armed conflict contains little guidance for resolving competing requests for the return of cultural objects removed from zones of conflict or occupation. Given the nature of cultural property, disputes can arise over whether such property should be returned to the situs of removal and also whether it should be returned to the State or, instead, to local authorities, a minority community, or victims.

[1] Patty Gerstenblith, 'The Disposition of Movable Cultural Property' in Anne-Marie Carstens and Elizabeth Varner (eds), *Intersections in International Cultural Heritage Law*, (OUP 2020) (Ch 1).

Elizabeth Varner then focuses on the legal protection of cultural heritage at a more granular level, assessing varying interpretations of rules protecting cultural property during armed conflict based on developments that have occurred within the last decade.[2] After several decades of relative dormancy, eleven States have joined the 1954 Hague Convention more than a half-century after the treaty was first adopted, including two major military powers: the United States and the United Kingdom. Nonetheless, State interpretations of their obligations toward cultural property during armed conflict still sometimes reflect disagreement, stemming from a variety of factors. These factors can include: whether States are Parties to the instrument that conveys the obligation; whether the obligation is one of customary international law, which is often contested; the individual State's interpretation; interpretation of tribunals; and a plethora of other factors. Given these discrepancies in interpretation, a review of States' military manuals is useful to see if they shed any light on the State's interpretation of their obligations toward cultural property under the law of armed conflict (LOAC) and international obligations in LOAC more generally. She analyzes and compares the military manuals of the United States and the United Kingdom to determine how they elucidate several key issues in the protection of cultural property during armed conflict, such as the definition of 'cultural property', requirements for 'respect', the doctrine of military necessity, and responsibilities in non-international armed conflicts.

Sabine von Schorlemer concludes this part with a case study of international responses to the destruction of historic mausoleums and other cultural heritage at the UNESCO World Heritage site of Timbuktu and elsewhere in Mali, from 2012 to 2013.[3] She outlines UNESCO's new strategy for responding to such threats, as well as the French military initiative, Operation Serval, that entered the territory of Mali to quell unrest and oust the militant extremists occupying Timbuktu, thereby preventing further destruction. In her view, these efforts serve as a possible example of military intervention to protect cultural property. She also observes that threats to cultural heritage were sufficiently dire that they prompted a series of UN Security Council resolutions, including the first resolution that expressly directed UN peacekeeping forces to assist national authorities in protecting Mali's historical and other cultural sites, in collaboration with UNESCO.

Anne-Marie Carstens and Elizabeth Varner

[2] Elizabeth Varner, 'Comparing Interpretations of States' and Non-State Actors' Obligations Toward Cultural Heritage in Armed Conflict and Occupation: Military Manuals and the Law of War' in Anne-Marie Carstens and Elizabeth Varner (eds), *Intersections in International Cultural Heritage Law* (OUP 2020) (Ch 2).

[3] Sabine von Schorlemer, 'Military Intervention, the UN Security Council, and the Role of UNESCO: The Case of Mali' in Anne-Marie Carstens and Elizabeth Varner (eds), *Intersections in International Cultural Heritage Law* (OUP 2020) (Ch 3).

1

The Disposition of Movable Cultural Heritage

*Patty Gerstenblith**

Introduction

The destruction of cultural, religious, and historic structures and sites in the Middle East has received considerable attention since the 2003 Gulf War. The legal instruments that aim to protect such sites, in particular the 1954 Hague Convention for the Protection of Cultural Property in the Event of Armed Conflict (1954 Hague Convention),[1] have received similar attention and additional ratifications as a result of these conflicts and their deleterious effect on cultural heritage. While rampant looting of archaeological sites throughout this region has contributed significantly to the destruction of cultural heritage, the international treaty regime that aims to prevent these losses is poorly equipped to deal with this type of destruction, which is carried out under the lure of the profits to be earned through the international market in art and antiquities. The failure of international law to confront this problem is in large measure the result of its bifurcation between those instruments that apply to armed conflict and those that apply to the movement of cultural objects, primarily during peacetime, as a part of the international art market.

Early in the development of the international legal regime that addresses protection of cultural heritage, a divide developed between the protection of cultural heritage during armed conflict and that which addresses illegal movement and trafficking in cultural objects. The first international legal instruments to address cultural heritage during armed conflict were the early Hague Conventions of 1899 and 1907 governing land warfare and their Regulations,[2] which were formulated at

* I want to thank Lois Wetzel (DePaul Law '19) for her research assistance.

[1] Convention for the Protection of Cultural Property in the Event of Armed Conflict (adopted 14 May 1954, entered into force 7 August 1956) 249 UNTS 240 (1954 Hague Convention).

[2] Convention (IV) Respecting the Laws and Customs of War on Land and its Annex: Regulations concerning the Laws and Customs of War on Land (opened for signature 18 October 1907, entered into force 26 January 1910) 187 CTS 227 (1907 Hague Convention (IV)); Hague Convention (II) with Respect to the Laws and Customs of War on Land and its Annex: Regulations concerning the Laws and Customs of War on Land (adopted 29 July 1899, entered into force 4 September 1900) 187 CTS 429 (1899 Hague Convention (II)) (collectively, the 1899 and 1907 Hague Conventions). The

Patty Gerstenblith, The Disposition of Movable Cultural Heritage In: *Intersections in International Cultural Heritage Law.*
Edited by Anne-Marie Carstens and Elizabeth Varner. © Oxford University Press 2020. The several contributors
DOI: 10.1093/oso/9780198846291.003.0002

a time when the connection between destruction and theft, on the one hand, and an international market, on the other, was not of particular concern. However, the connection between theft and looting and the promotion of armed conflict became apparent during the Second World War when the theft of art works for sale on the international market became a means of funding the Nazi war effort while also enriching the collections and pockets of the Nazi leadership.[3]

Following the Second World War, the 1954 Hague Convention was promulgated to address exclusively the protection of cultural property during armed conflict and occupation. Despite what was known about the sales of stolen art works onto the international market, the provisions of the main Convention were limited to prohibiting the theft and destruction of cultural property. The question of what happened to objects after they had been illegally removed was relegated to the Convention's First Protocol,[4] adopted at the same time as the main Convention, but its provisions are limited to very narrow circumstances concerning military occupation by a State. On the other hand, the primary legal instrument for preventing illegal trafficking in cultural objects, the UNESCO Convention on the Means of Prohibiting and Preventing the Illicit Import, Export and Transfer of Ownership of Cultural Property (1970 UNESCO Convention),[5] which focuses on illegal movement through the market, was not adopted until 1970 and pays relatively little attention to the fate of cultural objects during armed conflict.

Both the legal treatment of and the attention paid to the movement of cultural objects for sale on the international art market as the result of armed conflict and military occupation are not as robust as those that apply to the protection of immovable heritage. Or, to rephrase this, damage to and destruction of immovable heritage do not implicate the related issues of financial incentive provided by the international art market and the consequent funding of armed conflict. The existing legal provisions that pertain to movable heritage within the armed conflict context are now seen to be woefully inadequate to confront the reality of contemporary theft and looting in the Middle East and North Africa (MENA) region. Brodie has concluded that between 1990 and 2015, '[a] large if not the major cause of damage [to cultural property] … was theft from cultural institutions and illegal

provisions governing cultural heritage in the two treaties are substantially verbatim, with the 1907 Hague Convention (IV) supplanting the earlier 1899 Hague Convention (II) for Parties to both treaties.

[3] Lynn Nicholas, *The Rape of Europa* (Alfred A Knopf 1994) 5–6, 23–25; Uwe Fleckner, 'Marketing the Defamed: On the Contradictory Use of Provenances in the Third Reich' in Gail Feigenbaum and Inge Reist (eds), *Provenance: An Alternate History of Art* (Getty Publications 2012) 137, 144–49 (discussing the sale abroad of art works removed from German museums).

[4] Protocol for the Protection of Cultural Property in the Event of Armed Conflict (adopted 14 May 1954, entered into force 7 August 1956) 249 UNTS 358 (1954 First Protocol).

[5] Convention on the Means of Prohibiting and Preventing the Illicit Import, Export and Transfer of Ownership of Cultural Property (adopted 14 November 1970, entered into force 24 April 1972) 823 UNTS 231 (1970 UNESCO Convention).

digging of archaeological sites to feed the voracious demand of the international market in cultural objects' rather than intentional or collateral damage caused during military activities.[6] Yet, Brodie also points out that 'the illegal trade is not something driven by the military necessity of armies or the fanaticism of ideologues. It is a commercial construct. Of all causes of damage to cultural property, it is to all appearances the one most open to control'.[7]

The recent conflicts in the MENA region thus illustrate that this bifurcation in the international legal regime between wartime and peacetime treaties has severely hampered our ability to protect archaeological sites from looting and has necessitated several *sui generis* legal instruments, including three UN Security Council Resolutions.[8] This chapter will examine the various international legal instruments, and the interpretations and implementations given to them by various States, that attempt to control the disposition of movable cultural objects removed during armed conflict and will explore their shortcomings. In particular, the role that looting and theft[9] of cultural objects for sale on the international market have played in the ongoing conflicts in the MENA region demonstrates that the law of armed conflict is poorly equipped to deal with the international trade in stolen and looted cultural objects, while the law concerning international movement is poorly equipped to deal with the problems of cultural objects looted and stolen during armed conflict and occupation. This chapter suggests that the lack of intersection among the treaties that address wartime circumstances and those that address peacetime movement and the functioning of the international art market of cultural objects creates these gaps in international law. Thus, this lack of intersection among relevant law is responsible for the failure to remove effectively the incentives to loot and steal cultural objects and for the failure to protect adequately our cultural heritage.

[6] Neil Brodie, 'Protection Not Prevention: The Failure of Public Policy to Prevent the Looting and Illegal Trade of Cultural Property from the MENA Region (1990–2015)' in Jane Anderson and Haidy Geismar (eds), *The Routledge Companion to Cultural Property* (Routledge 2017) 89, 89.

[7] ibid.

[8] UNSC Res 2347 (24 March 2017) UN Doc S/RES/2347; UNSC Res 2199 (12 February 2015) UN Doc S/RES/2199; UNSC Res 1483 (22 May 2003) UN Doc S/RES/1483.

[9] The terms 'looting' and 'theft' are often used interchangeably. I will use the term 'theft' to refer to an illegal removal of known cultural objects that are documented in either a private or public collection, such as that of a museum, archives, library, or religious institution. The term 'looting' refers to the unscientific removal of archaeological objects from their original context, typically underground or under water. Hart and Chilton define the looting of archaeological sites and cultural objects as 'the act of digging up artifacts for private collection or sale without the concomitant record of excavation, context and lab work associated with scientific archaeology'. Siobhan M Hart and Elizabeth S Chilton, 'Digging and Destruction: Artifact Collecting as Meaningful Social Practice' (2014) 21 Intl J Heritage Studies 318. Such looting is often also illegal under the laws of the State where the site is located, but the emphasis here is on the loss of associated context and, with it, the loss of knowledge that results from the looting of archaeological sites. Archaeological objects for which ownership is vested in the State and are illegally exported are characterized as stolen property under the laws of the United States and other countries. *United States v Schultz* 333 F3d 393 (2d Cir 2003).

I. The Hague Convention Regime and the Law of Armed Conflict

The 1899 and 1907 Hague Conventions[10] prohibit pillage and seizure of cultural objects by invading and occupying forces.[11] Article 56 of the Regulations of the 1907 Hague Convention, for example, which substantially repeats the corollary article from the 1899 treaty, states:

> The property of municipalities, that of institutions dedicated to religion, charity and education, the arts and sciences, even when State property, shall be treated as private property.
>
> All seizure of, destruction or wilful damage done to institutions of this character, historic monuments, works of art and science, is forbidden, and should be made the subject of legal proceedings.[12]

A. The 1954 Hague Convention

Following the Second World War, the 1954 Hague Convention was promulgated as the first international treaty to address exclusively cultural property.[13] While Article 1 defines 'cultural property' to include immovable property, such as monuments of architecture, historic structures, and archaeological sites, the definition also refers to movables, such as 'works of art, manuscripts, books and other objects of artistic, historical or archaeological interest, scientific collections and important collections of books and archives' as well as repositories for these types of cultural objects.

[10] 1899 Hague Convention (II); 1907 Hague Convention (IV). The 1899 and 1907 Hague Conventions prohibit pillage in general during armed conflict (art 28) and prohibit pillage during occupation (art 47).

[11] The earlier *Instructions for the Government of Armies of the United States in the Field*, General Orders No 100 (24 April 1863) , drafted for the Union Army during the US civil war and known as the Lieber Code, prohibited seizure and appropriation of what we would today call cultural property:

> If such works of art, libraries, collections, or instruments belonging to a hostile nation or government, can be removed without injury, the ruler of the conquering state or nation may order them to be seized and removed for the benefit of the said nation. The ultimate ownership is to be settled by the ensuing treaty of peace. In no case shall they be sold or given away, if captured by the United States, nor shall they ever be privately appropriated, or wantonly destroyed or injured.

ibid, art 36.

[12] 1907 Hague Convention (IV) art 56. See also ibid, arts 23(g), 28.

[13] The Treaty on the Protection of Artistic and Scientific Institutions and Historic Monuments (Roerich Pact) (adopted 15 April 1935, entered into force 26 August 1935) 167 LNTS 289, was the first treaty drafted to address exclusively cultural property. However, it is of limited viability and was ratified only by States in the Americas.

The 1954 Hague Convention in Article 4(3) imposes an obligation 'to prohibit, prevent and, if necessary, put a stop to any form of theft, pillage or misappropriation of, and any acts of vandalism directed against, cultural property'. This provision is worded without specifying to which actor it applies, and, until the looting of the Iraq Museum in Baghdad in April 2003, this provision received relatively little commentary.[14] The wording in the passive voice without specifying an actor causes an ambiguity in its interpretation. On the one hand, this provision may be interpreted to mean that a military is required to prevent its own troops from engaging in theft, pillage, or misappropriation, not that it is required to prevent third Parties from doing so.[15] On the other hand, Roger O'Keefe argues that international law obliges an occupying power to also prevent the local populace from engaging in such theft and misappropriation.[16] In doing so, he relies on other international law sources that impose an obligation to maintain general order, such as Article 43 of the Regulations annexed to the 1899 and 1907 Hague Conventions and Article 64 of the 1949 Geneva Convention relative to the Protection of Civilian Persons in Time of War (1949 Fourth Geneva Convention), as well as customary international law. He also suggests that while Article 4(3) does not explicitly prohibit archaeological excavation during occupation, excavation without the permission of the local governing authority by an occupying power would violate this provision if national law vests ownership of archaeological artifacts in the State.[17] In addition, the large-scale looting of archaeological sites, as seen in Syria, would likely constitute a violation of Article 4(1) as the deliberate targeting of cultural property. Regardless of the interpretation of the obligations imposed by Article 4(1) and Article 4(3), the main Convention does not address the status of cultural objects after their removal and their subsequent transport either through the international art market or otherwise.

[14] See eg Jiří Toman, *The Protection of Cultural Property in the Event of Armed Conflict: Commentary on the Convention for the Protection of Cultural Property in the Event of Armed Conflict and its Protocol* (UNESCO/Dartmouth 1996) 70–71.

[15] See eg Patty Gerstenblith, 'From Bamiyan to Baghdad: Warfare and the Preservation of Cultural Heritage at the Beginning of the 21st Century' (2006) 37 Geo J Intl L 245, 308–11.

[16] Roger O'Keefe, *The Protection of Cultural Property in Armed Conflict* (CUP 2006) 132–34. In his argument, however, O'Keefe fails to address whether the obligation to prevent looting, based as it is on an obligation during occupation to maintain order, also applies during conflict itself, as occurred with the looting of the Iraq Museum in Baghdad in early April 2003. In fact, the obligation is contained in art 4 of the 1954 Hague Convention and is not referred to in art 5, which specifically addresses obligations during occupation. Benvenisti suggests that 'in a post-invasion, pre-occupation phase, it is *sensible* to give cultural property a higher degree of protection and oblige the invading power actively to secure cultural artifacts against looting'. Eyal Benvenisti, *The International Law of Occupation* (2nd edn, OUP 2012) 251 (emphasis added). However, imposing an obligation that arises only during occupation on armed forces during the conflict does not seem sensible.

[17] R O'Keefe (n 16) 133–34.

B. The First Protocol (1954)

The subject of legality of cultural objects that were illegally removed during armed conflict or occupation and their subsequent disposition was separated from the main Convention and is treated primarily in the First Protocol, which was written at the same time as the main Convention.[18] This separation was the result of objections raised by the United States and the United Kingdom and to make it easier for these States to ratify the main Convention without having to confront the legal status of movable objects and the question of restitution.[19] The 1954 First Protocol, and to the extent that it is elaborated by the 1999 Second Protocol to the 1954 Hague Convention, is the primary means for and, in fact, is limited to preventing illegal removal of cultural objects only from occupied territory. The extent of its applicability is thus severely restricted. As of 2019, 110 States have ratified the First Protocol, which is fewer than those that have ratified the main Convention, which has 133 States Parties.[20] There are several reasons why the First Protocol has proved less popular.[21] In particular, both transit and ultimate market nations dislike the obligation to return movable cultural objects and other obligations that might interfere with the operation of their art markets.

The first part of the Protocol addresses the prevention of export of cultural objects from occupied territory and the return of any such exported cultural objects. It does so by imposing four obligations: (1) that the occupying power must prevent the export of cultural objects from occupied territory;[22] (2) a State Party (regardless of whether it is the occupying power) must take into custody any cultural

[18] 1954 First Protocol. For a more detailed discussion, see Patrick J O'Keefe, 'The First Protocol to the Hague Convention Fifty Years On' (2004) 9 Art Antiquity and Law 99.

[19] Toman (n 14) 344; Ana Vrdoljak, *International Law, Museums and the Return of Cultural Objects* (CUP 2008) 149; Kevin Chamberlain, *War and Cultural Heritage: A Commentary on the Hague Convention 1954 and its Two Protocols* (2nd edn, IAL 2013) 144. At the time President Clinton transmitted the main Convention and1954 First Protocol to the Senate for ratification in 1999, the transmittal was accompanied by a recommendation to utilize the opt-out provision of the First Protocol to ratify only the second part, which would have relieved the United States of the responsibility to return cultural property removed from occupied territory. Transmittal of the Hague Convention for the Protection of Cultural Property in the Event of Armed Conflict and, for Accession, the Hague Protocol to the Senate Foreign Relations Committee, S Treaty Doc No 106–1, III–IV, IX (1999). The United States has not taken any steps toward ratification of the First Protocol. It seems incongruous that at the same time that the United States was leading an effort to return cultural objects stolen by the Nazis to their original owners and heirs, the United States seemed to be concerned that it not have any responsibility for restoring stolen cultural objects to their owners in future wars.

[20] Several nations that attended the conference and signed the main Convention did not sign the Protocol, including the United States, the United Kingdom, Australia, and Israel. Toman (n 14) 349. Several countries, including Canada and Israel, first ratified the Convention and later acceded to the First Protocol.

[21] P J O'Keefe, 'Fifty Years On' (n 18) 100–03.

[22] Paragraph 1 states: 'Each High Contracting Party undertakes to prevent the exportation, from a territory occupied by it during an armed conflict, of cultural property as defined in Article 1 of the Convention.' This provision seems to apply regardless of whether the occupied territory belongs to a Party to the Protocol. Toman (n 14) 344; Chamberlain (n 19) 103.

objects imported either directly or indirectly from occupied territory;[23] (3) a State Party must return at the end of hostilities any cultural objects illegally removed from occupied territory;[24] and (4) the occupying power must compensate any good faith possessor of such cultural objects.[25] Section II of the Protocol requires that any cultural property removed from one State Party and placed in the territory of another State Party for safekeeping during armed conflict must be returned at the end of the conflict, which raises questions that are discussed in greater detail in Part III, below.[26]

C. The Second Protocol (1999)

The Second Protocol to the 1954 Hague Convention was adopted at a multilateral conference in 1999 and came into effect in 2004.[27] As of 2019, it has eighty-two States Parties. It updates the main Convention, primarily with respect to the definition of military necessity (Article 6), introducing the concepts of proportionality and feasibility (Article 7), establishing command responsibility (Article 15(2)), and requiring States Parties to adopt specific criminal provisions (Article 15). An intentional violation of Article 4(3) of the main Convention constitutes a serious violation of the Second Protocol and is one of the acts for which a State Party must establish a criminal offense within its domestic law (Article 15(1)(e) and (2)).[28]

[23] Paragraph 2 states: 'Each High Contracting Party undertakes to take into its custody cultural property imported into its territory either directly or indirectly from any occupied territory. This shall either be effected automatically upon the importation of the property or, failing this, at the request of the authorities of that territory.'

[24] Paragraph 3 states: 'Each High Contracting Party undertakes to return, at the close of hostilities, to the competent authorities of the territory previously occupied, cultural property which is in its territory, if such property has been exported in contravention of the principle laid down in the first paragraph. Such property shall never be retained as war reparations.'

[25] Paragraph 4 states: 'The High Contracting Party whose obligation it was to prevent the exportation of cultural property from the territory occupied by it shall pay an indemnity to the holders in good faith of any cultural property which has to be returned in accordance with the preceding paragraph.'

[26] Paragraph 5 states: 'Cultural property coming from the territory of a High Contracting Party and deposited by it in the territory of another High Contracting Party for the purpose of protecting such property against the dangers of an armed conflict, shall be returned by the latter, at the end of hostilities, to the competent authorities of the territory from which it came.' The remaining articles comprise Part III of the Protocol and cover procedural aspects.

[27] Second Protocol to the Hague Convention of 1954 for the Protection of Cultural Property in the Event of Armed Conflict (adopted 26 March 1999, entered into force 9 March 2004) 253 UNTS 172 (1999 Second Protocol).

[28] Under Article 28 of the main Convention, States Parties are to pursue criminal actions against violators of the Convention 'within the framework of their ordinary criminal jurisdiction'. However, there is no requirement to enact specific implementing legislation and the Convention does not define specific criminal acts. The Rome Statute of the International Criminal Court makes the intentional destruction of cultural property a war crime but does not address theft or looting. Rome Statute of the International Criminal Court (adopted 17 July 1998, entered into force 1 July 2002) 2187 UNTS 3, art 8(2)(b)(ix) (applying to international armed conflict), art 8(2)(e)(iv) (applying to non-international armed conflict) (Rome Statute).

The Second Protocol establishes new substantive law with respect to movable objects in Article 9. In part, it reiterates Article 4(3) of the main Convention by prohibiting any illicit export, removal, or transfer of ownership of cultural property (Article 9(a)). Perhaps of greater interest is a prohibition on 'any archaeological excavation, save where this is strictly required to safeguard, record or preserve cultural property' (Article 9(b)). This article also prohibits 'any alteration to, or change of use of, cultural property which is intended to conceal or destroy cultural, historical or scientific evidence' (Article 9(c)). These last two provisions seem to recognize the particular problems caused by long-term occupations, such as that of the Palestinian Territories and of northern Cyprus—problems that did not arise in the course of the Second World War.

D. Implementation and Enforcement of the Hague Regime

Enforcement of the 1954 First Protocol has met with obstacles due to limited ratifications[29] and, even more so, limited implementation into domestic national law among those countries that do not regard the First Protocol as self-executing and so require adoption of implementing legislation; it has therefore rarely been invoked.[30] In *The Autocephalous Greek Orthodox Church in Cyprus v Willem OA Lans*,[31] the Autocephalous Greek Orthodox Church of Cyprus was unable to recover four icons located in the Netherlands that had been stolen from the Antiphonitis Church in the northern part of the island after it fell under Turkish occupation in 1974. The court held that the Protocol did not grant a private right of action, and the rights of the defendant, particularly as a good faith purchaser, were protected under Dutch civil law. The Court of Appeal further held that the claim was time-barred, regardless of whether the defendant had acted in good or bad faith.[32] This outcome prompted the Netherlands to enact the Cultural Property

[29] According to the International Committee of the Red Cross, the core provisions of the 1954 First Protocol are accepted as part of customary international law: 'Rule 41. The occupying power must prevent the illicit export of cultural property from occupied territory and must return illicitly exported property to the competent authorities of the occupied territory.' According to Rule 40, article 4(3) of the main Convention is a part of customary international law, as is the second paragraph of article 56 of the 1907 Hague Regulations (prohibiting seizure of 'works of art and science'). Jean-Marie Henckaerts, 'Study on Customary International Humanitarian Law: A Contribution to the Understanding and Respect for the Rule of Law in Armed Conflict' (2005) 87 International Review of the Red Cross 201–02 <https://www.icrc.org/en/doc/assets/files/other/irrc_857_henckaerts.pdf> accessed 20 December 2019.

[30] On the problem of domestic implementation of the 1954 First Protocol, see Stephan Matyk, 'The Restitution of Cultural Objects and the Question of Giving Direct Effect to the Protocol to the Hague Convention for the Protection of Cultural Property in the Event of Armed Conflict' (2000) 9 IJCP 341.

[31] *Autocephalous Greek Orthodox Church in Cyprus v Lans*, Rb (First Instance Ct) Rotterdam 4 February 1999, NJ 1999, 37; *Autocephalous Greek Orthodox Church in Cyprus v Lans*, Hof (Appeals Ct) The Hague 7 March 2002, NIPR 2002, No 248.

[32] ibid. See also P J O'Keefe, 'Fifty Years On' (n 18) 110; Nout van Woudenberg and Liesbeth Lijnzaad (eds), *Protecting Cultural Property in Armed Conflict* (Martinus Nijhoff 2010) 153–54; Evelien

Originating from Occupied Territory (Return) Act in March 2007 in order to implement the First Protocol.[33] Germany enacted similar implementing legislation also in 2007.[34] In both cases, the legislation applies to objects removed illegally from occupied territory after the date when the country ratified the First Protocol (1967 for Germany and 1959 for the Netherlands). Germany and the Netherlands are among the few destination market countries, now joined by the United Kingdom, that have enacted specific implementing legislation for the First Protocol.

The United Kingdom is the most recent major military power to ratify all three Hague instruments, and it enacted detailed implementing legislation.[35] Its implementation of the First Protocol is worth examining. In some respects the implementation is quite broad in that the prohibition on dealing in illegally exported cultural property[36] applies to objects illegally exported any time after 1956, when the First Protocol went into effect and more than sixty years before the United Kingdom became a State Party.[37] 'Unlawful' is defined as 'in contravention of the laws of the territory from which the property is exported' or 'in contravention of any rule of international law'.[38]

However, the accepted definition of occupied territory, specifically adopted by the UK legislation, imposes a significant limitation on the First Protocol's applicability.[39] Unlawful export is restricted to unlawful export 'from a territory which at the time was occupied by a state that was a party to the First or Second Protocol' or 'from a territory which at the time was territory of a state that was a party to the First or Second Protocol, and was occupied by another state'.[40] In other words, the unlawful export provisions apply only if the occupying power was a party to one

Campfens, 'Whose Cultural Heritage? Crimean Treasures at the Crossroads of Politics, Law and Ethics' (2017) 22 Art Antiquity and Law 193, 204–05.

[33] Stb 2007, 123, currently codified as Sections 6.9–6.15 of the Act of 9 December 2015, Relating to the Combining and Amendment of Rules Regarding Cultural Heritage (Heritage Act 2016) <https://www.eui.eu/Projects/InternationalArtHeritageLaw/Documents/NationalLegislation/Netherlands/actof2007coveringoccupiedterritory.pdf> accessed 20 December 2019.

[34] Transformation Act of 25 April 2007; Act of 18 May 2007 Implementing the UNESCO Convention of 14 November 1970 on the Means of Prohibiting and Preventing the Illicit Import, Export and Transfer of Ownership of Cultural Property (Implementation Act) 18.5.2007, BGBl I, 2007, p 757, art 4.

[35] Cultural Property (Armed Conflicts) Act 2017 (United Kingdom).

[36] The act of dealing in unlawfully exported cultural property includes acquiring in, disposing in, importing into, or exporting from the United Kingdom. ibid, s 17(1). When a perpetrator has been convicted, the property involved in the offense may be forfeited. ibid, s 18. Illegally exported cultural objects may be forfeited even if an offense is not established. ibid, s 19. In some cases, a court may condition forfeiture on the payment of compensation in case the object was acquired in good faith. ibid, s 21.

[37] ibid, s 16(2). However, the prohibition on dealing applies only to illegally exported objects that enter the United Kingdom after the legislation went into effect. ibid, s 17(2).

[38] ibid, s 16(3).

[39] This limitation accords with other limitations on responsibilities to protect and safeguard cultural property that apply only in cases of occupation by a State. See Anne-Marie Carstens, 'The Hostilities–Occupation Dichotomy and Cultural Property in Non-International Armed Conflicts' (2016) 52 Stanford J Intl L 1, 6.

[40] Cultural Property (Armed Conflicts) Act 2017 (n 35) s 16(1)(a)(b).

of the Protocols or if the occupied territory was that of a State Party, but in both cases the occupier must be a State. In assessing applicability to the recent situation in Syria, although Syria is a Party to the First Protocol, unlawful export of cultural objects from Syrian territory occupied by the Islamic State of Iraq and the Levant (ISIL) or by other non-State actors would not fall under the UK legislation because ISIL is not itself a State.

The wording of the first section of the First Protocol, imposing an obligation to prevent export from occupied territory, explicitly refers to occupation by a State Party upon whom this obligation falls. However, sections two and three refer to the obligations of a State Party that is not the occupying power but, rather, is a 'third party' into which the illegally exported cultural objects have been imported. These obligations are to take such objects into custody and to return them at the end of hostilities.[41] It would seem logical that the imposition of these obligations on a 'third party' does not need to depend on the status of the occupier, whether as a State or a non-State.

The explanatory notes that accompany the UK legislation explain this limitation to States as based on the definition of belligerent occupation given in the 1907 Hague Regulations Article 42, which states 'Territory is considered occupied when it is actually placed under the authority of the hostile army. The occupation applies only to territory where such authority is established and in a position to assert itself.' Although this provision refers to the fact that the occupier must have effective authority over the territory for which it is responsible as a function of its status as an occupier, Article 42 does not explicitly require that the occupier be a State.[42] Admittedly, only a State could become a Party to the Convention and the Convention was viewed as applying only to international armed conflict. Most commentators have perpetuated the traditional view that only a State can be an occupying power and that therefore the First Protocol only applies where occupation is carried out by a State. However, some have also questioned the view that only a State can be an occupying power, particularly in light of the fact that the Hague Convention itself and the Second Protocol otherwise specifically apply to non-State actors.

The primary concern of the law regulating military occupation is the status of protected persons, and applicability of this body of law to the protection of cultural property is not an easy fit. Nonetheless, the limitation of the law of occupation to circumstances where the occupier is a State has been criticized, and it has been suggested that the qualifying factor, following the text of Article 42, should be whether the occupier has control over the occupied territory, not whether the

[41] 1954 First Protocol, paras 2 and 3.

[42] For discussion of the generally accepted requirement that occupation must be carried out by a State and does not exist in non-international armed conflict, see R O'Keefe (n 16) 98–99; Carstens (n 39) 9.

occupier is a State.[43] Benvenisti suggests that the law of occupation should apply to situations of non-international armed conflict as well as to international armed conflict. He would therefore extend the definition of occupation to 'the case when an organized secessionist government which has established its authority within a state is engaged in armed conflict with the metropolitan state during which it seizes territory'.[44]

This limitation to occupation by a State may be the product of a time when conflict with non-State actors was less common and when non-State actors were not considered subject to or beneficiaries of international law.[45] It may also be based on the reluctance of States to grant any degree of legitimacy to non-State actors. However, subjecting non-State actors to international law, at least in this context, would seem more to be a source of obligations than of privileges or legitimacy. A definition of occupation should be based on whether any party has effective control over specific territory. Any such party would be subject to this additional obligation under the First Protocol, as it already is subject to other provisions relating to the obligation of respect in the 1954 Hague Convention.[46]

The drafters of the UK legislation were not obliged to adopt this limitation and could, instead, have chosen a more realistic and contemporary approach to this definition. We now see the unfortunate effect of this limitation in that illegal export of cultural objects from territory occupied by ISIL would not trigger an obligation in the United Kingdom to return these cultural objects under the 1954 Hague Convention regime. Thus, under the UK interpretation and example, the initial illegality of theft and misappropriation under the main Convention does not follow these objects onto the international art market and into destination countries, even if they are Parties to these instruments, thus necessitating enactment of additional legislation to prevent this trade. While, as discussed in Section II.B below, such provisions have been enacted with respect to Syria and Iraq, this is an inefficient, unreliable, and under-productive approach. This produces a result similar to that under Article 4(3) of the main Convention, as well as under other provisions of international law that prohibit the theft and looting of civilian objects, including cultural objects. While it is a violation of international law to pillage and steal, the

[43] With respect to the status of protected persons, Benvenisti wrote:

> The protections of the law should not be cast into doubt because the belligerents dispute the status of territory. The better test would focus not on the occupant's characterization as an enemy of the population, but on the relationships between the administrations and the individuals and communities subject to its rule.

Benvenisti (n 16) 59.

[44] ibid 61.

[45] See M Cherif Bassiouni, 'The New Wars and the Crisis of Compliance with the Law of Armed Conflict by Non-State Actors' (2008) 98 J Crim L & Criminology 711.

[46] Article 19 provides that 'In the event of an armed conflict not of an international character occurring within the territory of one of the High Contracting Parties, each party to the conflict shall be bound to apply, as a minimum, the provisions of the Convention which relate to respect for cultural property.'

illegality of the initial theft and looting do not attach to the object and follow it into international commerce.[47]

E. Other Sources of International Humanitarian Law

The humanitarian law conventions adopted in the post-Second World War era, such as the Geneva Conventions of 1949, do not specifically address the theft and looting of movable cultural objects. However, they have provisions prohibiting the theft and pillage of civilian property in general. For example, the 1949 Fourth Geneva Convention prohibits pillage. It also identifies the 'appropriation of property, not justified by military necessity and carried out unlawfully and wantonly', as a 'grave breach' of international law and requires its States Parties to recognize it accordingly in their domestic regimes.[48] Neither the subsequent 1977 Additional Protocols to the Geneva Conventions nor the 1998 Rome Statute of the International Criminal Court specifically addresses the theft or misappropriation of movable cultural objects. However, similar to the 1949 Fourth Geneva Convention, the Rome Statute classifies the destruction and appropriation of civilian property when not justified by military necessity as a war crime.[49]

Only by defining the large-scale theft and looting of cultural objects as a form of targeted destruction or by addressing theft and looting of cultural objects under general provisions governing pillage or seizure of property would these activities fall under these other legal instruments. Though not specific to cultural objects, these instruments have been a principal legal source for efforts to redress large-scale looting including, for example, the United Nations Security Council (UNSC) resolution demanding that Iraq return Kuwaiti cultural objects in the early 1990s.[50] Similar to the 1954 Hague Convention and its Protocols, the shortcoming of these

[47] For example, 1899 and 1907 Hague Conventions, arts 28, 47; 1949 Fourth Geneva Convention, arts 33, 147; Protocol Additional to the Geneva Conventions of 12 August 1949, and Relating to the Protection of Victims of Non-International Armed Conflicts (adopted 8 June 1977, opened for signature 12 December 1977, entered into force 7 December 1978) 1125 UNTS 609 (Additional Protocol II).

[48] 1949 Fourth Geneva Convention, arts 33, 147. Pillage and theft of movable property was also prohibited by the early Hague Conventions. 1899 and 1907 Hague Conventions, arts 28, 47. The indictment of Alfred Rosenberg, the head of the Einsatzstab Reichsleiter Rosenberg, at the Nuremberg trials included the charge of wanton confiscation of property. Much of this property consisted of cultural objects, but these were not specifically mentioned. *Trial of the Major War Criminals Before the International Military Tribunal (Nuremberg 14 November 1945 – 1 October 1946)* (42 vols, Intl Military Tribunal 1947–49) vol I, 29, 55–56.

[49] The Rome Statute includes as war crimes: 'Extensive destruction and appropriation of property, not justified by military necessity and carried out unlawfully and wantonly' (art 8(2)(a)(iv)); 'Pillaging a town or place, even when taken by assault' (art 8(2)(b)(xvi) (in international armed conflict) and art 8(2)(d)(v) (in non-international armed conflict)). Rome Statute of the International Criminal Court (adopted 17 July 1998, entered into force 1 July 2002) 2187 UNTS 3 (Rome Statute).

[50] UNSC Res 686 (2 March 1991) UN Doc S/RES/686, art 2(d) (calling on Iraq to return all Kuwaiti property seized by Iraq, including thousands of cultural objects seized from Kuwait's libraries, archives, and museums); Bruce P Montgomery, 'The Rape of Kuwait's National Memory' (2015) 22 IJCP 61.

instruments, particularly in the application of these instruments to trafficking in cultural objects, is that they largely prohibit only pillage and misappropriation. They criminalize such actions (in international law) or require Member States to criminalize it (in domestic law). However, they do not criminalize or prohibit the subsequent trafficking in these illegally removed cultural objects.

This demonstrates, at least in part, why reliance on provisions concerning general property, for which there is a limited or no subsequent market, does not fit the theft and appropriation of cultural objects, much of which is motivated by the potential of subsequent sales on the international market. Further, the separation of the treatment of cultural property into a different convention (the 1954 Hague Convention), rather than its inclusion in the 1949 Geneva Conventions, reinforces the lower status accorded by the international community to the protection of cultural property in the post-Second World War era. This produces the ironic result that the theft and pillage of ordinary movable property is treated more seriously than the theft and looting of cultural objects. Only by attaching illegality to the subsequent trafficking in cultural objects illegally removed during armed conflict and occupation can the motivation for such looting and theft be diminished and these activities deterred.

II. Regulation of International Movement of Cultural Objects

A. The 1970 UNESCO Convention and the 1995 UNIDROIT Convention

The international community has adopted two conventions that have as their purpose regulation of the international movement of cultural objects, particularly by removing or reducing incentives for illegal export and theft: the 1970 UNESCO Convention and the 1995 UNIDROIT Convention on Stolen or Illegally Exported Cultural Objects (1995 UNIDROIT Convention),[51] adopted under the auspices of the International Institute for the Unification of Private Law (UNIDROIT), an independent, intergovernmental organization. While these conventions would apply to all illegal movement of cultural objects, whether the movement began during armed conflict or during peacetime, their efficacy in the context of armed conflict is limited by two factors. The first is what a State must do in advance, in addition to ratification and implementation, for these conventions to be of use during periods

51 UNIDROIT Convention on Stolen or Illegally Exported Cultural Property (adopted 24 June 1995, entered into force 1 July 1998) 34 ILM 1322 (1995 UNIDROIT Convention). For additional discussion of the principal features of the 1970 UNESCO Convention and 1995 UNIDROIT Convention, and their use in claims for restitution of cultural objects not directly tied to armed conflict, see Janet Blake, 'Trafficking in Cultural Property: Where Cultural Heritage Law and the International Fight against Transnational Organized Crime Coincide' (Ch 6) in this volume.

of armed conflict? To restate this, does the convention and its various forms of implementation take a proactive or reactive approach? The second criterion is to what extent are these conventions useful for confronting the specific problems of illegal movement of previously undocumented objects and whose documentation is precluded either by the exigencies of armed conflict or by other factors, such as the appearance of previously unknown objects that are looted from an archaeological site or of indigenous objects. This latter difficulty is particularly relevant in light of the 1970 UNESCO Convention's requirement that cultural property be 'specifically designated' by each State Party.[52] The underlying question is whether a cultural object's illegal status, which may have been established under one of the Hague Convention instruments, follows the object onto the international market and into transit and final market countries through the mechanisms of either the 1970 UNESCO Convention or the 1995 UNIDROIT Convention.

The 1970 UNESCO Convention is the primary mechanism by which international law attempts to regulate the market in cultural objects.[53] Article 11 applies specifically to the theft and illegal removal of cultural objects from occupied territory, stating: 'The export and transfer of ownership of cultural property under compulsion arising directly or indirectly from the occupation of a country by a foreign power shall be regarded as illicit.' This provision carries an explicit limitation to removal from territory occupied by a State. It does not seem to have been specifically implemented by any of the major market countries, and it has not been utilized in any claim for restitution of cultural objects.

In 1995, at the request of UNESCO, UNIDROIT finalized its convention governing the trade in stolen or illegally exported cultural objects, the 1995 UNIDROIT Convention.[54] The Convention has forty-two States Parties. This Convention was intended to appeal to the States that have adopted some form of the good faith purchaser doctrine, which mandates that a good faith purchaser can acquire title to stolen property or is, at the least, entitled to compensation if the purchaser is required to return a stolen object to its original owner. Unlike the 1970 UNESCO Convention, which permits considerable variation in the method of implementation adopted by the different States Parties but then has equally varying efficacy, the UNIDROIT Convention requires full implementation of its provisions with little variation, which has proven to be an obstacle to wider State ratification. Another difference between the two conventions is that the UNIDROIT Convention pertains to private international law, and implementing legislation creates private rights of action for recovery of stolen and illegally exported cultural objects, whereas the 1970 UNESCO Convention operates exclusively on a State-to-State basis.

[52] 1970 UNESCO Convention, art 1.

[53] For a comprehensive review of the Convention, see Patrick J O'Keefe, *Protecting Cultural Objects: Before and After 1970* (IAL 2017).

[54] For a comprehensive review of the Convention, see Lyndel V Prott, *Commentary on the UNIDROIT Convention* (IAL 1997).

In analyzing the two conventions from the perspective of the issues outlined above, one needs to consider the different modes of implementation of the 1970 UNESCO Convention utilized by various market countries.[55] These models are (1) reciprocal import restrictions; (2) bilateral agreements implementing Article 3 (Switzerland) or Article 9 (United States); (3) hybrid approaches incorporating principles of the 1995 UNIDROIT Convention; and (4) reliance on an inventory or list principle. There are two fundamental flaws with utilization of the 1970 UNESCO Convention, depending on the model of implementation utilized. One flaw results from reliance on a list or inventory approach to satisfy the designation requirement and thereby determine which cultural objects are subject to import restriction. The second arises from those countries that have chosen primarily a reactive, rather than proactive, approach.

1. Designation requirement

One obstacle in utilizing the 1970 UNESCO Convention, particularly in the context of armed conflict and the looting of archaeological sites, is that it defines 'cultural property' in part as 'property which, on religious or secular grounds, is *specifically designated* by each State as being of importance for archaeology, prehistory, history, literature, art or science' and which belongs to one of an enumerated list of types of cultural objects.[56] The methods by which different countries have dealt with the specific designation requirement are important in evaluating the usefulness of the 1970 UNESCO Convention.

The implementing legislation of the United States explicitly removes the designation requirement from the definition of cultural property.[57] Those countries utilizing a reciprocal approach prohibit the import of cultural objects whose export is prohibited by another State Party.[58] This approach utilizes designation by category or type

[55] See Patty Gerstenblith, 'Implementation of the 1970 UNESCO Convention by the United States and Other Market Nations' in Jane Anderson and Haidy Geismar (eds), *The Routledge Companion to Cultural Property* (Routledge 2017) 70.

[56] Art 1 (emphasis added).

[57] Convention on Cultural Property Implementation Act, 19 USC s 2601(6).

[58] Pursuant to this form of implementation, any cultural property illegally exported from its country of origin, if that country is a 1970 UNESCO Convention State Party, cannot be imported. Australia enacted its implementing legislation in 1986 before becoming a State Party to the 1970 Convention in 1989. Read literally, the export controls of the Protection of Movable Cultural Heritage Act, as amended in 2011, apply to all illegally exported cultural objects, regardless of whether the State of origin is a Party to the 1970 UNESCO Convention. <http://www.comlaw.gov.au/Details/C2012C00239> accessed 1 November 2017. The export control that was violated only needs to be a 'law of that country relating to cultural property' (s 14(1)). In addition, it does not matter when the object was illegally exported from its country of origin, so long as the import into Australia occurred after the effective date of the legislation. Such an object is subject to forfeiture. However, this interpretation has been criticized on the ground that it would impose retroactive liability. Susan M Crennan, 'Review: Asian Art Provenance Project' National Gallery of Australia (17 February 2016) <https://nga.gov.au/AboutUs/press/pdf/NGAIndependentReview.pdf> accessed 1 November 2017. A person who knowingly violates the import prohibition commits an offense punishable by a fine not exceeding $100,000 (AUD) or imprisonment not exceeding five years or both (s 14(2)). However, the acquisition of cultural objects illegally removed from India and purchased by the National Gallery of Australia seems to indicate

rather than documentation in an inventory or on a list. In the case of Canada, which follows the category model of implementation,[59] when confronted with the question of what constitutes designation, a Canadian court held that the categorization of cultural objects for the purpose of export control by a State Party constitutes designation in compliance with the 1970 UNESCO Convention's requirement. In *R v Yorke*,[60] the court held that the Bolivian Decree, which restricted the export of the category of textiles, had thereby designated the category of textiles and was in compliance with the 1970 UNESCO Convention. The court understood the difficulty posed by a specific designation requirement, particularly as applied to archaeological and ethnographic objects that were undocumented before their illegal removal, stating:

> [T]he appellant's submission that, to 'specifically designate' cultural property something more was required of Bolivia than what was specified in the Decree, is not tenable. It would not be possible for a nation to create an itemized list of every piece of property to be protected. The categories have been made clear in the Decree …, and they apply to the items seized from the appellant. Likewise, the suggestion that the term 'weavings' is somehow overly broad and fails to distinguish those 'weavings' which are of cultural significance from those which are not, is not persuasive. The term 'weavings' is one of common usage and the Decree distinguishes them from property of other types of manufacture.… Textiles that are cultural property reveal valuable information regarding ethnic groups and their religious practices.[61]

This approach has not as yet been judicially evaluated in other destination or transit market nations.

When Germany first ratified the 1970 UNESCO Convention and enacted implementing legislation in 2007, it adopted the list or inventory principle and restricted the import of only those illegally exported cultural objects that had been individually classified in an accessible inventory by the country of origin. In an attempt to take account of the difficulties of inventorying freshly looted archaeological objects, the country of origin was given one year to inventory an archaeological object after learning of the illegal excavation.[62] However, in recognition

that Australia's law is not well enforced or lacks adequate enforcement mechanisms. Crennan, 20–25; Calla Wahlquist, 'National Gallery of Australia Returns Indian Antiquities Worth More than $2m' *The Guardian* (19 September 2016) <https://www.theguardian.com/culture/2016/sep/19/national-gallery-of-australia-returns-indian-antiquities-worth-more-than-2m> accessed 11 November 2017.

[59] Cultural Property Export and Import Act, RSC 1985, c C-51, s 37(2).

[60] *R v Yorke* [1998] 166 NSR (2d).

[61] ibid 150. This may be the only judicial interpretation of the specific designation requirement and how it can be satisfied.

[62] Act of 18 May 2007 Implementing the UNESCO Convention of 14 November 1970 on the Means of Prohibiting and Preventing the Illicit Import, Export and Transfer of Ownership of Cultural Property (Implementation Act) 18.5.2007, BGBl I, 2007, p 757, s 6(2) sentences 1–3.

that the list principle does not work for objects that cannot be inventoried, such as freshly looted archaeological materials or ethnographic objects, and other difficulties with the 2007 implementation,[63] in 2016 Germany amended its legislation[64] to require evidence of legal export from another State Party to the Convention if the object was exported after 2007.[65] On the other hand, Japan adopted and still applies the list principle in that its import restrictions apply only to 'cultural property that has been stolen from an institution' in accordance with Article 7(b)(i) of the Convention.[66] As such, Japan has implemented neither Article 3 nor Article 9 of the 1970 UNESCO Convention.

The 1995 UNIDROIT Convention deals with the problem of undocumented archaeological objects not only by removing any requirement of listing or designation but by providing at Article 3(2) that 'a cultural object which has been unlawfully excavated or lawfully excavated but unlawfully retained shall be considered stolen, when consistent with the law of the State where the excavation took place'. States that have ratified the 1995 UNIDROIT Convention have incorporated this provision, thereby eliminating any question of the legal status of looted undocumented archaeological objects. While clarifying the status of undocumented archaeological objects, this provision leaves less clear the status of undocumented non-archaeological objects.

The United Kingdom adopted its own approach, which may be viewed as a hybrid between the two Conventions. The Dealing in Cultural Objects (Offences) Act of 2003 prohibits dealing in 'tainted cultural objects'.[67] A tainted cultural object is one that '(a) is removed from a building or structure of historical, architectural or archaeological interest where the object has at any time formed part of the building or structure, or (b) it is removed from a monument of such interest'.[68]

[63] Robert Peters 'The Protection of Cultural Property: Recent Developments in Germany in the Context of New EU Law and the 1970 UNESCO Convention' (2016) 2 Santander Art & Culture L Rev 85, 96–97.

[64] Act on the Protection of Cultural Property (Cultural Property Protection Act – KGSG) 31.7.2016, BGBl I, 2016, p 1914. This was, at least in part, a response to the widespread looting that was occurring in Middle Eastern countries, particularly in Iraq and Syria, which is discussed in more detail in Section II.C.

[65] Federal Government Commissioner for Culture and the Media, *Key Aspects of the New Act on the Protection of Cultural Property in Germany*, p 7 (September 2016) <https://www.bundesregierung.de/Content/DE/_Anlagen/BKM/2016/2016-09-23-kulturgutschutz-informationen-englisch.pdf?__blob=publicationFile&v=2> accessed 1 November 2017. This shifts the burden to the importer to present such documentation; in the absence of such documentation, the cultural property is considered to have been unlawfully removed. The burden is further shifted onto the importer because the legislation creates a presumption that, in the absence of documentation that establishes otherwise, cultural objects were unlawfully exported from the relevant State Party after 2007.

[66] P J O'Keefe, *Protecting Cultural Objects* (n 53) 204–07. Article 7(b)(1) refers to objects that have been stolen from a 'museum or a religious or secular public monument or similar institution'.

[67] Dealing in Cultural Objects (Offences) Act 2003, ch 27, art 1. This legislation is not technically an implementation of the 1970 UNESCO Convention, as the United Kingdom took the position that it did not need to enact new legislation when it ratified the Convention. However, it adopted this legislation soon after ratification.

[68] ibid, art 4. Monument is defined to include any work, cave or excavation, and any site. ibid, art 5.

This legislation goes further than the UNIDROIT Convention because its prohibition is not limited to archaeological objects, although it is not clear whether it is broad enough to cover other categories of cultural objects that are often undocumented, such as ethnological objects.

2. Proactive and reactive approaches

Both the United States and Switzerland require a supplementary bilateral agreement to prevent the import of illegally exported cultural materials under the 1970 UNESCO Convention. Switzerland implements Article 3 of the Convention, so its import restrictions apply to the broader range of cultural property as defined in Article 1 of the Convention,[69] while the United States' agreements implement Article 9, thus applying only to archaeological and ethnological objects. United States import restrictions apply to the broader category of cultural property only under Article 7 of the Convention and thus require that the cultural property has been documented in the inventory of a public, either religious or secular, institution.[70] The United States currently has bilateral agreements with twenty[71] of the 1970 UNESCO Convention States Parties, while Switzerland has agreements with eight.[72]

The fundamental problem with the approach of the United States is that it is reactive in nature. Despite provisions for emergency situations, it requires a foreign State to initiate the process for a bilateral agreement by first bringing a request to the United States. The request must include supporting documentation for the statutory criteria required for an agreement, as well as for an emergency action.[73] The need for a request means that the United States and the requesting State have diplomatic relations, by which the request is submitted. This system seems intentionally designed to prevent the United States, the world's largest art market, from acting effectively even in emergency situations.

This process nullifies the idea of a proactive response even in the face of a crisis of looting and theft, such as in Iraq in 2003 and in Syria and Libya post-2011. This means that a country that is in crisis or falls into crisis may not be able to request an agreement or renew existing import restrictions. In the case of Iraq and Syria,

69 Federal Act on the International Transfer of Cultural Property (Cultural Property Transfer Act) (20 June 2003), art 7.

70 19 USC s 2607.

71 The US agreements are with: Algeria, Belize, Bolivia, Bulgaria, Cambodia, China, Colombia, Cyprus, Ecuador, Egypt, El Salvador, Greece, Guatemala, Honduras, Italy, Jordan, Libya, Mali, Nicaragua, and Peru. As of the end of 2019, requests for bilateral agreements with Chile, Morocco, Tunisia, Turkey, and Yemen are pending. The United States has imposed import restrictions on cultural materials from Iraq and Syria under its legislation's emergency provisions pursuant to special acts of Congress.

72 Switzerland's agreements are with Italy (2008), Greece (2011), Colombia (2011), Egypt (2011), Cyprus (2014), China (2014), Peru (2016), and Mexico (2017). Federal Office of Culture, 'Bilateral agreements' <https://www.bak.admin.ch/bak/en/home/cultural-heritage/transfer-of-cultural-property/bilateral-agreements.html> accessed 9 May 2018.

73 19 USC s 2603(c)(1).

the United States Congress had to enact special legislation to prohibit the import of illegally removed cultural objects given the difficulties of submitting a request to the United States under the US implementing legislation. On the other hand, Switzerland does not require that a country initiate a request for a bilateral agreement and, in the case of a crisis, may impose import restrictions under Article 9 on archaeological and ethnological materials without an agreement.[74]

The reactive approach of the United States is exacerbated by the need for a State Party to renew emergency restrictions after five years, and the renewal may last for only an additional three years. In addition, all bilateral agreements must be renewed every five years.[75] In contrast, Switzerland's agreements last for an indefinite period of time with no set date for expiration or requirement of a renewal process.

B. European Union Import Controls

The European Union has had controls on the export of cultural goods since 1992. The Council Regulation[76] deals with the question of export of cultural objects from the European Union by requiring an export license from the competent Member State.[77] Council Directive 93/7/EEC of 15 March 1993 on the Return of Cultural Objects Unlawfully Removed from the Territory of a Member State requires EU Member States to return cultural objects that have been unlawfully removed from another Member State.[78] However, this left unregulated the import of cultural

[74] Cultural Property Transfer Act (n 69) art 8 (allowing Switzerland to 'participate in common international actions in terms of Article 9, UNESCO Convention of 1970'). In early 2018, Libya succeeded in finalizing a bilateral agreement with the United States. 'Libya (18-223)—Memorandum of Understanding on Categories of Archaeological and Ethnological Materials' <https://www.state.gov/18-223/> accessed 19 June 2019.

[75] 19 USC s 2603(c)(3) (imposing eight-year limit on emergency actions); 19 USC s 2602(b) (imposing five-year limit on bilateral agreements); 19 USC s 2602(e) (allowing extensions of bilateral agreements for five years).

[76] The Council Regulation was originally adopted in 1992, Council Regulation (EEC) 3911/92 of 9 December 1992 on the export of cultural goods. In order to update the Regulation and incorporate several amendments into a single document, it was restated in 2008 as Council Regulation (EC) 116/2009 of 18 December 2008 on the export of cultural goods [2009] OJ L39/1 (Reg 116/2009).

[77] Reg 116/2009 (n 76) art 2(2). A competent Member State is defined as either the State 'in whose territory the cultural object in question was lawfully and definitively located on 1 January 1993' or 'in whose territory it is located following either lawful and definitive dispatch from another Member State, or importation from a third country, or re-importation from a third country after lawful dispatch from a Member State to that country.' Directive 2014/60/EU sets minimal standards for the issuance of an EU export license.

[78] Council Directive 93/7/EEC was recast as Directive 2014/60/EU with four substantial modifications: elimination of the annex with age or financial thresholds, thereby allowing each Member State to define its national cultural property; extension of the time limit to three years in which Member States must substantiate their claim for return; improving administrative cooperation among the Member States by using the Internal Market Information System; and shifting of the burden of proof so that a possessor must demonstrate due diligence in order to receive compensation as a good faith purchaser when relinquishing a cultural object. The Directive's due diligence provisions correspond to those in the 1995 UNIDROIT Convention. Peters (n 63) 94–95.

objects from non-EU Member States into the European Union[79] with the exception of cultural goods imported from Iraq[80] or Syria.[81]

In 2019, the European Parliament and the Council of the European Union adopted the Regulation on the Import of Cultural Goods to deal with the problem of illicitly trafficked cultural property imported into the European Union from non-EU Member States.[82] In Articles 3–5, the Regulation sets out the requirements, depending on the category of cultural goods, for an importer to obtain an import license from the EU State through which the cultural goods are introduced into the European Union, or to make an importer statement. Article 3 sets out the general principle that the import of cultural goods (Annex Part A), which were removed from the territory of the country where they were created or discovered in breach of the laws and regulations of that country, shall be prohibited. Article 4 (import license) applies to the types of cultural goods listed in Annex B[83] and includes (1) products of archaeological excavations and discoveries on land and underwater (including regular and clandestine) and (2) elements of artistic or historical monuments or archaeological sites that have been dismembered; for both categories the minimum age threshold of 250 years applies, however, without any financial threshold.[84] All other categories of cultural objects, namely cultural objects that are more than 200 years old and above the minimum financial threshold of €18,000 per item (Annex, Part C), do not require an import license but, rather, an importer statement.[85] When applying for an import license or submitting an importer statement, the importer must provide evidence or a signed declaration that the goods have been exported from their country of creation or discovery, in accordance with the laws and regulations of that country, or that the country does not have such laws or regulations.[86] However, in the alternative, evidence may be presented that the goods have been legally exported from an intermediary country where they have been located for more than five years and for purposes other than temporary use, transit, re-export or transshipment. This exception applies, however, only if the country of creation or discovery cannot be reliably determined or if the cultural goods were exported from the country of creation or discovery before 1972.[87] The limitation of the derogation to objects for which the country of origin cannot be reliably determined

[79] Peters (n 63) 98.

[80] Council Regulation (EC) 1210/2003 of 7 July 2003 concerning certain specific restrictions on economic and financial relations with Iraq and repealing Regulation [2003] OJ L169/6.

[81] Council Regulation (EU) 1332/2013 of 13 December 2013 concerning restrictive measures in view of the situation in Syria and amending Regulation (EU) 36/2012 concerning restrictive measures in view of the situation in Syria [2013] OJ L335/3, p 3.

[82] Regulation (EU) 2019/880 of the European Parliament and of the Council of 17 April 2019 on the introduction and the import of cultural goods [2019] OJ L151/1 (EU Import Regulation).

[83] ibid, Annex Part B.

[84] This provision may be modeled on the US implementation of Article 9 of the 1970 UNESCO Convention, 19 USC § 2601(2)(C)(i)(II), but is not a part of the Convention itself.

[85] EU Import Regulation, art 5.

[86] EU Import Regulation, art 4(4).

[87] ibid.

is an improvement over the draft proposal, which would have allowed import in any case in which an object was legally exported from an intermediary country. However, this still may provide a significant loophole in the effectiveness of the Regulation as it is often difficult to determine the country of modern discovery because ancient cultures and modern territorial boundaries often do not coincide.[88]

C. UN Security Council Resolutions

The patchwork quilt of ratifications and implementation of the 1970 UNESCO Convention and of the 1995 UNIDROIT Convention and the limited provisions of the 1954 Hague Convention regime with respect to stolen or looted cultural objects translate into an international treaty regime that is weak in controlling the movement of illegally obtained cultural objects. The international community has determined that the existing legal regime is insufficient to meet recent emergency threats to cultural heritage. As a result, on three occasions the United Nations Security Council has taken the unprecedented step of requiring its Member States to restrict the import of cultural objects outside the existing treaty regime and to bypass the ratification and implementation process of international treaties.

The first UNSC resolution to address specifically the status of cultural objects was Resolution 1483 adopted on 22 May 2003, in the wake of the looting of the Iraq Museum in Baghdad and of other cultural sites during the US-led invasion of Iraq. Paragraph 7 of UNSC Resolution 1483 states that the Security Council

> Decides that all Member States shall take appropriate steps to facilitate the safe return to Iraqi institutions of Iraqi cultural property and other items of archaeological, historical, cultural, rare scientific, and religious importance illegally removed from the Iraq National Museum, the National Library, and other locations in Iraq since the adoption of resolution 661 (1990) of 6 August 1990, including by establishing a prohibition on trade in or transfer of such items and items with respect to which reasonable suspicion exists that they have been illegally removed, and calls upon the United Nations Educational, Scientific, and Cultural Organization, Interpol, and other international organizations, as appropriate, to assist in the implementation of this paragraph.[89]

[88] For more detailed discussion of the Regulation, see Robert Peters 'Nationalism versus Internationalism: New Perspectives Beyond State Sovereignty and Territoriality in the Protection of Cultural Heritage' (Ch 15) in this volume.

[89] UNSC Res 1483 (22 May 2003) UN Doc S/RES/1483. One may note that most of the looting of cultural institutions in Iraq occurred during April 2003, while the armed conflict was still ongoing and before the United States was recognized as an occupying power. Thus, regardless of whether the 1954 First Protocol is considered part of customary international law, artifacts stolen from those institutions would not fall under the First Protocol's prohibitions. Looting of archaeological sites stretched into a longer period, at least into 2004 and possibly up until 2008. See Elizabeth C Stone, 'Patterns of Looting

Resolution 1483 was adopted under Chapter VII of the United Nations Charter and was therefore legally binding on all UN Member States. As a result, the United States, the United Kingdom, the European Union, and Switzerland, among market nations, adopted specific provisions implementing this resolution to prevent the import of and trade in cultural materials illegally removed from Iraq after the time of the initial trade sanctions that were imposed on Iraq in 1990.[90] It was the first time that States were required to prohibit import and trade in a defined category of cultural objects, not as a matter of their specific consent to be bound to a treaty provision but through membership in the United Nations.

The international community took a similar approach after the civil war in Syria, which began in March 2011, morphed first into armed conflict not of an international character, then into the sweeping territorial expansion of ISIL in eastern Syria and northwestern Iraq beginning in 2014, and then into international armed conflict with the entry of multiple State actors.[91] Multiple Parties to the conflict destroyed cultural heritage, both intentionally and as collateral damage, stole objects from institutions and looted from archaeological sites. Anecdotal reports,[92] confirmed through satellite imagery,[93] and documents recovered from a raid on an ISIL compound[94] indicated that ISIL had orchestrated large-scale looting of sites and thefts from institutions in order to provide a stream of income to fund its terrorist activities and armed conflict. There has been considerable debate as to the extent of funding ISIL has realized or may realize in the future from looted cultural objects. However, at this time, such a figure is inherently 'unknowable'. Based on

in Southern Iraq' (2008) 82 Antiquity 125; 'An Update on the Looting of Archaeological Sites in Iraq' (2015) 78 Near Eastern Archaeology 178.

[90] Emergency Protection for Iraqi Cultural Antiquities Act of 2004, Pub L No 108-429, 118 Stat 2434, ss 3001–03 (United States); Iraq (United Nations Sanctions) Order 2003, SI 2003/1519, s 8 (United Kingdom); Council Regulation (EC) 1210/2003 of 7 July 2003 concerning certain specific restrictions on economic and financial relations with Iraq and repealing Regulation (EC) 2465/96 [2003] OJ L169/6, art 3 (European Union); Ordonnance instituant des mesures économiques envers la République d'Irak RS 946.206, art 1a, modified 28 May 2003 (Switzerland).

[91] For more detailed discussion of the effect of the Syrian conflict on cultural heritage, see Patty Gerstenblith, 'The Destruction of Cultural Heritage: A Crime against Property or a Crime against People?' (2016) 15 John Marshall Rev Intellectual Prop L 336, 372–77.

[92] Amr al-Azm, Salam al-Kuntar, and Brian I Daniels, 'ISIS' Antiquities Sideline' Op-Ed, *NY Times* (2 September 2014) <http://www.nytimes.com/2014/09/03/opinion/isis-antiquities-sideline.html?_r=0> accessed 1 November 2017.

[93] Susan Wolfinbarger and others, 'Ancient History, Modern Destruction: Assessing the Status of Syria's World Heritage Sites Using High-Resolution Satellite Imagery' (American Association for the Advancement of Science 2014) <http://www.aaas.org/page/ancient-history-modern-destruction-assessing-current-status-syria-s-world-heritage-sites-using> accessed 1 November 2017; Jesse Casana, 'Satellite Imagery-Based Analysis of Archaeological Looting in Syria' (2015) 78 Near Eastern Archaeology 142; Jesse Casana and Elise Jakoby Laugier, 'Satellite Imagery-Based Monitoring of Archaeological Site Damage in the Syrian Civil War' (2017) 12 PLoSOne <https://doi.org/10.1371/journal.pone.0188589> accessed 1 November 2017.

[94] US Department of State, Bureau of Educational and Cultural Affairs, 'ISIL Leader's Loot' <http://eca.state.gov/cultural-heritage-center/iraq-cultural-heritage-initiative/isil-leaders-loot> accessed 1 November 2017.

information obtained from the raid on the ISIL compound in May 2015, US government officials estimated that ISIL earned several million dollars during an approximate year from mid-2014 to mid-2015. Receipts found on Abu Sayyaf's hard drive, for example, indicate a tally of US$265,000 as being realized from the sale of antiquities. However, it is not known over how long a period of time these profits were gained or over how large a territory.[95]

In response to this information and upon recommendation of the ISIL (Daesh) and Al-Qaida Sanctions Committee and Monitoring Team,[96] in February 2015, the Security Council adopted Resolution 2199. This Resolution reaffirmed the commitment of Resolution 1483 to prevent trade in cultural materials illegally removed from Iraq after August 1990 and called for new prohibitions on trade in cultural materials illegally removed from Syria after March 2011, the beginning of the civil war.[97] Resolution 2199 also condemned the destruction of cultural heritage in

[95] Remarks of Andrew Keller, Deputy Assistant Secretary Bureau of Economic Affairs, US Department of State (29 September 2015) <http://eca.state.gov/video/conflict-antiquities-panel-1-video/transcript> accessed 1 November 2017. For an early discussion of unreliable media reporting on the extent of ISIL's revenue from antiquities looting and smuggling, see 'Danti's Inference: The Known Unknowns of ISIS and Antiquities Looting' (*Chasing Aphrodite*, 18 November 2014) <http://chasingaphrodite.com/2014/11/18/dantis-inference-the-known-unknowns-of-isis-and-antiquities-looting/> accessed 1 November 2017.

[96] The Al-Qaida and Taliban Sanctions Committee was originally established in 1999, pursuant to Security Council Resolution 1267. In 2011, pursuant to Resolutions 1988 and 1989, it was split into two separate Committees. United Nations Security Council Subsidiary Organs: Security Council Committee Pursuant to Resolutions 1267 (1999), 1989 (2011) and 2253 (2015) concerning ISIL (Daesh), Al-Qaida and Associated Individuals, Groups Undertakings and Entities <https://www.un.org/sc/suborg/en/sanctions/1267> accessed 1 November 2017. The 1267 Sanctions Regime, monitored by the ISIL (Daesh), Al-Qaida and Taliban Monitoring Team, is the only sanctions regime that applies to transnational non-State actors who constitute a global, regional, or local threat or an evolving and asymmetric threat using unconventional methods and weapons. In Resolution 2170, the Security Council directed the sanctions monitoring team to report on the continuing threat posed by ISIL and Al-Nusra Front and their sources of funding and to present recommendations to the Security Council. UNSC Res 2170 (15 August 2017) UN Doc S/RES/2170, para 22. This resolution also notes that ISIL and Al-Nusra Front are splinter groups of Al-Qaida. Para 18.

[97] UNSC Res 2199 (12 February 2015) UN Doc S/RES/2199, paras 15–17. The resolution has been implemented by the European Union, Council Regulation (EU) 1332/2013 of 13 December 2013 amending Regulation (EU) 36/2012 concerning restrictive measures in view of the situation in Syria, art 4 adding art 11c, Annex XI; by the United Kingdom as a criminal provision, The Export Control (Syria Sanctions (Amendment)) Order 2014, SI 2014/1896, para 2 (inserting art 12A) <http://www.legislation.gov.uk/uksi/2014/1896/made> accessed 1 November 2017; and by Switzerland, *Verordnung über Massnahmen gegenüber Syrien* (Ordinance on Sanctions against Syria) revised on 17 December 2014, art 9A, para 1 <http://www.admin.ch/opc/de/official-compilation/2015/45.pdf> accessed 1 November 2017. The United States finally implemented Resolution 2199 in 2016 with the Protect and Preserve International Cultural Property Act, Pub L 114-151, 130 Stat 369 (2016). This legislation provides for import restrictions on cultural materials illegally removed from Syria after March 2011. In 2016, the US Department of Justice took the unusual step of issuing a forfeiture complaint for antiquities that were recorded in the Abu Sayyaf documents but were not found in his compound. *United States v One Gold Ring with Carved Gemstone*, Case 1:16-cv-02442 (DDC 15 December 2016) <https://www.justice.gov/usao-dc/press-release/file/918536/download> accessed 28 January 2020. The items include a gold ring and several gold coins, of the Hellenistic to Roman period, and the top of a carved stele of the Neo-Assyrian period, dated to approximately the mid-ninth century BCE. The Department of Justice issued an amended complaint in 2017, adding three antiquities but also stating that there was probable cause to believe that the previously identified ring had been sold in Turkey for approximately US$250,000. Turkish authorities have confiscated the ring. 'United States Seeks Warrant to Seize Ring Trafficked by

Iraq and Syria, 'whether such destruction is incidental or deliberate, including targeted destruction of religious sites and objects'.[98] This Security Council Resolution marked a significant change in how the international community perceives theft and looting of movable cultural objects based on the recognition that such objects could be sold on the market to provide funding for armed conflict within Syria and Iraq and terrorist activity both in the Middle East and abroad. The condemnation of incidental destruction also marks a departure from the narrower provisions of the 1954 Hague Convention, which do not clearly define what is meant by military necessity and might be interpreted to excuse incidental destruction that results from military action. By condemning incidental destruction, the Security Council Resolution indicates incorporation of the principles of proportionality, feasibility, and distinction, perhaps as a reflection of customary international law as well as of the 1999 Second Protocol to the 1954 Hague Convention.

In March 2017, the UN Security Council took another landmark step in adopting Resolution 2347, which focuses almost exclusively on the theft, looting, and movement of cultural objects from Syria and Iraq.[99] As with UNSC Resolution 2199, this resolution was largely motivated by data indicating that the theft, looting, and sale onto the international market of cultural objects were sources of income to ISIL and that cultural objects had become intertwined with trafficking networks and other forms of cross-border movement of contraband goods, such as drugs and weapons.[100] Resolution 2347 has three main elements: a recognition of the general international law principles[101] that aim to protect cultural heritage and prevent destruction; general concern with terrorism and its financing through international networks; and the specific role in terrorism finance of the looting of archaeological sites and thefts from cultural institutions, whether directly or indirectly orchestrated by ISIL, al-Nusra Front, or other terrorist groups.

ISIS' (6 December 2017) <https://www.justice.gov/usao-dc/pr/united-states-seeks-warrant-seize-ring-trafficked-islamic-state-iraq-and-syria-isis> accessed 11 December 2017.

[98] UNSC Res 2199 (n 98) para 15. The Security Council had also condemned cultural heritage destruction in Mali in Resolutions 2085 and 2100. UNSC Res 2085 (20 December 2012) UN Doc S/RES/2085; UNSC Res 2100 (25 April 2013) UN Doc S/RES/2100.

[99] UNSC Res 2347 (24 March 2017) UN Doc S/RES/2347.

[100] For a discussion of the international legal regimes dedicated to combatting organized transnational crime, including the trafficking of cultural objects and other contraband goods by organized transnational criminal networks, see Janet Blake, 'Trafficking in Cultural Property: Where Cultural Heritage Law and the International Fight against Transnational Organized Crime Coincide' (Ch 6) in this volume.

[101] As one would expect, Resolution 2347 cites a litany of cultural property/heritage conventions: the 1954 Hague Convention and its two Protocols, the 1970 UNESCO Convention, the 1972 UNESCO Convention on the World Cultural and Natural Heritage, the 2003 Convention for the Safeguarding of the Intangible Cultural Heritage, and the 2005 Convention on the Protection and Promotion of the Diversity of Cultural Expressions. In contrast, it does not refer to the 1995 Unidroit Convention, although, as previously noted, this convention focuses on illegal trafficking of cultural objects. UNSC Res 2347 Preamble, para 12.

For the most part, Resolution 2347 focuses on the role of looted and stolen cultural objects in financing terrorism and associated criminal activities, money laundering, bribery, and corruption, but it also cites other elements of international law that aim to protect cultural heritage more generally. The resolution acknowledges that 'the attempt to deny historical roots and cultural diversity in this context can fuel and exacerbate conflict and hamper post-conflict national reconciliation, thereby undermining the security, stability, governance, social, economic and cultural development of affected States'.[102] The resolution also recognizes the prosecution at the International Criminal Court of Ahmad Al Faqi Al Mahdi for directing the destruction of mosques and shrines at the World Heritage Site of Timbuktu in Mali[103] and affirms that directing unlawful attacks against cultural sites and structures may constitute a war crime.[104]

Despite the expansive sentiments expressed in Resolution 2347, it is limited on substantive provisions and even more limited on requirements for Member States. The resolution '*[r]equests*' that Member States take appropriate steps to fulfill the provisions of the earlier two resolutions on trafficking in cultural materials from Syria and Iraq, which is arguably a derogation from the mandatory language of UNSC Resolution 1483 and UNSC Resolution 2199,[105] and recalls a general requirement that States ensure that no funds or economic resources be provided to ISIL, Al-Qaida, and those affiliated with them.[106] Several provisions call for, urge, or encourage cooperation among States and various intergovernmental organizations, such as UNESCO, UNODC, and INTERPOL,[107] and preventive measures within States.[108]

Even Paragraph 17, which comes the closest to having substantive content, '*Calls upon* Member States . . . to *consider* adopting' the outlined measures.[109] These measures include improving inventories; adopting regulations on export and import; contributing to and updating the World Customs Organization Harmonized System Nomenclature and Classification of Goods;[110] establishing specialized units

[102] UNSC Res 2347 Preamble, para 5.

[103] *Prosecutor v Al Mahdi* (Trial Judgment and Sentence) ICC-01/12-01/15-171 (27 September 2016). In March 2018, a second defendant was referred to the International Criminal Court for prosecution for destruction of cultural heritage in Mali as well as crimes against humanity, including torture, rape, sexual slavery, and persecution on religious and gender grounds. *Prosecutor v Al Hassan* (Arrest Warrant) ICC-01/12-01/18 (27 March 2018); *Prosecutor v Al Hassan* (Decision constituting Trial Chamber X and referring to it the case of *Prosecutor v. Al Hassan*) ICC-01/12-01/18 ICC-01/12-01/18 (21 November 2019).

[104] UNSC Res 2347, para 4.

[105] ibid, para 8. The 'request' language of UNSCR 2347 contrasts with the language of UNSC Res 1483, which states that the Security Council '*Decides* that all Member States *shall* . . .' (emphases added). UNSC Res 2199 uses the same mandatory language.

[106] UNSC Res 2347, para 8.

[107] ibid, paras 11, 12.

[108] ibid, paras 9, 12, 16.

[109] ibid, para 17 (emphasis added).

[110] The Harmonized Tariff Schedule has a single statistical breakout for 'Archaeological, historical, or ethnographic pieces' (9705.00.00.70), which means that it is not possible to determine the extent of imports in any one of these categories. See 19 USC s 1202, Harmonized Tariff Schedule (2017

among law enforcement and national databases; contributing to databases maintained by intergovernmental organizations, such as UNESCO, INTERPOL, and WCO, which track criminal activity and law enforcement efforts; engaging museums and the trade in improving provenance documentation and due diligence standards; inventorying cultural objects removed from areas of armed conflict, and undertaking efforts to educate and raise awareness concerning illegal trafficking in cultural objects. While encouraging cooperation, information sharing, and better documentation among the various national agencies and intergovernmental organizations is positive, this resolution is remarkably short on substantive requirements. In particular, the focus on documentation is likely to be frustrated because antiquities looted from the ground and sold directly onto the international market cannot be documented—a feature that makes freshly looted antiquities particularly well-suited as a vehicle for money laundering, terrorism finance, and other criminal activity.

Even these Security Council resolutions are themselves insufficient. They are reactive in nature and are targeted to specific countries.[111] Therefore, like the domestic legislation of some market countries (such as that of the United States in implementing the 1970 UNESCO Convention), the resolutions do not prepare us to deal with the *next* crisis—especially if the next crisis does not share a link with funding of armed conflict and international terrorism or if the situation has not captured the world's attention through the media. When taken together, the three resolutions constitute a striking acknowledgement by the international community that the existing treaty regime is inadequate to prevent trade in cultural objects illegally removed from areas of armed conflict.

This inadequacy is the result of a failure to link sufficiently the armed conflict treaties (that is, the 1954 Hague Convention and its Protocols), even given their shortcomings as previously discussed, with those treaties that aim to regulate the international market, particularly the 1970 UNESCO Convention and the 1995 UNIDROIT Convention. What is needed is a mechanism to create an intersection among these treaty regimes whereby illegal removal during armed conflict or occupation renders the object illegal on the international market and in transit and destination countries, so this illegality follows and stays with the object, rather than having the object enter into a different legal regime as it travels through the world.

HTSA Revision 1 Edition). In 2018, sub-categories were added so that an importer must distinguish among the three categories (archaeological, historical, ethnographic). This is intended to improve recordkeeping and analysis of the archaeological and ethnographic objects imported into the United States. See Harmonized Tariff Schedule of the United States 9705.00.00.80 and the Statistical Notes defining 'Archaeological pieces' and 'Ethnographic pieces'.

[111] For discussion of these failures, see Neil Brodie, 'Syria and its Regional Neighbors: A Case of Cultural Property Protection Policy Failure?' (2015) 22 IJCP 317.

This situation also constitutes a failure because, while the link to terrorism finance is real enough in Syria and Iraq, Resolution 2347 indicates that the world is not concerned with preserving cultural heritage for its own sake and broadly throughout the world (despite the resolution's hortatory statements in that regard). Rather, the world community is moved to action to compensate for a weak treaty regime only when other criminal activity and funding of terrorism and armed conflict are specifically implicated. A good example of this failure is the lack of mechanisms for dealing with the similar crisis in Libya, which has simply not received the same level of attention as the cultural heritage destruction perpetrated in Syria and Iraq.[112]

It is neither politically feasible nor realistic to expect the Security Council to continuously adopt resolutions on a country-by-country basis. Nor is it realistic for market and other States to adopt legislation on a country-by-country basis. Furthermore, given the haphazard nature of such resolutions and implementing legislation, this approach fails in the essential function of deterring the market through dampening demand, which, in turn, would reduce the incentive to supply the market. International conventions exist to provide a relatively uniform mechanism for carrying out stated objectives upon which the international community has reached consensus. Reliance on Security Council resolutions to fulfill this function and to fill the lacunae that the current international treaty regime has created is doomed to fail within the broader scope of the goal of protecting cultural heritage.

III. Remaining Questions

Two questions remain to be addressed concerning how the international treaty regime treats movable cultural objects. The first of these is to whom or to where should a cultural object be returned. The second is how the international treaty regime can be modified to link the armed conflict instruments with the international trade treaties.

A. To Whom or to Where Should Cultural Objects Be Returned?

The First Protocol is clear in stating that an object removed illegally from occupied territory should be returned to that territory at the end of the occupation. This establishes the basic norm of territoriality—that an object should be returned to the place from which it was last illegally removed, even if it had previously been

[112] Neil Brodie 'Why Is No One Talking about Libya's Cultural Destruction?' (2015) 78 Near Eastern Archaeology 212.

illegally removed from a different location. However, given the limited applicability of the First Protocol, this issue requires closer examination.

1. Place of last removal versus original location

A paradigmatic example is presented by the story of the horses of St Mark's (San Marco).[113] Although the origin of the four horses is unknown, they were located in Constantinople (modern Istanbul), possibly in the Hippodrome, as of the time of Constantine the Great in the first third of the fourth century. They were plundered during the Fourth Crusade and brought to Venice in 1204 where they were placed in the Basilica of St Mark. They remained there until Venice fell to Napoleon. Napoleon brought them to Paris in 1798 where they entered the city as part of a triumphal procession, mimicking those of the Roman emperors.[114] After Napoleon's defeat, the Venetian sculptor Antonio Canova succeeded in having the horses returned to Venice and St Mark's Basilica in 1815. They are now housed inside the basilica to protect them from air pollution, and copies stand in their place on the balcony. At the time of their return to Venice, the question of return to Istanbul, rather than to Venice, does not seem to have been considered as an option. While this may reflect a Eurocentric approach and reinforces the nineteenth-century principle that international laws applied only to European countries,[115] it also fit the pattern that art works taken during armed conflict are returned to the place from which they were last taken. This result has a relative advantage of certainty. It is likely known whence an object was most recently taken but perhaps the original location is not known, as also demonstrated by the St Mark's horses. However, several examples test this principle and, in some cases, bring it into serious question.

2. State versus local authorities

An example that raises the question of proper return involves the disposition of 565 objects, including jewelry, weapons, decorative objects, and a Chinese lacquer box, that were on loan from museums in Crimea first to Bonn and then to the Allard Pierson Museum in Amsterdam in 2014.[116] The loan agreements stipulated that the artifacts would be returned to the respective museums, one in Kyiv and four in Crimea, at the end of the exhibition. In March 2014, while the works were

[113] For more detailed discussion, see Charles Freeman, *The Horses of St. Mark's* (Overlook 2004).

[114] Andrew McClellan, *Inventing the Louvre: Art, Politics, and the Origins of the Modern Museum in Eighteenth-Century Paris* (CUP 1994) 122–23, 149.

[115] Vrdoljak points out that indigenous and colonized peoples, as well as non-Europeans in general, were excluded from the protections of international law over the course of the nineteenth century. Vrdoljak (n 19) 47–50. Thus art works that Napoleon took from outside Europe, such as from Egypt, were not returned.

[116] For an in-depth discussion of this case, see Campfens (n 32). See also Evelien Campfens and Irina Tarsis, 'Cri-Me-A-River! Crimean Gold in the Crosshairs of Geopolitics' (2017) 18 IFAR J 36; Maria Nudelman, 'Who Owns the Scythian Gold? The Legal and Moral Implications of Ukraine and Crimea's Cultural Dispute' (2015) 38 Fordham Intl L J 1262 (this discussion predated the December 2016 court ruling).

in Amsterdam, Russia annexed Crimea. The Ukrainian Ministry of Culture then cancelled the loan agreements and, claiming that the State is the rightful owner, requested the early return of the objects to Kiev, rather than to Crimea. In November 2014, the four Crimean museums filed suit in Amsterdam to recover the objects and Ukraine entered the case a few months later. The Crimean museums and Russian authorities argued that 'valuables can only be kept in the region where they were found. . . . They are Crimea's heritage'.[117] On the other hand, Ukraine argued that the artifacts 'are part of its national patrimony, protected by international conventional laws' based on its sovereign rights.[118]

In December 2016, the Amsterdam District Court ruled that the works should be returned to Ukraine, rather than to Crimea,[119] apparently affirming that it is the State that operates, at least on the international level, as the owner and responsible party for cultural heritage. The District Court first held that the loan agreements had been terminated, due to a 'material change in circumstances' as provided for under both Ukraine and the Netherlands law, thereby cancelling the obligation to return the artifacts to the museums from which they had come. Ukraine argued that the artifacts were State property based on laws making the collections of the Crimean museums State property and vesting ownership of all archaeological finds in the State.[120]

The Amsterdam court sidestepped the question of ownership, on the grounds that ownership should be decided after the artifacts are returned, and decided the case, instead, on the basis of the Heritage Act of 2016, the Netherlands' law implementing the 1970 UNESCO Convention.[121] The court held that the cancellation of the loan agreements and therefore also of the export licenses from Ukraine, along with the non-return of the objects, effectively made the export of the artifacts from Ukraine illegal. This, in turn, made their import into the Netherlands illegal under the Dutch Heritage Act. The court found this to be consistent with Ukraine's law as well as with the goals of the 1970 UNESCO Convention to prevent illegal export of cultural objects. The court also cited the 2014 European Directive on unlawfully removed cultural objects and the 1995 UNIDROIT Convention, 'both

[117] 'Crimean Museums Appeal Court Ruling Returning Scythian Gold To Kyiv' (Radio Free Europe/Radio Liberty, 26 January 2017) <www.rferl.org/a/crimean-museums-appeal-dutch-court-ruling-scythian-gold-return-to-kyive/28260071.html> accessed 1 November 2017 (quoting Natalya Poklonskaya, a Russian parliament deputy). Of course, political considerations may have entered into the decision, given that the West has not recognized Russia's annexation of Crimea as legitimate. Russia has filed an appeal with the Dutch Supreme Court.

[118] Campfens (n 32) 198.

[119] *Tavrida Central Museum and others v Universiteit van Amsterdam*, Rb (First Instance Ct) Amsterdam 16 March 2018, rolnr HA ZA 14-1179; Nina Siegal, 'Museum Pieces on Loan from Crimea Belong to Ukraine, Dutch Court Rules' *NY Times* (14 December 2016) <www.nytimes.com/2016/12/14/arts/design/crimea-ukraine-allard-pierson-museum-amsterdam.html?mcubz=3> accessed 1 November 2017.

[120] Campfens (n 32) 199.

[121] Act of 9 December 2015, Relating to the Combining and Amendment of Rules Regarding Cultural Heritage.

of which include in their definition of "unlawfully removed" cultural objects, objects that were not returned at the end of a period of lawful temporary removal'.[122] This decision reaffirms that the law of the State of origin (*lex originis*) determines what constitutes unlawful transfer of cultural objects, which, in turn, defines illegal import for other UNESCO Convention State Parties. Although not resolving the question of ownership, the District Court held that the return claim of the State would have priority over that of a third party.[123] While a decision in the appeal has been postponed until at least 2020, the resolution to this point illustrates the tension between local or regional governments and a national government.[124]

A variation on the problem posed by the change in the status of Crimea may result when a country undergoes extreme regime change so that, arguably, the government is no longer the same as the previous government. In such a case, the 'people' of a State may be viewed as distinct from the State itself. An example would be the transfer of the Hungarian Crown of St Stephen and other royal regalia to the United States at the end of the Second World War to protect them from the Soviets. However, the United States refused to return the regalia for three decades on the grounds of its (political) opposition to the Communist government of Hungary.[125] In this case, even distinct from the case of Crimea, it seems clear that the regalia should have been returned to Hungary, once asked to do so and where a return would not have threatened the safety of the objects. The refusal of the United States to do so was a result of geopolitical, rather than cultural or legal, considerations.

3. State versus minority community

International treaties, such as the 1970 UNESCO Convention, exacerbate this problem because they operate exclusively on a State-to-State basis. Questions of proper disposition also arise when a national government is not viewed as adequately representing the interests of a local, often minority or indigenous, population or, conversely, when the community with cultural connections no longer

[122] Campfens (n 32) 201.

[123] ibid 202, citing Article 1012 of the Dutch Code of Civil Procedure, which states that 'ownership of the cultural object that is subject to a return request by a State Party will be decided upon after return by the national laws of the state that claimed for its return.' This provision of the Code of Civil Procedure implements article 13 of the 2014 EU Regulation.

[124] According to one news report of the postponement of the decision, the appeals court rejected the rationale behind the earlier court's decision. In its statement, the appeals court said the four Crimean museums could claim ownership on the basis of their appointment by the Ukraine government as the custodians of the objects. However, according to this statement, any ownership rights of the Crimean museums would be derivative from the ownership rights of the State by means of Ukrainian administrative law. Bart Meijer, 'Dutch Appeals Court Postpones Verdict on Crimean Gold' *Reuters* (16 July 2019) <https://www.reuters.com/article/us-russia-ukraine-crimean-gold/dutch-appeals-court-postpones-verdict-on-crimean-gold-idUSKCN1UB0TV> accessed 19 September 2019.

[125] Paul Hofmann, 'Crown of St. Stephen Formally Returned to Hungary' *NY Times* (7 January 1978) <www.nytimes.com/1978/01/07/archives/crown-of-st-stephen-formally-returned-to-hungary-emotion-was.html> accessed 16 March 2018.

resides for the most part within that State. In both cases, restitution to a national government may conflict with cultural connections.

When an object is returned to a country of origin, the object then may not be returned to the community with the closest cultural connections to the objects but may, instead, be housed in a national museum in the capital city or elsewhere. The local community may have little control over this disposition. This problem is particularly acute where a minority indigenous or descendant community is located within a territorial sovereign that has a predominantly distinct majority culture. For example, when the United States returns an archaeological or ethnological artifact under its implementation of Article 9 of the 1970 UNESCO Convention, the object is returned to the national government,[126] rather than to a local or indigenous community from which it may have originated and which has the closest cultural connections to the objects.

In this regard, Campfens points to the United Nations Declaration of Rights of Indigenous Peoples, which states that 'States shall provide redress through effective mechanisms, which may include restitution, developed in conjunction with indigenous peoples, with respect to their cultural, intellectual, religious and spiritual property taken without their free, prior and informed consent or in violation of their laws, traditions and customs.'[127] The acknowledgement by the Special Rapporteur for the UN Human Rights Council in the field of Cultural Rights, Karima Bennoune, of the need for intersection between the fields of human rights and cultural heritage provides a path toward reconciling the rights of minority communities within larger States to control and have access to their cultural heritage. It may also provide a justification for overriding concerns of sovereignty in particular cases involving the rights of indigenous groups.[128]

Another tension arises when the geographic extent of an ancient or modern cultural group is outside the modern State that controls that territory. One example of this is the conflict over the disposition of what has been dubbed the 'Iraqi Jewish archive'. In April 2003, as American forces fought to take Baghdad, they discovered in the flooded basement of the headquarters of Saddam Hussein's secret police (the *mukhabarat*) a cache of some 2,700 books and several thousand other documents belonging to the remnants of the Iraqi Jewish community.[129]

[126] 19 USC s 2609(b) (stating that '[a]ny designated archaeological or ethnological material which is imported into the United States in violation of section 2606 ... and which is forfeited to the United States under this chapter shall—(1) first be offered to the State Party').

[127] Campfens (n 32) 206 (citing UNGA Res 61/295 (13 September 2007) UN Doc A/RES/61/295, art 11(2)).

[128] UNHRC 'Report of the Special Rapporteur in the field of cultural rights' (2016) UN Doc A/HRC/31/59 (3 February 2016); UNHRC, Report of the Special Rapporteur in the field of Cultural Rights (2016) UN Doc A/71/317 (9 August 2016).

[129] Edward Rothstein, 'The Remnants of a Culture's Heart and Soul: Iraqi Jewish Documents at the National Archives' *NY Times* (10 November 2013) <www.nytimes.com/2013/11/11/arts/design/iraqi-jewish-documents-at-the-national-archives.html?mcubz=3.> accessed 1 November 2017. A first-hand account is given by Harold Rhode, at the time a policy analyst with the Office of Net Assessments in the Office of the Secretary of Defense, then assigned to the Coalition Provisional Authority. Harold Rhode,

An unexploded coalition bomb had pierced the water pipes of the building and caused the flooding. The United States government decided to preserve the documents through freezing and drying processes and brought them to the United States where, after some preservation efforts carried out by the National Archives, they remain and their ultimate disposition is contested. Portions of the collection have been digitized and are available online; a smaller number have been exhibited at various locations.[130]

The United States, although neither a State Party nor signatory to the First Protocol to the 1954 Hague Convention, seemed to acknowledge that removal from occupied territory without the consent of Iraq would violate international law.[131] At the time of the removal in the summer of 2003, the United Nations Security Council, under Resolution 1483, had recognized the United States as the occupying power of Iraq.[132] While the First Protocol was not technically applicable, unless it is viewed as a part of customary international law, Article 56 of the 1907 Hague Convention, forbidding seizure of works of art and science, was still binding on the United States.

The US National Archives and Records Administration signed an agreement with the Coalition Provisional Authority, acting as the occupying power on behalf of the Iraqi government, allowing the removal of the archive but requiring return of the materials after two years.[133] However, the agreement to return the archive was ignored for several years and then extended with successive Iraqi governments.[134] The continuation of the agreement is a recognition by the United States that the archive belongs to Iraq based on a territorial understanding of cultural

'Outrage: U.S. Returning Artifacts Looted from Iraqi Jews to Iraq, Instead of Lawful Owners' *PJ Media* (26 August 2013) <https://pjmedia.com/blog/outrage-u-s-returning-artifacts-looted-from-iraqi-jews-to-iraq-instead-of-lawful-owners/?singlepage=true.> accessed 1 November 2017

[130] 'Discovery and Recovery: Preserving Iraqi Jewish Heritage' (Preserving the Iraqi Jewish Archive) <https://ija.archives.gov/exhibit/exhibit.> accessed 1 November 2017. The online database has some 3,846 entries.

[131] It is worth noting that the United States did not seem to be equally concerned about several other archives removed from Iraq both in the early 1990s and in 2003 and still retained in the United States. See Arbella Bet-Shimon, 'Preservation or Plunder? The ISIS Files and History of Heritage Removal in Iraq' Middle East Research and Information Project (8 May 2018) <www.merip.org/mero/mero050818> accessed 10 May 2018.

[132] UNSC Res 1483 (22 May 2003) UN Doc S/RES/1483, Preamble, para 13 (recognizing the United States and United Kingdom and their 'specific authorities, responsibilities, and obligations … as occupying powers').

[133] 'Iraq Urges U.S. to Give Back Iraqi Jewish Archive' *The Associated Press* (16 January 2010) <https://www.haaretz.com/jewish/news/iraq-urges-u-s-to-give-back-iraqi-jewish-archive-1.261536> accessed 1 November 2017.

[134] Each time the agreement is close to expiring, public pressure is brought on the United States not to return the archive and the agreement is renewed. For example Rhode (n 129); Carole Basri and David Dangoor, 'The Iraqi Jewish Archive is Stolen Property that Should Go Back to Its Original Owners' *The Hill* (27 April 2018) <http://thehill.com/opinion/international/385072-the-iraqi-jewish-archive-is-stolen-property-that-should-go-back-to-its> accessed 7 May 2018.

heritage. However, this contradicts the cultural connection between the archive and the communities of Iraqi Jews, who were persecuted and expelled from Iraq and now live primarily in Israel and the United States and, to a lesser extent, in the United Kingdom.

One can speculate what would be the solution in light of the political pressure in the United States against return if, at some point, the United States and Iraq are unable to agree to further extensions of the agreement. Because the documents have been digitized and are available on the internet, the question of disposition is not about their contents and historical information, but rather about what possession of the original work signifies. The lack of congruity between cultural connection and territorial domain is found in other examples but is, perhaps, particularly poignant in this regard. One could suggest a three-part solution, based on the character of the materials.

To the extent that materials in the archive are identifiable as belonging to or related to specific individuals, such as school records, these should be returned to the individual or to immediate family members. In the case of particularly significant historical and religious manuscripts and books with sacred meaning, such as a Torah scroll, perhaps the cultural connection should be honored, and these should be given to the descendant community of expatriate Iraqi Jews. In the case of other records and a representative group of religious and historical documents, the territorial principle could govern disposition, based as well on the cultural and historical tie between these documents and the territory of Iraq. The rationale for returning some of the Jewish materials to Iraq, despite the lack of Jewish presence, was stated by Saad Eskander, at that time director of the Iraq National Library and Archives, 'Iraqis must know that we are a diverse people, with different traditions, different religions, and we need to accept this diversity.... To show it to our people that Baghdad was always multiethnic.'[135] Equally, having documents available for display in the United States and perhaps other countries means that the multi-religious, multi-ethnic character of Iraq would be on view for those outside Iraq to appreciate.

A negotiated compromise could also be devised by using a combination of ownership principles and long-term (even permanent) loans, an approach that has been used to resolve other cultural heritage disputes. One such resolution was the disposition of a group of gold jewelry purchased by the University of Pennsylvania Museum of Archaeology and Anthropology in 1966, which therefore predated adoption of the 1970 UNESCO Convention. Without conclusive evidence that the objects originated from the Troad region of Turkey, the Museum nonetheless agreed to return the objects on a long-term, indefinite loan to Turkey. The

[135] Quoted in 'Iraq Urges U.S. to Give Back Iraqi Jewish Archive' (n 133).

Museum and Turkey entered into an agreement for cultural collaboration that included loans of materials from the site of Gordion and continued support for the Museum's excavation at Gordion.[136]

This melding of the rights of lineal descendants, descendant communities, and territorial sovereignty is foreign to international law, which operates on a State-to-State basis. However, it finds a parallel in the determination of ownership of human remains and cultural items under the Native American Graves Protection and Repatriation Act (NAGPRA), which regulates disposition of human remains, associated and unassociated funerary objects, sacred objects, and objects of cultural patrimony that are culturally affiliated with Indian tribes and Native Hawaiian organizations.[137] This statute establishes a 'pecking' order of ownership rights, first, in the lineal descendants, second, in 'the Indian tribe or Native Hawaiian organization on whose tribal land such objects or remains were discovered' or, third, with the closest cultural affiliation, or, finally, with the 'Indian tribe recognized as aboriginally occupying the area in which the objects were discovered'.[138]

A similar problem arises when an ancient culture or indigenous group spans more than one modern State. If an object is identified only by the ancient culture that produced it, it is difficult to determine to which State to return it or, more problematic, whether a particular State's national ownership law is applicable to the object or whether the object is covered by a bilateral agreement between the particular State and the United States or Switzerland. This problem also occurs with repatriation of Native American human remains and cultural items under NAGPRA, which limits repatriation to federally recognized tribes and therefore does not apply to remains and cultural items that belong to a group located outside the United States.[139]

NAGPRA has been recognized as civil rights legislation within the United States. Similarly, international human rights law should be brought to bear on resolving conflicts between a State and a minority community that lives within the State or that may live outside that State, whether as the result of population displacement or exile. Developing an intersection between cultural heritage law and human rights law may allow partnerships and sharing arrangements to be devised that would help determine the proper disposition of cultural objects and also to heal some of the divisions between minority populations and States.

[136] Ece Velioglu, Anne Laure Bandle, and Marc-André Renold, 'Case Troy Gold—Turkey and the University of Pennsylvania Museum of Archaeology and Anthropology' *ArThemis* (May 2013) <https://plone.unige.ch/art-adr/cases-affaires/troy-gold-2013-turkey-and-the-university-of-pennsylvania-museum-of-archaeology-and-anthropology/case-note-troy-gold-turkey-and-the-university-of-pennsylvania-museum-of-archaeology-and-anthropology/view> accessed 21 May 2018.

[137] 25 USC ss 3001–13.

[138] 25 USC s 3002.

[139] 25 USC s 3001 (7) (defining 'Indian tribe').

4. State versus victims of cultural losses

At the conclusion of the Second World War, Soviet troops looted cultural objects from German and other Eastern European repositories.[140] These included works that the Germans had stolen from the Soviet Union, objects the Soviets took from German museums and private collections, and art works that the Germans had taken from Western Europe. The Soviets dubbed this 'trophy art' and decided to keep the art works in the Soviet Union (now Russia) as compensation for the looting of cultural objects and other destruction inflicted by the Germans. The Soviet Union returned some objects to the Soviet-friendly German Democratic Republic (East Germany) during the 1950s. The full extent of the holdings in Russian institutions only became apparent after the collapse of the Soviet Union.[141] While it is clear that this approach violates Article 56 of the 1899 and 1907 Hague Conventions,[142] Russia has persisted in retaining these objects as a unilateral decision of reparation and self-compensation.

In 1998, the Russian Federation adopted a law that provides that all such cultural objects taken by the Soviet military will become federal property with two primary exceptions.[143] One exception is that national property from the former Soviet Republics of Belorussia, Moldova, Ukraine, and the Baltic States will be returned to the rightful owner. The second exception is property that belonged to religious organizations or private organizations and 'those that used to belong to individuals who were deprived of said objects on account of their active fight against Nazism, including occupation regimes, collaborationist regimes and/or on account of their race, religion, or ethnicity'.[144] However, due to onerous conditions imposed for return of the latter group of objects, so far as can be determined, no claims have been made under this procedure.

While this law violates the principle of return to the State from which cultural objects were removed, the concept of returning objects to those who were

[140] Nicholas (n 3) 362–67.

[141] The rest went into deep storage at the Hermitage Museum in Leningrad, the Pushkin Museum in Moscow, and possibly other museums, not to surface until the collapse of the Soviet Union. Konstantin Akinsha and Gregorii Kozlov, *Beautiful Loot: The Soviet Plunder of Europe's Art Treasures* (Random House 1995).

[142] Article 56 states that '[a]ll seizure of … works of art and science [] is forbidden, and should be made the subject of legal proceedings'. In other words, the final disposition of any works of art should be decided through a treaty of peace at the end of hostilities, as apparently Germany and the other Allies expected at the end of the Second World War and as was binding on the Soviet Union. Article 4(3) of the 1954 Hague Convention prohibits the 'requisitioning [of] movable cultural property situated in the territory of another High Contracting Party'. While the 1954 Hague Convention post-dates the Second World War, given the history of similar provisions going back to the Lieber Code, this provision would seem to be a part of customary international law.

[143] Wilfried Fiedler, 'Russian Federal Law of 13 May 1997 on Cultural Values that have been Displaced to the USSR as a Result of World War II and are to be Found in the Russian Federation Territory' (1998) 7 IJCP 512.

[144] ibid 513. The criteria for bringing a claim were quite onerous, including a time limit of eighteen months, agreement to cover all costs associated with the restitution, and various agreements by other States to treat Russian claims with equal deference.

themselves victims of cultural theft seems to have merit, particularly within the context of the Second World War, as these objects would have been returned to the victims of Nazi Germany. One may also compare this to the policy of external restitution adopted by the Allies at the end of the Second World War by which cultural objects were turned over to the State from which they had been removed rather than to individual victims. Those States then had the responsibility to return the cultural objects to their original owners.[145] While following a principle of territoriality, this policy of external restitution had only moderate success in achieving the ultimate goal of returning cultural objects to the theft victims and their descendants.[146]

B. Unification of Law of Armed Conflict Treaties and International Trade Treaties

The second identified problem is the failure of the initial illegality that arises from removal of cultural objects during armed conflict and military occupation to follow these objects as they pass onto the international market and to ultimate destination countries. It is problematic that the recognition following the Second World War that cultural objects needed to be returned to their owners was not codified into any of the postwar international humanitarian law treaties, including the 1954 Hague Convention. As has previously been discussed, the 1954 Hague Convention itself does not have a general prohibition on removal of cultural objects from areas of armed conflict during the conflict. The term 'occupation' in the First Protocol, which prohibits removal during occupation, has been interpreted narrowly so that it does not apply to circumstances such as the occupation of parts of Syria and Iraq by ISIL. While the 1970 UNESCO Convention also prohibits removal during occupation, no State Party has specifically implemented this provision. The remedy requires modification of the international treaty regime, whether through new enactment or through reinterpretation.

I am reluctant to propose any new international instrument, including a new Protocol to the 1954 Hague Convention, in light of the difficulty of achieving widespread ratification. Nonetheless, the 1954 Hague Convention requires a more explicit statement that *any* removal of cultural objects during armed conflict

[145] For example Vrdoljak (n 19) 141–43; *Von Saher v Norton Simon Museum of Art at Pasadena*, 592 F 3d 954, 961–63 (9th Cir 2010).

[146] For example Ignaz Seidl-Hohenveldern, 'The Auction of the "Mauerbach Treasure"' (1997) 6 IJCP 247 (discussing disposition of unclaimed artworks located in Austria's territory at the end of the war); Les MNR ou les oeuvres issues de la spoliation artistique confiées aux musées de France, Site Rose-Valland Musées Nationaux Récupération, <http://www.culture.gouv.fr/documentation/mnr/MnR-pres.htm> accessed 13 November 2017 (collection of art works in France at the end of the war, which were incorporated into French national museum collections).

or occupation, regardless of the actor, is prohibited. The only exception would be for the purpose of temporary safeguarding of the objects when strictly necessary and with strong requirements for return at the end of the conflict.[147] This could be achieved, in part, by characterizing the widespread and systematic theft of cultural objects from repositories and looting of archaeological sites as destruction and an act of hostility directed against cultural property under Article 4(1) of the Hague Convention. While this conclusion may already be recognized, more importantly, all States Parties to the 1954 Hague Convention would have an obligation to prohibit the import, export, and trade in cultural objects removed during armed conflict and that appear within their territory. They would also have an accompanying obligation to return the cultural objects once any situation of hostilities and occupation has ended. Such objects would be considered the 'fruit' of the original war crime of intentional destruction of cultural property and therefore as inherently illegal.

The international community has demonstrated its willingness to take such measures through United Nations Security Council resolutions under narrow circumstances, such as existed during the 2003 Gulf War and in Syria and Iraq from 2011. But such provisions should be broadened to encompass all circumstances of armed conflict and without reference to a specific conflict or specific countries. The obligation could be triggered either through a formal declaration of war from any of the Parties to a conflict or through a determination by the Security Council or by the International Committee of the Red Cross (ICRC) that a state of armed conflict, whether international or non-international in scope, exists.[148] From that point on, the removal of any cultural objects from within the conflict zone would

[147] The term 'safeguarding' is often viewed with negative connotations because it has sometimes been used to disguise cultural theft and plunder. The second part of the 1954 First Protocol to the 1954 Hague Convention establishes a system of safekeeping whereby cultural objects may be deposited with another country and the latter is obligated to return the objects at the conclusion of hostilities. This provision of the First Protocol was codified to a limited extent in the Protect and Preserve International Cultural Property Act, which implemented UNSC Res 2199. Protect and Preserve International Cultural Property Act, Pub L No 114-151, 130 Stat 369 (2016). This legislation allows the US government to accept for deposit cultural objects from Syria, upon request from the owner or lawful custodian or, if no owner or lawful custodian is identified, when the President determines that the object should be temporarily located in the United States for the purpose of protecting and preserving the object. Such objects may be placed temporarily in a US cultural or educational institution but must be returned upon request of the owner or lawful custodian. ibid, s 3(e).

[148] In 1994, the International Criminal Tribunal for the former Yugoslavia offered a comprehensive definition of armed conflict as 'protracted armed violence between governmental authorities and organized armed groups or between such groups within a State'. Laurie R Blank and Geoffrey S Corn, 'Losing the Forest for the Trees: Syria, Law and the Pragmatics of Conflict Recognition' (2013) 46 Vanderbilt J Transnational L 693, 698 (quoting *Prosecutor v Tadić* (Decision on Defence Motion for Interlocutory Appeal on Jurisdiction) ICTY-94-0 (2 October 1995) 70). In July 2012, the ICRC concluded that the situation in Syria, which began with a rebellion in March 2011, constituted a non-international armed conflict. Stephanie Nebehay, 'Exclusive: Red Cross Ruling Raises Questions of Syrian War Crimes' *Reuters* (Geneva, 15 July 2012) <https://www.reuters.com/article/us-syria-crisis-icrc/exclusive-red-cross-ruling-raises-questions-of-syrian-war-crimes-idUSBRE86D09H20120714> accessed 1 November 2017.

be considered illegal *ab initio*, unless done with the consent of the owner, whether a State, an institution, or an individual, for the purpose of safekeeping. Such a declaration of armed conflict would also remove the defense of good faith under the good faith purchaser doctrine so that cultural objects could be recovered without payment of compensation, even after they had been sold through the international art market.

While a modest step, this mechanism would start to heal the divide between protection of cultural heritage during armed conflict and military occupation, on the one hand, and the problems of international trafficking in cultural objects, on the other hand. It would remove or reduce the incentive to loot and pillage cultural objects during armed conflict if the objects were to retain their initial illegality in the international art market and if buyers know that they are at risk of forfeiting such objects or of criminal liability, in appropriate circumstances. This uniting of disparate aspects of international law dealing with armed conflict and international trade might provide a more effective means of protection for cultural heritage—an urgent step whose necessity has become apparent in light of the current conflicts in the Middle East and that is suited to the contemporary realities of trafficking in cultural objects.

Conclusion

This chapter has demonstrated the lack of intersections among the various international legal instruments and their varying adoption into domestic law, which impedes the ability of the world community to protect adequately the world's cultural heritage, particularly its archaeological heritage. Unifying the wartime legal regime and the peacetime legal regimes that address international movement of cultural heritage would significantly aid in protecting this heritage through a mechanism such as a declaration of armed conflict that would make all objects removed illegally from conflict zones illegal on the international market.

This chapter has also demonstrated the inability or inadequacy of international law, based as it is exclusively on State-to-State mechanisms, to respond to problems of minority populations that live within a State or that live outside a modern State so that the State is not able to adequately represent the interests of the minority group. States are not typically enthusiastic about recognizing the rights of minority population groups and even less enthusiastic about these rights when they are recognized through international legal mechanisms. Particularly in the cultural heritage field, this lack of recognition and enforceability of human rights principles demonstrates another failure of intersection between human rights instruments and the legal instruments that aim to protect cultural heritage. However, recent moves to incorporate human rights approaches within both the law of armed conflict and the treaties addressing international movement of cultural objects may assist in resolving this second type of inadequate intersection among different sources of international law that aim to protect cultural heritage.

2

Comparing Interpretations of States' and Non-State Actors' Obligations Toward Cultural Heritage in Armed Conflict and Occupation

Military Manuals and the Law of War

*Elizabeth Varner**

Introduction

The 1954 Hague Convention on the Protection of Cultural Property in the Event of Armed Conflict (1954 Hague Convention)[1] remains the leading treaty on the treatment of cultural heritage during armed conflict and occupation. After several decades of relative dormancy, eleven States have joined the 1954 Hague Convention in the last decade: Afghanistan, Angola, Benin, Djibouti, Ethiopia, Ireland, Palestine, Togo, Turkmenistan, and two major military powers: the United States and the United Kingdom.

In addition to the 1954 Hague Convention, a host of laws touch on the protection of cultural property in armed conflict, including the 1907 Convention and Regulations respecting the Laws and Customs of War on Land (1907 Hague Convention),[2] the 1949 Convention relative to the Protection of Civilian Persons

* This chapter reflects the author's view in her private capacity. Nothing included within reflects the views or is endorsed by the US government or any groups with which the author is associated. Thanks to Dick Jackson for taking the time, as always, to discuss the law of war as well as the issues covered by this chapter. Any mistakes are mine.

[1] Convention for the Protection of Cultural Property in the Event of Armed Conflict (adopted 14 May 1954, entered into force 7 August 1956) 249 UNTS 240 (1954 Hague Convention).

[2] Convention Respecting the Laws and Customs of War on Land and its Annex: Regulations concerning the Laws and Customs of War on Land (opened for signature 18 October 1907, entered into force 26 January 1910) 187 CTS 227 (1907 Hague Convention). Given the parallels and relationship between the 1899 and 1907 Hague Conventions, only the 1907 Hague Convention will be discussed. See Hague Convention with Respect to the Laws and Customs of War on Land and its Annex: Regulations concerning the Laws and Customs of War on Land (adopted 29 July 1899, entered into force 4 September 1900) 187 CTS 429.

Elizabeth Varner, Comparing Interpretations of States' and Non-State Actors' Obligations Toward Cultural Heritage in Armed Conflict and Occupation In: *Intersections in International Cultural Heritage Law.* Edited by Anne-Marie Carstens and Elizabeth Varner. © Oxford University Press 2020. The several contributors DOI: 10.1093/oso/9780198846291.003.0003

in Time of War (1949 Fourth Geneva Convention),[3] 1977 Protocols Additional to the 1949 Fourth Geneva Convention (1977 Additional Protocols I and II),[4] and the 1999 Second Protocol to the 1954 Hague Convention (1999 Second Protocol),[5] as well as those under customary international law. Of these, the United States is a Party to the 1907 Hague Convention, the 1949 Fourth Geneva Convention, and the 1954 Hague Convention. The United Kingdom is a Party to those same treaties and also a Party to the 1977 Additional Protocols I and II and to the 1954 First Protocol and 1999 Second Protocol to the 1954 Hague Convention.[6]

Nonetheless, there are disagreements in interpretations of States' obligations toward cultural property during armed conflict stemming from a variety of factors. These factors can include: whether States are Parties to the instrument that conveys the obligation or if the obligation is one of customary international law, which of itself is often contested; the individual State's interpretation; interpretation by tribunals, such as the International Criminal Tribunal for the former Yugoslavia (ICTY); and a plethora of other factors.

Given these discrepancies in interpretation, a review of States' military manuals is useful to see if they shed any light on the State's interpretation of their obligations toward cultural property under the law of armed conflict (LOAC) and international obligations in LOAC more generally.[7] This chapter will analyze and

[3] Geneva Convention Relative to the Protection of Civilian Persons in Time of War (adopted 12 August 1949, entered into force 21 October 1950) 75 UNTS 287 (1949 Fourth Geneva Convention).

[4] Protocol Additional to the Geneva Conventions of 12 August 1949, and Relating to the Protection of Victims of International Armed Conflicts (adopted 8 June 1977, opened for signature 12 December 1977, entered into force 7 December 1978) 1125 UNTS 3 (Additional Protocol I); Protocol Additional to the Geneva Conventions of 12 August 1949, and Relating to the Protection of Victims of Non-International Armed Conflicts (adopted 8 June 1977, opened for signature 12 December 1977, entered into force 7 December 1978) 1125 UNTS 609 (Additional Protocol II).

[5] Second Protocol to the Hague Convention of 1954 for the Protection of Cultural Property in the Event of Armed Conflict (adopted 26 March 1999, entered into force 9 March 2004) 253 UNTS 172 (1999 Second Protocol).

[6] The States Parties to the 1907 Hague Convention, the 1949 Fourth Geneva Convention, and the 1977 Additional Protocols I and II are provided in the ICRC IHL Database. IRCR, 'Treaties, State Parties, and Commentaries' <https://ihl-databases.icrc.org/ihl> accessed 27 December 2018.

The States Parties to the 1954 Hague Convention and to its 1954 and 1999 Protocols are provided in the UNESCO Database on Armed Conflict and Heritage. UNESCO, 'Armed Conflict and Heritage: States Parties' <http://www.unesco.org/new/en/culture/themes/armed-conflict-and-heritage/convention-and-protocols/states-parties/> accessed 21 December 2018.

[7] Military manuals are useful as one kind of evidence of State practice and/or *opinio juris*, though they are not dispositive because customary international law needs more evidence than just military manuals. See US Department of Defense, *Law of War Manual* (2015) (US LOW Manual) 31–32 ('Although manuals or other official statements may provide important indications of State behavior, they cannot replace a meaningful assessment of operational State practice' (citing John B Bellinger III and William J Haynes II, 'A US Government Response to the Int'l Committee of the Red Cross Study *Customary International Humanitarian Law*' (2006) 89 Intl Review of the Red Cross 515 (omitting 'and *opinio juris*' after 'State behavior', which was in Bellinger's and Haynes' response.) The *US LOW Manual* relies heavily on the official US response to the ICRC study by Bellinger and Haynes for its discussion of the relevance of military manuals to customary international law, which includes, inter alia, that *opinio juris* is not established through evidence consisting 'predominantly of military manuals'; positions in the manual can be a result of treaty requirements or national policy rather than customary legal obligation; and *opinio juris* cannot 'be inferred from practice'. US LOW Manual 33–34 nn 145 and 148 (internal quotations and citations omitted).

compare the military manuals of two major military powers—the United States and the United Kingdom—to determine how they elucidate several key issues in the protection of cultural property during armed conflict, such as the definition of 'cultural property', requirements for 'respect', the doctrine of military necessity, and laws applicable in non-international armed conflicts (NIAC).

In June of 2015, the US Department of Defense (DOD) released the over 1,000-page[8] Law of War Manual (US LOW Manual), which had been decades in the making. After seeking comment, the revised version was released in May 2016. The stated intent of the US LOW Manual is to 'provide not only the black letter rules, but also discussion, examples of State practice, and references to past manuals, treatises, and other documents to provide explanation, clarification, and elaboration.'[9] This manual is intended to provide information on the US DOD's interpretation of laws of war, including treaties and international customary law, to US DOD personnel and not to create any enforceable rights.[10] This is the first law of war manual to address the United States' ratification of the 1954 Hague Convention in 2009, as well as the heightened issue of NIAC.

The United Kingdom's equivalent to the US LOW Manual is the United Kingdom Ministry of Defence, Joint Service Publication 383, The Joint Service Manual of the Law of Armed Conflict (UK LOAC Manual),[11] which was published in 2004. Since then, there have been seven amendments, the most recent of which was in 2013.[12] At the time that the UK LOAC Manual and subsequent amendments were released, the United Kingdom was not a Party to the 1954 Hague Convention nor its 1954 First Protocol or 1999 Second Protocol. The United Kingdom did not become a Party to the 1954 Hague Convention and its two protocols until 2017, though the UK LOAC Manual does reference the 1954 Hague Convention and its 1999 Second Protocol throughout.[13] The UK LOAC Manual notes that 'it is intended to ratify the [1954 Hague] Convention when implementing legislation has been introduced and passed by Parliament' and that the UK forces therefore, 'though not strictly bound by the terms of the Convention, should apply the principles it contains. There are also provisions for the protection of cultural property in 1977 Additional Protocol I, which UK forces are required to apply.'[14]

[8] The Manual includes 1,147 pages without preface or appendices.

[9] US LOW Manual v.

[10] ibid iii, 1. As such, this chapter declines to speculate if the States themselves are agreeing to customary international law unless the manual so states. Rather, this chapter will focus on debated issues to see where key military powers are on the spectrum.

[11] UK Ministry of Defence, *Joint Service Manual of the Law of Armed Conflict* (JSP 383) (2004) (UK LOAC Manual).

[12] UK Ministry of Defence, *The Manual of the Law of Armed Conflict: Amendments (JSP 383)*, <https://www.gov.uk/government/publications/the-manual-of-the-law-of-armed-conflict-amendments-to-the-text?> accessed 15 December 2018.

[13] UNESCO, '1954 Hague Convention State Parties' (n 6). UNESCO, 'State Parties to 1st Protocol' (n 6); UNESCO, 'State Parties to 2nd Protocol' (n 6).

[14] UK LOAC Manual 15 n 52.

While the UK LOAC Manual was drafted about twelve years earlier than the US LOW Manual (two to three years if the amendments are included), and is less than half of the pages of that Manual, both Manuals have a similar layout and, to a certain extent, substantive content, which is not surprising given that the US LOW Manual lists the UK LOAC Manual as a resource used in preparing the Manual.[15] These Manuals are relevant to understanding these State's interpretation of international legal obligations more generally. They also clarify conventional obligations, and to the extent they set out obligations for which the State is not bound by a treaty, they can contribute to establishing the existence of customary legal obligations, as discussed below.

This chapter will first review the US DOD's understandings of its obligations toward cultural property through an analysis of the new US LOW Manual. To best contextualize the US LOW Manual's treatment of cultural property, these sections will analyze the issues in the order in which they are covered in the US LOW Manual. This context aids in a nuanced analysis of the United States' interpretation of their obligations. Following this structure, this chapter will compare the US DOD's understanding of its obligations to the UK LOAC Manual and UNESCO's Protection of Cultural Property Military Manual (UNESCO Military Manual),[16] thereby providing recent interpretations of international law. While there are many rules, general and specific, throughout the manuals that will affect cultural property, including, but not limited to general property rules, this chapter will only focus on *a few* provisions in the manuals, either to give a general flavor or to address specific issues, as discussed previously.

I. 'General Background'

The US LOW Manual 'focuses on *jus in bello*—law relating to the conduct of hostilities and the protection of war victims' that is applicable to the United States.[17] It provides rules, principles, discussion, and examples of State practice. While the US LOW Manual states that it 'does not necessarily reflect the views of any other department or agency of the U.S. Government or the views of the U.S. Government as a whole', it 'provides information on the law of war to DOD personnel responsible

[15] The manuals might use different words and a different order of sections. The United States does seem to have a separate chapter on cyber conflict that is not fully embodied in the UK LOAC Manual. Additionally, both the manuals address preparation or safeguarding in the hostilities section, rather than an independent section for preparation for armed conflict.

[16] UNESCO, *Protection of Cultural Property Military Manual* (2016) xiii (UNESCO Military Manual) (stating that the purpose of the manual is 'to outline the practical implementation of the 1954 Hague Convention and its Second Protocol' so that Member States can 'include in their military directives guidelines and instruction on the protection of cultural property').

[17] US LOW Manual 1–50. See ibid v, 1 for the 'Preface' and 'Purpose and Scope of This Manual' sections.

for implementing the law of war and executing military operations' and 'represents the legal views of the Department of Defense'.[18] The US LOW Manual built upon multiple antecedents, including various services' manuals, and benefitted from consultation with other governmental actors and also international experts, particularly those in Australia, Canada, New Zealand, and the United Kingdom.[19] The *jus in bello*, or law of war, applies in 'international and non-international armed conflict; belligerent occupation; and the relationships between belligerent, neutral, and non-belligerent States.'[20]

II. 'Principles'

The US LOW Manual noted that principles such as distinction, honor, humanity, military necessity, and proportionality[21] provide the foundation for the law of war rules, are used to interpret treaties and customary rules, and fill in gaps when no rule exists.[22] The UK LOAC Manual focused on four principles: military necessity, humanity, distinction, and proportionality.[23] While all of these principles are relevant for cultural property protection, those most discussed in debates regarding cultural property include distinction, military necessity, and proportionality. The US LOW Manual states that the additional principle of humanity bars actions that are not necessary, and honor 'supports the entire system and gives parties confidence in it'.[24]

Military necessity, as interpreted by the US LOW Manual, permits actions to 'defeat the enemy as quickly and efficiently as possible that are not prohibited by the law of war'.[25] In the UK LOAC Manual section, 'Basic Principles of the Law of Armed Conflict', military necessity is 'the principle whereby a belligerent has the right to apply any measures which are required to bring about the successful conclusion of a military operation and which are not forbidden by the laws of war'.[26]

[18] ibid. This caveat does not reduce the Manual's value in showing State practice and/or *opinio juris*, as it is just one factor to consider along with operational State practice.

[19] ibid iii-vi.

[20] ibid 7–8. See ibid 7–15 for the 'Definition of the Law of War' section. Dieter Fleck (ed), *The Handbook of International Humanitarian Law* (3rd edn, OUP 2013) 12 ('whereas the older treaties applied only in a "war", today humanitarian law is applicable in any armed conflict, even if the parties to that conflict have not declared war and do not recognize that they are in a situation defined under law of war').

[21] US LOW Manual 50–70.

[22] ibid 51.

[23] UK LOAC Manual 21.

[24] US LOW Manual 51–52.

[25] ibid 51. See also UK LOAC Manual 21–22.

[26] UK Ministry of Defence, *The Manual of the Law of Armed Conflict Amendment 3* (September 2010) 5 (citing UK and NATO definitions, explaining 'a state engaged in an armed conflict may use that degree and kind of force, not otherwise prohibited by the law of armed conflict, that is required' for the 'complete or partial ... submission of the enemy at the earliest possible moment with the minimum expenditure of life and resources').

The UK LOAC Manual only permits this defense if 'express allowance is made for military necessity within the provision allegedly breached' and comports with the proportionality principle.[27] According to the US LOW Manual, '[a]lthough military necessity cannot justify actions that have been prohibited by the law of war, some law of war rules expressly incorporate military necessity',[28] such as Article 4(2) of the 1954 Hague Convention, which permits the waiver of obligations to respect and not direct hostilities toward cultural property if 'military necessity imperatively' requires it. Additionally, the UK LOAC Manual cites the 1949 Geneva Conventions and 1977 Additional Protocol I for express military necessity provisions.[29] The famous quote from US General Eisenhower's *Memorandum Regarding the Protection of Historical Monuments in Italy* during the Second World War was included in the US LOW Manual to support the proposition that '*military necessity* must not be conflated with mere convenience'.[30]

The US LOW Manual also utilized 'feasibility', generally for affirmative obligations, such as 'feasible precautions', and to temper obligations as seen in language such as 'only to the extent feasible or consistent with *military necessity*'.[31] The Manual further noted that the law of war 'permit[s] consideration of the broader imperatives of winning the war as quickly and efficiently as possible'; some actions are 'inherently militarily necessary'; and military necessity is determined 'in good faith based on the information available to them at the relevant time'.[32]

Two other important principles that are integral to LOAC, as applied to cultural property in the US LOW Manual and UK LOAC Manual, include distinction, which is critical for separating protected from unprotected objects or military objectives, and proportionality, which requires that actions are not 'unreasonable or excessive' even if justified by military necessity.[33] Of interest, both of these principles are found in the 1977 Additional Protocol I, to which the United Kingdom is a Party and which the UK LOAC Manual cites.[34] The United States is not a Party, so

[27] UK LOAC Manual 444.
[28] US LOW Manual 55.
[29] UK LOAC Manual 23 n 6 (citing Waldemar A Solf and J Ashley Roach (eds), *Index of International Humanitarian Law* (ICRC 1987) 152).
[30] US LOW Manual 55 and n 30 (citing General Dwight D Eisenhower, 'Memorandum Regarding the Protection of Historical Monuments in Italy'(29 December 1943) (internal citation omitted, explaining that although 'the phrase "military necessity" is sometimes used where it would be more truthful to speak of military convenience or even personal convenience', military necessity should not 'cloak slackness or indifference' to discerning whether law of war obligations, such as the protection of cultural property, may be fulfilled without any detriment to operational needs).
[31] US LOW Manual 55–56.
[32] ibid 56.
[33] ibid 51.
[34] See UK LOAC Manual 24–26. UK LOAC Manual 24 n 10 (citing 1977 Additional Protocol 1, arts 48 and 49(3)). UK LOAC Manual 25 nn 15 (citing Additional Protocol I, art 51(5)(b)) and 16 (citing Additional Protocol I, arts 57(2)(a)(iii) and (b)).

the US LOW Manual does not cite this source, though it does use the language for proportionality found in the 1977 Additional Protocol I and considers a provision in the 1977 Additional Protocol I for distinction.[35]

III. 'The Conduct of Hostilities'

A. General Property

The US LOW Manual includes sections specifically for cultural property protection that are applicable in three distinct stages/kinds of conflict: 'The Conduct of Hostilities',[36] which features 'Protection of Cultural Property During Hostilities'; 'Military Occupation', which includes 'Protection of Cultural Property During Occupation', and 'Non-International Armed Conflict (NIAC)', which has a section 'Protection of Cultural Property in NIAC'.[37] The UK LOAC Manual includes two sections specifically for cultural property protection in 'The Conduct of Hostilities' section: 'Protection of Cultural Objects and Places of Worship' and 'Cultural Property Convention'. However, numerous sections throughout both Manuals affect the protection of cultural property, many of which are not within the specific above-named sections. Given the debate on the definition of 'cultural property' and the subjective nature of the determination, this chapter will highlight some examples of how the Manuals interpret the protection of civilian property, but the analysis is by no means complete or exhaustive.

In the section 'The Conduct of Hostilities', the US LOW Manual addresses general rules for civilian property,[38] feasible precautions to reduce the risk of harm to civilian property,[39] and then special provisions for cultural property and feasible precautions to protect cultural property in 'Protection of Cultural Property During Hostilities'. The UK LOAC Manual's same-named section, 'The Conduct

[35] US LOW Manual 60–65 and n 80 (considering Additional Protocol I, art 48). See also Additional Protocol I, arts 51–52. Cf US LOW Manual 61 to Additional Protocol I, arts 51(5) and 57.

[36] US LOW Manual 184–336.

[37] Specific sections that also address cultural property protection include 'Classes of People, Personnel Engaged in Duties Related to the Protection of Cultural Property'. ibid 136.

[38] See ibid 207–93 (eg sections on 'Discrimination in Conducting Attacks', 'Military Objectives', 'Proportionality in Conducting Attacks', 'Proportionality—Prohibition on Attacks Expected to Cause Excessive Incidental Harm', 'Prohibition on Using Protected Persons and Objects to Shield, Favor, or Impede Military Operations', and 'Seizure and Destruction of Enemy Property').

[39] See ibid 250–76 (eg sections on 'Proportionality—Feasible Precautions in Planning and Conducting Attacks to Reduce the Risk of Harm to Protected Persons and Objects' and 'Feasible Precautions to Reduce the Risk of Harm to Protected Persons and Objects by the Party Subject to Attack').

of Hostilities', addressed not attacking civilian objects in its 'Immunity of Civilian Objects' section and then cultural property in the 'Protection of Cultural Objects and Places of Worship' section and in a subsequent section covering the 1954 Hague Convention.[40] The sections on civilian protection in the US LOW Manual are relevant to cultural property protection as the law of war utilizes a tiered framework of protection for objects such that even if an object does not fit within a State's interpretation of 'cultural property', regardless of which convention they are Party to, it can still potentially have protections afforded civilian or enemy property.

In the 'Overview of Rules for the Protection of Civilians' section, the US LOW Manual provides a general framework for the military's obligations to civilians, noting that there are 'negative duties to respect civilians and to refrain from directing military operations against them' and 'affirmative duties to take feasible precautions to protect civilians and other protected persons and objects'.[41] The language in this provision is useful for later interpretations of obligations as 'respect' is interpreted for the military to not act while 'feasible precautions' requires the military to act.

The US LOW Manual states that the 'party controlling civilians and civilian objects has the primary responsibility for the protection of civilians and civilian objects'[42] such that, cumulatively, there are two qualifiers for affirmative protection—control of the civilian objects and feasibility. Later, the US LOW Manual expands on affirmative duties to take feasible precautions for the protection of civilians and other protected objects, the language of which recalls that of the 1977 Additional Protocol I.[43] In explaining what precautions are feasible, the US LOW Manual and UK LOAC Manual define 'feasible' as that which is 'practicable or practically possible, taking into account all circumstances ruling at the time, including humanitarian and military considerations' such that it is a matter of 'due regard or diligence, not an absolute requirement to do everything possible'.[44]

[40] UK LOAC Manual 70.

[41] US LOW Manual 187.

[42] ibid. See also United States, Statement on Ratification of the 1954 Hague Cultural Property Convention (13 March 2009) 2575 UNTS 7, 8 ('the primary responsibility for protection of cultural objects rests with the party controlling that property').

[43] US LOW Manual 190–91. See ibid nn 35 and 40 (providing an example and citing Michael J Matheson, 'Remarks on the United States Position on the Relation of Customary International Law to the 1977 Protocols Additional to the 1949 Geneva Conventions at the Sixth Annual American Red Cross-Washington College of Law Conference on International Humanitarian Law' (1987) 2 American U Intl L Rev 419, 426–27 ('We support the principle that all practicable precautions, taking into account military and humanitarian considerations, be taken in the conduct of military operations to minimize' harm to 'civilian objects, and that effective advance warning be given of attacks which may affect the civilian population, unless circumstances do not permit.')). Compare Additional Protocol I, art 57.

[44] US LOW Manual 192-93; UK LOAC Manual 81 n 191.

The UNESCO Military Manual interpreted feasibility to be 'everything' armed forces 'can reasonably do'.[45]

In the section on 'Discrimination in Conducting Attacks', the US LOW Manual applies the principle of discrimination to civilian property noting that objects that are not military objectives may not be attacked, especially cultural property, historic monuments, museums, scientific, artistic, educational, cultural institutions, and places of worship.[46] Similar to the US LOW Manual, the UK LOAC Manual states that '[c]ivilian objects shall not be the object of attack or of reprisals'.[47] 'Civilian objects' include 'buildings and facilities used by civilians (so long as they do not fall within the definition of military objectives) such as ... museums, places of worship, and other similar buildings'.[48]

The US LOW Manual does allow this property to be an object of attack if that 'protection is specifically forfeited under the circumstances', which will be covered later in military necessity discussions.[49] Feasible precautions are then expounded upon and connected to the principle of proportionality, which considers 1977 Additional Protocol I to support this obligation.[50] Feasible precautions include 'advance warning before an attack that may affect civilians' and 'selecting weapons that "reduce risk of harm to civilians and civilian objects"'.[51] In addition to these precautions, the UK LOAC Manual also includes determining that the target is a military objective and that the harm is not excessive in relation to the military advantage anticipated.[52]

In the US LOW Manual section 'Prohibition on Using Protected Persons and Objects to Shield, Favor, or Impede Military Operations', there is an express prohibition on using protected objects, 'especially cultural property', inter alia to shield military objectives or 'impede the adversary's military operations'.[53] Interestingly, the Manual notes '[t]his rule does not prohibit a party from using what would

[45] UNESCO Military Manual 29, para 96. But see 'it will be only in exception cases, if at all,' that defensive destruction of cultural property occurs. ibid 38, para 126.

[46] US LOW Manual 207–08 (citing The Treaty on the Protection of Artistic and Scientific Institutions and Historic Monuments (Roerich Pact) (adopted 15 April 1935, entered into force 26 August 1935) 167 LNTS 289, art 1)).

[47] UK LOAC Manual 69 n 100 (citing Additional Protocol I, art 52(1)).

[48] ibid n 102 (citing Additional Protocol I, art 52(3)).

[49] US LOW Manual 207. For more information, see ibid 208–20 ('Military Objectives'), 241–50 ('Proportionality in Conducting Attacks').

[50] ibid 250 and nn 334 (considering Additional Protocol I, art 57(2)) and 336 (citing, inter alia, 1907 Hague Convention, Regulations, art 27). The Manual also cites statements from Harold Koh, then Legal Adviser to the Department of State, noting that although the United States is not a Party to Additional Protocol I, provisions 'are an accurate statement of the fundamental law of war principle of discrimination'. ibid 251 n 336. Cf Additional Protocol I, art 57(2) (providing obligations for precautions in attack).

[51] ibid 251–58. Given space constraints, this chapter skips the sections on 'Proportionality—Prohibition on Attacks Expected to Cause Excessive Incidental Harm' and 'Feasible Precautions to Reduce the Risk of Harm to Protected Persons and Objects by the Party Subject to Attack'. See ibid 260–76.

[52] UK LOAC Manual 81 n 190 (citing Additional Protocol I, art 57(2)).

[53] US LOW Manual 282 and n 489.

otherwise be a civilian object for military purposes and thereby converting it to a military objective that is not protected by the law of war',[54] which could simply be a restatement of military necessity. Using cultural property as a shield does not obviate the principle of discrimination, but 'may impair the attacking force's ability to discriminate and increase the risk of harm to protected persons and objects'.[55]

Even if the object is not a protected object that fits within the protections above (ie the object did not fit within the State's definition of 'cultural property', or even within the State's interpretation of a 'protected object' above), the object might still be afforded protection as 'enemy property', as demonstrated in the 'Seizure and Destruction of Enemy Property' section.[56] Citing the 1907 Hague Convention Regulations, the US LOW Manual noted that '[e]nemy property may not be seized or destroyed unless imperatively demanded by the necessities of war'.[57]

Pillage was also covered in the section 'Seizure and Destruction of Enemy Property'. Pillage is not allowed, particularly when it involves cultural property.[58] The US LOW Manual notes that '[i]n certain cases, there is an affirmative obligation to prohibit and prevent pillage',[59] which is an important clarification for the debate over obligations to protect cultural property, specifically whether States have affirmative obligations under Article 4(3) of the 1954 Hague Convention, discussed in Section III.B.5., to prohibit pillaging or looting from their respective armed forces or from third Parties. While the US LOW Manual does not expound upon what those 'certain cases' are, it does cross reference the section 'Obligation to Stop or Prevent Theft, Pillage, or Misappropriation of, and Acts of Vandalism Against, Cultural Property', which will be discussed in depth in Section III.B. Of additional interest, citing the 1958 UK war manual, the US LOW Manual noted that 'there is no obligation to protect abandoned property in the area of active obligations',[60] which could further suggest that the United States does not interpret that they have an affirmative obligation to protect cultural property as most remaining cultural property, particularly buildings housing cultural property, will likely be abandoned in areas of active conflict.

B. Cultural Property

In the section, 'Protection of Cultural Property During Hostilities', the US LOW Manual incorporates wholesale many 1954 Hague Convention provisions to the

[54] ibid.
[55] ibid 284 and n 507, 261 n 410.
[56] ibid 286–89.
[57] US LOW Manual 286 (citing 1907 Hague Convention, Regulations, art 23(g)).
[58] ibid 289 and n 538.
[59] ibid 290.
[60] ibid 292 (citing Hersch Lauterpacht, *The Law of War on Land: Being Part III of the Manual of Military Law*, War Office Pub No 12333 (HMSO 1958) para 615).

exclusion of other conventions, save a brief reference to Additional Protocol I at the end of the section. The Manual notes that 'cultural property, the areas immediately surrounding it, and appliances in use for its protection should be safeguarded and respected' during hostilities and there are '[s]ome obligations with respect to cultural property' during peacetime, occupation, and NIAC.[61] The UK LOAC Manual includes a similar summation, noting that the 1954 Hague Convention 'places an equal obligation on defenders and attackers by requiring States to refrain from uses of cultural property that would expose it to danger in armed conflict and to refrain from acts of hostility against cultural property'.[62] In addressing the 1954 Hague Convention in the 'Conduct of Hostilities' section, the UK LOAC Manual further expounds that 'States must avoid using cultural property for military purposes, must not direct hostilities against it, and must protect it from theft, misappropriation, vandalism, requisitioning, or reprisals'.[63] These obligations 'can be waived only' by a certain staff position within the respective armed forces (that increases in rank concomitantly with the protection afforded the cultural property) if 'the property has become a military objective, there is no feasible alternative method for dealing with the situation and, unless it is a case of immediate self-defence, a prior warning is given with a reasonable time-limit for compliance'.[64]

Restrictions in the Manuals on hostilities against cultural property are of even greater relevance in light of the recent decision in *Prosecutor v Al Mahdi*, holding that destruction of the protected historic and religious buildings in Timbuktu, Mali, constituted a war crime of 'intentionally directing attacks against buildings dedicated to religion, education, art, science or charitable purposes, [and] historic monuments' that are not military objectives.[65] Al Mahdi was found guilty of committing this war crime under the Rome Statute of the International Criminal Court (Rome Statute), which is particularly relevant to the United Kingdom because it is a Party to the Rome Statute.[66]

The US LOW Manual further states that the United States has identified parts of the 1954 Hague Convention as customary international law such that the United

[61] ibid 293.

[62] UK LOAC Manual 15.

[63] ibid 72 n 120 (adding that such protection can only be waived by imperative military necessity) and n 121 (citing 1954 Hague Convention, art 4).

[64] UK LOAC Manual 73 n 132 (citing 1954 Hague Convention, arts 4, 11; 1999 Second Protocol, art 13).

[65] *Prosecutor v Al Mahdi* (Trial Judgment and Sentencing) ICC-01/12-01/15 (27 September 2016).

[66] Rome Statute of the International Criminal Court (adopted 17 July 1998, entered into force 1 July 2002) 2187 UNTS 3 (Rome Statute); ICRC (n 6). See also Sabine von Schorlemer 'Military Intervention, the UN Security Council, and the Role of UNESCO: The Case of Mali' (ch 3) and Karolina Wierczyńska and Andrzej Jakubowski, 'The *Al Mahdi* Case: From Punishing Perpetrators to Repairing Cultural Heritage Harm' (ch 5) in this volume for in-depth coverage of the destruction of cultural property in Mali and the *Al Mahdi* case. Note that while the Rome Statute, art 8(2)(e)(iv) applies to intentionally attacking cultural property in NIAC, the corresponding provision of the Rome Statute, art 8(2)(b)(ix), applies in international armed conflict (IAC). Of course, 1954 Hague Convention, art 28, requires Parties to establish sanctions for violation of the Convention within their 'ordinary criminal jurisdiction'.

States should act as if the State on whose territory US forces are operating is a Party to the 1954 Hague Convention, regardless of whether such State has ratified the Convention. The referenced customary international law 'prohibits the use of any cultural property to shield any legitimate military targets from attack and ... allows all property to be attacked using any lawful and proportionate means, if required by military necessity and notwithstanding possible collateral damage to such property'.[67]

1. Definition of cultural property

The US LOW Manual spends considerable time on the definition of 'cultural property'—over three pages. The US LOW Manual's definition of cultural property is from the 1954 Hague Convention, Article 1, which defines three categories of cultural property 'irrespective of origin or ownership': (1) 'movable or immovable property of great importance to the cultural heritage of every people'; (2) 'buildings intended to shelter cultural property'; and (3) 'centers containing monuments'.[68] The US LOW Manual notes that the 1954 Hague Convention's definition for cultural property is likely more limited than other international instruments for which the Manual lists a series of definitions, including those from the Lieber Code, 1907 Hague Convention, Roerich Pact, and Additional Protocol I; notes that 'the scope of objects being protected by each instrument is not the same (although there may be overlap)', and then states that the 1954 Hague Convention supplements earlier treaties.[69] The US LOW Manual emphasizes that '[o]rdinary property (such as churches or works of art) that are not of great importance to the cultural heritage of every people' would not qualify as cultural property, but might fit within the protections afforded civilian or enemy property discussed above.[70] This appears contrary to the requirement in the 1907 Hague Convention, to which the United States is a Party, to 'protect "buildings dedicated to religion, art, science, or charitable purposes, historic monuments"', the scope of which was not limited in the US LOW Manual, unlike that of the 1977 Additional Protocol I.[71]

The UK LOAC Manual's coverage of the definition for cultural property was more abbreviated than the US LOW Manual, which might just be a factor of the disparities in scale of the two Manuals.[72] The United Kingdom's definition of cultural property is similar to the US LOW Manual in that both include terminology

[67] US LOW Manual 293, n 565 (citing 1954 Hague Convention, art 4(1)) and n 566 referring to 'Special Protection for International Property' clarified at ibid 305 n 645 (citing United States, 'Statement on Ratification of the 1954 Hague Cultural Property Convention' (13 March 2009) 2575 UNTS 7, 8).

[68] US LOW Manual 293–94 n 568 (paraphrasing 1954 Hague Convention, art 1).

[69] ibid 294–95 nn 573 (citing 1907 Hague Convention, Regulations, art 27), 575 (citing Roerich Pact, art 1) and 576 (citing Additional Protocol I, art 53).

[70] ibid 295.

[71] ibid 294 (citing 1907 Hague Convention, Regulations, art 27, but using the term 'protect' rather than 'spare' that is the language used in the 1907 Hague Convention). But see ibid 311.

[72] This definition was also expounded upon in the Manual's 'Hostilities' section.

from the 1954 Hague Convention and the 1977 Additional Protocol I, though the United States (unlike the United Kingdom) is not a Party to the 1977 Additional Protocols and makes no statement of the binding effect of its provisions governing cultural property.[73] The United Kingdom, as it was not a Party to the 1954 Hague Convention at the time of the UK LOAC Manual publication, focused initially on Additional Protocol I and then the 1954 Hague Convention.

The UK LOAC Manual limited the definition of 'cultural property' under the 1954 Hague Convention to property of international importance, while the US LOW Manual requires a 'delicate and somewhat subjective judgment' explaining that those materials that can be replaced would be less important regardless of financial value, while some irreplaceable objects with high intrinsic value might have less financial value.[74] Consequently, it appears that the handling of the threshold question to access the protections of the 1954 Hague Convention in the US LOW Manual is more flexible, and potentially more expansive, than the UK LOAC Manual.

Of interest, although the United States is a Party to the 1907 Hague Convention, the US LOW Manual only relies on the 1907 Hague Convention for purposes of proffering an example of a description of cultural property that is broader than that in the 1954 Hague Convention, and not for the content of its requirement to 'protect "buildings dedicated to religion, art, science, or charitable purposes, historic monuments"'.[75] Beyond proffering the definition in the list above, this article is not addressed in this section of the US LOW Manual, suggesting that the 1954 Hague Convention definition has superseded that of the 1907 Hague Convention in the US LOW Manual. Conversely, while the United States is not a Party to Additional Protocol I, that instrument's coverage of cultural property was addressed in this section as well as later in the US LOW Manual to limit the scope of the 1977 Additional Protocol I's protection for cultural property. Skipping ahead to the end of this section, the US LOW Manual addresses cultural property in the 1977 Additional Protocol I, specifically Article 53, which requires protection of 'historic monuments, works of art or places of worship which constitute the cultural or spiritual heritage of peoples.'[76] Citing statements of the US delegation during negotiations of 1977 Additional Protocol I, Article 53, the US LOW Manual advises that this provision is not interpreted as broadly as the wording appears, suggesting that those objects that achieved 'special protection' under the 1977 Additional Protocol I were those that would also qualify for 'special protection' under Article 8 of the 1954 Hague Convention.[77]

[73] UK LOAC Manual 15 and nn 52 and 54 (citing 1954 Hague Convention, art 1); ibid 71–72 and nn 104 (citing Additional Protocol I, art 53), 117, and 118 (citing 1954 Hague Convention, art 1(a)–(c)). See also US LOW Manual 311.

[74] UK LOAC Manual 70, 71 n 116. US LOW Manual 579–81.

[75] US LOW Manual 294 (citing 1907 Hague Convention, Regulations, art 27).

[76] ibid 311 n 684 (citing Additional Protocol I, art 53).

[77] ibid n 685. See 1954 Hague Convention, art 8.

Interestingly, while the 1954 Hague Convention employs a two-tier protection schema of 'general protection' and 'special protection',[78] the 1977 Additional Protocols do not. 'Special protection' under the 1954 Hague Convention applies heightened protection to refuges of moveable cultural property and centers containing immoveable cultural property of 'very great importance', which is a higher threshold than the 'great importance' required for 'general protection'. It also entails restrictions that bar protection if used to shield military objectives or for military purposes and depends upon entry in an international register established in the treaty, the International Register of Cultural Property under Special Protection.[79] Consequently, while the United States is not a Party to 1977 Additional Protocol I and makes no indication that it intends to be so bound by that provision, the US LOW Manual interprets objects protected under the 1977 Additional Protocol I to meet a higher requirement than that of 'cultural property' afforded general protection under the 1954 Hague Convention.[80] The UK LOAC Manual also limited the definition in the 1977 Additional Protocol I stating that its interpretation of protected cultural property 'only applies to very important cultural property of international stature'.[81] The Commentary to Additional Protocol I and II noted, however, that despite the differences in language between the two definitions in the 1954 Hague Convention and Additional Protocol I, 'the basic idea is the same'.[82]

Meanwhile, the UNESCO Military Manual notes that the determination of whether an object is 'cultural property' is 'a question for the state on whose territory it is situated'.[83] If there is doubt as to the status of property because the State has not conveyed this information, the Manual notes that armed forces 'should proceed on the assumption that' the movable or immovable property of historic, artistic, or architectural significance 'is of great importance' to the State 'protected by the 1954 Hague Convention and its two Protocols and by customary international law'.[84] The UNESCO Military Manual then echoes the Commentary to Additional Protocol I and II adding that despite the difference in language, the 'property of cultural significance' under the 1977 Additional Protocols I and II is 'effectively the same' as 'cultural property' under the 1954 Hague Convention and its Protocols.[85] The UNESCO Military Manual's approach is a significant departure from that of the US LOW and UK LOAC Manual, finding that the determination of 'cultural property' was of State, not international importance, or even a nuanced balancing

[78] 1954 Hague Convention, arts 2, 8.

[79] ibid, arts 8, 12.

[80] US LOW Manual 311 (citing Additional Protocol I and including language from art 53 of that instrument) and n 685 (citation omitted). Cf 1954 Hague Convention, art 1.

[81] UK LOAC Manual 70 n 105.

[82] Yves Sandoz, Christophe Swinarski, and Bruno Zimmerman (eds), *Commentary on the Additional Protocols of 8 June 1977 to the Geneva Conventions of 12 August 1949* (Martinus Nijhoff 1987) 646, para 2064.

[83] UNESCO Military Manual 13, para 45.

[84] ibid 14, para 47.

[85] ibid, para 48.

test under the US LOW Manual such that the UNESCO Military Manual interpretation requires a far lower threshold for property to receive protections under the 1954 Hague Convention, its Protocols, and Additional Protocol I.

2. Safeguarding and respect

The US LOW Manual inserted 1954 Hague Convention, Article 2, stating that '[t]he protection of cultural property comprises the safeguarding of and respect for such property' and noting that '[s]afeguarding consists of the affirmative acts that are to be taken to ensure the protection of cultural property', while 'respect . . . requires parties to refrain from certain acts, such as placing cultural property in peril or causing damage to it'.[86] The US LOW Manual included the 1954 Hague Convention duties to 'safeguard' cultural property within the subsection '1954 Hague Convention Peacetime Obligations to Prepare for the Safeguarding of Cultural Property',[87] which is interesting both in that it is distinguishing affirmative obligations to protect in peacetime from negative obligations for 'respect' during hostilities, but also because peacetime obligations are within the hostilities section of the US LOW Manual. The UK LOAC Manual also included measures to safeguard cultural property in the 'Conduct of Hostilities Section'.[88] Of course, neither Manual has a dedicated peacetime section.

In regard to respect, the negative obligations, the US LOW Manual states that '[n]o use should be made of cultural property, its immediate surroundings, or appliances in use for its protection, for purposes that are likely to expose it to destruction or damage in the event of armed conflict' unless there is imperative military necessity.[89] The UK LOAC Manual similarly notes that '[t]his Convention places an equal obligation on defenders and attackers by requiring states to refrain from uses of cultural property that would expose it to danger in armed conflict and to refrain from acts of hostility against cultural property'.[90] The US LOW Manual states

[86] US LOW Manual 297 nn 591 (citing 1954 Hague Convention, art 2), 592, and 593 (citing 'Jiří Toman, Cultural Property in Wartime, 57 (1996)'). It appears that the publication referenced is Jiří Toman, *The Protection of Cultural Property in the Event of Armed Conflict* (UNESCO/Dartmouth 1996). For additional analysis of Toman's interpretation of Parties' obligations to cultural property in armed conflict, see Elizabeth Varner, 'The Art of Armed Conflicts: An Analysis of the United States' Legal Requirements Towards Cultural Property Under the 1954 Hague Convention' (2011) 44 Creighton L Rev 28.

[87] US LOW Manual 297 and n 594 (citing 1954 Hague Convention, art 3 (duties of 'safeguarding')). See also ibid 297–98 n 596 (citing 1954 Hague Convention, art 4(5) (obligations of 'respect' apply even where safeguarding measures are not applied)) and ibid 1085 (citing 1954 Hague Convention, art 7 (requiring peacetime introduction of military regulations or instructions to ensure observance of the treaty 'and to foster in the members of their armed forces a spirit of respect for the culture and cultural property of all peoples')).

[88] UK LOAC Manual 73.

[89] US LOW Manual 298–300 and nn 597-98 (citing 1954 Hague Convention, art 4(1), (2)). The US LOW Manual explains that '(1) using the cultural property for military purposes; (2) placing military objectives near cultural property; or (3) using the cultural property in such a way that an adversary would likely regard it as a military objective' would likely be uses that would expose the cultural property to damage or destruction. ibid.

[90] UK LOAC Manual 15.

there is no waiver for military necessity for the prohibition against using 'the threat of potential harm to cultural property to shield military objectives from attack, or otherwise to shield, favor, or impede military operations'.[91]

3. Feasible precautions

The US LOW Manual explains that 'feasible precautions should be taken to reduce the risk of harm to cultural property' including: alerting armed forces about the location of cultural property, creating no-strike lists of cultural property, and creating civil authorities to plan and 'ensure respect for cultural property under its control'; 'physically shielding cultural property from harm'; and 'establishing refuges and evacuating movable cultural property to them'.[92] The UK LOAC Manual notes that the 1954 Hague Convention Protocol II incorporated some of the 1977 Additional Protocol I's precautions in attack.[93]

4. Imperative military necessity and proportionality

When covering what 'imperative military necessity' means for protection of cultural property, the US LOW Manual notes that it is similar to 'the requirement that enemy property may only be seized if imperatively required by the necessities of war'.[94] It also provides examples of imperative military necessity, including when cultural property is being used for military purposes, when the enemy uses cultural property to shield military objectives, or when a military objective is in close proximity to cultural property.[95] This explanation in the US LOW Manual suggests that the US DOD does not see an appreciable difference between 'military necessity' and 'imperative military necessity' in regards to cultural property.

The UK LOAC Manual notes that the United Kingdom made a declaration when ratifying Additional Protocol I that cultural property no longer enjoys protected status from attacks if used for military purposes.[96] Citing the 1999 Second Protocol to the 1954 Hague Convention, the UK LOAC Manual states that '[t]here may be *rare* cases where it is essential to use cultural property for military purposes,

[91] US LOW Manual 298.

[92] ibid 298–99, n 606 (citing examples of cultural property identified for protection in Iraq during Operation Desert Storm and Angkor Wat in Cambodia during the conflict in Vietnam) and n 607 (eg 'museum curators and staff, local fire and law enforcement authorities, and civil defense personnel').

[93] UK LOAC Manual 73.

[94] US LOW Manual 300.

[95] ibid nn 613 (comparing, inter alia, Roerich Pact, art 5 and 1907 Hague Convention, Regulations, art 27 focusing on language regarding not using cultural property for military purposes); 614 (citing US Department of Defense, *Conduct of the Persian Gulf War: A Report to Congress* (1992) 610 finding 'imperative military necessity' can occur when cultural property or its immediate surroundings are used to protect military objectives); 615 (citing Strobe Talbot, 'Letter of Submittal' (12 May 1998) in Transmittal of the Hague Convention for the Protection of Cultural Property in the Event of Armed Conflict and, for Accession, the Hague Protocol to the Senate Foreign Relations Committee, S Treaty Doc No 106-1, III–IV, IX (1999) (finding that proximity of cultural property does not immunize military objectives under 1954 Hague Convention)).

[96] UK LOAC Manual 70 and n 107.

for example, an historic bridge that is the only available river crossing' but that such cases 'only occur where there is no choice possible between the use of cultural property for military purposes and another feasible method for obtaining a similar military advantage'.[97] The UK LOAC Manual states '[t]he prohibition in the Protocol of the use of cultural property for military purposes is important because if it is not so used, there is no need to attack it.'[98]

Interestingly, the United Kingdom 'has reserved the right to take reprisals against cultural property in certain circumstances'.[99] The UK LOAC Manual explains that while reprisals are prohibited against cultural property under the 1977 Additional Protocol I as well as under the 1954 Hague Convention, the United Kingdom made a reservation upon ratifying the 1977 Additional Protocol I, which permits reprisals to the extent required to get the other party to cease particular 1977 Additional Protocol I violations.[100] This is different than the US LOW Manual, which notes that Parties to the 1954 Hague Convention must refrain from reprisals, citing the 1954 Hague Convention.[101] Of course, at the time of the UK LOAC Manual, the United Kingdom was not a Party to the 1954 Hague Convention. The United Kingdom did not make any such similar reservations upon becoming a Party to the 1954 Hague Convention or its Protocols.[102]

An additional point of interpretation regarding military necessity is the 1999 Second Protocol's impact on military necessity—specifically whether the narrower definition of military necessity in the 1999 Second Protocol clarifies that term in the 1954 Hague Convention or, rather, if it is only applicable to those States that are Parties to the 1999 Second Protocol. Regardless, when the 1999 Second Protocol comes into play it modifies the 1954 Hague Convention, stating that a waiver pursuant to military necessity under the 1954 Hague Convention can only be invoked to direct hostile acts against cultural property when the cultural property is, 'by its function', a military objective and 'there is no feasible alternative available to obtain a similar military advantage to that offered by directing an act of hostility

[97] ibid 71 n 112 (citing 1999 Second Protocol, art 6) (emphasis in original).

[98] ibid 71.

[99] ibid 70 n 104.

[100] ibid (citing Additional Protocol I, art 53); 422–23; and 422 n 58 (citing Additional Protocol I, art 53(c) and 1954 Hague Convention, art 4(4)).

[101] US LOW Manual 1115 and n 218 (citing 1954 Hague Convention, art 4(4)). While not specifying the binding effect, the US LOW Manual lists a series of objects and places from which Additional Protocol I prohibited reprisal, notes that such prohibitions are 'counter-productive' and 'remove[s] a significant deterrent that protects civilians', and lists a series of States, including the United Kingdom, that have made reservations or declarations limiting this provision. ibid 1115–16 nn 220–24 (citing Additional Protocol I, arts 51–52 and 54–56). Article 53 of Additional Protocol I, which protects cultural objects and places of worship, was conspicuously absent.

[102] UNESCO, 'Ratification and accession by the United Kingdom of Great Britain and Northern Ireland to the Convention for the Protection of Cultural Property in the Event of Armed Conflict and accession to, its 1954 First Protocol (The Hague, 14 May 1954) and its Second Protocol (The Hague, 26 March 1999)' <http://portal.unesco.org/en/ev.php-URL_ID=49438&URL_DO=DO_TOPIC&URL_SECTION=201.html> accessed 22 December 2018.

against that objective'.[103] Further, imperative military necessity can only be invoked to 'use cultural property for purposes which are likely to expose it to destruction or damage when and for as long as no choice is possible between such use of the cultural property and another feasible method for obtaining a similar military advantage'.[104]

The United Kingdom references the 1999 Second Protocol in the UK LOAC Manual, noting that it has a 'stricter definition of military necessity', and includes its Article 6 in the 'Hostilities' section discussion on utilizing cultural property for military purposes.[105] The United Kingdom has since ratified the 1999 Second Protocol and made a reservation that it understands the term 'feasible', as used in the Second Protocol, to mean 'that which is practicable or practically possible, taking into account all circumstances ruling at that time, including humanitarian and military considerations',[106] which comports with the US LOW Manual's interpretation above, using 'feasible' as tempering obligations rather than as an absolute requirement. The UNESCO Military Manual also utilizes the 'no feasible alternative' language found in the Second Protocol that restricts 'imperative military necessity' in the 1954 Hague Convention, but takes a stricter view of feasibility noting that 'attacking cultural property is a last resort'.[107]

The interpretation of military necessity, as applied to cultural property, elucidated in the US LOW Manual and UK LOAC Manual fits within that adopted in one of the final cases in the ICTY's jurisprudence, *Prosecutor v Prlić*. In a three-volume judgment issued in November 2017, the ICTY Appeals Chamber in *Prlić* dealt with military necessity in its discussion of the claim of wanton destruction of cities, towns, or villages, or devastation not justified by military necessity arising out of the destruction of the Old Bridge of Mostar.[108] The Tribunal found that once the bridge had been deemed to be a valid military target, there could not be wanton destruction not justified by military necessity.[109] However, the dissent argued that being a military objective was just one prong of the discussion and that military necessity could not violate the laws of armed conflict such that principles of

[103] Cf 1954 Hague Convention, art 4 and 1999 Second Protocol, art 6.

[104] ibid.

[105] See UK LOAC Manual 15, 73, 394.

[106] UNESCO, 'Convention for the Protection of Cultural Property in the Event of Armed Conflict with Regulations for the Execution of the Convention 1954: Declarations and Reservations' <http://portal.unesco.org/en/ev.php-URL_ID=13637&URL_DO=DO_TOPIC&URL_SECTION=201.html> accessed 9 December 2018. See also UK LOAC Manual 81.

[107] UNESCO Military Manual 28, para 94.

[108] See Maurice Cotter, 'Military Necessity, Proportionality and Dual-Use Objects at the ICTY: A Close Reading of the *Prlić et al.* Proceedings on the Destruction of the Old Bridge of Mostar' (2018) 23 J Conflict & Security L 283. In regard to the issue of dual-use objects, the US LOW Manual notes that either an object is a military objective or it is not. 'However, it will be appropriate to consider in applying the principle of proportionality the harm to the civilian population that is expected to result from the attack on such a military objective.' US LOW Manual 209.

[109] *Prosecutor v Prlić* (Appeals Judgment) ICTY-04-74-A (29 November 2017) 172–73, para 411.

distinction, proportionality, and precaution must also be complied with, which he did not think the Tribunal adequately addressed.[110] While the Tribunal restricted its analysis to destruction of property, the Trial Chamber and the dissent expanded the scope of effects to include the psychological effect of isolating the Muslim population. Within this discussion, the dissent relied on the UNESCO Military Manual—noting that UNESCO claimed the contents of their manual reflect customary international law—for the proposition that cultural property can only be attacked if it is a military object and 'there is no feasible alternative for obtaining a similar military advantage'.[111] Reliance on the UNESCO Military Manual is interesting as it, and the feasibility language that is similar to that in the 1999 Second Protocol and referred to in the UNESCO Military Manual as being reflected in customary international law, post-dates the 1993 destruction of the bridge.[112] Regarding proportionality analyses, the UNESCO Military Manual further states that 'only the promise of very considerable concrete and direct military advantage, in many cases overwhelming,' will 'justify an attack that is likely to cause incidental damage to cultural property'.[113]

The US LOW Manual explicitly notes that the ICTY decisions, while influential, do not, 'as a strictly legal matter, "bind" other courts'.[114] Nonetheless, it is likely that both the US LOW Manual's and the UK LOAC Manual's handling of military necessity fit within the Tribunal's determination. Even if there is a waiver of protection to respect cultural property and environs because of imperative military necessity under the 1954 Hague Convention, the US LOW Manual notes that the principle of proportionality will apply such that the 'risk of harm to the cultural property must be considered … and feasible precautions should be taken to reduce the risk of harm to the cultural property'.[115] Moreover, 'as a matter of policy, decision-makers may still seek to refrain from harming cultural property'.[116] However, the UK LOAC Manual fits better within the dissent's higher bar that tracks the 1999 Second Protocol, which, as noted earlier, has been joined by the United Kingdom but not the United States. Including the psychological impact of the destruction of a dual-use bridge that was a military objective in a proportionality analysis is another matter entirely.

[110] *Prosecutor v Prlić* (Appeals Judgment, Dissenting Opinions of Judge Pocar) ICTY-04-74-A (29 November 2017) 3–11, paras 5–23.

[111] ibid (citing UNESCO Military Manual 29, 55).

[112] See 1999 Second Protocol, art 6. UNESCO Military Manual 4 ('customary international law of armed conflict mirrors to a large extent the rules embodied in treaty form in the 1954 Hague Convention and its two Protocols') 11. Note also that Judge Pocar's dissent echoed the 1999 Second Protocol's language of 'enhanced protection', stating that 'it is clear that cultural property is subject to enhanced protection under IHL.' *Prosecutor v Prlić* (Dissenting Opinions by Judge Pocar) 9 , para 17.

[113] UNESCO Military Manual 35, para 114.

[114] US LOW Manual 35 (citation omitted).

[115] ibid 301.

[116] ibid n 618.

5. 1954 Hague Convention Article 4(3)

The US LOW Manual includes the text of the 1954 Hague Convention, Article 4(3), noting that '[a]ny form of theft, pillage, misappropriation of, or requisition of, and any acts of vandalism directed against, cultural property is prohibited' and further notes that requisitions of cultural property in the territory of another State Party, waivers from 'imperative military necessity', and pillage are not permitted.[117] The Manual includes a requirement to take 'reasonable measures' to prevent or stop the aforementioned actions, which is 'part of the obligation to take feasible precautions to reduce risk of harm to cultural property'.[118] Reasonable efforts depend on 'availability of forces, the commander's mission, ... enemy threats,' and 'information available to the commander at the time'.[119]

Different interpretations exist as to whether the associated provision of the 1954 Hague Convention conveys an affirmative duty to stop third Parties or merely the armed forces' own combatants. The US LOW Manual does not explicitly state whether it recognizes an affirmative obligation to stop third Parties. The examples listed primarily refer to the United States stopping harm to cultural property from its own troops (eg training and issuing and enforcing orders). Moreover, the Manual previously notes that the obligation of 'respect' under the 1954 Hague Convention requires Parties to refrain from certain acts.[120] However, this Manual also states that 'efforts to identify cultural property within an area of operations and to secure it from theft or pillage are a prudent part of the planning process of military operations' and that 'such efforts may deny opposing forces the opportunity to exploit harm to cultural property for propaganda purposes'.[121] Any obligation would be limited pursuant to 'reasonable measures'. These provisions, as well as the earlier statements in the US LOW Manual on preventing pillage, suggests that while the US DOD might not interpret Article 4(3) of the 1954 Hague Convention as a requirement to affirmatively stop third Parties, it is a good idea to do so, which represents a shift in tone from previous DOD documents.[122] The UK LOAC Manual spends less time on obligations of 'respect' than the US LOW Manual and does not give much insight into whether 'respect' is a negative obligation to prevent the UK military from harming cultural property or if it is an affirmative obligation to protect cultural property from third Parties.

[117] ibid n 619 (quoting 1954 Hague Convention, art 4(3)).
[118] ibid.
[119] US LOW Manual 301–02.
[120] ibid 187.
[121] ibid 302.
[122] See Varner (n 86) 33–36, for an analysis of DOD's previous handling of 1954 Hague Convention, art 4(3). This volume does not cover a variety of topics within this section, such as marking and displaying emblems on cultural property, special protection, and transportation of cultural property, due to space limitations.

IV. 'Military Occupation'

A. 'Introduction'

The US LOW Manual[123] defines occupation as 'a temporary measure for administering territory under the control of invading forces' and notes that the occupier 'has obligations related to the maintenance of public order and safety, and the protection of civilians and property in occupied territory'.[124] The Manual includes a host of rules that are applicable during occupation, including from the 1907 Hague Convention, 1949 Geneva Conventions, and 1954 Hague Convention, noting that the 1954 Hague Convention applies to occupation, partial or total, regardless of lack of armed resistance.[125]

The US LOW Manual notes that belligerent occupation does not exist during invasions, 'liberation of friendly territory', NIAC, and in some postwar situations.[126] Rather, it, and the UK LOAC Manual, observe that there must be occupation 'in fact' such that the territory 'is actually placed under the authority of the hostile forces', pursuant to the customary international law standard codified in Article 42 of the 1907 Hague Convention, which additionally limits occupation to 'where such authority has been established and can be exercised'.[127] While noting that a proclamation of occupation is not required for occupation to exist, and that 'territory may be occupied even though no proclamation has been issued', the US LOW Manual notes that such a proclamation might be useful in setting a date for the start of occupation.[128] The Manual's cited example for the utility of such a proclamation was the opinion of a former US Assistant Attorney General, that 'the United States became an occupying power [in Iraq] no later than April 16, 2003'.[129] The term 'no later than' suggests that the occupation, a fact-based inquiry, could have started earlier. However, the example proffered for setting a date for beginning occupation was after the looting of the Iraqi Museum occurred, approximately before 10 April until 13 April 2003, suggesting that the

[123] US LOW Manual 754–839.

[124] ibid 754–55.

[125] ibid 757 (citing 1949 Geneva Conventions, common art 2 for similar language) and n 16 (citing 1954 Hague Convention, art 18). See UK LOAC Manual 275–76. The US LOW Manual notes that the 1954 Hague Convention supplements the 1907 Hague Convention provisions regarding occupation if both are applicable. In addition, it states that many provisions in the 1907 Hague Convention arts 42 through 56 reflect customary international law and, and as such, potentially apply to non-Party States, as well as NIACs discussed in Section IV.B. ibid 756–57.

[126] ibid 759.

[127] ibid 764, 767 and nn 54, 55, and 72 (citing 1907 Hague Convention, Regulations, art 42).

[128] ibid 767–68.

[129] ibid 767–68 n 75 (citing Jack L Goldsmith III's opinion in applying a standard of 'actual authority', based on the date that General Tommy Franks announced the creation of the 'Coalition Provisional Authority to exercise powers of government temporarily' (citations omitted)).

US DOD does not interpret the law of occupation to have applied during the looting of the Iraqi Museum.[130]

B. 'Enemy Property During Occupation'

The US LOW Manual in its 'Enemy Property During Occupation' section[131] advises that '[p]illage is forbidden' and that enemy private property may not be seized or destroyed during occupation 'unless imperatively demanded by necessities of war'.[132] The UK LOAC Manual echoes the prohibition on destroying private or state enemy property unless there is absolute necessity, citing the 1907 Hague Convention and the 1949 Fourth Geneva Convention.[133] The US LOW Manual also includes the applicable quotes from the Fourth Geneva Convention within the text.[134] Moreover, the US LOW Manual and the UK LOAC Manual both incorporated language from the 1907 Hague Convention, Article 56, which requires that

> The property of municipalities, that of institutions dedicated to religion, charity, and education, and the arts and sciences, even when State property, shall be treated as private property. All seizure of, destruction of, or willful damage done to institutions of this character, historic monuments, works of art, and science, is forbidden, and should be made the subject of legal proceedings.[135]

C. 'Protection of Cultural Property During Occupation'

For cultural property, the US LOW Manual notes the 'general rules for the protection of cultural property during hostilities also apply during occupation'.[136] The US LOW Manual then inserts language from the 1954 Hague Convention for obligations toward cultural property in occupation, including obligations to support

[130] See eg John F Burns, 'A Nation at War: Looting; Pillagers Strip Iraqi Museum of Its Treasure' *NY Times* (New York, 13 April 2003). For additional information, see the section 'When Military Occupation Law Applies' in US LOW Manual 763–69. Sources differ on the date looting began.

[131] US LOW Manual 806–16.

[132] ibid 806 (citing 1907 Hague Convention, Regulations, art 47).

[133] UK LOAC Manual 299 n 129 (citing 1907 Hague Convention, Regulations, art 23(g), 1949 Geneva Convention IV, art 53).

[134] US LOW Manual 806 n 300 (citing 1949 Geneva Convention IV, art 53 ('Any destruction by the Occupying Power of real or personal property belonging individually or collectively to private persons, or to the State, or to other public authorities, or to social or cooperative organizations, is prohibited, except where such destruction is rendered absolutely necessary by military operations')).

[135] See US LOW Manual 813 n 343 and UK LOAC Manual 303 n 146 (quoting from 1907 Hague Convention, Regulations, art 56).

[136] US LOW Manual 816.

competent national authorities of the occupied country 'as far as possible' with safeguarding and preserving cultural property and to take 'the most necessary measures of preservation' when the competent national authorities are unable to do so.[137]

While the UK LOAC Manual did not have a section within 'Occupied Territory' dedicated to cultural property, it did cite a 1907 Hague Convention provision related to sparing cultural property from attack during hostilities and the 1977 Additional Protocol I for the premise that cultural property is protected during occupation as well as echoing another 1977 Additional Protocol I provision for the proposition that '[c]ultural property is not to be used for military purposes'.[138] Earlier in the UK LOAC Manual, in the 'Cultural Property Convention' sub-section within the 'Conduct of Hostilities' section, the Manual noted that occupiers 'have a duty to safeguard and preserve cultural property'.[139]

V. 'Non-International Armed Conflicts (NIAC)'

A. 'Introduction'

In its Introduction to this section,[140] the US LOW Manual defines a non-international armed conflict, or NIAC, as 'armed conflicts that are not between States' explaining that a NIAC can take place across more than one State—the key issue is the Parties, not the geographical location.[141] The comparable section in the UK LOAC Manual, as noted in its section title, focuses on 'Internal Armed Conflict'. An amendment to the UK LOAC Manual notes that while 'throughout history, and today, non-international armed conflict is the predominant form of conflict, traditionally, international law has been principally concerned with relations between states and not with internal matters within states', but that 'focus is changing' especially in NIAC.[142] Consequently, while much of the information in this section is similar to that in the US LOW Manual, the scope potentially is more limited.[143] The US LOW Manual further states that some 'baseline rules' apply to NIAC, citing common article 3 of the 1949 Geneva Conventions on 'Conflicts Not of an International Character' to which the United States and United Kingdom are Parties, and law of war principles, such as humanity.[144]

[137] ibid n 362 (citing 1954 Hague Convention, art 5(1)).

[138] UK LOAC Manual 303 nn 147 (citing 1907 Hague Convention, Regulations, art 27 and Additional Protocol I, art 53) and 148 (citing Additional Protocol I, art 53).

[139] ibid 72.

[140] US LOW Manual 1027–32.

[141] ibid 1027–28.

[142] See UK LOAC Manual Amendment 3 (n 26) 1 (revising UK LOAC Manual 3 n 6).

[143] For the purposes of this chapter, the remainder of this section will continue to evaluate the UK LOAC Manuals for insight into NIAC.

[144] US LOW Manual 1030 nn 14 (citing art 3 common to all four 1949 Geneva Conventions) and 15 (quoting *Prosecutor v Tadić* (Appeals Chamber) ICTY-94-1-AR72 (2 October 1995) for insight that

B. 'Application of International Law to NIACs'

In general, both Manuals reflect the premise to apply LOAC to NIAC (or 'internal armed conflict', in the case of the United Kingdom),[145] including treaty rules that expressly state applicability in NIAC (or internal armed conflict), which obviously only bind States Parties, and customary international law.[146] The United States is a Party to some treaties that have provisions that explicitly apply to NIAC, including Common Article 3 of the 1949 Geneva Conventions and the 1954 Hague Convention.[147] The United Kingdom is a Party to those same Conventions and the 1977 Additional Protocol II.[148]

Since the publication of the US LOW Manual, a former Legal Advisor to the US State Department clarified the United States' interpretation of international law applicable in NIAC, noting that the principle of distinction applied as 'parties must distinguish between military objectives' and 'civilian objects' as Parties can only attack military objectives.[149] After using the language for the definition of a military objective found in the 1977 Additional Protocol I, he clarified that military objectives 'include objects that make an effective contribution to the enemy's war-fighting or war-sustaining capabilities.'[150] In regard to feasibility, he noted that precautions must be taken to reduce the risk of harm to civilians in an attack, such as providing warnings.[151] Further, he noted that customary international law bars targeting civilian objects and indiscriminate attacks, which includes indiscriminate weapons.[152] Finally, Egan recognized the principle of proportionality

'[w]hat is inhumane, and consequently proscribed, in international wars, cannot but be inhumane and inadmissible in civil strife'). See also Brian Egan, 'International Law, Legal Diplomacy, and the Counter-ISIL Campaign: Some Observations' (2016) 92 Intl L Studies 242.

[145] US LOW Manual 1032–40.

[146] See ibid 1031–33, 1039. UK LOAC Manual 383–84. The US LOW Manual noted that the 'law of war applicable in a non-international armed conflict is binding upon all parties to the armed conflict, including State armed forces and non-State armed groups.' US LOW Manual 1039. The US LOW Manual noted that some treaties 'may apply implicitly to non-international armed conflict.' US LOW Manual 1033–35 (citing conventions and protocols prohibiting genocide, torture, chemical and biological weapons, and child soldiers).

[147] US LOW Manual 1033 n 30 (citing Commentary to the 1949 Geneva Conventions for the proposition that common Article 3 is like a "'Convention in miniature'" that applies to non-international conflicts only) and n 33 (citing 1954 Hague Convention, art 19(1) (In NIAC 'occurring within the territory of one of the High Contracting Parties, each party to the conflict shall be bound to apply, as a minimum, the provisions of the present Convention which relate to respect for cultural property').

[148] UK LOAC Manual 383 n 1. The UK LOAC Manual notes that the 1999 Second Protocol to the 1954 Hague Convention also explicitly applies in internal armed conflict. ibid 394.

[149] Egan (n 144) 242. Compare Additional Protocol I, art 48. See ibid, arts 51–52.

[150] Egan (n 144) 242. Compare Additional Protocol 1, art 52(2). See also, inter alia, US LOW Manual 210 n 157 (considering Additional Protocol I art 52(2)) and n 164 (citing Commentary to the 1977 Additional Protocols I and II)) 635 (finding that when the two elements cited in the US LOW Manual for the two-part test for military objectives are present, 'there is a military objective in the sense of the Protocol').

[151] Egan (n 146) 242. Compare Additional Protocol I, art 57.

[152] ibid 243. Compare Additional Protocol I, arts 51–52.

applied in NIAC to prohibit attacks against military objectives that 'are expected to cause incidental harm to civilians that would be excessive in relation to the concrete and direct military advantage anticipated'.[153] Of interest, this language tracks that found in the 1977 Additional Protocol I for IAC rather than that in the 1977 Additional Protocol II for NIAC, suggesting that these obligations may be interpreted to be customary legal obligations.

C. 'Protection of Cultural Property in NIAC'

Egan further noted that attacks against cultural property are not allowed unless the 'protection has been forfeited'.[154] The US LOW Manual observes that the 1954 Hague Convention explicitly applies to protect cultural property in NIAC in territories of Parties to the Convention through Article 19 of the 1954 Hague Convention.[155] Interestingly, the Manual states that the obligation to 'respect' cultural property includes 'essentially negative duties, ie, duties to refrain from acts of hostility directed against cultural property and duties to refrain from the use of cultural property in support of military operations where such use is not imperatively necessary'.[156] This language suggests that the United States' interpretation of 'respect' does not require affirmative actions to protect cultural property from third Parties.

The UK LOAC Manual reviews some of the applicable customary international law within the subsection on 'Immunity of Civilian Objects', noting that civilian property can only be destroyed pursuant to military necessity.[157] The UK LOAC Manual states, within the subsection on 'Protection of cultural objects and places of worship', that acts of hostility against cultural property are prohibited unless it is being used for military purposes; that uses that would expose cultural property to harm are prohibited 'unless there is no feasible alternative', as is 'stealing, misappropriating, confiscation of, or willful damage to, cultural property'; and that cultural property includes religious, charitable, educational, art, and science institutions and historic monuments.[158] Of interest, the UK LOAC Manual cites this 1907 Hague Convention provision that lists cultural property to spare in this 'Internal Armed Conflict' section and the 'Occupied Territory' section, not the 'Conduct of Hostilities' section, and, similar to the US LOW Manual, does not appear to proscribe any limitations to this provision as was done with the 1954 Hague Convention and 1977 Additional Protocol I.

[153] ibid. Compare Additional Protocol, art 51(5).
[154] Egan (n 144) 242. Compare 1954 Hague Convention, art 4, and Additional Protocol I, art 53.
[155] US LOW Manual 1055 n 147 (citing 1954 Hague Convention, art 19(1)).
[156] ibid 1056 n 148 (considering Additional Protocol II, art 16).
[157] UK LOAC Manual 393.
[158] ibid 393–94 and n 40 (citing 1907 Hague Convention, Regulations, art 27).

Conclusion

The last few years have seen continued armed conflict and damage and destruction to cultural property as a result, whether intentional or incidental. Armed conflict has evolved, including the manner in which it is fought and who is fighting it, concomitantly with interpretations of States' obligations. With the ready proliferation of horrific images of destruction resulting from armed conflict across a plethora of media platforms, dissatisfaction of the protections afforded civilians, their property, and cultural property has continued to grow apace. These concerns, developments in law and State practice, discrepancies in views, and the inherently chaotic nature of armed conflict have led to differing interpretations of obligations to cultural heritage.

Within the last decade, two major military powers—the United States and United Kingdom—have joined the 1954 Hague Convention. Analyzing their military manuals and other recent developments provides insights into the States' interpretations of their obligations. Some key takeaways include both States' recognition of a tiered level of protection for property, such that even if the property does not reach the level of protection afforded by the 1954 Hague Convention or the 1977 Additional Protocol I, it still is afforded some protection. The United States utilizes a nuanced balancing approach to determine if property fits within the cultural property definition in the 1954 Hague Convention, while the United Kingdom only considers property of international importance to fit within the 1954 Hague Convention and 1977 Additional Protocol I. Both States utilize key LOAC principles of distinction, proportionality, and military necessity, though there are differences in interpretation. It appears also that while the US LOW Manual notes the benefit of protecting cultural property from third Parties, there is no requirement to do so. Finally, the US LOW Manuals notes customary international law applies to NIAC, as does the 1954 Hague Convention in the territory of State Parties, with which the UK LOAC Manual concurs in respect to Internal Armed Conflict, in addition to applying Additional Protocol II.

3

Military Intervention, the UN Security Council, and the Role of UNESCO

The Case of Mali

*Sabine von Schorlemer**

Introduction

Annihilation of cultural heritage is gradually evolving into an issue of peace and security in the twenty-first century. Destructive ideologies are not new in history, as the UNESCO Strategy, entitled 'Reinforcement of UNESCO's Action for the Protection of Culture and the Promotion of Cultural Pluralism in the Event of Armed Conflict', acknowledges; but today 'threats to cultural heritage in the event of armed conflict result from intentional destruction, collateral damage, forced neglect, as well as from the organized looting and illicit trafficking of cultural objects ... at an unprecedented scale'.[1] Intentional destruction of cultural heritage by extremist non-State actors, such as the Taliban in Afghanistan, the so-called Islamic State (Islamic State of Iraq and the Levant, or ISIL, or Daesh) in Syria, Iraq, and Libya, or Boko Haram in Nigeria, may be seen as part of 'ideological warfare against cultural property'.[2]

Against this background, events in Mali, a former French colony, demonstrate to what extent precious tangible and intangible cultural heritage, such as monuments,

* This chapter was presented at the international conference on 'Intersections in International Cultural Heritage Law', hosted by Georgetown University Law Center (Washington DC) on 29 March 2016.

[1] UNESCO General Conference, 'Reinforcement of UNESCO's Action for the Protection of Culture and the Promotion of Cultural Pluralism in the Event of Armed Conflict' (2 November 2015) UNESCO Doc 38/C/49. See also UNESCO General Conference, 'Strategy for the Reinforcement of UNESCO's Action for the Protection of Culture and the Promotion of Cultural Pluralism in the Event of Armed Conflict' (24 October 2017) UNESCO Doc 39/C/57, para 1.

[2] Kirsten Schmalenbach, 'Ideological Warfare against Cultural Property: UN Strategies and Dilemmas' (2016) 19 Max Planck YB UN L 1, 10; regarding 'identity-based violence' cf Sabine von Schorlemer, *Kulturgutzerstörung: Die Auslöschung von Kulturerbe in Krisenländern als Herausforderung für die Vereinten Nationen* (Nomos 2016) 79ff (Schorlemer, 'Kulturgutzerstörung') with further references. See also Sabine von Schorlemer, 'Cultural Heritage Protection as a Security Issue in the 21st Century: Recent Developments' (2018) 16 Indonesian Journal of International Law 28 (Schorlemer, 'Cultural Heritage Protection'); Sabine von Schorlemer, 'Der Schutz von Kulturerbestätten als Aufgabe der UN-Sicherheitspolitik' (2016) 64 Vereinte Nationen 3ff.

Sabine von Schorlemer, Military Intervention, the UN Security Council, and the Role of UNESCO In: *Intersections in International Cultural Heritage Law*. Edited by Anne-Marie Carstens and Elizabeth Varner. © Oxford University Press 2020. The several contributors DOI: 10.1093/oso/9780198846291.003.0004

mosques, manuscripts, and cultural practices, suffers from willful attacks by non-State actors. When extremist forces tried to forcefully create an independent state named Azawad in the north of Mali in 2012–13, this incursion seemed to become a test case for the will and capacity of the United Nations (UN) to react.

The present chapter intends to explore in more detail the security-related intersections in international cultural heritage law. The Security Council established the United Nations Multidimensional Integrated Stabilization Mission (MINUSMA) and gave it a remarkably broad mandate that was also 'the first to include the protection of cultural and historical sites in the mandate of a peacekeeping operation'.[3]

This chapter will review critically not only the mandate of the UN peace mission in Mali, set out in UN Security Council (UNSC) Resolution 2100 (2013),[4] but also its possible relevance to future culture-embedded UN missions in general. At the same time, it aims to contribute to the debate on the legitimacy of robust cultural protection action, asking in particular to what extent the 2013 unilateral French military Operation Serval, which was established a short time before UN troops actually arrived on the ground, was helpful for the preservation of Malian cultural heritage as well.

Furthermore, the chapter addresses the role of the United Nations Educational, Scientific and Cultural Organization (UNESCO)—the Paris-based UN specialized agency—regarding the preservation of cultural heritage both in times of peace and emergencies. This chapter will elucidate to what extent UNESCO is promoting a 'new international agenda'[5] regarding the comprehensive role of culture for resilience, peace, and security.

I. UNESCO Peacetime Support for the Preservation of Malian Cultural Heritage

Mali, a state in sub-Saharan Africa with roughly 18 million inhabitants, is historically known for its rich cultural heritage. According to experts, Mali possesses some of the 'best-known archaeological sites in sub-Saharan Africa'.[6] In particular, the mosques and mausoleums in Timbuktu, one of Mali's main cities, are seen as outstanding witnesses to the important commercial, spiritual, and cultural role of Mali

[3] UNHRC, 'Report of the Independent Expert on the Situation of Human Rights in Mali, Suliman Baldo' (10 January 2014) UN Doc A/HRC/25/72, 16, para 89 (UNHRC, 'Report of the Independent Expert').

[4] UNSC Resolution 2100 (25 April 2013) UN Doc S/RES/2100.

[5] See <https://en.unesco.org/The-role-of-culture-for-resilience-peace-and-security> accessed 4 February 2020.

[6] With further references, see Elizabeth A Klesmith, 'Nigeria and Mali: The Case for Repatriation and Protection of Cultural Heritage in Post-Colonial Africa' (2014) 4 Notre Dame J Intl and Comparative L 45, 72; Timothy Insoll, 'The Archaeology of Islam in Sub-Saharan Africa: A Review' (1996) 10 J World Prehistory 439.

and its traditional construction techniques. Timbuktu was an intellectual capital and Islamic center throughout Africa in the fifteenth and sixteenth centuries, with its mosques Djingareyber, Sankoré, and Sidi Yahya recalling the so-called 'golden age'.[7] It has been an 'important part of the region's belief system'[8] and a traditional place of pilgrimage for the whole West African region.[9]

For decades, numerous efforts have been made to preserve the Malian heritage with the help of UNESCO. In 1974, UNESCO had supported the establishment of the Institut des hautes études et de recherches islamiques Ahmed Baba (Ahmed Baba Institute of Higher Learning and Islamic Research). The Institute became the largest repository of ancient manuscripts in West Africa with about 40,000 objects, about 10,000 of which are digitized.

From 1980 to 2012, the year when a military coup d'état ousted the President of the Republic of Mali (on 22 March), UNESCO adopted about forty decisions concerning the peacetime preservation of cultural properties in Mali.[10] In 1988, not only the Old Towns of Djenné but also Timbuktu, with its three large mosques and sixteen cemeteries and mausoleums, were inscribed on the World Heritage List.[11] One year later the World Heritage Committee acknowledged the Cliff of Bandiagara (Land of the Dogons) as an exceptional combination of natural and cultural elements and put it on the World Heritage List as well, despite concerns regarding the impact of tourism on the cultural and natural values of the site.[12] When Timbuktu was classified as a World Heritage Site in 1988, the World Heritage Committee was already viewing the sand encroachment as a threat and suggesting that the Malian authorities consider the inscription of this property on the List of World Heritage in Danger. Consequently, in 1990 the Committee decided to place Timbuktu on the List of World Heritage in Danger, the so-called 'Red List'.[13]

At the same time, a program to safeguard the property was set up, including the consolidation of the famous Djiangareyber Mosque and the improvement of the terrace rainwater drainage systems.[14] In 1995, Malian authorities signed a contract with the UNESCO World Heritage Centre to launch a pilot project concerning the

[7] For the description of Timbuktu as a World Heritage Site, see UNESCO World Heritage Centre <http://whc.unesco.org/en/list/119/> accessed 4 February 2020. See also Patty Gerstenblith, 'The Destruction of Cultural Heritage: A Crime Against Property or a Crime Against People?' (2016) 165 John Marshall Rev Intellectual Property L 336, 357.

[8] UNESCO World Heritage Centre News, 'Director-General Praises the People of Timbuktu for the Reconstruction of the City's Mausoleums' (19 July 2015) <http://whc.unesco.org/en/news/1324> accessed 4 February 2020.

[9] UNESCO World Heritage Centre, 'World Heritage List, Timbuktu' <http://whc.unesco.org/en/list/119> accessed 4 February 2020.

[10] See overview at UNESCO World Heritage Centre, 'Mali' (Documents) <http://whc.unesco.org/pg_friendly_print.cfm?cid=246&documents=1&id=ml&> accessed 4 February 2020.

[11] UNESCO, 12th session of the World Heritage Committee, Decision COMF001 XIV.A (1988).

[12] UNESCO, 13th session of the World Heritage Committee, Decision CONF 004 XV.A (1989).

[13] UNESCO, 14th session of the World Heritage Committee, Decision CONF 004 VII.C (1990).

[14] ibid.

maintenance of the three mosques of Djiangareyber, Sankoré, and Sidi Yahya.[15] The Tomb of Askia in Gao, another cultural property of outstanding universal value, was inscribed on the World Heritage List in 2004 not only because it reflected the local building traditions and the distinctive architectural tradition of the West African Sahel, but also because it represented important remains of the Empire of Songhai.[16]

Mali has also joined most of the relevant UNESCO treaties governing the protection and preservation of cultural heritage. In 1961, Mali ratified the 1954 Convention on the Protection of Cultural Heritage in the Event of Armed Conflict (1954 Hague Convention),[17] and it acceded to its Second Protocol in 2012, the latter being applicable also to internal conflicts as in the present case.[18] Furthermore, Mali joined the 1970 Convention on the Means of Prohibiting and Preventing the Illicit Import, Export and Transfer of Ownership of Cultural Property (1970 UNESCO Convention) in 1987, the 1972 Convention Concerning the Protection of the World Cultural and Natural Heritage (1972 World Heritage Convention) in 1977, and the 2003 Convention for the Safeguarding of the Intangible Cultural Heritage (2003 ICH Convention) in 2005. In this way, Malian heritage came under the umbrella of UNESCO cultural heritage law.

II. Threats to Malian Cultural Heritage (from 2011)

A. The Political Conflict in Mali

Rebel groups threatening Malian cultural treasures in recent years were mostly composed of ethnic Tuaregs who predominantly live in the northern part of the country.[19] In 2011, when President Gaddafi in Libya was defeated, some of his combatants escaped southward to Mali and joined forces with Malian rebels, whereupon the security situation in Mali became 'very volatile'.[20] Mali was confronted

[15] UNESCO, World Heritage Committee Decision: CONF 201 VI.21: Timbuktu (Mali), <http://whc.unesco.org/en/decisions/5487> accessed 4 February 2020.

[16] UNESCO, 28th Session of the Word Heritage Committee, Decision 28 COM 14B.20 (2004).

[17] Convention for the Protection of Cultural Property in the Event of Armed Conflict (adopted 14 May 1954, entered into force 7 August 1956) 249 UNTS 240 (1954 Hague Convention).

[18] Second Protocol to the Hague Convention of 1954 for the Protection of Cultural Property in the Event of Armed Conflict (adopted 26 March 1999, entered into force 9 March 2004) 253 UNTS 172, art 22(1) (1999 Second Protocol).

[19] International Criminal Court, Office of the Prosecutor, 'Situation in Mali, Article 53(1) Report' (16 January 2013) 8ff (quoting, inter alia: CIA World Factbook, Mali, February 2012; UNDP Human Development Index, UNDP Human Development Report 2011; World Bank Country Data, Mali 2011) (Office of the Prosecutor, 'Situation in Mali').

[20] Joris Kila, 'Mission Report: Civil-Military Assessment Mission for Malian Heritage' (2014) 11 J of Art Crime 73, 74. See also International Crisis Group, CrisisWatch Database, Mali (January 2012) <https://www.crisisgroup.org/crisiswatch/database> accessed 4 February 2020 (stating a 'regional spillover from Libyan conflict'); Marina Lostal, *International Cultural Heritage Law in Armed*

with a profound crisis that put its 'national unity, territorial integrity and its tradition as a multi-ethnic, secular democracy' at stake, as set forth in the Report of the UN Secretary-General on the situation in Mali of 28 November 2012.[21]

On 17 January 2012, an attack by the MNLA (Mouvement national de libération de l'Azawad/National Movement for the Liberation of Azawad) on the Malian Forces military base in Menaka, Gao region, took place. As a result, the Malian armed forces withdrew from the north, and non-State armed groups, including the MNLA, the Ansar Dine (Defenders of Faith), Al-Qaeda in the Islamic Maghreb (AQIM), and the Movement for Unity and Jihad in West Africa (MUJAO), occupied the northern part of the country.[22] Between 30 March and 2 April 2012, the rebels took over the main cities and military bases of Timbuktu, Gao, and Kidal[23] and declared the independence of the territory of Azawad. The Tuareg-MNLA occupation of northern Mali ended when military and financially superior forces of Al-Qaeda of the Islamic Maghreb and MUJAO took control while at the same time Ansar Dine started controlling Kidal.[24] The situation was aggravated by a coup d'état by the military junta in Bamako, which forced President Touré to resign at the beginning of April 2012, shortly before the presidential elections, which were originally scheduled for 20 April 2012, could take place.[25]

The framework agreement of 6 April 2012 resulted in the establishment of transitional institutions. Dioncounda Traoré, the former spokesman of Parliament, was elected as interim President and Cheick Modibo Diarra was nominated as Prime Minister of the new transitional government—a process supported by the Economic Community of West African States (ECOWAS), the African Union, and the United Nations. Following the coup d'état, the UN Secretary-General's Representative for West Africa, Said Djinnit, offered the support of the United Nations to the Malian authorities.[26]

Thus, the situation in Mali was characterized by the occupation of the northern territories and the overthrow of its constitutional order. As a result, the country suffered from severe 'human rights violations and acts of violence committed in

Conflict: Case-studies of Syria, Libya, Mali, the Invasion of Iraq, and the Buddhas of Bamiyan (CUP 2107) 128.

[21] UNSC, 'Report of the Secretary-General on the Situation in Mali' (28 November 2012) UN Doc S/2012/894, para 2.

[22] UNHRC, 'Report of the Independent Expert' (n 3) 5, para 9.

[23] See Office of the Prosecutor, 'Situation in Mali' (n 19) 9.

[24] See Arthur Boutellis, 'Can the UN Stabilize Mali? Towards a UN Stabilization Doctrine?' (2015) 4 Intl J of Security & Development, art 33, 3. However, on 19 September 2015, the armed Tuareg coalition 'Coordination of Movements of Azawad' (CMA) announced it had resumed control of the northern town Anéfis. See International Crisis Group, CrisisWatch Database, Mali (October 2015) <https://www.crisisgroup.org/crisiswatch/database> accessed 4 February 2020.

[25] For details see Office of the Prosecutor, 'Situation in Mali' (n 19) 4, 9, 11. See also UNHRC, 'Report of the Independent Expert' (n 3) 5, para 10.

[26] UNSC, 'Report of the Secretary-General' (n 21) para 11.

particular by the rebels, terrorist groups and other organized transnational criminal networks, including … *theft and destruction of religious and cultural sites*', as a report of the UN Human Rights Council (UNHRC) emphasized.[27]

B. The Cultural Heritage of Mali under Threat

Various factors affected Malian heritage sites, mainly civil unrest, illegal activities, and armed conflict. The crisis had considerable cultural consequences, threatening many rich cultural treasures of Mali and creating a state of emergency.

During the occupation of northern Mali by armed groups, World Heritage Sites became 'prime targets of systematic and generalized attacks', not only in Timbuktu but also in Gao where the Tomb of Askia is located.[28] The two other World Heritage properties, the Old Towns of Djenné and the Cliff of Bandiagara (Land of the Dogans), are located in the region of Mopti in the center of Mali. When on 30 June 2012 Ansar Dine destroyed several mausoleums in Timbuktu, there was wide media coverage of these events. These acts of vandalism were claimed to be part of Ansar Dine Salafist ideology, the branch of Sunni Islam found in Saudi Arabia, with strong iconoclastic grounds.[29]

The overall damage to cultural heritage was considerable, for example:

1) In Timbuktu, approximately 4,200 manuscripts from the Ahmed Baba Institute of Higher Learning and Islamic Research were burned; much of the digitization equipment was destroyed. Also, fourteen of sixteen mausoleums on the List of World Heritage Sites were annihilated. Two mausoleums of the famous Djingareyber mosque, which itself was constructed from mud and brick by Emperor Kankou Moussa after his return from Mecca in 1327, were equally lost. The emblematic El Farouk independence monument in the shape of a horse at the entrance of Timbuktu was razed to the ground.
2) In the Gao region, the Cheikh El-Kebir mausoleum was destroyed in September 2012. Kebir's tomb was venerated by the Kunta tribe whose members live not only in Mali, but also in Algeria, Mauritania, and Niger.
3) In Douentza, the big toguna—a fascinating public building with a low roof, erected in the middle of the village by the Dogon people in order to discuss public affairs—was pillaged and its sculpted pillars burned.

[27] UNHRC, 'Human Rights Situation in Mali' (17 July 2012) UN Doc A/HRC/RES/20/17, para 2 (emphasis added).

[28] UNHRC, 'Report of the Independent Expert' (n 3) 16, para 88; for details, see Jadranka Petrovic, 'What Next for Endangered Cultural Treasures? The Timbuktu Crisis and the Responsibility to Protect' (2013) 11 New Zealand J of Public and Intl L 381, 387.

[29] For details, see Klesmith (n 6) 73; Lostal (n 20) 130.

Urgent conservation measures were needed not only for the built heritage but also for movable property. A large number of historically important manuscripts, some of them from the late thirteenth century that have been preserved for centuries, were in a fragile state.[30] In addition, there were high risks of illicit trafficking of an estimated 300,000 manuscripts,[31] many of them having been in long-standing private possession by Malian families.

III. The UNESCO Response, French Military Intervention, and the UN Security Council

A. UNESCO Emergency Assistance

Since the beginning of the crisis, former UNESCO Director-General Bokova repeatedly condemned the acts of deliberate destruction of cultural heritage in Mali and expressed her concern. Ten appeals were made between April 2012 and January 2013[32] urging all Parties to respect the cultural sites and property. In particular, Bokova urged respect for the preservation of the World Heritage Site of Timbuktu[33] and appealed for concerted action to prevent loss or destruction of Timbuktu's documentary heritage.[34] The Director-General also drew the attention of the President of the African Union Commission to the state of Malian cultural heritage, including the World Heritage Sites in Timbuktu and Gao, and mobilized Mali's neighbouring countries to avoid possible thefts and illicit exports of Malian cultural property.

[30] UNESCO, Committee for the Protection of Cultural Property in the Event of Armed Conflict, 'Report of the Secretariat on its activities' (5 December 2013) UNESCO Doc CLT-13/8. COM/CONF.203/INF.2, para 31. See also Kila (n 20) 75ff; UNESCO World Heritage Committee, 'State of conservation of World Heritage properties inscribed on the World Heritage List' (1 June 2012) UNESCO Doc WHC-12/36.COM/7B.Add, 214; concerning restoration, see Section V.

[31] See UNESCO, 'International Experts Meeting for the Safeguarding of Mali's Cultural Heritage: Final Report and Action Plan for the Rehabilitation of Cultural Heritage and the Safeguarding of Ancient Manuscripts in Mali' (18 February 2013) 5, para 9 ('Final Report and Action Plan').

[32] UNESCO, Committee for the Protection of Cultural Property in the Event of Armed Conflict, 'Report of the Secretariat on its activities' (5 December 2013) UNESCO Doc CLT-13/8. COM/CONF.203/INF.2, 3, para 7. See also the overview given by Mr Lazare Eloundou (Chief of the African Unit of the UNESCO World Heritage Centre) in International Experts Meeting, 'Final Report and Action Plan' (n 31) 7, para 15.

[33] UNESCOPRESS, Press Release: 'Director-General of UNESCO urges respect for the preservation of World Heritage site of Timbuktu (Mali)' (5 April 2012) <http://www.unesco.org/new/en/media-services/single-view/news/director_general_of_unesco_urges_respect_for_the_preservatio/> accessed 4 February 2020. Information about UNESCO emergency actions in Mali is available on the UNESCO website <http://www.unesco.org/new/en/culture/themes/illicit-trafficking-of-cultural-property/emergency-actions/mali/> accessed 4 February 2020.

[34] UNESCOPRESS, Press Release: 'UNESCO Director-General appeals for concerted action to prevent loss or destruction of Timbuktu's documentary heritage' (15 April 2012) < http://www.unesco.org/new/en/media-services/world-heritage-37th-session/whc37-details/news/unesco_director_general_appeals_for_concerted_action_to_prev/> accessed 4 February 2020.

On 6 May 2012, the Malian State Party addressed a letter to the Director-General to request UNESCO assistance in case the situation further deteriorated. From 18 to 20 May 2012, a UNESCO emergency mission was sent to Bamako in order to gather information on the current state of conservation and explore options to save the cultural heritage.[35] As a result of the mission, the World Heritage Centre encouraged Mali to draft a state of conservation report and request technical and financial assistance. Mali requested the inscription of the World Heritage Site of Timbuktu and the Tomb of Askia on the List of World Heritage in Danger and finalized the documents of adhesion to the Second Protocol relating to the 1954 Convention for the Protection of Cultural Property in the Event of Armed Conflict. UNESCO, in turn, pledged to assist the government of Mali in reinforcing protection and to cooperate closely with all UN organizations engaged in humanitarian action in Mali to ensure the safeguarding of the country's cultural heritage.[36]

Just a few days before the Ansar Dine terrorist group attacked Timbuktu, the World Heritage Committee accepted the request of the government of Mali to place Timbuktu and the Tomb of Askia in the city of Gao on the so-called Red List.[37] Petrovic criticized, however, that despite the inscription of the Timbuktu mausoleums, 'there was no direct international action against this acknowledged threat to the city's treasures'.[38]

Still, UNESCO was actively involved and helped to prevent further deterioration of Malian cultural treasures. Mali's requests for international assistance have been quite successful in Paris. For example, a 'Special Fund Account' for the safeguarding of World Heritage in Mali was created[39] to support the Malian government in assessing the damage and carrying out reconstruction and rehabilitation projects of the properties affected.[40] The ad hoc allocation of the sum of US$40,500 to the Fund for the Protection of Cultural Property in the Event of Armed Conflict that was granted as an emergency assistance to Mali in December 2012 enabled the country to take some important measures in the northern regions, including restoration of parts of

[35] UNESCO World Heritage Centre News, 'Government of Mali and UNESCO move to protect Timbuktu and other heritage sites in the north of Mali', (24 May 2012) <http://whc.unesco.org/en/news/877/?www.unesco.org/fr/prospective=&> accessed 4 February 2020.

[36] UNESCO World Heritage Centre News, 'Government of Mali and UNESCO Move to Protect Timbuktu and Other Heritage Sites in the North of Mali' (24 May 2012) <http://whc.unesco.org/en/news/877> accessed 4 February 2020.

[37] UNESCO World Heritage Committee, 'Decisions adopted by the World Heritage Committee at its 36th session' (24 June–6 July 2012) UNESCO Doc WHC-12/36.COM/19; UNESCO World Heritage Centre News, 'Heritage Sites in Northern Mali Placed on List of World Heritage in Danger' (28 June 2012) <http://whc.unesco.org/en/news/893/> accessed 4 February 2020. Timbuktu, which had been removed from the Danger List where it was placed for environmental reasons in 2005 (UNESCO 29th session of the World Heritage Committee, Decision 29 COM 7 A.14 (2005)) was placed on the Danger List again in 2012, together with the Tomb of Askia (UNESCO, 36th session of the Word Heritage Committee, Decision 36 COM 7B.106 (2012)).

[38] Petrovic (n 28) 383.

[39] UNESCO World Heritage Centre News, 'Creation of a Special Fund for the Safeguarding of Mali's World Heritage sites' (25 July 2012) <http://whc.unesco.org/en/news/913> accessed 4 February 2020.

[40] Decision 36 COM 7B.107.

the roof of the Tomb of Askia and the treatment of the premises of the museum of Sikasso in the south of Mali to get rid of insects that were threatening the exhibits.

A detailed report on the state of preservation, which was described as precarious, was prepared.[41] Conservation measures were urgently needed not only due to violence or negligence but also due to difficult climate conditions (including dust, heat, and moisture). For that reason, the Director-General of UNESCO granted US$140,000 from the Emergency Fund for safeguarding measures for cultural property;[42] another US$70,000 stemmed from the World Heritage Fund.[43] Thanks to the funding from UNESCO and the Prince Claus Fund, a programme was implemented to reinforce security and convince the local people of the value of their heritage, including a broadcast on the radio and television in Mali.[44]

Furthermore, UNESCO has developed a 'Heritage Passport' in order to facilitate the implementation of Malian laws on heritage and of UNESCO's international conventions ratified by Mali. In November 2012, the Ministry of Culture in Mali published the *Passeport pour le patrimoine* with the support of UNESCO, a document that facilitated protection and rehabilitation measures. It contains a 'questionnaire' concerning tangible and intangible heritage that asks observers on the ground to send information they have collected about the state of the objects ('very good', 'good', 'average', 'bad', 'destroyed') to the ministry.[45]

In early 2013, when the potential for military conflict was rising, more than 200 experts had been convened for a meeting at UNESCO's Headquarters.[46] An Action Plan for Mali's Cultural Heritage and Manuscripts was adopted in February 2013. Specific actions were envisaged for Timbuktu, the Tomb of Askia in Gao, the Old Towns of Djenné, and the Cliff of Bandiagara (Land of the Dogons), as well as several museums. The start of the UNESCO programme of assistance to rebuild Mali's cultural heritage was said to 'spearhead' UNESCO's commitment to safeguard and rebuild Mali's cultural heritage.[47]

[41] For more details, see UNESCO Committee for the Protection of Cultural Property in the Event of Armed Conflict, 'Report on the Use of Financial Assistance Granted to Mali from the Fund for the Protection of Cultural Property in the Event of Armed Conflict' (24 September 2013) UNESCO Doc CLT-13/8.COM/CONF.203/5.

[42] UNESCO, Committee for the Protection of Cultural Property in the Event of Armed Conflict, 'Report of the Secretariat on its Activities' (5 December 2013) UNESCO Doc CLT-13/8.COM/CONF.203/INF.2, para 10.

[43] ibid, para 11.

[44] International Experts Meeting, 'Final Report and Action Plan' (n 31) 6, para 11.

[45] The 'Passeport' for Mali is available online via <http://www.unesco.org/new/fileadmin/MULTIMEDIA/HQ/BPI/EPA/images/media_services/Director-General/Passeport-pour-le-Mali.PDF> accessed 4 February 2020.

[46] See International Experts Meeting, 'Final Report and Action Plan' (n 31). See also UNESCO World Heritage Centre News, 'International Experts and Decision-Makers Gathered at UNESCO Adopt Action Plan for Mali's Cultural Heritage and Manuscripts' (19 February 2013) <http://whc.unesco.org/en/news/987> accessed 4 February 2020.

[47] UNESCO World Heritage Centre News, 'UNESCO Director-General Irina Bokova in Mali to Spearhead UNESCO's Commitment to Safeguard and Rebuild Mali's Extraordinary Cultural Heritage' (2 February 2013) <http://whc.unesco.org/en/news/978> accessed 4 February 2020.

B. Operation Serval (January–July 2013): Too Little—Too Late?

Shortly before the United Nations deployed the African-led International Support Mission in Mali (AFISMA) on 17 January 2013, France launched Operation Serval on 11 January 2013 with approximately 3,700 French ground troops.[48]

Once the French military Operation Serval had started, the UNESCO Director-General urged military forces to protect cultural sites in Mali during air raids and ground interventions.[49] Together with Malian and African Union Forces, and also with the help of the MNLA, the French military took over Gao on 26 January 2013; Timbuktu on 27 January; and Kidal on 30 January. A few days later, they had regained control of the rest of northern Mali territories held so far by Ansar Dine. The French forces 'quickly re-conquered the northern towns of Gao and Timbuktu, then Kidal with support from Chadian AFISMA troops'.[50] Apparently, the French troops and their allied forces met little resistance as armed groups disappeared into the inaccessible northern Mali region of Adrar des Ifoghas and into southern Libya.[51]

The UNHRC acknowledged that the French operation 'halted the offensive of armed jihadi groups towards the south and liberated localities in the north of the country'.[52] Operation Serval was characterized as a 'counterterrorism force'[53] that helped to stabilize the situation within the country, including that of cultural treasures and World Heritage Sites. 'France did step in and help take Timbuktu back from the rebels... [T]housands of manuscripts were saved', as experts observed.[54] Lostal views Operation Serval even as a 'rapid success'.[55]

At the International Experts Meeting for the Safeguarding of Mali's Cultural Heritage in February 2013, at UNESCO Headquarters in Paris, the French intervention was commended as it had 'put an end to destruction in Timbuktu and Gao'.[56] Finally, in a ceremony at the Headquarters of UNESCO (5 June 2013),

[48] International Crisis Group, CrisisWatch Database, Mali (February 2013) <https://www.crisisgroup.org/crisiswatch/database> accessed 4 February 2020.

[49] UNESCO World Heritage Centre News, 'The Director-General of UNESCO Urges Military Forces to Protect Cultural Sites in Mali During Air Raids and Ground Interventions' (14 January 2013) <http://whc.unesco.org/en/news/975/> accessed 4 February 2020.

[50] Boutellis (n 24) 3. See also Raphaël van Steenberghe, 'Les interventions Française et Africaines au Mali au nom de la lutte armée contre le terrorisme' (2014) 118 Revue Générale de Droit Intl Public 273, 274.

[51] Boutellis (n 24) 3.

[52] Human Rights Council, 'Report of the Independent Expert' (n 3) 5, para 11. See also Kila (n 20) 74.

[53] Boutellis (n 24) 6.

[54] Klesmith (n 6) 74.

[55] Lostal (n 20) 131.

[56] Ambassador and Permanent Delegate of Côte d'Ivoire (Ivory Coast) at the International Experts Meeting for the safeguarding of Mali's Cultural Heritage, see International Experts Meeting, 'Final Report and Action Plan' (n 31) para 8.

President Hollande was presented with the UNESCO Félix Houphouët-Boigny award as a sign of recognition of his contributions to peace.[57]

To sum up, the French military intervention had some positive effects as it brought more stability to the region and ended the control of the insurgents in the northern territories.[58] Further damage to cultural heritage—both tangible and intangible—was avoided. With improved security conditions, UNESCO and its partners were also able to begin reconstruction work at the cultural sites.[59] Still, the French intervention came too late to prevent the outright destruction of a large part of important cultural sites and historic architecture, such as the magnificent mausoleums in Timbuktu.

C. The Role of the UN Security Council

The legal basis for the unilateral French military intervention (Operation Serval) was quite unclear in the beginning. Apparently, the Malian president Dioncounda Traoré asked the French president to intervene militarily because AFISMA was not ready to be deployed.[60] Still, the backing from the Security Council seemed to be missing.

In UN Security Council Resolution 2056, which was submitted by France, Germany, Morocco, South Africa, Togo, the United Kingdom, and the United States and adopted unanimously on 5 July 2012, the Council stressed 'that attacks against buildings dedicated to religion or historic monuments can constitute violations of international law which may fall under Additional Protocol II to the 1949 Geneva Convention and the Rome Statute of the International Criminal Court'.[61] The Council urged 'all parties in Mali to immediately take appropriate steps to ensure the protection of Mali's World Heritage Sites'[62] and strongly condemned the 'desecration, damage and destruction of sites of holy, historic and cultural significance'.[63] The explicit reference to Malian cultural heritage was rightly seen as 'of the utmost importance'.[64] However, the Council did not explicitly mention external intervening actors such as France.

[57] The Félix Houphouët-Boigny Peace Prize is intended to honor living individuals and active public or private bodies or institutions that have made a significant contribution to promoting, seeking, safeguarding, or maintaining peace, in conformity with the Charter of the United Nations and the Constitution of UNESCO < https://en.unesco.org/prizes/felix-houphouet-boigny > accessed 4 February 2020; other laureates are Lula da Silva (2008), Martti Ahtisaari (2007), Mary Robinson (2000), Yitzhak Rabin, Shimon Peres, and Yassir Arafat (1993), and Nelson Mandela (1991).

[58] As to the remaining problems, see below, Section IV.

[59] Regarding UNESCO's role in heritage rehabilitation, see Section V.

[60] Lostal (n 20) 131.

[61] UNSC Res 2056 (5 July 2012) UN Doc S/RES/2056, para 16.

[62] ibid.

[63] ibid, preambular part, para 14.

[64] Petrovic (n 28) 420; however, it is not quite clear why the Security Council mentioned neither movable cultural property nor archaeological sites.

In UN Security Council Resolution 2085 (2012), the Council confirmed that the situation in Mali posed a threat to international peace and security.[65] The Council strongly condemned the 'destruction of cultural and religious sites'[66] and encouraged the international community 'to provide support to resolve the crisis in Mali through coordinated actions for immediate and long-term needs, encompassing security, development and humanitarian issues'.[67] For that reason, the Council authorized the deployment of AFISMA.[68] Here for the first time, the Council called upon UN Member States 'to contribute troops to AFISMA'[69] and 'to provide coordinated support to AFISMA, including … any necessary assistance in efforts to reduce the threat posed by terrorist organizations'.[70]

Again, France was not mentioned in UN Security Council Resolution 2085—despite the fact that Operation Serval started on 11 January 2013, only three weeks after the adoption of the Resolution. There would have been enough time to officially authorize the French military mission and also to define the exact mandate of Operation Serval if political consensus of the P-5 had existed. This seems not to have been the case. As the French military intervention was not mentioned in Resolution 2085 (2012), this resolution is no solid legal basis for it either.[71]

However, the French military Operation Serval may be legitimate despite the fact that it has not been explicitly authorized by the United Nations. Interestingly enough, the Council members themselves have argued in this direction: In a Press Statement of the Council of 10 January 2013—only one day before the French intervention—the Council called upon Member States henceforth 'to assist the settlement of the crisis in Mali and, in particular, to provide assistance to the Malian Defence and Security Forces in order to reduce the threat posed by terrorist organizations and associated groups'.[72] Thus, the statement expressed the will of all Council members to now have military action on the ground *before* AFISMA officially started. It was made clear that UN Member States' support ought to be given directly to Malian forces.

This procedure is rather unusual, all the more so as the Council modified what it had stated in the previous basic Resolution 2085. Doubts were expressed, therefore,

[65] UNSC Res 2085 (20 December 2012) UN Doc S/RES/2085.

[66] ibid, preambular part, para 6.

[67] ibid. See also Berenika Drazewska, 'The Human Dimension of the Protection of the Cultural Heritage from Destruction during Armed Conflicts' (2015) 22 IJCP 205, 218.

[68] The mission of AFISMA was described in UNSC Res 2085 (20 December 2012) UN Doc S/RES/2085, para 9 (a)–(f).

[69] UNSC Res 2085 (20 December 2012) UN Doc S/RES/2085, para 13.

[70] ibid, para 14.

[71] van Steenberghe (n 50) 284: 'S'agissant de l'intervention française, il est clair … qu'elle ne peut en aucun cas trouver un fondement juridique valable dans l'autorisation d'employer la force contenue dans la résolution 2085 (2012) du Conseil de sécurité', with reference to Théodore Christakis and Karine Bannelier, 'Volenti non fit injuria? Les effets du consentement à l'intervention militaire' (2004) 50 Annuaire Français de Droit Intl 102, 133ff.

[72] UNSC, 'Press Statement on Mali' (10 January 2013) UN Doc SC/10878-AFR/2502.

whether a non-binding press statement can have any effect on a previously taken resolution.[73] The regular way to proceed would have been the adoption of a new or modified resolution, complementing Resolution 2085 (2012), to authorize the French mission on the ground.

Instead, the Security Council members chose a more pragmatic approach, presumably in fear of a veto and in view of the dramatic situation on the ground. Council Members apparently had wished to give a new meaning to its Resolution 2085 (2012) in order to authorize one of its P-5 members (France) to assist the Malian Forces and to react swiftly to Islamist threats. Thus, the subsequent press statement may be seen as a sort of 'auto-interpretation' of the will of Council members having the function of a stepping-stone in order to prepare new, more comprehensive action.

This specific procedure did not meet much resistance in state practice. In contrast to what could have been expected—given the general problems with state sovereignty of a unilateral intervention in a foreign country—there was no open protest. On the contrary—several States, among them the United Kingdom, the United States, and also various organs of the United Nations, even reacted positively.[74] Also, the ECOWAS Chairman thanked the French government for its 'expeditious reaction aimed to stabilize the military situation in Mali'.[75] Another more discrete sign of 'approval' of the French military action within the UN system was of a rather practical nature: On 3 February 2013, shortly after Operation Serval had started on the ground, UNESCO Director-General Bokova and French President Hollande visited Mali.[76] Consequently, it may be said that Operation Serval was welcomed by UNESCO and accepted broadly by the international community.

Interestingly enough, several months *after* Operation Serval had been deployed on the ground, the UN Security Council approved this unilateral intervention retroactively. In its Resolution 2100, which was adopted unanimously on 25 April 2013, the Council recalled earlier resolutions concerning Mali, among them Resolution 2085, and welcomed 'the swift action by the French forces . . . to stop the offensive of terrorist, extremist and armed groups towards the South of Mali'.[77] In clear words, the Council stressed also that 'terrorism can only be defeated by a sustained and comprehensive approach involving the active participation and collaboration *of all States*',[78] implicitly including France.

[73] See eg van Steenberghe (n 50) 283.

[74] With further reference, ibid 275.

[75] Communiqué of the ECOWAS Chairman on Mali (No 005/2013, 11 January 2013).

[76] UNESCOPRESS, 'Director-General Visits Mali with French President François Hollande' (03 February 2013).

[77] UNSC Res 2100 (25 April 2013) UN Doc S/RES/2100, preambular part, para 5.

[78] ibid, preambular part, para 4 (emphasis added).

To conclude, this wording in a subsequent UN Security Council resolution may exceptionally be interpreted as an *ex post* approval of a unilateral military mission. Apparently, the massive terrorist threat outweighed legal concerns in the end.

D. The Stabilization Period (from April 2013): The UN Peace Mission in Mali (MINUSMA)

In April 2013, France began to withdraw its forces, leaving 'a sizeable element in Mali' to support the Malian national forces.[79] Officially, Operation Serval ended on 15 July 2013, while the French Operation Barkhane started subsequently on 1 August. In parallel, a consent-based UN peacekeeping force was established: On 25 April 2013, the Security Council adopted Resolution 2100, creating the UN Multidimensional Integrated Stabilization Mission in Mali (MINUSMA).

On 1 July 2013, MINUSMA took over from AFISMA, following the signature of the Ouagadougou Preliminary Peace Agreement of 18 June 2013 between rebel groups of northern Mali and the interim government. The Agreement provided for an 'immediate ceasefire' and established a 'framework for inclusive peace talks with all communities of the North of Mali'.[80]

The cultural dimension was clearly taken into account in the mandate of MINUSMA. According to Resolution 2100 (2013), MINUSMA's task is to 'assist the transitional authorities of Mali, as necessary and feasible, in protecting from attack the cultural and historical sites in Mali'.[81] The fact that the Council did not mention 'religious sites' does not mean they are excluded: According to Gerstenblith, 'they are presumably subsumed within the categories of cultural and historic heritage'.[82] Still, the mandate given by the Council is weakened because of the 'feasibility proviso', that is, 'the caveat that the mission only protects cultural heritage to the extent feasible' as Schmalenbach emphasized.[83]

When the Security Council extended the mandate of MINUSMA and established a troop ceiling of 11,200 military personnel/1,449 police personnel in June 2014,[84] it was decided that, apart from 'priority tasks', MINUSMA should have some 'additional tasks', such as support for cultural preservation. Later, the Security Council developed a new approach regarding MINUSMA's mandate of cultural heritage protection and eliminated the distinction between 'priority tasks' and 'additional (cultural) tasks'. Instead, *all* tasks of MINUSMA were supposed to be on an equal footing henceforth: As para 14 and especially para 14(h) of UN

[79] Kila (n 20) 74.
[80] UNSC Res 2164 (25 June 2014) UN Doc S/RES/2164, preambular part, para 6.
[81] ibid, para 16(f).
[82] Gerstenblith (n 7) 385.
[83] Schmalenbach (n 2) 32.
[84] UNSC Res 2164 (25 June 2014) UN Doc S/RES/2164.

Security Resolution 2227 (2015) set forth, MINUSMA should have the task 'to assist the Malian authorities, as necessary and feasible, in protecting from attack the cultural and historical sites in Mali, in collaboration with UNESCO'.[85]

MINUSMA being the first comprehensive culture-embedded peacekeeping mission established by the UN, its personnel had to be trained accordingly. The 'Environmental and Culture Unit' of MINUSMA focused on training,[86] while UNESCO cooperated in this new task.[87] For example, the Secretariat of the 1954 Hague Convention and its two Protocols developed a brochure for personnel in training and a handbook for trainers. Moreover, a PowerPoint presentation was made available to MINUSMA military, police, and civilian personnel before they were deployed to Mali in order to explain the applicable rules of national and international law.[88]

Even though MINUSMA was not directly involved in any act of military defence of Malian heritage sites, the mission was useful in supporting and protecting UNESCO's early restoration efforts on the ground. MINUSMA engaged in a number of activities that included supporting the programme coordinated by UNESCO and the Ministry of Culture in Malito rehabilitate the heritage sites in the north of the country and to support the resumption of cultural events related to intangible heritage in order to promote social cohesion.[89] Together with UNESCO, MINUSMA also supported early investigations of the ICC's Office of the Prosecutor in the *Al Mahdi* case.[90]

To conclude, MINUSMA is to be seen as an exemplary case for future robust cultural heritage protection by the United Nations. The mission's mandate is important 'not merely for UNESCO and the issue itself but also for the expansion of the possible scope of future peace operations and wider involvement in them by other parts of the UN system' as Weiss and Connelly rightly emphasized.[91] In such a way, international cultural heritage protection is evolving gradually into a comprehensive cross-cutting issue in UN law and policy, emphasizing its nexus to security and peace.

[85] UNSC Res 2227 (29 June 2015) UN Doc S/RES/2227.

[86] United Nations General Assembly (UNGA), 'Cash Position of the United Nations Multidimensional Integrated Stabilization Mission in Mali as at 9 October 2015' (23 October 2015) UN Doc A/70/443.

[87] See UNSC Res 2227 (29 June 2015) UN Doc S/RES/2227, para 14.

[88] UNESCO, Committee for the Protection of Cultural Property in the Event of Armed Conflict, 'Report of the Secretariat on its Activities' (5 December 2013) UNESCO Doc CLT-13/8.COM/CONF.203/INF.2, para 25.

[89] See the website of MINUSMA <https://minusma.unmissions.org/en/cultural-heritage> accessed 4 February 2020. For more detail, see Olabiyi Yai, 'Perspectives Africaines sur le Patrimoine Culturel' in Janet Blake (ed), *Safeguarding Intangible Cultural Heritage: Challenges and Approaches* (IAL 2007) 73.

[90] Concerning the ICC Judgment, see eg Karolina Wierczyńska and Andrzej Jakubowski, 'The *Al Mahdi* Case: From Punishing Perpetrators to Repairing Cultural Heritage Harm' (Ch 5) in this volume.

[91] Thomas G Weiss and Nina Connelly, 'Cultural Cleansing and Mass Atrocities: Protecting Cultural Heritage in Armed Conflict Zones' (2017) 1 *J Paul Getty Trust Occasional Papers in Cultural Heritage Policy* 20.

IV. Ongoing Problems

Shortly after the French Operation Serval, presidential elections were held in Mali on 28 July and 11 August 2013, bringing President Ibrahim Boubacar Keïta into office. Only six weeks later, however, the armed groups resumed their destabilizing activities and started a new series of attacks.[92] The President launched an 'Inter-Malian Inclusive Dialogue' by appointing a High-Representative on 23 April 2014 to consult with national and international actors on the peace process[93] and a cease-fire agreement was signed on 23 May 2014.[94]

Still, the security situation in the north of Mali remained fragile and violence continued. MNLA members who before had supported the French troops in ousting the extremist groups even became targets of 'regular abductions and assassinations'.[95] The continuing activities of terrorist organizations in the Sahel region, including Al-Qaida in the Islamic Maghreb, Ansar Dine, the Movement for Unity and Jihad in West Africa, and Al-Mourabitoun, 'constitute a threat to peace and security in the region and beyond', as the Security Council emphasized in its Resolution 2164 (2014).[96] At the same time, the Security Council noted 'with growing concern the transnational dimension of the terrorist threat in the Sahel region',[97] condemning strongly 'all abuses and violations of human rights and violations of international humanitarian law'.[98] The members of the Security Council expressed their concern about the expansion of terrorist and criminal activities into central and southern Mali while stressing the relevance of the implementation of the Agreement on Peace and Reconciliation in Mali.[99]

Against this background, MINUSMA's mandate was difficult to fulfill right from the beginning. On the one hand, MINUSMA was criticized as being 'partial to the government'; on the other hand, the process of developing UN projects with the help of MINUSMA was disapproved of as 'legitimizing' rebel groups.[100] An increasing number of asymmetric terrorist attacks were directed against both

[92] For details, see UNHRC, 'Report of the Independent Expert' (n 3) 6, para 15.

[93] See UNSC Res 2164 (25 June 2014) UN Doc S/RES/2164, preambular part, para 8.

[94] See ibid, preambular part, para 10.

[95] Boutellis (n 24) 7.

[96] UNSC Res 2164 (25 June 2014) UN Doc S/RES/2164, preambular part, para 11. See also UNSC Res 2227 (29 June 2015) UN Doc S/RES/2227, on the extension of the mandate of the UN Multidimensional Integrated Stabilization Mission in Mali (MINUSMA) until 30 June 2016.

[97] UNSC Res 2164 (25 June 2014) UN Doc S/RES/2164, preambular part, para 15.

[98] ibid, preambular part, para 19.

[99] UNSC, 'Press Statement on Mali' (12 January 2016) UN Doc SC/12198-AFR/3300-PKO/555; when extending MINUSMA's mandate in June 2017, the Security Council recognized the recent progress achieved in the implementation of the Agreement on Peace and Reconciliation, including the holding of a *Conference d'Entente nationale* in March 2017, but also expressed deep concern over the persistent delays for its full implementation two years after its conclusion. See UNSC Res 2364 (29 June 2017) UN Doc S/RES/2364, preambular part.

[100] Boutellis (n 24) 6.

Malian Forces and MINUSMA.[101] As of May 2018, 170 fatalities of MINUSMA had been reported.[102] Reacting to the serious attacks on UN troops' members, the UN Security Council stressed the importance of ensuring adequate protection of MINUSMA personnel.[103]

Therefore, it remains quite unclear whether the UN mission will finally succeed in achieving the overall objective of stabilization in the interest of the Malian government. Meanwhile, responsibility for violence was reaffirmed to be the obligation of the Malian state,[104] an obligation including the protection of cultural heritage as well.

V. UNESCO's Role Concerning the Rehabilitation of the Malian Cultural Heritage

Since its formation in 1945, UNESCO has played a lead role in standard-setting.[105] In addition, and to an increasing extent, the organization assumes operational responsibility for culture in emergencies as well.[106] The handbook published in 2016 by UNESCO and the International Centre for the Study of Preservation and Restoration of Cultural Property (ICCROM), *Endangered Heritage*, deals with practical problems in emergency situations, for example.[107]

UNESCO officials consider heritage restoration in Mali essential for national unity, reconciliation, and a source of strength for the people of Mali. When the UNESCO Director-General visited Timbuktu on 18 July 2015, she declared that the reconstruction work done by UNESCO with the support of the Malian population was 'a lesson in tolerance, dialogue and peace',[108] adding proudly: 'Here we

[101] See UN News Centre, 'UN Strongly Condemns Deadly Terrorist Attack on Mali Peacekeeper' (17 January 2015) <https://www.un.org/apps/news/story.asp?NewsID=49825#.WZ7jiulpzIU> accessed 4 February 2020; UN News Centre, 'UN Strongly Condemns Attack on Base in Northern Mali that Kills Two 'Blue Helmets' and a Civilian Contractor' (28 November 2015) <https://www.un.org/apps/news/story.asp?NewsID=52680#.WZ7i_OlpzIU> accessed 4 February 2020.

[102] UN Peacekeeping, 'Fatalities by Mission, Year and Incident Type', <https://peacekeeping.un.org/en/fatalities> accessed 4 February 2020.

[103] UNSC, 'Press Statement on Mali' (12 January 2016) UN Doc SC/12198-AFR/3300-PKO/555.

[104] ibid.

[105] Cf Abdulqawi A Yusuf (ed), *Standard-setting in UNESCO, Vol I: Normative Action in Education, Science and Culture* (UNESCO/Martinus Nijhoff 2007); *Standard-setting in UNESCO, Vol II: Conventions, Recommendations, Declarations and Charters* (1948-2006) (UNESCO/Martinus Nijhoff 2007).

[106] Cf the work of the Emergency Preparedness and Response Unit, established in 2014 within the Culture Sector of UNESCO (CLT/EPR), which acts as a focal point under the Strategy for the Reinforcement of UNESCO's Action for the Protection of Culture and the Promotion of Cultural Pluralism in the Event of Armed Conflict. For more information see <https://en.unesco.org/themes/culture-emergencies> accessed 4 February 2020.

[107] Aparna Tandom (ed), *Endangered Heritage: Emergency Evacuation of Heritage Collections* (UNESCO/ICCROM 2016).

[108] UNESCO World Heritage Centre News, 'Director-General Praises the People of Timbuktu for the Reconstruction of the City's Mausoleums' (19 July 2015) <http://whc.unesco.org/en/news/1324> accessed 4 February 2020.

have our response to extremism ... an example of the successful integration of culture in peace building'.[109]

To advise on the international rehabilitation efforts in Mali, UNESCO had established an expert group, composed of representatives from UNESCO, ICCROM, the International Council of Museums (ICOM), the International Council on Monuments and Sites (ICOMOS), the International Federation of Library Associations and Institutions (IFLA), École du Patrimoine Africain (EPA), African World Heritage Fund (AWHF), and Centre de recherche et d'application en terre (CRAterre). The former UNESCO Assistant Director-General for Culture, Francesco Bandarin, encouraged the government of Mali to incorporate the Action Plan in the national development plan to mobilize potential donors.[110] The costs of the Action Plan were estimated at some US$11 million. To prepare for the rehabilitation period, a donor conference for Mali was organized in Paris on 15 May 2013.

Furthermore, an expert mission with the support of MINUSMA, including experts from ICOMOS, ICCROM, AWHF, CRAterre, ICOM, IFLA, EPA, the Aga Khan Trust for Culture (AKTC), the national library of France, the French government, and the EU was sent to Mali to evaluate Mali's cultural heritage in more detail on 7 June 2013. Apparently, the Malian cultural heritage was damaged more severely than expected.[111]

Important conservation measures were undertaken for documentary heritage, specifically manuscripts, in Mali. Under the title 'Ancient Manuscripts Facing Modern Day Challenges', a conference took place in January 2015, organized by the UNESCO Office in Bamako together with the Ministry of Higher Education and Scientific Research of Mali, the Ahmed Baba Institute of Higher Learning and Islamic Research, the Malian Ministry of Culture, and the NGO SAVAMA-DCI.[112] The conference aimed at improving the efficiency of management and conservation of manuscripts. With the help of several donor countries, among them Norway and Luxembourg, safeguarding activities took place. Germany, for example, provided 350,000 EUR for the preservation of ancient manuscripts from Timbuktu.[113]

[109] ibid.

[110] International Experts Meeting, 'Final Report and Action Plan' (n 31) 10, para 27.

[111] UNESCO World Heritage Centre News, 'World Heritage Committee to Inscribe New Sites on UNESCO World Heritage List and Examine Conservation of Sites Already on the List' (7 June 2013) <http://whc.unesco.org/en/news/1021> accessed 4 February 2020.

[112] For details, see UNESCO World Heritage Centre News, International Conference on Ancient Manuscripts of Mali <http://whc.unesco.org/en/events/1215> accessed 4 February 2020.

[113] Federal Foreign Office, 'Cultural Preservation in Crisis Regions—Federal Foreign Office Provides 350,000 Euros to Help Save Historic Manuscripts from Mali', press release (29 June 2015) <http://www.auswaertiges-amt.de/EN/Infoservice/Presse/Meldungen/2015/150629_Mali.html?nn=354316> accessed 4 February 2020. In close cooperation with the German Federal Foreign Office, the Gerda Henkel Foundation provided, from 2013 to 2019, funds of approx. 900,000 euros to secure, digitalize and restore the manuscripts and to ensure their accessibility for Malian and international research (<https://40jahre.gerda-henkel-stiftung.de/2014> accessed 04 February 2020). A detailed overview of the project is provided by the Centre for the Study of Manuscripts Cultures, University of Hamburg, at <https://www.manuscript-cultures.uni-hamburg.de/timbuktu/> accessed 04 February 2020.

In May 2013, shortly after the mausoleums' destruction, the government of Mali had turned to UNESCO and requested support in their reconstruction. After long and thorough planning[114] and research (including on the history, architecture, the techniques, the material, the qualified masons, etc) the work started in August 2013 with the reconstruction of the Djiangareyber Mosque in Timbuktu, the largest of three mosques at the World Heritage Site sheltering two mausoleums that were destroyed. A setback occurred while construction was underway: On 28 September 2013, a suicide attack took place near the Djiangareyber Mosque killing two citizens and causing substantial new damage to the building under reconstruction.[115]

Furthermore, UN stabilization efforts concentrated on the establishment of a comprehensive inventory of Mali's intangible cultural heritage, specifically knowledge and practices related to nature, oral traditions, rituals, festivals, and traditional crafts. On 28 October 2013, the UNESCO Bureau of the Intergovernmental Committee for the Safeguarding of Intangible Heritage approved emergency funds of US$307,307 for the preparation of an inventory. The project helped to evaluate the state of the intangible heritage in all parts of Mali, starting in the northern regions (Gao, Kidal, and Timbuktu) and the east-central region of Mali (Mopti), continuing in the South (Kayes, Koulikoro, Ségou, and Sikasso). The UN Human Rights Council's report welcomed the inventory.[116]

In this context, the 'Imzad musical tradition' of the Tuareg communities, often female groups, was presented as a joint nomination from Mali, Niger, and Algeria in 2013, and adopted for the UNESCO Representative List of Intangible Cultural Heritage.[117] As the Islamic groups had issued restrictions on both—music and the movement of women—while they had been in control of northern Mali,[118] the subsequent UNESCO inscription explicitly celebrated the importance of music and the role of women as a defense of human rights. The listing was part of UNESCO's endeavors to react to Islamist human rights violations while at the same time fostering universal values and mutual understanding. In November

[114] When a World Heritage Site or part of it is completely destroyed and its original building material is lost, authenticity must be analyzed in every single case from the point of view of experts for monument preservation, see Birgitta Ringbeck, *Management Plans for World Heritage Sites: A Practical Guide* (German Commission for UNESCO 2008) 17ff. See also the 'Nara Document on Authenticity' (1998), which is annexed to the Operational Guidelines of the 1972 World Heritage Convention, *Operational Guidelines for the Implementation of the World Heritage Convention*, UNESCO Doc WHC.17/01 (12 July 2017), Annex 4.

[115] UNESCO World Heritage Centre News, 'UNESCO Director-General Deplores Suicide Attack near Djingareyber Mosque in Timbuktu' (30 September 2013) <http://whc.unesco.org/en/news/1072> accessed 4 February 2020.

[116] UNHRC, 'Report of the Independent Expert' (n 3) 16, para 9.

[117] Henrike Florusbosch, 'Mali's Heritage: Beyond Timbuktu, Leiden Anthropology Blog' (4 June 2015) <http://www.leidenanthropologyblog.nl/articles/malis-heritage-beyond-timbuktu> accessed 4 February 2020.

[118] On 22 August 2012, MUJO announced the banning of 'profane music', see International Crisis Group, CrisisWatch Database, Mali (September 2012) <https://www.crisisgroup.org/crisiswatch/database> accessed 4 February 2020.

2015, UNESCO Member States adopted a landmark decision to provide assistance to States in developing strategies to prevent violent extremism.[119]

Most needed was action against illicit trade. The 1970 Convention on the Means of Prohibiting and Preventing the Illicit Import, Export and Transfer of Ownership of Cultural Property calls upon the States Parties 'to participate in a concerted international effort to determine and carry out the necessary concrete measures, including the control of exports and imports and international commerce'.[120] The UNESCO Director-General urged national authorities of Mali and countries of the region to implement this provision.[121] Experts who participated in an early mission to Mali during the crisis emphasized that 'Mali has to be supported in order to stop illicit trade'.[122] An important signal was seen in this context by the United States 'by banning the import of unauthorized Malian antiquities'.[123] A binding trade moratorium of the UN Security Council on the traffic of cultural objects from countries at war—so far nonexistent—would certainly be another useful measure for future cultural heritage protection.[124]

Conclusion

To conclude, the integration of culture within international humanitarian, security, and peacebuilding policies and operations is a means to promote dialogue and peace among nations. Protecting culture and promoting cultural pluralism is seen nowadays as a 'key to lasting peace'.[125] Related to that view, the 2015 UNESCO Strategy 'Reinforcement of UNESCO's Action for the Protection of Culture and the Promotion of Cultural Pluralism in the Event of Armed Conflict'[126] highlights 'the strong connections between the cultural,

[119] UNESCO Executive Board Decision 197EX/46 (23 November 2015). See also the UN Secretary-General's Plan of Action to Prevent Violent Extremism that warned that 'items and sites of great historical, religious and cultural significance are being wantonly destroyed in violation of the protection afforded to the cultural heritage under international humanitarian law', UNGA, Report of the Secretary-General (24 December 2015) UN Doc A/70/674, para 19.

[120] Convention on the Means of Prohibiting and Preventing the Illicit Import, Export and Transfer of Ownership of Cultural Property (adopted 14 November 1970, entered into force 24 April 1972) 823 UNTS 231, art 9 (1970 UNESCO Convention).

[121] UNESCOPRESS, 'UNESCO Director-General Appeals for Concerted Action to Prevent Loss or Destruction of Timbuktu's Documentary Heritage' (15 April 2012) <http://www.unesco.org/new/en/general-conference-38th/single-view/news/unesco_director_general_appeals_for_concerted_action_to_prev/> accessed 4 February 2020.

[122] Kila (n 20) 73.

[123] See Klesmith (n 6) 75.

[124] Schorlemer, 'Kulturgutzerstörung' (n 2) 395ff.

[125] See in this context UNESCO General Conference, 'Protecting Culture and Promoting Cultural Pluralism: The Key to Lasting Peace' (24 October 2017) UNESCO Doc 39 C/57, Annex II.

[126] UNESCO General Conference, 'Reinforcement of UNESCO's Action for the Protection of Culture and the Promotion of Cultural Pluralism in the Event of Armed Conflict' (2 November 2015) UNESCO Doc 38/C/49, 38th session. See also UNESCO General Conference, 'Strategy for the Reinforcement of

humanitarian and security dimensions of conflicts', stressing at the same time that ultimately attacks against cultural heritage and diversity are attacks against people.[127]

Events in Mali demonstrate that in such cases, comprehensive protection measures are needed for the survival of cultural heritage, not only in the field of prevention and risk reduction but also concerning emergency action and post-conflict rehabilitation. In that sense, despite ongoing security problems, Mali may be seen as a positive 'test case' for the system of the United Nations to provide a broad range of measures.

The clear placement of cultural heritage protection in a peacekeeping mandate is unprecedented in the history of the United Nations. Both the UNESCO Executive Board and the General Conference emphasized the 'positive results' of MINUSMA.[128] Based also on that experience, the UN Security Council adopted Resolution 2347 (2017),[129] which itself is the first resolution to focus exclusively on the protection of cultural heritage and its necessity for peace and security.[130] Resolution 2347 stresses the need to include the protection of cultural heritage in future UN peacekeeping missions, thus 'assisting relevant authorities, upon their request, in the protection of cultural heritage from destruction, illicit excavation, looting and smuggling in the context of armed conflict, in collaboration with UNESCO'.[131]

Whenever the Council may establish culture-embedded UN peacekeeping missions along these lines in the future, the integration of a realistic module on the protection of cultural heritage within the standard training of a peacekeeping force is important. Close cooperation between cultural heritage experts and the military needs to be developed with the support of UNESCO, while at the same time mechanisms for the rapid mobilization of national experts who are willing to cooperate with UNESCO in the implementation of relevant international legal instruments (such as the Hague 1954 Convention)[132] should be improved.

UNESCO's Action for the Protection of Culture and the Promotion of Cultural Pluralism in the Event of Armed Conflict' (24 October 2017) UNESCO Doc 39/C/57.

[127] UNESCO General Conference, 'Strategy for the Reinforcement of UNESCO's Action for the Protection of Culture and the Promotion of Cultural Pluralism in the Event of Armed Conflict' (24 October 2017) UNESCO Doc 39/C/57, para. 4.

[128] Resolution adopted on the report of the CLT Commission at the 17th plenary meeting on 17 November 2015, UNESCO, Records of the General Conference, 38th Session (3–18 November 2015) 42: Reinforcement of UNESCO's action for the protection of culture and the promotion of cultural pluralism in the event of armed conflict, para 6. See also UNESCO, Executive Board, Decisions adopted by the Executive Board at its 197th session (23 November 2015) UNESCO Doc 197 EX/SR.8, para 10.

[129] UNSC Res 2347 (24 March 2017) UN Doc S/RES/2347.

[130] Circular letter from Irina Bokova on UNSC Resolution 2347 (9 June 2017) UNESCO Doc CL/4210, at 1. For more details, see Schorlemer, 'Cultural Heritage Protection' (n 2) 39ff.

[131] UNSC Res 2347 (24 March 2017) UN Doc S/RES/2347, para 19.

[132] UNESCO World Heritage News Centre, Italy Creates a UNESCO Emergency Task Force for Culture (16 February 2016) <https://whc.unesco.org/en/news/1436/> accessed 4 February 2020.

Given the chances of more timely and better-coordinated heritage protection action in cases of crises, as was reflected upon in this chapter in the context of Mali, the intersections of international cultural heritage law and security issues should rank high on the future research agenda of the international epistemic community.

PART II

CULTURAL HERITAGE-BASED OFFENSES IN INTERNATIONAL CRIMINAL LAW AND IN THE INTERNATIONAL LEGAL REGIME FOR COMBATTING TRANSNATIONAL ORGANIZED CRIME

This part focuses on the intersections of cultural heritage law and both international criminal law and more recent developments in international law for combatting transnational organized crime. The intersection of international cultural heritage law and international criminal law has developed directly from—and thus intersects directly with—the law of armed conflict. The historical development of crimes against cultural heritage and recent developments in the International Criminal Court are discussed in the Chapters 4 and 5, respectively. Chapter 6 evaluates the international legal regime designed to combat transnational organized crime, partly by establishing joint initiatives to investigate, criminalize, and facilitate prosecution of various participants involved in the illicit trafficking of cultural artifacts.

Anne-Marie Carstens begins this part by arguing that the inclusion of cultural heritage-based 'war crimes'—offenses based on the unnecessary destruction of cultural sites and sometimes also on the misappropriation of cultural objects—was never a foregone conclusion in international criminal law.[1] She suggests, however, that the 'swinging pendulum' as to whether or not to include cultural property-based offenses resulted not only from a persistent view that property-based crimes

[1] Anne-Marie Carstens, 'The Swinging Pendulum of Cultural Heritage Crimes in International Criminal Law' in Anne-Marie Carstens and Elizabeth Varner (eds), *Intersections in International Cultural Heritage Law* (OUP 2020) (Ch 4).

were less serious than other grave offenses. Drafters also likely were influenced by contemporaneous developments at other intersections of international law. In particular, they often considered and took into account whether other institutions or regimes, such as the International Court of Justice or instruments for protecting human rights and minority rights, were better suited to redressing violations of the law of armed conflict governing cultural property protection. In the end, though, the international criminal regime recognized heritage-based offenses, while not fully embracing the concept of cultural genocide. Prosecutions before the International Criminal Tribunal for the Former Yugoslavia (ICTY) and the International Criminal Court (ICC) established the prevailing view that cultural heritage offenses are sufficiently serious to qualify as 'war crimes' on their own. They also confirm that under specific circumstances, deliberate attacks on cultural property can mutually reinforce or corroborate other war crimes, crimes against humanity, and even genocide.

Karolina Wierczyńska and Andrzej Jakubowski delve into the relevant jurisprudence from both the ICTY and ICC to confirm the role of cultural heritage crimes within the wider panorama of international criminal law.[2] They focus, in particular, on the *Al Mahdi* case in the ICC to explore the evolving system of individual criminal responsibility for cultural heritage crimes. They also extrapolate from the case to examine the Court's approach in defining the contours and gravity of cultural heritage crimes for the future.[3] Wierczyńska and Jakubowski discuss Al Mahdi's sentence of imprisonment but focus more extensively on a distinctive feature of the *Al Mahdi* case: the assessment and imposition of reparations to victims for a cultural heritage crime. They observe that the reparations reinforced the Rome Statute's provision for victim reparations, which was itself a landmark development that deviated from the practice of the prior ad hoc criminal tribunals, and reflected the increasing influence of international human rights law.

The final chapter by Janet Blake examines how international law has begun to address a different kind of criminality involving cultural heritage. While recent cases in the ICC highlight the destruction of cultural sites as a war crime, Blake examines developments for curbing the illicit trafficking of cultural objects through transnational criminal networks.[4] Blake provides a comparative analysis of two different regimes for redressing the illicit international trade in artifacts. Specifically, she starts by surveying the 'cultural heritage-based approach', represented primarily by the 1970 UNESCO Convention and the 1995 UNIDROIT Convention on Stolen

[2] Karolina Wierczyńska and Andrzej Jakubowski, 'The *Al Mahdi* Case: From Punishing Perpetrators to Repairing Cultural Heritage Harm' in Anne-Marie Carstens and Elizabeth Varner (eds), *Intersections in International Cultural Heritage Law* (OUP 2020) (Ch 5).

[3] See eg *Prosecutor v Al Mahdi* (Trial Judgment and Sentence) ICC-01/12-01/15-171 (27 September 2016); *Prosecutor v Al Mahdi* (Reparation Order) ICC-01/12-01/15-236 (17 August 2017).

[4] Janet Blake, 'Trafficking in Cultural Property: Where Cultural Heritage Law and the International Fight against Transnational Organized Crime Coincide' in Anne-Marie Carstens and Elizabeth Varner (eds), *Intersections in International Cultural Heritage Law* (OUP 2020) (Ch 6).

or Illegally Exported Cultural Objects (1995 UNIDROIT Convention).[5] She then compares this approach with the more recent, alternative approach of investigating and punishing the illicit trafficking in cultural objects as a form of transnational organized crime, represented primarily by the 2000 United Nations Convention Against Transnational Organized Crime (2000 Palermo Convention).[6] She concludes that a purely cultural heritage-based approach does not sufficiently address the challenge of illicit trafficking in cultural objects. As a result, the international law enforcement regime is an appropriate and long-overlooked avenue for addressing the trafficking in cultural property as an emerging transnational crime. This approach brings new tools to the effort that include joint international investigations, extradition agreements, and obligations to including trafficking in cultural objects as a domestic criminal offense.

Anne-Marie Carstens and Elizabeth Varner

[5] UNIDROIT Convention on the International Return of Stolen or Illegally Exported Cultural Objects (adopted 24 June 1995, entered into force 1 July 1998) 34 ILM 1322 (1995 UNIDROIT Convention).

[6] United Nations Convention Against Transnational Organized Crime (adopted 15 November 2000 in UNGA Res 55/25, entered into force 29 September 2003) 2225 UNTS 209 (2000 Palermo Convention).

4

The Swinging Pendulum of Cultural Heritage Crimes in International Criminal Law

Anne-Marie Carstens

Introduction

Recent prosecutions in the International Criminal Court (ICC) for cultural heritage crimes committed at the World Heritage site of Timbuktu, in Mali, have raised anew a debate over how far international criminal law and international criminal tribunals should go in redressing attacks on cultural heritage. The 2016 prosecution of Ahmad Al Mahdi Al Faqi (Al Mahdi) was seized as fodder for critics arguing against prosecuting perpetrators of these property-related crimes. Al Mahdi, a leader within the Al-Qaida-affiliated Ansar Dine,[1] was prosecuted, convicted, and sentenced by the Court to nine years' imprisonment, plus ordered to pay reparations, for his role in the 2012 orchestrated destruction of Timbuktu's historic mausoleums.[2] As noted in the subsequent chapter by Wierczyńska and Jakubowski, the case against Al Mahdi was not only the Court's first effort at prosecuting a crime against cultural heritage. It was also the first time that any international criminal tribunal had pursued such an offense that was not accompanied or supplemented by charges of other war crimes or crimes against humanity.[3]

The pending prosecution of Al Hassan Ag Abdoul Aziz Ag Mohamed ag Mahmoud (Al Hassan) is more traditional in that respect, in comparison with previous prosecutions in other international criminal tribunals. The arrest warrant, which issued in March 2018 (just weeks after the Court finalized the reparations order in the *Al Mahdi* case), cited crimes against cultural heritage on a longer list of crimes against humanity and war crimes committed during the occupation of Timbuktu by militant

[1] The ICC alternatively refers to the movement as Ansar Eddine.

[2] *Prosecutor v Al Mahdi* (Trial Judgment and Sentence) ICC-01/12-01/15-171 (27 September 2016); *Prosecutor v Al Mahdi* (Reparation Order) ICC-01/12-01/15-236 (17 August 2017). Sabine von Schorlemer presents a detailed discussion of the 2012 destruction in Mali in Chapter 3 of this volume, and Karolina Wierczyńska and Andrzej Jakubowski amply discuss the judgments and orders in the *Al Mahdi* case in Chapter 5.

[3] Wierczyńska and Jakubowski (ch 5).

Anne-Marie Carstens, The Swinging Pendulum of Cultural Heritage Crimes in International Criminal Law In: *Intersections in International Cultural Heritage Law*. Edited by Anne-Marie Carstens and Elizabeth Varner. © Oxford University Press 2020. The several contributors DOI: 10.1093/oso/9780198846291.003.0005

extremists in 2012 and 2013. In particular, it alleged that Al Hassan, also a member of Ansar Dine and de facto chief of the Islamic police, directed the Islamic police forces to carry out the same series of attacks on the historic mausoleums, as well as having assisted in implementing policies that resulted in, inter alia, torture, rape, sexual slavery, religious and gender persecution, and outrages on personal dignity.[4]

Critics decried the Court's earlier prosecution of Al Mahdi for its singular focus on a cultural property-related crime in the face of widespread and varied outrages committed in Mali and elsewhere.[5] Certainly the prosecution of Al Hassan covers a broader terrain of offenses. Still, critics might lob a corollary argument, maintaining that the inclusion of cultural property-related crimes diminishes the significance of the accompanying charges.

Defenders of prosecuting cultural heritage crimes in international criminal tribunals strongly counter that the deliberate destruction of cultural property often appears as part of a campaign of persecution, designed to diminish and eradicate the signs of a culture and its represented populations. The truth of this assertion has been borne out both in armed conflicts and in facts established in international criminal prosecutions. Following this argument, perpetrators of such destruction should be prosecuted alongside the perpetrators of other atrocities committed against protected persons and targeted communities.[6] The fact that the low

[4] *Prosecutor v Al Hassan* (Arrest Warrant), ICC-01/12-01/18 (27 March 2018). See also *Prosecutor v Al Hassan* (Decision constituting Trial Chamber X and referring to it the case of *Prosecutor v. Al Hassan*) ICC-01/12-01/18 ICC-01/12-01/18 (21 November 2019) (constituting trial chamber after Pre-Trial Chamber I confirmed charges of war crimes and crimes against humanity); Rosemary Grey, *Prosecuting Sexual and Gender-Based Crimes at the International Criminal Court* (CUP 2019) 241–46 (listing and discussing offenses); UNSC, 'Informal Expert Group on Women and Peace and Security: Summary of the meeting on Mali and the Sahel, 5 June 2018' (11 July 2018) UN Doc S/2018/688, Annex, 3.

[5] See eg Reuters, 'Mali War Crimes Suspect in Custody: International Criminal Court' (31 March 2018) <https://www.reuters.com/article/us-icct-mali/mali-war-crimes-suspect-in-custody-international-criminal-court-idUSKBN1H70QB> accessed 14 November 2018 (observing that '[v]ictims' groups had been critical of the court for the limited scope of al-Mahdi's indictment', though also observing that the case 'was widely viewed as a landmark because it was the first time a person has been convicted of a war crime solely for destruction of cultural artifacts'); Owen Bowcott, 'ICC's First Cultural Destruction Trial to Open in The Hague' *The Guardian* (28 February 2016) <https://www.theguardian.com/law/2016/feb/28/iccs-first-cultural-destruction-trial-to-open-in-the-hague> accessed 14 November 2018 (noting criticisms of the decision 'to make obliteration of heritage a priority in dealing with the aftermath of Mali's conflict' and 'that no major figure in the Tuareg uprising has been charged'); Valérie V Suhr, 'The ICC's Al Mahdi Verdict on the Destruction of Cultural Heritage: Two Steps Forward, One Step Back?' (3 October 2016) Völkerrechtsblog (blog) <https://voelkerrechtsblog.org/the-iccs-al-mahdi-verdict-on-the-destruction-of-cultural-heritage-two-steps-forward-one-step-back/> accessed 14 November 2018 (arguing that the ICC Prosecutor should file charges related to additional allegations 'to counteract the possible impression that "stones are more important than humans"'); FIDH Worldwide Movement for Human Rights, 'Press Release: Mali: The Hearing of Al Mahdi before the ICC is a Victory, but Charges Must Be Expanded' (30 September 2015) <https://www.fidh.org/en/issues/international-justice/international-criminal-court-icc/mali-the-hearing-of-abou-tourab-before-the-icc-is-a-victory-but> accessed 14 November 2018 (insisting, based on field missions by human rights organizations, that the ICC Prosecutor also consider allegations of his criminal responsibility 'for additional international crimes committed against civilians').

[6] Al Mahdi was one of the first high-level perpetrators who could be located. See eg UNHRC, 'Report of the Independent Expert on the situation of human rights in Mali, Suliman Baldo' (9 January 2015) UN Doc A/HRC/28/83, paras 11, 37, 40, 54–102 (observing that a 'legal loophole in the fight against impunity' had allowed the release of persons detained in connection with the armed conflict).

number of cultural heritage-related prosecutions is dwarfed by the volume of prosecutions of other war crimes, crimes against humanity, and the crime of genocide moreover suggests that attention to cultural heritage seizure and destruction has neither diluted nor crowded out humanitarian protections or ideals. Such cultural heritage-related prosecutions, when they do occur, also highlight a context that establishes cultural heritage crimes as part of this larger narrative. Indeed, far from distancing the Court from cultural heritage offenses in light of the criticism precipitated by the Al Mahdi prosecution, the ICC Prosecutor further emphasized the Court's attention to cultural heritage crimes by signing a Letter of Intent with the United Nations Educational, Scientific and Cultural Organization (UNESCO) to increase collaborative efforts between the ICC and UNESCO in addressing destructive attacks on cultural heritage.[7]

The crux of this debate—when and whether international cultural heritage offenses should be included in an international criminal code or prosecuted by international criminal tribunals—predates the prosecutions in the ICC and, in fact, extends as far back as the interwar period following the First World War. The prolonged lack of consensus, in turn, forced the development of international cultural heritage crimes on a non-linear journey. Specifically, the willingness of the drafters, prosecutors, and jurists in contemporary international criminal law to include cultural heritage crimes in the work of international criminal tribunals does *not* represent the culmination of a cumulative, mounting development toward embracing such crimes. Instead, the current inclusion of cultural heritage crimes in our leading international criminal statutes (and the recent prosecutions of perpetrators of such attacks) merely stands at one point on the arc of a pendulum, which has swung back and forth over the past century.

This chapter explores this evolution of international criminal law concerning the destruction, plunder, and pillage of cultural heritage, from the 1899 and 1907 Hague Conventions up until the end of the twentieth century, when the Statute of the International Criminal Tribunal for the Former Yugoslavia (ICTY Statute) and the Rome Statute of the International Criminal Court (Rome Statute) were adopted.[8] It argues that the progress and status of cultural heritage crimes as part of an emerging international criminal code differed significantly across three critical periods, each of which are analyzed in this chapter:

1) the period following the First World War and the interwar period, during which the first international criminal code was formally suggested but not adopted;

[7] ICC, 'Press Release: The ICC Office of the Prosecutor and UNESCO sign Letter of Intent to strengthen Cooperation on the Protection of Cultural Heritage' (6 November 2017).

[8] Rome Statute of the International Criminal Court (adopted 17 July 1998, entered into force 1 July 2002) 2187 UNTS 3 (Rome Statute); Statute of the International Criminal Tribunal for the Former Yugoslavia (adopted 25 May 1993 in UNSC Res 827, as amended) (ICTY Statute).

2) a second period that took place after the Second World War, which included the first international criminal tribunal established at Nuremberg but that did not include specific offenses for destruction or seizure of cultural property; and
3) a third period that began in the 1980s after relative dormancy and continued through the adoption of the Statutes governing the ICTY and ICC, during which cultural heritage-related offenses achieved lasting permanence.

The first of these periods favored the inclusion of cultural property offenses among a longer list of proposed offenses, all drawn from the example of the 1899 and 1907 Hague Conventions. The First World War highlighted deficiencies in enforcing the laws and customs of war that had been recently codified in the 1899 and 1907 Hague Conventions. The proposed establishment of an international criminal code and international criminal court attempted to respond to these perceived deficiencies and reflected a prevailing view among the victorious Allies that vanquished States would not prosecute their own nationals for violations to a meaningful extent.[9] The second period arguably was not, or at least was considerably less in favor of including specific cultural property offenses in the wake of the Second World War, despite the vast devastation and spoliation that accompanied that conflict. By the 1980s, however, movement shifted again in a third period toward including cultural heritage crimes, at least with respect to the intentional destruction of cultural sites. This decision prevailed and proved instrumental in the prosecutions that took place before the ICTY until its conclusion in 2017, as well as in the ICC today.

These vacillating positions, as to whether or not to include such offenses, however, reflect more than just differing perspectives and priorities with respect to which offenses were considered sufficiently egregious or posed a significant enough threat to international security, as the contemporary debate discussed above would suggest. This chapter argues that contemporaneous developments happening at other intersections of international law served as an important driver of the indecision and controversy as to whether cultural heritage destruction or seizure should be recognized as a 'war crime'. In particular, it reveals an underlying dialogue that considered whether other international institutions or instruments might better provide the appropriate mechanism(s) to address attacks on

[9] Convention (IV) Respecting the Laws and Customs of War on Land and its Annex: Regulations concerning the Laws and Customs of War on Land (open for signature 18 October 1907, entered into force 26 January 1910) 187 CTS 227; Hague Convention (II) with Respect to the Laws and Customs of War on Land and its Annex: Regulations concerning the Laws and Customs of War on Land (adopted 29 July 1899, entered into force 4 September 1900) 187 CTS 429 (collectively, the 1899 and 1907 Hague Conventions). The provisions governing cultural heritage in the two treaties are substantially verbatim, except that 'historic monuments' was added to the relevant provisions in the 1907 Hague Convention. The 1907 Hague Convention (IV) supplants the earlier 1899 Hague Convention (II) for parties to both treaties. The codified laws and customs of war are appended to the treaties as Regulations.

cultural property during armed conflict. This argument presents an alternative lens through which to view the criticisms challenging the prosecution of cultural heritage crimes: not just as challenges to the mere idea of prosecuting cultural heritage crimes in international tribunals, but also (or even instead) as a second-guessing of whether international criminal tribunals are the most suitable or effective fora. The chapter additionally argues that this dialogue had an underappreciated influence on cultural heritage-based offenses as they are codified and prosecuted in international criminal law today.

I. The Swing Toward Codifying Cultural Heritage Crimes: The First World War through the Interwar Period

Following the First World War, an intergovernmental commission included the 'wanton destruction of religious, charitable, educational, and historic buildings and monuments' and other property-based offenses that should be tried before a specially created postwar tribunal.[10] The victorious powers had established this commission, the Commission on the Responsibilities of the Authors of the War and on Enforcement of Penalties (Commission on Responsibilities), at the Preliminary Peace Conference at Paris in 1919 and had tasked it both with determining 'breaches of the laws and customs of war committed by the forces of the German Empire and their Allies' during the war and with pursuing the creation of 'a tribunal appropriate for the trial of these offences'.[11] The laws and customs of war had long existed as customary obligations that governed the conduct of belligerents during armed conflict. At the time of the First World War, they had also been recently codified for the first time in a binding treaty in the 1899 and 1907 Hague Conventions.

Pursuant to its mandate, the Commission proposed 'a high tribunal' of an international character to try any of thirty-two proposed offenses stemming from the war.[12] Though the Commission did not expressly state that the list was organized by importance or priority, the first nine offenses in pole position all pertained to atrocities committed against civilians, including murders and massacres, systematic terrorism, torture, deliberate starvation, rape and abduction for prostitution, deportation and internment, and forced labor.[13]

Property-related crimes were contained in the middle section of the list and included offenses that could apply to the seizure or destruction of cultural heritage

[10] Commission on the Responsibilities of the Authors of the War and on Enforcement of Penalties, *Report Presented to the Preliminary Peace Conference* (29 March 1919), in (1920) 14 AJIL 95 (Report of the Commission on Responsibilities) 114–15, enumerated offenses nos 13–20.

[11] ibid.

[12] ibid 114, 117, Annex I.

[13] ibid 114, enumerated offenses nos 1–12.

either directly (with the express reference to destruction of 'historic buildings and monuments') or indirectly (through general offenses based on the misappropriation or destruction of property). Specifically, the Commission's list expressly included the following five enumerated offenses: pillage, confiscation of property; wanton devastation and destruction of property; deliberate bombardment of undefended places; and wanton destruction of religious, charitable, educational, and historic buildings and monuments.[14]

The list was rounded out by specific rules relating to merchant ships and hospital vessels, the breach of rules 'relating to the Red Cross', use of certain weapons (such as deleterious and asphyxiating gases), perfidy, poisoning of wells, and ill-treatment of prisoners of war.[15]

The proposed list of offenses reflects that the government representatives on the Commission on Responsibilities embraced the inclusion of cultural heritage-based offenses in a codified international criminal code. The proposed offenses unsurprisingly tracked the related laws and customs of war codified in the Regulations appended to the 1899 and 1907 Hague Conventions governing land warfare.[16] The codified Hague rules that govern active hostilities (as opposed to the later section with rules that govern occupation[17]) provide that belligerents must take 'all necessary steps ... to spare, as far as possible, buildings dedicated to religion, art, science, or charitable purposes, [and] historic monuments'.[18] Like the offenses set out by the Commission on Responsibilities, the Hague Regulations' specific reference to cultural heritage was limited to destruction of cultural sites. Movable cultural property was protected from destruction or seizure only by the *lex generalis* barring pillage and unnecessary destruction or seizure of property.[19]

In determining the mandate of an international tribunal, the Commission considered whether the proposed tribunal should entertain prosecutions for violations of both the *jus ad bellum* and the *jus in bello*.[20] The Commission concluded that the proposed offenses based on the *jus in bello* should be prosecuted before the proposed tribunal, but that any efforts to redress the acts of aggression that precipitated and exacerbated the conflict should instead be handled in the anticipated, forthcoming peace process.[21] This latter recommendation was not sufficient to quell the concerns of the US delegation, though, which was less keen on pursuing prosecutions before an international criminal tribunal and submitted forcefully

[14] ibid 114–15, enumerated offenses nos 13–20.
[15] ibid, enumerated offenses nos 21–32.
[16] 1899 and 1907 Hague Conventions, Regulations.
[17] 1899 and 1907 Hague Conventions, Regulations, s 3.
[18] ibid, art 27.
[19] ibid, arts 23, 28.
[20] Report of the Commission on Responsibilities (n 10) 118 (identifying the two 'classes of culpable acts' as those that 'provoked the world war and accompanied its inception' and those that violated 'the laws and customs of war and the laws of humanity').
[21] ibid 120, 123–24.

worded reservations, in the form of a published 'dissent' from the recommendations of the Commission.[22] This resistance had significant bearing on the ultimate decision to abandon plans for an international criminal court and for developing an international criminal code at this time.[23]

In the end, the official efforts to establish an international criminal tribunal and to codify international criminal offenses, based on violations of the laws and customs of war, faltered in the years after the First World War.[24] Some of the Allied Powers had sent a warning to Ottoman authorities early in the war, warning them that they would hold *all* Ottoman authorities responsible for the 'crimes of Turkey against humanity and civilization', namely massacres of the Armenian population, and the victorious Allies also inserted provisions in the Treaty of Versailles providing both for a 'special tribunal' to try German Kaiser Wilhelm II and for their military tribunals to prosecute 'persons accused of having committed acts in violation of the laws and customs of war'.[25] None of these anticipated prosecutions came to be. The Allies ultimately agreed for the vanquished Parties to prosecute violations in their respective domestic systems, a decision largely attributable to the lack of any governing international norms for prosecutions before an international body.[26]

The postwar treaties contained provisions on cultural property that called for the restitution, repatriation, or other transfer of movable cultural property—some of which required distributing cultural property to new governments in the wake of the breakup of the Hapsburg empire, for example, while other provisions called for the restitution of cultural objects stemming from previous conflicts or

[22] Memorandum of Reservations Presented by the Representatives of the United States to the Report of the Common on Responsibilities (4 April 1919) in ibid, Annex II, 127–51.

[23] The US resistance to the outcomes of the 1919 Paris Peace Conference went further, with the United States additionally refusing to join the sixty-three-member League of Nations established by the Conference in the Treaty of Versailles. The Covenant of the League of Nations succeeded in establishing the first permanent international court, the Permanent Court of International Justice (PCIJ), and gave it competence to adjudicate 'any dispute of an international character which the parties thereto submit to it', but the PCIJ was not a criminal tribunal. Treaty of Peace between the Allied and Associated Powers and Germany (opened for signature 28 June 1919, entered into force 10 January 1920), in (1919) 13 AJIL Supp 27 (Treaty of Versailles). Sixty-three Member States participated in the League of Nations for at least part of its duration before it was replaced by the United Nations after the Second World War.

[24] See eg Harry M Rhea, 'Paris 1919 and Rome 1998: Different Treaties, Different Presidents, Different Senates, and the Same Dilemma' (2011) 20 Trans L & Contemporary Problems 411, 415–18; M Cherif Bassiouni, 'From Versailles to Rwanda in Seventy-Five Years: The Need to Establish a Permanent International Criminal Court' (1997) 10 Harvard Human Rights J 11, 12–21, 26–27.

[25] United Nations War Crimes Commission, 'Information Concerning Human Rights Arising from Trials of War Criminals: Report Prepared by the United Nations War Crimes Commission in Accordance with the Request Received from the United Nations' (1948) UN Doc E/CN.4/W.19 (15 May 1948) 7 (warning by Russia, Great Britain, and France); Treaty of Versailles (n 23) arts 227–30.

[26] Kaiser Wilhelm II had taken refuge in the Netherlands, which refused to surrender him for that purpose, and the Allies ultimately agreed that Germany could prosecute a select list of offenders in special courts that it established at Leipzig. See eg Treaty of Versailles (n 23) arts 227–30; 'Notes to Part VII, Articles 227 to 230' in *Foreign Relations of the United States, The Paris Peace Conference, 1919* (GPO 1947) vol XII, 372–80.

controversies.[27] None set out a code of international criminal offenses based on the law of armed conflict.

By the 1920s, the mantle for bolstering protection of cultural property during armed conflict and redressing violations of applicable protections instead shifted to two parallel movements: (a) efforts to establish a convention that would codify and elaborate the laws and customs of war for protecting cultural property during armed conflict, and (b) private initiatives to include the destruction of cultural property within the nascent concept of 'genocide'. During the interwar period, public efforts on this first front included the 1923 Draft Hague Rules for Air Warfare,[28] the 1935 Treaty on the Protection of Artistic and Scientific Institutions and Historic Monuments (the Roerich Pact or the Washington Pact),[29] and the 1938 Draft Convention (later reduced to a Declaration) from the International Museums Office of the League of Nations.[30] The 1923 Draft Hague Air Rules included greater protections for cultural property as part of a larger attempt to adapt the laws of armed conflict to aerial warfare,[31] while the Roerich Pact and the draft convention from the International Museums Office were both standalone instruments dedicated exclusively to protecting cultural property. Only the Roerich Pact succeeded as a binding treaty, joined by most countries on the North and South American continents.[32] With provisions that applied during both conflict and peace, it originated as a private initiative from the Belgium-based International Union for the Roerich Pact (*Union Internationale pour le Pact Roerich*) but was later modified and taken up by the Pan-American Union. Unfortunately, the Pact was never implemented in any meaningful way.[33]

[27] See eg Treaty of Versailles (n 23) arts 131, 245–47; Treaty of Peace between the Allied and Associated Powers and Austria (signed 10 September 1919, entered into force 16 July 1920), in 14 AJIL Supp 1 (1920) Annex I, III. See also Ana Vrdoljak, 'Enforcement of Restitution of Cultural Heritage through Peace Agreements' in Francesco Francioni and James Gordley (eds), *Enforcing International Cultural Heritage Law* (OUP 2013) 22, 24–27.

[28] [Draft] Rules of Aerial Warfare, in John Bassett Moore (ed), *International Law and Some Current Illusions* (Macmillan 1924) 225 (Draft Hague Air Rules).

[29] Additional private initiatives included a questionnaire for foreign governments that was commissioned by the Netherlands Archaeological Society (*Nederlandsche Oudheidkundige Bond*) and a proposal from the Geneva Zones (*Lieux de Genève*) organization for combined zones of protection by designating historic centers as civilian refuges. See eg 'Projet de questionnaire relatif à la protection des oeuvres d'art en temps de guerre' (1919) 10 Rev Générale de Droit Intl Public 329, 330–31; Georges Saint-Paul, *Le Lieu de Genève: Exposé général (Extrait de Strasbourg Médical)* (Imprimerie Arrault 1938), in Papers of Liddell Hart, Liddell Hart Centre for Military Archives, King's College London, File 15/3/243a; Pascal Gondrand, 'The International Civil Defence Organisation (ICDO) from 1931 to 2001' 13 (June 2001) Intl Civil Defence J 61. For further discussion of these initiatives, see Anne-Marie Carstens, *Safeguarding Cultural Property During Armed Conflict* (OUP forthcoming 2020) (Ch 2).

[30] See eg Preliminary Draft Convention on the Protection of Historic Buildings and Works of Art in Times of War, 19 LNOJ 937 (1938), Annex; Draft Declaration Concerning the Protection of Historic Buildings and Works of Art in Time of War (1939), in United States Department of State, *Documents & State Papers* (June 1949) vol I, App A.

[31] Draft Hague Air Rules (n 28) 244–47.

[32] See 'Status of the Treaties and Conventions Signed at the International Conferences of American States and at Other Pan American Conferences' (1938) 32 AJIL (Supp) 102–04.

[33] Although several European states initially considered the developing instrument with interest, this interest dissipated by the time of its adoption, in part because it came to be seen chiefly as a regional

None of these efforts to expand conventional rules for the wartime protection of cultural property, however, included provisions for redress, enforcement, or penal sanctions. After all, the law of armed conflict has traditionally been prescriptive by nature, focused on establishing rules of belligerent conduct rather than on enforcement. Still, for the protection of cultural property, the failure to provide for prosecution or sanctions in these interwar instruments was a bit of an anomaly. In the 1899 and 1907 Hague Conventions, the rule expressly applicable to protecting cultural property during occupation was unusual in requiring prosecution of violations, which was not expressly required for violations of any other provisions in these two instruments. It provided that seizure and destruction of institutions dedicated to religion and to the arts and sciences, of historic monuments, and of works of art and science 'is forbidden, *and should be made the subject of legal proceedings*'.[34]

This uncharacteristic mandate for prosecuting cultural heritage crimes, set forth already in an international convention, provided one of the clearest (albeit isolated) bases for a critical element found lacking after the First World War: an international norm for prosecuting violations of the laws and customs of war. An attempt to codify an international criminal offense based on destruction or seizure of cultural property therefore arguably would have stood on stronger footing than would corollary offenses based on other violations, though the subtle significance of the mandate meant that it could also have been used as the entrée for establishing offenses more generally.

Instead, the coinciding movement to develop an international criminal code during this period was proceeding on an entirely different track. The Conference for the Unification of Penal Law, for example, had begun in 1927 to draw up a series of what its members considered offenses against the law of nations (*delicta juris gentium*). The list began with seven offenses, including piracy and any trade in slaves, women, or children, and an early attempt to define terrorism as an international crime, and the list grew over successive conferences.[35]

For the fifth such conference held in 1933, Lemkin, a Polish jurist and public prosecutor, was not in attendance but submitted a provocative proposal for adding five more offenses to the list, including the two linked offenses of 'barbarity' and 'vandalism'.[36] Barbarity consisted principally of acts of extermination against

treaty for the Americas. See Anne-Marie Carstens, *Safeguarding Cultural Property During Armed Conflict* (OUP forthcoming 2020) (ch 2).

[34] 1899 and 1907 Hague Conventions, Regulations, art 56 (emphasis added).

[35] See Resolutions of the Conference for the Unification of Penal Law (1927).

[36] Raphael Lemkin, 'Les actes constituant un danger général (interétatique) considérés comme délites des droit des gens' (Special Report presented to the 5th Conference for the Unification of Penal Law in Madrid) (14–20 October 1933), translated and reproduced at <http://www.preventgenocide.org/lemkin/madrid1933-english.htm> accessed 10 November 2018; Raphael Lemkin, *Totally Unofficial: The Autobiography of Raphael Lemkin* (Donna-Lee Frieze ed, Yale 2013) 22, 64. See also

religious, ethnic, or social groups, also known as 'collectivities'—Lemkin had the Armenian genocide of the First World War in mind[37]—while vandalism referred to the 'systemic and organized destruction of the art and cultural heritage' of a targeted collectivity. In Lemkin's characterization, the perpetrator of such an attack causes not only an immediate irrevocable loss to the property and culture of the people directly concerned, but 'it is also all humanity which experiences a loss by this act of vandalism'.[38]

Lemkin thus became one of the first authors to formally articulate a stark view of the destruction of cultural property as one facet of the extermination and persecution of a targeted cultural group. This articulation provided an alternate justification for prosecuting such violations as an international offense, challenging the then-prevalent view that such property should be spared from destruction on account of its historic, religious, or aesthetic character, which was based on the formulation presented in the 1899 and 1907 Hague Conventions.

After the outbreak of the Second World War, Lemkin coined the term 'genocide' and crystallized both barbarism and vandalism within a newly conceived crime of genocide. This time, his proposed doctrine touched him personally and directly. Lemkin escaped German-occupied Poland in 1939 and emigrated to the United States during the war, while dozens of his relatives at home perished in the Holocaust.[39] He identified cultural genocide as one of eight 'techniques of genocide'.[40] Lemkin's concept of 'cultural genocide' included the vandalism that he previously described—the destruction of cultural monuments, museums, and libraries, for example.[41]

II. The Swing Away from Codifying Cultural Heritage-Based Crimes: The Postwar Period and Cold War

The mass atrocities and vast devastation of the Second World War led the four Allied Powers to return to the question of establishing an international criminal tribunal in the postwar period. By the end of 1945, these powers had established

Vesselin Popovski, 'Raphael Lemkin: Inventing and Codifying Genocide' (2018) 3 Jus Gentium: J Intl L Hist 181, 196–99.

[37] Interview with Raphael Lemkin, 'UN Casebook' (television series, CBS News) (February 1949); Lemkin, *Autobiography* (n 36) 19–20. See also Popovski (n 36) 192–94; Peter Balakian, 'Raphael Lemkin, Cultural Destruction, and the Armenian Genocide' (2013) 27 Holocaust and Genocide Studies 57; William Schabas, *Genocide in International Law: The Crime of Crimes* (CUP 2000) 25.

[38] Lemkin, 'Les actes constituant un danger général'(n 36).

[39] Popovski (n 36) 190–91.

[40] Raphael Lemkin, *Axis Rule in Occupied Europe: Laws of Occupation, Analysis of Government, Proposals for Redress* (Carnegie Endowment for Intl Peace 1944).

[41] ibid. See also Elisa Novic, *The Concept of Cultural Genocide: An International Law Perspective* (OUP 2016) 18–22.

the International Military Tribunal at Nuremberg (Nuremberg Tribunal), where the prosecutions of high-level officers and perpetrators were governed by the Charter of the International Military Tribunal (Nuremberg Charter).[42] The war had emphasized the extent to which entire regimes employed the destruction and seizure of cultural property as a tool of oppression and persecution, as well as how indiscriminate warfare could decimate entire communities, both lives and property. The war's unprecedented destruction of religious and historic buildings and the widespread policies used to wrest cultural objects from Jewish communities and other persecuted groups became the watershed examples of destruction and seizure of cultural property to eradicate the outward manifestations and cultural identity of minority communities.

Still, the postwar period arguably witnessed the lowest support for recognizing deliberate cultural heritage destruction as a distinct offense in an international criminal code. This was true not only for the statute that governed the ad hoc Nuremberg Tribunal and efforts by the United Nations (UN) to establish a permanent criminal code.[43] It was also ultimately true for the Convention on the Prevention and Punishment of the Crime of Genocide (1948 Genocide Convention), which represented the culmination of Lemkin's agitation for an international criminal offense of 'genocide' and which was adopted by the UN General Assembly in 1948.[44]

This reality, however, must take into account not only how the instruments on international criminal law during this period addressed cultural heritage-based violations, but also the larger development of public international law happening at the same time. Viewed in isolation, the early draft criminal codes suggest that actors working toward developing international criminal law placed lower priority on violations of cultural heritage-based protections in light of the horrific atrocities committed against civilians and cultural groups during the war. Yet several developments were occurring at the same time in other legal regimes that bore on efforts to improve the protection of cultural property in any one of them, including in international criminal law. Viewed together, these overlapping efforts show, sometimes directly and sometimes implicitly, that determinations to exclude cultural heritage crimes from international criminal law also took account of the broader developments in public international law to address cultural property protection in future conflicts.

[42] Charter of the International Military Tribunal, in *Trial of the Major War Criminals Before the International Military Tribunal (Nuremberg 14 November 1945–1 October 1946)* (42 vols, International Military Tribunal 1947–49) vol I, 10–18 (Nuremberg Charter). See also UNGA Res 3(I) (13 February 1946) UN Doc A/RES/1.

[43] Nuremberg Charter; ILC, 'Draft Code of Offences against the Peace and Security of Mankind' (1954) UN Doc A/CN.4/85.

[44] Convention on the Prevention and Punishment of the Crime of Genocide (adopted 9 December 1948, entered into force 21 January 1951) 78 UNTS 277 (1948 Genocide Convention).

The Nuremberg Charter was the immediate postwar effort to establish an international criminal regime and contained no express references to cultural heritage. It notably failed to incorporate the 1899 and 1907 Hague Conventions' express formulation of prohibiting unnecessary destruction of 'institutions dedicated to religion, art, science, or charitable purposes' or 'historic monuments' despite the fact that the Tribunal declared that the laws and customs of war contained in those treaties had passed into customary law at the time of the war.[45] In fact, during the early drafting of the Nuremberg Charter, the drafters contemplated excluding not just cultural heritage crimes, but any violations of the laws and customs of war stemming from property destruction or seizures. Lauterpacht, the principal drafter, acknowledged that the destruction of property, and even of certain cultural property specifically, could constitute 'war crimes'. Yet he specifically advised against prosecuting these 'less grave war crimes'—property destruction, unlawful requisitions, or the 'destruction of buildings and monuments of religious, charitable, scientific and historic character'—at Nuremberg because they did not 'present those elements of political and moral urgency as in the case of the other war crimes'.[46] Certainly this assessment suggests a bias against addressing property-based violations of the law of armed conflict. Perhaps, but it was also the case that Lauterpacht looked outside international criminal law to consider two alternate fora for such offenses: the recently established International Court of Justice (ICJ) and a possible 'International Criminal Court to be created as part of the general international settlement'.[47]

In its final form, the Nuremberg Charter adopted a less stringent position and did not exclude property crimes altogether. The Charter's list of war crimes included 'plunder of public or private property', the 'wanton destruction of cities, towns or villages', and 'devastation not justified by military necessity'.[48] Destruction or seizure of cultural sites or cultural objects thus were encompassed by these general provisions on property and thus only implicitly within the definition of 'war crimes'.

The Nuremberg Charter's limitation of property-based offenses to general property crimes did not prove fatal, however. The Tribunal used the definitions of 'war crimes' as the basis for adjudicating several crimes against cultural property, while it certainly focused overwhelmingly and foremost on atrocities committed against civilians. The prosecutors presented extensive evidence of the roles played by Rosenberg, Goering, von Ribbentrop, and others in the deliberate destruction and seizure of cultural sites and movable works,[49] and the Tribunal relied on this evidence in its judgment to reinforce the link between destruction and cultural

[45] *Trial of the Major War Criminals* (n 42) vol I, 254.
[46] Hersch Lauterpacht, *International Law: Collected Papers* (CUP 2004) vol V, 540.
[47] ibid.
[48] Nuremberg Charter, art 6(b).
[49] See eg *Trial of the Major War Criminals* (n 42) vol V, 48, 53–104.

extermination. Keitel and Bormann, too, were found guilty of war crimes and crimes against humanity, in part for their complicity in the orchestrated confiscation of movable works.[50] All were sentenced to death.[51]

The Nuremberg judgment also served as an effective precedent in establishing that the destruction and seizure of cultural sites and movable works constituted an important violation of the law of war. The Nuremberg Tribunal interpreted 'plunder of public or private property' under the Charter to include the prohibitions on unnecessary destruction and seizure of 'historic monuments', 'works of art and science', and 'institutions dedicated to religion, charity and education', as provided in Article 56 of the 1899 and 1907 Hague Conventions, which it quoted in its entirety.[52] Still, such offenses were always conjoined with other offenses against persons.[53]

After the Nuremberg Tribunal dissolved, the international community resolved to address the threats to cultural heritage during armed conflict, but a debate continued to brew over which international institutions and which kinds of instrument were best equipped to address these threats. UNESCO, established in 1945 as the cultural arm of the UN,[54] quickly developed a plan of action in which the organization aimed to achieve three coinciding and overlapping aims: improving protection of cultural property during armed conflict; establishing an international fund of 'very considerable sums' to subsidize the protection, preservation, and restoration of cultural sites; and facilitating the incorporation of cultural heritage crimes in any international penal code.[55] UNESCO appointed an expert committee to study these tasks.[56]

The 1950 report of the UNESCO-appointed experts advised against a major multilateral convention on the protection of cultural property during armed conflict. The experts felt that the emerging Cold War effectively precluded 'a broad multilateral treaty entered into by some forty or so powers' for protecting cultural property.[57] The report included draft articles that reflected customary international law obligations for cultural property protection during armed conflict, but a multilateral treaty was not their intended use. The experts instead primarily hoped their draft provisions would be incorporated in 'a draft code of offenses against the peace and security of mankind' that was then being drawn up by the United Nation's International Law Commission (ILC)—the principal vehicle established in the

[50] ibid 289, 339.
[51] ibid, Tabulation of Sentences, 366–67.
[52] *US and others v Goering and others*, Judgment, in *Trial of the Major War Criminals* (n 42) vol I, 171, 239 (quoting 1907 Hague Convention, Regulations, art 56).
[53] eg ibid 287–96.
[54] Constitution of the United Nations Educational, Scientific and Cultural Organization (UNESCO) (adopted 16 November 1945, entered into force 4 November 1946).
[55] UNESCO Doc 5C/PRG/6, Annex I (8 March 1950) 4–5 (National Archives (UK), FO 371/88915).
[56] ibid 1, 4–5 (quoting 1949 General Conference proceedings).
[57] ibid 1–2, 21

postwar period that was tasked with developing a permanent international criminal code and for creating an International Criminal Court.[58]

The Director-General of UNESCO subsequently submitted the draft articles on cultural property protection to the ILC, which agreed with UNESCO that destruction of cultural sites and objects fell within the general concept of war crimes.[59] In other discussions also held in 1950, the ILC additionally suggested that plunder, wanton destruction, and devastation not justified by military necessity qualified as 'war crimes' based on the example of the Nuremberg Tribunal.[60]

In the meantime, the United Nations had confirmed 'genocide' as a 'crime under international law' and begun considering drafts for an international convention on genocide.[61] The Preamble to the first draft convention, prepared by the Secretary-General with Lemkin serving as one of three assisting experts, proclaimed:

> Genocide, which is the intentional destruction of a group of human beings, defies universal conscience, inflicts irreparable loss on humanity by depriving it of the cultural and other contributions of the group so destroyed, and is in contradiction with the spirit and aims of the United Nations.[62]

The draft convention identified three categories of conduct that would qualify as 'genocide' under the treaty: physical genocide, biological genocide, and cultural genocide.[63] Physical genocide and biological genocide both consisted of deliberate acts committed against members of a group, with the former directed at acts causing death or injury to health or integrity (such as group massacres, conditions likely to result in debilitation or death, and mutilations and biological experiments), and the second directed at acts restricting birth.[64] The draft's definition of physical genocide also extended to deprivation of 'all means of livelihood' including through property confiscations and looting.[65]

Cultural genocide consisted of measures aimed at '[d]estroying the specific characteristics of the group'.[66] Such acts included transfers of children to another human group, as well as forced and systematic exile 'of individuals representing

[58] ibid 1–2, 11–14. See also UNGA Res 177(II) (21 November 1947) UN Doc A/RES/177(II), para b.

[59] ILC, 'Report of the International Law Commission' UN Doc A/1316 (1950) Supp 12, para 153, in [1950] YB ILC, vol 2, 380.

[60] ibid, paras 118–19.

[61] UNGA Res 96(I) (11 December 1946) UN Doc A/RES/96; UNGA Res 180(II) (21 November 1947) UN Doc A/RES/180.

[62] Draft Convention on the Crime of Genocide (including Comments on the Draft Convention), UN Doc E/447 (26 June 1947), Preamble, Comments at 15.

[63] ibid, art 1, and Comments at 17–18, 26–28.

[64] ibid, arts 1(1), 1(2).

[65] ibid, art 1(II)(1). The rationale was that depriving one of a means of livelihood condemns a group to death 'at the end of a medium period instead of to a quick death in concentration camps', a difference only of degree as to the ultimate result. ibid, Comments at 26.

[66] ibid, art 1(II)(3).

the cultural of a group'.[67] But it also included systematic destruction of books, religious materials, and historic or religious monuments, as well as 'destruction or dispersion' of documents and of historical, artistic, and religious objects.[68] The appended Comments noted that including 'cultural genocide' was controversial, even among the three expert advisers. Lemkin favored the inclusion, but the other two were against it, except as to forced transfers of children, on the grounds that other instruments on protection of human rights and minority rights better covered the conduct concerned.[69] The concept of cultural genocide (including the associated systematic destruction of certain cultural property) prevailed in the next draft, though forced segregation of children from parents was recast as a form of physical genocide.

In a twist of events, though, the mechanisms for developing international law to protect cultural property during armed conflict proceeded contrary to what might have been anticipated from these early developments. The concept of cultural genocide was dropped from later drafts for a convention on genocide, as were several of the acts originally proposed, including the reference to property deprivations and looting as capable of establishing physical genocide. In the end, the 1948 Genocide Convention, adopted by the UN General Assembly, defined 'genocide' as encompassing only physical and biological genocide and provided that persons charged with genocide could be prosecuted by competent courts in the territory where the acts were committed or by an envisioned 'international penal tribunal'.[70] Opposition to including cultural genocide rested partly on the argument that it simply did not fit the mold of the 'horrifying aspects' that had rendered a convention on genocide so urgent.[71] At the same time, the drafters did not necessarily disagree in principle to redressing the acts presented as 'cultural genocide' so much as they considered the availability of other instruments—particularly instruments addressing human rights, discrimination, or minority rights—as more suitable vehicles for the purpose.[72]

Not only was cultural heritage destruction excluded from the 1948 Genocide Convention, but when the ILC finally produced its first Draft Code of Offences against the Peace and Security of Mankind in 1954, the draft included no provisions referencing cultural property—or even property at all.[73] It conformed to Lauterpacht's earlier inclinations.

[67] ibid, art 1(II)(3)(a)–(b).

[68] ibid, art 1(II)(3)(d)–(e).

[69] ibid, Comments at 28.

[70] 1948 Genocide Convention, arts II, VI.

[71] Report of the Committee and Draft Convention Drawn Up by the Committee, UN Doc E/794 (24 May 1948) 17–18.

[72] ibid.

[73] ibid 6; ILC, 'Draft Code of Offences against the Peace and Security of Mankind' (1954) UN Doc A/CN.4/85, 112.

Yet that same year, a multinational conference adopted the 1954 Hague Convention for the Protection of Cultural Property in the Event of Armed Conflict (1954 Hague Convention),[74] the leading treaty on cultural property protection during conflict and occupation to date. The adoption of this large, multilateral treaty disproved the skepticism of the UNESCO experts who drafted the 1950 report, even if Cold War politics played a part in shaping the treaty. The 1954 Hague Convention was based, in part, of several rounds of revisions, expert roundtables, and input from UNESCO Member States that evolved from the draft articles previously set out in the 1950 report.[75] In addition, though, the 1954 Hague Convention added provisions on criminal responsibility and penal sanctions for violations:

> The High Contracting Parties undertake to take, within the framework of their ordinary criminal jurisdiction, all necessary steps to prosecute and impose penal or disciplinary sanctions upon those persons, of whatever nationality, who commit or order to be committed a breach of the present Convention.[76]

This provision, which admittedly calls for domestic criminal responsibility or court-martial rather than international criminal liability, followed the model of the 1949 Geneva Convention Relative to the Protection of Civilian Persons in Time of War (1949 Fourth Geneva Convention).[77] The 1949 Fourth Geneva Convention required States Parties to provide effective penal sanctions for 'grave breaches' of the Convention. Grave breaches consisted primarily of atrocities against persons, such as willful killing and torture, but could also include destruction and seizure of cultural property when it could be characterized as extensive, wanton, and unlawful destruction or appropriation of property, not justified by military necessity.[78] This same model of domestic criminal responsibility was followed again when rules for civilian protection and cultural property protection merged in the 1977 Protocols Additional to the Geneva Conventions of 12 August 1949 (1977 Additional Protocols I and II).[79] Additional Protocols I and II

[74] Convention for the Protection of Cultural Property in the Event of Armed Conflict (adopted 14 May 1954, entered into force 7 August 1956) 249 UNTS 240 (1954 Hague Convention).

[75] See Records of the Conference Convened by the United Nations Educational, Scientific and Cultural Organization Held at The Hague from 21 April to 14 May 1954 (The Netherlands 1961); One concern was that the treaty provisions would be ineffectual in the event of nuclear warfare. See eg Jiří Toman, *The Protection of Cultural Property in the Event of Armed Conflict: Commentary on the Convention for the Protection of Cultural Property in the Event of Armed Conflict and its Protocol* (UNESCO/Dartmouth 1996) 23–24; A Noblecourt, *Protection of Cultural Property in the Event of Armed Conflict* (UNESCO 1958) (translated from 1956 French ed).

[76] 1954 Hague Convention, art 28.

[77] Convention Relative to the Protection of Civilian Persons in Time of War (adopted 12 August 1949, entered into force 21 October 1950) 75 UNTS 287, arts 146–47 (1949 Fourth Geneva Convention).

[78] ibid.

[79] Protocol Additional to the Geneva Conventions of 12 August 1949, and Relating to the Protection of Victims of International Armed Conflicts (adopted 8 June 1977, opened for signature 12 December 1977, entered into force 7 December 1978) 1125 UNTS 3 (Additional Protocol I); Protocol Additional

provided for penal sanctions and prosecutions for violations committed in international and non-international conflicts, respectively, and Additional Protocol I also provided for mutual legal assistance in criminal matters, extradition, and reparations.[80] None made reference to prosecution by an international criminal tribunal.

Through the postwar and Cold War periods, the international community therefore showed itself disinclined to include cultural heritage-based crimes as specific offenses in international criminal law. It even seemed to close the door on recognizing generalized property offenses, such as plunder and pillage, that could encompass destruction of cultural property as used at Nuremberg. Instead, the adoption of the 1954 Hague Convention suggested that the preferred avenue was to secure better protection for cultural property through new treaties on the law of armed conflict that prescribed rules applicable to cultural property protection, with provisions that called for enforcement.

III. A New Era of International Criminal Tribunals, with Cultural Heritage Crimes: The 1980s through Today

The ILC recommenced efforts in the early 1980s on the Draft Code of Offences against the Peace and Security of Mankind,[81] which had been ostensibly shelved since 1954. The early revisions contained no references to either property or cultural property,[82] just like their 1954 predecessor.[83] After a series of drafts and consultations, however, specialized rules for cultural property appeared for the first time in the 1989 revision and were included in all subsequent revisions thereafter.[84] The ILC's 1991 Draft Code of Crimes against the Peace and Security of Mankind, for example, identified willful attacks on property of exceptional religious, historical, or cultural value as an 'exceptionally serious war crime'.[85] Though the modifier of 'exceptionally serious' was later dropped, a revised version of the Draft Code with a cultural heritage-based offense was adopted by the UN Security Council

to the Geneva Conventions of 12 August 1949, and Relating to the Protection of Victims of Non-International Armed Conflicts (adopted 8 June 1977, opened for signature 12 December 1977, entered into force 7 December 1978) 1125 UNTS 609 (Additional Protocol II).

[80] Additional Protocol I, arts 75(4), 75(7), 88, 89, 91; Additional Protocol II, art 6.

[81] UNGA Res 36/106 (10 December 1981) UN Doc A/RES/36/106.

[82] See eg ILC, 'Report of the ILC on the work of its 36th Session, Draft code of offences against the peace and security of mankind' (1984) UN Doc A/39/10 8–17; UNGA 'Fourth report by Special Rapporteur Doudou Thiam on the draft code of offences against the peace and security of mankind' (11 March 1986) UN Doc A/CN.4/398 61–62.

[83] ILC, 1954 'Draft Code' (n 73).

[84] ILC, 'Report of the International Law Commission on the Work of its 41st Session', 2 YB ILC (1989) UN Doc A/CN.4/SER.A/1989/Add.1 (Pt 2) 63, paras 189–92.

[85] ILC Report UN Doc A/46/10 (1991), art 22(2)(f).

in 1993 as the ICTY Statute.[86] Five years later, the Rome Statute was adopted, establishing the first permanent international criminal tribunal. It provided that intentional attacks on cultural sites and historic monuments constituted a 'war crime', unless the site was a military objective, with a corollary provision applicable in non-international armed conflicts.[87]

By the end of the twentieth century, developing international criminal law thus had swung in favor of incorporating cultural heritage violations as offenses, including in the ICTY Statute and the Rome Statute. They were also incorporated in the law governing the Extraordinary Chambers in the Courts of Cambodia (ECCC), which was established as a hybrid domestic–international criminal tribunal to redress violations that occurred during the reign of the Khmer Rouge, which included attacks against the rich cultural tapestry of Cambodia.[88]

Cultural heritage crimes therefore appear to have secured a lasting place in the statutes governing both the permanent ICC and ad hoc international criminal tribunals, in the latter instance at least for conflicts in which attacks on cultural heritage feature prominently. (The Statutes governing the conflicts in Rwanda and Sierra Leone, for example, did not include express provisions for the destruction or seizure of cultural property.) Several indictments in the ICTY alleged the offense covering destruction of or damage to cultural institutions, including in high-profile prosecutions of Jokić and Strugar for their roles in the shelling of the Old City of Dubrovnik, a World Heritage site, and in the *Prlić* case for destruction of the Old Bridge of Mostar, though the latter case was ultimately decided on the basis of other provisions.[89] The corollary rule in the

[86] ICTY Statute, art 3(d). See also *Prosecutor v Tadić* (Trial Judgment, Separate Opinion of Judge Robinson) ICTY-94-1-Tbis-R117 (11 November 1999) 6 (describing differences between proposed 'exceptionally serious war crimes' and offenses set out in the ICTY Statute).

[87] Rome Statute, arts 8(b)(ix), 8(e)(iv); ICTY Statute, art 3(d).

[88] Agreement between the United Nations and the Royal Government of Cambodia Concerning the Prosecution under Cambodian Law of Crimes Committed during the Period of Democratic Kampuchea (adopted 6 June 2003, entered into force 29 April 2005) 2329 UNTS 41723; Law on the Establishment of the Extraordinary Chambers, with inclusion of amendments as promulgated on 27 October 2004 (NS/RKM/1004/006), art 7 (stating that the ECCC 'shall have the power to bring to trial all Suspects most responsible for the destruction of cultural property during armed conflict pursuant to the 1954 Hague Convention for Protection of Cultural Property in the Event of Armed Conflict' committed during the relevant time period). See eg Caroline Ehlert, *Prosecuting the Destruction of Cultural Property in International Criminal Law: With a Case Study on the Khmer Rouge's Destruction of Cambodia's Heritage* (Martinus Nijhoff 2013); Federico Lenzerini, 'The Role of International and Mixed Criminal Courts in the Enforcement of International Norms Concerning the Protection of Cultural Heritage' in Francesco Francioni and James Gordley (eds), *Enforcing International Cultural Heritage Law* (OUP 2013).

[89] *Prosecutor v Prlić* (Appeals Judgment) ICTY-04-74-A (29 November 2017); *Prosecutor v Strugar* (Appeals Judgment) ICTY-01-42-A (17 July 2008); *Prosecutor v Jokić* (Sentencing Appeal Judgment) ICTY-01-42/1-A (30 July 2005); *Prosecutor v Jokić* (Sentencing Judgment) ICTY-01-42/1-S (18 March 2004). In November 2017, the Appeals Chamber reversed the Trial Court's finding that Prlić and others committed the crime of wanton destruction not justified by military necessity in destroying the Old Bridge, on the grounds that the bridge constituted a military objective at the time of the destruction, and thus also reversed convictions of persecution and unlawful infliction of terror 'insofar as they concern

Rome Statute is the basis for the Al Mahdi and Al Hassan prosecutions in the ICC.[90]

A comparison of the Rome Statute and the ICTY Statute, however—both with each other and with the previous proposals—reveals two ways in which international criminal law today does not recognize cultural heritage crimes to their full potential. The most obvious is that like the 1948 Genocide Convention, both the ICTY Statute and Rome Statute confine the crime of genocide to the physical or biological destruction of a group, and therefore continue to reject 'cultural genocide' as an international crime.[91] The ICTY later confirmed this reading in the *Krstić* case, observing that developments in protection for cultural heritage had not expanded the reach of 'genocide' to include cultural genocide. The ICJ has likewise ruled that the 'destruction of historical, cultural and religious heritage' does not fall within the categories of acts that constitute genocide.[92] The ICJ made clear that the conclusive evidence of the destruction of historical, cultural, and religious heritage of Bosnian Muslims could not be shoehorned into the provision of the 1948 Genocide Convention on 'deliberate infliction of conditions of life calculated to bring about the physical destruction of the group'.[93]

Nonetheless, the tribunals in these same cases embraced Lemkin's conception of 'cultural genocide' to a limited degree, even if not as a standalone crime: both tribunals endorsed the view that systematic attacks on cultural property as symbols of a targeted group can be considered as evidence of the requisite *mens rea* when they coincide with physical and biological destruction of a group.[94] In addition, the ICTY Trial Chamber in *Blaškić* held that destruction of cultural heritage can serve as the *actus reas* for the crime of persecution on political, racial, and religious grounds, which is classified as a crime against humanity, though the Appeals

the Old Bridge'. *Prlić*, paras 423, 798. See also Elizabeth Varner, 'Comparing Interpretations of States' and Non-State Actors' Obligations Toward Cultural Heritage in Armed Conflict and Occupation: Military Manuals and the Law of War' (Ch 2) in this volume.

[90] *Prosecutor v Al Mahdi* (Trial Judgment and Sentence) ICC-01/12-01/15-171 (27 September 2016); *Prosecutor v Al Hassan* (Arrest Warrant), ICC-01/12-01/18 (27 March 2018) <https://www.icc-cpi.int/itemsDocuments/CR2018_01863_FRA.PDF> accessed 6 October 2018.

[91] ICTY Statute, art 4; Rome Statute, art 6.

[92] *Application of the Convention on the Prevention and Punishment of the Crime of Genocide (Bosnia and Herzegovina v Serbia and Montenegro)* (Judgment) [2007] ICJ Reports 43, paras 335–44; *Prosecutor v Krstić* (Trial Judgment) ICTY-98-33-T (2 August 2001) para 580. Both tribunals pointed to the *travaux préparatoires* of the 1948 Genocide Convention. For more discussion of these cases and their consideration of cultural heritage destruction, see Gabriele Gagliani, 'The ICJ and Cultural Heritage: International Cultural Heritage Law Through the Lenses of the World Court Jurisprudence?' (Ch 9) in this volume; Karolina Wierczyńska and Andrzej Jakubowski, 'The *Al Mahdi* Case: From Punishing Perpetrators to Repairing Cultural Heritage Harm' (Ch 5) in this volume.

[93] *Application of the Convention on the Prevention and Punishment of the Crime of Genocide (Bosnia and Herzegovina v Serbia and Montenegro)* (Judgment) [2007] ICJ Reports 43, para 344. See also *Application of the Convention on the Prevention and Punishment of the Crime of Genocide (Croatia v Serbia)* (Judgment) [2015] ICJ Reports 3, paras 386–90.

[94] ibid, paras 335–44; *Krstić* (n 92) para 580.

Chamber declined to either confirm or reject that holding.[95] The qualifier is that the nature of the destruction must place it on par with the acts necessary to establish crimes against humanity more generally.[96] (As with genocide, the crimes against humanity in the ICTY Statute all refer to acts committed against persons and do not includes acts against their property.) As a result, acts of destruction of cultural property of a group can be considered in the international criminal regime in the context of establishing genocide and persecution of a group, much in line with the original conception of cultural genocide and vandalism. These interpretations, combined with international instruments on human rights and minority rights, provide an alternate avenue for recognizing the gist of cultural genocide, even in the absence of an express offense.[97]

But as compared to the ICTY Statute, the Rome Statute also reveals a slight shift of the pendulum away from recognizing cultural heritage crimes in international criminal law in one key respect: while the ICTY Statute recognized both the unnecessary seizure and destruction of cultural property as an express offense, the Rome Statute is much more restrictive because it only recognizes destruction of cultural sites. The ICTY Statute thus fully embraced cultural heritage-based violations of prohibitions on unnecessary destruction *and seizure* of cultural property, thereby reaching both immovable cultural sites *and movable cultural objects* in a single provision.[98] The relevant offense in the ICTY Statute is as follows:

> Seizure of, destruction or willful damage done to institutions dedicated to religion, charity and education, the arts and sciences, historic monuments and works of art and science.[99]

Adopted just five years later to govern international criminal prosecutions on a permanent basis, the Rome Statute recognizes only deliberate and unnecessary attacks on cultural sites (and incorporates express reference to the doctrine of military necessity):

[95] *Prosecutor v Blaškić* (Trial Judgment) ICTY-95-14-T (3 March 2000); *Prosecutor v Blaškić* (Appeals Judgment) ICTY-95-14-A (29 July 2004).

[96] *Prosecutor v Kordić & Čerkez* (Trial Judgment) ICTY-95-14/2-T (26 February 2001) para 20. For additional discussion of these cases, see Karolina Wierczyńska and Andrzej Jakubowski, 'The *Al Mahdi* Case: From Punishing Perpetrators to Repairing Cultural Heritage Harm' (Ch 5) in this volume.

[97] In the next chapter, Wierczyńska and Jakubowski argue that the ICC's recognition of cultural heritage destruction as a crime against humanity or genocide is probably 'a question of time'. The premise of this chapter—namely that any reluctance to recognize or expand cultural heritage offenses can harden where alternate avenues are perceived by the principal actors as available and potentially more suitable—means that I am not optimistic that such change will occur in the near future.

[98] ICTY Statute, art 3(d). For a discussion of ways in which the law of armed conflict has not always provided comparable protection to movable cultural objects and to cultural sites, and of shortcomings in the protection governing cultural objects generally, see Patty Gerstenblith, 'The Disposition of Movable Cultural Heritage' (Ch 1) in this volume.

[99] ICTY Statute, art 3(d).

> Intentionally directing attacks against buildings dedicated to religion, education, art, science or charitable purposes, historic monuments ... provided they are not military objectives.[100]

The difference is attributable to the sources in the law of armed conflict from which the provisions originate. While the drafters of the ICTY Statute elected to adopt the formulation from Article 56 in the 1899 and 1907 Hague Conventions, which appears in the section on occupation, the drafters of the Rome Statute ultimately retreated to the more limited Article 27, which applies during bombardment and siege.[101]

Two reasons support the ICTY's inclusion of a broader cultural heritage-based offense. First and foremost, the 1954 Hague Convention includes prohibitions on the destruction and seizure of movable and immovable cultural property, in all stages of conflict, and in both international and non-international armed conflict.[102] Former ICTY President Meron recognized that the former Yugoslavia had joined the 1954 Hague Convention and that the subject matter of the provision in the ICTY Statute and 1954 Hague Convention were roughly comparable, so the broader reach could be explained as based on a broader conventional obligation for the particular conflict for the particular ad hoc tribunal.[103] But even without relying on conventional law, a strong basis existed at the time of the adoption of the ICTY Statute for also recognizing negative rules of restraint against destruction *and* seizure of cultural property as customary obligations that applied across all stages of a conflict. This position had been recognized by the Nuremberg Tribunal (notwithstanding the absence of a specific provision in the Nuremberg Charter), as well as by many States, including military powers that were then still holdouts to the 1954 Hague Convention.[104] As a result, the ICTY Statute's broader formulation reflected the unremarkable proposition that unnecessary destruction and seizure

[100] Rome Statute, art 8(b)(ix). See also ibid, art 8(e)(iv) (applicable in non-international armed conflict). The ICTY in its jurisprudence nonetheless qualified protection by reference to the doctrine. See eg Theodor Meron, 'The Protection of Cultural Property in the Event of Armed Conflict within the Case-law of the International Criminal Tribunal for the Former Yugoslavia' (2005) 57 Museum Intl 41, 45 (stating that the Trial Chamber in *Blaškić* did not explain its rationale for holding that 'the institutions must not have been in the immediate vicinity of military objectives' but speculating that it was to ensure that the property was not being used for a military purpose).

[101] See 1899 and 1907 Hague Conventions, Regulations, arts 27, 56.

[102] 1954 Hague Conventions, arts 4, 19.

[103] Meron (n 100) 44–47.

[104] US Dept of Defense, Conduct of the Persian Gulf Conflict: An Interim Report to Congress (July 1991); US Dept of Defense, Department of Defense Report to Congress on the Conduct of the Persian Gulf War (1991) app O; Hersch Lauterpacht, *The Law of War on Land: Being Part III of the Manual of Military Law*, War Office Pub No 12333 (HMSO 1958) 170, para 613 (UK War Office Manual observing that enemy property belonging to cultural and religious institutions, 'for instance, crown jewels, pictures, collections of works of art and archives', cannot be appropriated). Cf Joseph R Baker, and Henry G Crocker, *The Laws of Land Warfare Concerning the Rights and Duties of Belligerents as Existing on August 1, 1914* (November 1918) (GPO 1919) (Department of State publication) 416, 420 (applying rule against appropriation as applicable to 'occupant').

of immovable and movable cultural property violate both conventional and customary rules in the law of armed conflict.

The Rome Statute, on the other hand, adopts a much more conservative view. It follows the original century-old articulation of the 1899 and 1907 Hague Conventions. It also follows the example of the Nuremberg Tribunal, in which seizure of cultural property was addressed under a general prohibition on 'plunder' rather than as a stand-alone offense.[105] In fact, the Rome Statute contains more general property-based offenses that can be applied to cultural property in certain circumstances, by comparison with the ICTY Statute and the Nuremberg Charter.[106] Finally, it arguably follows the approach of the 1977 Additional Protocols, if one parses the differences between the two protocols and determines that only Additional Protocol II reflects those rules that the negotiating Parties could agree constituted customary law, and thus applicable to non-international armed conflicts. Additional Protocol II similarly fails to include an express rule barring seizure of cultural property. Instead, it prohibits use of cultural property for the military effort but otherwise only prohibits a party to a non-international armed conflict from committing 'any acts of hostility directed against historic monuments, works of art or places of worship which constitute the cultural or spiritual heritage of peoples'.[107] The Commentary on whether 'acts of hostility' can embrace seizure is internally contradictory, or at least inconsistent. After comparing the 1954 Hague Convention's prohibition on destruction, vandalism, pillage, and appropriation, it states that the rule applies to acts of hostility that threaten the 'physical integrity' of the protected objects.[108]

Nonetheless, the Rome Statute and the ICC provide more expansive protection in its cultural heritage-based offense in a few key respects. As observed by Wierczyńska and Jakubowski, the Rome Statute provides for prosecution of attacks against cultural property, regardless of whether they result in damage or destruction, while the ICTY Statute is limited, on its face, to destruction, damage, or seizure of cultural property.[109] Even as to attacks on civilian objects, which can

[105] See Section II of this chapter; Nuremberg Charter, art 6(b).

[106] For international armed conflicts, general property-based offenses include art 8.2(a)(iv) (extensive destruction and appropriation of property, not justified by military necessity and carried out unlawfully and wantonly), art 8.2(b)(ii) (intentionally directing attacks against civilian objects), art 8.2(b)(iv) (intentionally launching attack knowing incidental damage to civilian objects will result), art 8.2(b)(v) (attacking or bombarding undefended towns or buildings), and 8.2(b)(xiii) (destroying or seizing enemy property, except by imperative military necessity); art 8.2(b)(xvi) (pillage). For non-international armed conflicts, the Rome Statute's general provisions that can apply to cultural property include art 8.2(e)(5) (pillage) (destroying an adversary's property, art 8.2(e)(xii) absent imperative military necessity).

[107] 1977 Additional Protocol II, art 16.

[108] Yves Sandoz, Christophe Swinarski, and Bruno Zimmerman (eds), *Commentary on the Additional Protocols of 8 June 1977 to the Geneva Conventions of 12 August 1949* (ICRC/Martinus Nijhoff 1987) 4845.

[109] ICTY Statute, art 3(d); Rome Statute, arts 8(b)(ix), 8(e)(iv); Wierczyńska and Jakubowski (Ch 5) in this volume. This is true as well for the 1977 Additional Protocols. Sandoz, Swinarski, and Zimmerman (n 108) 4845.

encompass cultural property, the ICTY held in *Kordić and Čerdez* that while the customary prohibition reflected in the 1977 Additional Protocols did not require a result requirement, insufficient state practice and *opinio juris* existed to establish definitively that *imposing criminal responsibility* in the absence of a result requirement had passed into customary law.[110]

More important, though, the ICC has demonstrated that it recognizes the importance of prosecuting violations of the law of armed conflict protecting cultural property, especially when committed against a broader backdrop of attacks designed to erase a group and their culture. It has underlined this importance in a critical way that no other international criminal tribunal has done: by prosecuting cultural heritage crimes without marrying them to other charges.[111]

Conclusion

Two important themes emerged during the historical development of cultural heritage-based crimes in international criminal law that have had lasting influence on contemporary cultural heritage-based offenses. First, drafters of an international criminal code vacillated from the very beginning as to whether such a code should include offenses that expressly referred to destruction or seizure of cultural property, including of artistic, historic, and scientific property and of historic monuments. Disinclinations sometimes could be attributed to principled views of the relative priority of cultural heritage-based offenses, and even property violations generally, as compared to offenses aimed at redressing attacks on persons and groups. Yet at each critical juncture, they also reflected attentive consideration to developments at other intersections of international law that were considered potentially more suitable, whether that was the perceived preference for violations to be resolved by the ICJ, through means of enforcement provided in new treaties on the law of armed conflict, or through other regimes, such as instruments governing international human rights and minority rights. In the end, the ultimate inclusion of cultural heritage crimes reflects a final determination that redressing violations through international criminal law, the law of armed conflict, and other avenues need not be mutually exclusive. Cultural heritage-based offenses have achieved a lasting place in international criminal law, despite the availability of other fora and other means of enforcement.

Second, though, neither the ICTY Statute nor the Rome Statute—the two international criminal codes that embrace cultural heritage crimes more than any other, to date—has incorporated the full panoply of cultural heritage-based crimes that

[110] *Prosecutor v Kordić and Čerdez* (Appeals Judgment) ICTY-95-14/2-A (17 December 2004) paras 55–68.

[111] See text accompanying nn 1–7.

have been contemplated previously for inclusion in an international criminal code. In fact, the ICC Statute represents a partial retreat even from the ICTY Statute, thus refuting the notion that the trend in contemporary international criminal law continues only toward greater recognition of cultural heritage-based offenses, at least as a statutory matter. Redressing violations of the law of armed conflict governing cultural property protection, and affirming the relationship between attacks on cultural property and attempts to oppress or eradicate groups, therefore relies on a broad array of international tools to enforce the protections: the ability to resort to other tribunals, the availability of other instruments, and the ability to prosecute or cite cultural heritage-based violations under other offenses. All of these avenues supplement the demonstrated commitment to prosecuting cultural heritage crimes in international criminal tribunals.

5

The *Al Mahdi* Case

From Punishing Perpetrators to Repairing Cultural Heritage Harm

*Karolina Wierczyńska and Andrzej Jakubowski**

Introduction

On 21 July 356 BC, a poor shoemaker, seeking notoriety and immortal fame, burned down the Temple of Artemis in Ephesus, one of the Seven Wonders of the Ancient World. For this outrageous act, Ephesian authorities sentenced him to death and also forbade others from mentioning his name, in order to dissuade those of similar intent. Yet the name Herostratus was well remembered. A few decades later, Greek historian Theopompus brought the event and name of the perpetrator back into the light. Thus, despite the stigma that was placed on Herostratus, his name survived and today symbolizes a wrongdoer praying for *nomen omen* herostratic fame.[1]

Crime as a mean of self-glorification and fame is not only part of ancient history. While the destruction of the Temple of Artemis, an important place of worship and an artistic masterpiece, had been aimed at shocking the ancient Greek civilization, the current widely broadcast and promoted online attacks against cultural heritage sites cherished by all humankind have, essentially, been intended to intimidate and humiliate local populations. Yet recent attacks also aim to show the helplessness of the international community before brutal strength. The impunity of crimes contributes to the black legend of perpetrators and encourages their followers. Cultural heritage as a target of crime constitutes a deliberate choice because heritage is a powerful, value-laden notion linking 'the past, the present and the future as it encompasses things inherited from the past that are considered to be of such value or significance today, that individuals and communities want to transmit

* The authors wish to acknowledge that some of the research for this article was carried out and co-funded by the European Union within the project *HEURIGHT—The Right to Cultural Heritage—Its Protection and Enforcement through Cooperation in the European Union*, ERA-NET, JPI Heritage Plus 'Cultural Heritage and Global Change'.

[1] See Albert Borowitz, *Terrorism for Self-Glorification. The Herostratos Syndrome* (Kent State U Press 2005) 4 ff.

Karolina Wierczyńska and Andrzej Jakubowski, The *Al Mahdi* Case In: *Intersections in International Cultural Heritage Law*. Edited by Anne-Marie Carstens and Elizabeth Varner. © Oxford University Press 2020. The several contributors
DOI: 10.1093/oso/9780198846291.003.0006

them to future generations'.[2] The key role of cultural heritage in building people's identities is crucial for asserting rights and legitimacy to control determined territories, people's beliefs, conscience, and ways of life. Therefore, cultural heritage has constantly been exposed to intentional destruction, suppression, and plunder that dramatically affects human communities.[3] Indeed, the history of mankind is profoundly marked by systematic cultural cleansing performed in the name of ethnic, national, religious, or cultural 'purity', driven by ideological foundations of power.

Since the Nuremberg Trial, international criminal law has gradually recognized that such intentional acts against protected cultural heritage may amount to war crimes and crimes against humanity, thus requiring adequate mechanisms of persecution and conviction of perpetrators. Yet the issue of remedies and reparations for cultural heritage destruction has long gone beyond the objectives of international criminal law. In this regard, the present chapter aims to explore the current shift from the mere struggle against the impunity of individual perpetrators of international crimes toward broader objectives of bringing justice to victims of international cultural heritage crimes. Particularly, it focuses on the role of the most recent practice of the International Criminal Court (ICC or Court) in the case of Mr Ahmad Al Mahdi Al Faqi (Al Mahdi), a member of Ansar Dine who headed an Islamic militant group—*Hesbah*—responsible for destroying cultural heritage sites in Timbuktu.[4] *Al Mahdi* was the first case brought before the ICC concerning the destruction of cultural property. Hence it has been perceived as a landmark case, paving the way for a more efficient enforcement of international justice with respect to cultural heritage crimes.[5] Moreover, it is also the first case by an international criminal tribunal that provided for reparations to victims of a cultural heritage crime.[6] This chapter begins with a general overview of international criminal law and jurisprudence in relation to cultural heritage crimes, with a particular focus on the case law of the International Criminal Tribunal for the former Yugoslavia (ICTY). This background outlines the limited provisions of the Rome Statute of the ICC[7] and offers some critical observations in relation to the evolving system of individual criminal responsibility for cultural heritage crimes. Second, it scrutinizes the approach taken by the ICC in convicting Al Mahdi for the crime of intentionally directing attacks against buildings dedicated to religion

[2] United Nations Human Rights Council, 'Report of the independent expert in the field of cultural rights Farida Shaheed' (21 March 2011) UN Doc A/HRC/17/38, para 5.

[3] Janet Blake, 'On Defining the Cultural Heritage' (2000) 49 ICLQ 61, 84.

[4] *Prosecutor v Al Mahdi* (Trial Judgment and Sentence) ICC-01/12-01/15-171 (27 September 2016).

[5] It is to be noted that another case concerning the crime of intentionally directing attacks against buildings dedicated to religion and historic monuments, allegedly committed in Timbuktu, is currently before the ICC. See *Prosecutor v Al Hassan* (Decision constituting Trial Chamber X and referring to it the case of *Prosecutor v. Al Hassan*) ICC-01/12-01/18 ICC-01/12-01/18 (21 November 2019).

[6] *Prosecutor v Al Mahdi* (Reparation Order) ICC-01/12-01/15-236 (17 August 2017) (*Al Mahdi*, Reparation Order).

[7] Statute of the International Criminal Court (adopted 17 July 1998, entered into force 1 July 2002) 2187 UNTS 90 (Rome Statute).

and/or historical monuments. Third, this chapter considers the issue of remedies and reparations for cultural harm suffered in light of the relevant provisions of the Rome State and doctrinal discussion on this matter. Next, it analyzes the approach taken by the ICC in *Al Mahdi* regarding methodology of determining reparations. Finally, it offers a set of conclusions as to possible ways in which international criminal law could evolve in response to intentional destruction of cultural heritage.

I. Criminalizing and Prosecuting Cultural Heritage Crimes under International Law

The safeguarding of cultural heritage has indeed become an important part of international law.[8] Cultural heritage has been conceptualized as a global common good, and its protection perceived as an essential element for the full realization of all human rights.[9] For these reasons, cultural heritage law is now considered 'an established branch of international law'.[10]

A. International Humanitarian Law

Undoubtedly, the most developed legal framework within this domain of international law relates to the protection of cultural heritage in armed conflict.[11] In fact, the general humanitarian regime established by the Convention for the Protection of Cultural Property in the Event of Armed Conflict (the 1954 Hague Convention)[12] has become nearly universal. The First Protocol to the 1954 Hague Convention,[13] regarding the restitution of cultural property unlawfully removed in connection with armed conflict, and the 1999 Second Protocol to the Convention,[14] establishing a new category of enhanced protection for cultural heritage that is

[8] For more on the question of criminal responsibility for crimes against cultural heritage property, see, for instance, Karolina Wierczyńska and Andrzej Jakubowski, 'Individual Responsibility for Deliberate Destruction of Cultural Heritage: Contextualizing the ICC Judgement in Al-Mahdi Case' (2017) 16 Chinese JIL 695.

[9] Compare Janet Blake, *International Cultural Heritage Law* (OUP 2015) 1–22.

[10] See Alessandro Chechi, 'Evaluating the Establishment of an International Cultural Heritage Court' (2013) 18 Art, Antiquity & Law 31, 32.

[11] See Anne-Marie Carstens and Elizabeth Varner, 'Intersections in Public International Law for Protecting Cultural Heritage: Past, Present, and Future' in this volume; also see Marina Lostal, *International Cultural Heritage Law in Armed Conflict: Case-studies of Syria, Libya, Mali, the Invasion of Iraq, and the Buddhas of Bamiyan* (CUP 2017) 48 ff.

[12] Convention for the Protection of Cultural Property in the Event of Armed Conflict (adopted 14 May 1954, entered into force 7 August 1956) 249 UNTS 240.

[13] Protocol to the Convention of 1954 for the Protection of Cultural Property in the Event of Armed Conflict (adopted 14 May 1954, entered into force 7 August 1956) 249 UNTS 358.

[14] Second Protocol to the Convention for the Protection of Cultural Property in the Event of Armed Conflict (adopted 26 March 1999, entered into force 9 March 2004) 2253 UNTS 172.

particularly important for humankind, have also received a large number of ratifications. Accordingly, the legal regime set up by the 1954 Hague Convention and its Protocols, supported and supplemented by other humanitarian law instruments, in particular the 1977 Additional Protocols to the 1949 Geneva Conventions,[15] today form a consistent universal legal framework for the protection of cultural heritage in armed conflict.[16] The binding nature of these obligations is also seen as stemming from customary international law.[17]

B. International Criminal Law and Jurisprudence

Notwithstanding the wide recognition of the international obligations to protect cultural heritage in armed conflicts, such properties are still subject to attacks and plunder. Alongside the actual fulfillment of the obligation to protect cultural heritage during armed conflicts, particularly in those involving terrorist groups,[18] the other major consideration refers to the consequences of the violation of such obligations. The volume of crimes against cultural heritage committed in current armed conflicts raises the question of how to ensure efficient measures to counteract such offenses and eliminate the impunity of perpetrators. Although penal provisions concerning the attacks against cultural heritage—enshrined in the 1954 Hague Convention, in its Second Protocol, and in the 1977 Additional Protocols to the 1949 Geneva Conventions—have been implemented in the internal law of many States of the world, domestic jurisdiction often fails to prosecute and punish individual perpetrators, especially when criminalized acts have been committed in internal (non-international) conflicts. Hence many expectations are usually associated with the role of international criminal tribunals. Indeed, before the *Al Mahdi* case, most of the international jurisprudence concerning war cultural heritage crimes came from the case law of ad hoc international tribunals or mixed criminal courts. Since the time of the Nuremberg Trial, such acts

[15] Protocol Additional to the Geneva Conventions of 12 August 1949, and Relating to the Protection of Victims of International Armed Conflicts (adopted 8 June 1977, entered into force 7 December 1987) 1125 UNTS 3, art 85(4)(d) (1977 Additional Protocol I); Protocol Additional to the Geneva Conventions of 12 August 1949, and Relating to the Protection of Victims of Non-International Armed Conflicts (adopted 8 June 1977, entered into force 7 December 1978) 1125 UNTS 609, art 16 (1977 Additional Protocol II).

[16] See Micaela Frulli, 'The Criminalization of Offences against Cultural Heritage in Times of Armed Conflict: The Quest for Consistency' (2011) 22 EJIL 203, 216–17.

[17] See, inter alia, Jean-Marie Henckaerts and Louise Doswald-Beck, *Customary International Humanitarian Law* (CUP 2005) vol I, 127–38, 523–25 and vol II, 723–813, 3452 *passim*; UNSG, 'Secretary-General's Bulletin: Observance by United Nations Forces of International Humanitarian Law' (6 August 1999) UN Doc ST/SGB/1999/13 para 6(6).

[18] See Elizabeth Varner, 'Comparing Interpretations of States' and Non-State Actors' Obligations Toward Cultural Heritage in Armed Conflict and Occupation: Military Manuals and the Law of War' (Ch 2) in this volume; Kristin Hausler, 'The UN Security Council, the Human Rights Council, and the Protection of Cultural Heritage: A Matter of Peace and Security, Human Rights, or Both?' (Ch 8) in this volume.

committed by individuals during armed conflicts may be considered as international crimes and give rise to individual criminal responsibility.[19] Although the practice of the International Military Tribunal in Nuremberg had been pivotal for the development of international criminal law in this regard, the subsequent practice occurred only a few decades later on the occasion of the war in the former Yugoslavia.[20]

1. The legacy of the ICTY

Under the Statute of the ICTY,[21] 'seizure of, destruction or wilful damage done to institutions dedicated to religion, charity and education, the arts and sciences, historic monuments and works of art and science' were criminalized as war crimes.[22] The practice of this international ad hoc tribunal offers the most comprehensive case law to date in the area of individual criminal responsibility for international cultural heritage crimes, paving the way for other international adjudicating bodies which have competence in the matter of cultural heritage crimes.[23]

With the *Kordić and Čerkez* case, the ICTY confirmed that the intentional destruction of religious objects may amount to 'an attack on the identity of people and as such, it manifests a nearly pure expression of the notion of "crimes against humanity", for all of humanity is indeed injured by the destruction of a unique religious culture and its concomitant cultural objects'.[24] Moreover, the ICTY addressed the issue of intent in a few cases involving the destruction of protected cultural heritage. In particular, in *Blaškić* it emphasized that the only reasons to explain the acts of attacking religious properties 'were reasons of discrimination'.[25] Thus it found that ethnic and religious discrimination could give rise to an analysis through the prism of 'persecution which justifies a more severe penalty'.[26] More importantly, in *Krstić* the ICTY, while analyzing the provisions of the ICTY Statute concerning the crime of genocide and specifically the special intent of the perpetrator, noticed that the deliberate destruction of a group does not have to be caused

[19] *US and others v Goering and others* (Judgment) in *Trial of the Major War Criminals before the International Military Tribunal (Nuremberg 14 November 1945–1 October 1946)* (42 vols, International Military Tribunal 1947–49) vol I, 113–14.

[20] In fact, contrary to the Nuremberg Trial, the systematic destruction, plunder, and seizure of cultural property were not mentioned separately in the trial of Japanese war criminals before the International Military Tribunal for the Far East. See <http://werle.rewi.hu-berlin.de/tokyo.anklageschrift.pdf> accessed 11 July 2019.

[21] Statute of the International Criminal Tribunal for the Former Yugoslavia (adopted 25 May 1993, UNSC Res 827, as amended) (ICTY Statute).

[22] ICTY Statute, art 3(d).

[23] Federico Lenzerini, 'The Role of International and Mixed Criminal Courts in the Enforcement of International Norms Concerning the Protection of Cultural Heritage' in Francesco Francioni and James Gordley (eds), *Enforcing International Cultural Heritage Law* (OUP 2013) 40, 58 ff.

[24] *Prosecutor v Kordić & Čerkez* (Trial Judgment) ICTY-95-14/2-T (26 February 2001) para 207. For a general discussion of the role of the ICTY in adjudicating the crimes against cultural heritage see, for instance, Lenzerini (n 23) 44 ff.

[25] *Prosecutor v Blaškić* (Trial Judgment) ICTY-95-14-T (3 March 2000) para 421.

[26] ibid, para 785.

only by physical destruction, but also 'through purposeful eradication of its culture and identity resulting in the eventual extinction of the group as an entity distinct from the remainder of the community'.[27] Thus, the attacks directed at cultural or religious institutions and properties simultaneous to biological and physical destruction can be used to establish the intent of the perpetrator (*mens rea*), although the cultural destruction of a group cannot be perceived as a constituent element of genocide taking into account its definition.[28] In other words, the intentional destruction of mosques and houses belonging to members of a certain group can be the evidence of intent to destroy such group.

In the *Jokić*[29] and *Strugar*[30] cases concerning military attacks on the Old City of Dubrovnik—inscribed on the UNESCO World Heritage List in 1979—the ICTY held that those were 'not only against the history and heritage of the region, but also against the cultural heritage of humankind'.[31] It found that since an 'attack on civilian objects is a very serious violation of humanitarian law, it is a crime of even greater seriousness to direct an attack on an especially protected site'.[32] This holding could lead to the conclusion that the attack against a World Heritage site needs therefore to be viewed as a graver crime than an attack on other civilian objects. The tribunal also found that a critical factor in imposing criminal liability on the military leaders who ordered bombardments of the protected cultural heritage site arose from the fact that its historical substance enjoyed international protection.[33]

As already mentioned, the experience of the ICTY has given grounds for other international or mixed adjudicating bodies having competence in the matter of cultural heritage crimes.[34] Indeed, the Rome Statute defines, as war crimes, acts committed in the event of international or non-international conflict and which consist in 'intentionally directing attacks against buildings dedicated to religion, education, art, science or charitable purposes, historic monuments, hospitals, and places where the sick and wounded are collected, provided they are not military objectives'.[35] Such war crimes do not have to amount to the destruction of the attacked properties, but the perpetrators must have been acting with intent and

[27] *Prosecutor v Krstić* (Trial Judgment) ICTY-98-33-T (2 August 2001) para 574.

[28] ibid, para 580, *Prosecutor v Krstić* (Appeals Judgment) ICTY-98-33-A (19 April 2004) para 25.

[29] *Prosecutor v Jokić* (Sentencing Judgment) ICTY-01-42/1-S (18 March 2004).

[30] *Prosecutor v Strugar* (Trial Judgment) ICTY-01-42-T (31 January 2005).

[31] *Jokić* (n 29) para 51.

[32] ibid, para 53.

[33] *Strugar* (n 30) paras 327–29 and 461.

[34] For general discussion see Lenzerini (n 23) 58 ff. It is also important to mention that in two genocide cases the International Court of Justice (ICJ) referred to the ICTY's judgment in *Krstić* as to the cultural dimension of genocide. Accordingly, it held that attacks on cultural and religious property in armed conflict constitute a violation of international law. Furthermore, such acts may be considered as evidence of a genocidal intent aimed at the extinction of a group. See *Application of the Convention on the Prevention and Punishment of the Crime of Genocide (Bosnia and Herzegovina v Serbia and Montenegro)* (Judgment) [2007] ICJ Reports 43, para 344; *Application of the Convention on the Prevention and Punishment of the Crime of Genocide (Croatia v Serbia)* (Judgment) [2015] ICJ Reports 3, para 390.

[35] Rome Statute, arts 8(2)(b)(ix) and 8(2)(e)(iv).

knowledge[36] of attacking those non-military targets, and finally they must have been aware that their acts are associated with armed conflict.[37] Yet, contrary to the Statute of the ICTY, the provisions of the Rome Statute do not require the destruction or willful damage done to protected properties.[38] Hence the provisions of the ICC's Statute go further than those of the ICTY: even lesser attacks or acts of vandalism can be classed a war crime; intentionally directed attacks, even if not successful, fulfill the elements of a war crime as defined in the Rome Statute.

2. Al Mahdi—contours and gravity of international cultural heritage crimes

The *Al Mahdi* case before the ICC is important for a number of particular reasons which will be developed below. What is the most important factor here is the fact that it was not only a first case based solely on one article of the Rome Statute adjudging crimes against cultural heritage and a case based on admission of guilt, but additionally this case defined the contours of future cases concerning the protection of cultural heritage under international law, and clarified the question of the gravity of the crimes against cultural objects, consequently being a voice in discussion on admissibility of the case before the ICC.

a. The ICC's approach

In September 2015, following the conclusion of the official investigation into the situation in Mali by Fatou Bensouda, ICC Chief Prosecutor, the ICC issued the arrest warrant against Al Mahdi, the head of *Hesbah*.[39] He was deemed responsible for individually and jointly with others facilitating or otherwise contributing to the commission of war crimes of intentionally directing attacks on monuments under the international protection of the United Nations Educational, Scientific and Cultural Organization (UNESCO).[40] Yet it needs to be underlined that the ICC acts on the basis of the principle of complementarity, which generally means that the priority in exercising prosecution was left to States Parties to the Rome Statute, while the ICC acts as a court of 'last resort' in situations where a State is not acting at all or its actions are not genuine, and where that State is in fact unable or unwilling to prosecute the case. The mechanism of admissibility of a case before the ICC requires not only an assessment of complementarity (specifically whether a State is properly, genuinely exercising its jurisdiction in a concrete case), but also an assessment of the gravity of a case, that is, whether a given case is sufficiently grave to justify further action by the ICC.[41] If the assessment is that a case is indeed

36 As prescribed in Rome Statute, art 30.

37 See 'Elements of Crimes' (ICC, 2011) <https://www.icc-cpi.int/NR/rdonlyres/336923D8-A6AD-40EC-AD7B-45BF9DE73D56/0/ElementsOfCrimesEng.pdf> accessed 11 July 2019.

38 ICTY Statute, art 3(d).

39 *Prosecutor v Al Mahdi (Arrest Warrant)* ICC-01/12-01/15-1-Red (28 September 2015).

40 ibid, para 6.

41 Rome Statute, art 17.

sufficiently grave, the key factor becomes whether the State is genuinely acting.[42] Accordingly, before the case of Al Mahdi could be submitted to the ICC, the Prosecutor had to decide whether Mali was acting in the case (or if acting, whether its actions were genuine) and whether the case was of sufficient gravity to warrant further proceedings before the Court.

Since the Malian Government referred the situation in Mali to the ICC, with respect to alleged crimes committed on its territory, the Court, recognizing the crimes' gravity, found itself competent to prosecute and adjudicate the case.[43] On 26 September of the same year, Al Mahdi was surrendered to the ICC by the authorities of Niger. In March 2016, Pre-Trial Chamber I of the ICC confirmed against Ahmad Al Faqi Al Mahdi the war crime charge related to the attacks on historical and religious monuments in Timbuktu.[44] The destroyed institutions, as underlined in the decision of the Chamber, did not constitute military objectives, were protected as a significant part of the cultural heritage of Timbuktu, were classified as world heritage and thus under the protection of UNESCO, and were also protected sites under the regime of the World Heritage Convention.[45] Moreover, the acts were directed against a local community, and concerned the general interest of the international community as a whole.[46] His trial began on 22 August 2016, and he pleaded guilty to a charge of intentional attacks against historic monuments of the city. On 27 September 2016, he was sentenced to imprisonment.

The evidence collected by the Prosecutor allowed for the confirmation of charges against Al Mahdi. The defendant himself also admitted guilt as to the war crime, which resulted in the destruction of historical and religious monuments in Timbuktu, between around 30 June 2012 and 11 July 2012.[47] Specifically, in the agreement Al Mahdi acknowledged his guilt and accepted his criminal responsibility for his criminal actions and confirmed that he would not appeal the conviction and the sentence imposed.[48] The Prosecutor also confirmed that she would not appeal the sentence and recommended a sentence range between 9 and 11 years of imprisonment.[49] Besides that, by making the admission, Al Mahdi gave up some

[42] See, for instance, Markus Benzing, 'The Complementarity Regime of the International Criminal Court: International Criminal Justice between State Sovereignty and the Fight against Impunity' (2003) 7 Max Planck YB UN L 591.

[43] ICC, *Arrest Warrant* (n 39) paras 11–12.

[44] *Prosecutor v Al Mahdi* (Decision on the confirmation of charges against Ahmad Al Faqi Al Mahdi (24 March 2016) ICC-01/12-01/15). It is worth noting that the purpose of a confirmation hearing is not to conclusively determine issues of probative value of evidence, including with respect to credibility of witnesses, but rather the Chamber competence is limited to what it considers necessary and sufficient for its determination on the charges.

[45] Convention Concerning the Protection of the World Cultural and Natural Heritage (adopted 16 November 1972, entered into force 17 December 1975) 1037 UNTS 151.

[46] ICC, Decision of the confirmation of charges (n 44) 22–27.

[47] ibid, para 36. See the information on the website of the ICC: <https://www.icc-cpi.int/Pages/item.aspx?name=pr1236> accessed 10 July 2019.

[48] *Prosecutor v Al Mahdi* (Agreement Regarding Admission of Guilt) ICC-01/12-01/15-78-Anx1-Red2 (19 August 2016) para 13.

[49] ibid, para 19.

important procedural opportunities such as the right to plead not guilty, remain silent, or the right to raise defenses excluding his criminal responsibility.[50] He could, however, appeal the sentence if it exceeded the one proposed by the Prosecutor.[51] The agreement connected with the admission of guilt was accompanied by many benefits as mentioned above, but also meant a faster procedure, sparing time and resources, and a more acceptable procedure to victims who do not wish to testify.[52]

The Court concluded that facts demonstrated that Al Mahdi as head of moral police *Hesbah* was put in charge during the phase of destruction of mausoleums and mosques mentioned above (violating Article 8(2)(e)(iv) of the Rome Statute). These buildings are classed not only as historic or religious institutions, but a major part of them forms UNESCO World Heritage Sites. Thus they are buildings of unique meaning and special importance for international cultural heritage.[53] The ICC also assessed that the destruction took place during the non-international armed conflict.[54]

Al Mahdi was found responsible for the executive phase of attack, determining the sequence of destruction, supporting with necessary logistical arrangements, and justifying those attacks and destructions it caused through media interviews. The Chamber found that the mode of liability, as formulated in the provisions of the Rome Statute on criminal responsibility,[55] best reflects the full scope of Al Mahdi's criminal responsibility as co-perpetrator for attacking the protected objects in Timbuktu.[56] The Court decided to sentence the defendant to nine years of imprisonment, taking into account Al Mahdi's intent to commit the crime, the degree of participation, means deployed to commit the crime, the fact that there were no aggravating circumstances, and five mitigating circumstances (Al Mahdi's admission of guilt, his remorse and cooperation with the Prosecutor, his initial reluctance to commit the crime, together with the steps he took to limit the damage caused, and his good behavior).[57]

The *Al Mahdi* judgment is for many reasons a special and unique decision, as already mentioned. First, the case was grounded on only one article—specifically the violation of the provision of the Rome Statute regarding the war crime of attacking protected objects,[58] so it refers to damage not related to the physical harm of an

[50] ibid, para 21.

[51] ibid, para 22.

[52] See elaboration of the ICC on the issue: *Prosecutor v Al Faqi Al Mahdi* (Trial Judgment and Sentence) ICC-01/12-01/15-171 (27 September 2016) para 28.

[53] ibid, paras 45–46.

[54] ibid, para 49.

[55] Rome Statute, art 25(3)(a), which reads: 'In accordance with this Statute, a person shall be criminally responsible and liable for punishment for a crime within the jurisdiction of the Court if that person commits such a crime, whether as an individual, jointly with another or through another person, regardless of whether that other person is criminally responsible'.

[56] See considerations of the Court, *Al Mahdi* (Trial Judgment and Sentence) (n 4) paras 57–63.

[57] ibid, para 109.

[58] Rome Statute, art 8(2)(e)(iv).

individual. Clearly, the Court defined the contours of the protection of cultural heritage, which consequently must from now on be treated as one of the objectives of the criminal justice system. The Court's findings will affect the way the international community responds to attacks on protected objects, and the judgment demonstrates that international criminal justice (and so the international community) could prevent and punish crimes aimed at destroying cultural heritage.

Second, it was the first case before the ICC applying the admission of guilt, which resulted in a fast and effective trial: Al Mahdi accepted his responsibility and demonstrated remorse for his actions. Without doubt, his guilty plea saved valuable time and resources. It also avoided secondary stigmatization of victims. It is true that the charges included only war crimes as destruction of protected objects—but the Timbuktu people were deeply devoted to the destroyed buildings; for them the destruction was a real tragedy, and they are the true victims of those crimes. The trial, if conducted without the admission of guilt agreement, would have lasted longer and could have stigmatized again all those people who would have been forced to testify before the Court and relive the moments of destruction of such valuable institutions.

Third, it is worth noting that in determining the sentence, the ICC had to also assess the gravity of the crime. In doing so, the Court referred to the findings made in the *Katanga* case,[59] where the Chamber noted the difference of gravity between crimes committed against persons and crimes committed against property.[60] In *Al Mahdi*, the Chamber referred to this finding by confirming that crimes against objects 'even if inherently grave …, are generally of lesser gravity than crimes against persons.'[61] The Court noticed that those crimes affected not only the community of Mali ('the fact that the targeted buildings were not only religious buildings but had also a symbolic and emotional value for the inhabitants of Timbuktu is relevant in assessing the gravity of the crime committed'[62]) but the whole international community, adding that the 'entire international community, in the belief that heritage is part of cultural life, is suffering as a result of the destruction of the protected sites'.[63] The Court noted that because of the special value of the destroyed objects, the crimes aimed at the destruction of such objects are the crimes of significant gravity.[64]

Countering all the critics for whom 'the judgment did not go far enough'[65] it must be noted that the Court assigned special value to the cultural heritage

[59] *Prosecutor v Katanga* (Decision on Sentence Pursuant to Article 76 of the Statute) ICC-01/04-01/07 (23 May 2014).

[60] ibid, para 43.

[61] *Al Mahdi*, Judgment and sentence (n 4) para 72.

[62] ibid, para 79.

[63] ibid, para 80.

[64] ibid, para 82.

[65] For instance, see Lucas Lixinski and Sarah Williams, 'The ICC's Al-Mahdi Ruling Protects Cultural Heritage, but Didn't Go Far Enough', *The Conversation* (19 October 2016) <https://theconversation.

property. According to this judgment, destruction of cultural heritage is a crime of significant gravity besides the fact that it is a crime against property, and its special value is connected with the special meaning of destroyed buildings for the international community as a whole. Such an evaluation of the gravity of a crime will also have an impact on the future admissibility assessments made by the Court, where the crimes against cultural property would be qualified as sufficiently grave to 'justify further action by the Court'.[66]

b. International cultural heritage crimes—beyond the realm of armed conflict?

The *Al Mahdi* case raises another important question as to uneven protection of cultural heritage under international law. As already highlighted, over the last few decades UNESCO has elaborated the unique instruments in order to protect cultural heritage in times of armed conflict.[67] This protection has been strengthened by the practice of the ICC in *Al Mahdi*. In fact, if the destruction has taken place in armed conflict, the ICC's response is connected with its jurisdiction over war crimes against cultural property committed during international and non-international armed conflicts. It refers to '[i]ntentionally directing attacks against buildings dedicated to religion, education, art, science or charitable purposes, historic monuments, hospitals, and places where the sick and wounded are collected, provided they are not military objectives'[68] and to '[d]estroying or seizing the property of an adversary unless such destruction or seizure be imperatively demanded by the necessities of the war'[69] and, more generally, to '[p]illaging a town or place, even when taken by assault'.[70]

Accordingly, from literal reading of the provisions of the Rome Statute, it seems that the responsibility for the deliberate destruction of cultural heritage can only be enforced under the rubric of the war crime, as cultural heritage is directly protected only under Article 8 of the Rome Statute. However, the practice of other international criminal tribunals shows that such interpretations limiting the crime of destruction only to armed conflicts are unfounded.[71] In the last few decades, all the main

com/the-iccs-al-mahdi-ruling-protects-cultural-heritage-but-didnt-go-far-enough-67071> accessed 11 July 2019.

66 See Rome Statute, art 17.

67 Also see Guido Carducci, 'The Role of UNESCO in the Elaboration and Implementation of International Art, Cultural Property, and Heritage Law' (Ch 7) in this volume.

68 Rome Statute, arts 8(2)(b)(ix) and 8(2)(e)(iv).

69 See Rome Statute, arts 8(2)(b)(xiii) and 8(2)(e)(xii), respectively.

70 ibid, arts 8 (2)(b)(xvi) and 8(2)(e)(v).

71 So far the decision whether the destruction of cultural heritage could be also treated as a crime against humanity (a crime not necessarily connected with war or international conflict) was not confirmed by the ICC. But, for example, the ICTY decided that acts aimed at intentional destruction or wilful damage of buildings, institutions dedicated to religion or education may amount to acts of persecution and as such a crime against humanity. See ICTY, *Prosecutor v Kordić & Čerkez*, Judgment (n 24) paras 206–07. See also UNESCO, *Protection of Cultural Property Military Manual* (2016) 5 ff; Elizabeth Varner, 'Comparing Interpretations of States' and Non-State Actors' Obligations Toward Cultural Heritage in Armed Conflict and Occupation: Military Manuals and the Law of War' (Ch 2) in this volume;

principles of humanitarian law have also been extended to internal conflicts. The ICTY confirmed the customary character of humanitarian norms and principles, adding that '[p]rinciples and rules of humanitarian law reflect "elementary considerations of humanity" widely recognized as the mandatory minimum for conduct in armed conflicts of any kind'.[72] It would probably be *reductio ad absurdum* if such a protection of cultural heritage would not be mandatory also in times of peace.[73]

Therefore, a broader perspective is needed while addressing the issue of how to respond when the crime against cultural heritage has in fact been committed, but no statutory qualification of war crime could be applied. According to the provisions of the Rome Statute, the destruction of cultural property with discriminatory intent can be also treated as the evidence of intent to destroy the religious, national, racial, or ethnic group under the provisions of the Rome Statute governing genocide, and subsequently a crime could be qualified as genocide.[74] Classing the destruction of cultural heritage as a 'crime against humanity' as provided in Article 7 of the Rome Statute might be a more complex issue, as it seems that among the crimes such as murder, extermination, or enslavement mentioned in Article 7,[75] only the crime of persecution[76] or 'other inhumane acts'[77] could be useful to assess the destruction of cultural heritage,[78] if committed as part of a widespread or systematic attack directed against any civilian population with knowledge of the attack as enshrined under the chapeau of Article 7. Additionally, persecution is not an autonomous crime, and it must be committed in connection with any act referred in Article 7 or any crime within the jurisdiction of the Court.[79] This nexus requirement weakens the gravity of such crime, although beside some sporadic acts of degradations or humiliation there are many examples of acts of persecution that amount to the gravest crimes within the jurisdiction of the ICC. Also,

Anne-Marie Carstens, 'The Swinging Pendulum of Cultural Heritage Crimes in International Criminal Law' (Ch 4) in this volume.

[72] See *Prosecutor v Tadić* (Decision on the Defence Motion for Interlocutory Appeal on Jurisdiction) ICTY-94-0 (2 October 1995) paras 129, 134.

[73] See, for instance, Francesco Francioni and Federico Lenzerini, 'The Destruction of the Buddhas of Bamiyan and International Law' (2003) 14 EJIL 619.

[74] Rome Statute, art 6. See the Trial Judgment of ICTY: *Prosecutor v Krstić* (n 27) para 574.

[75] Rome Statute, art 7.

[76] According to Article 7(1)(h) of the Rome Statute, the crime of persecution refers to '[p]ersecution against any identifiable group or collectivity on political, racial, national, ethnic, cultural, religious, gender as defined in paragraph 3, or other grounds that are universally recognized as impermissible under international law, in connection with any act referred to in this paragraph or any crime within the jurisdiction of the Court'.

[77] Article 7(1)(k) of the Rome Statute states: '[o]ther inhumane acts of a similar character intentionally causing great suffering, or serious injury to body or to mental or physical health'.

[78] In that context we could definitely refer to the experience of the ICTY, specifically: *Prosecutor v Kordić and Čerkez* (Appeals Judgment) ICTY-95-14/2-A (17 December 2004) para 105, where the Chamber stated: 'the Appeals Chamber finds that unlawful attack launched deliberately against civilians or civilian objects may constitute a crime of persecutions without the requirement of a particular result caused by the attack(s)'.

[79] Rome Statute, art 7(h).

the qualification 'other inhumane acts' would be useful to absorb the broad range of criminal behavior, including the destruction of cultural heritage in the time of peace, especially as the ICC has already considered whether the destruction of property could cause 'serious injury to mental health'[80] as prescribed in the Rome Statute. [81] The Chamber decided that evidence failed to establish that, but the situation was different as it did not refer to the destruction of objects with special legal value as cultural heritage, but to ordinary property.

Arguably, it is probably a question of time whether the ICC will regard the destruction of cultural property not only as a war crime, but also as a crime against humanity or as a necessary element to establish genocidal intent to cover the crimes committed with no nexus with an armed conflict under the jurisdiction of the ICC.

II. Cultural Heritage Crimes and the Issue of Reparations

As already mentioned, the *Al Mahdi* case is also unique as it is followed by the reparation order concerning the destruction of protected objects, which actually confirms that cultural heritage is an internationally important issue regardless of its location, origin, or material value. Indeed, alongside effective mechanisms to prosecute and punish perpetrators, the issue of adequate modalities of redressing cultural heritage harm has gradually been raised within the body of international criminal law. In fact, one may legitimately ask whether the purposes of international criminal justice would be met if victims of international crimes had no avenues to redress the harm they suffered. Originally, the issue of reparations had been the primary concern of human rights adjudicating bodies, whereas it was rarely addressed in international criminal law and jurisprudence. With the signing of the Rome Statute, the debate on reparations in international criminal law has accelerated. Accordingly, under Article 75(1), the Court 'shall establish principles relating to reparations to, or in respect of, victims, including restitution, compensation and rehabilitation'.[82] Reparations may be ordered 'directly against a convicted person' or awarded through the Trust Fund,[83] specially created for this purpose.[84] Accordingly, such principles and procedures applied to reparations were established by the ICC in the case of Thomas Lubanga Dyilo (further as *Lubanga*).[85] To date, there have been three reparations orders, including that issued in *Al Mahdi*.

[80] *Prosecutor v Muthaura* (Decision on the Confirmation of Charges Pursuant to Article 61(7)(a) and (b) of the Rome Statute) ICC-01/09-02/11-382-Red (29 January 2012) para 279.

[81] Rome Statute, art 7(1)(k).

[82] Rome Statute, art 75(1).

[83] ibid, art 75(2)

[84] ibid, art 79.

[85] *Prosecutor v Lubanga* (Decision establishing the principles and procedures to be applied to reparations) ICC-01/04-01/06-2904 (7 August 2012); *Prosecutor v Lubanga* (Judgment on the appeals against the 'Decision establishing the principles and procedures to be applied to reparations' of 7 August 2012

A. Reparations and International Criminal Law

Although the Rome Statute was the first international criminal law instrument that provided for the principles concerning reparations to, or in respect of, victims, including restitution, compensation, and rehabilitation, it must be noted that it was not the sole initiative in international criminal law that actually referred to the question of reparations.[86] Rather, it constituted the apogee of previous works and discussions undertaken on various international law fora. Already before the Second World War, the International Association of Penal Law (*l'Association Internationale de Droit Penal, or* AIDP) discussed the necessity of establishing an international criminal court. Within this debate, reparations for victims played a key role.[87] Subsequently, the topic of reparations returned in reference to civil responsibility of States for international crimes in the context of the discussion on a new criminal chamber to be established within the structure of the ICJ.[88] The issue was also debated at the time of drafting the future Genocide Convention.[89] Accordingly, the draft presented by the United Nations (UN) Secretariat[90] provided for reparations to victims of genocide. Yet the obligation to redress the crime of genocide was imposed on States, and not on individual perpetrators:

> When genocide is committed in a country by the government in power or by sections of the population, and if the government fails to resist it successfully, the State shall grant to the survivors of the human group that is a victim of genocide redress of a nature and in an amount to be determined by the United Nations.[91]

Moreover, such redress was of a civil rather than penal character and it was addressed not only to direct but also indirect victims of the crime since compensation was intended to support family and persons maintained by the victims.[92]

Certain initiatives as to reparations for victims of international crimes were undertaken under the auspices of the UN General Assembly and the UN

with amended order for reparations (Annex A) and public annexes 1 and 2) ICC-01/04-01/06-3129 (3 March 2015).

86 For a general discussion see, inter alia, Christine Evans, *The Right to Reparation in International Law for Victims of Armed Conflict* (CUP 2012); Conor McCarthy, *Reparations and Victim Support in the International Criminal Court* (CUP 2012).

87 'Memorandum présenté par le Secrétariat' (24 November 1950) UN Doc A/CN.4/39 (1950) 2 YILC 283, para 6.

88 ibid 362, para 167.

89 Adopted as the Convention on Prevention and Punishment of the Crime of Genocide (adopted 9 December 1948, entered into force 12 January 1951) 78 UNTS 277.

90 First Draft of the Genocide Convention, prepared by the UN Secretariat (May 1947) UN Doc E/447 <http://www.preventgenocide.org/law/convention/drafts> accessed 12 July 2019.

91 ibid, Article XIII.

92 Hirad Abdahi and Philippa Webb, *The Genocide Convention: The Travaux Préparatoires* (Martinus Nijhoff 2008) vol I, 250.

Commission on Human Rights. These directly referred to offenders' obligations to make restitution to victims, their families and dependents, including 'return of property or payment for the harm or loss suffered, reimbursement of expenses incurred as a result of the victimization, the provision of services and the restoration of rights';[93] and States' obligations to establish and implement procedures for reparations.[94] These documents, despite their non-binding character, should be treated as a point of reference for States, which should periodically review their existing legislation and practices to ensure their responsiveness to the principles formulated in UN legal instruments. In this regard, it needs to be remembered that international obligations of States in the context of their responsibility for reparations was already a widely recognized principle in the 1940s.[95] The debate on modalities of redress to victims of international crimes was also continued in the 1990s during the work of the International Law Commission (ILC) on the international responsibility of States, not individual perpetrators.[96]

The topic of individual liability as a ground for compensatory claims by the victim of an international crime reappeared in the context of the discussion concerning the possible establishment of international criminal jurisdiction as the 'objective and uniform implementation of the Code of Crimes against the Peace and Security of Mankind'.[97] Accordingly, the nature of proceedings relating to compensation to victims was recalled among other questions such as the law to be applied by the envisaged international criminal court and its jurisdiction *ratione materiae*.[98] However, the Statutes of the ICTY and of the International Criminal Tribunal for Rwanda (ICTR)[99] did not provide any significant progress in the context of the recognition of victims, who were solely passive participants in the proceedings before these ad hoc tribunals.[100] The issue of reparations to the victims was not addressed in the Statutes, in which the references to the victims of the crimes were rather marginal.[101] Moreover, the jurisprudence of the ICTY and ICTR is very limited as to the situation of victims. Some judgments of these Tribunals only stated that one

[93] Declaration of Basic Principles of Justice for Victims of Crime and Abuse of Power, UN Doc A/RES/40/34 (29 November 1985); see principle 8.

[94] Basic principles and guidelines on the right to reparation for victims of [gross] violations of human rights and international humanitarian law, UN Doc E/CN.4/1998/34 (22 December 1997) para 5 et seq.

[95] As visible in the works of the ILC (n 87).

[96] Report of the ILC on the work of its forty-second session (1 May–20 July 1990) UN Doc A/45/10.

[97] Report of the ILC on the work of its forty-fourth session (4 May–24 July 1992) UN Doc A/47/10. Official Records of the General Assembly, Forty-seventh session, Supplement No 10, Extract from the Yearbook of the International Law Commission:1992 vol II, 10, para 29.

[98] ibid.

[99] Statute of the International Criminal Tribunal for Rwanda (adopted 8 November 1994, UNSC Res 955, as amended) (ICTR Statute); ICTY Statute.

[100] Evans (n 86) 91.

[101] See arts 15, 18, 20, 22 of the ICTY Statute, and similar provisions in the ICTR Statute in arts 14, 17, 19, 21. Some of those provisions actually referred to the rights of victims but only in the context of fair proceedings, not the compensation issue; see also Evans (n 86) 91.

of the objectives of sentencing is reconciliation,[102] and that 'the expression of condemnation of grave violations of fundamental human rights … is also recognition of the harm and suffering caused to the victims'.[103] However, both Tribunals had their Victims and Witness Support Units, which aimed at providing help and support to witnesses rather than compensation or rehabilitation.[104]

Hence, it was only the Rome Statute that explicitly recognized the right of a victim to obtain reparation, and in that context statutory provisions must be treated as a landmark development of the international criminal law as reaffirming the right of a victim to reparation. The reparation order is made directly against the perpetrator of the crime specifying appropriate reparations in respect of the victims of those crimes. State responsibility to award compensation was not regulated in the Rome Statute; its provisions are designed to exercise individual criminal responsibility.[105] Not to diminish the role of States in their responsibility for serious violations of international law, a proper clause appeared in the Rome Statute, which states that 'no provision in this Statute relating to individual criminal responsibility shall affect the responsibility of States under international law'.[106]

For decades one would observe gradual incorporation of reparations in debates on the nature of international criminal law and its social impact. Arguably, this has not been the result of the progressive development of international criminal law, but rather it has been caused by the impact of the international human rights law and jurisprudence and its experience of granting reparations to victims of serious violations of human rights, which allows emphasis on the rights of victims and the role of victims in the criminal proceedings.

B. Reparations for Cultural Heritage Harm—A Broader Picture

The practice of human rights bodies is particularly important in terms of determining reparations for cultural heritage harm suffered. Such a harm is usually collective or communal in nature, thus entailing collective reparations.[107] Traditionally, it has been addressed and repaired within the framework of inter-state arrangements following armed conflicts and territorial reconfigurations in terms of reparation, restitution, or restoration of dispersed national cultural

[102] See, for instance, *Prosecutor v Furundzija* (Judgment) ICTY-95-17/1-T (10 December 1998) para 288.

[103] See *Prosecutor v Nikolić* (Judgment) ICTY-02-60/1 (2 December 2003) para 86.

[104] See <http://www.icty.org/en/about/registry/witnesses> accessed 11 July 2019.

[105] Luke Moffett, 'Reparations for Victims at the International Criminal Court: A New Way Forward?' (2017) 21(9) Intl J Hum Rts 1204, 1205–06.

[106] Rome Statute, art 25(4).

[107] See Elisa Novic, *The Concept of Cultural Genocide: An International Law Perspective* (OUP 2016) 192 ff; Ana Filipa Vrdoljak, 'Reparations for Cultural Loss' in Federico Lenzerini (ed), *Reparations for Indigenous Peoples* (OUP 2007) 197.

treasures.[108] However, the access to mechanisms of redressing cultural harm suffered by non-State human collectives has essentially been articulated by human rights law. To date, the most developed jurisprudence as to redressing collective harm comprising cultural harm has been offered by the Inter-American Court of Human Rights (IACtHR). In a number of cases concerning violations of indigenous communities' rights, including cultural rights, it decided on collective reparations involving communal development funds, educational programmes, and so on.[109] In particular, in the famous case *Yakye Axa Indigenous Community v Paraguay*,[110] concerning the State's failure to ensure the ancestral property rights of the Yakye Axa Indigenous Community and its members, the IACtHR explicitly linked traditional lands with the notion of cultural identity:

> The culture of the members of indigenous communities directly relates to a specific way of being, seeing and acting in the world, developed on the basis of their close relation with their traditional territories and the resources therein, not only because they are their main means of subsistence, but also because they are part of their worldview, their religiosity, and therefore, of their cultural identity.[111]

In terms of reparations, alongside the restitution of the ancestral lands to the community, the IACtHR also ordered that a community development fund was to be established, comprising education, housing, agricultural, and health programs, to be implemented in participation with the affected indigenous community.[112]

An instructive example of reparations for the destruction of religious heritage was offered by the Human Rights Chamber for Bosnia and Herzegovina (HRCBiH), a *sui generis,* mixed national–international court, operating in 1996–2003,[113] as an element of post-conflict transitional justice in the Balkans. Its jurisdiction covered violations of human rights obligations contained in the European Convention on Human Rights (ECHR) and its Protocols.[114] Interestingly, in the case brought by the Islamic Community in Bosnia and Herzegovina against Republika Srpska, involving the destruction of mosques in Zvornik,[115] the HRCBiH held that the

[108] See, in particular, Ana Filipa Vrdoljak, 'Enforcement of Restitution of Cultural Heritage through Peace Agreements' in Francioni and Gordley (eds) (n 23) 22.

[109] See Kristin Hausler, 'Collective Cultural Rights in the Inter-American Human Rights System' in Andrzej Jakubowski (ed), *Cultural Rights as Collective Rights: An International Law Perspective* (Brill 2016) 222.

[110] IACtHR, *Yakye Axa Indigenous Community v Paraguay* (Judgment on Merits, Reparations and Costs) IACHR Series C No 125 (17 June 2005).

[111] ibid, para 135.

[112] ibid, para 205.

[113] See Ana Filipa Vrdoljak, 'Genocide and Restitution: Ensuring Each Group's Contribution to Humanity' (2011) 22 EJIL 17, 42–46.

[114] Convention for the Protection of Human Rights and Fundamental Freedoms (adopted 4 November 1950, entered into force 3 September 1953) 213 UNTS 222, as amended.

[115] HRCBiH, *Islamic Community in Bosnia Herzegovina v The Republika Srpska* (Decision on admissibility and merits) CH/98/1062 (9 November 2000).

latter was responsible for the destruction of a mosque and construction on its site of an Orthodox church. Accordingly, the Republika Srpska violated the Islamic Community's right to freedom of religion, under Article 9 of the ECHR, right to the peaceful enjoyment of its possessions, as guaranteed by Article 1 of Protocol No 1 to the ECHR,[116] and 'discriminated against the Islamic Community in its enjoyment of these protected rights by preventing the Islamic Community from using the sites of destroyed mosques and reconstructing the destroyed mosques in Zvornik'.[117] Accordingly, Republika Srpska was required to pay monetary compensation and to allocate 'in consultation with the Islamic Community, and for its use only, a suitable building site (. . .) to permit, upon request of the Islamic Community, the construction of a mosque to replace' the destroyed one.[118] The HRCBiH held that '[s]uch compensation in kind is necessary under the circumstances because the respondent Party, by permitting construction of the Serb Orthodox church on the site, has effectively divested the Islamic Community of its right to ownership of the land'.[119] Thus, it applied a restitution-in-kind form of reparation for the destruction of cultural heritage enjoyed by the religious community.

In relation to the latter example, it is worth recalling that recovery (restitution) and reconstruction are considered primary modalities of repairing cultural heritage harm, suffered in armed conflicts.[120] As Bokova, the former UNESCO Director-General, said: '[l]ike destruction, restoration is not only about buildings. It is about history, identity, culture and the promise of the future'.[121] In fact, since the conflicts in Bosnia and Herzegovina and in Kosovo, the reconstruction of destroyed heritage has constituted an important element of both international peacekeeping programs and restorative, transitional justice. The most recent experience of the reconstruction of cultural heritage in Mali appears to the best and most successful example.[122] Indeed, the Environment and Culture Unit of the UN Multidimensional Integrated Stabilization Mission in Mali (MINUSMA), in cooperation with UNESCO, has not only been engaged in training the personnel and in safeguarding and restoring damaged heritage, but it has also supported the resumption of cultural events in Mali, contributing to the transmission and enhancement of intangible heritage and social cohesion. Importantly, the current Director

[116] Protocol No 1 to the Convention for the Protection of Human Rights and Fundamental Freedoms (adopted 20 March 1952, entered into force 18 May 1954) 213 UNTS 262.

[117] See HRCBiH, *Islamic Community in Bosnia Herzegovina v Republika Srpska* (Zvornik Mosques) (Decision on review) CH/98/1062 (12 October 2001) para 1.

[118] ibid, paras 34, 39.

[119] ibid, para 34.

[120] Cf Vrdoljak, 'Genocide and Restitution' (n 113) 44 ff.

[121] UN Press Release, 'Protecting Cultural Heritage Threads through United Nations Peacekeeping Strategy, Secretary-General Tells Yale University Colloquium' (12 April 2016) SG/SM/17664 <https://www.un.org/press/en/2016/sgsm17664.doc.htm> accessed 11 July 2019.

[122] See Sabine von Schorlemer, 'Military Intervention, the UN Security Council, and the Role of UNESCO: The Case of Mali' (Ch 3) in this volume.

of the Division of Culture in Emergencies at UNESCO, Lazare Eloundou Assomo, who in 2014 served as Chief of UNESCO's Africa section, said in Bamako:

> Our strategy is to work with the community (. . .). We use local people—they have the knowledge, they are the custodians. We also want to try to improve their living conditions: through our activities we are able to create 140 jobs just in the reconstruction of the mausoleums, then you can add the mosques and the rest.[123]

In such a spirit, the forum of experts representing thirty countries and several international organizations, under the auspices of UNESCO's World Heritage Centre, adopted on 8 May 2018 the 'Warsaw Recommendation on Recovery and Reconstruction of Cultural Heritage'.[124] This, while fully acknowledging the value of cultural heritage in the processes of peacebuilding and post-conflict and post-disaster recovery and reconstruction, calls for the full participation of communities concerned in decision-making that would regard their cultural life and heritage. It also promotes the idea of the 'time for reflection' necessary to address and assess the real needs of societies, considering 'the evolving nature of values post-trauma, the challenges of ensuring a fully inclusive and participatory process of consultation and the complex interrelations between heritage and other societal needs in the context of post-conflict and post-disaster recovery and reconstruction'.[125]

III. Reparations Order in *Al Mahdi*: A New Avenue of International Criminal Justice?

Undoubtedly, the Reparation Order rendered by the ICC in *Al Mahdi* needs to be seen within this broader context of redressing cultural wrongs and repairing cultural heritage harm. The Court referred to the value of cultural heritage as the transmitter of cultural practice, customs, and traditions—all those resources that enable the cultural identification of a community.[126] The ICC noticed that '[b]ecause of their purpose and symbolism, most cultural property and cultural heritage are unique and of sentimental value. As a result, they are not fungible or readily replaceable.'[127] It also noted that '[w]orld cultural heritage is a most important category. Greater interest vested in an object by the international community reflects

[123] See 'Timbuktu's Embattled Citizens Head Home Despite Mali's Uncertain Future' *The Guardian* (22 October 2014) <https://www.theguardian.com/global-development/2014/oct/22/timbuktu-refugees-return-mali-future> accessed 11 July 2019.

[124] <https://whc.unesco.org/en/news/1826> accessed 12 July 2019.

[125] ibid.

[126] *Al Mahdi*, Reparation Order (n 6) paras 13–20.

[127] ibid, para 22.

a higher cultural significance and a higher degree of international attention and concern'.[128]

This excerpt, however, raises questions relating to the degree of value placed on cultural heritage: A higher cultural significance than *what*? A higher degree of international attention and concern than *what*? The wording used by the Court calls for clarification of what is less valuable. One could be disappointed as the Court should provide the answers, not leave doubts. Why not admit simply that crimes against world cultural heritage are more serious than crimes against cultural property and consequently graver than crimes against ordinary property (as the Court did in the judgment)? The Court must constantly assess the gravity of a case when assessing its admissibility,[129] so why not to refer to the gravity in the reparation order?

In the subsequent part of the *Al Mahdi* Reparation Order, the Court set the principles and concrete responsibility of Al Mahdi. Determining principles on reparations and applicable law the Court decided to refer to relevant principles formulated by the Appeals Chamber in the case of *Lubanga*,[130] in the judgment on the appeals against the 'Decision establishing the principles and procedures to be applied to reparations'[131] and Order for reparations.[132] The judgment referred to the minimum content of a reparation order, noting its five essential elements as follows:

1) it must be directed against the convicted person;
2) it must establish and inform the convicted person of his or her liability with respect to the reparations awarded in the order;
3) it must specify, and provide reasons for, the type of reparations ordered, either collective, individual or both, (. . .);
4) it must define the harm caused to direct and indirect victims as a result of the crimes for which the person was convicted, as well as identify the modalities of reparations that the Trial Chamber considers appropriate based on the circumstances of the specific case before it; and
5) it must identify the victims eligible to benefit from the awards for reparations or set out the criteria of eligibility based on the link between the harm suffered by the victims and the crimes for which the person was convicted.[133]

[128] ibid, para 17.

[129] Rome Statute, arts 17, 19.

[130] Additionally, it must be noted that the Reparation Order in the case of *Katanga* before the ICC was also heavily focused on the principles discussed in *Lubanga*. *Prosecutor v Katanga* (Order for Reparations pursuant to Article 75 of the Statute) ICC-01/04-01/07-3728 (24 March 2017) paras 29–30.

[131] *Lubanga* (Appeals Judgment) (n 85) para 1.

[132] *Prosecutor v Lubanga* (Order for reparations) ICC-01/04-01/06-3129-AnxA (3 March 2015).

[133] *Lubanga* (Judgment on the appeals) (n 85) para 32, similarly *Al Mahdi*, Reparation Order (n 6) para 38.

The Chamber in *Al Mahdi* case applied exactly the same elements.

The main principles mentioned by the Court refer to the obligation of the convicted person to remedy the harm caused by the crimes of which he was convicted. Any person found to be criminally responsible before the ICC can be simultaneously held liable for reparations. Reparations are to repair the harm caused by the perpetrator of the crime, to the possible extent they are to relieve the suffering caused by the serious crime.[134] Moreover, all victims are to be treated fairly and equally as regards reparations, irrespective of whether they participated in the trial proceedings.[135] Also, reparations should be granted taking into account the principle of non-discrimination as they shall not be based on any distinction such as religion, gender, language, ethnicity, nationality, etc. Additionally, reparations shall be effective, adequate, and prompt.

All principles refer generally to the principles worked out in the *Lubanga* case. Interestingly, not even one principle mentioned in *Al Mahdi*'s Reparation Order can be assessed as referring exclusively to the question of heritage goods. It does not mean, however, that those principles do not refer generally to the destroyed heritage goods, but it would be extremely important to develop more concrete and specific principles and guidelines referring solely to the destroyed objects. It would act as the point of reference for future cases concerning cultural heritage. Many factors distinguish this case from two previous cases in which reparation orders were issued, namely the *Katanga* and *Lubanga* cases. For instance, just because *Al Mahdi* was based solely on the destruction of cultural heritage and the secondary victim of his crimes was the whole international community,[136] the general principle guiding the granting of reparations must be formulated to cover the expenses of reconstructing destroyed heritage goods for the benefit of future generations. Such a principle refers specifically only to heritage goods and would depict the will, responsibility, and intergenerational solidarity of the international community, especially when the destruction concerned objects from the World Heritage List. In this regard, the ICC referred to renovations already performed by UNESCO and the future enjoyment of reconstructed monuments. It considered that 'the harm caused by the destruction of the Protected Buildings will be satisfactorily addressed by measures for their protection and maintenance'.[137] It also noted that 'the appropriate modality of reparations shall be measures aimed at rehabilitating the Protected Sites with effective measures to guarantee non-repetition of the attacks directed against them'.[138]

In the part of the Reparation Order referring to the obligations of Al Mahdi, the specificity of crimes of cultural heritage was noted and developed. The Court

134 See *Al Mahdi*, Reparation Order (n 6) paras 27 ff.
135 ibid, paras 29 ff.
136 ibid, paras 51–53.
137 ibid, para 67.
138 ibid.

addressed all types of harm suffered by the victims through its awards of individual, collective, and symbolic reparations. The order addressed damage to the protected buildings granting the collective reparations; assessed the economic loss granting individual reparations for those whose livelihoods exclusively depended upon the protected buildings and collective reparations for the community of Timbuktu as a whole; and assessed the moral harm suffered by the victims.[139] One Euro was granted to the Malian State and international community represented by UNESCO.[140] As to the personal liability of Al Mahdi, the Court made an attempt to assess the damage to protected buildings, the economic loss connected with protected buildings (including, for example, the loss of income from tourism), and moral harm. Noting the problems connected with assessing the moral harm, the ICC concluded 'the Chamber does not have enough information to quantify this harm at the same level as the economic loss'.[141] Ultimately, the Chamber held that Al Mahdi is liable for 2.7 million Euros in expenses for individual and collective reparations.[142]

The determination that reparation for the people of Timbuktu suffices as reparation for the harm suffered by the people of Mali and the international community demonstrates respect for the cultural heritage of victims. Additionally, by providing reparations, the Court created the precedent for the application of remedies for cultural loss in order to preserve the spiritual, religious, and symbolic connection between the victimized communities and protected heritage.

Conclusion

The aim of this chapter was to examine the ongoing process of consolidating the international criminal law regime for counteracting international cultural heritage crimes, with particular focus on reparations for cultural harm. More precisely, it attempted to explain and substantiate the role of the *Al Mahdi* case before the ICC in this process. Accordingly, the effect of this case may be seen as threefold.

First, the approach taken by the Prosecutor and Chamber has enhanced the significance and gravity of deliberate attacks against cultural heritage. It needs to be stressed that after *Al Mahdi* intentional attacks against cultural heritage, under certain conditions, can no longer be seen as less heinous than other international crimes. The destruction of cultural heritage as referring to common goods and values cherished by all humankind is sufficiently grave to justify the action of the

[139] ibid, para 104.

[140] ibid, paras 106–07. Beside that the Chamber also decided as a symbolic measure to ensure that all victims have access to Mr Al Mahdi's apology, by ordering the Registry to produce an excerpt of the video of Mr Al Mahdi's apology, see ibid, para 71.

[141] ibid, para 130.

[142] ibid, para 135.

ICC, no matter under which 'label' of international law (as war crime, genocide, or crime against humanity), and such acts of destruction deserve the ICC's attention as well as any other crime within its jurisdiction. Thus the ICC confirmed and consolidated the approach already taken by the ICTY in recognizing the gravity of crimes aimed at cultural annihilation within international criminal law.

Second, the Court in Al Mahdi's Reparation Order attempted to identify the victims of the destruction of cultural heritage. These findings are extremely important as the Court referred both to direct victims—who have the closest inherent link with the targeted heritage—and the international community as a whole, which has a general interest in protecting and enjoying cultural heritage of outstanding universal value. In this regard, the ICC substantiated the nature of harm caused by the destruction of cultural heritage. It also concerned the types of modality of collective reparations to be applied for the harm caused by the destruction of protected cultural heritage: rehabilitation, protection, and maintenance. Yet the Court failed to specify any specific principles referring to the reparations addressing solely the heritage crimes. It would be necessary to formulate such a catalog, as a point of reference for future cases, and lack of formulation of such a catalog must be viewed as an omission on the Court's part. Perhaps the practice of human rights bodies could serve as a guideline in the future.

Third, both the 2016 judgment and 2017 Reparation Order concerning deliberate attacks against cultural heritage in Timbuktu can undoubtedly be seen as an important step in international criminal law. However, it is also clear that the ICC will never offer the best forum to address cultural heritage crimes. The jurisdiction of the Court is not widely recognized. As of January 2020, only 123 States are party to the Rome Statute, and importantly this number does not include Syria, Iraq, and three permanent members of the UN Security Council (China, Russia, and the United States). Next, decisions on admissibility refer to one, two, or three cases a year, and as already mentioned, the ICC's assessment of the gravity of cultural heritage crimes can be difficult beyond those directed toward World Heritage Sites. It is also important to mention that the ICC would not provide answers to some of the most difficult problems related to cultural heritage crimes, that is, corporate (group) criminal responsibility of non-State actors such as Daesh (ISIL) or Ansar Dine. Reflecting the current state of international law, it provides only for jurisdiction over natural persons—not their collectives, since there are so far no 'accepted rules or standards' for corporate criminal responsibility under international law.[143]

Finally, the *Al Mahdi* case is unique because the conviction of the perpetrator was based on his guilty plea, which resulted in a rather quick and smooth trial and no lodging of appeals, but it is unlikely that future trials would go so smoothly. The ICC can act only as a court of 'last resort', when the State is fragile, but beside that,

[143] James Crawford, *State Responsibility: The General Part* (CUP 2013) 81.

because of its limited powers, its actions will be more preventive and supportive than merely prosecutorial. Therefore, it remains the prime responsibility of States to prosecute international cultural heritage crimes before their respective domestic courts. Indeed, without closer cooperation between States as to the prosecution, extradition, and punishment of those committing crimes against cultural heritage, the fight against the impunity of those perpetrators will be lost. Moreover, the non-repetition of such crimes will not be ever possible without carefully designed and properly funded assistance programs aimed at victims. Such schemes must not be focused solely on rehabilitating and maintaining cultural heritage, they also need to provide sound, inclusive, and participatory educational and heritage governance programmes.

6

Trafficking in Cultural Property

Where Cultural Heritage Law and the International Fight Against Transnational Organized Crime Coincide

Janet Blake

Introduction

This chapter will concentrate primarily on the peacetime regime for the prevention of illegal movement of cultural objects and their return to countries of origin. It complements the chapter by Patty Gerstenblith, who addresses the treatment of movable cultural heritage during armed conflict and occupation and the regimes that regulate the illicit trade in objects removed from conflict areas. As Gerstenblith notes, the current distinction between wartime and peacetime legal regimes is mostly the product of an historical dichotomy in international law that no longer matches the realities on the ground.[1] Consistent with the focus of this volume on the intersections of cultural heritage law with other areas of international law, this chapter provides a comparative analysis of the principal cultural heritage-based approach to curbing the illicit movement of cultural objects and the more recent, alternative approach that treats the illicit trafficking in cultural objects as a form of transnational organized crime subject to international law enforcement regimes. Given the limited effectiveness of cultural heritage treaty regimes in preventing this illicit trade and/or supporting the return of illicitly trafficked items and the interchangeable character of transnational trafficking (ranging from animals and plants to people, toxic waste, and cultural artifacts), this approach has become increasingly favored as a more attractive route for combating the illicit trade.

[1] See Patty Gerstenblith, 'The Disposition of Movable Cultural Heritage' (Ch 1) in this volume. Similarly, the traditional distinction between human rights law (as being applied predominantly in peacetime) and humanitarian law (law of war) is becoming blurred in the face of modern non-State conflicts.

Janet Blake, Trafficking in Cultural Property In: *Intersections in International Cultural Heritage Law*. Edited by Anne-Marie Carstens and Elizabeth Varner. © Oxford University Press 2020. The several contributors
DOI: 10.1093/oso/9780198846291.003.0007

The large-scale illegal movement of and trade in art and antiquities is a worldwide phenomenon, often fed by illicit excavation.[2] For instance, the number of cultural property items recorded by the United Nations Office on Drugs and Crime (UNODC) as illegally trafficked from Turkey alone between 2003 and 2008 ranged from an annual total of 1,161 (in 2008) to 1,416 (in 2006).[3] Given that the recorded cases are likely to be only a small proportion of the total, these figures demonstrate the scale of the problem facing INTERPOL and national law enforcement forces. They also starkly illustrate the economic and geopolitical realities of a trade where the poverty of some communities around the world feeds markets in the world's richest nations.[4]

The value of this illicit trade is enormous,[5] and large profits can be made by middlemen in particular. Brodie and colleagues have estimated that over 98 percent of the final price of smuggled antiquities ends up in the pockets of the middlemen.[6] A classical period table-leg depicting Marsyas being flayed by Apollo provides a good example: discovered by a farmer at Philadelphia near Antalya (southern Turkey) on an unspecified date, it was bought by a dealer for US$7,000 and subsequently placed at auction in New York with an asking price of US$540,000.[7] Italian tomb-robbers (*tombaroli*) receive only a small fraction of the final profits on looted objects, selling items for a low fixed price to an international go-between (*ricettatore*), who will realize a much larger return on the object.[8]

These exorbitant mark-ups on cultural objects demonstrate clearly that the profits to be made by criminals engaged in smuggling and selling illegally looted antiquities and stolen works of art can be huge and that this illegal trade likely will continue for as long as criminal gangs are able to operate. Alongside the cultural heritage treaties designed to prevent the illicit export and movement of cultural property and to facilitate its return, international law must also confront the criminality involved in this illegal trade. This requires effective strategies for

[2] Past instances of reported site destruction (for major sites) in Belize have been estimated at 74.3 percent. Mark A Gutchen, 'The Destruction of Archaeological Resources in Belize, Central America' [1993] J of Field Archaeology 217.

[3] UN Office on Drugs and Crime (UNODC), Illicit Trafficking in Cultural Property and Related Offences, Number of Police-recorded Offences (2008) <www.unodc.org/documents/data-and-analysis/Crime-statistics/Illicit_trafficking_in_cultural_property.xls> accessed 30 January 2020.

[4] Subsistence digging (a term generally preferred over 'subsistence looting') has been well covered in the archaeological literature. See eg David Matsuda, 'Subsistence Diggers' in Karen Fitz Gibbons (ed), *Who Owns the Past? Cultural Policy, Cultural Property, and the Law* (Rutgers UP 2005) 225–65.

[5] UNESCO has estimated the annual turnover of illicit trade in antiquities at US$2.6 billion. See UNESCO, *The Fight Against the Illicit Trafficking of Cultural Objects: The 1970 Convention: Past and Future*, UNESCO Doc CLT/2011/CONF.206/6 (15–16 March 2011) 3.

[6] Neil Brodie, Jenny Doole, and Peter Watson, *Stealing History: The Illicit Trade in Cultural Material* (McDonald Institute for Archaeological Research 2000) 13.

[7] Özgen Acar and Melik Kaylan, 'The Turkish Connexion: An Investigative Report on the Smuggling of Classical Antiquities' [1990] Connoisseur 30–137.

[8] Simon Mackenzie, 'Organised Crime and Common Transit Networks', Trends and Issues in Crime and Criminal Justice No 233 (Australian Institute of Criminology 2002) 1.

international cooperation, especially in the areas of policing and judicial action, and for individual States to take the necessary action on the domestic level.

The prevailing international legal regime for the 'cultural heritage' approach to combatting illegal movement of cultural objects comprises (a) the 1970 UNESCO Convention on the Means of Prohibiting and Preventing the Illicit Import, Export and Transfer of Ownership of Cultural Property (1970 UNESCO Convention),[9] which was developed under the auspices of the United Nations Educational, Scientific and Cultural Organization (UNESCO), and (b) the 1995 UNIDROIT Convention on Stolen or Illegally Exported Cultural Objects (1995 UNIDROIT Convention),[10] which was developed under the auspices of the International Institute for the Unification of Private Law (UNIDROIT). The 1970 UNESCO Convention represented the first concerted effort by the international community to address the illicit trade in movable cultural property,[11] while the 1995 UNIDROIT Convention aimed at providing an acceptable framework for international claims for the restitution of stolen cultural artifacts and the return of those illegally exported. The alternative approach to combatting the illicit trafficking in cultural objects, by treating it as a form of transnational crime, relies primarily on the 2000 United Nations Convention Against Transnational Organized Crime (2000 Palermo Convention).[12] The 2000 Palermo Convention confronts the illegal trafficking in cultural property by criminalizing a number of actions (such as participation in an organized criminal group) that are an intrinsic part of committing such a crime. The new Council of Europe Convention on Offences relating to Cultural Property (2017 Nicosia Convention)[13] further enriches this body of law and provides a hybrid approach by focusing specifically on trafficking in cultural artifacts as a transnational crime.[14]

[9] Convention on the Means of Prohibiting and Preventing the Illicit Import, Export and Transfer of Ownership of Cultural Property (adopted 14 November 1970, entered into force 24 April 1972) 823 UNTS 231 (1970 UNESCO Convention). For a general overview of the legal tools available, see UNESCO, *Legal and Practical Measures Against Illicit Trafficking in Cultural Property* (UNESCO 2006).

[10] UNIDROIT Convention on the International Return of Stolen or Illegally Exported Cultural Objects (adopted 24 June 1995, entered into force 1 July 1998) 34 ILM 1322 (1995 UNIDROIT Convention).

[11] Lyndel V Prott, 'The Fight Against the Illicit Traffic of Cultural Property: The 1970 Convention: Past and Future, 15–16 March 2011' (2011) 18 IJCP 437.

[12] United Nations Convention Against Transnational Organized Crime (adopted 15 November 2000 in UNGA Res 55/25, entered into force 29 September 2003) 2225 UNTS 209 (2000 Palermo Convention).

[13] Council of Europe Convention on Offences relating to Cultural Property (adopted 19 May 2017) (2017) CETS 221 (2017 Nicosia Convention).

[14] This chapter does not discuss the 2001 UNESCO Convention on the Protection of the Underwater Cultural Heritage (adopted 2 November 2001, entered into force 2 January 2009) 2562 UNTS 3 (2001 UCH Convention), although it does identify a provision specifically addressing the disposal of and preventing the clandestine movement of artifacts retrieved from underwater sites. See text accompanying n 125. For discussion of the 2001 UCH Convention, see Sarah Dromgoole, 'The 2001 UNESCO Convention on the Protection of the Underwater Cultural Heritage and Its Principles Relating to the Recovery and Disposition of Material from Shipwrecks' (Ch 12) in this volume.

I. The Cultural Heritage-Based Approach: Relevant Treaties

This section introduces the two main cultural heritage treaties aimed at preventing illegal movement of cultural property in peacetime and facilitating its return, namely the 1970 UNESCO Convention and the 1995 UNIDROIT Convention. Together these treaties form a regime that concentrates on international cooperation for the return and restitution of stolen and illegally exported cultural items, as well as prevention of illicit trafficking through internal measures.

A. 1970 UNESCO Convention

The 1970 UNESCO Convention establishes a diplomatic framework, based on international cooperation, for the return of stolen and/or illegally exported cultural property. It was adopted in order to respond to increasing theft from museums and archaeological sites in the late 1960s and 1970s, particularly in developing countries. There are now 140 States Parties to the Convention,[15] suggesting unwillingness among some States to recognize other States' rights to retrieve stolen or illegally exported cultural property.[16] Until recently, most major market States were not ready to ratify the Convention in the belief that it favored the interests of countries of origin. However, positive moves in this direction have occurred since the late 1990s with France, the United Kingdom, Switzerland, Germany, and Belgium all acceding to the Convention since 1997.[17] These recent additions are extremely important to the operation of the 1970 UNESCO Convention because without the participation of market States, the treaty cannot provide a useful framework for preventing illicit movement and transfer of ownership of cultural property and facilitating its return due to its primarily diplomatic approach.

The Preamble sets out the following three approaches, namely: (1) 'every state [must] protect the cultural property existing within its territory against the dangers of theft, clandestine excavation, and illicit export'; (2) the *true value* of cultural property can only be understood in relation to 'the fullest possible information' regarding its provenance; and (3) protection of cultural heritage can only be fully effective if organized both nationally and internationally amongst States working in cooperation.[18] The 1970 UNESCO Convention attempts to strike an appropriate balance between the duties of market States to prevent the illicit importation and sale of cultural property, and the responsibility of countries of origin to protect

[15] The treaty's status is available online at: <www.unesco.org/eri/la/convention.asp?KO=13039&language=E> accessed 30 January 2020.

[16] For a reappraisal of the implementation of this Convention, see Prott (n 11).

[17] The dates for ratification/acceptance area: France (1997), United Kingdom (2002), Switzerland (2003), Germany (2007), Belgium (2009), and the Netherlands (2009).

[18] Preamble to the 1970 UNESCO Convention at recitals 4, 3, and 8, respectively.

their cultural property within their borders and to prevent its looting, theft, and illegal export. Duties imposed on countries of origin include introducing a system of export certification,[19] providing for the appropriate national services and staff,[20] drafting legislation where necessary,[21] keeping a national inventory of protected property,[22] and establishing ethical codes for, inter alia, curators, dealers, and collectors. They are also obliged to bear all the costs relating to the return and delivery of cultural property of which they have requested the return.[23]

As a counterbalance, the main duties imposed on importing States include preventing museums and similar institutions from acquiring items illegally exported from another State Party after the entry into force of the Convention and, where possible, informing other States of any offers of such property.[24] State Parties must also prohibit the importation of inventoried cultural property stolen from a museum or similar institution after the Convention's entry into force (on the request of another State Party), take appropriate steps to recover and return such cultural property stolen,[25] and provide the necessary documentation and evidence to establish a claim for its recovery.[26] Further duties on receiving States include admitting legal actions for the recovery of lost or stolen items of cultural property, recognizing the right of each State Party to declare certain cultural property inalienable and not subject to exportation, and preventing transfers of ownership likely to promote its illicit import or export.[27] This last provision implies a further obligation on importing States to control the internal market in such items.

A steady number of stolen items have been traced, identified, and returned worldwide under the terms of the 1970 UNESCO Convention. For example, Italy returned over 12,000 pre-Columbian objects to Ecuador in 1983 following a seven-year litigation process. In this case, the moral support of the Convention's Intergovernmental Committee for Promoting the Return of Cultural Property to its Countries of Origin or its Restitution in Case of Illicit Appropriation (ICPRCP) was recognized by the Ecuadorian authorities as a significant factor in the success of this case.[28] In another case showing the influence that the ICPRCP can bring to bear, the United States of America, one of the world's leading art market States, returned the Phra Narai lintel to Thailand in 1988 following mediation facilitated by

[19] 1970 UNESCO Convention, art 6.
[20] ibid, art 5.
[21] ibid, art 5(a).
[22] ibid, art 5(b).
[23] ibid, art 7(b)(ii).
[24] ibid, art 7.
[25] Subject to an obligation to pay just compensation 'to an innocent purchaser' or any other person with valid title to the property. ibid.
[26] ibid, art 7.
[27] ibid, art 13.
[28] On the website of the intergovernmental committee of the 1970 Convention, online at <http://www.unesco.org/new/en/culture/themes/restitution-of-cultural-property/return-or-restitution-cases/> accessed 22 September 2018.

the Committee.[29] Germany, which ratified the 1970 Convention in 2007, agreed to return to Turkey a stone Hittite sphinx excavated at Boğazköy in the 1910s and removed to Germany post-excavation. The return of the Boğazköy Sphinx followed a recommendation made by the ICPRCP in September 2010.[30] In another case, the Makondé Mask was returned to Tanzania under a bilateral agreement reached in 2010 between Tanzania and the Barbier-Mueller Museum in Geneva, following a request lodged by Tanzania in 2006 with ICPRCP.[31] However, despite such cases where source countries have succeeded in retrieving cultural objects that have been illegally removed and traded overseas, numerous other cases persist where diplomatic approaches have not borne fruit.[32]

B. 1995 UNIDROIT Convention

The 1995 UNIDROIT Convention is aimed at responding to the difficulties associated with litigation for the return of cultural heritage and at addressing more effectively the private law aspects of cultural property protection. While the 1970 UNESCO Convention has generally been seen as favorable to countries of origin, the 1995 UNIDROIT Convention was designed to create a text more acceptable to both source *and* market countries. It provides a framework for international litigation[33] and supplements the 1970 UNESCO Convention by setting out minimal legal standards for the restitution and return of cultural objects. It also provides guarantees for the private international law rules and international procedure. In this way, the two Conventions are, at the same time, both compatible

[29] ibid.

[30] The sphinx was sent to Germany *on a temporary basis* to be cleaned, restored, and catalogued in 1917. In 1987, ICPRCP invited both Parties to hold comprehensive bilateral negotiations as soon as possible with a view to bringing this issue to a mutually acceptable solution. See Alessandro Chechi, Anne Laure Bandle, and Marc-André Renold, 'Case Boğazköy Sphinx—Turkey and Germany', Platform ArThemis (Art-Law Centre, University of Geneva) <https://plone.unige.ch/art-adr/cases-affaires/bogazkoy-sphinx-2013-turkey-and-germany> accessed 21 April 2018. The return of the sphinx in 2011 is noted on the website of the Intergovernmental Committee of the 1970 Convention, <http://www.unesco.org/new/en/culture/themes/restitution-of-cultural-property/return-or-restitution-cases/ accessed 22 September 2018.

[31] ICOM Press Release available online at <http://archives.icom.museum/press/MM_Dossierdepresse_fr.pdf> accessed 22 September 2017.

[32] Examples include the failure of the Government of Nigeria to secure the restitution of the 'Benin Bronzes' in 1987 from the British Museum, see Folarin Shyllon, 'The Nigerian and African Experience on Looting and Trafficking in Cultural Objects' in Barbara T Hoffman (ed), *Art and Cultural Heritage: Law, Policy and Practice* (CUP 2006). Another example concerns the failed attempts by Iran to retrieve from the University of Ghent Museum in Belgium a very valuable collection of 349 ceramics and one bronze (dating from 1300 to 800 BC) from the necropolis of Khurvin. This was subject to a long-running court case *Iran v Wolfcarius* (1981–2011) in which the relevance of the 1970 Convention was examined and denied by the Court since Belgium had not become a party until 2009. See *Iran v Wolfcarius* [Case Report, 1981–2011] Tribunal de 1re Instance de Bruxelles, R.G. o.114.084.

[33] UNIDROIT, 'Overview—UNIDROIT Convention on Stolen or Illegally Exported Cultural Objects (Rome, 1995)' (updated 9 June 2014) <www.unidroit.org/overviecp/english> accessed 18 April 2018.

and complementary.[34] The 1995 UNIDROIT Convention has thus far secured only forty-two States Parties, of which the large majority are States of origin; the absence of the leading art market States (the United States, United Kingdom, Switzerland, Germany, France, and Japan) is notable, and these absences reduce its effectiveness.[35]

The 1995 UNIDROIT Convention responds to a set of issues avoided by the 1970 treaty regime.[36] Hence, it recognizes pre-existing public and private international law rules, including trade law rules, making it an extremely difficult and complex set of requirements to negotiate.[37] This recognition of both public and private law rules is necessary because potential litigants in international suits for the return of cultural objects face multiple obstacles, even apart from the huge cost and length of such cases. Among these challenges is the *lex situs* rule, which provides that the law of the place where the item is or was situated at the material time governs any litigation concerning it. This rule is problematic in litigation concerning cultural property because '[p]ossession of the item is paramount and the role of the law should be to establish who is entitled to it, based on an assessment of the competing values and not a mechanical rule'.[38] The *lex situs* rule is interpreted differently in different jurisdictions,[39] with the result that some are much more favorable for such litigation than others.

The private law rules of conflict of laws and extraterritoriality can also be inimical to cultural heritage because they govern whether a court will apply the public law of a foreign jurisdiction, such as export regulations, and were developed for international trade and commerce.[40] Other traditional private law rules that often do not support cultural heritage-related litigation are statute of limitations rules, other common law doctrines that can bar claims (such as the laches doctrine), and the civil law rules of prescription.[41] These rules come into play because

[34] Lyndel V Prott, 'UNESCO and UNIDROIT: A Partnership against Illicit Trafficking' (1996) Uniform L Rev 59.

[35] The treaty status is online at <www.unidroit.org/status-cp> accessed 18 April 2018.

[36] See generally Lyndel V Prott, *Commentary of the UNIDROIT Convention* (IAL 1998). See also UNESCO, Information Note submitted to the Conference Celebrating the 10th Anniversary of the 1995 UNIDROIT Convention on Stolen or Illegally Exported Cultural Objects UNESCO Doc CLT-2005/Conf/803/2 (16 June 2005).

[37] A working group representing both 'exporting' and 'importing' states was established during the final week of the discussions.

[38] Oliver Sandrock, 'Foreign Laws Regulating Export of Cultural Property: The Respect Due to the Lex Fori' in Pierre Lalive (ed), *International Sales of Works of Art* (International Chamber of Commerce/Faculté de droit de Genève 1985).

[39] In France, the law of the place of the litigation is applied, while under English law, the law of the last transaction is applied.

[40] Extraterritoriality was an important issue in the case of *Attorney-General of New Zealand v Ortiz* concerning some Maori carvings offered for sale in Sotheby's (London) in 1978, which the New Zealand government claimed had been illegally exported. [1982] QB 349 and [1984] AC 1.

[41] See Lyndel V Prott, 'Problems of Private International Law for the Protection of the Cultural Heritage' (1989) Recueil des Cours de l'Académie de Droit Intl 224. Statute of limitations rules set out the maximum time (which varies according to the jurisdiction) after an event within which related legal proceedings may be initiated; the laches doctrine in common law systems concerns cases where a lack of diligence in making a legal claim or in moving forward with legal enforcement of a right is asserted,

it is not uncommon for a case to be brought many years, if not decades, after the actual theft or illegal movement of a cultural object.[42] It is also often extremely hard to prove the provenance of objects from ancient cultures and civilizations, and this lack of provenance can be further exacerbated by the lack of consonance between modern State boundaries and the cultural boundaries of the ancient world.[43]

By recognizing that 'a proper role for legal trading' in cultural objects must be safeguarded alongside measures to combat illicit trade, the 1995 UNIDROIT Convention signals a shift in attitude toward both accepting a controlled licit trade in cultural objects as a necessary part of the global control of the market and seeking a reasonable compromise between the interests of market and 'source' States.[44] In the interests of the latter, the treaty counters the strong protection of a good faith purchaser found in civil law regimes by treating objects acquired through clandestine excavation as stolen, if in accordance with the law in that State. This presumption responds to the fact that stolen cultural objects are frequently placed on the market with convincingly fake provenances that would protect the interests of 'good faith' purchasers in such jurisdictions. As a counterbalance, it limits the claims for restitution and return that can be covered by the Convention[45] and sets a three-year time limit for restitution claims, from the time the claimant knew the location of the cultural object and the identity of its possessor. This takes account of the difficulties faced by claimants in ascertaining the whereabouts of cultural objects that may have been hidden from public view for many years.[46] The provision of compensation for a person returning a stolen cultural object to its true owner, if they could prove due diligence in its acquisition, represents a compromise between the competing interests of a good faith purchaser and the original owner. In the

resulting in an unreasonable delay that may prejudice the defendant(s); and civil law rules of prescription require almost all lawsuits to be brought within a legally determined period and may be either acquisitive or extinctive in character.

[42] This was the case of much art looted during the Nazi era. See eg Evelien Campfens (ed), *Fair and Just Solutions? Alternatives to Litigation in Nazi Looted Art Disputes: Status Quo and New Developments* (Eleven 2014); Charlotte Woodhead, 'Nazi Era Spoliation: Establishing Procedural and Substantive Principles' [2013] AAL 167. Principle VIII of the Washington Conference Principles On Nazi-Confiscated Art, adopted at the Washington Conference on Holocaust-Era Assets, Washington (3 December 1998), calls for achieving 'a just and fair solution' in cases of 'art that is found to have been confiscated by the Nazis and not subsequently restituted'.

[43] A good illustration of this problem is the case *Government of Peru v Johnson*, 720 FSupp 810 (CD Cal 1989), a suit brought by Peru for return, from a US-based dealer and collector, of eighty-nine artifacts it alleged were looted in Peru from the Moche site of Sipán. Despite considerable sympathy for the claimant, the court was not persuaded that the undocumented pre-Columbian items in question could conclusively be proved to have originated from Peru.

[44] 1995 UNIDROIT Convention, Preamble. Proponents of this view include Clemency Chase Coggins, 'A Licit International Trade in Ancient Art: Let There be Light!' (1995) 4 IJCP 61, and Hugo Keith Wiehe, 'Licit International Traffic in Cultural Objects for Art's Sake' (1995) 4 IJCP 81.

[45] 1995 UNIDROIT Convention, arts 4, 5, and 7.

[46] By applying the so-called discovery rule. This rule was relevant in *Autocephalous Greek Orthodox Church of Cyprus v Goldberg*, 717 F Supp 1374 (S D Ind 1989). The claimants remained unaware of the location of the stolen Byzantine mosaic for approximately ten years after its removal.

interests of securing the support of market States, the non-retroactive character of the Convention is made explicit.[47]

Taken cumulatively, the treaty attempts to make litigation for return of such items easier and, importantly, receiving States readier to facilitate such claims in their courts. In this sense, it operates as a 'Protocol' to the 1970 UNESCO Convention by complementing that treaty's predominantly diplomatic framework by ensuring more effective and accessible litigation in cases where a diplomatic approach may prove less effective.[48] However, the coverage of the treaty is not extensive, and its lack of acceptance by market States renders it largely ineffective. Moreover, it has not achieved greater uniformity in national measures taken, and a 2011 study noted that the 'existing differences in national policies are frequently exploited by criminals not just to transfer and eventually legitimise stolen property, but also to escape punishment and sanction'.[49]

II. An Alternative Approach: Treating Illegal Movement of Cultural Objects as an International or Transnational Crime

In contrast to the cultural heritage-based approach discussed above, this section examines the possibilities of a more recent, alternative approach offered by treating illegal movement of cultural objects as an international or transnational crime. It focuses on two complementary efforts to combat cultural property trafficking in this regard: the 2000 Palermo Convention, which addresses the great diversity of criminal activity crossing international borders that represents a substantial and growing global challenge; and complementary international regimes for countering illegal movement of cultural objects, including the 2017 Nicosia Convention.

A. The Relationship Between Cultural Objects and Organized Transnational Crime

An analysis of this regime requires understanding the mechanics of this illegal international trade and how it relates to other forms of organized transnational criminality.[50] In a great many cases, transnational smuggling networks

[47] Article 10. For stolen items, the State in which a claim is brought must be a party at the time of the theft; for illegally exported items, the Convention only applies to objects illegally exported after the Convention entered into force both in the requesting State and the State where a claim is brought.

[48] eg Prott 'UNESCO and UNIDROIT: A Partnership against Illicit Trafficking' (n 34).

[49] Siobhán Ní Chonaill, Anaïs Reding, and Lorenzo Valeri, *Assessing the Illegal Trade in Cultural Property* (RAND 2011) viii.

[50] Blythe Bowman Proulx, 'Organized Criminal Involvement in the Illicit Antiquities Trade' (2011) 14 Trends in Organized Crime 1.

are interchangeable. The same criminal organization may operate counterfeiting, money laundering, extortion, arms deals, drug trafficking, prostitution, theft, bribery, smuggling, fraud, tax evasion, contract killing, and even toxic waste dumping.[51] In view of the specialist character of the cultural heritage regime, the interchangeable character of organized transnational criminality is a point of great importance because it signals the need to look beyond that regime to find effective means of controlling this illegal trade. Cultural heritage law intersects directly with international criminal law at this point.

Moreover, the extent of the illicit trade in cultural objects remains huge and must be addressed as part of a larger picture of transnational organized criminality. Indeed, the more traditional cultural heritage approaches have proved inadequate to this task.[52] A consensus has emerged in the international community that cultural property is falling victim to transnational organized criminal activity and that this development requires a coordinated international response.[53] As the Secretariat of the 2000 Palermo Convention noted in 2010:

> [Trafficking in cultural property] has links to organized crime, as it relies on *modus operandi* used by organized criminal groups; the strong demand for illicit objects is highly lucrative for those participating in the trade; its complex nature often requires the involvement of many actors, legal entities and third parties, who tend to operate in a structured and organized way; and the use of modern and sophisticated technologies. There is also evidence that transnational trafficking in antiquities is linked to other illicit activities in which organized criminal groups are involved, including drugs and arms smuggling, violence, corruption and money-laundering.[54]

Most modern transnational criminal groups are 'fluid network structures' that have no central leadership. In fact, the 2000 Palermo Convention, discussed more fully below, describes an organized criminal group as a 'Structured group,' which means that it 'is not randomly formed for the immediate commission of an offence' and 'does not need to have formally defined roles for its members, continuity of its membership or a developed structure'.[55] In such organizations, each

[51] Peter B Campbell, 'The Illicit Antiquities Trade as a Transnational Criminal Network: Characterizing and Anticipating Trafficking of Cultural Heritage' (2013) 20 IJCP 113.

[52] Folarin Shyllon, 'Extraordinary Meeting of States Parties to the Convention on the Means of Prohibiting and Preventing the Illicit Import, Export and Transfer of Ownership of Cultural Property' (2013) 20 IJCP 499.

[53] Greg Borgestede, 'Cultural Property, the Palermo Convention, and Transnational Organized Crime' (2014) 21 IJCP 281.

[54] Conference of the Parties to the UN Convention against Transnational Crime, *Use of the UN Convention against Transnational Crime for Protection against Trafficking in Cultural Property*, Vienna, 18–22 October 2010, <www.unodc.org/documents/treaties/organized_crime/COP5/CTOC_COP_2010_17/CTOC_COP_2010_17_E.pdf> accessed 21 March 2017.

[55] Palermo Convention, art 2(a).

participant has a clearly defined role to play and is linked to the others through a series of criminal relationships that have been compared to a 'plate of spaghetti [where] every piece seems to touch each other, but you are never sure where it all leads'.[56] The flexibility of criminal networks creates a myriad of challenges for law enforcement. These networks are vast because conducting trafficking activities that involve moving illicit goods—whether hazardous wastes, people, or illicit cultural artifacts—from source to market requires a large number of participants with their own specializations. They include Afghanistan's Haqqani network, the Turkish mafia, Armenian human traffickers, Bulgarian drug dealers, Lebanese weapons smugglers, and other traditional crime organizations.[57]

The specific roles can range from transport specialists through farmers to antiquities experts, with the sole thing binding them together being criminality and the opportunity for large profits. Such specialization is a function of collaboration, and participants accept the sharing of profits in order to benefit from the specialist knowledge and skills of others. In antiquities trafficking, the relevant specialist knowledge and skills include locating sites, transporting objects, providing false customs documents, laundering, and even creating false provenances for cultural items. Campbell identifies four principal participants in the different general stages of the illicit cultural property trade, who are: (1) looter or thief who initially acquires the items; (2) early-stage intermediary who transports the items; (3) late-stage intermediary who launders the items; and (4) buyer and/or collector.[58]

Comparison is sometimes made with the trade in illicit drugs, another internationally trafficked material. This comparison is superficially attractive because the same networks often traffic in both goods, using established smuggling routes. Indeed, the same countries are often sources for both trades, such as Colombia and Peru (for cocaine and pre-Columbian artefacts to the United States) and Turkey, Afghanistan, Iran, and Pakistan (for heroin and Greek, Roman, and Islamic-era objects). Nonetheless, the structural differences between the two trades remain significant, and this distinction must affect the approach to policing and control: In the drugs trade, a limited number of suppliers provide for a virtually unlimited market, and it is easier for the authorities to control suppliers and sellers. In contrast, the art and antiquities market is a small and limited one, with a large potential number of suppliers where it is more effective to police the buyers (and dealers). For this reason, litigation against private collectors or, more commonly, against museums and similar institutions for the return of stolen antiquities proves so important.

[56] Timothy Green, *The Smugglers* (Walkers 1969) 9.

[57] Peter B Campbell, 'How Crime, Corruption, and Murder Are Hidden in the Elusive Black Market Stages of Antiquities Trafficking' *Archaeology Blogs*, University of Southampton (4 July 2013) <https://generic.wordpress.soton.ac.uk/archaeology/2013/07/04/antiquities-trafficking/> accessed 2 March 2017.

[58] ibid.

A more appropriate comparison, on many levels, can be made with the trade in endangered species regulated by the 1973 Convention on the International Trade in Endangered Species of Fauna and Flora (CITES Convention).[59] As with antiquities, the species concerned are a potentially non-renewable resource, and their extinction would represent partial destruction of the biological record, comparable with the destruction of the archaeological record caused by illegal excavation. Both trades also share the problem of laundering through third-party States, as in the case of wild cyclamen, exported from Turkey (a non-Party to the CITES treaty) to Holland (a State Party) and then sold on as the 'Produce of Holland'. Since all species of cyclamen are included in Appendix II of CITES, and so subject to export controls in trade between States Parties, this practice demonstrates the danger of non-signatory States to treaties regulating international trade; the practice is the functional equivalent of the laundering of antiquities through transit States to supply them with a good title.[60]

Trafficking in cultural objects from Afghanistan demonstrates the role of organized crime in the illicit antiquities trade. Afghanistan has become a major victim of the illicit antiquities trade as a consequence of war, political instability, and poverty. Local communities turn to looting archaeological artifacts due to economic hardship, and these subsistence diggers sell the artifacts to middlemen who visit their villages. The primary exit route for Afghani antiquities appears to be into Pakistan through an unmanned border crossing at Baramcha used by narcotics smugglers.[61] A number of smuggling organizations operating along the Afghan–Pakistani border are engaged in trafficking narcotics, arms, humans, antiquities, and other commodities. On arrival in Pakistan, illicit antiquities are then sold on to Pakistani-based criminal groups in border towns and then transported to major cities, where they are then generally shipped to the United Arab Emirates.[62]

A large quantity of smuggled goods is included among the legitimate Afghani goods passing through the Pakistani port of Karachi.[63] Once they have reached Sharjah, the smuggled antiquities are purchased by individuals with connections overseas, who export them by hiding them in legitimate items such as furniture, under falsified cargo manifests, or in false compartments.[64] When they arrive in Europe or North America, the artifacts are usually sold on to further middlemen or dealers and eventually introduced onto the market:[65] A Belgian documentary

[59] Convention on the International Trade in Endangered Species of Fauna and Flora (adopted 3 March 1973, entered into force 1 July 1975) 993 UNTS 243 (CITES Convention).

[60] Falsely labelled in Turkey, either as being of a non-protected species or as 'cultivated', they are then exported to Holland (a party to CITES) apparently legitimately. See Linda Warren, 'Trade in Endangered Species' (1989) 3 Environmental L 239.

[61] Gretchen Peters, *Seeds of Terror: How Heroin is Bankrolling the Taliban and al Qaeda* (Oneworld 2011).

[62] ibid.

[63] Facilitated by the Afghan Transit Trade Agreement that waives import taxes between Afghanistan and Pakistan. Campbell, 'The Illicit Antiquities Trade as a Transnational Criminal Network' (n 51) 121.

[64] ibid.

[65] Peters (n 61).

film showed how one dealer has a 'safe house' off a main gallery street where newly smuggled antiquities are brought and are either sold to other dealers or placed in his gallery.[66]

In recent years, the Internet has become a major conduit for criminal activities, and illicit antiquities are available online.[67] Online sales allow criminals to reach the wider population, and the privacy afforded by a personal computer provides the criminals with impersonal and anonymous contacts. Both high- and low-end antiquities are now being sold with relative ease through websites such as Ebay,[68] and may even be netting large profits. It has been estimated that, in the period 2011 through 2013, '[o]n average . . . a minimum of 6,285 lots of pre-Columbian antiquities were sold online each year', with some lots including multiple objects. This netted an estimated annual aggregate value of more than US$3.6 million, although this figure is likely to be an underestimate.[69] The advantages of online trading mean that legitimate dealers, even well-known galleries and auction houses, are also gravitating towards Internet sales. However, the Internet has always attracted illicit as well as licit forms of commercial activities, and it is becoming an important conduit for dealers to sell large quantities of looted cultural objects. The 2017 Operational Guidelines to the 1970 UNESCO Convention note 'worrisome trends, such as the proliferation of pillage and clandestine excavations of archaeological and paleontological sites and related sales on Internet, are posing further challenges to the protection of cultural heritage'.[70]

New technologies can also be a useful tool in preventing illicit trade in cultural artifacts, and inventories and databases of cultural property are essential tools for tracking down and recovering stolen cultural items. Noting the challenge posed to national authorities by this newly emerging threat, the aforementioned Operational Guidelines advise them to use the available Internet tools and expertise to find means of confronting it.[71] These Guidelines also refer to the *Basic Actions concerning Cultural Objects being offered for Sale over the Internet*, jointly developed by the International Criminal Poice Organization (INTERPOL), UNESCO, and the International Council of Museums (ICOM) in 2006,[72] and note

[66] *Blood Antiquities* (Journeyman TV 2010), a television documentary on the illegal smuggling of Afghanistan's cultural heritage to finance terrorism and the Taliban.

[67] Meg Lambert and Donna Yates, 'Crime, Controversy and the Comments Section: Discussing Archaeological Looting, Trafficking, and the Illicit Antiquities Trade Online' (2015) Internet Archaeology 39 <http://intarch.ac.uk/journal/issue39/index.html> accessed 1 December 2017.

[68] ibid.

[69] Brodie and others (n 6).

[70] UNESCO, *Operational Guidelines for the Implementation of the Convention on the Means of Prohibiting and Preventing the Illicit Import, Export and Transfer of Ownership of Cultural Property (UNESCO, Paris, 1970)* (2017) <www.unesco.org/new/fileadmin/MULTIMEDIA/HQ/CLT/pdf/OPERATIONAL_GUIDELINES_EN_FINAL_FINAL.pdf> accessed 18 April 2018, para 2.

[71] The Operational Guidelines advise Member States 'to marshal the support of all Internet providers and promote the supervision by the public (specialists or other individuals interested in particular cultures) to be vigilant concerning Internet offers'. ibid, para 69.

[72] ibid, paras 69 and 70.

the 'need to consider ways and means to keep improving' them or to explore 'other ways to contribute to countering the illicit sale of cultural property through the Internet'.[73] Examples of national databases for publicizing stolen cultural property include the Carabinieri National Stolen Cultural Property Database (Italy), the Antiquities sites Database (Jordan), and the National Stolen Art File (United States).[74]

International databases also provide a powerful tool for preventing trafficking in cultural property, providing evidence in court cases, and as the basis for police action. INTERPOL has established the Stolen Works of Art database, which, by March 2018, contained around 51,000 records submitted by 125 countries. Approximately 2,000 stolen items have been recovered since the database was created.[75] In 2003, UNESCO and INTERPOL also jointly established a database for stolen Iraqi cultural property.[76]

B. The 2003 Palermo Convention

Adopted by a UN General Assembly Resolution in 2000,[77] the Palermo Convention is the main international treaty for combating transnational organized crime. It has secured 189 Parties,[78] which shows a real determination on the part of States to address the challenges associated with transnational organized criminality. Even if trafficking in cultural property may not be the leading priority,[79] the adoption of the 2000 Palermo Convention does demonstrate the importance now accorded to this growing problem. In view of the nature of the transnational crimes it addresses, its dual-track approach based on national measures and international cooperation provides an effective framework for challenging such crimes, including cultural property trafficking. Since criminal networks often use established routes and operations for different types of trafficking, this

[73] ibid, para 70.

[74] UNESCO, 'Illicit Trafficking of Cultural Property: Databases' <www.unesco.org/new/en/culture/themes/illicit-trafficking-of-cultural-property/databases/> accessed 12 March 2017.

[75] UNESCO/INTERPOL Special Arrangement in Accordance with Article 4(4) of the Cooperation Agreement (8 July 2003 <https://www.interpol.int/Search-Page?search=UNESCO> accessed 30 January 2020.

[76] UNESCO, 'Stolen Cultural Property Database' <http://portal.unesco.org/culture/en/ev.php-URL_ID=17373&URL_DO=DO_PRINTPAGE&URL_SECTION=201.html> accessed 12 March 2017.

[77] UNGA Res 55/25 (15 November 2000) UN Doc A/RES/55/25.

[78] Details on the treaty status are online at <https://treaties.un.org/Pages/ViewDetails.aspx?src=TREATY&mtdsg_no=XVIII-12&chapter=18&lang=en> accessed 21 April 2018.

[79] Two Protocols were adopted with the treaty, namely the Protocol to Prevent, Suppress and Punish Trafficking in Persons, especially Women and Children and the Protocol against the Smuggling of Migrants by Land, Sea and Air, both adopted by UN General Assembly Resolution 55/25 (15 November 2000) UN Doc A/RES/55/25. The Protocol against the Illicit Manufacturing of and Trafficking in Firearms, their Parts and Components and Ammunition, was later adopted by UN General Assembly Resolution 55/255 (31 May 2001) UN DOC A/RES/55/255.

treaty can be effective in reducing the illegal trade in cultural objects, both directly and indirectly.

The stated purpose of the treaty is 'to promote cooperation to prevent and combat transnational organized crime more effectively'.[80] According to the UNODC, which oversees the treaty's implementation, the convention is aimed at addressing a number of emerging transnational crimes that include trafficking in cultural property.[81] Notably, the treaty's drafters were not required to set out the specific crimes that would be targeted by its provisions, yet they did so and identified trafficking in cultural property as one. In the first few years after the Palermo Convention entered into force in 2003, however, cultural property trafficking was largely ignored by the States Parties, who focused instead on applying the Convention to such higher priority crimes as human trafficking, illegal movement of hazardous waste, and drugs and arms trafficking.[82]

Some years on from its adoption, however, the application of the 2000 Palermo Convention to cultural property trafficking has become more important. During the 2010 Conference of the Parties to the Palermo Convention, the States Parties announced a list of 'emerging' crimes on which the Parties should focus in the short term that included trafficking in cultural property.[83] Conference speakers noted that 'globalization and interconnectivity had contributed to the expansion of transnational organized criminal groups, allowing them to gain power, adapt their modus operandi and operate beyond national borders' and that their activities included increased trafficking in cultural property, as well as cybercrime, piracy, environmental crime, and other contemporary challenges.[84] Also in 2010, UNODC noted that cultural objects in source countries were subject to illegal 'removal', namely looting and theft, and that these objects were subsequently smuggled to rich market countries.[85]

[80] Palermo Convention, art 1.

[81] 'The Conference of the Parties to [UNODC] … identified cybercrime, identity-related crimes, trafficking in cultural property, environmental crime, piracy, organ trafficking, and fraudulent medicine as new and emerging crimes of concern.' UNODC, 'Emerging Crimes' <https://www.unodc.org/unodc/en/organized-crime/intro/emerging-crimes.html> accessed 2 December 2017. In Resolution 5/7 of the Conference of the Parties on *Combating Transnational Organized Crime against Cultural Property* (2010), it was stated that 'the Convention should be fully used for the purpose of combating criminal offences against cultural property, including by exploring other possible normative developments, when appropriate' (Preamble, recital 4).

[82] Conference of the Parties to the United Nations Convention against Transnational Organized Crime, 'Report of the Conference of the Parties to the United Nations Convention against Transnational Organized Crime adopted at its 5th session, held in Vienna from 18 to 22 October 2010' UN Doc CTOC/COP/2010/1 (2 December 2010).

[83] ibid.

[84] ibid, paras 24 and 25. Paragraph 12 notes, 'There is also evidence that transnational trafficking in antiquities is linked to other illicit activities in which organized criminal groups are involved, including drugs and arms smuggling, violence, corruption and money-laundering.'

[85] ECOSOC, Discussion Guide for the Thematic Discussion on Protection against Trafficking in Cultural Property: Note by the Secretariat, UN Doc E/CN.15/2010/6 (23 February 2010) para 11; Conference of the Parties to the United Nations Convention against Transnational Organized Crime, 'Use of the United Nations Convention against Transnational Organized Crime for Protection against

The approach taken in the Palermo Convention consists of three central pillars. First, the treaty requires States Parties to create domestic criminal offenses covering participation in an organized criminal group, money laundering, corruption, and obstruction of justice, all of which can be material to cases involving trafficked cultural property.[86] Second, it encourages and facilitates the adoption of the frameworks vital to international cooperation, which include extradition agreements, mutual legal assistance (MLA), and cooperation between law enforcement bodies through joint investigations.[87] Third, it promotes training and technical assistance for building the capacity of national authorities.[88] The whole approach of this treaty is therefore firmly based on the principle of international cooperation and in developing a number of means through which such cooperation can be achieved and improved, especially between national law enforcement and judicial bodies. Such efforts would occur in parallel with the strengthening of national legislative and administrative measures to prevent organized criminal activities.

The 2000 Palermo Convention operates, therefore, by targeting a number of different transnational organized crimes that require a specific framework of international cooperation to respond to them.[89] For the first pillar, it sets out criteria for criminal activity that are key to understanding the way the Convention operates and its applicability to any form of criminal activity, including trafficking in cultural property. To activate the Convention's provisions, the treaty specifies that the action in question must first qualify as *all* of the following:

1) an activity of an 'organized criminal group', which is defined as a 'structured group of three or more persons, existing for a period of time and acting in concert with the aim of committing one or more serious crimes';[90]
2) a transnational crime that is committed in more than one State or involves more than one State in its planning, commission, or effects;[91]
3) a 'serious crime', which is defined in terms of the penalty that it would incur, namely 'conduct constituting an offence punishable by a maximum deprivation of liberty of at least four years or a more serious penalty'.[92]

Trafficking in Cultural Property: Note by the Secretariat', UN Doc CTOC/COP/2010/12 (13 August 2010) para 30(e).

[86] Palermo Convention, arts 5, 6, 7, 8, and 23.
[87] ibid, arts 13, 16, 18, and 19.
[88] ibid, art 29.
[89] ibid, art 1. Article 1 sets out its purpose as to: 'promote cooperation to prevent and combat transnational organized crime more effectively'.
[90] ibid, art 2(a).
[91] ibid, art 2(b).
[92] ibid.

The Palermo Convention then enumerates the acts that it characterizes as criminal. These include the offense of participating in an organized criminal group,[93] which is understood to involve either (a) agreeing with one or more other persons to commit a serious crime for financial or other material benefit or (b) knowingly taking part in the criminal or related activities of an organized criminal group with a view to contributing to their criminal aim. This characterization of participation allows for the different approaches that may be taken toward conspiracy, association, and other criminal activities. Such approaches include criminalizing the laundering of the proceeds of crime and criminalizing the act of corruption, as well as taking the necessary measures to combat these activities, and treating any related obstruction of justice as a criminal act.[94] The Palermo Convention further provides that legal persons should be held liable for participating in the aforementioned serious crimes[95] and for seizure of the proceeds of these crimes, or property of an equivalent value, as well as of any 'property, equipment or other instrumentalities used in or destined for use in offences'.[96] Importantly, jurisdiction under the Convention can be asserted on all three jurisdictional bases, namely territorial, flag State, and nationality.[97]

The second pillar of the treaty involves developing the frameworks vital to international cooperation, including extradition agreements, MLA, and cooperation between law enforcement bodies. The adoption of such mechanisms operates in parallel with the domestic measures that Parties must establish to prevent the commission of transnational crimes and associated criminal organizations from operating. This cooperation is primarily through MLA, which can apply across many different types of crime, including criminal offenses relating to cultural property, and which can involve: taking evidence or statements from persons; executing searches and seizures; providing information and evidence; and any other type of assistance that is not contrary to the domestic law of the requested state.[98] The other main forms of international cooperation envisaged in the Convention are joint investigations, extradition, transfer of sentenced persons, cooperation between law enforcement bodies, and international cooperation for the seizure and confiscation of property and equipment.[99]

In 2012, the UNODC canvassed States Parties to the treaty and found that the Convention has not yet been widely applied to cases involving trafficking in cultural property.[100] A number of reasons were cited, in particular the lack of harmonized

[93] ibid, art 5.
[94] ibid, arts 6–9, and 23, respectively.
[95] ibid, art 10.
[96] ibid, art 12.
[97] ibid, art 15.
[98] ibid, art 18(3). With twenty-nine subparagraphs, this provision comprises a major component of the treaty's approach.
[99] ibid, arts 16, 17, 19, and 27.
[100] Conference of the Parties to the United Nations Convention against Transnational Organized Crime, Application of the United Nations Convention against Transnational Organized Crime by States

criminal legislation. Another reason was the failure to employ the aforementioned criteria in domestic legislation dealing with cultural property crime, especially that for a 'serious crime'. As a consequence, 'many countries do not generally apply [the Convention] to cases involving trafficking in cultural property'.[101]

UNODC can play a valuable role in improving this situation by providing its Member States with the necessary technical assistance for applying the Convention to trafficking in cultural property, developing national legislative responses to cultural property crime, setting up a web portal with tools for dealing with such criminality, and enhancing international cooperation. Member States have also tasked UNODC with the collection, analysis, and dissemination of data on cultural property crime as a transnational organized crime through its Crime Trends Survey. Collating data should constitute a fundamental approach toward addressing criminal activities with regard to cultural property, by analogy to the collating of corollary data for trafficking in endangered fauna and flora within the framework of the 1973 CITES Convention.[102]

C. Complementary International Regimes for Countering Illegal Movement of Cultural Objects as an International Crime

As a further UNODC instrument that can support implementation of the Palermo Convention through bilateral cooperation, the UNODC developed a Model Treaty on Mutual Assistance in Criminal Matters.[103] This instrument is primarily aimed at ensuring more effective international cooperation for the control of criminality, viewing 'a model treaty on mutual assistance in criminal matters as an effective way of dealing with the complex aspects and serious consequences of crime, especially in its new forms and dimensions'.[104]

In view of the fact that much transnational criminal activity directly involves customs violations, the World Customs Organization (WCO) has also developed a model bilateral agreement for providing mutual customs assistance.[105]

Parties with Respect to Criminal Offences against Cultural Property: Report of the Secretariat (31 July 2012) UN Doc CTOC/COP/WG.2/2012/3.

[101] ibid, para 32.

[102] This collating of data has been undertaken both by the Secretariat to CITES and by TRAFFIC, an international NGO. Such data has shown, for example, that South Africa in the 1980s underestimated the exports (licit and illicit) of ivory to East Asia by a factor of ten. See Simon Lyster, *International Wildlife Law* (OUP 1989, reprinted 2000).

[103] United Nations Model Treaty on Mutual Assistance in Criminal Matters (adopted by UNGA Res 45/117 on14 December 1994, amended by UNGA Res 53/112 on 9 December 1998) UN Doc A/RES/45/11.

[104] Preamble, at the tenth recital.

[105] World Customs Organization, Model Bilateral Agreement on Mutual Customs Assistance (as revised June 2004).

This agreement provides the means for administrative assistance in such areas as classification and origin, thus assisting the fight against transnational organized crime across borders. The Commentary to this Model Agreement notes that it complements the 2000 Palermo Convention 'in the area of mutual administrative assistance in Customs matters' just as that Convention provides for MLA.[106] This observation underlines the fact that the cooperation required to combat transnational crime against cultural property is not the domain of any single intergovernmental body.

Hence, the United Nations Economic and Social Council (ECOSOC) organized a series of meetings on the question of crime prevention and criminal justice responses to cultural property trafficking[107] and has encouraged UNODC 'to continue to contribute to the cooperative network established among the UNESCO, ICOM, INTERPOL, UNIDROIT, and WCO in the areas of trafficking in cultural property'.[108] The UN General Assembly has also adopted a Resolution that contains Guidelines for preventing trafficking in cultural property and providing appropriate criminal justice responses to the challenge it poses.[109] In this resolution, the UN body expresses its alarm

> at the growing involvement of organized criminal groups in all forms and aspects of trafficking in cultural property and related offences, and observing that ... such property is being unlawfully excavated and illicitly exported or imported with the facilitation of modern and sophisticated technologies.[110]

As further evidence supporting the view that a purely cultural heritage approach to this challenge is not sufficient alone, the Council of Europe in May 2017 adopted the Convention on Offences Relating to Cultural Property (2017 Nicosia Convention).[111] This new Convention is the sole international treaty to focus on criminal measures and sanctions specifically for illicit activities relating to cultural property. As such, it bridges the gap between the 1970 UNESCO Convention and the 1995 UNIDROIT Convention, which again concentrates on international co-operation for the return and restitution of stolen and illegally exported cultural items (and prevention of theft and illegal export through internal measures), and the 2000 Palermo Convention, which addresses a range of transnational crimes

[106] ibid 2.

[107] Including its fifth plenary held on this topic in July 2010, see ECOSOC, 'Crime Prevention and Criminal Justice Responses to Protect Cultural Property, Especially with Regard to its Trafficking' (22 July 2010) UN Doc 2010/19.

[108] ibid, para 17.

[109] UN General Assembly Resolution 69/196 (18 December 2014) UN Doc A/RES/69/196.

[110] ibid, Preamble, recital 4.

[111] Council of Europe Convention on Offences relating to Cultural Property (adopted 19 May 2017) (2017) CETS 221 (2017 Nicosia Convention).

and is not specifically targeted toward trafficking in cultural property.[112] Indeed, the 2017 Nicosia Convention sets out the challenge that it is intended to address, namely: growth in the number of offenses related to cultural property, and the concomitant destruction of the world's cultural heritage; the sale, in different ways, of unlawfully excavated and illicitly exported or imported cultural property, including over the Internet;[113] and the role played by organized crime in the trafficking of cultural property.[114] Moreover, the 2017 Nicosia Convention expresses concern that terrorist groups are not only deliberately destroying cultural heritage, but also using the trafficking of cultural property as a source of financing their activities, a concern confirmed more recently by a recent Resolution of the UN Security Council adopted in 2016.[115]

In view of these newly emerging threats, the 2017 Nicosia Convention sets out criminal sanctions and replaces the earlier European Convention on Offences relating to Cultural Property (1985 Delphi Convention),[116] serving as 'a criminal law convention to prevent and combat the intentional destruction of, damage to, and trafficking in cultural property by strengthening criminal justice responses while facilitating co-operation on an international level'.[117] The twin purposes of

[112] The Council of Europe's *Explanatory Report* makes this point: 'As none of these international instruments deal with criminal law issues, the Convention thereby enhances law enforcement capacity by requiring State Parties to implement several important provisions concerning cultural property into their criminal law, further ensuring the ability to investigate, prosecute, sentence and/or extradite persons suspected or convicted of offences falling under the ambit of the Convention.' Council of Europe, *Explanatory Report to the Council of Europe Convention on Offences relating to Cultural Property*, para 12 <https://rm.coe.int/1680710437> accessed 12 March 2017.

[113] According to the Council of Europe, *Explanatory Report*, ibid, para 3:

> [T]rafficking of cultural property is, by its nature, a transnational phenomenon with artefacts often being trafficked through organised crime networks. The black market trade in antiquities, art and artefacts by unscrupulous dealers who do not care about the illicit provenance of such cultural objects can end up funding corruption, terrorism, violence and other crimes. After arms and drugs trafficking, according to some estimates, the illicit trade in cultural objects is one of the most profitable forms of transnational organised crime.

[114] Preamble.

[115] UN Security Council Resolution 2322 (2016) urges States 'to develop, including, upon request, with the assistance of UNODC and in close cooperation with UNESCO and INTERPOL, broad law enforcement and judicial cooperation in preventing and combating all forms and aspects of trafficking in cultural property and related offences' and 'to introduce effective national measures at the legislative and operational levels ... to prevent and combat trafficking in cultural property and related offences'. UNSC Res 2322 (2016) UN Doc S/RES/2322, para 12. See also Patty Gerstenblith, 'The Disposition of Movable Cultural Heritage' (Ch 1) in this volume, for detailed discussion of the financing issues.

[116] Council of Europe Convention on Offences relating to Cultural Property (adopted 23 June 1985) CETS 119 (Delphi Convention). Other treaties mentioned are: European Cultural Convention (adopted in Paris on 19 December 1954) (1954) CETS 18; European Convention on the Protection of the Archaeological Heritage (adopted in London on 6 July 1969) (1969) CETS 66, as revised, CETS 143 (Valetta Convention); Convention for the Protection of the Architectural Heritage of Europe (1985) CETS 121 (Granada Convention); Framework Convention on the Value of Cultural Heritage for Society (2005) CETS 199 (Faro Convention); Convention on Mutual Assistance in Criminal Matters (adopted in Strasbourg on 20 April 1959 (1959) CETS 30; and the Convention on Extradition (adopted in Paris on 13 December 1957) (1957) CETS 24. The last two demonstrate newer thinking in this area, to include an international criminal law approach alongside one based more broadly on international cultural cooperation.

[117] Council of Europe, *Explanatory Report* (n 112) para 12.

the Convention are to protect cultural property by preventing and fighting against criminal activity and to strengthen international cooperation among States Parties to this end.[118] Its scope is limited to tangible items of cultural heritage, either movable or immovable. Movable cultural property should be defined or designated 'as being of importance for archaeology, prehistory, ethnology, history, literature, art or science' and must also fall into one of several enumerated categories; immovable cultural property must either be defined or designated 'as being of importance for archaeology, prehistory, ethnology, history, art or science' or be listed on the World Heritage List established by the 1972 World Heritage Convention.[119]

The essential substantive criminal law provisions are complementary to each other and are aimed at criminalizing the different elements of the crime of trafficking in cultural property:

1) theft and the other forms of unlawful appropriation of movable cultural property;[120]
2) unlawful excavation and removal, requiring Parties to criminalize the excavation of movable cultural property and its unlawful retention and of unauthorized excavation on land or underwater (including by clandestine diggers and treasure hunters);[121]
3) illegal importation of cultural property;[122]
4) illegal exportation of cultural property which should be criminalized under their domestic law when such export is prohibited or done without authorization;[123]
5) the acquisition of cultural property that has been stolen or unlawfully excavated, imported or exported (as per Articles 3, 4, 5, or 6);[124]
6) the placing on sale of cultural property that has been stolen or unlawfully excavated, imported or exported (as per Articles 3, 4, 5, or 6);[125] and

[118] Nicosia Convention, art 1(1), para 2, establishes a follow-up mechanism for effective implementation of the Convention.

[119] ibid, art 2(e).

[120] ibid, art 3.

[121] ibid, art 4.

[122] ibid, art 5, based on the presumption that a Party has put domestic legislation in place prohibiting importation of cultural property stolen or excavated or exported in violation of the export law of another State, in cases where the offender knew of the unlawful provenance of the cultural property.

[123] ibid, art 6. Paragraph 2 requires State Parties to consider taking additional measures in respect of illegally imported movable cultural property in order to prevent the onward export of such movable cultural property and in response to the increasing threat from trafficking in cultural items.

[124] ibid, art 7. As noted in Council of Europe, *Explanatory Report* (n 112) para 55, the definition given for 'acquisition' is broad and covers not only traditional forms of transfer of ownership, such as antique shops and auction houses, but also acquisition through donation, exchange, online markets, and social networks. Parties should require a higher level of due diligence from professional dealers and other experts than is expected of non-experts (para 2).

[125] ibid, art 8. The term 'placing on the market' is understood to include supplying illicitly traded cultural property and publicly offering such cultural property for sale and, as under Art.7, States Parties should criminalize such actions according to the level of due diligence regarding provenance they expect from experts.

7) the falsification of and tampering with documents relating to the origin and ownership history of movable cultural property.[126]

As noted, the 2017 Nicosia Convention also responds to a newer threat to cultural property, namely its unlawful destruction or damage especially by terrorist groups, as experienced especially in Mali, Syria, and Iraq in the five years preceding the treaty's adoption.

As with the Palermo Convention, the Nicosia Convention operates on the international and national levels in a way that seeks to create a synergy between the two. Hence, States Parties are required to establish jurisdiction[127] over the offenses covered in the Convention, at minimum criminalizing these offenses and giving their courts competence to try them,[128] and they have a legal ability to act domestically if they refuse to extradite a person on the basis of one of these offenses.[129] Some general principles governing international cooperation in criminal matters are also set out, including the relationship with other international law[130] and providing mutual assistance in criminal matters and extradition.[131]

The 2017 Nicosia Convention further sets out measures for the prevention of criminal activity and other administrative measures at the national and international levels.[132] At the national level, the States Parties must criminalize, under their domestic law, (a) the removal of movable or immovable cultural property without the owner's consent with a view to exporting, importing, or placing it on the market, and (b) intentionally aiding or abetting a criminal offense under the Convention.[133] The States Parties must adopt legislative and other necessary measures.[134] As a basic step, the cultural property in question must be inventoried and States Parties must facilitate sending out alerts over a particular cultural property at risk of being subject to trafficking. Both state and private cultural institutions also should be prevented from acquiring protected cultural property, and persons involved in the cultural property trade should show due diligence, such as keeping

[126] ibid, art 9.

[127] ibid, art 12. The jurisdictional bases applied include territorial, flag State, and nationality according to Art 12(1)(a)–(d).

[128] ibid, art 12. Parties may make reservations to this article and the bases set out here are not exhaustive.

[129] ibid, art 12(2).

[130] ibid, art 19(1) mentions the Convention on Extradition (ETS No 24), the Convention on Mutual Assistance in Criminal Matters (ETS No 30), the Convention on the Transfer of Sentenced Persons (ETS No 112), the Convention on Laundering, Search, Seizure and Confiscation of the Proceeds from Crime (ETS No 141), and the Convention on Laundering, Search, Seizure and Confiscation of the proceeds from Crime and on the Financing of Terrorism (CETS No 198) as well as the Palermo Convention.

[131] Nicosia Convention, art 19(2). This takes a similar approach to the Palermo Convention.

[132] ibid, arts 20 and 21, respectively.

[133] ibid, art 11. States Parties may reserve the right not to apply this provision, or to apply only in specific cases or conditions and its application should be proportional when distinguishing between an 'attempt' and preparatory acts that should not be treated as criminal acts.

[134] As set out in art 20(a)–(l).

records. Import and export certificates should be employed as a tool against trafficking,[135] and measures should be taken to ensure that free ports are not used to store cultural property that has been stolen, unlawfully appropriated, excavated, imported, or exported.[136] In recognition of the growing threat of this trade, national authorities should be enabled to monitor existing Internet platforms and Internet providers, and platforms and all actors involved in online sales should be required to take the necessary proactive measures.

To strengthen powers of investigation, these measures may be undertaken without a prior complaint, and sufficient expertise should also be available to professionals responsible for criminal proceedings concerning offenses relating to cultural property.[137] Sanctions and measures for offenses must be 'effective, proportionate and dissuasive'.[138] Hence, available remedies include imprisonment and/or monetary sanctions for individuals, as well as administrative sanctions or civil liability for other legal persons.[139] This treaty also provides for the seizure and confiscation of any vessels, tools, or other instrumentalities used to commit offenses, as well as any proceeds from these offenses or property of an equivalent value.[140] Moreover, the sanctions can take into account aggravating circumstances,[141] provided that they are not part of the constituent elements of the offense.

Taken together, the Palermo and Nicosia Conventions thus represent an important part of the global response to trafficking in cultural property by organized criminal groups. Their benefits include taking a broad and flexible view of what constitutes a transnational offense, what an organized criminal group is, and what constitutes serious crime. In addition, they provide for building national capacities to combat this growing threat, as well as developing better international cooperation mechanisms that should make individual States and the international community better equipped to deal with it. Although protection of cultural property should primarily be regarded as a cultural matter, and diplomacy litigation and other routes must always be pursued and strengthened, these are not sufficient alone. Addressing trafficking in cultural property as a transnational crime, in view

[135] As under CITES for species listed in Appendices I and II.

[136] In *Autocephalous Greek Orthodox Church of Cyprus v Goldberg* (n 46), a stolen mosaic changed hands in the Free Zone of Zurich Airport.

[137] Nicosia Convention, arts 17–18.

[138] Wording applied in both paras 1 and 2.

[139] Other measures which could be taken in respect of legal persons under art14(2) include: temporary or permanent disqualification from commercial activities; exclusion from entitlement to public benefits or aid; placing under judicial supervision; or a judicial winding-up order. See Council of Europe, *Explanatory Report* (n 112) para 89.

[140] Nicosia Convention, art 14, para 3.

[141] Article 15(2)(a)–(d) refers, inter alia, to abuse of trust placed by professionals, offenses committed by public officials responsible for the conservation or the protection of movable or immovable cultural property, offenses committed by a criminal organization, and offenses by repeat offenders. Article 16 allows for sentences passed by another party to be taken into account in assessing a sentence, a relatively new approach in international criminal law.

of its similarities with other such criminal activities, will continue to be a major legal tool for preventing and mitigating the impacts of this illicit trade.

Conclusion

Since the 1950s, the international community has attempted to provide an international legal framework to prevent criminal trafficking in cultural property and to facilitate the return of stolen, illicitly excavated, and/or illegally exported and traded cultural property. At first, this framework was seen as an adjunct to other damage to cultural heritage in the event of armed conflict and duly addressed within the framework of the 1954 Hague Convention on the Protection of Cultural Property in the Event of Armed Conflict.[142]

Subsequently, the historic despoliation of the cultural heritage of the newly independent countries of Asia and Africa by the colonial powers was seen to require redress. At the same time, the continued looting of the cultural wealth of poorer countries called for a response from the international community. The 1970 UNESCO Convention represented an attempt to resolve the sometimes-conflicting interests of source and market States. This treaty has been responsible for the return of many items of cultural heritage that are of importance to their country of origin, but its primarily diplomatic character was seen by many governments as insufficient against private dealers and collectors, museums, and even governments that proved reluctant to return stolen or illegally exported cultural objects. Hence, the 1995 UNIDROIT Convention was developed to facilitate international litigation for the return of cultural property and, again, to establish an appropriate balance between the multiple interests involved, even if this has not secured sufficient participation by market States Parties to be fully effective.

More recently, the trafficking of cultural property as a transnational criminal activity (and the associated theft, illegal excavation, and other illicit activities) has emerged as a major global challenge that is part of a wider challenge of combatting transnational organized crime. Because trafficking in cultural heritage can be linked to financing major terrorist activities, and may be conducted along the same routes and with the same criminal personnel as human trafficking, it can no longer be viewed simply as a challenge for cultural heritage law. The cultural heritage protection approach should be viewed as part of a wider picture of national and international efforts to address this serious form of international criminality.

[142] Convention for the Protection of Cultural Property in the Event of Armed Conflict (adopted 14 May 1954, entered into force 7 Aug 1956) 249 UNTS 240 (1954 Hague Convention); Protocol for the Protection of Cultural Property in the Event of Armed Conflict (adopted 14 May 1954, entered into force 7 Aug 1956) 249 UNTS 358 (1954 First Protocol).

PART III

THE UNITED NATIONS SYSTEM AND THE PROTECTION OF CULTURAL HERITAGE

The role of the United Nations (UN) and its bodies and specialized agencies feature throughout this volume, as they have acted as principal drivers for many of the developments that have occurred at various intersections of international cultural heritage law and public international law. Nonetheless, this part presents in-depth examinations of the distinct roles played by several actors within the UN system in the protection of cultural heritage: UNESCO, the UN Security Council, the UN Human Rights Council, and the International Court of Justice (ICJ).

In his chapter on the role of UNESCO, Guido Carducci, former Chief of the International Standards Section at UNESCO, explores how the cultural arm of the United Nations has served both to elaborate and implement international law for the protection of art, cultural property, and cultural heritage.[1] He begins by observing that international cultural heritage law has emerged relatively recently and has adopted several of the same values, trends, sources, and techniques as other areas of public international law. Nonetheless, he stresses that cultural heritage law also contains its own developments, such as specific rules governing post-conflict restitution. Moreover, UNESCO has codified and affirmed principles in the context of cultural heritage protection, such as universal jurisdiction, and thus fostered the development of those same principles outside a cultural heritage-specific context. The role of UNESCO in this process, he notes, takes several forms, including (but by no means limited to) facilitating intergovernmental negotiation of both conventional and soft law instruments, providing a forum for international discourse, and assisting in defining the scope of property covered by the relevant instruments. Carducci also discusses the collaborative approach UNESCO takes with other parts of the UN system, such as the UN Security Council, and other

[1] Guido Carducci, 'The Role of UNESCO in the Elaboration and Implementation of International Art, Cultural Property, and Heritage Law' in Anne-Marie Carstens and Elizabeth Varner (eds), *Intersections in International Cultural Heritage Law* (OUP 2020) (Ch 7).

international legal regimes. Finally, he notes that UNESCO plays a critical role in the implementation of cultural heritage law—which he emphasizes is distinct and separate from the role played by the Member States themselves—such as by setting up and maintaining reporting mechanisms or even by establishing committees to pursue implementation directives, such as the World Heritage Committee.

Kristin Hausler then examines two different UN bodies that have increasingly responded to threats to cultural heritage, but that have also viewed those threats through different lenses: the UN Security Council and the UN Human Rights Council.[2] She observes that the UN Security Council has addressed the destruction of cultural heritage, particularly in Syria and Iraq, as constituting a threat to international peace and security. The UN Human Rights Council and the Special Rapporteur in the Field of Cultural Rights, on the other hand, view such destruction as endangering human rights. Adopting a human rights-based approach for the protection of cultural heritage, she concludes, would help move the protective regime away from an object-centric focus and helpfully toward a more holistic regime that recognizes the connection between individuals and cultural objects.

In the final chapter, Gabriele Gagliani addresses the role played by the International Court of Justice (ICJ) in adjudicating cultural heritage-related public international law issues that extend well beyond the much-discussed territorial dispute between Cambodia and Thailand concerning the Temple of Preah Vihear, a UNESCO World Heritage site.[3] Gagliani observes that although the ICJ has not often been called upon to decide disputes that directly implicate cultural heritage as their primary object, cultural rights or other cultural heritage-related issues have nonetheless formed an undercurrent in several cases in the Court's jurisprudence. The Court has confronted several cases concerning access to and enjoyment of tangible and intangible cultural heritage, for example, in which the cultural heritage issues are framed as 'customary rights' or 'historic rights'. Gagliani additionally points to cases in which the Court considered the interests of indigenous communities in deciding questions concerning 'the right to self-determination' or considered long-standing cultural customs and practices in deciding territorial disputes, among others.

Anne-Marie Carstens and Elizabeth Varner

[2] Kristin Hausler, 'The UN Security Council, the Human Rights Council, and the Protection of Cultural Heritage: A Matter of Peace and Security, Human Rights, or Both?' in Anne-Marie Carstens and Elizabeth Varner (eds), *Intersections in International Cultural Heritage Law* (OUP 2020) (Ch 8).

[3] Gabriele Gagliani, 'The International Court of Justice and Cultural Heritage: International Cultural Heritage Law Through the Lenses of the World Court Jurisprudence?' in Anne-Marie Carstens and Elizabeth Varner (eds), *Intersections in International Cultural Heritage Law* (OUP 2020) (Ch 9).

7

The Role of UNESCO in the Elaboration and Implementation of International Art, Cultural Property, and Heritage Law

Guido Carducci

Introduction

This chapter aims to define the relevant context and focus on three essential terms, the UNESCO 'role', the 'elaboration', and the 'implementation' of international art, cultural property, and heritage law. Several monographs would be necessary (i) to analyze in detail each of UNESCO's legal instruments on culture; and (ii) to measure their impact, both when they were first adopted and currently, on international law, primarily treaty law and possibly on customary law, then on national law. Indeed, such UNESCO instruments are numerous and, in their legal nature, belong to both hard (binding) and soft (non-binding) law.

I. The Main UNESCO Conventions

Considering here only the former, the list of major binding UNESCO instruments includes the following multilateral instruments, in reverse chronological order:

- 2005 Convention on the Protection and Promotion of the Diversity of Cultural Expressions[1]
- 2003 Convention for the Safeguarding of the Intangible Cultural Heritage (2003 Intangible Cultural Heritage Convention)[2]
- 2001 Convention on the Protection of the Underwater Cultural Heritage (2001 Underwater Cultural Heritage Convention)[3]

[1] Convention on the Protection and Promotion of the Diversity of Cultural Expressions (adopted 20 October 2005, entered into force 18 March 2007) 2440 UNTS 311.

[2] Convention for the Safeguarding of the Intangible Cultural Heritage (adopted 17 October 2003 entered into force 20 April 2006) 2368 UNTS 3 (2003 Intangible Cultural Heritage Convention).

[3] Convention on the Protection of the Underwater Cultural Heritage (adopted 2 November 2001, entered into force 2 January 2009) 2562 UNTS 3 (2001 Underwater Cultural Heritage Convention).

Guido Carducci, The Role of UNESCO in the Elaboration and Implementation of International Art, Cultural Property, and Heritage Law In: *Intersections in International Cultural Heritage Law*. Edited by Anne-Marie Carstens and Elizabeth Varner. © Oxford University Press 2020. The several contributors DOI: 10.1093/oso/9780198846291.003.0008

- 1972 Convention Concerning the Protection of the World Cultural and Natural Heritage (1972 World Heritage Convention)[4]
- 1971 Universal Copyright Convention, as revised at Paris on 24 July 1971, with Appendix Declaration relating to Article XVII and Resolution concerning Article XI[5]
- 1970 Convention on the Means of Prohibiting and Preventing the Illicit Import, Export and Transfer of Ownership of Cultural Property (1970 UNESCO Convention)[6]
- 1954 Convention for the Protection of Cultural Property in the Event of Armed Conflict with Regulations for the Execution of the Convention (1954 Hague Convention), and First and Second Protocols[7]
- 1952 Universal Copyright Convention, with Appendix Declaration relating to Articles XVII and Resolution concerning Article XI[8]
- 1950 Agreement on the Importation of Educational, Scientific and Cultural Materials, with Annexes A to E and Protocol annexed[9]

II. Terminology

Some preliminary terminological observations seem necessary. The above-mentioned treaties do not have the term 'art' in their titles. Does it mean that 'art' is not covered by these treaties? It depends on the definitions retained in the treaty by its drafters—in principle the experts of Member States.

Outside the law, in common use the terms 'art', 'cultural property', and 'heritage' are, with some approximation, at times perceived or used as synonyms, unless the user has a particular knowledge or understanding of these terms, which leads to diversification. Among other elements, for instance, time certainly plays a role in distinguishing terminologies. Adding 'contemporary' to art could detach art, in

[4] Convention Concerning the Protection of the World Cultural and Natural Heritage (open for signature 16 November 1972, entered into force 15 December 1975) 1037 UNTS 151 (1972 World Heritage Convention).

[5] Universal Copyright Convention (revised version adopted 24 July 1971, entered into force 10 July 1974) 943 UNTS 178.

[6] Convention on the Means of Prohibiting and Preventing the Illicit Import, Export and Transfer of Ownership of Cultural Property (adopted 14 November 1970, entered into force 24 April 1972) 823 UNTS 231 (1970 UNESCO Convention).

[7] Convention for the Protection of Cultural Property in the Event of Armed Conflict (adopted 14 May 1954, entered into force 7 August 1956) 249 UNTS 240 (1954 Hague Convention); Protocol for the Protection of Cultural Property in the Event of Armed Conflict (adopted 14 May 1954, entered into force 7 August 1956) 249 UNTS 358 (1954 First Protocol); Second Protocol to the Hague Convention of 1954 for the Protection of Cultural Property in the Event of Armed Conflict (adopted 26 March 1999, entered into force 9 March 2004) 253 UNTS 172 (1999 Second Protocol).

[8] Universal Copyright Convention (adopted 6 September 1952, entered into force 16 September 1955) 216 UNTS 132.

[9] Agreement on the Importation of Educational, Scientific and Cultural Materials (adopted 17 June 1950) and Protocol (adopted 26 November 1976).

the minds of many, from cultural property and heritage, which are generally associated with time and history. The term 'heritage' leads also toward immovable sites, while property is common for movables and objects of an historical and/or cultural significance. Other features distinguish, from different perspectives, art, cultural property, and heritage.

When one turns to the legal value and significance of the terms 'art', 'cultural property', and 'heritage', what matters is the definition and the legal consequences that the legislation in each country has retained for 'art', cultural 'property', and 'heritage', no longer the user's, or a perceived common understanding of the term. Depending on the country and its legislation, or on international law if it is applicable and provides such distinctions in an instrument, art, cultural property, and heritage carry the legal definition and significance of the national legislation or of the applicable (if any) international law instrument. It follows, inter alia, that the term 'art' could take different forms and either be excluded (though rarely) from or included in the term 'cultural property', depending on the definition of the two notions in national and international law.

In spite of the idea of universalism in art and in culture, in the legal world the rules and their definitions are relative and may well vary from country to country or over time. In more unusual and extreme cases, the same object could be defined and protected at law as 'cultural property' in country A, but not in country B.

III. Interactions with International Law

This chapter is part of the entire volume whose main objective is to explore and discuss the interactions between the development of international cultural property and heritage law and international law. Focusing on such interactions, the following features of international cultural property and heritage law are to be noted:

- It has appeared relatively recently and was codified progressively starting from the first codifications of international law.
- It is part of international law and, as such, has naturally adopted the same leading values, trends, sources of law, and legal techniques. As to sources, within UNESCO treaties are the main source of international cultural property and heritage law, through the numerous UNESCO Conventions. Secondary sources are the UNESCO Recommendations or Declarations that codify soft law rules.
- It has known its own developments in international customary law. In the practice of States, the first forms of customary developments in the Renaissance consisted in a progressive distinction of art, understood broadly, from the international law (essentially the law of war at the time) governing ordinary objects. At a later stage, a complex and stimulating issue was, and

remains to some extent, the determination of the precise content and of the date of appearance of a rule of international customary law imposing the restitution of cultural property taken during an (international) armed conflict.[10] Those developments in international customary law that the international community within UNESCO regarded as well established and rooted in customary rules were then naturally codified in UNESCO instruments.

- It has, at times, retained and affirmed in the field of culture, and even codified in a multilateral treaty, a principle whose recognition was thus reinforced generally in international law, well beyond the specificity of art and culture. An interesting example is the so-called 'Universal Jurisdiction'. Indeed, States Parties to the 1999 Second Protocol to the 1954 Hague Convention shall take the necessary legislative measures to establish their jurisdiction over several serious offenses against cultural property under enhanced protection,[11] when such an offense is committed, not only in the territory of the State Party or by a national of that State, but also when the alleged offender is present in that State's territory.

IV. The Role of UNESCO

As with other international organizations, UNESCO's Constitution defines the Organization's purpose, essentially:

> to contribute to peace and security by promoting collaboration among the nations through education, science and culture in order to further universal respect for justice, for the rule of law and for the human rights and fundamental freedoms which are affirmed for the peoples of the world, without distinction of race, sex, language or religion, by the Charter of the United Nations.[12]

To realize this institutional purpose, UNESCO is, inter alia, to maintain, increase, and diffuse knowledge, 'by assuring the conservation and protection of

[10] On such determination, see Guido Carducci, 'L'obligation de restitution des biens culturels et des objets d'art en cas de conflit armé: droit coutumier et droit conventionnel, avant et après la Convention de La Haye de 1954. L'importance du facteur temporel dans les rapports entre les traités et la coutume' (2000) 104 Rev Générale de Droit Intl Public 288–357.

[11] Second Protocol (n 7) art 15. This obligation applies to the following offenses:

a. making cultural property under enhanced protection the object of attack;
b. using cultural property under enhanced protection or its immediate surroundings in support of military action; [and]
c. extensive destruction or appropriation of cultural property protected under the Convention and this Protocol.

[12] Constitution of the United Nations Educational, Scientific and Cultural Organization (adopted 16 November 1945, entered into force 4 November 1946) art I(1), para 1.

the world's inheritance of books, works of art, and monuments of history and science, and by recommending to the nations concerned the necessary international conventions'.[13]

Recommending international conventions to the nations concerned implies, firstly, intergovernmental negotiation and the adoption of such conventions. UNESCO represents the institutional and obvious forum within the system of the United Nations for this normative effort in cultural, educational, and scientific matters. In greater detail, in culture as in other sectors within its mandate, UNESCO's role in international standard-setting includes:

- collecting globally, through Member States, data as to the identification of new concerns, in the broad sense, and the desirability of new international legal instruments addressing such concerns;
- providing Member States with a suitable forum allowing them to identify and discuss globally such new concerns, and decide at the Headquarters in Paris whether to request the Secretariat to prepare a first draft of a legal instrument addressing the concerns, to be submitted to the attention of Member States;
- initiating, upon request of Member States if they regard the concerns and the Secretariat's first draft worthy to be further considered, an intergovernmental negotiation of a new legal instrument, either of hard law as a convention or protocol, or of soft law as a recommendation or declaration. Member States decide the form, the scope of application, and the content (provisions) of the instrument;
- adopting the instrument if Member States are satisfied with the outcome of the negotiation. Once adopted, the draft instrument becomes a UNESCO legal instrument. Depending on its typology the adopted instrument has its legal status and effects under international law. For instance, under the law of treaties, a treaty, and therefore a UNESCO Convention:
    - is binding and must be performed in good faith only when it is in force and only by the Parties to it;
    - is non-retroactive and thus non-applicable to acts or facts that took place before its entry into force, unless the treaty otherwise provides.

A new instrument can be completed in a shorter or longer period depending on various factors, mainly the sector (culture, education, science), the existence or not of a preliminary instrument in an interrelated sector (or at least of preliminary studies), and the kind and the degree of complexity of the issue, or underlying concern. For instance, the period of the negotiation and

[13] ibid, art I(b).

adoption of the 2003 Intangible Cultural Heritage Convention[14] was rather short. This has been possible also thanks to the adoption by UNESCO on 15 November 1989 of a Recommendation on the Safeguarding of Traditional Culture and Folklore,[15] and to the experience gained on such safeguarding in the countries that implemented the Recommendation. Such experience enabled experts to focus on the weaknesses of the Recommendation when the international community decided to upgrade the safeguarding of the intangible cultural heritage (ICH) by adopting a hard-law instrument, the multilateral Convention, in 2003.

Conversely, the negotiation of other UNESCO Conventions could not rely on an earlier UNESCO instrument in the same, or in a closely related, field. A clear example is the 2001 Convention on the Protection of the Underwater Cultural Heritage. Although the 1956 UNESCO Recommendation on International Principles Applicable to Archaeological Excavations[16] has proved a useful and then innovative instrument with regard to any research aimed at the discovery of objects of archaeological character, whether by means of digging of the ground or systematic exploration of its surface or of the bed or in the subsoil of inland or territorial waters of a Member State,[17] it is undisputed that the 1982 United Nations Convention on the Law of the Sea (UN Law of the Sea Convention, or UNCLOS)[18] was the most relevant international instrument, though not specific to underwater cultural heritage. Its articles 149 and 303 were the norms later regarded as too mild for an effective protection of such heritage[19] when the international community decided to negotiate and adopt within UNESCO an international convention specifically on the protection of the underwater cultural heritage, entailing a higher threshold of protection.[20]

The term 'international standards' may prove misleading at times. A variety of such standards exists at present in a variety of sectors and industries. However, if the focus is on intergovernmental international standards then standard-setting is by normative international instruments and States are the key actors. Member States are naturally the driving force, first collectively, in making and adopting new UNESCO international legal instruments, then individually, in making them

[14] 2003 Intangible Cultural Heritage Convention (n 2).

[15] Recommendation on the Safeguarding of Traditional Culture and Folklore (adopted 15 November 1989).

[16] UNESCO Recommendation on International Principles Applicable to Archaeological Excavations (adopted 5 December 1956).

[17] ibid, art 1.

[18] United Nations Convention on the Law of the Sea (adopted 10 December 1982, entered into force 16 November 1994) 1833 UNTS 397 (1982 Law of the Sea Convention, or UNCLOS).

[19] See generally, Anastasia Strati, *The Protection of the Underwater Cultural Heritage: An Emerging Objective of the Contemporary Law of the Sea* (Martinus Nijhoff 1995).

[20] Various articles are available in Tullio Scovazzi and Guido Camarda (eds), *The Protection of the Underwater Cultural Heritage* (Giuffrè 2002).

'binding' if a hard law instrument is at stake, as a convention, and a State decides to be bound by it.

UNESCO is an international organization, with its own legal entity, distinct from its Member States. When one refers to a treaty as a 'UNESCO Convention' it is meant generally that the treaty was negotiated, in principle in Paris,[21] and adopted by Member States within UNESCO. It does not mean that the treaty is negotiated and concluded by, and later binds upon, UNESCO as an organization that is distinct from Member States.

V. UNESCO's Role in the Elaboration of International Cultural Property and Heritage Law

As clarified above, UNESCO's role in the elaboration of international cultural property and heritage law is the result of the Member States' intergovernmental negotiation and adoption of the instrument, with the assistance of the Secretariat. The elaboration implies many decisions by Member States, as to form, scope, and, above all, content of each provision of the instrument.

Some selected examples of issues that Member States have to decide upon are illustrated below.

A. From Ordinary Property to Identifying, Defining, and Protecting Cultural Property

Nowadays, the terms 'cultural property' and 'heritage' are common. Nevertheless, it took several centuries before these two terms emerged as distinct, through a slow process distinguishing, first, 'art' and 'art objects' from ordinary property, and later, 'cultural' property and heritage from the broad term of 'art'. The 1954 Hague Convention and its First Protocol, adopted on the same day, are the first treaties to adopt an articulated definition of 'cultural property' in international law. So reads the Convention's definition:

> For the purposes of the present Convention, the term 'cultural property' shall cover, irrespective of origin or ownership:
>
> (a) movable or immovable property of great importance to the cultural heritage of every people, such as monuments of architecture, art or history, whether religious or secular; archaeological sites; groups of buildings which, as a whole, are of historical or artistic interest; works of art; manuscripts, books

[21] Unless Member States decide otherwise.

and other objects of artistic, historical or archaeological interest; as well as scientific collections and important collections of books or archives or of reproductions of the property defined above;

(b) buildings whose main and effective purpose is to preserve or exhibit the movable cultural property defined in sub-paragraph (a) such as museums, large libraries and depositories of archives, and refuges intended to shelter, in the event of armed conflict, the movable cultural property defined in sub-paragraph (a);

(c) centers containing a large amount of cultural property as defined in sub-paragraphs (a) and (b), to be known as 'centers containing monuments'.[22]

It is common in legal instruments, whether in national, EU, or international law, that definitions concentrate in a few lines several key words and determine the instrument's scope of application. For instance, this definition in the 1954 Hague Convention not only includes movables, immovable structures, and centers, but it makes irrelevant both the 'origin', whether religious or secular, and the 'ownership', whether private or public, of cultural property. Thus, some key preliminary questions are solved—are the provisions of the Convention suitable to all such cultural properties?—and have removed some uncertainties—as to the Convention's scope of application (*ratione materiae*)—that existed in the past, or still exist under instruments containing a less detailed definition.

Once the cultural property or heritage at stake is defined, Member States design and negotiate the provisions that they regard as best suited to protect the property or heritage at stake in each UNESCO instrument, and whether it has the form of a Convention, Protocol, Recommendation, or Declaration. This is, in essence, the international significance of each UNESCO instrument.

B. All-Encompassing or 'Selective' Instruments of Protection?

An old debate underlies the question whether all cultural property or heritage, or only the portion of it that has a greater cultural significance, should be covered by national legislation and, in international law, by UNESCO's legal instruments. The debate is known in each part of culture and heritage. The only reasonable and reliable answer at law from a general standpoint is that the suitable balance between the two extremes (all versus some property) is determined, case by case, either by Parliament or the Government in each country as to national law and with regard to the property located in its territory, or by States acting collectively

[22] 1954 Hague Convention (n 7) art 1.

when they negotiate and adopt an international legal instrument on cultural property.

Member States that have drafted UNESCO's instruments have adopted both positions over the years, depending on the type of property at stake, and the scope and objectives of the instrument.

The 'all property' position, without a given threshold of cultural significance, is found, for instance, in the 1970 UNESCO Convention.[23] Its definition reads:

> For the purposes of this Convention, the term 'cultural property' means property which, on religious or secular grounds, is specifically designated by each State as being of importance for archaeology, prehistory, history, literature, art or science and which belongs to the following categories:
> (a) rare collections and specimens of fauna, flora, minerals and anatomy, and objects of paleontological interest;
> (b) property relating to history, including the history of science and technology and military and social history, to the life of national leaders, thinkers, scientists and artist and to events of national importance;
> (c) products of archaeological excavations (including regular and clandestine) or of archaeological discoveries;
> (d) elements of artistic or historical monuments or archaeological sites which have been dismembered;
> (e) antiquities more than one hundred years old, such as inscriptions, coins and engraved seals;
> (f) objects of ethnological interest;
> (g) property of artistic interest, such as:
> (i) pictures, paintings and drawings produced entirely by hand on any support and in any material (excluding industrial designs and manufactured articles decorated by hand);
> (ii) original works of statuary art and sculpture in any material;
> (iii) original engravings, prints and lithographs;
> (iv) original artistic assemblages and montages in any material;
> (h) rare manuscripts and incunabula, old books, documents and publications of special interest (historical, artistic, scientific, literary, etc.) singly or in collections;
> (i) postage, revenue and similar stamps, singly or in collections;
> (j) archives, including sound, photographic and cinematographic archives;
> (k) articles of furniture more than one hundred years old and old musical instruments.[24]

[23] 1970 UNESCO Convention (n 6).
[24] ibid, art 1.

Having retained the 'all property' position, this definition lacks a 'threshold' or minimum cultural significance of property, below which the Convention would not apply to the property. However, a closer look at the definition shows that in addition to belonging to one of these categories, the 'cultural property' is such under the Convention if it has been specifically designated by each State as being of importance for archaeology, prehistory, history, literature, art, or science. And such specific designation, whose practice the Convention leaves to Member States, requires some degree of significance for the property at stake.

The other approach is openly selective and addresses solely cultural property or heritage that not only belongs to one or more categories of property listed in the treaty, but also captures a given degree of cultural significance. UNESCO Member States have developed this approach in three main variations.

A first variation was adopted in the 1954 Hague Convention, with its Regulations for the Execution of the Convention. It addresses only cultural property which is movable or immovable property of great importance to the cultural heritage of every people.[25]

A second variation was adopted in the 1972 World Heritage Convention, which covers only monuments, groups of buildings, and sites of outstanding universal value and, in addition, adopts a list system.[26] The Convention applies to such heritage of outstanding universal value which is inserted in the 'World Heritage List,' or exceptionally in the 'list of World Heritage in Danger'.[27] The Convention wisely distinguishes the requirement of an outstanding universal value from the insertion on these lists by clarifying that the fact that a cultural or (natural) heritage has not been included in either of the two lists does not mean that it does not have an outstanding universal value for purposes other than those resulting from inclusion in these lists.[28]

A third variation in setting up a selective treaty and protection system was adopted more recently in the 2003 Intangible Cultural Heritage Convention.[29] Also, this Convention has adopted a two-list system, the 'Representative List of the Intangible Cultural Heritage of Humanity' and the 'List of Intangible Cultural Heritage in Need of Urgent Safeguarding'.[30] However, its definition of ICH does not require a particular degree of cultural significance.[31] This feature reflects also the self-evident difference between tangible and intangible cultural heritage and how the identification and the legal protection are more direct, ordinary, and effective, as to the former, tangible property, be it movable or immovable.

[25] 1954 Hague Convention (n 7) art 1.
[26] 1972 World Heritage Convention.
[27] ibid, art 11.
[28] ibid, art 12.
[29] 2003 Intangible Cultural Heritage Convention (n 2).
[30] ibid, arts 16–17.
[31] ibid, art 2.

Conversely, as the Convention's definition clarifies, intangible cultural heritage

i) means the practices, representations, expressions, knowledge, skills—as well as the instruments, objects, artefacts and cultural spaces associated therewith—that communities, groups and, in some cases, individuals recognize as part of their cultural heritage. This intangible cultural heritage, transmitted from generation to generation, is constantly recreated by communities and groups in response to their environment, their interaction with nature and their history, and provides them with a sense of identity and continuity, thus promoting respect for cultural diversity and human creativity. For the purposes of this Convention, consideration will be given solely to such intangible cultural heritage as is compatible with existing international human rights instruments, as well as with the requirements of mutual respect among communities, groups and individuals, and of sustainable development; [and]

ii) is manifested inter alia in the following domains:
   (a) oral traditions and expressions, including language as a vehicle of the intangible cultural heritage;
   (b) performing arts;
   (c) social practices, rituals and festive events;
   (d) knowledge and practices concerning nature and the universe; [and]
   (e) traditional craftsmanship.[32]

C. Relationships between UNESCO Conventions and the Codification of International Law

Among the thousands of existing treaties, whether bilateral or multilateral, the great majority of treaties govern only the rights and obligations of the States Parties. Some treaties are meant to 'codify' international law, and under Article 13 of the Charter of the United Nations (UN Charter), the General Assembly is mandated to encourage its progressive development and codification.[33] Under its Statute, the International Law Commission (ILC) is to promote the progressive development of international law and its codification, primarily in public international law, and possibly in private international law.[34]

UNESCO Conventions progressively codify international cultural and property law at the multilateral level. Outside UNESCO's standard-setting activity, at

[32] ibid.

[33] Charter of the United Nations (adopted 26 June 1945, entered into force 24 October 1945) 1 UNTS XVI, art 13, para 1(a) (UN Charter).

[34] Statute of the International Law Commission (adopted 21 November 1947) UNGA Res 174(II) art 1.

times the 'general' codification of international law has codified rules concerning, directly or indirectly, cultural property or heritage. So did, rather indirectly, the UN Law of the Sea Convention with regard to underwater cultural heritage.[35] This is why, some twenty years later, when the international community of States adopted within UNESCO a *lex specialis*, the 2001 Underwater Cultural Heritage Convention,[36] it clarified its relationships with the *lex generalis* of the law of the sea, UNCLOS, and excluded that the new Convention may prejudice the rights, jurisdiction, and duties of States under international law, including UNCLOS, and set the principle that it shall be interpreted and applied in the context of and in a manner consistent with international law, including UNCLOS.[37]

This provision concerns interpretation, while the 2001 Underwater Cultural Heritage Convention naturally provides provisions specific to underwater cultural heritage as distinct from UNCLOS. An example among others is the regime of law of finds and salvage law, which is in principle declared non-applicable to underwater cultural property law under the UNESCO Convention,[38] while UNCLOS did not affect the ordinary operation of the law of salvage as to archaeological and historical objects found at sea.[39]

D. Relationships between UNESCO Conventions and International Customary Law

Treaty law and customary law are two distinct sources of international law. Each source operates under its conditions and with its legal effects. This distinction is one of principle and should not allow confusion between the two sources. The current focus within the ILC is on the 'identification of customary international law' and seeks a proper identification of the 'potential sources of evidence of customary law'.[40] Such identification of potential sources of evidence does not replace, and in principle facilitates, the necessary preliminary determination of whether a rule of customary law exists, in principle by evidence of the traditional requirements of State practice and *opinio juris*.

This being noted for the sake of clarity, any UNESCO Convention may intervene in a field of international cultural property and heritage law in which international

[35] UN Law of the Sea Convention (n 18) arts 149, 303.

[36] Guido Carducci, 'New Developments in the Law of the Sea: the UNESCO Convention on the Protection of Underwater Cultural Heritage' (2002) 96 AJIL 419–34; Roberta Garabello and Tullio Scovazzi (eds), *The Protection of the Underwater Cultural Heritage (Before and After the 2001 UNESCO Convention)* (Martinus Nijhoff 2003).

[37] 2001 Underwater Cultural Heritage Convention (n 3) art 3.

[38] ibid, art 4.

[39] Guido Carducci, 'The Crucial Compromise on Salvage Law and the Law of Finds' in Roberta Garabello and Tullio Scovazzi (eds), *The Protection of the Underwater Cultural Heritage (Before and After the 2001 UNESCO Convention)* (Martinus Nijhoff 2003) 193–206.

[40] See 70th session of the International Law Commission (2018) UN Doc A/CN.4/710, para 6.

customary law was developing or is formed and exists, and may thus codify such customary rules in the way the drafters of the Convention identify the rules. One example, is the sensitive issue of whether, and since when, international customary law exists so as to impose upon States the obligation to return cultural property removed during an (international) armed conflict.[41] At present, the only UNESCO instrument in force with provisions on this issue is the First Protocol to the 1954 Hague Convention.[42]

Summarizing here several complex issues, it is a fact that States decided to deal with the sensitive issue of restitution only in the First Protocol and not in the main Convention, knowing that the former was distinct from the latter and subject to a separate ratification. Pragmatically, any hesitation on this issue and fewer ratifications of the First Protocol would thus not affect the objective of a widely ratified Convention outside this issue. This fact seems to confirm that in 1954 the international community of States did not feel that general international customary law was firmly established and clearly imposed upon the generality of States a well-defined obligation to return cultural property removed during an armed conflict.[43]

E. The Growing Diversification of the Sources of International Cultural Property and Heritage Law: The Example of the United Nations (UN) Security Council

Composed of fifteen Members, the UN Security Council has primary responsibility for the maintenance of international peace and security and operates under Chapter V of the UN Charter.[44] Its decisions are binding and Members of the United Nations agree to accept and carry them out in accordance with the Charter.[45]

The role of UNESCO implies naturally cooperation within the UN system and may extend to drawing the attention of the UN Security Council to issues that are within the Council's mandate and relate to the protection of cultural property or heritage. The Security Council decides independently and under its own rules whether to include and deal with such issues in a resolution.

Three clear and interesting examples of positive decisions by the Council that include express reference to cultural property and to the role UNESCO are: UN Security Resolution 1483, adopted 22 May 2003; UN Security Resolution 2199, adopted 12 February 2015; and UN Security Council Resolution 2347, adopted

[41] See Patty Gerstenblith, 'The Disposition of Movable Cultural Heritage' (Ch 1) in this volume.
[42] First Protocol (n 7).
[43] For a detailed historical perspective, Carducci, 'L'obligation de restitution des biens culturels ' (n 10).
[44] UN Charter, ch V.
[45] ibid, art 25.

24 March 2017.[46] Resolution 1483, adopted in response to reports of looting during and following international conflict in Iraq in the early 1990s and again from 2003, not only referred specifically to the need for Member States to take steps to facilitate the return of Iraqi cultural property and related items, but also called upon UNESCO to assist in this effort. Its paragraph 7 provides that the UN Security Council:

> Decides that all Member States shall take appropriate steps to facilitate the safe return to Iraqi institutions of Iraqi cultural property and other items of archaeological, historical, cultural, rare scientific, and religious importance illegally removed from the Iraq National Museum, the National Library, and other locations in Iraq since the adoption of resolution 661 (1990) of 6 August 1990, including by establishing a prohibition on trade in or transfer of such items and items with respect to which reasonable suspicion exists that they have been illegally removed, and *calls upon the United Nations Educational, Scientific, and Cultural Organization, Interpol, and other international organizations, as appropriate, to assist in the implementation of this paragraph*.[47]

Resolution 2199, adopted in the wake of reports of widespread destruction in both Syria and Iraq, contained three paragraphs dedicated to cultural heritage by condemning its destruction and noting concern for the looting and smuggling of cultural property, as well as again calling on UNESCO to assist in efforts by Member States. Its paragraphs on 'Cultural Heritage' so read that the UN Security Council:

> 15. *Condemns* the destruction of cultural heritage in Iraq and Syria particularly by ISIL and ANF, whether such destruction is incidental or deliberate, including targeted destruction of religious sites and objects;
>
> 16. *Notes with concern* that ISIL, ANF and other individuals, groups, undertakings and entities associated with Al-Qaida, are generating income from engaging directly or indirectly in the looting and smuggling of cultural heritage items from archaeological sites, museums, libraries, archives, and other sites in Iraq and Syria, which is being used to support their recruitment efforts and strengthen their operational capability to organize and carry out terrorist attacks; [and]
>
> 17. *Reaffirms* its decision in paragraph 7 of resolution 1483 (2003) and *decides* that all Member States shall take appropriate steps to prevent the trade in Iraqi and Syrian cultural property and other items of archaeological, historical, cultural, rare scientific, and religious importance illegally removed from Iraq since 6

[46] UNSC Res 1483 (22 May 2003) UN Doc S/RES/1483; UNSC Res 2199 (12 February 2015) UN Doc S/RES/2199; UNSC Res 2347 (24 March 2017) UN Doc S/RES/2347.

[47] UNSC Res 1483 (22 May 2003) UN Doc S/RES/1483 para 7 (emphasis added).

> August 1990 and from Syria since 15 March 2011, including by prohibiting cross-border trade in such items, thereby allowing for their eventual safe return to the Iraqi and Syrian people and *calls upon the United Nations Educational, Scientific, and Cultural Organization, Interpol, and other international organizations, as appropriate, to assist in the implementation of this paragraph*[.][48]

Resolution 2347, which was adopted after reports that the Islamic State in Iraq and the Levant, Al-Qaida, and associated Parties were engaging in looting and smuggling of cultural property to finance terrorism activities, calls upon UNESCO to assist Member States in protecting cultural property, as with the earlier resolutions. Yet Resolution 2347 notes and supports many more of UNESCO's functions, beginning at the outset of the resolution with an invitation to the UNESCO Director-General 'to elaborate on an action plan in order to implement' UNESCO's strategy for protecting culture and promoting cultural pluralism during armed conflict.[49] It then notes additional responsibilities of UNESCO, including:

i. Welcoming the 'central role played by UNESCO in protecting cultural heritage and promoting culture as an instrument to bring people closer together and foster dialogue';[50]
ii. Urging Member States to develop, with assistance of the United Nations Office of Drugs and Crime (UNODC) and in cooperation with UNESCO and INTERPOL, law enforcement and judicial efforts to prevent and counter 'trafficking in cultural property and related offences that benefit or may benefit organized criminal groups, terrorists or terrorist groups';[51]
iii. Welcoming UNESCO's actions to 'safeguard and preserve cultural heritage in peril and actions for the protection of culture and the promotion of cultural pluralism' during armed conflict;[52]
iv. Encouraging Member States to enhance cooperation 'through joint initiatives within the scope of relevant UNESCO programmes';[53]
v. Taking note of 'the UNESCO Heritage emergency fund' and encouraging Member States to provide financial support, fight against illicit trafficking of cultural property, and assist in recovery of cultural heritage, 'in the spirit of the principles of the UNESCO Conventions';[54]

[48] UNSC Res 2199 (12 February 2015) UN Doc S/RES/2199 paras 15–17 (emphasis added with respect to the role of UNESCO in assisting Member States).
[49] UNSC Res 2347 (24 March 2017) UN Doc S/RES/2347 preamble, 2nd recital.
[50] ibid, preamble, 14th recital.
[51] ibid, para 11. See also Janet Blake, 'Trafficking in Cultural Property: Where Cultural Heritage Law and the International Fight against Transnational Organized Crime Coincide' (Ch 6) of this volume.
[52] UNSC Res 2347 (24 March 2017) UN Doc S/RES/2347, para 13.
[53] ibid, para 14.
[54] ibid, para 15.

vi. Encouraging Member States 'to take preventive measures to safeguard their nationally owned cultural property and their other cultural property of national importance in the context of armed conflicts' with reference to 'the draft UNESCO Action Plan, which contains several suggestions to facilitate these activities';[55]
vii. Encouraging Member States, 'in order to prevent and counter trafficking of cultural property illegally appropriated and exported in the context of armed conflicts, notably by terrorist groups', inter alia to use and contribute to the UNESCO Database of National Cultural Heritage Laws;[56]
viii. Affirming that UN peacekeeping operations mandated by the UN Security Council may assist relevant authorities 'in the protection of cultural heritage from destruction, illicit excavation, looting and smuggling in the content of armed conflicts, in collaboration with UNESCO';[57]
ix. Calling upon UNESCO and other international organizations 'to assist Member States in their efforts to prevent and counter destruction and looting of and trafficking in cultural property in all forms';[58] and
x. Requesting that the UN Secretary-General, with the support of UNESCO and other relevant monitoring teams and UN bodies, submit a report on the implementation of Resolution 2347 before the end of 2017.[59]

All three Resolutions are clear examples of how the importance of the protection of cultural property and heritage from various threats, including looting or destruction, can lead to the adoption of normative instruments, and sometimes interrelated instruments,[60] adopted within the system of the United Nations, not by UNESCO. Nevertheless, UNESCO plays in principle a role, in various ways, in the process. A Security Council Resolution has its own legal status under the UN Charter. It remains distinct from the ordinary UNESCO international standard-setting instruments and thus contributes directly to the growing diversification of the sources of international cultural property and heritage law.[61] At the same time, these Resolutions acknowledge the role played by UNESCO in assisting Member States and facilitating the protection of cultural property.

[55] ibid, para 16.
[56] ibid, para 17(f).
[57] ibid, para 19.
[58] ibid, para 20.
[59] ibid, para 22.
[60] UN Security Resolution 2199 refers expressly to UN Security Resolution 1483.
[61] On such growing diversification of the sources and its consequences, Guido Carducci, 'The Growing Complexity of International Art Law: Conflict of Laws, Uniform Law, Mandatory Rules, UNSC Resolutions and EU Regulations' in Barbara T Hoffman (ed), *Art and Cultural Heritage: Law, Policy and Practice* (CUP 2005) 68–86

F. Relationships between Public and Private International Law in the UNESCO Conventions

UNESCO Conventions are treaties, naturally public international law instruments. UNESCO Conventions do touch upon public and private law situations or relationships. A distinction between the two s necessary.

As to the latter, one example is when the 1970 UNESCO Convention considers the acquisition in good faith of a stolen and/or illegally exported cultural property. UNESCO Conventions touch upon private law situations or relationships by substantive rules. They do not contain rules of private international law, meaning conflict of laws rules designate the law applicable, and thus govern, the private law situations or relationships having an international character. One instance is the acquisition in London by an American collector of a painting sold by a French collector, gallery, or museum. The lack of any conflict of laws rules in the Convention leaves unaffected, in case of litigation, the operation of the tribunal's rules on conflict of laws. Such operation is particularly relevant as to the complex issues of restitution of stolen and/or illegally exported cultural property that international art trade regularly raises to the attention of the public. Such issues include whether the good faith purchaser has acquired title and/or is entitled to compensation for acquisition in the country where possession was lost[62] or elsewhere.[63]

VI. Implementation of International Cultural Property and Heritage Law

In the legal world, the terms of implementation and enforcement are distinct, both in national and international law. The former refers to making a given legal provision effective, ensuring its application, in its legal system. The latter assumes a non-compliance with the provision by its addressee and compels obedience to it. An example is a court compelling a party to pay a given amount or return a chattel.

This distinction is naturally relevant with regard to the UNESCO Conventions. These are binding upon their States Parties, and they are in charge, at the national level, of their implementation and, where necessary, enforcement. Under international law, as the ILC has confirmed,[64] a State commits an internationally

[62] On private international law and its interactions with the UNESCO and UNIDROIT Conventions and the EU Regulation and Directive, Guido Carducci, *La restitution internationale des objets d'art et des biens culturels volés ou illicitement exportés. Droit commun, Directive CEE, Conventions d'Unesco et d'Unidroit* (LGDJ 1997).

[63] Guido Carducci, 'Acquisition a non domino, prescription acquisitive, possession vaut titre, conflit mobile et circulation d'une res extra commercium (droit commun des biens et droit des biens culturels)' (2015) 1 Travaux du Comité Français de Droit Intl Privé 137–82.

[64] ILC, Draft Articles on Responsibility of States for Internationally Wrongful Acts (2001) (Annex to UNGA Res 56/83 of 12 December 2001, and corrected by UN Doc A/56/49(Vol. I)/Corr.4) arts 1, 2.

wrongful act entailing its international responsibility each time that its action or omission constitutes a breach of an international obligation—including the obligation arising out of a treaty in force—of the State and is attributable to it under international law.

Like other international organizations, UNESCO is a legal entity in itself, distinct from its Member States. UNESCO is not bound as such by a 'UNESCO' Convention, that is, a treaty that Member States adopted within the General Conference. The implementation (and enforcement where necessary) of the UNESCO Convention or treaty by States Parties are their responsibility, not UNESCO's.

Usually the drafters of UNESCO Conventions set up a reporting system under which States Parties commit to report periodically. The reporting system can be organized and set up in different ways to obtain different levels of information and related control on States Parties' implementation of a treaty. Within the UNESCO instruments on culture, the reporting is to UNESCO,[65] or to an intergovernmental committee set up by a Convention,[66] or to the General Assembly of UNESCO and involving also an intergovernmental committee,[67] as to the implementation of the Convention at the national level. Depending on the subject matter and the scope of each Convention, such implementation reports include information as to implementing legislation and/or measures taken by government, primarily the Ministry of Culture, and/or decisions by national courts.

A variation concerning the implementation of a convention by States Parties may consist of setting up a Committee entitled to adopt its own implementation directives, self-evidently more detailed than the provisions of the convention. Indeed, the Convention Concerning the Protection of the World Cultural and Natural Heritage, which is the most ratified UNESCO treaty, has set up the World Heritage Committee, which stands as the main body in charge of the implementation of the Convention. Such Committee has developed over the years its Operational Guidelines, which are the criteria for the proper implementation of the Convention, in particular with regard to the inscription of properties on the World Heritage List and for the provision of international assistance under the World Heritage Fund.[68] The Guidelines represent a remarkable example of a flexible and in-progress tool assisting States Parties to better and more uniformly implement the Convention.[69] Self-evidently, the Guidelines do not replace the Convention itself, its authority and its binding nature upon States Parties. The Committee is also

[65] An example is the 1970 UNESCO Convention (n 6) art 16.

[66] An example is the 2003 Intangible Cultural Heritage Convention (n 2) arts 7, 29.

[67] An example is the 1972 World Heritage Convention, art 29.

[68] World Heritage Committee, *Operational Guidelines for the Implementation of the World Heritage Convention*, UNESCO Doc WHC.17/01 (12 July 2017).

[69] The Guidelines also assist other stakeholders, primarily the World Heritage Committee and Centre, the Advisory Bodies.

responsible for reviewing annually the state of conservation of properties on the List of World Heritage in Danger[70] and has established a procedure for the eventual deletion of properties from the World Heritage List.[71]

Conclusion

While implementation of treaties is in the hands, and under the responsibility, of States Parties, the greatest UNESCO contribution to international cultural property and heritage law is, since its inception, its normative and international standard-setting action. Such action invites currently 195 Member States to contribute directly to the intergovernmental negotiation of new instruments, by their cultural property and legal experts. The Member States participating in the negotiation undertake an in-depth analysis as to the identification of the international (hard or soft) law standards, ensuring a legal and material protection which is suitable and specific to each type of cultural property or heritage at stake. Such negotiation implies important discussions and decisions, with distinguished national experts, on a variety of legal and cultural issues. If the outcome of the negotiation is satisfactory for the majority of Member States, the agreed text is adopted as a UNESCO instrument (convention, recommendation or declaration) and gains its status under international law.

[70] 1972 World Heritage Convention, art 11(4).
[71] *Operational Guidelines* (n 68) para 192.

8

The UN Security Council, the Human Rights Council, and the Protection of Cultural Heritage

A Matter of Peace and Security, Human Rights, or Both?

*Kristin Hausler**

Introduction

In recent years, attacks against cultural heritage have often made headline news with the deliberate targeting by armed non-State actors (ANSAs) of high-profile sites, many of them bearing World Heritage status because of their 'outstanding universal value'. For example, in January 2017, during a brief period when the Islamic State of Iraq and the Levant (ISIL, or Daesh) regained control over Palmyra, the ancient site which has been inscribed on the World Heritage List since 1980 was again the object of attacks, with the tetrapylon being partially destroyed and parts of the ancient Roman amphitheater damaged.[1] This followed the 2015 destruction by ISIL of the 2,000-year-old Baalshamin Temple and the beheading of Palmyra's head of antiquities, Khaled al-Asaad, for his reported refusal to divulge the location of valuable hidden artifacts to his captors.[2]

Reacting to these attacks, the Security Council, the United Nations (UN) body that has primary responsibility for the maintenance of international peace and security, issued a press statement reaffirming 'grave concern for the protection of

* The author is thankful to John Grainger for having commented on an earlier draft of this chapter.

[1] UNESCO, 'News Release: UNESCO Director-General condemns destruction of the Tetrapylon and severe damage to the Theatre in Palmyra, a UNESCO World Heritage site' (20 January 2017) <https://whc.unesco.org/en/news/1620/> accessed 12 November 2018.

[2] UNESCO, 'News Release: Director-General Irina Bokova firmly condemns the destruction of Palmyra's ancient temple of Baalshamin, Syria' (24 August 2015) <https://en.unesco.org/news/director-general-irina-bokova-firmly-condemns-destruction-palmyra-s-ancient-temple-baalshamin> accessed 12 November 2018; UNESCO, 'News Release: Director-General Irina Bokova deplores the loss of two leading scholars of Syrian antiquity' (20 August 2015) <https://en.unesco.org/news/director-general-irina-bokova-deplores-loss-two-leading-scholars-syrian-antiquity> accessed 12 November 2018; <https://www.icomos.org/images/DOCUMENTS/Secretariat/2016/Memoire_Khaled_al_Asaad_18082016/Khaled_al_Asaad_Booklet_DGAM_2016.pdf> accessed 12 November 2018.

Kristin Hausler, The UN Security Council, the Human Rights Council, and the Protection of Cultural Heritage In: *Intersections in International Cultural Heritage Law*. Edited by Anne-Marie Carstens and Elizabeth Varner. © Oxford University Press 2020. The several contributors DOI: 10.1093/oso/9780198846291.003.0009

the World Heritage Site of Palmyra and the systematic campaign of destruction of cultural heritage in Syria by ISIL/Daesh'.[3] It also reiterated its 'condemnation of the destruction of cultural heritage in Syria by ISIL/Daesh, including targeted destruction of religious sites and objects, and noted with concern that ISIL and other individuals, groups, undertakings, and entities associated with Al-Qaida have generated income from engaging directly or indirectly in the looting and smuggling of cultural heritage items'.[4]

The partial destruction of the tetrapylon and damage to the theater in Palmyra in 2017 were also addressed by mechanisms established by the UN Human Rights Council, which seeks to promote and protect human rights around the world. These mechanisms include the Independent International Commission of Inquiry on the Syrian Arab Republic), which was established by the Human Rights Council in 2011 to investigate alleged violations of international human rights law in the country since March 2011.[5] In its first report, the Commission described the attack on the tetrapylon as 'a particular blow to Syrian culture as in addition to its historic value, the structure has been described by UNESCO as symbolising the spirit and openness of Palmyra'.[6] The Human Rights Council Advisory Committee referred to the Security Council's statement, further asking the Human Rights Council to 'take a more pro-active stance before this concerning trend and contribute to the debate to the intentional destruction of cultural heritage by highlighting the human rights related concerns and issues which are involved'.[7]

It is clear that in situations of armed conflict, the destruction of cultural monuments or sites can constitute a violation of international humanitarian law. Cultural objects are protected as a result of their civilian status, as well as through provisions that take into account their specific cultural value. According to the 1977 Additional Protocol I to the 1949 Geneva Conventions,[8] which applies in international armed conflicts, attacks against civilian objects are prohibited unless they have been turned into military objectives.[9] In addition, its Article 53 specifically provides that it is prohibited 'to commit any acts of hostility directed against the

[3] UNSC, Press Release: 'Security Council Press Statement on Destruction of Cultural Heritage, Executions in Palmyra', SC/12690 (20 January 2017) <https://www.un.org/press/en/2017/sc12690.doc.htm> accessed 12 November 2018.

[4] ibid.

[5] UNHRC, Res S-17/1 on Situation of human rights in the Syrian Arab Republic (22 August 2011) UN Doc A/HRC/S-17/2 (18 October 2011) para 13.

[6] UNHRC, Conference Room Paper of the Independent International Commission of Inquiry on the Syrian Arab Republic: Human Rights Abuses and International Humanitarian Law Violations in the Syrian Arab Republic, 21 July 2016–28 February 2017, UN Doc A/HRC/34/CRP.3 (10 March 2017) para 85. See also ibid, paras 84, 110.

[7] UNHRC Advisory Committee, Research Proposal: Destruction of Cultural Heritage and its Effects on the Enjoyment of Economic, Social and Cultural Rights (2017) UN Doc A/HRC/AC/18/2 (27 March 2017) Annex III.A, paras 3, 12.

[8] Protocol Additional to the Geneva Conventions of 12 August 1949, and Relating to the Protection of Victims of International Armed Conflicts (adopted 8 June 1977, adopted 12 December 1977, entered into force 7 December 1978) 1125 UNTS 3 (Additional Protocol I).

[9] ibid, art 52. However, it can be argued that art 13(1) is vague enough to encompass all civilian objects.

historic monuments, works of art or places of worship which constitute the cultural or spiritual heritage of peoples' and 'to use such objects in support of the military effort',[10] a prohibition that is reiterated in Article 16 of Additional Protocol II to the 1949 Geneva Conventions, which applies in non-international armed conflicts (NIAC).[11] Under the 1954 Hague Convention on the Protection of Cultural Property in the Event of Armed Conflict,[12] all Parties to a conflict, whether States or ANSAs must respect cultural property by refraining from exposing it to possible damage or destruction.[13] This includes a prohibition on using cultural property in a manner likely to cause it to become a military objective.[14] Therefore, attacks against cultural monuments or sites that are committed in the context of an armed conflict constitute a violation of humanitarian law, except in the case of imperative military necessity.[15]

As noted by the Human Rights Council Advisory Committee, the destruction of cultural heritage can also give rise to human rights concerns. Furthermore, both in situations of armed conflicts and in peacetime, the destruction of cultural heritage itself can amount to a violation of the human right to participate in cultural life, as enshrined in Article 15 of the 1966 International Covenant on Economic, Social and Cultural Rights (ICESCR),[16] which has been interpreted as including the right 'to benefit from the cultural heritage ... of other individuals and communities'.[17]

[10] ibid, art 53.

[11] Protocol Additional to the Geneva Conventions of 12 August 1949, and Relating to the Protection of Victims of Non-International Armed Conflicts (adopted 8 June 1977, opened for signature 12 December 1977, entered into force 7 December 1978) 1125 UNTS 609 (Additional Protocol II) art 16. Note that Additional Protocol I also prohibits making cultural objects the object of reprisals (art 53(c)) and considers that making clearly recognized historic monuments, works of art, or places of worship the object of attack and causing extensive destruction thereof, under certain circumstances, a grave breach of the Protocol (art 85(4)(d)). To qualify as a 'grave breach', the property must constitute the cultural or spiritual heritage of peoples and been given special protection by special arrangement (for example, within the framework of a competent international organization) and not been used militarily or located close to military objectives. ibid. However, neither of these provisions were adopted in Additional Protocol II.

[12] Convention for the Protection of Cultural Property in the Event of Armed Conflict (adopted 14 May 1954, entered into force 7 August 1956) 249 UNTS 240 (1954 Hague Convention).

[13] 1954 Hague Convention, arts 2, 3, 4(1), 7(1), and 7(2). See also Rule 40 of the International Committee of the Red Cross study on Customary International Humanitarian Law. Jean-Marie Henckaerts and Louise Doswald-Beck (eds), *Customary International Humanitarian Law* (CUP 2003) vol I (Rules), r 40 (ICRC, Customary IHL Study).

[14] 1954 Hague Convention, art 4; 1977 Additional Protocol I, art 53; and 1977 Additional Protocol II, art 16. See also ICRC, Customary IHL Study, r 39. For example, a mobile broadcasting infrastructure was placed next to a cultural heritage site in Iraq.

[15] 1954 Hague Convention, art 4(2).

[16] International Covenant on Economic, Social and Cultural Rights (adopted 16 December 1966, entered into force 3 January 1976) 999 UNTS 3, art 15 (ICESCR). Iraq, Mali, and Syria are among its 164 State Parties.

[17] UN Committee on Economic, Social and Cultural Rights (CESCR) General Comment No 21 on the right of everyone to take part in cultural life (ICESCR art 15, para 1(a)) (2–20 November 2009) UN Doc E/C.12/GC/21 (21 December 2009) para 15(b). For an extended discussion of the relationship of cultural heritage to the right to participate in cultural life, see Vanessa Tünsmeyer, 'Bridging the Gap Between International Human Rights and International Cultural Heritage Law Instruments: A Functions Approach' (Ch 13) in this volume.

As with all human rights treaties, State Parties to the ICESCR must respect, protect, and fulfil the rights contained therein.[18] According to the UN Committee on Economic, Social and Cultural Rights (CESCR), 'the obligation to respect [the right to take part in cultural life] includes the adoption of specific measures aimed at achieving respect for the right of everyone, individually or in association with others or within a community or group', to have access to their own cultural heritage 'and to that of others'.[19] The CESCR added that, in times of both peace and armed conflict, State Parties must '[r]espect and protect cultural heritage in all its forms':

> Cultural heritage must be preserved, developed, enriched and transmitted to future generations as a record of human experience and aspirations, in order to encourage creativity in all its diversity and to inspire a genuine dialogue between cultures. Such obligations include the care, preservation and restoration of historical sites, monuments, works of art and literary works, among others.[20]

This means that States must prohibit the willful destruction of cultural heritage.[21] The obligation to protect also means that States must apply due diligence and take measures to prevent third parties, including ANSAs, from interfering with the exercise of this right and from damaging or destroying cultural heritage.[22] In addition, ANSAs exercising governmental functions and control over a territory could also have to respect human rights norms, because individuals located on the territory in question would otherwise not benefit from any human rights protection.[23]

Given that the destruction of cultural heritage can not only amount to a violation of international humanitarian law but also of international human rights law, this chapter seeks to assess the efforts undertaken so far by the Human Rights

[18] See generally CESCR, General Comment No 3 on the Nature of States Parties' Obligations (ICESCR art 2, para 1) UN Doc E/1991/23 (14 December 1990) Annex 3; Tünsmeyer (n 17).

[19] CESCR, General Comment No 21 (n 17) para 49(d). The CESCR has also stated that this right entails an obligation for States Parties to adopt measures aimed at the preservation of 'mankind's cultural heritage', Revised General Guidelines Regarding the Form and Contents of Reports to the Submitted by States Parties under Articles 16 and 17 of the ICESCR: 17/06/91, UN Doc E/C.12/1991/1 (17 June 1991), with regard to Article 15 of the Covenant, para 1(d).

[20] CESCR, General Comment No 21 (n 17) para 50(a). See also art 7 of the 2001 UNESCO Universal Declaration on Cultural Diversity, which adopts the same language. Convention on the Protection and Promotion of the Diversity of Cultural Expressions (adopted 20 October 2005, entered into force 18 March 2007) 2440 UNTS 311, art 7.

[21] Roger O'Keefe, *The Protection of Cultural Heritage in Armed Conflict* (CUP 2006) 305.

[22] CESCR, General Comment No 21 (n 17) para 50.

[23] See Daragh Murray, *Human Rights Obligations of Non-State Armed Groups* (Hart 2016) 10. See also eg UNHRC, 'Report of the Special Rapporteur on Extrajudicial, Summary or Arbitrary Executions on Armed Non-State actors: The Protection of the Right to Life' (5 June 2018) A/HRC/38/44, in particular paras 9–18, which include Human Rights Council and Security Council resolutions pertaining to the human rights obligations of non-State actors. Note that the extent to which ANSAs have human rights obligations is the object of ongoing debate but that there is growing acceptance that those groups have at least to *respect* (if not protect and fulfill) human rights.

Council, a subsidiary organ of the UN General Assembly but the key UN organ in the field of human rights, in highlighting the destruction of cultural heritage within the international human rights framework. It thus starts with an analysis of the key Human Rights Council resolutions addressing the destruction of cultural heritage, as well as the work of its special procedures in particular the Special Rapporteur in the Field of Cultural Rights. This section also discusses references made by the Human Rights Council to the recommendations of the UN Security Council on the matter.

After having considered the destruction of cultural heritage from a human rights' perspective, the chapter then adopts another lens for looking at the destruction of cultural heritage, namely peace and security, for which the UN Security Council has primary responsibility. It thus draws attention to the resolutions of the UN Security Council on the same issue in order to determine on what basis the Council has determined that the destruction of cultural heritage can amount to a threat to peace and security. It concludes by identifying possible synergies between these two bodies, and between two of the UN pillars set forth in the UN Charter, the maintenance of international peace and security and respect for human rights.

I. The Destruction of Cultural Heritage Before the Human Rights Council

Before being replaced by the UN Human Rights Council in 2006, the UN Commission on Human Rights had already addressed the destruction of cultural heritage as part of its role as the main human rights body within the United Nations to promote and protect human rights around the world. For example, in a resolution focused on the human rights situation in Afghanistan in 1998, the Commission noted reports of heritage destruction and urged the Afghan Parties to 'protect and safeguard the cultural and historical heritage' of the country.[24]

The Commission also expressed its concern in relation to the illicit trafficking of cultural property in thematic (rather than country-specific) resolutions concerned with the 'Promotion of the enjoyment of the cultural rights of everyone and respect for different cultural identities'.[25] In those resolutions, it presented damage to the 'cultural heritage of nations' through trafficking as a threat to cultural diversity, 'a cherished asset for the advancement and welfare of humanity at large' that

[24] UN Commission on Human Rights, Res 1998/70 on Situation of Human Rights in Afghanistan (1998) UN Doc E/CN.4/1998/70 (21 April 1998) paras 2(g) and 5(h).

[25] UN Commission on Human Rights, Res 2003/26 on Promotion of the Enjoyment of the Cultural Rights of Everyone and Respect for Different Cultural Identities (22 April 2003) UN Doc E/CN.4/2003/L.11/Add.3 (2 May 2003) Preamble; UN Commission on Human Rights, Res 2004/20 on Promotion of the Enjoyment of the Cultural Rights of Everyone and Respect for Different Cultural Identities (16 April 2004) UN Doc E/CN.4/2004/127, Preamble; and UN Commission on Human Rights, Res 2005/20 (14 April 2005) UN Doc E/CN.4/2005/134 (Part I) Preamble.

'should be valued, enjoyed, genuinely accepted and embraced as a permanent feature which enriches our societies'.[26]

A. Linking Cultural Heritage Destruction and Human Rights

In 2007, the year following its establishment, the Human Rights Council adopted a resolution exclusively focused on the 'Protection of cultural rights and property in situations of armed conflict'.[27] It affirmed the link between human rights and 'the destruction of, or any other form of damage to, cultural property' which 'may impair the enjoyment of cultural rights, in particular of article 15 of the International Covenant on Economic, Social and Cultural Rights', and noted 'that the protection of cultural property during armed conflicts can contribute to the full enjoyment of the right of everyone to take part in cultural life'. [28] It thus called on States not only to respect the rules of international humanitarian law, including those pertaining to cultural property, but also to 'respect human rights law'.[29] It also requested 'the Secretary-General to bring the present resolution to the attention of all Governments, the competent UN bodies, the specialized agencies, regional intergovernmental organizations and international humanitarian organizations'.[30]

That same year, the Human Rights Council also adopted a more general resolution on the 'Protection of cultural heritage as an important component of the promotion and protection of cultural rights'.[31] In this key resolution, adopted a few years after the adoption of the 2003 UNESCO Declaration concerning the Intentional Destruction of Cultural Heritage,[32] the Council expressed its '*grave concern* about continuing acts of intentional destruction of cultural heritage that take place in various parts of the world', affirming that 'cultural heritage is an important component of the cultural identity of communities, groups and individuals, and of social cohesion, so that its intentional destruction may have adverse consequences on human dignity and human rights' and that 'intentional destruction of cultural heritage may violate the principles of international law'.[33] It also reaffirmed 'the importance of the protection of cultural heritage and the commitment to fight against its intentional destruction in any form so that such

[26] ibid.

[27] UNHRC, Res 6/1 on Protection of Cultural Rights and Property in Situations of Armed Conflict (27 September 2007) UN Doc A/HRC/RES/6/1 (27 September 2007).

[28] ibid, Preamble.

[29] ibid, para 1.

[30] ibid, para 6.

[31] UNHRC, Res 6/11 on Protection of Cultural Heritage as an Important Component of the Promotion and Protection of Cultural Rights, UN Doc A/HRC/RES/6/11 (28 September 2007) Preamble.

[32] UNESCO Declaration Concerning the Intentional Destruction of Cultural Heritage (17 October 2003) UNESCO Doc 32/Res 33.

[33] UNHRC, Res 6/11 (n 31) Preamble.

cultural heritage may be transmitted to the succeeding generations', acknowledging the transgenerational aspect of heritage, and that 'respect for the diversity of belief, culture and language promotes a culture of peace and dialogue among all civilizations', linking heritage protection and cultural diversity.[34] As part of this reaffirmation, the Council recognized 'that intentional destruction of cultural heritage may constitute advocacy and incitement to national, racial or religious hatred and thereby violates fundamental principles of international human rights law',[35] thus highlighting that destruction of cultural heritage may amount to a violation not only of Article 15 of the ICESCR but also of Article 20 of the International Covenant on Civil and Political Rights (ICCPR),[36] which prohibits incitement to hatred.[37]

Given that intentional destruction of heritage may violate human rights, the Council then underlined the responsibility of States if they fail to take appropriate measures to prohibit, prevent, stop, and punish any such destruction of cultural heritage of great importance for humanity, to the extent provided for by international law.[38] Again, the Council sought some linkage with other UN bodies, as it requested 'the High Commissioner for Human Rights to bring the present resolution to the attention of all Governments, the competent UN organs, programmes and specialized agencies, as well as regional intergovernmental organizations',[39] which may of course include the Security Council.

B. Elaborating a Human Rights Approach to Cultural Heritage Destruction

In subsequent resolutions on the protection of cultural heritage,[40] the Council developed a 'human rights-based approach' to the protection of cultural heritage, noting that its destruction may have an 'irreversible impact on the enjoyment of cultural rights, in particular the right of everyone to take part in cultural life,

[34] ibid.

[35] ibid, paras 1, 3–4.

[36] International Covenant on Civil and Political Rights (adopted 16 December 1966, entered into force 23 March 1976) 999 UNTS 171 (ICCPR).

[37] ibid, art 20(2).

[38] UNHRC, Res 6/11 (n 31) para 5. In para 6, the Council encouraged 'all States, relevant intergovernmental and non-governmental organizations and the media to promote a culture of tolerance and respect for the diversity of cultures, civilizations and religions and for cultural and religious sites, which represent an important aspect of the collective heritage of humankind'. ibid, para 6.

[39] ibid, paras 9–10, where it also encouraged 'the High Commissioner for Human Rights to enhance consultations with the Council and cooperation with relevant international and regional organizations and bodies concerned with the issue of protection of cultural heritage in order to address human rights-related aspects of this issue'.

[40] UNHRC, Res 33/20 on Cultural Rights and the Protection of Cultural Heritage (30 September 2016) UN Doc A/HRC/RES/33/20 (6 October 2016) in which it acknowledged the Special Rapporteur 2016 report, and Res 37/17 on Cultural Rights and the Protection of Cultural Heritage (19 March 2018) UN Doc A/HRC/37/L.30.

including the ability to access and enjoy cultural heritage'.[41] Developing the concept of heritage itself, the Council also highlighted the importance of the protection not only of tangible cultural heritage, but also of intangible cultural heritage, which is particularly at risk in NIAC with an ethnic or religious component.[42] As there is no specific rule protecting intangible cultural heritage in armed conflict (except for those protecting religious practices or those offering an indirect form of protection through the concept of dignity), the respect and protection of cultural rights are particularly relevant.[43]

The Council also pinpointed the link between illicit trafficking and the financing of terrorism, adding that safeguarding cultural rights may in turn contribute to fighting terrorism, among other global challenges.[44] More in general, it reiterated that violation of the right to access and enjoy cultural heritage 'may threaten stability' and constitutes 'an aggravating factor in conflict and a major obstacle to peace'.[45] It also recognized the crucial contribution of UN peacekeeping missions, which are authorized by the Security Council, without specifically referring to the latter.[46] However, it specifically mentions the United Nations Educational, Scientific and Cultural Organization (UNESCO), the United Nations Office on Drugs and Crime (UNODC), the International Criminal Police Organization (INTERPOL), and the World Customs Organization, in its call for enhanced international cooperation in the fight against trafficking.[47] In any case, it did call for 'the recognition of the protection of cultural heritage as an important component of humanitarian assistance' in the view to mainstream 'the protection of cultural heritage into humanitarian actions, security strategies and peacebuilding processes, and in post-conflict reconciliation initiatives',[48] which is directly relevant to the mandate of the Security Council.

The Human Rights Council even requested that the UN High Commissioner for Human Rights convene a seminar to identify ways to address the negative impact of heritage destruction on the upholding of human rights and to discuss concrete actions to be taken.[49] When opening the discussions of the resulting intersessional

[41] See eg UNHRC, Res 37/17 on Cultural Rights and the Protection of Cultural Heritage (19 March 2018) UN Doc A/HRC/37/L.30, Preamble.

[42] ibid.

[43] See also UNHRC 'Report of the United Nations High Commissioner for Human Rights on the Intersessional Seminar on Cultural Rights and the Protection of Cultural Heritage' (27 December 2017) UN Doc A/HRC/37/29, paras 27–30 (intervention of Ms Johannot-Gradis) (UNHRC, Intersessional Seminar Report). For further discussion of the link between the illicit trafficking of cultural goods and the financing of terrorism, see Patty Gerstenblith, 'The Disposition of Movable Cultural Heritage' (Ch 1), and Janet Blake, 'Trafficking in Cultural Property: Where Cultural Heritage Law and the International Fight against Transnational Organized Crime Coincide' (Ch 6) in this volume.

[44] UNHRC, Intersessional Seminar Report (n 43).

[45] ibid.

[46] ibid.

[47] ibid, para 4.

[48] ibid, para 8.

[49] UNHRC, Res 33/20 on Cultural Rights and the Protection of Cultural Heritage (30 September 2016) UN Doc A/HRC/Res/33/20 (6 October 2016).

seminar, a representative of the Office of the United Nations High Commissioner for Human Rights noted the significance of cultural heritage 'as a resource for the identity and development of individuals and groups, and the negative impact that its destruction had on several human rights and on people's capacity for resilience and peace'.[50] On that occasion, the Special Rapporteur in the Field of Cultural Rights, Bennoune, also highlighted the need to 'mainstream' the 'human rights approach to cultural heritage across the United Nations system'.[51] Among the recommendations, there was a call to adopt a 'human rights approach' to the protection of cultural heritage, one that is based on the realization of cultural rights and that includes women, minorities, and local populations in decision-making.[52]

This approach includes the ratification and domestic implementation of relevant treaties, such as the 2003 Convention for the Safeguarding of the Intangible Cultural Heritage[53] and the ICESCR. Through those widely ratified instruments, intangible cultural heritage is protected both in peacetime and in situations of armed conflict. It thus safeguards a dimension of cultural heritage that is not protected by international humanitarian law, except for the protection of 'convictions and religious practices'.[54] This approach further complements humanitarian rules by protecting, through the human right to participate in cultural life, the access to and enjoyment of tangible heritage in situations that do not meet the threshold of armed conflict. It can also protect those sites that may not be deemed significant enough to deserve special protection under international humanitarian law. While international humanitarian law focuses on cultural property 'of great importance to the cultural heritage of every people', including (but not limited to) World Heritage sites, 'often monuments that appear to be "minor" in the eyes of outsiders acted as the glue that kept a community together'.[55]

A human rights approach also means that all of the rights allowing for the realization of cultural rights must be protected. At the Human Rights Council intersessional seminar, the Council also highlighted the need 'to preserve the conditions that enabled the creation of cultural goods and practices, such as the enjoyment of cultural rights and the rights to health, education, security and sustainable socioeconomic development, rather than the cultural goods and practices themselves'.[56] In order to implement such a human rights approach, calls were made to States to adopt legal frameworks capable of addressing the protection of cultural heritage in all its forms.[57]

[50] UNHRC, Intersessional Seminar Report (n 43) para 5 (statement by Ms Peggy Hicks). The seminar on cultural rights and the protection of cultural heritage was held on 7 July 2017.

[51] ibid, para 13 (statement by Ms. Karima Bennoune).

[52] ibid, paras 92, 100(b), and 101(e).

[53] UNESCO Convention for the Safeguarding of the Intangible Cultural Heritage (adopted 17 October 2003, entered into force 20 April 2006) 2368 UNTS 1.

[54] See 1977 Additional Protocol I, art 75(1), and 1977 Additional Protocol II, art 4(1).

[55] UNHRC, Intersessional Seminar Report (n 43) para 67.

[56] ibid, para 59.

[57] ibid, para 21.

At the intersessional seminar, there was also a call to implement in full the recommendations contained in Security Council Resolutions 2199 (2015) and 2347 (2017), which included protecting cultural heritage in peacekeeping and providing for measures to curb the illicit trafficking of cultural objects.[58] While recommendations pertaining to curbing the illicit trade in cultural objects were naturally limited to tangible heritage,[59] the recommendations which emanated from the intersessional seminar pertaining to peacekeeping included the recognition of the protection of cultural heritage *and cultural rights* as 'an important aspect of humanitarian assistance, peacekeeping and peacebuilding before, during and after conflict', as well as the systematic incorporation of cultural heritage considerations in the mandate of peacekeeping missions,[60] which can be established by the Security Council. In terms of cooperation between various UN mechanisms and States, the establishment of a contact group of interested Parties was mentioned,[61] as well as the strengthening of cooperation between various UN entities, in order to promote considerations of cultural rights in security and peacebuilding operations, but not with the Security Council. Nevertheless, and more generally, a recommendation was made to 'integrate the protection of cultural heritage and cultural rights in the mandate of the UN peacekeeping operations, in accordance with paragraph 19 of Security Council resolution 2347 (2017)'.[62]

Recommendations made at the intersessional seminar built not only on those made by the Security Council but also on those made by the Special Rapporteur in the Field of Cultural Rights,[63] a thematic procedure that was established in 2009.[64] As an independent expert reporting to both the Human Rights Council and the General Assembly, the Special Rapporteur has been actively addressing the issue of cultural heritage destruction, building on the work of her predecessor, Farida Shaheed, who had conceptualized access to and enjoyment of cultural heritage within the right to participate in cultural life in her pivotal 2011 report.[65]

[58] See Section II.A. below.

[59] UNHRC, Intersessional Seminar Report (n 43) para 105.

[60] ibid, para 104.

[61] ibid, para 106.

[62] ibid, para 107(b).

[63] UNHRC 'Report of the Independent Expert in the Field of Cultural Rights, Farida Shaheed' (2011) UN Doc A/HRC/17/38 (21 March 2011); UNHRC 'Report of the Special Rapporteur in the Field of Cultural Rights' (3 February 2016) UN Doc A/HRC/31/59 and Corr.1; and UNHRC 'Report of the Special Rapporteur in the Field of Cultural Rights' (9 August 2016) UN Doc A/71/317. It also referred to the Expert Mechanism on the Rights of Indigenous Peoples, see UNHRC 'Study on the Expert Mechanism on the Rights of Indigenous Peoples' (19 August 2015) UN Doc A/HRC/30/53.

[64] UNHRC, Res 10/23 Independent Expert in the Field of Cultural Rights (26 March 2009) Doc A/HRC/RES/10/23. See also UNHRC, Res 6/6 on Promotion of the Enjoyment of the Cultural Rights of Everyone and Respect for Cultural Diversity (28 September 2007) Doc A/HRC/RES/6/6, para 1, where the Human Rights Council reiterated that 'cultural rights are an integral part of human rights, which are universal, indivisible, interrelated and interdependent'.

[65] UNHRC 'Report of the Independent Expert in the Field of Cultural Rights, Farida Shaheed' (21 March 2011) UN Doc A/HRC/17/38. The Report itself expanded on General Comment No 21 on the Right of everyone to take part in cultural life from the UN Committee on Economic, Social and Cultural Rights. See CESCR, General Comment No 21 (n 17). See also UNHRC, Res 17/15 on Promotion of the

In that report, the Special Rapporteur had already tackled the issue of cultural heritage destruction in armed conflict, stating that it 'has important human rights implications'.[66] She also hinted at a shift from the protection of cultural heritage based on its intrinsic outstanding value for humanity to a protection based on its value 'for individuals and communities in relation to their cultural identity'.[67]

Although the current Special Rapporteur, Bennoune, did not issue a statement following the January 2017 attacks on Palmyra, this special procedure of the Human Rights Council has been particularly active over the last few years in highlighting the protection of cultural heritage as a human rights issue. In 2016, she reported specifically on the intentional destruction of cultural heritage as a violation of human rights.[68] In affirming that the destruction of cultural heritage amounts to a violation of the right to take part in cultural life, she observed that it thus violates the 'right to maintain and develop the cultural practices of one's choice, and to access cultural heritage including one's own history, and the right to freedom of artistic expression and creativity'.[69] She further highlighted that it may also violate other human rights, such as the right to freedom from discrimination and the right to freedom of thought, conscience, and religion.[70]

More particularly, the Special Rapporteur stated that a failure to address the destruction of cultural heritage as 'a question of human rights generally, or of cultural rights in particular',[71] has contributed in practice to insufficient education and awareness-raising on the importance of cultural heritage from the human rights perspective,[72] as well as to a lack of consideration for the stakeholders in such heritage, including the frontline defenders of cultural heritage.[73] Importantly, she highlighted the need to protect not only tangible forms of cultural heritage, which have long been the object of specific rules of protection under international humanitarian law, for example, but also intangible forms of cultural heritage, which have often been left out of the discourse on the protection of cultural heritage, in

Enjoyment of the Cultural Rights of Everyone and Respect for Cultural Diversity (14 July 2011) UN Doc A/HRC/RES/17/15, para 10, where it noted the work of the Special Rapporteur on the topic and the expert meeting held on 10 February 2011.

[66] UNHRC 'Report of the Independent Expert in the Field of Cultural Rights, Farida Shaheed' (21 March 2011) UN Doc A/HRC/17/38, para 15.

[67] ibid, para 20.

[68] UNHRC 'Report of the Special Rapporteur in the Field of Cultural Rights' (2016) UN Doc A/HRC/31/59 (3 February 2016) (Report of the Special Rapporteur to UNHRC); UNHRC 'Report of the Special Rapporteur in the Field of Cultural Rights' (2016) UN Doc A/71/317 (9 August 2016) (Report of the Special Rapporteur to the UNGA).

[69] Report of the Special Rapporteur to the UNGA (n 68) para 34.

[70] ibid.

[71] Report of the Special Rapporteur to UNHRC (n 68) para 69, citing a memorandum submitted by Elsa Stamatopoulou.

[72] ibid, para 79.

[73] ibid, paras 73-75.

particular in situations of armed conflict.[74] As examples, she noted that 'ancient languages and religious practices tied to sacred spaces and structures and cultural landscapes of northern Iraq and the Syrian Arab Republic are being lost as populations are displaced and objects, texts and historic structures are destroyed'.[75] She therefore advocated an approach that 'is holistic, contemplating both prevention and punishment, targeting acts by State and non-State actors, in conflict and non-conflict situations and of tangible and intangible heritage'.[76] This 'human rights approach to cultural heritage' is meant to consider the rights of individuals and groups in relation to cultural heritage, thus looking beyond preservation and safeguarding.[77]

Her recommendations included the integration of the 'protection of cultural heritage and of cultural rights as a critical component of humanitarian assistance, including in conflict', as well as investigating 'the use of funds from looting and the illicit traffic of cultural objects for the financing of terrorism and consider requiring increased due diligence with regard to cultural objects being sold from at-risk regions', the systematic inclusion of 'cultural awareness, the safeguarding, restoration and memorialization of cultural heritage and the respect and protection of cultural rights in the mandate of peacekeeping missions, in peacebuilding policies and initiatives and in post-conflict reconciliation', and further 'international exchange of best practices in the field of protection of cultural heritage and of the right to access and enjoy cultural heritage'. As will be explained in Section II.A. below, those recommendations were followed by the Security Council in its Resolution 2347.

C. What else Can the Human Rights Council Do?

While cultural rights are legally binding obligations for States Parties to the relevant treaties, their enforcement has long been a challenge for those victims of violations. In addition to the Special Rapporteur, who can receive individual complaints of alleged violations of cultural rights, the CESCR can now also hear such complaints. In 2008, the Human Rights Council adopted Resolution 8/2, which established the 'Optional Protocol to the International Covenant on Economic, Social and Cultural Rights' (Optional Protocol)[78] The Optional Protocol was

[74] ibid, para 77, where she underlined that 'attacks on one form of heritage are often accompanied by assaults on the other'. See also Report of the Special Rapporteur to the UNGA (n 68) para 6.

[75] ibid, para 7.

[76] UNHRC 'Report of the Special Rapporteur in the Field of Cultural Rights' (2016) UN Doc A/HRC/31/59 (3 February 2016) and Corr.1, para 88.

[77] UNHRC 'Report of the Special Rapporteur in the Field of Cultural Rights' (2016) UN Doc A/71/317 (9 August 2016) para 53.

[78] UNHRC, Res 8/2 'Optional Protocol to the International Covenant on Economic, Social and Cultural Rights' (18 June 2008, subsequently adopted 10 December 2008 by UNGA Res 63/117) Annex (Optional Protocol). At the time of writing, the Optional Protocol had twenty-four States Parties.

subsequently adopted also by the UN General Assembly and put an end to the lack of enforcement mechanisms for cultural rights at the UN level. This mechanism allows for individual complaints regarding alleged violations of the right to participate in cultural life; it may thus include alleged violations of the right to access and enjoy cultural heritage, whether in peace or wartime, by a State Party to the Optional Protocol. However, this is only applicable with regard to individuals under the jurisdiction of a State Party to the Optional Protocol and, as of yet, this instrument has not been widely ratified. Neither does it address violations committed by non-State actors, unless their actions could be attributed to a State or a State had failed in its duty to exercise due diligence to protect the human rights of all under its jurisdiction.

The Universal Periodic Review may also play a role in strengthening the realization of cultural rights. Within the recommendations made at the intersessional seminar, civil society was asked to submit more reports and individual complaints related to Article 15 of the ICESCR 'to help expand the Committee's jurisprudence regarding the right to take part in cultural life and the right to access and enjoy cultural heritage', as well as to 'submit further contributions to the universal periodic review process on these issues', in the same way as States were asked to make better use of this review process, which has so far seldom addressed cultural rights.[79]

Since its creation in 2006, the Human Rights Council has also established commissions of inquiry, fact-finding missions, and investigations with regard to twenty-two countries,[80] including the Commission of Inquiry on Syria, which has noted instances of cultural heritage destruction in its reports.[81] By contrast, during the same period, the Security Council mandated only one international commission of inquiry to investigate events in the Central African Republic, in

[79] UNHRC, Res 33/20 on Cultural Rights and the Protection of Cultural Heritage (30 September 2016) UN Doc A/HRC/RES/33/20 (6 October 2016), and UNHRC, Intersessional Seminar Report (n 43) para 51 (intervention of Mr Mancisidor) and para 110.

[80] They include Yemen, Democratic Republic of the Congo, Myanmar, Burundi, South Sudan, Cameroon, Chad, Niger, Nigeria, Libya, Iraq, Syria, Palestine/Israel, Eritrea, Sri Lanka, Mali, Democratic People's Republic of Korea, Côte d'Ivoire, Honduras, Sudan (Darfur), and Lebanon. See UN, 'Research Guide on International Commissions of Inquiry: Fact-finding Missions' <http://libraryresources.unog.ch/c.php?g=462695&p=3162812#21493516> accessed 12 November 2018. The fact-finding mission pertaining to Mali has, for example, highlighted the destruction of cultural and religious sites in Timbuktu by Ansar Dine, see UNHRC 'Twenty-second session, Report of the United Nations High Commissioner for Human Rights on the Situation of Human Rights in Mali' (7 January 2012) UN Doc A/HRC/22/33 (7 January 2013) para 45.

[81] See UNHRC 'Report of the Independent International Commission of Inquiry on the Syrian Arab Republic' (8 August 2017) UN Doc A/HRC/36/55, paras 52–61; UNHRC 'Human Rights Abuses and International Humanitarian Law Violations in the Syrian Arab Republic, 21 July 2016–28 February 2017: Conference Room Paper of the Independent International Commission of Inquiry on the Syrian Arab Republic' (10 March 2017) UN Doc A/HRC/34/CRP.3, paras 84–85; UNHRC, '"They Came to Destroy": ISIS Crimes Against the Yazidis' (15 June 2016) UN Doc A/HRC/32/CRP.2, para 157; UNHRC 'Report of the Independent International Commission of Inquiry on the Syrian Arab Republic' (11 February 2016) UN Doc A/HRC/31/68, paras 85–93; UNHRC 'Report of the Independent International Commission of Inquiry on the Syrian Arab Republic' (18 July 2013) UN Doc A/HRC/23/58, para 116ff.

2013, a situation for which the Human Rights Council also set up a fact-finding mission.[82] As a result, the Human Rights Council may possibly benefit from more first-hand evidence of international law violations,[83] including cultural rights, than the Security Council, which nevertheless has also been actively addressing cultural heritage protection.

II. The UN Security Council and Cultural Heritage

According to Article 24 of the UN Charter,[84] the UN Security Council's primary responsibility is the maintenance of international peace and security.[85] Over the years, the Security Council has slowly established that protecting cultural heritage from destruction and looting is part of its mandate, affirming the destruction and looting of cultural heritage as a threat to peace and security.

A. Attacks Against Cultural Heritage as a Threat to Peace and Security

In 2017, the Security Council adopted Resolution 2347, its first resolution exclusively dedicated to cultural heritage.[86] However, it was not the first time that the Security Council had considered attacks against cultural heritage as a threat against peace and security. Like the Human Rights Council, it had already adopted several resolutions addressing country-specific situations of armed conflicts, such as in 1999, when it called for 'respect for Afghanistan's cultural and historical heritage'.[87]

While the protection of cultural heritage in situations of armed conflict has been a growing concern for the Security Council over the past two decades, it has failed to recommend specific measures in certain contexts, such as Libya or Yemen. In Yemen, several historic buildings have been bombed, including in the Old City of Sana'a, a site which was inscribed on the List of World Heritage in Danger in

[82] UNHRC, Res 23/18 on Technical Assistance to the Central African Republic in the Field of Human Rights (13 June 2013) in 'Report of the Human Rights Council' (2013) UN Doc A/68/53, 168–70.

[83] However, note that the Security Council may gain first-hand evidence not only from commissions of inquiry but also from special representatives and peacekeeping operations, among others, which may also report back to it.

[84] Charter of the United Nations (adopted 26 June 1945, entered into force 24 October 1945) 1 UNTS XVI (UN Charter).

[85] ibid, ch V.

[86] UNSC Res 2347 (24 March 2017) UN Doc S/RES/2347.

[87] UNSC Res 1267 (15 October 1999) UN Doc S/RES/1267. See also text accompanying n 24 (observing that the Human Rights Council similarly passed a country-specific resolution in 1998 for Afghan Parties to 'protect and safeguard the cultural and historical heritage' of Afghanistan).

2015.[88] Despite its inconsistent approach to cultural heritage destruction, the Security Council has nevertheless gradually established cultural heritage protection as a key element in the maintenance of international peace and security. In particular, the Security Council specifically addressed the illicit trade in antiquities as a threat to peace and security, as well as incorporating the protection of cultural heritage within peacekeeping.

In 2003, following the Iraq invasion, the Security Council stressed 'the need for respect for the archaeological, historical, cultural, and religious heritage of Iraq' and decided that States should take measures 'to facilitate the safe return to Iraqi institutions of Iraqi cultural property' and to prohibit 'trade in or transfer of such items'.[89] As the prohibition of trade in Iraqi cultural property was framed as a binding obligation, Member States had to adopt import bans with regard to those objects. This illicit trade in antiquities was eventually linked to the funding of terrorism, which is one of the most serious threats to international peace and security.[90] In Resolution 2199, the Security Council noted that terrorist groups

> are generating income from engaging directly or indirectly in the looting and smuggling of cultural heritage items from archaeological sites, museums, libraries, archives, and other sites in Iraq and Syria, which is being used to support their recruitment efforts and strengthen their operational capability to organize and carry out terrorist attacks.[91]

It then extended the prohibition of trade of cultural objects, already in place with regard to Iraq, to Syrian antiquities.[92]

Concerns over terrorism financing also explain the broad support received by Resolution 2347, as reference was made to Abu Sayyaf, a now deceased high-ranking ISIL official, who had illicitly traded in antiquities to finance terrorism at the time of voting.[93] In Resolution 2347, the Security Council requested that States

[88] For more examples on the destruction of cultural heritage in Yemen, see Mwatana for Human Rights, 'The Degradation of History'(November 2018) <http://mwatana.org/en/the-degradation-of-history-2/> accessed 12 November 2018.

[89] UNSC Res 1483 (22 May 2003) UN Doc S/RES/1483, para 7. Note that trade sanctions with regard to all Iraqi goods (which has now been lifted), including cultural goods, had already been imposed under UNSC Res 661 (1990). See Patty Gerstenblith, 'From Bamiyan to Baghdad: Warfare and the Preservation of Cultural Heritage at the Beginning of the 21st Century', 37 Georgetown J Intl L 245 (2006) nn 158 and 329–34 on implementation of UNSC Res 1483 in the United States, United Kingdom, and Switzerland.

[90] This link was first explicitly made in UNSC Res 2195 (19 December 2014), where the Security Council expressed concern at terrorists in Africa benefiting from transnational organized crimes including trafficking in artifacts.

[91] UNSC Res 2199 (12 February 2015) UN Doc S/RES/2199, paras 15–16.

[92] ibid, para 17. Note that while the Syrian civil war broke out in 2011, the Security Council only raised its concern with regard to its cultural heritage from 2014 onwards.

[93] Ambassador Michele J Sison, US Deputy Permanent Representative to the United Nations, US Mission to the United Nations, 'Explanation of Vote at the Adoption of UN Security Council Resolution 2347 on the Destruction and Trafficking of Cultural Heritage by Terrorist Groups and in Situations of Armed Conflict' (24 March 2017) <https://usun.state.gov/remarks/7721> accessed 12 November 2018.

'take appropriate steps to prevent and counter the illicit trade and trafficking' in cultural objects beyond those originating from Iraq or Syria to items originating from any context of armed conflict.[94] Although not a binding obligation, this request recalls previous resolutions which contained similar provision with regard to objects from Iraq and Syria, calling on States to address all situations of armed conflict, such as Yemen.

Despite having specifically addressed the illicit trade in cultural objects, the Security Council did not encourage the ratification of the UNESCO Convention on the Means of Prohibiting and Preventing the Illicit Import, Export and Transfer of Ownership of Cultural Property (1970) in Resolution 2347, only recalling it. It also failed to mention the UNIDROIT Convention on Stolen or Illegally Exported Cultural Objects (1995) to which only one permanent member of the Security Council is a party (China).[95] While Resolution 2347 encourages ratification of the Hague Convention,[96] countering the trafficking in antiquities requires increased cooperation among States, which is also addressed in the UNESCO Convention, for example. Nevertheless, Resolution 2347 has led to increased efforts to curb the illicit trade in cultural objects, such as through the creation of specialized units or the integration of heritage personnel within police and customs authorities, the provision of training to police and customs officials, or the development of databases for information collection and sharing, as well as strengthened international cooperation.[97]

Having incorporated threats against cultural heritage within its mandate, the Security Council has also extended the mandate of the UN peacekeeping mission in Mali, the United Nations Multidimensional Integrated Stabilization Mission in Mali (MINUSMA), to 'support for cultural preservation' by assisting the transitional authorities in protecting the heritage sites 'as necessary and feasible', thus allowing it to use force to do so.[98] The Security Council had already strongly condemned 'the desecration, damage and destruction of sites of holy, historic and cultural significance, especially but not exclusively those designated UNESCO World Heritage sites, including in the city of Timbuktu' when considering threats to peace and security in Mali in 2012.[99] As mentioned, integrating considerations of

[94] UNSC Res 2347 (24 March 2017) UN Doc S/RES/2347, para 8 (where States 'have a reasonable suspicion that the items originate from a context of armed conflict').

[95] Although the work of UNIDROIT is on the agenda of the UNGA Sixth (Legal) Committee, it has limited visibility at the UN as it addresses private (rather than public) international law matters.

[96] It is worth noting that the United Kingdom ratified the 1954 Hague Convention a few months after the adoption of this Resolution.

[97] UNSC Res 2347 (24 March 2017) UN Doc S/RES/2347, paras 12–18, 49–71.

[98] UNSC Res 2100 (25 April 2013) UN Doc S/RES/2100, para 16(f), to be read with para 17. See also Guido Carducci, 'The Role of UNESCO in the Elaboration and Implementation of International Art, Cultural Property, and Heritage Law' (Ch 7) in this volume (discussing the role of UNESCO, including as observed in recent Security Council Resolutions).

[99] UNSC Res 2056 (5 July 2012) UN Doc S/RES/2056. A few months later, the Security Council again condemned the destruction of cultural and religious sites in UNSC Res 2071 (12 October 2012) UN

cultural heritage in peacekeeping missions had been recommended by the Human Rights Council. However, when renewing the mandate of MINUSMA in 2018, the Security Council did not extend its protective role with regard to cultural heritage, only requesting the peacekeeping mission to continue 'to operate mindfully in the vicinity of cultural and historical sites'.[100]

B. Linking International Peace and Security to Human Rights

While the Security Council has affirmed that attacks against cultural heritage can amount to a threat to peace and security, this section considers whether it has also considered attacks against cultural heritage as human rights violations, linking the two UN pillars. Over the past three decades, the Security Council has integrated the promotion of the respect for human rights within its considerations, after having largely left it outside its scope as it was deemed principally a matter of State sovereignty, as well as falling outside the scope of its mandate.[101] This change in attitude followed the increasing occurrence of NIAC, which are often preceded by mass human rights' violations,[102] and thus could act as indicators of threats to international peace and security, which the Security Council is specifically mandated to identify.[103] The situations which have been referred to by the Security Council, which is concerned with the destruction of cultural heritage, have all been NIAC.

In Resolution 2347, the UN Under-Secretary-General for Political Affairs noted that the protection of cultural heritage 'is not only a cultural issue, it is also a security and humanitarian imperative',[104] underlining that terrorists groups do not only 'exploit cultural sites to finance their activities' but also 'destroy and traffic

Doc S/RES/2071, UNSC Res 2085 (20 December 2012) UN Doc S/RES/2085, and UNSC Res 2100 (25 April 2013) UN Doc S/RES/2100.

[100] UNSC Res 2423 (28 June 2018) UN Doc S/RES/2423, para 67. While this could be interpreted as a reversal of the extent of power the Security Council may provide peacekeeping operations with regard to cultural preservation, it may also be due to a change in the circumstances on the ground, according to which cultural preservation may no longer be seen as a priority.

[101] For rare examples of earlier resolutions referring to human rights, in particular those adopted in the decolonization context, see Daphna Shraga, 'The Security Council and Human Rights—from Discretion to Promote to Obligation to Protect' in Bardo Fassbender (ed), *Securing Human Rights? Achievements and Challenges of the UN Security Council* (OUP 2011). See also UNSC, *Security Council Report, Human Rights and the Security Council: An Evolving Role* (25 January 2016) 2–3.

[102] ibid 2.

[103] See Vera Gowlland-Debbas, 'The Security Council as Enforcer of Human Rights' in Fassbender (n 101).

[104] UNSC, Meeting on Maintenance of International Peace and Security: Destruction and Trafficking of Cultural Heritage by Terrorist Groups and in Situations of Armed Conflict (24 March 2017) UN Doc S/PV.7907, 2–3 (intervention of Mr Feltman). At the same meeting, UNESCO Director-General Bokova echoed his words when she said that 'defending cultural heritage is more than a cultural issue; it is a security imperative that cannot be separated from the protection of human lives', ibid, 4.

cultural heritage to undermine the power of culture as a bridge between generations and people of different backgrounds and religions'.[105] Despite this broad conceptualization of culture as a bridge between different generations and cultures, Resolution 2347 does not explicitly make the link between the destruction of cultural heritage and human rights. While it does refer to the 2003 Convention for the Safeguarding of the Intangible Cultural Heritage and the 2005 Convention on the Protection and Promotion of the Diversity of Cultural Expressions,[106] there is no clear reference to direct attacks against intangible forms of cultural heritage.[107] To the contrary, it highlights tangible forms of cultural heritage noting the 'destruction of religious sites and artefacts, as well as the looting and smuggling of cultural property from archaeological sites, museums, libraries, archives and other sites'.[108]

Nevertheless, the destruction of cultural heritage is noted as an attempt to deny historical roots and cultural diversity, thus pointing to a link between the destruction and smuggling of tangible heritage and human rights, even if only implicitly. Furthermore, it also states that the destruction and looting of cultural heritage may undermine not only peace and security but also the 'social, economic and cultural development of affected States'.[109] However, it still falls short of clearly connecting the destruction and looting of tangible cultural heritage with human rights' violations, or addressing all forms of cultural heritage. Yet, the Security Council had clearly made the link between the destruction of cultural heritage and human rights in previous resolutions. For example, with regard to Mali, it condemned 'strongly the abuses of human rights committed in the north of Mali by armed rebels, terrorist and other extremist groups, including violence against its civilians, notably women and children, killings, hostage-taking, pillaging, theft, destruction of cultural and religious sites'.[110] There is thus some ongoing inconsistency in the way the Security Council has linked the destruction of cultural heritage with human rights violations, despite having done so clearly in the past.

While the Security Council has played a role in promoting respect for human rights, it has not yet addressed cultural rights and the right of access to and enjoyment of cultural heritage, in all its forms, in a comprehensive and systematic manner. While this may be explained by the various delegations drafting the Security Council resolutions and the urgency of their writing process, it may partially also be due to the lack of direct links, and thus of coordination, between the Security Council and the Human Rights Council. At the time when the Human

[105] ibid 2–3 (intervention of Mr Feltman).

[106] UNSC Res 2347 (24 March 2017) UN Doc S/RES/2347, Preamble.

[107] Note that in UNSC Res 2170 (15 August 2014) UN Doc S/RES/2170, para 6 the Security Council had called on states to prevent the subversion of cultural institutions by terrorists and their supporters, which thus appeared to be concerned with intangible forms of culture and possibly cultural heritage.

[108] UNSC Res 2347 (24 March 2017) UN Doc S/RES/2347, para 1.

[109] ibid, Preamble, 5th recital.

[110] UNSC Res 2071 (12 October 2012) S/RES/2071. See also UNSC Res 2085 (20 December 2012) S/RES/2085.

Rights Council was established, although the three pillars of the UN, including peace and security and human rights (as well as development), were described as 'interlinked and mutually reinforcing', no direct links were foreseen between the two bodies.[111] This does not mean that there has not been any interaction between the two bodies, but only that it has been sporadic. Although the Security Council has regularly taken into account human rights over the past three decades, it has not done so systematically, giving rise to criticism and calls to include them in all the deliberations and decisions of the Security Council.[112] While considering human rights is not explicitly part of its mandate, it can be deemed to be part of it when the human rights violations in question amount to a threat to international peace and security.[113]

The Security Council has also not systematically used the resources emanating from the Human Rights Council with regard to human rights violations, including from its fact-finding and special procedures.[114] For example, while the Security Council refers in Resolution 2347 to efforts made by other intergovernmental organizations, such as UNESCO, UNODC, INTERPOL, or the Council of Europe, it makes no reference to the Human Rights Council or the work of its special procedures. There is thus still a need to correct the fragmented manner in which the three pillars of the United Nations are currently addressed as this would also improve its approach to cultural heritage matters.

Conclusion

Given the increased attention paid by the Human Rights Council, and its special procedure in the field of cultural rights, and by the Security Council, which has affirmed that such attacks constitute a threat to peace and security, to attacks against cultural heritage, the two bodies should better coordinate their respective efforts. On the one hand, members of the Human Rights Council should ask the Secretary-General to bring to the attention of the Security Council its decisions and reports pertaining to the destruction of cultural heritage and, on the other hand, members of the Security Council should consider the reports of the Human Rights Council and its mechanisms, including the Special Rapporteur in the field of cultural rights,

[111] UNGA Res 60/251 (15 March 2006) UN Doc A/RES/60/251 (3 April 2006).

[112] See, for example, Security Council 7926th Meeting, which was the first thematic debate on human rights violations in relation to peace and security. During the meeting, UN Secretary-General António Guterres stressed the need for a UN-wide coherent approach to human rights, noting that 'Human rights are intrinsically linked to peace and security, and their inclusion in the deliberations and decisions of the Security Council is of great importance'. UNSC, Meeting on Maintenance of International Peace and Security: Human Rights and Prevention of Armed Conflict (18 April 2017) UN Doc S/PV.7926.

[113] See, for example, Hersch Lauterpacht, *International Law and Human Rights* (Archon 1950) 185.

[114] UNSC, Security Council Report Human Rights and the Security Council: An Evolving Role (25 January 2016) 4-6.

in its decision-making process. [115] Any possible existing institutional barrier should be removed to permit those synergies.

The Special Rapporteur in the Field of Cultural Rights and the Human Rights Council, in particular through Resolution 33/20 (2016),[116] have called for a human rights-based approach to the protection of cultural heritage. This human rights approach is underpinned by an acknowledgment that the destruction of cultural heritage can amount to a violation of the right to take part in cultural life, as it denies the rights-holders access to, and enjoyment of, cultural sites. In times of armed conflict, the protection of cultural *property* (in the sense of tangible objects) does not require a human rights approach. Cultural objects, including archaeological sites, historic buildings, and works of art, for example, are clearly protected as civilian objects under international humanitarian law, many of them benefitting from an additional layer of protection due to their 'great importance to the cultural heritage of every people'. However, this form of protection places a focus on the object itself, a focus that has also been reflected in the way the UN Security Council has so far considered cultural heritage, overshadowing the link that communities have with that heritage and leaving out other forms of cultural heritage, whether tangible cultural heritage that may be deemed of lesser importance (in particular for a State that may not value a minority heritage) or intangible cultural heritage.

While a so-called 'human rights approach' is not needed for the protection of cultural property in armed conflict, which already benefits from specific humanitarian rules, it may have an impact on prevention and peacebuilding efforts, where the cultural rights of the relevant communities should be taken into account. It may also complement the existing humanitarian rules by highlighting the obligation to protect also properties of less importance, that is, those only protected as civilian objects under humanitarian law (and not specially protected as cultural properties), as well as intangible forms of cultural heritage, which are part of cultural rights and which are for the most part not protected under humanitarian law. While humanitarian law protects 'convictions and religious practices', other forms of intangible cultural heritage are not protected. When providing training to peacekeepers, the importance of intangible cultural heritage, manifested through the performance of rituals (which may not necessarily be religious) around cultural sites, for example, should also be made clear. While protecting a site in a situation of armed conflict may mean that the party in control of the territory where it is located may limit its access, such limitation should not curtail the exercise of cultural rights. Finally, the 'human rights approach' also seeks to highlight the specific risks facing those defending cultural heritage, such as Palmyra's head of

[115] See, for example, the Appeal of June 13th 2016, 'To Put Human Rights at the Heart of Conflict Prevention', presented at the thirty-second session of the Human Rights Council (2016) <https://www.eda.admin.ch/dam/eda/en/documents/aussenpolitik/internationaleorganisationen/20160613_Appel.pdf> accessed 12 November 2018.

[116] (30 September 2016) UN Doc A/HRC/RES/33/20.

antiquities, Khaled al-Asaad. Although these individuals are protected as civilians during armed conflicts, their close link to cultural heritage may turn them into targets and thus may require specific protection too.

As the Security Council will only consider attacks against cultural heritage when they threaten international peace and security, it will not consider all attacks against cultural heritage but will limit its focus to those that are particularly grave or widespread. Nevertheless, ensuring that the Security Council considers the destruction of cultural heritage as a human rights violation in situations where it may amount to a threat to international peace and security may reduce the protection gap, given that the Security Council can issue binding resolutions, whilst the Human Rights Council is limited to recommendations with no legal effect. It may also assist to divert slightly the spotlight that has so far been put on the protection of tangible heritage, and World Heritage sites more specifically.

As mentioned by the Human Rights Council,

> the violation or abuse of the right of everyone to take part in cultural life, including the ability to access and enjoy cultural heritage, may threaten stability, social cohesion and cultural identity, and constitutes an aggravating factor in conflict and a major obstacle to dialogue, peace and reconciliation.[117]

An approach to attacks against cultural heritage that considers their human rights implications may thus not only be welcome but also necessary in order to maintain peace and security. However, and in line with the UN pillars, it may perhaps be preferable to adopt a 'holistic' approach which incorporates human rights, rather than being strictly limited to them. Cultural heritage matters should be addressed in a coordinated manner not just by the Human Rights Council and the Security Council but by all the UN organs, and include the UN's three pillars: international peace and security, human rights, but also development.

[117] UNHRC Res 33/20 (2016) on Cultural Rights and the Protection of Cultural Heritage, Preamble.

9

The International Court of Justice and Cultural Heritage

International Cultural Heritage Law Through the Lens of World Court Jurisprudence?

Gabriele Gagliani

Introduction

The International Court of Justice (ICJ or the Court), the 'principal judicial organ of the United Nations',[1] has been confronted with cultural heritage issues and likely will continue to confront them in the future. In analyzing the Court's treatment of cultural heritage issues, one can distinguish between cultural heritage 'treaty disputes' regarding the interpretation and the application of UNESCO or other cultural heritage conventions within the Court's competence, and cultural heritage 'extra-treaty disputes', not 'covered' by UNESCO conventions or other agreements.[2] Nonetheless, such a dichotomous distinction seems to fail to catch the spectrum and variety of cultural heritage issues that have emerged in front of the ICJ, which go beyond any labeling. Indeed, under international law, the ICJ is a general court dealing potentially with a multitude of problems of the international legal order, and cultural property elements considered by the Court have always been entangled with other questions.[3] This reality mirrors the very nature and evolution of international cultural heritage law as an open and composite field of international law, which partly stems from, and overlaps with, other branches of the law.

[1] Statute of the International Court of Justice, San Francisco, 24 October 1945, art 1 (Statute of the ICJ).

[2] Alessandro Chechi, *The Settlement of International Cultural Heritage Disputes* (OUP 2014) 147; Ann P Prunty, Note, 'Toward Establishing an International Tribunal for the Settlement of Cultural Property Disputes: How to Keep Greece from Losing its Marbles' (1984) 72 Georgetown L J 1155–82.

[3] Here, the two terms 'cultural heritage' and 'cultural property' will be used interchangeably. However, this is not to overlook or diminish in any way the 'terminological' debate in international cultural heritage law. See Lyndel V Prott and Patrick J O'Keefe, '"Cultural Heritage" or "Cultural Property"?' (1992) 1 IJCP 311.

Gabriele Gagliani, The International Court of Justice and Cultural Heritage In: *Intersections in International Cultural Heritage Law*. Edited by Anne-Marie Carstens and Elizabeth Varner. © Oxford University Press 2020. The several contributors
DOI: 10.1093/oso/9780198846291.003.0010

Some scholarly attention has focused on cultural rights before the ICJ[4] or on cultural disputes before the Court, especially the extensive commentary on the Court's 1962 and 2013 decisions in the *Temple of Preah Vihear* case[5] and in the context of discussing the viability and opportunity of an international cultural heritage tribunal.[6] However, for the considerations above, an analysis both of cultural heritage issues before the ICJ and of the possible contribution of the Court to international cultural heritage law deserves more careful consideration. In particular, the Court's focus on certain points and arguments and an examination of the positions advanced by the Parties in dispute might provide significant insights into the role of the ICJ in international cultural heritage law, beyond insights that can be gleaned from studying only the final decisions of the Court. Moreover, it is worth noting that although the Court 'states the existing law and does not legislate', it also specifies the scope of the law and its general trends.[7] Interpreting the law often involves a part of creation by the interpreter,[8] who has some 'praetorian' powers.[9] And this creation by the interpreter occurs regardless of, and besides, any possible consideration on judicial activism. Taking these considerations into account, this chapter discusses whether, and in what way, the ICJ has contributed to international cultural heritage law.

I. The ICJ, International Law, and Cultural Heritage: Customary Rights and Sovereignty

The ICJ, commonly considered a 'continuation' of the Permanent Court of International Justice (PCIJ),[10] is an integral part of the United Nations (UN) system[11] and has a key role in international law. The Court has a potentially broad jurisdiction, comprising all cases that Parties refer to it.[12] In its role, beyond

[4] Eleni Polymenopoulou, 'Cultural Rights in the Case Law of the International Court of Justice' (2014) 27 Leiden J Intl L 447.

[5] See eg Victor Katta, 'The Ghosts of the Temple of Preah Vihear/Phra Viharn in the 2013 Judgment' (2015) 5 Asian J Intl L 16; Juan J Quintana, *Litigation at the International Court of Justice—Practice and Procedure* (Brill Nijhoff 2015) 961 ff; Yoshifumi Tanaka, 'A New Phase of the Temple of Preah Vihear Dispute Before the International Court of Justice: Reflections on the Indication of Provisional Measures of 18 July 2011' (2012) 11 Chinese J Intl L 191.

[6] Alessandro Chechi, 'Evaluating the Establishment of an International Cultural Heritage Court' (2013) 18 AAL 31.

[7] *Legality of the Threat or Use of Nuclear Weapons (Advisory Opinion)* [1996] ICJ Rep 226, para 18.

[8] Ingo Venzke, *How Interpretation Makes International Law—On Semantic Change and Normative Twists* (OUP 2012).

[9] Olivier Corten, *Méthodologie du Droit International Public* (Editions de l'Université de Bruxelles 2009) 198.

[10] James Crawford, *Brownlie's Principles of Public International Law* (8th edn, OUP 2012) 721; Martin Dixon, Robert McCorquodale, and Sarah Williams, *Cases and Materials on International Law* (5th edn, OUP 2011) 632.

[11] Charter of the United Nations (adopted 26 June 1945, entered into force 24 October 1945) 1 UNTS XVI, art 92 (UN Charter).

[12] Statute of the ICJ, art 36.1.

deciding the single cases at hand, the Court gives guidance and provides clarifications on relevant issues of international law.[13] As such, the ICJ has been the subject of detailed studies focusing on nearly every aspect of its activity,[14] and has not been immune from criticism.[15] In reality, the Court's position as one of the main organs of the United Nations and its concurrent need for judicial independence generate tensions.[16] And the Court provides an effective way of disposing of certain kinds and certain stages of disputes.[17]

In several cases, the ICJ has been confronted with rights concerning access to and enjoyment of tangible and intangible cultural heritage. Different terms have been employed in these cases, from 'customary rights' to 'historic rights'. However, despite terminological differences, these cases have all revolved around cultural heritage-related rights issues, entangled with a variety of questions. In its position, the ICJ, and the PCIJ before it, have contributed to the development of certain relevant cultural heritage concepts and have dealt with a number of cases that show the breadth of possible relations between communities' and States' cultural heritage rights.

The PCIJ had already had to deal with several questions on cultural rights, including the right to one's own traditions and language, in the context of a treaty dispute.[18] For instance, in *The Greco-Bulgarian Communities* case, the PCIJ was asked to address, inter alia, the definition of a 'community' within the scope of the Convention Between Greece and Bulgaria Respecting Reciprocal Emigration.[19] Before referring specifically to this Convention, the PCIJ remarked that, in general, elements such as race, religion, language, and traditions combine to define a 'community'.[20] Likewise, the *Minority Schools in Albania* case before the PCIJ concerned cultural rights of minorities.[21] In that case, the Permanent Court upheld the

[13] Pieter Kooijmans, 'The ICJ in the 21st Century: Judicial Restraint, Judicial Activism, or Proactive Judicial Policy' (2007) 56 ICLQ 741.

[14] John G Merrills, *International Dispute Settlement* (4th edn, CUP 2005) 127 ff.

[15] 'Contributions of the Court to the Resolution of International Tensions: Presentation by Sir Robert Jennings' in Connie Peck and Roy S Lee (eds), *Increasing the Effectiveness of the International Court of Justice—Proceedings of the ICJ/UNITAR Colloquium to Celebrate the 50th Anniversary of the Court* (Kluwer 1997) 81; Robert O Keohane, Andrew Moravcsik, and Anne-Marie Slaughter, 'Legalized Dispute Resolution: Interstate and Transnational' (2000) 54 Intl Organization 457, 480; for a different view, Thomas M Franck, *Fairness in International Law and Institutions* (OUP 1995) 346; James A Green, *The International Court of Justice and Self-Defence in International Law* (Hart 2009) 188.

[16] Robert Y Jennings and Rosalyn Higgins, 'General Introduction' in Andreas Zimmermann, Christian Tomuschat, Karin Oellers-Frahm, and Christian J Tams (eds), *The Statute of the International Court of Justice: A Commentary* (OUP 2012) 4, 18.

[17] ibid 41–45.

[18] *Certain German Interests in Polish Upper Silesia (Germany v Poland)* (Judgment) [1926] PCIJ Rep Series A No 7; *The Greco-Bulgarian 'Communities'* (Advisory Opinion) [1930] PCIJ Rep Series B No 17; *Minority Schools in Albania* (Advisory Opinion) [1935] PCIJ Rep Series A/B No 64.

[19] *The Greco-Bulgarian 'Communities'* (n 18); Convention between Greece and Bulgaria Respecting Reciprocal Emigration (signed at Neuilly-Sur-Seine on 27 November 1919) 1 LNTS 68.

[20] *The Greco-Bulgarian 'Communities'* (n 18) 21.

[21] *Minority Schools in Albania* (n 18).

right of minorities 'to have their own charitable, religious and educational institutions' in Albania.[22]

Though the significance of cases such as *The Greco-Bulgarian Communities* or the *Minority Schools in Albania* has to be measured against the specific context of territorial reorganization after the First World War and the related concerns for the protection of religious, ethnic, and linguistic minorities,[23] this case law has silently paved the way for the full recognition of cultural diversity under international law. Cultural rights and cultural diversity are strongly connected,[24] and it is precisely in the framework of cultural rights that the idea of cultural diversity has emerged and developed[25] through to its consecration in the 2005 UNESCO Convention on the Protection and Promotion of the Diversity of Cultural Expressions.[26] It is difficult to imagine cultural diversity becoming a value to be protected in and of itself at the international level,[27] without the 'hidden pillar' provided by the PCIJ's early consideration of certain rights.

In a similar fashion, in the wake of decolonization, the ICJ has addressed questions related to the right to self-determination, such as that of Namibia,[28] and touched also on sensitive issues, including the acquisition of territories inhabited by indigenous communities or tribes as *terra nullius*.[29] This latter inquiry is a highly sensitive point in light of the important or even sacred dimension that specific areas might assume in some cultures.

The Court case law on cultural heritage-related rights has not ceased there, however. Several territorial disputes have involved cultural heritage rights. This is not surprising, since cultural arguments and justifications have often been wielded to support territorial claims.[30] Both in the *Delimitation of the Maritime Boundary*

22 ibid, para 73.

23 Antonio Cassese, *I Diritti Umani Oggi* (4th edn, Editori Laterza 2005) 17–18.

24 Convention on the Protection and Promotion of the Diversity of Cultural Expressions (adopted 20 October 2005, entered into force 18 March 2007) 2440 UNTS, art 2(1) (Convention on Cultural Diversity); *Human Rights Are Essential Tools for an Effective Intercultural Dialogue*, Statement by a Group of UN Experts on the World Day for Cultural Diversity for Dialogue and Development, 21 May 2010; Yvonne Donders, 'The Cultural Diversity Convention and Cultural Rights: Included or Ignored?' in Toshiyuki Kono and Steven van Uytsel (eds), *The Convention on the Promotion and the Protection of the Diversity of Cultural Expressions* (Intersentia 2012).

25 Hélène Ruiz Fabri, 'Droit du Commerce et Culture: La Portée de la Convention sur la Diversité des Expressions Culturelles', UN Audiovisual Library of International Law, New York, May 2012.

26 Convention on Cultural Diversity (n 24).

27 On cultural diversity and human rights, Silvia Borrelli, 'Of Veils, Crosses and Turbans: The European Court of Human Rights and Religious Practices as Manifestations of Cultural Diversity' in Silvia Borrelli and Federico Lenzerini (eds), *Cultural Heritage, Cultural Rights, Cultural Diversity: New Developments in International Law* (Martinus Nijhoff 2012) 55.

28 *Legal Consequences for the States of the Continued Presence of South Africa in Namibia (South West Africa) Notwithstanding Security Council Resolution 276 (1970)* (Advisory Opinion) [1971] ICJ Rep 16; *Western Sahara* (Advisory Opinion) [1975] ICJ Rep 12.

29 *Western Sahara* (Advisory Opinion) [1975] ICJ Rep 12, para 81.

30 Brian T Sumner, 'Territorial Disputes at the International Court of Justice' (2004) 53 Duke L J 1779, 1782, 1785–86.

in the Gulf of Maine[31] and in the *Maritime Delimitation in the Area Between Greenland and Jan Mayen*[32] cultural arguments were used by the States in disputes as reasons to adjust or shift the boundary line(s) in one direction or the other. In the *Delimitation of the Maritime Boundary in the Gulf of Maine Area*, a groundbreaking case among border delimitation disputes,[33] Canada and the United States quarreled over the delimitation of the geographical area of the Gulf of Maine, on the eastern coast of North America.[34] The United States explicitly requested the Court to take into account, inter alia, the 'long established practices of fisheries and activities,' when drawing the delimitation line.[35] Fishing traditions represent a form of intangible cultural heritage, as proved by the Argungu fishing festival in Nigeria and the technique of shrimp fishing on horseback in Oostduinkerke.[36] In order to reach an equitable result,[37] the Court paid attention to the 'historic rights' invoked by the United States, which had allegedly taken the form of fishing and conservation and management of fisheries by the United States and its nationals, even before the United States gained independence.[38] Canada, in turn, had insisted on socio-economic aspects and fishing practices.[39]

The Court did not attribute decisive importance, for the purposes of the delimitation, to the antiquity or continuity of fishing activities carried out in the past within that part of the delimitation area. Rather, it factored in that until very recently, these expanses were part of the high seas and as such freely open to the fishermen of several countries.[40] The Court made it clear that its concern was to avoid a 'radically inequitable' result, such as 'catastrophic repercussions for the livelihood and economic well-being of the population of the countries concerned'.[41]

Similar considerations were made in the *Maritime Delimitation in the Area Between Greenland and Jan Mayen*, a dispute between Denmark and Norway.[42] In applying the relevant provisions of international law, the Court determined that the existence of 'special' or 'relevant circumstances' might have led to the shift or adjustment of a provisional median line adopted for the delimitation of both the

[31] *Delimitation of the Maritime Boundary in the Gulf of Maine Area (Canada/United States of America)* (Judgment) [1984] ICJ Rep 246.

[32] *Maritime Delimitation in the Area Between Greenland and Jan Mayen (Denmark v Norway)* (Judgment) [1993] ICJ Rep 38.

[33] *Delimitation of the Maritime Boundary in the Gulf of Maine Area* (n 31) paras 25–26.

[34] ibid, paras 28–29.

[35] ibid, paras 16–17.

[36] Both the Argungu International Fishing and Cultural Festival (Nigeria) and shrimp fishing on horseback in Oostduinkerke (Belgium) are inscribed as intangible cultural heritage of humanity in the Representative List of the Intangible Cultural Heritage of Humanity under Article 16 of the Convention for the Safeguarding of the Intangible Cultural Heritage (adopted 17 October 2003, entered into force 20 April 2006) 2368 UNTS 3.

[37] *Delimitation of the Maritime Boundary in the Gulf of Maine Area* (n 31) para 230.

[38] ibid, para 233.

[39] ibid, para 234.

[40] ibid, para 235.

[41] ibid, paras 237–38.

[42] *Maritime Delimitation in the Area Between Greenland and Jan Mayen* (n 32).

continental shelf and the fishery zone of the two States.[43] The Court held that while the disparity of coastal length was a relevant factor in this sense, socio-economic and cultural heritage arguments were not. The Court initially based this exclusion on neither Party having presented such arguments, although for different reasons, in the context of the possible adjustment of the median line provisionally drawn.[44]

Cultural arguments nonetheless came back at a later stage of the proceedings when the Court assessed whether access to the resources of the area of overlapping claims constituted a factor relevant to the delimitation.[45] Both States claimed practices, such as sealing and whaling, were fundamental for the survival of the Inuit community in Greenland and for the fragile economy of Norwegian coastal communities.[46] The Court noted that the conflict was essentially on access to fishery resources and, quoting its decision in the *Gulf of Maine* case and its concern in avoiding 'catastrophic repercussions,'[47] established that access to fishery resources for the vulnerable fishing communities concerned was enough to shift the provisional median line.[48] The Court further rejected 'cultural factors' summoned by Denmark, such as 'the attachment of the people of Greenland to their land and the surrounding sea,' in order to prevent the curtailment of the sea area in the 200-mile zone off the coast.[49]

The questions that emerged in these two disputes in front of the ICJ are not new in international law. Arguments based on the local communities' (cultural) practices and access to land, sea, and natural resources have been dealt with extensively by international human rights bodies and tribunals as cultural rights deserving protection.[50] Denmark itself had to face a claim brought to the European Court of Human Rights (ECtHR) by members of the Inughuit (Inuit) tribe of Greenland, who claimed that the deprivation of their traditional land and access to their livelihood (hunting and fishing activities) had violated several rights under the European Convention of Human Rights (ECHR).[51] However, the ECtHR rejected some of the tribe's claims and gave special relevance, inter alia, to the compensation that the tribe had been afforded for the eviction and loss of hunting rights.[52]

[43] ibid, paras 48–56.
[44] ibid, paras 60 ff.
[45] ibid, para 72.
[46] ibid, para 74.
[47] ibid, para 75.
[48] ibid, paras 75–76.
[49] ibid, paras 79–80, also quoting *Continental Shelf (Libyan Arab Jamahiriya/Malta)* (Judgment) [1985] ICJ Rep 13, para 50.
[50] See eg UNHRC, *Lubicon Lake Band v Canada*, Communication No 167/1984 (26 March 1990) UN Doc Supp No 40 (A/45/40) (1990) 1; IACtHR, *Yakye Axa Indigenous Community v Paraguay* (Judgment) Series C No 125 (17 June 2005); IACtHR, *Sawhoyamaxa Indigenous Community v Paraguay* (Judgment) Series C No 146 (29 March 2006) paras 73, 124–30, 180, 2482.
[51] ECtHR, *Hingitaq 53 and Others v Denmark* (Admissibility Decision) App no 18584/04 (12 January 2006).
[52] ibid 20; violations of human rights including the right to education and/or the right to access land have also been dealt with by the ICJ, although in a different context: *Legal Consequences of the*

Further, the *Gulf of Maine* and *Jan Mayen* cases point to the possible overlap and coincidence of States' interests and historic or customary rights with the interests and rights of their communities, beyond the dichotomy often featured in human rights cases. In the same vein, in the case *Racial Discrimination*, the Court had been at least 'virtually' confronted with alleged claims of destruction of Georgian culture and identity by Russia, as declared by Georgia 'on its own behalf and as *parens patriae* for its citizens'.[53] Unfortunately, the case did not reach the merits phase since the Court found that it had no jurisdiction to entertain Georgia's application.[54]

These cases might lead to the conclusion that, given the exclusive State-to-State nature of ICJ proceedings, a State-centric perspective must prevail in these disputes. However, this is not always the case. In the *Frontier Dispute (Burkina Faso/Niger)*, the Court was confronted with a dispute on the demarcation of the frontier between Burkina Faso and Niger.[55] Niger had stressed that a previously established boundary between the two colonies had created problems for nomadic populations, who had to pass from one colony to the other to 'retain their customary transhumant routes, or even to cultivate their croplands which overlapped the boundary'.[56] Once it determined the course of the frontier between the two countries, the Court 'expressed its wish' that each Party exercise its jurisdiction in the territory under its sovereignty having regard for the needs of the populations concerned, in particular of nomadic or semi-nomadic populations, 'and to the necessity to overcome difficulties that may arise for them because of the frontier'.[57] Further, Judge Bennouna and Judge Cançado Trindade supported the conclusion of the Court and brought its reasoning even further: one stressed the need to go beyond the Westphalian model and frontier demarcation, which does not take into account the particular cultural heritage of that region of the world;[58] the other highlighted that 'people and territory go together' and thus emphasized the need to respect the regime of transhumance and the 'solidarity' between peoples on the same territory.[59]

All these cases show that the Court has dealt with a wide spectrum of situations where cultural heritage-related rights have emerged in connection with, or in opposition to, national interests and historic rights. The State might be just one

Construction of a Wall in the Occupied Palestinian Territory (Advisory Opinion) [2004] ICJ Reports 136, paras 130–37.

53 *Application of the International Convention on the Elimination of All Forms of Racial Discrimination (Georgia v Russian Federation)* (Preliminary Objections, Judgment) [2011] ICJ Rep 70, paras 16 ff.

54 ibid, para 187.

55 *Frontier Dispute (Burkina Faso/Niger)* (Judgment) [2013] ICJ Rep 44, paras 12–19.

56 *Frontier Dispute (Burkina Faso/Niger)* (Memorial of Niger of 20 April 2011) para 2.5.

57 ibid, para 112.

58 *Frontier Dispute (Burkina Faso/Niger)* (Declaration of Judge Bennouna of 16 April 2013) 96.

59 *Frontier Dispute (Burkina Faso/Niger)* (Separate Opinion of Judge Cançado Trindade of 16 April 2013) para 87.

among several entities seeking access to justice to protect them,[60] and, of course, the key subject in the context of disputes before the ICJ.[61] Yet, cultural rights and cultural heritage-related rights might be recognized with varying degrees of access and enjoyment in different subjects.[62]

The ICJ, together with the PCIJ, has attached some relevance to cultural heritage arguments. The Courts supported the emergence of some prominent concepts of international cultural heritage law, such as the idea of 'community', and has paid some attention to whether States' interests overlap with communities' interests, such as in the case of nomadic communities' traditions and frontier demarcation. Yet, the Court's consideration of these issues has been indirect and limited, due to the Court's specific jurisdiction on the matters at issue and the application of general international law. In this context, as already noted, the ICJ might be regarded as an effective forum for the resolution of some, but not all, disputes.[63] Other dispute settlement fora might be useful for a different standpoint on certain interests and rights at stake.[64]

II. Cultural Heritage and the Environment

Several ICJ cases have featured the link between the environment and cultural heritage. This link had already been 'revealed' in the 1972 UNESCO Convention Concerning the Protection of the World Cultural and Natural Heritage (the World Heritage Convention).[65] Nevertheless, the Court has explored the breadth of the relationship between cultural heritage and the environment and has pushed for some development. The *Whaling in the Antarctic* case is emblematic in this sense.[66] The dispute arose out of Japan's issuance of special permits to catch whales in the framework of a Japanese whaling program (JARPA II), which Japan maintained was for scientific purposes and as such lawful under the 1946 International Convention for the Regulation of Whaling (ICRW), contrary to Australia's allegations.[67] As

[60] Ana P Vrdoljak, 'Standing and Collective Cultural Rights' in Andrzej Jabkubowski (ed), *Cultural Rights as Collective Rights: An International Law Perspective* (Brill Publishers 2012).

[61] The Court is not able to accept an *actio popularis*. *South West Africa (Second Phase) (Ethiopia v South Africa)* (Judgment) [1966] ICJ Rep 6, para 88.

[62] UNGA, Report of the Independent Expert in the Field of Cultural Rights, Farida Shaheed, UN Doc A/HRC/17/38, 16.

[63] Jennings and Higgins (n 16) 18.

[64] See eg ICSID, *Southern Pacific Properties (Middle East) Limited v Arab Republic of Egypt* (Award) ICSID case No ARB/84/3 (20 May 1992); WTO Appellate Body Report, European Communities—Measures Prohibiting the Importation and Marketing of Seal Products, WT/AB/DS400, WT/AB/DS401, circulated on 22 May 2014.

[65] Convention Concerning the Protection of the World Cultural and Natural Heritage (adopted 16 November 1972, entered into force 17 December 1975) 1037 UNTS 151.

[66] *Whaling in the Antarctic (Australia v Japan: New Zealand Intervening)* (Judgment) [2014] ICJ Rep 226.

[67] ibid, para 30.

stressed in the Preamble of the ICRW, the Convention pursues the double goal of ensuring the conservation of all whale species while allowing for their sustainable exploitation.[68] The Court concluded that the killing, taking, and treating of whales under the special permits granted by Japan was not for scientific research purposes falling within the relevant provisions of the ICRW.[69]

As some scholars included in this volume have noted elsewhere, the use and preservation of endangered species is the subject of cultural clashes, and whales and whaling are no exception.[70] The UNESCO World Heritage List, established in the 1972 World Heritage Convention, testifies to the range of (even conflicting) cultural heritage interests for whales and whaling. The World Heritage List sites range from the Wadi Al-Hitan (Whale Valley) in Egypt, containing fossils of whales, to the Whale Sanctuary of El Vizcaino in Mexico, relevant for its ecosystem, and the Red Bay Basque Whaling Station in Canada, an archeological site that testifies to the European whaling tradition. In this context, the *Whaling in the Antarctic* case epitomizes disputes where cultural heritage and environmental protection are at the same time allies, being the protection of whales an objective of both, and foes, for the environmental harm that too much whaling might cause. The International Whaling Commission, established under the ICRW in 1946, has granted an exemption to indigenous communities on the prohibition of killing of certain whales.[71] The exemption has not included whaling communities in countries such as Japan and Norway, which have therefore opposed the Convention.[72] Reconciling such competing claims,[73] or conflicting interests and goals, is a complex and difficult task.

Similarly, the *Dispute Regarding Navigational and Related Rights* case concerned opposing interests.[74] There, the Court seemed to privilege, at least in principle, environmental protection measures over riparian communities' rights. The case revolved around several incidents that had occurred between Costa Rica and Nicaragua. The two countries had concluded a Treaty of Limits in 1858 fixing the course of the boundary between them and partly overlapping with the course of the San Juan River.[75] That notwithstanding, the Court had to deal with the legal basis and scope of Costa Rica's right of free navigation[76] and Nicaragua's power to

[68] ibid, para 56.

[69] ibid, paras 223–27.

[70] James A R Nafziger, Robert Kirkwood Paterson, and Alison Dundes Renteln, *Cultural Law: International, Comparative and Indigenous* (CUP 2010) 74–77.

[71] In *Whaling in the Antarctic*, the same Court noted that whaling that fell outside art VIII, para 1, other than aboriginal subsistence whaling, was subject to the three Schedule provisions invoked by Australia. *Whaling in the Antarctic* (n 66) para 230.

[72] ibid, para 77.

[73] ibid.

[74] *Dispute Regarding Navigational and Related Rights (Costa Rica v Nicaragua)* (Judgment) [2009] ICJ Rep 213.

[75] ibid, para 15 ff.

[76] ibid, para 31 ff.

regulate navigation on the San Juan River.[77] Through an evolutionary interpretation of the 1858 Treaty, the Court recognized the protection of the environment as a relevant public interest and legitimate public purpose pursued by Nicaragua in its regulations[78] even though not all of its powers of regulation had been exercised in conformity with that Treaty.[79] Turning to the question of subsistence fishing of the riparian communities of the Costa Rican bank of the River,[80] the Court concluded that Costa Rica had a customary right, but that this right would have been subject to any Nicaraguan regulatory measures relating to fishing adopted for proper purposes, particularly for the protection of natural resources and the environment.[81]

In a recent related judgment, the Court found, inter alia, that Costa Rica had violated its obligations under general international law to carry out an environmental impact assessment (EIA) concerning the construction of a road along the San Juan River.[82] Both Parties-in-dispute had agreed that under international law an obligation existed to conduct an EIA for activities with cross-border effects.[83]

Given this obligation under international law, should an EIA take into account cultural heritage elements? This point was discussed in the *Pulp Mills* case[84] where the authorization, construction, and commissioning of two pulp mills by Uruguay had pushed Argentina to initiate Court proceedings. Argentina had alleged a breach of both procedural and substantive obligations under the Statute of the River Uruguay,[85] a treaty that entered into force between the two States in 1976.[86] In particular, Argentina had emphasized the negative impact of these activities on the quality of the waters of the river Uruguay and on the areas affected by the river.[87]

The Court found that Uruguay had breached certain procedural obligations,[88] but it rejected Argentina's claims on the violation of substantive obligations.[89] Appraising Uruguay's alleged violation of the substantive obligation to prevent pollution and preserve the aquatic environment under the 1975 Statue of the River Uruguay,[90] the Court assessed the EIA conducted by Uruguay.[91] Uruguay

[77] ibid, para 85 ff.
[78] ibid, para 89.
[79] ibid, para 133.
[80] ibid, para 134 ff.
[81] ibid, para 141.
[82] *Certain Activities Carried out by Nicaragua in the Border Area (Costa Rica v Nicaragua) & Construction of a Road in Costa Rica Along the San Juan River (Nicaragua v Costa Rica)* (Judgment) [2015] ICJ Rep 665, paras 146–62.
[83] ibid, para 101.
[84] *Pulp Mills on the River Uruguay (Argentina v Uruguay)* (Judgment) [2010] ICJ Rep 14.
[85] ibid, para 67.
[86] ibid, para 1.
[87] ibid.
[88] ibid, paras 111, 122, 158.
[89] ibid, para 282.
[90] ibid, para 190 ff.
[91] ibid, para 200 ff.

had argued that the EIA had to take into consideration, among other factors, the presence of historical and cultural sites.[92] The performance standards of the International Finance Corporation, a part of the World Bank Group participating in the investment in one of the mill plants, addressed cultural heritage concerns and incorporated, among others, the obligations of the World Heritage Convention.[93] The Court concluded that environmental and cultural factors had been given due consideration in the EIA.[94] As a result, even though the question was not central to the dispute at hand, the ICJ has set its seal on the relevance of cultural heritage aspects in EIAs, an issue until now discussed only marginally, and by technicians.[95]

These ICJ cases reflect the complex articulation of the relationship between cultural heritage and the environment. Even bearing in mind that cultural and natural heritage are very different,[96] the overlap and (at least partial) integration between cultural heritage and the environment seems undisputable. Still, this relationship is not always a 'mutually supportive' one, and the protection of the environment and cultural heritage has sometimes diverged.[97] For instance, it might well happen that the preservation of specific areas or endangered animal or plant species conflicts with the recognition and full exercise of cultural rights. Only in this context can one appreciate the sensitivity of the questions on cultural heritage and the environment that the Court has confronted and of the stances taken by the Court. In this sense, striking a balance between competing values and interests often entails 'political' choices.

III. Cultural Heritage and the Obligation to Cooperate

The Court has also taken some steps forward in favor of a less State-centric approach in the longstanding tension between national sovereignty and global protection of cultural heritage. If the domestic sovereignty model was a pillar of the 1970 UNESCO Convention on the Means of Prohibiting and Preventing the Illicit Import, Export and Transfer of Ownership of Cultural Property,[98] the World Heritage Convention started to change this perspective, leaving the tension between national sovereignty

[92] *Pulp Mills on the River Uruguay* (Counter-Memorial of Uruguay of 20 July 2007) para 4.113.

[93] ibid, paras 5.1–5.14.

[94] ibid, paras 209–10.

[95] See eg Alan Bond, Lesley Langstaff, Ross Baxter, Hans-Georg W J Kofoed, Katri Lisitzin, and Stina Lundström, 'Dealing with the Cultural Heritage Aspect of Environmental Impact Assessment in Europe' (2004) 22 Impact Assessment and Project Appraisal 37; Koji Tsunokawa and Christopher Hoban (eds), *Roads and the Environment: A Handbook* (1997) 376, World Bank Technical Paper 140 ff.

[96] Catherine Redgwell, 'Article 2: Definition of Natural Heritage' in Francesco Francioni and Federico Lenzerini (eds), *The 1972 World Heritage Convention: A Commentary* (OUP 2008).

[97] Janet Blake, *International Cultural Heritage Law* (OUP 2015) 117–18.

[98] Francesco Francioni, 'The 1972 World Heritage Convention: An Introduction' in Francioni and Lenzerini (eds) (n 96) 3.

and global ('humankind') interest unresolved.[99] Later international conventions backed the move away from a pure State-sovereignty model,[100] and the Court has given new significance to the obligation to cooperate and the need for negotiated solutions in the field of cultural heritage.

The *Case Concerning the Temple of Preah Vihear*[101] has been a goldmine for international law scholars and practitioners, beyond the borders of international cultural heritage law. The dispute between Cambodia and Thailand revolved around territorial sovereignty over the region of the Temple of Preah Vihear (the 'Temple'), and over the interpretation of the first ICJ decision on the controversy.[102]

The Temple is an ancient sanctuary, with considerable artistic and archaeological value.[103] It is located on a promontory on the border between Cambodia and Thailand, a border defined by a 1904 boundary Treaty between France and Siam (the old exonym of Thailand) and by a connected map that had left the Temple in Cambodia's territory. The map had been communicated to the Siamese authorities but had never been expressly approved. Following Cambodia's independence, Thailand had occupied the Temple and its vicinity. Both States had used several arguments to support their respective claims, based, inter alia, on religious, artistic, and historical heritage, as well as historical connections.[104] In its 1962 judgment, the Court, excluding the physical, historical, religious, and archaeological arguments used by both States that were dispositive of the matter,[105] had concluded that the Temple was situated in the territory under the sovereignty of Cambodia.[106] It further ruled that 'Thailand is under an obligation to withdraw any military or police forces, or other guards or keepers, stationed by her at the Temple, or in its vicinity on Cambodian territory'.[107]

Following the 1962 judgment, Thailand had withdrawn from the Temple buildings.[108] However, when in 2007 Cambodia requested the inscription of the Temple on the World Heritage List of the World Heritage Convention, Thailand contested

[99] Natasha Affolder, 'Democratising or Demonising the World Heritage Convention?' (2007) 38 Victoria U Wellington L Rev 41.

[100] Patrizia Vigni, 'The Enforcement of Underwater Cultural Heritage by Courts' in Francesco Francioni and James Gordley (eds), *Enforcing International Cultural Heritage Law* (OUP 2013) 135.

[101] *Case Concerning the Temple of Preah Vihear (Cambodia v Thailand)* (Merits, Judgment) [1962] ICJ Rep 6; *Request for Interpretation of the Judgment of 15 June 1962 in the Case Concerning the Temple of Preah Vihear (Cambodia v Thailand)* (Judgment) [2013] ICJ Rep 281.

[102] *Case Concerning the Temple of Preah Vihear (Cambodia v Thailand)* (n 101) 2; *Request for Interpretation of the Judgment of 15 June 1962 in the Case Concerning the Temple of Preah Vihear (Cambodia v Thailand)* (n 101).

[103] *Case Concerning the Temple of Preah Vihear (Cambodia v Thailand)* (n 101) 15.

[104] *Case Concerning the Temple of Preah Vihear (Cambodia v Thailand)* (Memorial of the Government of the Kingdom of Cambodia of 20 January 1960) paras 6–10.

[105] *Case Concerning the Temple of Preah Vihear (Cambodia v Thailand)* (n 101).

[106] ibid 34–35.

[107] ibid.

[108] *Request for Interpretation of the Judgment of 15 June 1962 in the Case Concerning the Temple of Preah Vihear (Cambodia v Thailand)* (n 101) para 22.

the border line between the two States in the map submitted by Cambodia.[109] Following the inscription (with the exclusion of the disputed area), several incidents occurred between the two countries.[110] These incidents had caused irreparable damage to the Temple along with the displacement of local people and loss of human life.[111] As a result, upon the request of Cambodia, the Court indicated a number of provisional measures including the withdrawal of military personnel.[112]

In its 2013 judgment, the Court interpreted the 1962 judgment and concluded that Cambodia had sovereignty over the whole territory of the promontory of the Temple.[113] It laid great emphasis on every State's obligation to respect the territorial sovereignty of all other States and the duty to settle any dispute between them by peaceful means.[114] In particular, given the religious and cultural relevance of the Temple for the peoples of the region and its inscription in the World Heritage List, the Court recalled that under Article 6 of the World Heritage Convention, Cambodia and Thailand, both Parties to the Convention, 'must co-operate between themselves and with the international community in the protection of the site as a world heritage.'[115] The Court also emphasized the need to ensure access to the Temple from Cambodia's plain.[116]

Although the importance of cooperation and negotiation between States has been reiterated by the ICJ in several contexts, such as for the joint management and prevention of any risk of damage to the environment,[117] its considerations in the *Temple of Preah Vihear* case appear innovative. After recalling States' duty to settle any dispute between them peacefully, the Court seems to vest Article 6 of the World Heritage Convention with a new function from the perspective of dispute settlement. Judge Cançado Trindade went further, pointing to the need to abandon a territorial sovereignty perspective and stating that the Court's 2011 order for provisional measures and its 2013 judgment had brought 'territory, people and human values together' in line with *jus gentium*, endorsing a process of 'humanization' of international law.[118]

[109] ibid, para 25.
[110] ibid, para 27.
[111] *Request for Interpretation of the Judgment of 15 June 1962 in the Case Concerning the Temple of Preah Vihear (Cambodia v Thailand)* (Provisional Measures—Order of 18 July 2011) [2011] ICJ Rep 537, para 48.
[112] *Request for Interpretation of the Judgment of 15 June 1962 in the Case Concerning the Temple of Preah Vihear (Cambodia v Thailand)* (n 101) para 69.
[113] ibid, para 107.
[114] ibid, para 105.
[115] ibid, para 106.
[116] ibid, para 106.
[117] *Pulp Mills on the River Uruguay* (n 84) paras 77, 218.
[118] *Request for Interpretation of the Judgment of 15 June 1962 in the Case Concerning the Temple of Preah Vihear* (Separate Opinion of Judge Cançado Trindade of 11 November 2013) paras 33, 64–65.

One cannot overstate the relevance of the need for Parties to cooperate in the context of ICJ disputes, where sensitive political situations mix with complex international law questions. In a similar fashion, in the *Application of the Interim Accord* case, which concerned Greece's opposition to the admission of the former Yugoslav Republic of Macedonia (FYROM) to the North Atlantic Treaty Organization (NATO), even after the conclusion of a specific interim accord between the two countries,[119] the Court put emphasis on the Parties' duty to negotiate under their interim accord. The ICJ dispute, which concerned the alleged use of historic and cultural patrimony (notably, the name 'Macedonia' and the use of the Vergina Sun, an ancient Greek art symbol in FYROM's flag) of one Party (Greece) by the other (FYROM),[120] was in fact the tip of the iceberg of complex political and cultural relations between the Parties.[121]

Likewise, the Court emphasized cooperation in the *Jurisdictional Immunities* case.[122] This dispute has marked the scholarly debate on State immunities and human rights violations.[123] Yet, the dispute has stood out also for its implications on cultural heritage. In this case, Germany had initiated proceedings against Italy claiming that the latter had violated its immunity from jurisdiction and its immunity from execution.[124] The case had arisen from Italian court decisions and the implementation in Italy of a Greek court decision, which had all granted relief to Italian and Greek citizens' claims for compensation against Germany for its conduct during the Second World War.[125] After a much-quoted discussion on State immunity,[126] the Court concluded that Italian courts had violated Germany's immunity under customary international law.[127] Pending claims by Italian citizens, the Court said, could be the subject of further negotiations between the two States, with a view to resolving the issue.[128]

The Court further concluded that Italy had violated Germany's immunity also by declaring enforceable, in Italy, the decisions of the Greek court against Germany.[129]

[119] *Application of the Interim Accord of 13 September 1995 (The former Yugoslav Republic of Macedonia v Greece)* (Judgment) [2011] ICJ Rep 644, paras 15–22.

[120] ibid, paras 148–65.

[121] *Application of the Interim Accord of 13 September 1995 (The former Yugoslav Republic of Macedonia v Greece)* (Dissenting Opinion of Judge ad hoc Roucounas of 5 December 2011) para 23.

[122] *Jurisdictional Immunities of the State (Germany v Italy: Greece Intervening)* (Judgment) [2012] ICJ Rep 99.

[123] Anne Peters, Evelyne Lagrange, Stefan Oeter, and Christian Tomuschat (eds), *Immunities in the Age of Global Constitutionalism* (Brill Nijhoff 2014); Michael Bothe, 'The Decision of the Italian Constitutional Court Concerning the Jurisdictional Immunities of Germany' (2015) 24 Ital YB Intl L Online 25; Bruno Simma, 'Human Rights Before the International Court of Justice: Community Interest Coming to Life?' in Christian J Tams and James Sloan (eds), *The Development of International Law by the International Court of Justice* (OUP 2013) 301.

[124] *Jurisdictional Immunities of the State* (n 122) paras 1, 15–16.

[125] ibid, paras 21–35.

[126] ibid, paras 60–93.

[127] ibid, para 107.

[128] ibid, para 104.

[129] ibid, para 131.

Before turning to this latter point, however, the Court discussed the inscription in the Land Registry of the Province of Como of a legal charge against Villa Vigoni, a property of Germany located near Lake Como.[130] The inscription followed the enforcement in Italy of a judgment rendered in Greece against Germany.[131] On this point, it is worth noting the positions of the Parties in dispute: while Germany had argued that this measure violated its immunity from enforcement, Italy had not sought to justify that measure but, on the contrary, had indicated to the Court that it had 'no objection to any decision by the Court obliging Italy to ensure that the mortgage on Villa Vigoni inscribed at the land registry is cancelled'.[132] Nonetheless, the Court proceeded in its analysis of this point.[133] The Court pointed that it was clear that Villa Vigoni, which was the seat of a cultural center for cooperation between Italy and Germany in the fields of research, culture, and education, was being used for governmental purposes that were entirely non-commercial and, as such, fell within Germany's sovereign functions.[134] The registration of the legal charge on Villa Vigoni constituted a violation of Italy's obligation to respect Germany's immunity from enforcement.[135]

The problem of preserving State immunity and cultural heritage on the one hand, and the need for justice on the other, is not uncommon in international disputes.[136] Cooperation and negotiation might provide the most effective means to resolve disputes given the difficulty in reconciling the sensitive interests at stake, as already observed with regard to cultural heritage and the environment. In this sense, the ICJ support for cooperation and negotiation allows an approach that not only goes beyond a purely 'national' perspective on cultural heritage under international law, but that also responds to a number of interests that legal disputes cannot accommodate.[137] This approach corresponds to recent trends in international cultural heritage law, for instance in the context of cultural heritage restitutions cases,[138] and might respond to the awareness that diplomatic means are sometimes the most practicable option when cultural heritage is involved.[139]

[130] ibid, paras 109 ff.
[131] ibid, para 109.
[132] ibid, para 110.
[133] ibid, para 112.
[134] ibid, paras 119–20.
[135] ibid, para 120.
[136] Stacie I Strong, 'Rubin Redux: Rights Balancing in Cultural Heritage Litigation' in Hildegard Schneider and Valentina S Vadi (eds), *Art and Heritage Disputes in International and Comparative Law* (2013) 5 Transnational Dispute Management <https://www.transnational-dispute-management.com/article.asp?key=2011> accessed 2 February 2020.
[137] For further discussion on national perspectives on cultural heritage see Robert Peters, 'Nationalism versus Internationalism: New Perspectives beyond State Sovereignty and Territoriality in the Protection of Cultural Heritage' (Ch 15) in this volume.
[138] Marie Cornu and Marc-André Renold, 'New Developments in the Restitution of Cultural Property: Alternative Means of Dispute Resolution' (2010) 17 IJCP 1, 12–13.
[139] Roger O' Keefe, 'World Cultural Heritage: Obligations to the International Community as a Whole?' (2004) 53 ICLQ 189, 207–08.

IV. The ICJ and Cultural Heritage: Is There any Jurisprudential Cross-Fertilization?

The complexity and variety of issues at stake in disputes involving cultural heritage make it possible for the same case or issue to be heard by different international courts and tribunals. The relations between these international dispute settlement fora can be conceptualized in a number of ways.[140] With this in mind, it appears worthwhile to consider whether any jurisprudential cross-fertilization has occurred between the ICJ and other international courts on matters concerning cultural heritage. This is relevant in order to assess whether the World Court has played any consistent role when addressing questions relating to cultural heritage under international law. For instance, the case on *Certain Property*[141] filed with the ICJ by Liechtenstein had been previously dealt with by the ECtHR. The facts giving rise to the two cases were exactly the same. After the Second World War, Czechoslovakia had confiscated German and Hungarian nationals' properties. The properties seized included a seventeenth-century painting owned by the then-monarch of Liechtenstein.[142] When in 1991, the painting was given on temporary loan by a museum in Brno (Czechoslovakia) to a museum in Cologne (Germany), the son of the former monarch of Liechtenstein, Prince Hans-Adam II, had filed claims with German courts for the sequestration and return of his property.[143] The claims were dismissed on the basis of the application of the special regime implemented for measures taken against German external assets in the aftermath of the Second World War.[144] In 1998, Prince Hans-Adam II instituted proceedings before the ECtHR against Germany, alleging violation of his right to a fair trial (Article 6), of his right to property (Article 1 of Protocol No. 1), and of the prohibition of discrimination (Article 14) of the ECHR.[145] All claims were rejected by the ECtHR. In particular, addressing the claim of violation of the right to property, the ECtHR established that it lacked jurisdiction *ratione temporis* to examine Czechoslovakia's expropriation and excluded any violation by German courts.[146]

Subsequently, in 2005, Liechtenstein brought a claim against Germany in front of the ICJ for the restitution of the seventeenth-century painting.[147] The ICJ found that it lacked jurisdiction *ratione temporis*.[148] According to the Court, the proceedings were instituted by Liechtenstein as a result of the decisions by German courts

[140] 'The Court and Other International Tribunals' in Peck and Lee (n 15) 280 ff.
[141] *Certain Property (Liechtenstein v Germany)* (Preliminary Objections, Judgment) [2005] ICJ Rep 6.
[142] ibid, para 13.
[143] ibid, paras 14–16.
[144] ibid.
[145] ECtHR, *Prince Hans-Adam II of Liechtenstein v Germany* (Judgment) App no 42527/98 (12 July 2001).
[146] ibid, paras 78–87.
[147] ibid, para 13 ff.
[148] ibid, para 54.

regarding the specific painting at issue in the 1990s, but the real cause of action was the specific measures taken by Czechoslovakia in 1945. According to the Court, these measures had been adopted before the 1957 European Convention for the Peaceful Settlement of Disputes entered into force between the Parties, which according to Liechtenstein was the basis of the Court's jurisdiction.[149] Although both the ICJ and the ECtHR determined they had no jurisdiction over Czechoslovakia's measures, this conclusion was reached for different reasons, such that it is difficult to assert that some jurisprudential cross-fertilization occurred.

Nonetheless, the observation remains that it is not rare for international courts and tribunals to refer to, and borrow from, each other's case law, thus generating cross-fertilization. In a number of cases involving cultural heritage, the ICJ has referred to other tribunals' jurisprudence. In 2002, the Court rendered its judgment in the *Land and Maritime Boundary* case, where the problem of the land boundary went back to the European portioning of Africa and involved treaties of protection concluded with indigenous peoples.[150] The Court did not attach great importance to these treaties, pointing out that these treaties were common in Sub-Saharan Africa and that Nigeria had not been able to prove its claims with regard to the presence of these tribes.[151] The Court supported its conclusions by referring to its previous jurisprudence and to the *Island of Palmas* arbitration case.[152] The *Island of Palmas* arbitration concerned a similar treaty in a different region of the world. In the dispute, the United States of America claimed sovereignty on the island of Palmas (or Mianga), which previously pertained to Spain and was situated near the Philippines, against the Netherlands.[153]

In a more prominent example, the ICJ referred extensively to other tribunals' jurisprudence in the *Genocide Convention* cases,[154] where cultural heritage was entangled with international humanitarian law, undoubtedly the first field of international law recognizing a special status for cultural heritage.[155] There, the Court referred substantively to the jurisprudence of the International Criminal Tribunal for the former Yugoslavia (ICTY). In the proceedings initiated by Bosnia and Herzegovina against Yugoslavia (later becoming Serbia and Montenegro), the former alleged violations of the Convention on the Prevention and Punishment of

[149] ibid, para 52 (citing European Convention for the Peaceful Settlement of Disputes (adopted 29 April 1957, entered into force 18 February 1980) 320 UNTS 243).

[150] *Land and Maritime Boundary between Cameroon and Nigeria (Cameroon v Nigeria: Equatorial Guinea intervening)* (Judgment) [2002] ICJ Rep 303, para 31 ff.

[151] ibid, paras 200–09.

[152] *Island of Palmas (USA v Netherlands)* (1928).

[153] ibid, para 205.

[154] *Application of the Convention on the Prevention and Punishment of the Crime of Genocide (Bosnia and Herzegovina v Serbia and Montenegro)* (Judgment) [2007] ICJ Reports 43; *Application of the Convention on the Prevention and Punishment of the Crime of Genocide (Croatia v Serbia)* (Judgment) [2015] ICJ Reports 3.

[155] Ana F Vrdoljak, 'Cultural Heritage in Human Rights and Humanitarian Law' in Orna Ben-Naftali (ed), *International Human Rights and Humanitarian Law* (OUP 2011) 250 ff.

the Crime of Genocide, adopted by the General Assembly of the United Nations on 9 December 1948 (Genocide Convention),[156] as well as various connected matters, in relation to the dissolution of the former Yugoslavia in 1991.[157] Inter alia, Bosnia and Herzegovina made a number of claims under Article II of the Genocide Convention, including deliberate destruction of historical, religious, and cultural property of the protected group in 'an attempt to wipe out the traces of their very existence'.[158] The Court made it clear that beyond the *actus reus*, it had to establish the existence of the *dolus specialis* in order to apply Article II of the Genocide Convention.[159]

The Court made extensive reference to the jurisprudence of the ICTY and further documents and reports, and it concluded that there existed 'conclusive evidence of the deliberate destruction of the historical, cultural and religious heritage of the protected group during the period' under analysis.[160] The Court held that this 'highly significant' destruction, even if aiming at the elimination of all traces of the cultural and religious presence of a group, did not fall within the scope of Article II of the Genocide Convention, which does not cover the notion of 'cultural genocide'.[161] Again, the Court quoted in support of its conclusion relevant ICTY jurisprudence[162] and concluded that genocide had occurred in Srebrenica and this event engaged Serbia's international responsibility.[163]

In its recent judgment on Croatia's and Serbia's mutual claims of violation of the Genocide Convention, the Court followed the same line of reasoning on cultural genocide.[164] It confirmed the occurrence of the events alleged by the Parties, by reference to ICTY's jurisprudence, but recalled its own conclusions in its 2007 judgment on the exclusion of cultural genocide from the scope of Article II of the Genocide Convention.[165] In both judgments, the Court pointed out that it might have nevertheless taken into account the 'attacks on cultural and religious property in order to establish an intent to destroy the group physically', as previously stated by ICTY.[166] Hence, the Court followed a well-established jurisprudence on the exclusion of cultural genocide from the Genocide Convention, consistent with ICTY's decisions, but did not overlook the significance of cultural heritage

[156] Convention on the Prevention and Punishment of the Crime of Genocide (adopted 9 December 1948, entered into force 21 January 1951) 78 UNTS 277 (Genocide Convention).

[157] *Application of the Convention on the Prevention and Punishment of the Crime of Genocide (Bosnia and Herzegovina v Serbia and Montenegro)* (n 154) para 1.

[158] ibid, para 335.

[159] ibid, para 242.

[160] ibid, paras 336–44.

[161] ibid, para 344.

[162] ibid.

[163] ibid, paras 278–97, 439–58.

[164] *Application of the Convention on the Prevention and Punishment of the Crime of Genocide (Croatia v Serbia)* (n 154).

[165] ibid, paras 386–89.

[166] ibid, para 390; *Application of the Convention on the Prevention and Punishment of the Crime of Genocide (Bosnia and Herzegovina v Serbia and Montenegro)* (n 154) para 344.

destruction as evidence of genocide. Despite recurrent criticism,[167] the Court's approach appears in line with current trends in international cultural heritage law.

Certainly, the plurality of judicial and quasi-judicial bodies at the international level allows for international cultural heritage disputes to be discussed in different fora and from different standpoints. This might push toward further fragmentation of international (cultural heritage) law,[168] but it might also be a way to address different actors' interests involved in contentious cases.[169] The ICJ case law is not extensive in this sense, and the Court seems to make an accurate selection when pointing to other adjudicatory bodies' decisions.[170] Hence, the Court has not shied away from referring to other international tribunals' jurisprudence dealing with similar issues, when appropriate. However, such cross-fertilization should not be taken for granted.

Conclusion

The vast and diverse range of cultural heritage issues heard by the Court complicates efforts to draw conclusions on the ICJ contribution to international cultural heritage law. The very structure and nature of the Court itself add a further layer of complexity to the questions dealt with here.

The Court is in a privileged position to hear (certain) interstate disputes. The considerations made by a US court in a recent international dispute over cultural heritage might help clarify this point. In the *Odyssey Maritime Exploration* case, a US court clarified that national proceedings were not the appropriate forum to address the dispute between the two sovereigns in dismissing Peru's claims over the cargo of a nineteenth-century sunken ship (the *Nuestra Señora de las Mercedes*), which allegedly pertained to its cultural and historical heritage, in a tripartite dispute with Spain and a private company.[171] In doing so, the US court acknowledged

[167] As noted by William A Schabas, *Genocide in International Law: The Crime of Crimes* (CUP 2009) 220.

[168] John G Merrills, 'The Mosaic of International Dispute Settlement Procedures: Complementary or Contradictory?' (2007) 54 NILR 361; Gilbert Guillaume, 'Advantages and Risks of Proliferation: A Blueprint for Action' (2004) 2 J Intl Crim Justice 300; Jorge E Viñuales and Pierre-Marie Dupuy, 'The Challenge of Proliferation: Legal and Normative Debates About International Adjudication' in Cesare Romano, Karen Alter, and Yuval Shany (eds), *The Oxford Handbook of International Adjudication* (OUP 2014); Laurence Boisson de Chazournes, Cesare Romano, and Ruth Mackenzie (eds), *International Organizations and International Dispute Settlement: Trends and Prospects* (Brill 2002); Thomas Buergenthal, 'Proliferation of International Courts and Tribunals: Is It Good or Bad?' (2001) 14 Leiden J Intl L 267.

[169] Antônio A Cançado Trindade, 'Prologue: An Overview of the Contribution of International Tribunals to the Rule of Law' in Geert De Baere and Jan Wouters (eds), *The Contribution of International and Supranational Courts to the Rule of Law* (Edward Elgar 2015) 17.

[170] The Court has, for instance, tended to ignore investment arbitral tribunal awards, Alain Pellet, 'The Case Law of the ICJ in Investment Arbitration' (2013) 28 ICSID Rev—Foreign Investment L J 223.

[171] *Odyssey Marine Exploration Inc v The Unidentified Shipwreck Vessel* No 8:07-CV-614-SDM-MAP, Magistrate Report and Recommendation (MD Fla 3 June 2009) 30 ff.

the need to consider the nature and interests involved in a specific dispute to understand which forum might be the most appropriate for its resolution. The ICJ might be the appropriate forum with regard to an inter-State dispute over cultural heritage of this kind. Only bearing in mind this caveat—that each international dispute settlement forum is apt to deal with certain kinds of dispute, and thus its structure and purpose will inevitably influence its contribution to international law—can one try to draw conclusions on the ICJ and international cultural heritage law.

One can safely conclude that the ICJ has given consideration, although with varying degrees, to cultural heritage and cultural heritage arguments and thus has contributed to the development of international cultural heritage law. Generally speaking, Parties in disputes before the ICJ have not leveraged strong cultural heritage law arguments. As a consequence, the ICJ itself has recognized relevance to cultural heritage arguments only when these have been coupled with other types of argument, such as access to natural resources or the immunity of historical monuments used for public purposes. Nonetheless, the Court, together with the PCIJ, has marked the emergence and expansion of international cultural heritage law. It has elaborated relevant concepts such as the one of 'community', and it has corroborated the relationship between cultural heritage and other fields of international law, such as environmental law and human rights. Moreover, it has allowed for the borders of cultural heritage law to expand, and it has somehow strengthened the 'international' approach to cultural heritage protection and management.[172] In this position, the ICJ has engaged in a 'dialogue' with other international tribunals.

This practice by the ICJ mirrors the open and composite nature of international cultural heritage law, which has developed from international humanitarian law, to encompass several international instruments, such as UNESCO Conventions, the Convention on Biological Diversity, and human rights conventions, among others. Just to take two examples, the World Heritage Convention and the UNESCO Convention on the Protection of Underwater Cultural Heritage expressly cut across such diverse international law branches as cultural heritage, environmental law, and law of the sea.[173]

In this sense, the ICJ jurisprudence has confirmed that international cultural heritage law is an integral part of public international law, at least when dealing with State-to-State and individual-to-State relations. Cultural heritage disputes are often, if not always, entangled with other sensitive and heterogeneous international law questions. For this reason, a general international court such as the ICJ might, unexpectedly, claim the lion's share in cultural heritage disputes under public international law.

[172] For further discussion of internationalism in cultural heritage law, see Robert Peters, 'Nationalism versus Internationalism: New Perspectives beyond State Sovereignty and Territoriality in the Protection of Cultural Heritage' (Ch 15) in this volume.

[173] Craig Forrest, 'A New International Regime for the Protection of Underwater Cultural Heritage' (2002) 51 ICLQ 511, 512. See Part IV, 'Special Legal Regimes for World Cultural Heritage and Underwater Cultural Heritage', in this volume.

PART IV

SPECIAL LEGAL REGIMES FOR WORLD CULTURAL HERITAGE AND UNDERWATER CULTURAL HERITAGE

The special interest of the international community in protecting cultural heritage has sometimes led to the creation of subject-specific regimes. This part focuses on two such regimes: the World Heritage program and the protection of underwater cultural heritage. The first two chapters focus on different aspects of the former, while the third chapter in this section presents a provocative, and potentially contested, argument concerning the direction of the *lex generalis* and *lex specialis* governing cultural heritage found at sea.

Lucas Lixinski and Vassilis Tzevelekos begin this part by addressing concurrent State responsibility for world cultural heritage.[1] They observe that instruments that protect cultural heritage by and large only determine obligations that States have toward heritage on their own territory that has been added to international inventories or toward the maintenance of an international system of safeguarding. Relatively little in these instruments speaks to State obligations regarding heritage that is not within their territory, and existing primary norms often do not set out sufficiently concrete obligations to allow other States to allege their breach. They suggest that under many UNESCO instruments, a disconnect exists between the language of the treaties and the mechanics of the positive law, on the one hand, and the actuality of international heritage management practice, on the other. They argue that although all States have a legitimate interest in the protection of heritage under various scenarios (thus all States may participate in the enforcement of the relevant rules at the international level), concurrent responsibility may apply only when cultural heritage protection develops a

[1] Lucas Lixinski and Vassilis P Tzevelekos, 'The World Heritage Convention and the Law of State Responsibility: Promises and Pitfalls' in Anne-Marie Carstens and Elizabeth Varner (eds), *Intersections in International Cultural Heritage Law* (OUP 2020) (Ch 10).

transnational (transboundary or extraterritorial) dimension. The analysis presented in this chapter highlights some of the weaknesses of the World Heritage system, in that its full operability and enforceability is premised on the fulfillment of aspirations about the importance of heritage beyond the territorial State's interest that are not supported by the traditional framework of international law within which the Convention is created. Lixinski and Tzevelekos conclude that as the Convention evolves, efforts to elevate it beyond territoriality seem to be a necessary step in bringing State actors to account for acts that harm World Heritage.

In the subsequent chapter on the overlap of international protection of tangible cultural heritage and the environment, Ottavio Quirico addresses how climate change raises questions that challenge the fundamentals of the World Heritage Convention.[2] Global warming critically affects cultural sites of outstanding universal value and depletes mixed cultural and natural sites inscribed on the World Heritage List. The root causes are rising temperatures and water levels and land alteration. He argues that the World Heritage Convention is *lex specialis* with respect to international environmental regulation concerning localized adaptation and mitigation measures protecting sites of outstanding universal value. By contrast, environmental regulation, notably the United Nations Framework Convention on Climate Change (UNFCCC)[3] regime as reviewed in Paris in December 2015, is *lex specialis* concerning general mitigation and adaptation, systemically integrating the protection of tangible cultural heritage. The fundamental right to culture has been invoked in international jurisdictions to protect intangible heritage, but still remains *lex generalis* with respect to the UNFCCC regime. As in a set of nested boxes, such an interactive pattern outlines a basic paradigm to shape the broader intersection between the regulatory regimes protecting tangible cultural heritage and the environment in international law.

In the concluding chapter of this part, Sarah Dromgoole evaluates the exploitation provisions in the 2001 UNESCO Convention on the Protection of Underwater Cultural Heritage.[4] She addresses the scope of the Convention and presents the provocative view that the Convention might bar recovery and disposition of fungible or toxic materials in shipwrecks. She draws attention to problems

[2] Ottavio Quirico, 'Nested Boxes: Tangible Cultural Heritage and Environmental Protection in Light of Climate Change' in Anne-Marie Carstens and Elizabeth Varner (eds), *Intersections in International Cultural Heritage Law* (OUP 2020) (Ch 11).

[3] UNGA, United Nations Framework Convention on Climate Change (adopted 9 May 1992, entered into force 31 March 2004) UN Doc A/RES/48/189.

[4] Sarah Dromgoole, 'The 2001 UNESCO Convention on the Protection of the Underwater Cultural Heritage and Its Principles Relating to the Recovery and Disposition of Material from Shipwrecks' in Anne-Marie Carstens and Elizabeth Varner (eds), *Intersections in International Cultural Heritage Law* (OUP 2020) (Ch 12); UNESCO Convention on the Protection of the Underwater Cultural Heritage (adopted 2 November 2001, entered into force 2 January 2009) 2562 UNTS 3.

that may arise when these provisions are applied in the specific context of shipwrecks under this strict interpretation. Finally, she explores why fungible and toxic materials in shipwrecks are not properly handled by the Convention under this interpretation and considers their potential impact in the future.

Anne-Marie Carstens and Elizabeth Varner

10

The World Heritage Convention and the Law of State Responsibility

Promises and Pitfalls

*Lucas Lixinski and Vassilis P Tzevelekos**

Introduction

The United Nations Educational, Scientific and Cultural Organization (UNESCO) was created in 1945. Since then, the body of international cultural heritage law has evolved greatly, occupying its own, thematically distinctive place in international law. Tools and concepts that are mostly associated with the regime of human rights protection have then been employed to equip cultural heritage law and endow it with certain systemic features that are absent from other areas and rules of international law. Thus, many speak of *erga omnes* obligations on cultural heritage,[1] or at least of a shift from negative obligations (not to destroy) to positive obligations (to protect).[2] A plethora of both hard and soft law rules have also been developed under the aegis of UNESCO and other international organizations.[3] Among these, one of the most important is the

* We are thankful to the editors and the audience and co-participants of the workshop where this chapter was first presented for their input, as well as to Matthew Kingsland for his research assistance. All errors remain our own.

[1] Francesco Francioni, 'Au-delà des traités: l'émergence d'un nouveau droit coutumier pour la protection du patrimoine culturel' (2007) 111 Rev Intl de Droit Intl Public 19; Gael M Graham, 'Protection and Reversion of Cultural Property: Issues of Definition and Justification' (1987) 21 Intl Lawyer 755, 756. *Erga omnes* obligations are discussed in more detail below. See Sections I.A. and II.A. of this chapter.

[2] Francesco Francioni, 'Beyond State Sovereignty: The Protection of Cultural Heritage as a Shared Interest of Humanity' (2003–04) 25 Michigan J Intl L 1209; and Graham (n 1) 756. Positive obligations are associated with the concept of protection, the principle of due diligence, and obligations of means that we discuss in more detail below. States are expected to be proactive, to the best of their ability, with a view to offering protection. See Section I.B. of this chapter and n 32.

[3] These organizations include, to name just the main ones, the International Institute for the Unification of Private Law (UNIDROIT), the International Council of Museums (ICOM), and the International Centre for the Study of the Preservation and Restoration of Cultural Property (ICCROM).

Lucas Lixinski and Vassilis P Tzevelekos, The World Heritage Convention and the Law of State Responsibility In: *Intersections in International Cultural Heritage Law.* Edited by Anne-Marie Carstens and Elizabeth Varner. © Oxford University Press 2020. The several contributors DOI: 10.1093/oso/9780198846291.003.0011

1972 Convention Concerning the Protection of the World Cultural and Natural Heritage (World Heritage Convention).[4]

In spite of its expansion and distinctiveness as a particular field of international law, the reach and effectiveness of cultural heritage law remain in a sense quite limited. In particular, this chapter investigates the relationship between international heritage law as a set of primary norms and the law of state responsibility as secondary norms, underscoring the disconnects between the two fields. Therefore, rather than exploring the relationships between different sets of primary norms, the way a number of contributors to this volume do, we focus instead on the relationships between primary and secondary norms in this field. Graphically, this would mean focusing on concentric circles on a vertical plane of sorts, rather than partly overlapping circles laid horizontally. The aforementioned disconnect between international heritage law and state responsibility essentially amounts to a disconnect between positive law and the everyday reality of international cultural heritage law, that is, a disengagement of the *law as it is* from the *need* for effective protection from a variety of threats, including those that are not linked to the conduct of states, such as natural phenomena and activities by non-State actors. Lack of effectiveness may be associated with a number of reasons that can be studied from different disciplinary standpoints (such as political science and law) and through varied methodological tools. This chapter contributes to the discussion by exploring one of the dimensions, namely state responsibility (seen as part of the broader concept of accountability) of the aforementioned mismatch between heritage law and the effects it produces in everyday life.

The chapter discusses how development in the law of state responsibility may influence the development of cultural heritage law and explores the intersecting relationship between international cultural heritage law and state responsibility, using—mainly—the World Heritage Convention as a case study. Section I focuses on the primary norms in the World Heritage Convention and identifies certain features that are of particular importance from the perspective of secondary norms on state responsibility. Section II identifies certain reasons relevant to the mismatch between positive law on state responsibility and its implementation. Section III gives a more positive tone by exploring how, in spite of its deficiencies, state responsibility is able to accommodate complex transnational scenarios, such as multinational heritage sites. The broader argument that transcends this analysis is that international cultural heritage law is at its strongest with respect to State responsibility when territoriality is challenged and sovereignty mitigated. Therefore, actors such as practitioners and communities should be re-engaged in the mechanics of international cultural heritage law, as a means of contesting state prerogative, and giving full effect to the aspirations of the field.

[4] Convention Concerning the Protection of the World Cultural and Natural Heritage (adopted 16 November 1972, entered into force 15 December 1975) 1037 UNTS 151 (World Heritage Convention).

I. Features of the World Heritage Convention Important for State Responsibility Purposes: Collective Enforcement, State Fault, and Special Rules

This section focuses on some of the key provisions under the World Heritage Convention and on how they have been articulated vis-à-vis state responsibility. The analysis identifies certain features of international cultural heritage law that have consequences in terms of state responsibility. Further, the section discusses the example of a Declaration, namely the 2003 Declaration concerning the Intentional Destruction of Cultural Heritage,[5] which contains more specific provisions (ie special rules) on responsibility for the destruction of cultural heritage. This instrument, even though not formally part of the World Heritage Convention, was largely seen in its drafting, and is now seen by subsequent commentators, as working to expand on the meaning of obligations under the World Heritage Convention, as we indicate below.

A. *Erga Omnes* Obligations and Types of Injured State

The key obligations in the World Heritage Convention are laid out in Articles 4 through 7 of the treaty. Particularly relevant are Articles 4 and 6,[6] which seemingly frame the obligation to protect heritage as a duty of the international community as a whole. Article 4 establishes 'the duty of ensuring the identification, protection, conservation, presentation and transmission to future generations', which falls 'primarily' with the territorial state. Article 6(3) determines the obligation 'not to take any deliberate measures which might damage directly or indirectly the cultural and natural heritage' situated in the territory of another state Party.[7] As such, Articles 4 and 6 each impose *erga omnes partes* obligations which, at least in theory, allow any state Party to invoke another's responsibility for breaches of these obligations.[8] This is the first feature of (certain) cultural heritage rules that is of importance from the perspective of the law of state responsibility. Because of its *erga omnes* quality, cultural heritage is susceptible to collective enforcement at the decentralized level.

The key to understanding who can invoke state responsibility as a matter of general international law is found in Articles 42 and 48 of the International Law

[5] UNESCO Declaration concerning the Intentional Destruction of Cultural Heritage (17 October 2003) UNESCO Doc 32/Res 33 (Declaration concerning the Intentional Destruction of Cultural Heritage).

[6] ibid, arts 4, 6.

[7] ibid.

[8] Gionata Buzzini and Luigi Condorelli, 'Article 11 List of World Heritage in Danger and Deletion of a Property from the World Heritage List' in Francesco Francioni (ed), *The 1972 World Heritage Convention* (OUP 2008) 175, 178; Roger O'Keefe, 'World Cultural Heritage: Obligations to the International Community as a Whole?' (2004) 53 ICLQ 189, 190.

Commission's (ILC) Articles on the Responsibility of States for Internationally Wrongful Acts (ARSIWA),[9] and the distinction they establish between injured and non-injured (or not directly injured)[10] states. If an obligation of general international law is owed *erga omnes*, all states in the world may invoke the responsibility of the wrongdoer, though they are not (directly) injured by the wrong.[11] *Mutatis mutandis*, if an obligation owed *erga omnes* has been established through a treaty (ie the obligation is *erga omnes partes*), all Parties to the treaty may invoke the responsibility of the wrongdoer, while they are not (directly) injured by the wrong.[12] Under both scenarios, the state invoking the responsibility may request the wrongdoer to cease its wrongful conduct and (offer guarantees of non-repetition),[13] and also repair the wrong in the interest of the injured subjects.[14] The same applies with regard to *jus cogens* rules, as these are all owed *erga omnes* (*partes*).[15]

Turning now to the right of the injured state to invoke the responsibility of the wrongdoer, Article 42 of ARSIWA recognizes that right when the obligation breached is bilateral(isable)[16] in nature (hence, reciprocal),[17] but also when, in case of *erga omnes* obligations, the breach specially affects a particular state.[18] As the ILC explains in its Commentary to ARSIWA, the term 'specially affected' is used to distinguish between the implications of wrongfulness for general interest (affecting the entire international community or the entire group of signatories to a treaty), as opposed to the particular adverse effects wrongfulness has on a specific state.[19] The latter is the individually injured state, which is 'affected by the breach in a way that distinguishes it from the generality of other states to which the obligation is owed'.[20] In the case of international cultural heritage law, a wrong affecting heritage of special interest to non-nominating and non-territorial states [21] *could* be seen as a basis justifying their involvement in the enforcement of the

[9] ILC, 'Articles on Responsibility of States for Internationally Wrongful Acts' (November 2001) (Annex to UNGA Res 56/83 of 12 December 2001, and corrected by UN Doc A/56/49(Vol. I)/Corr.4)10 Supp 10 ch IV.E.1 (ARSIWA).

[10] On the origins of the term, see Linos Alexandre Sicilianos, 'The Classification of Obligations and the Multilateral Dimension of the Relations of International Responsibility' (2002) 13 EJIL 1127, 1138.

[11] ARSIWA art 48(1)(b).

[12] ibid, art 48(1)(a).

[13] ibid, art 48(2)(a).

[14] ibid, art 48(2)(b).

[15] *Jus cogens* rules are absolute, peremptory rules that create international obligations from which States cannot escape. Rules that conflict with *jus cogens* are null and void. On the interrelationship between *jus cogens* and *erga omnes* norms, see M Byers, 'Conceptualising the Relationship between *Jus Cogens* and *Erga Omnes* Rules' (1997) 66 Nordic J Intl L 211, especially 236.

[16] Sicilianos (n 10) 1133–34.

[17] ARSIWA art 42(a).

[18] ibid, art 42(b)(1).

[19] ILC, 'Report of the International Law Commission on the Work of its 42nd Session' (23 April–1 June and 2 July–10 August 2001) UN Doc A/56/10, 31-143 (ARSIWA Commentary) 119.

[20] ibid.

[21] Lists exist under most heritage treaties, and properties are added to the lists if they go through a nomination process. A State in whose territory the heritage is located nominates the heritage for inclusion on the international heritage list.

rule that has been breached in their capacity as a specially affected state.[22] This practically means that, beyond the claims that any non-injured state can make in case of breach of an obligation owed *erga omnes (partes)*, the specially affected state may request reparation, and may also—provided the requirements established by ARSIWA are met[23]—resort to countermeasures. Nevertheless, our position is that non-injured states, too, are allowed to resort to countermeasures for the protection of general interest when the obligation breached is *erga omnes (partes)*.[24]

B. Due Diligence and State Fault

Outside of obligations *erga omnes* and collective enforcement, the second important feature of international cultural heritage law, in terms of state responsibility, is that obligations under the World Heritage Convention are primarily obligations of means.[25] Any obligation owed under Article 4 is limited by the qualification that the state must 'do all it can'.[26] This provision thus gives a wide margin of discretion to a state regarding action to comply with its obligations, requiring some unspecified conduct.[27] The obligation under Article 4 is not intended to amount to a rigid legal requirement to the level of a domestic statutory obligation,[28] and the World Heritage Committee's Operational Guidelines[29] support this interpretation of a qualified duty.[30] Each state Party must demonstrate a commitment to fulfilling this obligation 'within its means', as emphasized by Article 5's language, limited by the

[22] On specially affected States, see Giorgio Gaja, 'Is a State Specially Affected When its Nationals' Human Rights Are Infringed?' in Lal Chand Vohra, Fausto Pocar, Yvonne Featherstone, Olivier Fourmy, Michael F Graham, John Hocking, and Nicholas Robson (eds), *Man's Inhumanity to Man: Essays on International Law in Honour of Antonio Cassese* (Kluwer 2003) 373; Sicilianos (n 10) 1139.

[23] ARSIWA, arts 22, 26–27, and 49–53.

[24] Vassilis P Tzevelekos, 'Revisiting the Humanisation of International Law: Limits and Potential. Obligations Erga Omnes, Hierarchy of Rules and the Principle of Due Diligence as the Basis for Further Humanisation' (2013) 6 Erasmus L Rev 62, 68.

[25] Obligations of means are obligations to undertake certain activities as a best effort to achieving a desired outcome, therefore focusing on the instruments and processes used. They are contrasted with obligations of results, which are obligations to achieve the outcome. Obligations of means are associated with the principle of due diligence and the idea of protection through proactive involvement by State authorities. André Tunk, 'La Distinction des Obligations de Résultat et des Obligations de Diligence' [1945] La Semaine Juridique (Juris-Classeur Périodique) 449; PM Dupuy, 'Reviewing the Difficulties of Codification: On Ago's Classification of Obligations of Means and Obligations of Result in Relation to State Responsibility' (1999) 10 EJIL 371. See also n 32.

[26] World Heritage Convention, art 4.

[27] *Commonwealth v Tasmania* (1983) 158 CLR 1, para 72.

[28] Robert L Meyer, '*Travaux Preparatoires* for the World Heritage Convention' (1976) 2 Earth LJ 45, 51.

[29] The *Operational Guidelines* are created (and periodically revised) by the World Heritage Committee, for the implementation of the World Heritage Convention. While formally soft law, they are deeply influential in the interpretation and evolution of the Convention. World Heritage Committee, *Operational Guidelines for the Implementation of the World Heritage Convention*, UNESCO Doc WHC.17/01 (12 July 2017) para 53 (2017 World Heritage Operational Guidelines).

[30] ibid, para 53.

words 'in so far as possible and as appropriate for each country'.[31] In other words, the obligations in discussion amount to positive obligations under the principle of due diligence.[32] The close reading of the language explains why: (1) they are obligations of means; (2) standards of conduct are rather subjective, namely depending on each State's capacity;[33] and (3) states enjoy discretion in the fulfillment of their duties. These factors are important for state responsibility purposes as it requires shifting from objective responsibility to state fault.[34]

Ambiguity regarding the specific standards of diligence that a state is expected to demonstrate is inherent in all areas of law that establish duties of conduct, or obligations of means (the two terms meaning the same). Furthermore, certain subjective elements[35] need to be assessed for establishing the breach of the duty, which will consist in that case of negligence on behalf of the state. Such subjective elements include knowledge on behalf of the state that a threat or risk for cultural heritage exists,[36] but also state capacity to act in a protective way,[37] which depends on the means that are available in each nation. Therefore, under due diligence, the state is only required to perform to the best of its ability.[38] Instead of being obligated to achieve a given result, state authorities need to strive to achieve that result. As long as a state can prove that, given the circumstances of the case, it did everything it could have done within its means and as possible and appropriate, the effort suffices. Therefore, standards of conduct and proactive engagement with a problem are assessed on a case-by-case basis and depend on the particular circumstances, on the means that were available to the state and on other subjective criteria, such as knowledge on behalf of the state that a problem existed that required action from its side. This amounts to the so-called test of state fault.[39]

[31] ibid; cf Meyer (n 28) 51; World Heritage Convention, art 5.

[32] The literature on due diligence is vast. Among others, see Riccardo Pisillo-Mazzeschi, 'The Due Diligence Rule and the Nature of the International Responsibility of States' (1992) 35 German YB Intl L 9; Timo Koivurova, 'Due Diligence' in Rüdiger Wolfrum (ed), *Max Planck Encyclopedia of Public International Law* (OUP 2013).

[33] Compare Pisillo-Mazzeschi (n 32) 41–45, arguing that, although they are flexible, due diligence standards are objective.

[34] Among others, Andrea Gattini, 'La notion de faute à la lumière du projet de convention de la Commission du droit international sur la responsabilité international' (1992) 3 EJIL 253; Andrea Gattini, 'Smoking/No Smoking: Some Remarks on the Current Place of Fault in the ILC Draft Articles on State Responsibility' (1999) 10 EJIL 397.

[35] PM Dupuy, 'Le fait générateur de la responsabilité internationale des États' (1984) 188 Recueil des Cours de l'Académie de Droit Intl 9, 102; Pisillo-Mazzeschi (n 32) 18–21 and 49–50; Vassilis P Tzevelekos, 'Reconstructing the Effective Control Criterion in Extraterritorial Human Rights Breaches. Direct Attribution of Wrongfulness, Due Diligence, and Concurrent Responsibility' (2015) 36 Michigan Journal of International Law 129, 155–57.

[36] See for instance *Corfu Channel Case (United Kingdom v Albania)* (Judgment) [1949] ICJ Rep 4, 18; and *Case Concerning United States Diplomatic and Consular Staff in Tehran (United States of America v Iran)* (Judgment) [1980] ICJ Rep 3, 68.

[37] *Case Concerning United States Diplomatic and Consular Staff in Tehran* (n 36). See also *Application of the Convention on the Prevention and Punishment of the Crime of Genocide (Bosnia and Herzegovina v Serbia and Montenegro)* (Judgment) [2007] ICJ Rep 43, 430.

[38] This means that standards of conduct vary from one State to another. But see n 33.

[39] See n 34.

C. Special Rules on State Responsibility

Having finished with due diligence and state fault, we now move to a third point. International cultural heritage law very rarely addresses state responsibility. The overall impression is that its rules are created without having in mind state responsibility. We observe that the regime of cultural heritage law as a distinctive area of international law contains scarcely special rules (in the sense of *lex specialis* vis-à-vis the ILC rules) on state responsibility.[40] In the absence, in principle, of special rules and mechanisms of enforcement, cultural heritage law cannot but rely on the 'all-encompassing' tools that are available in general international law, that is to say the secondary norms on state responsibility, namely the ARSIWA. Yet, the example we discuss below differs in that it corresponds to a spasmodic, very uncharacteristic, and rather unfortunate instance of explicit reference to state responsibility by cultural heritage law.

As a means to expand the character of legal obligations under the World Heritage Convention and arguably expand their *erga omnes* character beyond *erga omnes partes*,[41] the UNESCO General Conference adopted in 2003 the Declaration concerning the Intentional Destruction of Cultural Heritage,[42] in the aftermath of the destruction of the Buddhas of Bamiyan. Even if not binding per se, the Declaration may be seen as enunciating binding customary obligations.[43] It is also seen as part of a greater moment in enabling the interaction among multiple legal regimes around the protection of cultural heritage.[44] The Declaration's text subscribes to universality and affirms that 'States should take all appropriate measures to prevent, avoid, stop and suppress acts of intentional destruction of cultural heritage, *wherever such heritage is located*'.[45] The language in this Declaration is the strongest erosion of sovereignty and territoriality (which is a topic we discuss in

[40] See, for instance, Article 3 of the Protocol to the Hague Convention of 1954 for the Protection of Cultural Property in the Event of Armed Conflict (adopted 14 May 1954, entered into force 7 August 1956) 249 UNTS 358, which prohibits retaining as war reparations cultural heritage exported from occupied territory. This provision may be seen as an example of *lex specialis* in the area of State responsibility. But see also discussion that follows in this section of the chapter. On the applicable law within the cultural heritage regime and more generally, see Alexandros Kolliopoulos, 'La destruction ciblée des monuments et sites archéologiques en période de conflit armé et la dimension culturelle de la paix internationalle' (2015) Annuaire Français de Droit Intl 119.

[41] Francesco Francioni and Federico Lenzerini, 'The Destruction of the Buddhas of Bamiyan and International Law' (2003) 14 EJIL 619, 633–35. For a contrary view, suggesting that the Declaration is meant to only restate the law, and not necessarily expand it, see Roger O'Keefe, *The Protection of Cultural Property in Armed Conflict* (CUP 2006) 359.

[42] Declaration concerning the Intentional Destruction of Cultural Heritage.

[43] But opinions on this matter diverge. See O'Keefe (n 8) 189–209; and Francioni and Lenzerini (n 41).

[44] Francesco Francioni, 'Plurality and Interaction of Legal Orders in the Enforcement of Cultural Heritage Law' in Francesco Francioni and James Gordley (eds), *Enforcing International Cultural Heritage Law* (OUP 2013) 9, 13.

[45] Declaration concerning the Intentional Destruction of Cultural Heritage, art III.1 (emphasis added).

Section III) when it comes to international responsibility of states,[46] and offers the most incisive language of all UNESCO instruments in this area, articulating clear obligations the breach of which by states activates ARSIWA. But what is of importance for the question that we are examining here is that this instrument contains a specific provision on the international responsibility of states in Article VI (titled 'State responsibility'), which reads:

> A State that *intentionally* destroys or *intentionally* fails to take appropriate measures to prohibit, prevent, stop, and punish any intentional destruction of cultural heritage of great importance for humanity, whether or not it is inscribed on a list maintained by UNESCO or another international organization, *bears the responsibility for such destruction, to the extent provided for by international law*.[47]

The requirement of intention is present for both the positive duty (namely the duty of states to take measures, that is, be proactive) and negative duty (namely the prohibition on states to destroy) fleshed out in the Declaration.[48] With respect to the negative obligation, the requirement of intention poses a subjective prong for the prohibitive rule and the obligation of result this establishes—that heritage be not destroyed through conduct directly[49] attributable to a state—to be breached. Apparently, under the Declaration it would not be a problem if the heritage was accidentally destroyed by state organs. Intention sets a threshold for the breach; thus, it conditions state responsibility for wrongfulness. With respect to the positive obligations of protection, which, as already argued, are, in essence, obligations of means under the principle of due diligence,[50] the notion of intentional negligence seems to be oxymoronic, as rather than intention, what is of significance in the case of state fault is knowledge.[51]

This example is given because, although clearly referring to state responsibility, in a sense this Declaration undermines it. Under the law on state responsibility, subjective elements such as intention and knowledge are only pertinent if the primary rule requires them;[52] they are a prerequisite for the existence of a breach only if and to the extent they are part of the primary rule. By adding intention, Article VI

[46] Alessandro Chechi, *The Settlement of International Cultural Heritage Disputes* (OUP 2014) 255.

[47] Declaration concerning the Intentional Destruction of Cultural Heritage, art VI (emphasis added).

[48] On the distinction between positive and negative obligations, see n 2 and 25.

[49] Direct attribution is juxtaposed against the concept of indirect attribution, which refers to indirect responsibility for lack of due diligence. See J Salmon (ed), *Dictionnaire de Droit International Public* (Bruylant 2001) 996 (defining indirect responsibility as 'incurred by a subject of law because of the conduct of another subject of law' [our translation]). See also JA Hessbruegge, 'The Historical Development of the Doctrines of Attribution and Due Diligence in International Law' (2004) 36 New York J Intl L and Politics 265, 268–69.

[50] On due diligence and obligations of means, see nn 25, 32, 34–38.

[51] See n 36.

[52] ARSIWA Commentary (n 19) 34. See Tzevelekos (n 35) 154–55.

narrowly circumscribes the duty of states. Thereby, it creates one extra requirement for a breach to exist. Overall, rather than enhancing the safeguarding of cultural heritage, it enfeebles it. The Declaration—to the extent that it corresponds to hard law—creates obligations the breach of which results in state responsibility in accordance with general international law. Seen from that perspective, it contains no *lex specialis*. Hence, it does not justify departing from ARSIWA. Yet, by introducing the subjective element of intention in the primary rule, it raises a higher (and rather unnecessary, especially in the case of positive obligations) threshold for the breach of the primary rule, which is a precondition for entering the field of state responsibility.

II. Factors Undermining the Effectiveness of State Responsibility within the World Heritage Regime

Irrespective of the threshold that may apply for entering the field of secondary obligations, namely the law of state responsibility, there are limits to the effectiveness of state responsibility. These limits can be classified in two categories: limits that are inherent to international law (thus, they apply to the international cultural heritage regime too); and limits that concern in particular the regime of international cultural heritage protection.

A. The Limits of Collective Enforcement

The study has already discussed obligations *erga omnes* and collective enforcement. However, invocation of responsibility is a right, and not a duty, of states. Especially non-injured states will often refrain from reacting to wrongfulness that does not affect them directly.[53] This reflects the reality of international relations in a decentralized legal system. Within such a system, in principle, enforcement operates in an equally decentralized way, state versus state. Yet most states will often refrain from paying the (political or economic) costs of the invocation of responsibility for something that only indirectly concerns them, in the sense that it is a matter of all states together and of none of them in particular. The naked truth is that, most times, collective enforcement at the decentralized level lacks effectiveness, and that states that are not (directly) injured often lack incentives to react to wrongfulness.[54]

[53] But see Eric A Posner, 'Erga Omnes Norms, Institutionalization, and Constitutionalism in International Law' (2009) 165 J of Institutional and Theoretical Economics 5.

[54] For a broader analysis see Alexander Thompson, 'The Rational Enforcement of International Law: Solving the Sanctioners' Dilemma' (2009) 1 Intl Theory 307. Thompson argues that 'the international community as a whole has an interest in punishing violators but no one state has an incentive to do so'. ibid 319.

But the enforcement potential is different with respect to states that may feel specially affected by certain wrongful conduct.

One battleground to test this doctrinal idea in the context of international cultural protection law is heritage of interest to non-nominating and non-territorial states. For instance, in 2002, the Saudi Arabian government demolished a 200-year-old Ottoman castle in its territory to make way for more tourist accommodation options around the site of Mecca.[55] Turkey repeatedly protested the destruction of the castle, which went ahead anyway. Does Turkey have any rights over the said castle (as the successor to the Ottoman Empire) because of its cultural and historical ties to it? Because the castle was on the territory of Saudi Arabia, that state exercises its territorial sovereignty, which is a barrier for other states (no matter how interested they are in the monument at issue) to directly interfere with the monument outside their territory. Yet, the question that remains open is whether, in spite of Turkey not being able to make an 'ownership' claim over the site (in the sense of having a legal title), it is owed any obligations by Saudi Arabia that would allow Turkey to prevent the destruction of the site or invoke the responsibility of Saudi Arabia and react to its wrongfulness through the means that are available under the law of state responsibility. Our view is that, although it is not in a position to directly prevent the destruction of the site without breaching Saudi Arabia's sovereignty, Turkey (apart from exercising other forms of jurisdiction, as we argue below) can invoke Saudi Arabia's responsibility for its conduct vis-à-vis the heritage in its capacity as a specially affected state. Yet, in scenarios like the one we are examining here, the best that can be hoped for are guarantees of non-repetition and reparation in the form of an apology (satisfaction), possibly also compensation, but no restitution. As we discuss below, these forms of reparation are of minor importance when unique and irreplaceable cultural heritage is at stake.

B. State Responsibility and the Particularities of Cultural Heritage

Enforcing the law within a decentralized, state-centric system comes with certain difficulties. States need to be both interested in enforcing the law and powerful enough to effectively do it. Especially when the duty is owed to all states and to none of them in particular, states are less willing to pay the 'cost' of enforcement. These are some of the reasons why, in general, state responsibility as a legal 'tool' is often proven to be of limited effectiveness. But, in the case of international cultural

[55] This situation is discussed in detail in Kanchana Wangkeo, 'Monumental Challenges: The Lawfulness of Destroying Cultural Heritage During Peacetime' (2003) 28 Yale J Intl L 183, 185–87. This specific site is not on the World Heritage List, but it is the kind of site that could be.

heritage law in general, and the World Heritage Convention in particular, one needs to add next to these general observations a number of factors impacting state responsibility that are special to the World Heritage regime. The factors discussed in the subsections below are rather selective, focusing on the most important particularities of cultural heritage law.

1. The challenge of reparations

An obvious point to make is that reparations for loss of cultural heritage are often impossible. The concepts of authenticity and integrity needed for inscription of World Heritage Sites,[56] for instance, only come to reinforce this idea of irreplaceability. The nature of cultural heritage is such that, even if (State) responsibility is triggered, there is a lingering question as to whether its legal regime is helpful. A factual scenario of ex post facto State responsibility in the context of heritage would in most cases imply destruction or damage, which is often conceived of as an 'irreparable loss'.[57] Irreplaceability creates a practical obstacle for the exigencies of the law of state responsibility regarding restitution to function in an effective manner in the area of heritage law, as the harm is more difficult to fully restitute,[58] whereas compensation,[59] supposing that the damage is financially assessable, does not truly remedy the problem. In a sense, the primary norms of cultural heritage law help articulate this status of irreplaceability as a means to attribute value to cultural heritage, but it reveals the limits of responsibility. Therefore, deterrence and, more generally, prevention (in light of the principle of due diligence) are of extreme importance in cultural heritage law.

2. Softness

The next point concerns the 'softness' of the law, not so much regarding the medium chosen to promote cultural heritage, namely through soft law rather than hard law instruments, but mainly in the loose and unclear way these soft and hard instruments prescribe the desirable conduct and the impact its breach may have on third states that would be entitled to invoke state responsibility. Cultural heritage is an area of law that owes a lot to soft law documents, such as the 2003 Declaration that we have already discussed, the Recommendation on the Historic Urban Landscape,[60] or the Recommendation on the Means of Prohibiting and Preventing the Illicit Export, Import and Transfer of Ownership of Cultural Property.[61] But

[56] 2017 World Heritage Operational Guidelines, paras 79–95.

[57] Guido Carducci, 'Articles 4–7' in Francesco Francioni (ed), *The 1972 World Heritage Convention: A Commentary* (OUP 2008) 103, 144–45.

[58] ARSIWA, art 35.

[59] ibid, art 36.

[60] UNESCO Recommendation on the Historic Urban Landscape, including a glossary of definitions (10 November 2011) UNESCO Doc 38C/71.

[61] UNESCO Recommendation on the Means of Prohibiting and Preventing the Illicit Export, Import and Transfer of Ownership of Cultural Property (19 November 1964).

there is also another form of softness.[62] Because they are not 'concrete', existing primary norms may not always set out obligations that can lead to an allegation of breach. Although some types of heritage lend themselves to clearer international obligations because of the very nature of the heritage, such as underwater heritage,[63] this is not always the case. The type of softness we are referring to here, namely lack of concreteness as to the prescribed conduct/duties, concerns both hard and soft law rules. To give an example stemming from soft law rules, paragraph 2 of the Recommendation concerning the Safeguarding and Contemporary Role of Historic Areas reads:

> The governments and the citizens of the States in whose territory they are situated should deem it their duty to safeguard this heritage and integrate it into the social life of our times. The national, regional or local authorities should be answerable for their performance of this duty in the interests of all citizens and of the international community, in accordance with the conditions of each Member State as regards the allocation of powers.[64]

What are the concrete legal obligations established here? And when could an (indirectly) injured state invoke state responsibility? In similar terms, to give also an example from hard law instruments, Article 5 of the World Heritage Convention, discussed above, states that:

> To ensure that effective and active measures are taken for the protection, conservation and presentation of the cultural and natural heritage situated on its territory, each state Party to this Convention shall endeavor, in so far as possible, and as appropriate for each country:
> (1) to adopt a general policy which aims to give the cultural and natural heritage a function in the life of the community and to integrate the protection of that heritage into comprehensive planning programmes;
> (2) to set up within its territories, where such services do not exist, one or more services for the protection, conservation and presentation of the cultural and natural heritage with an appropriate staff and possessing the means to discharge their functions;
> (3) to develop scientific and technical studies and research and to work out such operating methods as will make the State capable of counteracting the dangers that threaten its cultural or natural heritage;

[62] See the idea of *soft negotium* suggested by Jean d'Aspremont, 'Softness in International Law: A Self-Serving Quest for New Legal Materials' (2008) 19 EJIL 1075, 1084–87.

[63] Underwater heritage is often outside States' territories, and thus claims to it need to be resolved by other means, some of which are difficult to define, like cultural links.

[64] UNESCO Recommendation concerning the Safeguarding and Contemporary Role of Historic Areas (26 November 1976) para 2.

(4) to take the appropriate legal, scientific, technical, administrative and financial measures necessary for the identification, protection, conservation, presentation and rehabilitation of this heritage; and
(5) to foster the establishment or development of national or regional centres for training in the protection, conservation and presentation of the cultural and natural heritage and to encourage scientific research in this field.[65]

While that would not matter if one were to focus simply on the language of international heritage instruments, the effects of the use of ill-defined standards of conduct and this lack of clear obligations corresponding to interests that would affect concrete right-holders has consequences in terms of state responsibility.

3. Territoriality

Further, and particularly relevant for the World Heritage Convention, we need to consider cultural heritage and territoriality. This is a question that we discuss in more detail in the next section of the chapter, where we move beyond territoriality to capture the trans-boundary and transnational nature of heritage protection. For the purposes of the argument built here, suffice it to explain that, by and large, heritage protection rules focus on obligations that states have regarding heritage on their own territory that has been added to international inventories, or toward the maintenance of an international system of safeguarding. There is relatively little in cultural heritage instruments on state obligations regarding heritage that is not within their territory.

The World Heritage Convention, the most widely ratified heritage treaty, recognizes explicitly that the primary responsibility (in the sense of a duty) regarding heritage under its aegis lies with the state on whose territory the heritage is found.[66] The international community of states as a whole has a duty to cooperate in the protection of world heritage in other states as well, but only as long as it fully respects the sovereignty of the state on the territory of which the property is found.[67] The duty of cooperation is seen as eroding state sovereignty, but critics highlight that, in fact, there is too much sovereign control over those allegedly sovereign-eroding dimensions of World Heritage Convention processes. For instance, this duty of cooperation is defined as assisting the territorial state in their efforts to conserve and identify their heritage.[68] As to extraterritoriality, the key provision in the World Heritage Convention is Article 6.3, which determines that state Parties will not take *deliberate* measures against World Heritage

[65] World Heritage Convention, art 5.
[66] ibid, art 4.
[67] ibid, art 6.1.
[68] ibid, art 7.

Convention-listed properties situated in the territory of *other* parties.[69] As it has been rightly pointed out, Article 6.3 creates obligations among states Parties that may clearly engender state responsibility.[70] However, as we have argued above, the introduction of a subjective element, the criterion of intention, circumscribes the obligation and raises a threshold for the existence of a breach that is a pre-condition for the establishment of responsibility. This might be an extra factor explaining why the main avenue left to states Parties, at least before the aforementioned 2003 Declaration, was diplomacy outside traditional legal enforcement channels.[71]

Particularly in the context of the World Heritage Convention, one must consider that Article 4 of the World Heritage Convention obligates each state to 'do all it can' to ensure the protection of heritage in their territory.[72] Relevant practice under the treaty seems to suggest a requirement for appropriate heritage impact assessments to be undertaken prior to any development with the capacity to impact the site,[73] with a view to identifying any potential threats to the Outstanding Universal Value (OUV) of the property.[74] States in this respect can be expected to then take 'all possible measures' to address the specific risks identified.[75]

Failing that, there is also the possibility of using listing mechanisms to induce certain behaviors. For instance, states can ask that World Heritage Sites be added to the World Heritage in Danger List where they require 'major operations' to protect against the 'serious and specific dangers' to their OUV.[76] Addition to the list has the effect of imposing more stringent protective obligations under Article 4 of the World Heritage Convention, and of requiring that 'all necessary' corrective measures be undertaken to safeguard the site's OUV.[77]

[69] ibid, art 6.3 (emphasis added).

[70] Carducci (n 57) 127.

[71] O'Keefe (n 8) 208.

[72] World Heritage Convention, art 4.

[73] 2017 World Heritage Operational Guidelines, para 110 and Annex 13; Decision of the World Heritage Committee concerning the Archaeological Site of Sabratha (Libya) (2017) UNESCO Doc 39 COM 7A.39, para 4; Decision of the World Heritage Committee concerning Lamu Old Town (Kenya) (2010) UNESCO Doc 34 COM 7B.46, para 4.

[74] 2017 World Heritage Operational Guidelines.

[75] 2017 World Heritage Operational Guidelines, para 170; Decision of the World Heritage Committee concerning Iguaçu National Park (Brazil) (2000) UNESCO Doc CONF 202 IV.A.2, para 1; Decision of the World Heritage Committee concerning Robben Island (South Africa) (2003) UNESCO Doc 27 COM 7B.34, para 1.

[76] 2017 World Heritage Operational Guidelines, para 177; Decision of the World Heritage Committee concerning Liverpool—Maritime Mercantile City (United Kingdom of Great Britain and Northern Ireland) (C 1150) (2012) UNESCO Doc 36 COM 7B.93, paras 5–7.

[77] 2017 World Heritage Operational Guidelines, paras 176, 192; Decision of the World Heritage Committee concerning the Monitoring of the State of Conservation of the World Heritage Natural Properties and Related Technical Problems (1991) UNESCO Doc CONF 002 VIII, para 2; Decision of the World Heritage Committee concerning Bagrati Cathedral and Gelati Monastery (Georgia) (C 710) (2010) UNESCO Doc 34 COM 7B.88, para 7.

III. Moving Beyond Territoriality: Multiple Duty Bearers and Concurrent Responsibility

Although heritage law is in principle directed toward territoriality, the law of state responsibility (combined in the discussion that follows with due diligence) is equipped to address complex social phenomena that span across multiple jurisdictions. However, jurisdiction is in principle territorial,[78] meaning that the obligation to protect will primarily apply to the state on the territory of which heritage is found.[79] Yet, nothing precludes other states from being equally expected to demonstrate diligence, when other bases of jurisdiction[80] link them to a situation that calls for protection—especially on the basis of the active personality principle.[81] If, for instance, heritage is damaged by a non-state actor, such as a corporation operating overseas, it is not only the state on the territory of which the harmful activity is taking place that owes diligence, but also the home state, whose nationals engage in these activities.[82] In the case of the former state, jurisdiction will be territorial. The latter's jurisdiction will inevitably extend extraterritorially, yet, as long as the means that the state has chosen in order to comply with its due diligence obligations are not unlawful (for instance, enforcement cannot take place on the territory of another state without its consent),[83] the reach beyond territorial borders is fine. This leads to a scenario of multiple duty bearers[84] and of parallel and possibly overlapping jurisdiction[85] exercised by more than one state connected through different bases to the same situation.

[78] See for instance, ECtHR, *Banković v Belgium*, (Grand Chamber, Admissibility Decision) App no 52207/99 (12 December 2001) para 59. See also the references that the ECtHR makes to scholars supporting this point of view.

[79] See 1972 World Heritage Convention, art 4 as an example.

[80] On the bases of jurisdiction see, for instance, Christopher Stalker, 'Jurisdiction' in Malcolm D Evans (ed), *International Law* (4th edn, OUP 2014) 309; Rosalyn Higgins, *Themes and Theories* (OUP 2009) 801; Cedric Ryngaert, *Jurisdiction in International Law* (OUP 2008) Chs 3–4.

[81] Although the narrower version of the active personality principle requires for the exercise of jurisdiction that the conduct also be illegal within the legal order of the *locus delicti*, the place where the offense is committed. See for instance the separate opinion of the former President of the ICJ, Judge Guillaume in the *Arrest Warrant* case. *Arrest Warrant of 11 April 2000 (Democratic Republic of Congo v Belgium)* (Judgment—Separate Opinion of President Guillaume) [2002] ICJ Rep 35 para 5.

[82] For a similar argument in the area of investment law and the harmful conduct of corporations operating overseas, see Vassilis Tzevelekos, 'In Search of Alternative Solutions: Can the State of Origin be Held Internationally Responsible for Investors' Human Rights Abuses which are not Attributable to it?' (2010) 35 Brooklyn J Intl L 155.

[83] See for instance the dissenting opinion of Judge Van den Wyngaert in the *Arrest Warrant* case, distinguishing between prescriptive jurisdiction and enforcement jurisdiction and arguing that when the exercise of jurisdiction is permitted for States it cannot lead to acts of extraterritorial enforcement. *Arrest Warrant of 11 April 2000 (Democratic Republic of Congo v Belgium)* (Judgment—Dissenting Opinion of Judge Van den Wyngaert) [2002] ICJ Rep 137 para 49.

[84] On multiple duty bearers see the collection of studies edited by Wouter Vanderhole, *Challenging Territoriality in Human Rights Law: Building Blocks for a Plural and Diverse Duty-Bearer Regime* (Routledge 2015).

[85] See Ryngaert's idea about *reasonable jurisdiction* and the distinction he makes between primary and subsidiary jurisdictional bases. Ryngaert (n 80) 185 ff.

All involved states have a due diligence duty that demands them to deploy the pertinent means that are available in each one of them and allowed by international law. Ideally, states should coordinate their action and cooperate to achieve the best possible result. Often, the relevant legal framework will establish a duty of cooperation, such as, in the case of international cultural heritage law, the duty to provide technical assistance in the safeguarding of heritage,[86] and to cooperate in listing efforts.[87] But, even if this is not possible, the fact remains that transnational legal phenomena involve more than one jurisdiction connected to the same harmful situation simultaneously. The result is overlapping jurisdiction and, possibly, concurrent state responsibility too.[88] Whether a state is liable depends on whether it has breached its international obligations, including the duty to act in a protective manner under due diligence.

A variety of concurrent responsibility scenarios can be identified. The limits of this chapter do not allow us to examine them in a systematic way. Therefore, we limit ourselves to the matter of transboundary heritage. In the case of multinational heritage listing, at least two states are connected territorially with heritage to the extent that this heritage is on their territory. Unless other arrangements have been made between them, such as the creation of a bi-national organization to regulate shared water issues, such as the International Joint Committee of Niagara Falls by Canadian and US authorities,[89] each state contributes to the situation through its own conduct—consisting in acts or omissions. All involved states need to exercise diligence for the protection of the heritage at issue. They are equally expected to

[86] For instance, Convention for the Safeguarding of the Intangible Cultural Heritage (adopted 17 October 2003, entered into force 20 April 2006) 2368 UNTS 31, art 19:

> Article 19—Cooperation. 1. For the purposes of this Convention, international cooperation includes, inter alia, the exchange of information and experience, joint initiatives, and the establishment of a mechanism of assistance to States Parties in their efforts to safeguard the intangible cultural heritage. 2. Without prejudice to the provisions of their national legislation and customary law and practices, the States Parties recognize that the safeguarding of intangible cultural heritage is of general interest to humanity, and to that end undertake to cooperate at the bilateral, subregional, regional and international levels.

[87] World Heritage Convention, art 20: 'international assistance provided for by this Convention may be granted only to property forming part of the cultural and natural heritage which the World Heritage Committee has decided, or may decide, to enter in one of the lists mentioned in paragraphs 2 and 4 of Article 11 [the World Heritage List, and the List of World Heritage in Danger, respectively].'

[88] Tzevelekos (n 35) 129–78, esp 164 ff.

[89] See generally Melanie Hall, 'Niagara Falls: Preservation and the Spectacle of Anglo-American Accord' in Melanie Hall (ed), *Towards World Heritage: International Origins of the Preservation Movement 1870–1930* (Ashgate 2011) 23; and Robert G Healy, 'The Commons Problem and Canada's Niagara Falls' (2006) 33 Annals of Tourism Research 525. Save for specific regimes being created by the States involved, it would seem the administering institution could be the World Heritage Committee when World Heritage sites are involved. Having a separate legal personality, the World Heritage Committee and its conduct would be subject to the specific rules on the responsibility of international organizations, and the work of the ILC in this matter is particularly important. As in all similar cases, the thorny question is when can States be responsible for conduct linked with their participation in an international organization. At any rate, these situations need to be assessed on a case-by-case basis. See also n 106.

make use of all means available to them (including diplomatic and political means) to invite the other involved states to demonstrate the highest possible standards of diligence and to cooperate.

Another scenario might be when no author of wrongfulness exists. The risk or danger for heritage might be because of a natural phenomenon, like an earthquake, or a phenomenon caused by human activity that cannot be personified, such as air pollution.[90] More generally, what may in all those scenarios lead to concurrent responsibility is that more than one state is linked to the situation at issue. Although the subject that directly[91] breaks the law (if any) and the other(s) that failed to demonstrate diligence are breaking separate (ie each one its own) obligations, they all share liability over the same in essence harmful situation that is single and common to all. Finally it goes without saying that concurrent responsibility may exist even in the absence of a breach of the principle of due diligence. In the case, for instance, of heritage that crosses the borders of two or more states, all states shall refrain from damaging the heritage through conduct directly attributable to them. Each state has a duty not to directly damage heritage on its territory, and any state that directly causes or contributes to a common, single harm, is concurrently responsible together with the other states that directly cause harm—each one being responsible for its own wrongful conduct.[92]

In a nutshell, multiple duty bearers may exist. Sometimes, these can be found exercising parallel jurisdiction that may lead to their concurrent responsibility. The responsibility is concurrent,[93] and not joint and several,[94] because there is a plurality of wrongful acts by plural states, with each state being individually responsible for its own wrongful conduct, consisting either in state fault (ie breach of due diligence) or in wrongfulness directly[95] attributable to it.

[90] In these cases, and particularly disasters, principles of international cooperation seem to be paramount. The ongoing work of the International Law Commission in this area is particularly relevant in this context. See ILC Draft Articles on the Protection of Persons in the Event of Disasters with Commentaries. ILC, 'Report of the International Law Commission on the Work of its 68th Session' (2 May–10 June and 4 July–12 August 2016) UN Doc A/71/10 (2016) 12.

[91] In this chapter, by the terms wrong 'directly caused' or 'direct breach' we mean wrongfulness directly attributable to a State. See also n 49. For a more general and very thoughtful discussion on causality and State responsibility, treating both direct attribution and indirect omissions, fault, negligence etc., see Ilias Plakokefalos, 'Causation in the Law of State Responsibility and the Problem of Overdetermination: In Search of Clarity' (2015) 26 EJIL 471.

[92] For the use of the term 'directly' here, see nn 49 and 91.

[93] Tzevelekos (n 35) 164 and following. Compare the analysis by Khalfan, who characterizes responsibility as joint in the context of the International Covenant on Economic Social and Cultural Rights, Ashfaq Khalfan, 'Division of Responsibility amongst States' in Malcolm Langford, Wouter Vandenhole, Martin Scheinin, and Willem van Genugten (eds), *Global Justice, State Duties. The Extraterritorial Scope of Economic, Social and Cultural Rights in International Law* (CUP 2013) 299.

[94] The two terms, namely joint responsibility, and joint and several responsibility need to be distinguished. The latter also concerns the question of reparation; each responsible subject owes reparation in full, irrespective of its individual share of responsibility. See Jean Salmon (ed), *Dictionnaire de Droit International Public* (Bruylant 2001) 1039–40.

[95] See nn 49 and 91.

Concurrent responsibility will often present transnational or transboundary elements. In the context of heritage law these elements clearly appear in the case of multinational nominations on the World Heritage List.[96] At the moment, there are relatively few such nominations (34 transboundary world heritage sites, out of 1,052 sites at the time of writing).[97] A few examples are: the Jesuitic missions (in Argentina and Brazil);[98] the ancient Andean Road System (in Argentina, Bolivia, Chile, Colombia, Ecuador, and Peru);[99] the Waterton Glacier International Peace Park (on the border of Canada and the United States);[100] the Silk Roads (China, Kazakhstan, and Kyrgyzstan);[101] the Struve Geodetic Arc, which allowed for the first measurement of the size of the planet (Belarus, Estonia, Finland, Latvia, Lithuania, Norway, Moldova, Russia, Sweden, and Ukraine);[102] and the Historic Centre of Rome, the Properties of the Holy See in that City Enjoying Extraterritorial Rights, and San Paolo Fuori le Mura (Italy and the Holy See).[103] Some of these sites are serial sites (meaning parts are in multiple countries, and taken together, they reach the OUV threshold needed for inscription). A few are on the border of two states (with the Vatican corresponding to the entirety of one country plus its borders with Italy).[104]

[96] The competences of the World Heritage Committee are laid out in the World Heritage Convention, arts 8–14, particularly art 13. Most notable among these powers is the control over the World Heritage List. Addition to the World Heritage List engenders a number of consequences, most notably that States give the World Heritage Committee, with the assistance of specific NGOs (art 13(7)), the power to oversee the status of properties added to the World Heritage List, and to make recommendations to States on the management of these sites, as well as coordinate international assistance to the protection of world heritage. The issue of whether the World Heritage Committee could be internationally responsible is, to the best of our knowledge, untested. But it would seem that its responsibility might arise, for instance, in delaying decisions on international assistance that resulted in destruction or serious harm to a property on the World Heritage List; or it could be responsible for its failure to provide such assistance and directives to one State that is causing harm to a transboundary heritage site, to the detriment of the other State(s) involved in the listing.

[97] The World Heritage List is created by the World Heritage Convention, art 11(1) and is an international list of sites with 'outstanding universal value', as defined by the World Heritage Committee's Operational Guidelines. Multinational heritage consists of sites on the list that are jointly nominated by two or more States. UNESCO World Heritage List <http://whc.unesco.org/en/list/?&searchSites=&search_by_country=&region=&search_yearinscribed=&themes=&criteria_restriction=&type=&media=&order=country&description=&&transboundary=1> accessed 16 August 2018.

[98] UNESCO, Jesuit Missions of the Guaranis: San Ignacio Mini, Santa Ana, Nuestra Señora de Loreto and Santa Maria Mayor (Argentina), Ruins of Sao Miguel das Missoes (Brazil) <http://whc.unesco.org/en/list/275> accessed 16 August 2018.

[99] UNESCO, Qhapaq Ñan, Andean Road System <http://whc.unesco.org/en/list/1459> accessed 16 August 2018.

[100] UNESCO, Waterton Glacier International Peace Park <http://whc.unesco.org/en/list/354> accessed 16 August 2018.

[101] UNESCO, Silk Roads: the Routes Network of Chang'an-Tianshan Corridor <http://whc.unesco.org/en/list/1442> accessed 16 August 2018.

[102] UNESCO, Struve Geodetic Arc <http://whc.unesco.org/en/list/1187> accessed 16 August 2018.

[103] UNESCO, Historic Centre of Rome, the Properties of the Holy See in that City Enjoying Extraterritorial Rights and San Paolo Fuori le Mura <http://whc.unesco.org/en/list/91> accessed 16 August 2018.

[104] On the relationships between Italy and the Holy See, see John R Morss, 'The International Legal Status of the Vatican/Holy See Complex' (2015) 26 EJIL 927.

In these examples, because of the multinational nature of heritage, there clearly are the conditions for the presence of concurrent responsibility (in the sense of duty) to act in a protective manner, which may lead to the concurrent responsibility (in the sense of liability) of the involved states. The relevant obligations include the duty to establish joint management plans, which allocate duties between the signatories and set out the obligations of each Party in the conservation of the sites under their territorial jurisdiction, as well as conditions for assistance among the multiple states for conservation of the different parts. To be sure, each case is different, but the point here is that the conditions might be present for concurrent responsibility—in spite of the term 'joint' being used to describe these management plans.[105] Such plans also often involve the creation of multinational commissions for the protection of these sites.[106] The obligation of respect under Articles 4 through 7 of the World Heritage Convention, discussed earlier, is clearly owed in the event of World Heritage Convention sites on the border between two countries, given the relevant practice under the said Convention, which indicates that Article 4 obligations extend to the entirety of transboundary properties.[107] When it comes to serial sites, though, the situation is less clear-cut, as one cannot effectively measure how many parts, if any, of a serial site can be affected before the combination loses its OUV, a requirement for inscription. But the presumption is that an impact on one part of the serial site necessarily affects its totality. This assumption is reinforced by the relevant language of the Operational Guidelines, which suggests that '[e]ach component part should contribute to the Outstanding Universal Value of the property as a whole in a substantial, scientific, readily defined and discernible way'.[108]

[105] If there is harm caused by a plurality of States contributing through separate internationally wrongful conduct, responsibility is concurrent; if the harm has been caused by a plurality of States that are responsible for the same wrongful conduct, responsibility will be joint.

[106] The first question to be asked for the purposes of allocation of responsibility is whether such commissions are autonomous international legal persons, ie international organizations. Each case needs to be assessed in the light of its particular characteristics, including the competences and powers that have been transferred to the commission. States will be responsible for any breach of international law they commit, including breaches of their duties in the context of these commissions. Further, it might also be necessary to consider the responsibility of the commission itself as an independent legal body, but also the scenario of State responsibility associated with the conduct of the commission (in particular ILC Articles on the Responsibility of International Organizations, arts 17 and 61, see ILC, 'Report of the International Law Commission on the Work of its 63rd Session' (26 April–3 June and 4 July–12 August 2011) UN Doc A/66/10, para 87. See also n 89.

[107] 2017 World Heritage Operational Guidelines, paras 167, 200 and Annexes 2B, 7; Decision of the World Heritage Committee regarding Tyre (Lebanon) (1997) UNESCO Doc CONF 204 IV.B.46, para 2; Decision of the World Heritage Committee regarding Pyrénées Mont Perdu (France, Spain) (C/N 773bis) (2014) UNESCO Doc 38 COM 7B.57, paras 3–6.

[108] UNESCO, Operational Directives to the Convention for the Safeguarding of the Intangible Cultural Heritage (2015), as revised, UNESCO Doc ITH/18/7.GA/Resolutions (6 June 2018) Res 7.GA/10, Annex, para 137.

Conclusion

When it comes to the relationships between international cultural heritage law and the international law of state responsibility, it is clear that a disconnect exists between the law and practice of heritage management. The irreplaceability of heritage is an obstacle, because it implies confronting the damage to or loss of heritage, creating difficulties to thinking of state responsibility with respect to heritage and reparations in particular. Likewise, the softness of existing international law helps accommodate aspirations around heritage, without clearly articulating legal obligations.

In the process, state sovereignty and territoriality, as basic pillars of traditional international law, tend to occupy the void left by under-articulated values. Heritage that goes beyond the limits of territory, such as transboundary and serial sites, appears to be more protected. It seems, thus, that a way to ensure heritage is adequately covered by the body of secondary norms is to find ways of divorcing it from basic state attributes, and effectively achieve the aspirations of those committed to the protection of these resources.

A possible means of achieving this emancipation of heritage is to decrease territoriality further through, for instance, amendments to the World Heritage Convention's Operational Guidelines to divorce heritage from territory by, for instance, paying more attention to intangible and extraterritorial values in the statement of OUV, which could counter the strict territoriality in the delimitation of the property and its buffer zone. Lastly, the moral outrage around harm to or destruction of heritage needs to be grounded on possible legal strategies and responses, rather than the non-negotiable values of heritage, like its intrinsic value and irreplaceability. By bringing heritage closer to reality, the worth of heritage that currently impede the law's effectiveness can be better realized.

11

Nested Boxes

Tangible Cultural Heritage and Environmental Protection in Light of Climate Change

Ottavio Quirico

Introduction

There is overlap between the protection of culture and nature, as recognized by the 1972 Convention Concerning the Protection of the World Cultural and Natural Heritage (1972 World Heritage Convention).[1] Indeed, the Convention protects both cultural and natural sites of outstanding universal value, as well as mixed sites that are both naturally and culturally relevant.[2] By contrast, environmental treaties first address intangible heritage and only indirectly protect tangible cultural heritage.[3] For instance, the 1992 Convention on Biological Diversity[4] binds States to 'respect, preserve and maintain knowledge, innovations and practices of indigenous and local communities embodying traditional lifestyles relevant for the conservation and sustainable use of biological diversity'.[5] The Convention also requires Member States to 'protect and encourage customary use of biological resources in accordance with traditional cultural practices that are compatible with conservation or sustainable use requirements'.[6] There are, however, exceptions, such as the 1994 Convention to Combat Desertification,[7] whose Preamble takes a slightly broader stance and underscores the relationship between 'physical,

[1] Convention Concerning the Protection of the World Cultural and Natural Heritage (adopted on 16 November 1972, entered into force 17 December 1975), 1037 UNTS 151 (1972 World Heritage Convention).

[2] On the definition of 'cultural heritage', see Abdullah Yusuf, 'Article 1: Definition of Cultural Heritage' in Francesco Francioni and Federico Lenzerini (eds), *The 1972 World Heritage Convention: A Commentary* (OUP 2008) 23. On the definition of 'natural heritage', see Catherine Redgwell, 'Article 2: Definition of Natural Heritage', ibid 63.

[3] Janet Blake, *International Cultural Heritage Law* (OUP 2015) 124.

[4] Convention on Biological Diversity (adopted 5 June 1992, entered into force 29 December 1993) 1760 UNTS 79, art 8(j).

[5] ibid.

[6] ibid, art 10(c).

[7] Convention to Combat Desertification in those Countries Experiencing Serious Drought and/or Desertification, Particularly in Africa (adopted 17 June 1994, entered into force 26 December 1996) 1966 UNTS 415.

Ottavio Quirico, Nested Boxes In: *Intersections in International Cultural Heritage Law.* Edited by Anne-Marie Carstens and Elizabeth Varner. © Oxford University Press 2020. The several contributors DOI: 10.1093/oso/9780198846291.003.0012

biological, political, social, cultural and economic factors', whilst a later provision requires Member States to 'ensure adequate protection of local and traditional knowledge'.[8]

Among environmental threats to cultural heritage sites, climate change is particularly dangerous with respect to both cultural and natural heritage, which are intertwined.[9] The correlation is explicitly acknowledged in the case of 'mixed sites',[10] such as Tassili n'Ajjer in Algeria and Tongariro National Park in New Zealand. Tassili n'Ajjer is a vast plateau including rock painting and engraving from as long ago as 10,000 BCE to the beginning of the new era, as well as a set of geological formations with 'rock forests' of eroded sandstone resembling a lunar landscape.[11] Tongariro National Park includes diverse ecosystems, landscapes, and a set of mountains with cultural and religious significance for the Maori people, underscoring a spiritual link with the environment.[12] These are also examples of 'cultural landscape', representing the 'combined works of nature and man'.[13]

This chapter first outlines a taxonomy of the threats that climate change poses to World Heritage sites. Second, the chapter develops a literal, purposive, and systemic analysis of relevant provisions of the 1972 World Heritage Convention, according to the rules on treaty interpretation set forth in the 1969 Vienna Convention on the Law of Treaties (Vienna Convention) and the 1986 Vienna Convention on the Law of Treaties between States and International Organisations or between International Organisations.[14] Particularly in light of the Paris Agreement,[15] the aim is to analytically assess to what extent the legal framework established by the World Heritage Convention can compel Member States to take adaptation and mitigation measures with respect to anthropogenic greenhouse gas (GHG) emissions, so as to protect tangible cultural and mixed sites of outstanding universal value.

[8] ibid, art 16(g).

[9] World Heritage Committee, 'World Heritage Convention and Sustainable Development' (2010) WHC-10/34.COM/5D 3, para 8(b) (World Heritage Committee, 'World Heritage Convention').

[10] *Operational Guidelines for the Implementation of the World Heritage Convention*, UNESCO Doc WHC.17/01 (12 July 2017) para 46 (2017 World Heritage Operational Guidelines).

[11] UNESCO, 'World Heritage List: Tassili n'Ajjer' <http://whc.unesco.org/en/list/179> accessed 3 January 2018.

[12] UNESCO, 'World Heritage List: Tongariro National Park' <http://whc.unesco.org/en/list/421> accessed 3 January 2018.

[13] 2017 World Heritage Operational Guidelines, para 47.

[14] 1969 Vienna Convention on the Law of Treaties, adopted 23 May 1969, entered into force 27 January 1980, 1155 UNTS 331, and 1986 Vienna Convention on the Law of Treaties between States and International Organisations or between International Organisations, 21 March 1986, not yet in force, UN Doc A/CONF.129/15 art 31. Though the latter has not entered into force, it is authoritative in the matter of interpretation, and the 1972 World Heritage Convention and other international conventions are open to international organizations. Notably, the European Union is a Party to the UNFCCC, Kyoto Protoco, and the Paris Agreement.

[15] Paris Agreement (adopted 12 December 2015, entered into force 4 November 2016) C.N.63.2016. TREATIES-XXVII.7.d.

Under both the UN Framework Convention on Climate Change (UNFCCC)[16] and the 1972 World Heritage Convention, adaptation is considered to entail 'adjustment in natural or human systems in response to actual or expected climatic stimuli or their effects, which moderates harm or exploits beneficial opportunities'.[17] Mitigation is regarded as 'an anthropogenic intervention to reduce the sources of greenhouse gases or enhance their sinks'.[18] The same conduct is thus relevant to different regulatory regimes. Both adaptation and mitigation can be general or site-based, but adaptation by nature entails a targeted local dimension, whilst effective mitigation intrinsically requires a global approach.

From a literal and purposive perspective, core provisions of the 1972 World Heritage Convention are Articles 4, 5, and 6. In fact, these rules establish the basic substantive obligations of State Parties to ensure the preservation and protection of World Heritage sites, be they simply inscribed in the World Heritage List as provided in the World Heritage Convention or further included in the treaty's List of World Heritage 'in Danger'.[19] Systemically, the research balances core duties under the 1972 World Heritage Convention against the regime established by the UNFCCC, including the 1997 Kyoto Protocol[20] and 2015 Paris Agreement. Both regimes are quasi-universal, with the UNFCCC including 197 Parties, the Kyoto Protocol 192, the Paris Agreement 187, and the World Heritage Convention 193. Only a few States, such as the Bahamas, Bhutan, and the Democratic People's Republic of Korea, are Parties to the UNFCCC but not to the World Heritage Convention.[21]

The analysis of the intersection between core substantive duties established by the UNFCCC and the 1972 World Heritage Convention should also help to better understand how institutions under the two regimes can interact. As a set of nested boxes, exploring intersections between these regimes should allow a better understanding of the relationship between the protection of tangible cultural heritage and the environment more generally.

16 UN Framework Convention on Climate Change (adopted 9 May 1992, entered into force 21 March 1994) 1171 UNTS 107 (UNFCCC).

17 UNESCO World Heritage Centre, 'Policy Document on the Impacts of Climate Change on World Heritage Properties' (2008) 4 <whc.unesco.org/document/10046> accessed 3 January 2018 (reporting the definition of the Intergovernmental Panel on Climate Change (IPCC)).

18 ibid.

19 1972 World Heritage Convention, art 11(2) (World Heritage List) and 11(4) (List of World Heritage in Danger).

20 Kyoto Protocol (adopted 11 December 1997, entered into force 16 February 2005) 2303 UNTS 162.

21 UNFCCC, Status of Ratification of the Convention <https://unfccc.int/process-and-meetings/the-convention/status-of-ratification/status-of-ratification-of-the-convention> accessed 7 February 2020;; Kyoto Protocol, Status of Ratification <https://unfccc.int/process/the-kyoto-protocol/status-of-ratification> accessed 7 February 2020; Paris Agreement, Status of Ratification <https://unfccc.int/process/the-paris-agreement/status-of-ratification> accessed 7 February 2020; State Parties to the World Heritage Convention, Ratification Status <http://whc.unesco.org/en/statesparties> accessed 3 January 2018.

I. A Basic Taxonomy

Despite the absence of an exhaustive science-based taxonomy of the impact of climate change on World Heritage sites,[22] it is considered that global warming threatens the outstanding universal value of protected areas and thus their unique importance for humanity as a whole, so much so that climate change might drastically modify the current World Heritage List.[23] Because of its pervasive nature, climate change has environmental implications that comprehensively affect all types of World Heritage, including outdoor, indoor, and buried sites.[24]

Fundamentally, it is possible to distinguish three main effects of the impact of climate change on tangible cultural and mixed heritage, owing to:

(1) rising temperatures;
(2) rising water levels; and
(3) land alteration.

Rising temperatures affect buildings and change the composition of landscapes and biodiversity. For instance, cold temperatures keep archeological sites dry, protecting them from decay, preserve ice caps, and prevent drought. Rising water levels affect cultural and mixed heritage by causing flooding, increasing the intensity of storms and the possibility of earthquakes. The impact of these phenomena is further aggravated by chemical modification prompted by climate change in the composition of water, concerning, for instance, acidification and salinity. An extreme example of land alteration is desertification, inflicting sand encroachment and dryness on cultural monuments and natural ecosystems.[25] Historical buildings are particularly exposed to these changes because of the fragility of their fabric, which often dates back several centuries.

Of particular importance to tangible cultural heritage are changes in ground and water levels, storms, earthquakes, and landslides.[26] For instance, the centre of Prague includes some of the finest examples of architecture in Europe from the

[22] UNESCO, UCS, and UNEP, 'World Heritage and Tourism in a Changing Climate' (2016) 14 <whc.unesco.org/document/139944> accessed 3 January 2018.

[23] UNESCO, 'Case Studies on Climate Change and World Heritage' (2007) <http://whc.unesco.org/en/activities/473> accessed 3 January 2017. See the current World Heritage List at http://whc.unesco.org/en/list accessed 20 July 2019. On the effects of climate change, see IPCC, 'Climate Change: The Physical Science Basis' (2013) <https://www.ipcc.ch/report/ar5/wg1/> accessed 7 February 2020..

[24] UNESCO World Heritage Centre, 'Policy Document' (n 17) 11.

[25] See Stefan Gruber, 'The Impact of Climate Change on Cultural Heritage Sites: Environmental Law and Adaptation' (2011) 2 Carbon & Climate L Rev 209, 214–18. Cf also Cristina Sabbioni, Peter Brimblecombe, and May Cassar, *The Atlas of Climate Change Impact on European Cultural Heritage* (Anthem 2010); Jieh-Jiuh Wang, 'Flood Risk Maps to Cultural Heritage: Measures and Process' (2015) 16 J Cultural Heritage 210.

[26] UNESCO, 'Case Studies' (n 23) 54–77.

eleventh to the twentieth centuries. The site is affected by natural hazards, such as the 2002 flooding, which caused such serious damage as to collapse some historical buildings. Rising temperatures have significantly increased precipitation in most areas worldwide and are therefore a critical cause of flooding.[27]

The devastating impact that the Nepali earthquake had on cultural heritage sites in April and May 2015 is another tangible example. The earthquake caused irreparable damage to Indian, Tibetan, Hindu, and Buddhist iconography, including palaces, temples, and public spaces, such as Durbar square, the three cities of Hanuman Dhoka, Patan, and Bhaktapur, as well as the religious sites of Swayambhu, Bauddhanath, Pashupati, and Changu Narayan.[28]

Damage to mixed sites is caused by phenomena such as coastal flooding and biodiversity loss, ensuing from increasing average temperatures.[29] Notably, climate change is a major cause of loss of biodiversity,[30] which is an integral part of mixed World Heritage sites such as the Tasmanian Wilderness, where remains dating back to as far as 20,000 years ago lie amid parks and reserves protecting one of the last temperate rainforests in the world.[31]

The impact of the different risks created by climate change on tangible cultural and mixed sites varies depending on the specific location of a heritage area. Increased salinity and acidification of water is particularly dangerous for underwater cultural heritage.[32] Hué, Amsterdam, and Paris are amongst the World Heritage cities that are most exposed to multi-hazard risk generated by global warming. Aleppo, Moscow, and Venice rank high among the sites most threatened by flooding. Mostar, Oporto, and Macau are amongst the places most affected by landslide.[33]

The effect of climate change can also be indirect, as in the case of the impact of climate-induced migration on World Heritage sites or diminished tourism in World Heritage areas.[34] For instance, the monuments of the Heart of Neolithic Orkney site are an extraordinary testament to the culture of the Stone Age farmers who arrived in Britain about 6,000 years ago. The site is subject to extreme weather events, such as coastal erosion, storms, and flooding. In 2012–13, the tourism

27 ibid 72–73.

28 UNESCO, 'On Anniversary of Nepal Earthquake, A New Partnership for Heritage' (2016) <http://whc.unesco.org/en/news/1480> accessed 3 January 2018.

29 UNESCO, 'Case Studies' (n 23) 18–53.

30 ibid 40–41.

31 UNESCO, 'World Heritage List: Tasmanian Wilderness' <http://whc.unesco.org/en/list/181> accessed 3 January 2018.

32 On the impact of climate change on underwater cultural heritage, see Elena Perez-Alvaro, 'Climate Change and Underwater Cultural Heritage: Impacts and Challenges' (2016) 21 J Cultural Heritage 842–43.

33 Anthony Gad Bigio, Maria Catalina Ochoa, and Rana Amirtahmasebi, 'Climate-Resilient, Climate-Friendly World Heritage Cities' (2014) 3–7 <https://openknowledge.worldbank.org/handle/10986/19288> accessed 3 January 2018.

34 UNESCO, UCS, and UNEP, 'World Heritage' (n 22) 19. See also the Noah's Ark Project, 'Global Climate Change Impact on Built Heritage and Cultural Landscapes' (2007) SSPI-CT-2003-501837.

industry in Orkney generated a revenue of US$31 million, which is critical for both funding and the permanence of inhabitants in the area.[35]

Whilst the decisions of the World Heritage Committee have understandably so far focused more on the effect of climate change on natural heritage,[36] cultural heritage has also been taken into account.[37] For instance, the Committee recently underscored that 'the Gorham's Cave Complex is vulnerable to sea level rises, flooding and other effects of climate change'.[38] The Gorham complex includes four caves located in the steep limestone cliffs on the eastern side of the Rock of Gibraltar, with archaeological and paleontological deposits providing evidence of Neanderthal occupation over more than 100,000 years.[39]

Loss of tangible heritage has further relevant implications for the intangible dimensions of culture, not only in economic terms, but also because it involves irreplaceable spiritual loss and changed sense of a place.[40] Climate change thus entails the progressive disappearance of tangible heritage and interwoven intangible dimensions.[41]

II. Regulatory Intersections

A. Localized Measures: Site-Level Adaptation and Mitigation

The 1972 World Heritage Convention seems to accommodate site-level adaptation and mitigation measures. According to the principle of territoriality, Article 4 of the World Heritage Convention establishes for the State where World Heritage sites are situated an obligation of 'protection, conservation, presentation and transmission to future generations'.[42] Such a language embeds the concept of sustainable development,[43] whereby 'transmission' entails protection from damage,

35 UNESCO, 'Case Studies' (n 23) 78.

36 See, for instance, World Heritage Committee, 'Report of Decisions Taken at Its Forty-First Session' (2017) WHC/17/41.COM/18, Decision 41 COM 7, paras 20-21 (UNESCO, 'Report of Decisions Taken at Its Forty-First Session').

37 See the yearly Decisions of the World Heritage Committee at <http://whc.unesco.org/en/decisions> accessed 3 January 2018.

38 World Heritage Committee, 'Report of Decisions Taken at Its Fortieth Session' (2016) WHC/16/40.COM/19, Decision 40 COM 8B.29 para 3 (World Heritage Committee, 'Report of Decisions Taken at Its Fortieth Session').

39 UNESCO, 'World Heritage List, Gorham's Cave Complex' <http://whc.unesco.org/en/list/1500> accessed 3 January 2018.

40 Michael Hall, Tim Baird, Michael James, and Yael Ram, 'Climate Change and Cultural Heritage: Conservation and Heritage Tourism in the Anthropocene' (2017) 11 J Heritage Tourism 10, 13.

41 Leigh Welling, Marcy Rockman, James Watson, Brendan Mackey, and Andrew Potts, 'The Role of World Heritage Sites in a Changing Climate' (2015) 77 World Heritage Rev 4, 6–12; Blake (n 3) 275.

42 1972 World Heritage Convention, art 4.

43 World Commission on Environment and Development, 'Our Common Future' (1987) A/42/427 Annex.

destruction, and loss,[44] encompassing action against climate change. Furthermore, Article 5 of the World Heritage Convention spells out in detail general State obligations embedded in Article 4, specifically compelling the States Parties to adopt 'comprehensive planning programmes'[45] and 'appropriate legal, scientific, technical, administrative and financial measures'[46] to protect World Heritage sites. Extraterritorially, Article 6 of the World Heritage Convention provides that a State Party 'undertakes not to take any deliberate measures which might damage directly or indirectly cultural and natural heritage', within the framework of a general obligation of the 'international community as a whole to co-operate'.[47]

Under these core provisions, site-level GHG adaptation and mitigation measures can certainly be regarded as ad hoc remedies aiming at the 'protection', 'conservation', and 'transmission to future generations' of cultural and mixed World Heritage sites. Notably, local measures fit with the principle of territoriality, according to which the duty to take protective action is binding upon the State where World Heritage sites are situated. In this respect, it is worth mentioning that the 1972 World Heritage Convention confines the inscription of World Heritage sites on the List of World Heritage in Danger to properties threatened by '*specific* dangers'.[48] The concept of 'specific danger' seems to include indirect effects of climate change tackled by means of site-level adaptation and mitigation, such as thermal stress induced by increased atmospheric temperatures or calamities and cataclysms caused by climate change,[49] such as the earthquake that affected Nepali World Heritage sites in 2015. In this regard, the Operational Guidelines to the World Heritage Convention point out that the notion of 'specific danger' includes both 'natural events and human activities'.[50]

Furthermore, according to the Operational Guidelines for the implementation of the World Heritage Convention, climate change itself should be considered a 'serious and specific danger', requiring 'major operations necessary for the conservation of [a] property'.[51] In fact, climate change may be regarded as a 'cataclysm' or a 'calamity' under the 1972 World Heritage Convention.[52] A literal and purposive interpretation thus supports the adoption of site-level adaptation and

[44] Guido Carducci, 'Articles 4–7: National and International Protection of the Cultural and Natural Heritage' in Francioni and Lenzerini (n 2) 103, 107, 114–15.

[45] 1972 World Heritage Convention, art 5(a).

[46] ibid, art 5(d).

[47] ibid, art 6.

[48] 1972 World Heritage Convention, art 11(4) (emphasis added).

[49] Gionata P Buzzini and Lugi Condorelli, 'Article 11 List of World Heritage in Danger and Deletion of a Property from the World Heritage List' in Francioni and Lenzerini (n 2) 175.

[50] 2017 World Heritage Operational Guidelines, para 161.

[51] ibid, para 177(b) and (c).

[52] 1972 World Heritage Convention, art 11(4). See also Jean-François Pulvenis, 'The Framework Convention on Climate Change' in Luigi Campiglio, Laura Pineschi, Domenico Siniscalco, and Tullio Treves (eds), *The Environment after Rio: International Law and Economics* (Graham & Trotman and Martinus Nijhoff 1994) 71, 74.

mitigation strategies for anthropogenic GHG emissions under the World Heritage Convention, according to rules for treaty interpretation established in Article 31(1) of the Vienna Convention on the Law of Treaties.[53] In this respect, in 2008 the World Heritage Committee amended the Operational Guidelines, establishing the impact of climate change as a criterion for inclusion on the List of World Heritage in Danger, noting that the emphasis of corrective measures should be on adaptation rather than mitigation.[54]

The 1972 World Heritage Convention complements the UNFCCC regime as concerns site-level adaptation and mitigation. In fact, the UNFCCC, Kyoto Protocol, and Paris Agreement each compel the adoption of localized measures against climate change.[55] Therefore, the obligation to protect sites of outstanding universal value via site-level climate measures under the World Heritage Convention must be read consistently with subsequent UNFCCC obligations, according to Article 31(3)(c) of the Vienna Convention, which requires that a treaty be interpreted in light of 'any relevant rules of international law applicable in the relations between the parties'.[56] Site-level adaptation and mitigation is thus consistent with a systemic interpretation of the World Heritage Convention.

A similar approach should be taken with respect to environmental treaties compelling the adoption of site-level measures against climate change. For instance, the Conference of the Parties to the 1992 Convention on Biological Diversity, which is crucial to the preservation of mixed heritage sites,[57] recognized that the Parties should 'integrate climate change adaptation measures in protected area planning, management strategies, and in the design of protected area systems'.[58] Thus, the 1972 World Heritage Convention, other environmental treaties, and the UNFCCC regime systemically integrate with each other and can be interpreted harmoniously.[59]

Along these lines, with regard to both site-level adaptation and mitigation strategies, the urban development plan for the historic center of Vienna envisages the adoption of sustainable conservation policies. This cultural site is particularly rich in architecture, including Baroque castles and gardens, monuments, parks, and the late-nineteenth-century Ringstrasse. The site is inscribed on the List of World

53 Vienna Convention, art 31(1).

54 World Heritage Committee, 'Decisions Adopted at the Thirty-Second Session' (2009) WHC-08/32.COM/24Rev, Decision 32 COM 7A.32, paras 5–6.

55 UNFCC art 4(b) and (e); Kyoto Protocol art 10(b); Paris Agreement, art 7. See also the UNFCCC COP-13, Bali Action Plan (2008) FCCC/CP/2007/6/Add.1, para 1(c); UNFCCC COP-14, 'Copenhagen Accord' (2009) FCCC/CP/2009/11/Add.1, 2/CP.15, paras 1, 3, 8, 10, 11.

56 Vienna Conventions, art 31(3)(c).

57 UNESCO World Heritage Centre, 'Policy Document' (n 17) 10.

58 Conference of the Parties to the Convention on Biological Diversity, 'Protected Areas' (2004) Decision VII/28 para 1.4.5.

59 International Law Commission, 'Fragmentation of International Law: Difficulties Arising from the Diversification and Expansion of International Law' (2006) A/CN.4/L.682, paras 37ff (ILC, 'Fragmentation').

Heritage in Danger because of pressure arising from urban development.[60] More generally, most urban development plans for World Heritage cities address climate-related phenomena such as floods, saltwater intrusion, landslides, droughts, heat waves, and energy-efficiency.[61] This is the case, for instance, of the 2004–20 Paris Climate Protection Plan.[62] Edinburgh has also adopted a Biodiversity Action Plan, protecting the natural and cultural assets of the city.[63]

More specifically, it is consistently assumed that adaptation projects for World Heritage sites represent a critical test to assess optimal adaptive strategies to climate change.[64] A successful example of implementation of site-level adaptation measures is the adoption in 1997 of an emergency assistance fund allocated to devise immediate measures protecting the most significant and vulnerable parts of Chan Chan in Peru. Chan Chan is an extensive and hierarchically planned pre-Colombian city, including remnants of its industrial, agricultural, and water management systems. This archaeological area was inscribed on the List of World Heritage in Danger because of the precarious state of conservation of the earthen architecture and its vulnerability to the extreme climatic events caused by El Niño.[65] On-site protective measures have been adopted against the projected effects of El Niño, for instance, against flooding, whilst in the long-term adaptation strategies aim at reinforcing and stabilizing the foundations and structures of the main buildings and architecture surrounding the Tschudi Palace.[66]

Similarly, monitoring is conducted through the British Environment Agency's 'Thames Estuary 2100 Project' in a joint initiative between the Anglian, Southern, and Thames Regions, in order to determine the appropriate level of flood safety to protect London, the Thames Estuary, and related World Heritage sites over the next 100 years. The area includes monuments such as Westminster Palace, a fine example of neo-Gothic architecture, the Tower of London, the collection of buildings at Greenwich, and the surrounding park. Flooding threatens the integrity of the sites and is particularly aggravated by climate change, which causes more frequent and intense overflow of the River Thames through the City of London. It is predicted that unmitigated GHG emissions would determine a rise in average

[60] UNESCO, 'World Heritage List—Historic Centre of Vienna' <http://whc.unesco.org/en/list/1033> accessed 3 January 2018.

[61] Bigio, Ochoa, and Amirtahmasebi (n 33) 19.

[62] Available at <http://www.energy-cities.eu/IMG/pdf/Paris_climate_protection_plan_2007.pdf> accessed 3 January 2018.

[63] Available at <https://www.edinburgh.gov.uk/downloads/file/26216/edinburgh-biodiversity-action-plan-2019-2021> accessed 7 February 2020.

[64] World Heritage Committee, 'Issues Related to the State of Conservation of World Heritage Properties: The Impacts of Climate Change on World Heritage Properties' (2006) WHC-06/30.COM/7.1 55 (World Heritage Committee, 'Issues'). See also Helen Phillips, 'The Capacity to Adapt to Climate Change at Heritage Sites—The Development of a Conceptual Framework' (2015) 47 *Environmental Science and Policy* 118.

[65] UNESCO, 'World Heritage List—Chan Chan Archaeological Site' <http://whc.unesco.org/en/list/366> accessed 3 January 2018.

[66] UNESCO, 'Case Studies' (n 23) 57.

sea level and changes in storm patterns, increasing the incidence of flooding by storm surges affecting World Heritage properties located on the banks of the River Thames.[67]

With regard to the city of Venice and its Lagoon, the Italian Government implemented a system of mobile barriers to shield the city and its World Heritage sites from high waters. Founded in the fifth century and spread over several small islands, Venice is an architectural masterpiece displaying works by painters such as Canaletto, Lotto, Tiepolo, and Titian. The City and the Lagoon naturally attract artistic and literary events and traditions. These characteristics make Venice the symbol of harmony between art and environment. The particular geographical situation of the Lagoon naturally exposes Venice to the threats of climate change, notably rising sea level and ground subsidence. Work thus commenced to build mobile barriers protecting St Mark's Square and breakwaters at the Malamocco inlet.[68] This, however, did not prevent flooding in 2019.

Concerning mixed sites, Algeria passed cultural heritage legislation ensuring the sustainable management of Tassili in order to protect it, inter alia, from extreme weather conditions. The law ensures the sustainable development of Tassili by associating culture, local collectives, environment, and forests. Within this context, the Tassili Park Office has been established as an administrative body to ensure protection, conservation, and enhancement of cultural and natural heritage in the area. Climate change may have a significant impact on the natural component of the site, with particular regard to biodiversity, since Tassili n'Ajjer is part of an ecological belt, which includes plant and animal species typical of the Sahara, as well as tropical and Mediterranean species. Local programmes have thus been established to ensure on-site biodiversity management.[69]

However, localized adaptation measures put the World Heritage Convention framework under economic pressure. Indeed, adaptation work in Venice reportedly cost more than US$6 billion, whilst the United States allocated US$100 million to repair damages caused by Hurricane Sandy to the Statue of Liberty and adjacent areas as well as to prevent storm damage. These sums hugely exceed the overall amount available to States Parties to the World Heritage Convention requiring international assistance to support site management through the World Heritage Fund, which only totals US$4 million.[70] The World Heritage Committee recently emphasized 'the urgency of securing adequate financial resources to achieve the objectives of the 1972 Convention', specifically 'in light of the 2030 Agenda for Sustainable Development and unprecedented threats such as climate

[67] ibid 69.
[68] ibid 71.
[69] UNESCO, 'World Heritage List: Tassili n'Ajjer' <http://whc.unesco.org/en/list/179> accessed 3 January 2018.
[70] UNESCO, UCS, and UNEP, 'World Heritage' (n 22) 26.

change'.[71] These considerations are particularly significant by considering that site-level action is a small part of the overall problem. In fact, site-level adaptation and mitigation measures are obviously insufficient in the long term to resolve globally generated phenomena such as the threat of flooding to the city of Venice or loss of biodiversity in Tassili, which require more fundamentally the root causes of sea-level rise and biodiversity loss at the global level to be addressed.[72]

B. General Mitigation and Adaptation: Stretching the Limits of the World Heritage Convention

The question of whether the 1972 World Heritage Convention can compel the adoption of general adaptation and mitigation remedies against anthropogenic GHG emissions, thus protecting World Heritage sites as a whole in the long term, is a controversial one. The Preamble to the World Heritage Convention implicitly underscores that threats to World Heritage exist both at the site level and as a consequence of de-localized phenomena, requiring action not only 'by the State concerned', but also 'collective assistance'.[73] Similarly, Article 5(1) of the World Heritage Convention calls for Members to 'integrate the protection of ... heritage into *comprehensive planning programmes*'.[74] Furthermore, general measures could be justified under Article 4 of the World Heritage Convention, which establishes an obligation for the Sovereign Parties to do 'all [they] can' for 'ensuring the identification, protection and transmission to future generations of the cultural and natural heritage'.[75]

Therefore, according to a scholarly interpretation, general mitigation and adaptation measures would be one of the 'appropriate' legal, scientific, and technical undertakings under Article 5(d) of the World Heritage Convention.[76] These measures should be adopted in accordance with the principle of common but differentiated responsibility, since Article 4 of the World Heritage Convention provides that a Sovereign Party must protect World Heritage sites 'to the utmost of its own resources', and Article 5 of the World Heritage Convention further specifies that

[71] World Heritage Committee, 'Report of Decisions Taken at Its Forty-First Session' (n 36) Decision 41 COM 14, para 6.

[72] ibid. See also Colin Long and Anita Smith, 'Cultural Heritage and the Global Environmental Crisis' in Sophia Labadi and Colin Long (eds), *Heritage and Globalization (Key Issues in Cultural Heritage)* (Routledge 2010) 173–74.

[73] 1972 World Heritage Convention, Preamble.

[74] ibid, art 5(1) (emphasis added).

[75] Anna Huggins, 'Protecting World Heritage Sites from the Adverse Impacts of Climate Change: Obligations for States Parties to the World Heritage Convention' (2007) 14 Australian Intl L J 121, 125.

[76] Erica Thorson, 'On Thin Ice: The Failure of the United States and the World Heritage Committee to Take Climate Change Mitigation Pursuant to the World Heritage Convention Seriously' (2008) 38 Environmental L 139, 160.

States must endeavor to undertake appropriate measures 'in so far as possible'.[77] Such arguments, however, face the objection that, according to the principle of sovereignty, Articles 4 and 5 of the World Heritage Convention explicitly provide that each Party to the Convention assumes the primary responsibility for the preservation and protection of World Heritage sites situated 'on its territory'.[78]

The territorial objection may be overcome in light of the assumption that at least some cultural resources located within State boundaries are of 'common concern of humankind'.[79] Theoretically, following this pattern could lead to interpreting the concept so as to recognize collective sovereignty over sites of outstanding universal value, and thus universal protection. Whilst such an approach seems to be in contrast with the principle of sovereignty and the main responsibility for protection of the State where properties are situated under the World Heritage Convention, the notion of common heritage can be certainly relied upon to foster inter-State cooperation.

General mitigation is also justified under Article 6(3) of the World Heritage Convention, which establishes for Sovereign Members a duty 'not to *deliberately* cause harm' to other States' sites of outstanding universal value.[80] Some scholars note that GHG emissions should be characterized as deliberate State acts resulting in deterioration of other States' World Heritage properties.[81] In this respect, however, it can be argued that, in order to curb GHG emissions, States must adopt positive legislative measures. By contrast, not curbing GHG emissions is technically a failure to act, which does not fulfill the requirement of positive measures under Article 6(3) of the World Heritage Convention. Therefore, it is at least questionable that, if a State is aware of the widely available information that climate change affects World Heritage sites, deciding not to legislate to curb anthropogenic GHGs may be considered a deliberate measure. Indeed, in a position paper filed with the World Heritage Committee, the United States underscored that 'failure to take an action, such as not reducing greenhouse gases, does not constitute a "deliberat[e] measure which might damage a site" under Article 6(3) [of the 1972 World Heritage Convention]'.[82] Even more specifically, it is difficult to prove that GHG emissions 'deliberately' aim to damage World Heritage sites. In fact, GHG emissions are a collateral effect of conduct such as agricultural activities and the burning of fossil

[77] ibid, 168–69.

[78] 1972 World Heritage Convention, arts 4, 5.

[79] William Burns, 'Belt and Suspenders? The World Heritage Convention's Role in Confronting Climate Change' (2009) 18 Rev Eur, Comparative and Intl Environmental L 148, 156.

[80] Emphasis added.

[81] Huggins (n 75) 129; Thorson (n 76) 149. See also Belize, 'Petition to the World Heritage Committee' (2004) 31 <https://www.law.ufl.edu/_pdf/academics/centers-clinics/clinics/conservation/resources/belize.pdf> accessed 7 February 2020.

[82] United States, 'Position Paper on Climate Change with Respect to the World Heritage Convention and World Heritage Sites Filed with the World Heritage Committee in Advance of the Experts Meeting' (2006) 2 <www.elaw.org> accessed 3 January 2018.

fuels, mostly carried out by private industries in the energy sector.[83] Proof of such a 'deliberate intent' is particularly difficult with regard to the States Parties to the World Heritage Convention that respect their emission limits under the Kyoto Protocol and Paris Agreement.[84]

It thus seems that, whilst it is not impossible to interpret the World Heritage Convention as a means to impose general mitigation and adaptation measures against climate change on States Parties in order to ensure protection of cultural and mixed sites of outstanding universal value, this certainly requires an extensive interpretation of the language of the Convention. In this respect, it may be argued that climate change constitutes an unforeseen 'fundamental change of circumstances which has occurred with regard to those existing at the time of the conclusion of a treaty' and might be invoked by the Parties as a ground for 'terminating or withdrawing from' the World Heritage Convention, according to the Vienna Conventions.[85] This argument was indeed put forward by the United States in its position paper on Climate Change with Respect to the World Heritage Convention and World Heritage Sites.[86]

III. Practice

A. The Petitions to the World Heritage Committee: Protecting Tangible Cultural Heritage as a Means to Enforce Site-Level Adaptation and Mitigation

The relationship between climate change and tangible cultural heritage has been underscored in a set of petitions filed with the World Heritage Committee between 2004 and 2009, requesting the addition of several World Heritage sites to the List of World Heritage in Danger based on the effects of global warming.[87] Four petitions were filed in 2004 with regard to Sagarmatha National Park in Nepal, Huascarán National Park in Peru, the Great Barrier Reef in Australia, and Belize's Barrier Reef Reserve System. A fifth petition filed in 2006 addressed the Waterton Glacier International Peace Park in the United States and Canada, whilst another petition filed in 2007 targeted the Blue Mountains Area in Australia.[88] All the petitions

[83] UNEP and World Trade Organisation (WTO), 'Trade and Climate Change: A Report by the UNEP and WTO' (2009) 27 <https://www.wto.org/english/res_e/booksp_e/trade_climate_change_e.pdf> accessed 3 January 2018.

[84] Kyoto Protocol Annex B and Doha Amendment 2012; Paris Agreement, art 4(9);UNFCCC, 'Communications Received from the Parties on Nationally Determined Contributions' <http://unfccc.int/focus/ndc_registry/items/9981.php> accessed 3 January 2018.

[85] Vienna Convention, art 62. See Ottavio Quirico, 'Amidst Fragmentation and Coherence: A Systemic Interpretation of the World Heritage Convention and the UNFCCC Regime' (2012) 10 New Zealand YB Intl L 60–64.

[86] United States (n 82) 5–6.

[87] See the list of endangered sites at <http://whc.unesco.org/en/danger> accessed 3 January 2018.

[88] See the text of the petitions at <http://www.climatelaw.org> accessed 3 January 2018.

requested that the States Parties to the World Heritage Convention be constrained to critically reduce their general GHG emissions. None of the threatened sites is officially classified as 'cultural' or 'mixed', since all of them are considered 'natural' sites. However, the Petitions triggered a dynamic approach to the relationship between climate change and the protection of cultural and mixed sites under the 1972 World Heritage Convention.

The World Heritage Committee addressed the first four petitions in July 2005.[89] Whilst the Committee has not inscribed the sites in question on the List of World Heritage in Danger,[90] it generally acknowledged the effect of climate change on both 'natural and cultural sites' of outstanding universal value[91] and prompted the States Parties to the World Heritage Convention to 'seriously consider' its impact on management planning.[92] The Committee also requested the creation of a working group of experts on the risks posed by climate change to World Heritage sites,[93] which led to the publication of a Report on Predicting and Managing the Effects of Climate Change on World Heritage and a Strategy to Assist States Parties to Implement Appropriate Management Responses in 2006.[94]

The 2006 Strategy focuses on: (1) pre-emptive action, including monitoring, reporting and mitigation of climate change impacts; (2) corrective action, notably global, regional and local adaptation strategies; and (3) sharing of knowledge, including best practice, education and capacity building.[95] However, concerning mitigation, the Strategy underscores that whilst 'some mitigation opportunities could be contemplated in the context of the World Heritage Convention at the level of the World Heritage sites', the UNFCCC is 'the preferred international tool to address mitigation at the global and States Parties levels'.[96] Consistently, the Strategy addresses 'site managers' and fosters 'site-level action' for adaptation and mitigation measures.[97] Endorsing the Strategy, the World Heritage

[89] World Heritage Committee, 'Report of Decisions Adopted at the Twenty-Ninth Session' (2005) WHC-05/29.COM/22, Decision 29 Com 7B.a, 36-37 (World Heritage Committee, 'Report of Decisions Adopted at the Twenty-Ninth Session').

[90] At its thirty-third meeting, held in June 2009, the Committee did place the Belize Barrier Reef Reserve System on the List of World Heritage in Danger, but owing to mangrove cutting, not to climate change (World Heritage Committee, 'Report of Decisions Adopted at Its Thirty-Third Session' (2009) WHC-09/33.COM/20, Decision 33 COM 7B.33, paras 3 and 9 (World Heritage Committee, 'Report of Decisions Adopted at Its Thirty-Third Session').

[91] World Heritage Committee, 'Report of Decisions Adopted at the Twenty-Ninth Session' (n 89) Decision 29 Com 7B.a, paras 4 and 5.

[92] ibid, para 6.

[93] ibid, paras 7 and 9.

[94] World Heritage Committee, 'Report on Predicting and Managing the Effects of Climate Change on World Heritage and Strategy to Assist States Parties to Implement Appropriate Management Responses' (2006) <whc.unesco.org/document/8874> accessed 3 January 2018 (World Heritage Committee, 'Report' and 'Strategy').

[95] World Heritage Committee, 'Strategy' (n 94) 40–42.

[96] ibid 37.

[97] ibid 40.

Committee underscored that there are international instruments other than the 1972 World Heritage Convention coordinating the international response to climate change.[98]

The Strategy was followed in 2007 by the Policy Document on the Impact of Climate Change on World Heritage Properties, which was adopted by the Sixteenth General Assembly of State Parties to the World Heritage Convention.[99] The Policy confirms that the UNFCCC and IPCC are the 'key international organizations' to address climate change and highlights the importance for World Heritage sites to take localized adaptation and mitigation measures, whereby 'site-level adaptation' is the 'main focus of the response strategy'.[100] The Policy identifies Articles 4, 5, and 6 of the 1972 World Heritage Convention as the key rules to address the impact of climate change on cultural heritage and concludes that these norms compel monitoring the impact of global warming on World Heritage sites and taking adequate site-level adaptation and mitigation measures.[101]

The Policy is contextualized within the framework of a precautionary approach, in line with the UNFCCC,[102] and, more generally, the fundamentals of international environmental law.[103] More specifically, the Policy points out that, since it includes outdoor, indoor, and buried sites, World Heritage provides an ideal framework to develop model site-level adaptation measures.[104] Given that the effects of a threat are taken into account to determine whether a site is endangered, regardless of its origin, the Policy also highlights the possibility of inscribing World Heritage sites on the List of World Heritage in Danger because of climate change.[105]

Ten years after its adoption, the Policy remains, together with the Strategy, the key document for protecting World Heritage sites from the effects of climate change.[106] The Policy was endorsed by the World Heritage Committee in its answer to the Waterton petition[107] and, after the adoption of the Paris Agreement, in 2016 the Committee underscored the necessity of updating the document so as to 'make available the most current knowledge and technology

[98] World Heritage Committee, 'Report of Decisions Adopted at the Thirtieth Session' (2006) WHC-06/30.COM/19, Decision 30 COM 7.1 para 8 (World Heritage Committee, 'Report of Decisions Adopted at the Thirtieth Session').

[99] See UNESCO World Heritage Centre, 'Policy Document' (n 17).

[100] ibid 4 and 9.

[101] ibid 6–8.

[102] UNFCCC, art 3.

[103] UNESCO World Heritage Centre, 'Policy Document' (n 17) 8.. See also UN, Rio Declaration on Environment and Development (1992) UN Doc A/CONF.151/26, Principle 15.

[104] UNESCO World Heritage Centre, 'Policy Document' (n 17) 11.

[105] ibid 12.

[106] UNESCO, UCS, and UNEP, 'World Heritage' (n 22) 27.

[107] World Heritage Committee, 'Report of Decisions Adopted at Its Thirty-Third Session' (n 90) Decision 33 COM 7B.22, paras 7, 10, 12.

on the subject to guide the decisions and actions of the World Heritage community'.[108] In 2017, the Committee encouraged Italy to take into account the Policy in its management plan for the city of Venice, considering that Venice and its Lagoon are 'in a privileged position and might have the potential to influence monitoring and adaptation processes that can be applied elsewhere'.[109] More generally, addressing the Blue Mountains Petition, the Committee invited the Parties to the World Heritage Convention to 'exchange information on existing national policies, regulations and opportunities for immediate voluntary action to control the generation of black carbon that can affect World Heritage properties'.[110]

Recently, the World Heritage Committee prepared a Policy Document for the Integration of a Sustainable Development Perspective into the Processes of the 1972 World Heritage Convention.[111] The Policy Document broadly recognizes that the Convention 'contributes significantly to sustainable development'.[112] Whilst paying specific attention to the conservation of 'places of outstanding natural value', the new policy underscores that 'a concern for environmental sustainability, however, should *equally apply to cultural and mixed World Heritage properties*, including cultural landscapes', also 'strengthening resilience to disasters and *climate change*'.[113] Procedurally, this implies the adoption of 'environmental, social and cultural impact assessment tools' in policy planning.[114] Within this framework, World Heritage properties are seen as both 'an asset to be protected and a resource to strengthen the ability of communities and their properties to resist, absorb, and recover from the effects of a hazard'.[115] This ultimately leads to acknowledging that the States Parties to the World Heritage Convention should 'recognise and promote—within conservation and adaptation strategies—the inherent potential of the World Heritage properties for reducing disaster risks and adapting to climate change'.[116]

[108] World Heritage Committee, 'Report of Decisions Taken at Its Fortieth Session' (n 38) Decision 40 COM 7, para 16.
[109] World Heritage Committee, 'Report of Decisions Taken at Its Forty-First Session' (n 36) Decision 41 COM 7B.48, para 5.
[110] World Heritage Committee, 'Report of Decisions Adopted at Its Thirty-Third Session' (n 90) Decision 33 COM 7C, para 15.
[111] General Assembly of the State Parties to World Heritage Convention, 'Policy Document for the Integration of a Sustainable Development Perspective into the Processes of the World Heritage Convention' (2015) WHC-15/20.GA/INF.13.
[112] ibid, para 3.
[113] ibid, para 14 (emphasis added).
[114] ibid, para 7.
[115] ibid, para 16.
[116] ibid, para 16(i).

B. The Limits of Tangible Cultural and Mixed Heritage in Enforcing General Adaptation and Mitigation Seen Through the Lens of Human Rights

Civil society has pointed out that '[c]ultural heritage is a human right' and 'the changing climate puts some aspects of cultural heritage at additional risk'.[117] Linking cultural heritage and human rights theoretically lends support to the thesis that tangible cultural and mixed heritage should be relied upon to foster not only site-level measures, but also general mitigation and adaptation strategies against climate change. Prima facie, this approach seems viable, given that, among human rights regulatory instruments, the 1966 International Covenant on Economic, Social and Cultural Rights (ICESCR)[118] upholds the right of everyone to 'take part in cultural life' and compels States to 'achieve the full realisation of this right', including steps 'necessary for the *conservation*, the *development* and the *diffusion* of science and culture'.[119] More generally, the Universal Declaration of Human Rights (UDHR)[120] provides that 'everyone has the right freely to participate in the cultural life of the community'.[121] This facilitates viewing the duty to protect tangible cultural and mixed heritage as an *erga omnes* and possibly peremptory obligation, transcending national boundaries.[122] However, practice shows that this approach suits intangible rather than tangible cultural heritage.

The impact of climate change on cultural heritage has been envisaged from a human rights perspective in two petitions submitted by the Inuit people to the Inter-American Commission on Human Rights (IAComHR) in 2005 and 2012. The Inuit live in the Arctic Circle, and their culture is based on adaptation to cold conditions. The right to culture is the first of a list of fundamental rights invoked in the 2005 Petition,[123] which the Inuit filed against the United States for failing to adequately mitigate their GHG emissions.[124] On this basis, the Inuit argued that the United States should implement not only site-level adaptation policies, but most importantly mandatory measures capping GHG emissions globally.[125] A similar

[117] World Monuments Fund and Others, 'Pocantico Call to Action on Climate Impacts and Cultural Heritage' (2015) <https://www.ucsusa.org/sites/default/files/attach/2016/04/Pocantico-Call-to-Action-on-Climate-Impacts-Cultural-Heritage-4-11-2016.pdf> accessed 3 January 2018.

[118] International Covenant on Economic, Social and Cultural Rights (adopted 16 December 1966, entered into force 3 January 1976) 999 UNTS 3 (ICESCR).

[119] ibid, art 15 (emphasis added).

[120] Universal Declaration of Human Rights, UNGA Res 217A (10 December 1948) (UDHR).

[121] ibid, art 27. For more details, see Blake (n 3) 288 ff.

[122] See Francesco Francioni, 'The Human Dimension of International Cultural Heritage Law: An Introduction' (2011) 22 EJIL 9; Carducci (n 44) 103, 111, 121–22, 115, 119, 132–44; Buzzini and Condorelli (n 49) 175, 179.

[123] Inuit, *Petition to the Inter-American Commission on Human Rights Seeking Relief from Violations Resulting from Global Warming Caused by Acts and Omissions of the United States* [2005] P-1413–05 5.

[124] ibid.

[125] ibid 7, 103, 118.

stance was taken by the Arctic Athabaskan Council in the 2012 Petition, addressing black carbon emissions in Canada.[126]

The first Inuit petition was dismissed by the IAComHR in a short communication which assumes that 'the information provided [in the Petition] does not enable [the Commission] to determine whether the alleged facts would tend to characterize a violation of rights protected'.[127] The second petition has not (yet) been addressed by the IAComHR. However, whilst the petitions underscore a clear link between climate change and the human right to culture with respect to not only site-level undertakings, but also global strategies, the focus is on environmental protection as a necessary condition for the preservation of culture in general, not specifically on given cultural and mixed sites of outstanding universal value.

For the time being, available practice indicates that the most appropriate human rights framework to address general measures against climate change is afforded by intangible cultural heritage, whereas the regime established for the protection of tangible cultural heritage may only play a secondary role. In fact, the documents of the World Heritage Committee do not particularly foster a human rights approach to the protection of cultural and mixed heritage sites from climate change.

It must be noted that the language of the 2003 Convention for the Safeguarding of Intangible Cultural Heritage (2003 ICH Convention)[128] is similar to that of the 1972 World Heritage Convention. In fact, a State Party to the 2003 ICH Convention has an obligation to 'identify intangible cultural heritage *present in its territory*'[129] and to 'take the necessary measures to ensure the *safeguarding of the intangible cultural heritage present in its territory*'.[130] Likewise, the ICH Convention compels States to adopt '*measures aimed at ensuring the viability of the intangible cultural heritage*, including ... *preservation, protection, promotion, enhancement, transmission* ... of such heritage'.[131] Moreover, the Convention requires States to 'foster scientific, technical and artistic studies, as well as research *methodologies*, with a view to *effective safeguarding of the intangible cultural heritage*, in particular the intangible cultural heritage in danger' and to '*adopt appropriate legal, technical, administrative and financial measures* aimed at ... the *transmission* of such heritage'.[132]

Significantly, however, unlike the 1972 World Heritage Convention, with regard to the 2003 ICH Convention it is not possible to assume that climate change

[126] Arctic Athabaskan Council, *Petition to the Inter-American Commission on Human Rights Seeking Relief from Violations of the Rights of Arctic Athabaskan Peoples Resulting from Rapid Arctic Warming and Melting Caused by Emissions of Black Carbon by Canada* [2013] 2–3, 21, 54, 59, 49, and 87. See also Don McCrimmon, 'The Athabaskan Petition to the Inter-American Human Rights Commission: Using Human Rights to Respond to Climate Change' (2016) 6 Polar J 398.

[127] IAComHR, *Sheila-Watt Cloutier and Others* (Petition) P-1413-05 (16 November 2006).

[128] Convention for the Safeguarding of Intangible Cultural Heritage (adopted 17 October 2003, entered into force 20 April 2006) 2368 UNTS 3 (ICH Convention).

[129] ibid, art 11(b) (emphasis added).

[130] ibid (emphasis added).

[131] ibid, art 2(3) (emphasis added).

[132] ibid, art 13 (emphasis added).

constitutes an unforeseen 'fundamental change of circumstances' with respect to the conclusion of the treaty. First, the ICH Convention was adopted in 2003, when the international community had full cognizance of the phenomenon of climate change, and regulatory action against global warming had already been undertaken. Second, under the ICH Convention intangible cultural heritage is explicitly protected within the framework of 'sustainable development'.[133] Third, it is clear that protecting the environment as a necessary condition to safeguard the identity of entire groups of people, notably indigenous groups, is a much more compelling argument with respect to global GHG mitigation and adaptation measures than the necessity of protecting localized sites of outstanding universal value. If it is true that the tangible and intangible dimensions of cultural heritage are interwoven,[134] in practice the intangible element has so far been the primary focus of the human rights approach to climate change.

IV. An Integrated Approach

A. Systemic Cooperation

The relationship between the 1972 World Heritage Convention and the 2003 ICH Convention demonstrates that a correct understanding of the role of the World Heritage Convention in shaping GHG adaptation and mitigation strategies cannot be achieved in isolation, but requires contextualizing the Convention within the broader framework of international law.[135] From this perspective, environmental issues, and climate change in particular, are not only relevant to the World Heritage Convention, but also relate to other international regulatory regimes. As in a set of nested boxes, a network of regulatory intersections emerges between the 1972 World Heritage Convention, the 2003 ICH Convention, the UNFCCC, and environmental regulation.

For instance, the provisions of the 1992 Convention on Biological Diversity can be extensively interpreted in the same way as those of the 1972 World Heritage Convention to impose on States Parties not only local undertakings, but also general measures against GHG emissions. In fact, the biodiversity treaty provides that States have 'the responsibility to ensure that activities within their jurisdiction or control do not cause damage to the environment of other States or of areas beyond the limits of national jurisdiction'.[136] The Convention also provides for the development of 'national strategies, plans or programmes for the conservation

[133] 2003 ICH Convention, art 2(3).
[134] See text to nn 40 and 41.
[135] ILC, 'Fragmentation' (n 59).
[136] Convention on Biological Diversity, art 3.

and sustainable use of biological diversity'.[137] Furthermore, additional provisions of the Convention require that States Parties not only 'integrate consideration of the conservation and sustainable use of biological resources into national decision-making' and 'encourage cooperation between its governmental authorities and its private sector in developing methods for sustainable use of biological resources',[138] but also undertake monitoring and identification efforts 'in so far as possible and as appropriate',[139] which might be read as an implicit reference to the concept of 'common but differentiated responsibility' as in Articles 4 and 5 of the 1972 World Heritage Convention.[140] Envisaging site-level adaptation and mitigation within each regime is possible because of the de-localized nature of such action. By contrast, general mitigation and adaptation is centralized and does not allow the establishment of different 'self-contained regimes'.[141]

Consistent with this line of reasoning, the World Heritage Committee envisages a constant dialogue between institutions under the World Heritage Convention and the UNFCCC to define optimal measures for site-level adaptation to and mitigation of climate change with regard to World Heritage sites, whereby decisions are ultimately taken by managers of individual World Heritage properties within the framework of the 1972 World Heritage Convention.[142] In this respect, the World Heritage Convention is *lex specialis* and takes precedence over the UNFCCC.[143] The 2006 Strategy to assist the Members of the World Heritage Convention to implement appropriate management responses therefore requires that State Parties to the Convention 'take site level action' to '[i]dentify and promote synergies between adaptation and mitigation', whereby 'any adaptation measure should seek ways in which to mitigate' and '[e]ncourage site managers to reduce emissions of greenhouse gases at the level of the sites'.[144] However, the Strategy should be updated with a comprehensive review of the climate vulnerability of World Heritage sites,[145] integrating the interaction of climate change with factors such as tourism pressure, illegal harvesting of natural resources, oil and gas, armed conflict, and poverty, in collaboration with organizations such as the UN Development Programme, International Labour Organization, Industrial Development Organization, World Tourism Organization, and the UN Environment Programme.[146]

[137] ibid, art 6.
[138] ibid, art 10(a) and (e).
[139] ibid, art 7.
[140] See Alan Boyle, 'The Convention on Biological Diversity' in Luigi Campiglio , Laura Pineschi, Domenico Siniscalco, and Tullio Treves (eds),*The Environment after Rio—International Law and Economics* (Graham & Trotman/Martinus Nijhoff 1994) 111.
[141] ILC, 'Fragmentation' (n 59) para 172.
[142] World Heritage Committee, 'Report of Decisions Adopted at Its Thirtieth Session' (n 98) WHC-06/30.COM/19, Decision 30.COM/7.1, para 13.
[143] ILC, 'Fragmentation' (n 59) para 46.
[144] World Heritage Centre, 'Strategy' (n 94) 41.
[145] UNESCO, UCS, and UNEP, 'World Heritage' (n 22) 27.
[146] ibid 28.

Institutional dialogue should also take place with respect to general mitigation and adaptation measures, whereby decisions are ultimately taken by UNFCCC institutions.[147] In this regard, the UNFCCC regime is *lex specialis* and takes precedence over the 1972 World Heritage Convention. Within this framework, institutions under the World Heritage Convention should prompt UNFCCC decision-makers to outline GHG emission caps by taking into account the outstanding universal value of sites listed under the World Heritage Convention. Along these lines, the Strategy generally suggests that the World Heritage Committee '[p]rovide information to IPCC and UNFCCC on the impacts of climate change on World Heritage sites to assist them in tailoring mitigation strategies'.[148]

More specifically, the Strategy prompts the World Heritage Committee to 'collaborate with the UNFCCC secretariat on climate change issues by presenting information at the Conference of the Parties (COP) and subsidiary bodies meetings' and 'being involved in the SBSTA [Subsidiary Body for Scientific and Technological Advice] 5-year work programme, encouraging exchange of experts and by using UNFCCC guidelines.'[149] Consistently, in 2008 the Australia Climate Justice Program, Climate Action Network Australia, and Friends of the Earth Australia filed a submission with the Ad Hoc Working Group on Further Commitments for Annex 1 Parties under the Kyoto Protocol, arguing that World Heritage sites must play a meaningful role in the decision-making process leading to defining global GHG emission constraints beyond 2012.[150]

In 2015, the World Heritage Committee acknowledged that World Heritage properties are increasingly affected by climate change and prompted the States Parties to the World Heritage Convention to participate in UNFCCC COP21, with a view to achieving a universal climate agreement.[151] The Pocantico Call to Action also invokes cooperation, highlighting that '[n]either costs of addressing climate change impacts on cultural heritage, nor the knowledge we gain from understanding our cultural heritage, have been comprehensively addressed in climate policy responses at any level'.[152] The validity of this approach is also confirmed by the Sendai Framework for Disaster Risk Reduction 2015–2030, which underscores

147 World Heritage Committee, 'Issues' (n 64) paras 6–7; UNESCO World Heritage Centre, 'Policy Document' (n 17) 4. See also Burns (n 79) 158.

148 World Heritage Committee, 'Strategy' (n 94) 40.

149 ibid 28.

150 Australian Climate Justice Program, Climate Action Network Australia, and Friends of the Earth Australia, 'State Parties Responsibilities under the World Heritage Convention in the Context of Climate Change: Absolute Minimum Temperature Rise Necessary for Compliance with the World Heritage Convention', Submission to the Ad Hoc Working Group on Further Commitments for Annex 1 Parties under the Kyoto Protocol (2008) <whc.unesco.org/document/102033> accessed 3 January 2018.

151 World Heritage Committee, 'Report of Decisions Adopted at Its Thirty-Ninth Session' (2015) WHC-15/39.COM/19, Decision 39 COM 7, para 12.

152 World Monuments Fund and others (n 117) 1.

the importance of systematically envisaging 'environmental and cultural heritage impacts' to protect 'sites of historical, cultural heritage and religious interest'.[153]

Synergies are consistent with the 1972 World Heritage Convention, which establishes that 'the [World Heritage] Committee shall co-operate with international and national governmental and non-governmental organisations having objectives *similar* to those of this Convention'.[154] Such a policy would lead to establishing extra-systemic collaboration, a technique that is already largely exploited within the context of different multilateral environmental agreements.[155] Within a co-operative framework, the need to protect tangible cultural and mixed heritage should be integrated by and balanced against the necessity of defending other internationally protected interests, such as biodiversity.[156]

A systemic approach should more generally underpin the relationship between the 1972 World Heritage Convention and environmental regulation. Thus, for instance, whilst site-level measures to protect depletion of biodiversity in mixed World Heritage sites can be envisaged under the World Heritage Convention, the general framework for the preservation of biodiversity must be necessarily defined under the 1992 Convention on Biological Diversity, possibly integrating the need to protect World Heritage sites of outstanding universal value. In fact, the Strategy acknowledges that '[a]ddressing climate change issues at different levels requires the development of synergies and partnerships with other multilateral environmental agreements'.[157] The importance of this approach has been clearly underscored, for instance, with respect to the relationship between the 1971 Convention on Wetlands of International Importance Especially as Waterfowl Habitat (Ramsar Convention on Wetlands),[158] the 1992 Convention on Biological Diversity, and the UNFCCC.[159]

B. The Paris Agreement and Beyond

In practice, the IPCCC Reports and the Paris Agreement negotiations have not yet specifically referred to tangible cultural and mixed sites of outstanding universal

[153] UN, 'Sendai Framework for Disaster Risk Reduction 2015–2030' (2015) 5, 15, 19 <http://www.preventionweb.net/files/43291_sendaiframeworkfordrren.pdf> accessed 3 January 2018.

[154] 1972 World Heritage Convention, art 13(7) (emphasis added).

[155] Bharat Desai, *Multilateral Environmental Agreements* (CUP 2010) 60.

[156] World Heritage Committee, 'World Heritage Convention' (n 9) 3, paras 8(d) and 5.

[157] World Heritage Centre, 'Strategy' (n 94) 28.

[158] Convention on Wetlands of International Importance Especially as Waterfowl Habitat (adopted 2 February 1971, entered into force 21 December 1975) 996 UNTS 245 (Ramsar Convention on Wetlands).

[159] Ger Bergkamp and Brett Orlando, 'Wetlands and Climate Change: Exploring Collaboration between the Convention on Wetlands and the UN Framework Convention on Climate Change' (1999) 11 ff <https://www.ramsar.org/sites/default/files/documents/library/dn1999-9papere.pdf> accessed 3 January 2018.

value protected under the 1972 World Heritage Convention.[160] Whilst in 2006 the Strategy invited the UNESCO World Heritage Centre to 'engage with key climate change researchers from the Intergovernmental Panel on Climate Change to encourage them to address cultural heritage issues more directly',[161] no explicit reference is made in the Paris Agreement to the necessity of protecting tangible cultural and mixed heritage from the effects of climate change. Only an indirect reference is included in the Preamble to the Agreement, which recognizes that 'Parties should, when taking action to address climate change, respect, promote and consider their respective obligations on human rights', including 'the rights of indigenous peoples'. This seems nevertheless to be more a reference to intangible than tangible cultural heritage. However, a Policy Document jointly elaborated by United Nations Environment Programme (UNEP), UNESCO, and the Union of Concerned Scientists (UCS) in 2016 acknowledges the need to 'reduce greenhouse gas emissions in line with the Paris Agreement' and to provide the 'financial resources, support and expertise necessary to ensure the resilience of World Heritage properties over the long term'.[162]

The 2016 Policy Document positively underscores that the Paris Agreement has relevant implications for the protection of cultural and mixed World Heritage sites, to the extent that it focuses on risk assessment, adaptation planning and resilience building, in line with the Sendai Framework.[163] In this respect, the UN 2030 Agenda for Sustainable Development is more explicit, since it recognizes the need to '[s]trengthen efforts to protect and safeguard the world's cultural and natural heritage',[164] within the context of the necessity of taking 'urgent action on climate change'.[165] It has thus been argued that reading the Paris Agreement through the lens of the 2030 Agenda for Sustainable Development provides a road map for States to protect cultural heritage from the effects of climate change.[166] This approach confirms that a systemic view integrating different regulatory instruments can bring cultural and mixed sites of outstanding universal value within the focus of the UNFCCC regime.

Along the lines outlined by UNEP, UNESCO, and UCS, in 2016 the World Heritage Committee requested the World Heritage Centre to 'strengthen its relations with other organizations working on Climate Change, particularly with the UNFCCC and the Intergovernmental Panel on Climate Change (IPCC)' and asked the States Parties to the World Heritage Convention, the World Heritage Centre, and Advisory Bodies to work with the IPCC so as to include 'a specific

160 UNESCO, UCS, and UNEP, 'World Heritage' (n 22) 28–29.
161 World Heritage Committee, 'Strategy' (n 94) 31.
162 UNESCO, UCS, and UNEP, 'World Heritage' (n 22) 5.
163 ibid 17; Paris Agreement, arts 8(1) and 9(4).
164 UNGA Res 70/1 (2015) UN Doc A/RES/70/1, para 11.4.
165 ibid, Preamble and Goal 13.
166 UNESCO, UCS, and UNEP, 'World Heritage' (n 22) 18.

chapter on natural and cultural World Heritage in future IPCC assessment reports'.[167] In 2017, the Committee invited the Members of the 1972 World Heritage Convention to 'ratify the Paris Agreement at the earliest possible opportunity' and recalled the importance of 'undertaking the most ambitious implementation', that is, possibly limiting 'the global average temperature increase to 1.5 [degrees Celsius] above pre-industrial levels'.[168] Meaningfully, the Committee underscored that the Members of the 1972 World Heritage Convention must 'undertake actions to address Climate Change under the Paris Agreement consistent with their common but differentiated responsibilities and respective capabilities', which is 'fully consistent with their obligations within the World Heritage Convention to protect the OUV [Outstanding Universal Value] of all World Heritage properties'.[169] The Committee further requested the World Heritage Centre and Advisory Bodies to report on progress in relation to action on World Heritage and climate change,[170] considering the implementation of measures against climate change 'a priority'.[171]

In 2017, UNESCO adopted a Strategy for Action on Climate Change (SACC) for the period 2018–21.[172] In this context, UNESCO considers 'climate change as a cross-sectoral and interdisciplinary issue in an overall sustainable development context'[173] and promotes a '[s]ystem-wide Approach to Climate Action',[174] notably within the framework of the UN. The organization invites 'all Member States to engage fully with the UNESCO Secretariat' for effective action, including 'in relation to the preparation and achievement of their nationally determined contributions (NDC) under the Paris Agreement on Climate Change'.[175] According to the SACC, '[p]romoting cultural diversity and cultural heritage safeguarding for climate change mitigation and adaptation' is a thematic priority.[176]

The SACC envisages cultural heritage as a crucial driver for 'societal transformation and resilience needed in order to respond to climate change and promote sustainable development'.[177] UNESCO provides 'support to States Parties to its Conventions in the field of culture, especially those that are particularly vulnerable to the adverse effects of Climate Change, in strengthening their capacities to safeguard their heritage, both natural and cultural (tangible and intangible)' via

[167] World Heritage Committee, 'Report of Decisions Taken at Its Fortieth Session' (n 38) Decision 40 COM 7, para 15.

[168] World Heritage Committee, 'Report of Decisions Taken at Its Forty-First Session' (n 36) Decision 41 COM 7, para 22.

[169] ibid.

[170] ibid, para 25.

[171] ibid, para 19.

[172] UNESCO General Conference, 'Strategy for Action on Climate Change', Item 4.9 of the Provisional Agenda (2017) 39 C/46.

[173] ibid, para 7(c).

[174] ibid, para 10(7).

[175] ibid, para 10(8).

[176] ibid, Annex III(C).

[177] ibid, para 40.

'preventive and corrective measures to combat Climate Change impacts on their heritage', including 'pilot projects towards Climate Change mitigation, adaptation and resilience building'.[178] Notably, UNESCO 'plans to support Member States to mainstream sustainable development policy, including climate change, in the conservation and management of World Heritage properties under the 1972 Convention'.[179] Synergies are envisaged with UN partner organizations and the UNFCCC Secretariat on actions of mutual interest.[180]

Within this framework, UNESCO-designated sites allow 'effectively linking efforts under the Paris Agreement and the 2030 Agenda' and 'creating synergies among them and other UNESCO Conventions in the field of Culture'.[181] This approach ties in with the idea that all UNESCO's Cultural Conventions foster sustainable development via a cooperative approach. For instance, in line with the 2030 Agenda, the 2005 Convention on the Protection and Promotion of the Diversity of Cultural Expressions[182] is underpinned by the idea that cultural diversity, including traditional knowledge, creates a varied world that is essential to sustainable development.[183] Consistently, the Convention requires Parties to integrate culture in all their development policies and foster sustainability.[184]

Financial resources needed for the implementation of the SACC, however, depend to a significant degree on the availability of extrabudgetary resources.[185] Systemic integration and cooperation prove therefore fundamental for the success of adaptation and mitigation policies. For instance, it is argued that the World Bank has a pivotal role in financing the rehabilitation of historic cities, since it reportedly invested US$1.8 billion in operations aiming to protect World Heritage cities in the last forty years and is involved in financing climate change mitigation and adaptation.[186] The Clean Development Mechanism under the UNFCCC, the Global Environmental Facility, and Multilateral Development Banks are considered essential to financing conservation policies in developing countries.[187]

Conclusion

The negative impact of climate change on tangible cultural and mixed heritage is a proven fact and may have critical effects. This is particularly due to rising

178 ibid, para 41.
179 ibid, para 42.
180 ibid, para 74.
181 ibid, para 78.
182 Convention on the Protection and Promotion of the Diversity of Cultural Expressions (adopted 20 October 2005, entered into force 18 March 2007) 2440 UNTS 311.
183 ibid, Preamble and art 2(6).
184 ibid, art 13.
185 UNESCO General Conference, 'Strategy for Action' (n 172) para 85.
186 Bigio and others (n 33) 15.
187 ibid 18.

temperatures and water levels, and increased land alteration, as well as further implications in terms, for instance, of water acidification, storms, and earthquakes.

A literal and purposive interpretation of the 1972 World Heritage Convention certainly supports the view that States Parties should take site-based adaptation and mitigation measures against GHG emissions, whilst compelling general measures under the Convention would require stretching the limits of the text and possibly undermining it under the doctrine of the 'fundamental change of circumstances' embedded in the Vienna Convention.[188] A systemic interpretation supports the argument that tangible cultural and mixed heritage affords the right framework to take site-based adaptation and mitigation measures with respect to climate change to protect sites of outstanding universal value. Intangible cultural heritage, instead, provides a more suitable framework for the adoption of general mitigation and adaptation strategies, including a human rights perspective in line with the ICESCR.[189]

As in a set of nested boxes, climate change is not only a global problem from the territorial viewpoint, but is also multidisciplinary from the standpoint of legal regulation. In other words, climate change affects not only cultural heritage and the environment, but also several other regulatory frameworks, including critical instances such as biodiversity, the right of peoples to self-determination, free trade, and investment.

Invoking general mitigation and adaptation measures within the context of each regime is practically unfeasible and likely to lead to inconsistent regulation. To avoid fragmentation, whilst the 1972 World Heritage Convention can be relied upon as *lex specialis* to impose upon States Parties site-based adaptation and mitigation strategies, tangible cultural and mixed World Heritage sites should contribute to the implementation of general mitigation and adaptation by being taken into account as *lex generalis* within the UNFCCC regime and balanced with needs arising from different regulatory systems. This interactive pattern is established in the World Heritage Centre's 2006 Strategy and 2007 Policy on Climate Change and World Heritage and was particularly highlighted by the World Heritage Committee in critical decisions taken in 2017, after the adoption of the Paris Agreement. Such a pattern is not only valid to shape the intersection between the World Heritage Convention and UNFCCC regimes, but can also apply to the intersection between the 1972 World Heritage Convention and other environmental conventions, notably the 1992 Convention on Biological Diversity.

188 Vienna Convention, art 62.
189 1966 ICESCR, art 15.

12

The 2001 UNESCO Convention on the Protection of the Underwater Cultural Heritage and Its Principles Relating to the Recovery and Disposition of Material from Shipwrecks

*Sarah Dromgoole**

Introduction

'Underwater cultural heritage' (UCH) is the term now commonly applied to archaeological heritage found under the sea. Shipwrecks are by far the largest component of UCH, although evidence in the marine environment of past human life comes in many forms, including early aircraft and other types of vehicle; submerged coastal settlements and structures; isolated objects; and traces of prehistoric human life. During the twentieth century, UCH tended to be treated as a poor relation of land archaeology: a marginal area of the archaeological discipline and an outlier in the heritage management sector. The situation is now improving, in no small part because technological advances in the marine field since the 1990s have been leading to a constant stream of new UCH discoveries that are attracting professional and public attention. International recognition for the area has also come in the form of a purpose-built UNESCO treaty, the 2001 UNESCO Convention on the Protection of the Underwater Cultural Heritage (2001 UCH Convention),[1] to regulate activities directed at UCH. The treaty, adopted in 2001 and in force internationally since 2009, has attracted sixty States Parties to date.

Today it is generally accepted that maritime archaeological heritage should be subject to the same, or at least equivalent, principles and protective standards and measures as terrestrial heritage. While the marine environment certainly presents

* The author would like to acknowledge that, in writing this chapter, she has benefitted from information and insights provided by Mike Williams, Antony Firth, Dave Parham, and Toby Gane relating to some of the issues raised. The views expressed, and any errors, are the author's alone.

[1] UNESCO Convention on the Protection of the Underwater Cultural Heritage (adopted 2 November 2001, entered into force 2 January 2009) 2562 UNTS 3 (2001 UCH Convention).

Sarah Dromgoole, The 2001 UNESCO Convention on the Protection of the Underwater Cultural Heritage and Its Principles Relating to the Recovery and Disposition of Material from Shipwrecks In: *Intersections in International Cultural Heritage Law*. Edited by Anne-Marie Carstens and Elizabeth Varner. © Oxford University Press 2020. The several contributors
DOI: 10.1093/oso/9780198846291.003.0013

special challenges to archaeologists and others interested in accessing UCH—and, it should be noted, is also capable of affording certain advantages over the terrestrial environment as far as the preservation of archaeological material is concerned—archaeological heritage itself is a continuum: there are no distinct divisions, or differences in inherent value, between heritage assets found on land and those found at sea. The remains of ships and boats can be found not just at sea but in the inter-tidal zone and inland locations.[2] Equally, settlement sites and other remnants of past human occupation can be found in marine areas that were once dry land, most notably the millions of square kilometers of continental shelf that were exposed at intervals before the end of the Last Glacial Period.[3] However, because the main component of UCH is shipwrecks, some distinct issues of a legal and practical nature arise in the UCH context. These need to be taken into full account in framing principles that are to apply to UCH, not least principles relating to the recovery of material, and the eventual disposition of recovered material.

The 2001 UCH Convention provides a potentially globally applicable, modern, and—for the most part—comprehensive, legal framework to govern UCH and to set standards for the conduct of activities directed at UCH. Interestingly, there is no equivalent treaty with respect to terrestrial archaeological heritage, at least in part because terrestrial archaeological heritage is generally located in areas under national sovereignty. By contrast, substantial areas of the sea fall outside national territorial boundaries; therefore, international legal regulation and cooperation can often be the only means to control activities that may harm or destroy UCH. In providing for such regulation and cooperation, the 2001 UCH Convention is a most welcome development. Nevertheless, as will be shown below, the principles and standards it adopts give rise to some potentially problematic issues when applied to at least some of the shipwrecks falling within the scope of the Convention.

The purpose of this chapter is essentially two-fold: first, to introduce the 2001 UCH Convention and outline its principles and regulatory framework relating to the recovery and disposition of UCH; and, second, to draw attention to certain problems that may arise when these provisions are applied in the specific context of shipwrecks. Section I summarizes the background to the 2001 UNESCO Convention and its material scope of application, and then goes on to outline the Convention's provisions with respect to the recovery and disposition of UCH. Using some British examples as illustrations, Section II points out difficulties that may arise when these provisions are applied to shipwreck assemblages falling

[2] For example, in 1992 construction workers building a road through the port of Dover, England, discovered what is believed to be the world's oldest known seafaring vessel, thought to have been in use in around 1500 BCE. See Dover Museum and Bronze Age Boat Gallery, <www.dovermuseum.co.uk> accessed 6 September 2018.

[3] See Geoffrey N Bailey, Jan Harff, and Dimitris Sakellariou, 'Archaeology and Palaeolandscapes of the Continental Shelf: An Introduction' in Geoffrey N Bailey, Jan Harff, and Dimitris Sakellariou (eds), *Under the Sea: Archaeology and Palaeolandscapes on the Continental Shelf* (Springer 2017) (ch 1).

within the scope of the Convention. In the concluding section, some explanation is put forward for why these issues are not properly catered for by the Convention and some consideration given to their potential impact in the future.

I. 2001 UNESCO Convention

A. Background to the 2001 UNESCO Convention and Its Scope of Application

The original motivation behind the initiative to develop an international treaty governing UCH was to create mechanisms to enable States to control commercial treasure hunting on the continental shelf beyond the 12-mile territorial sea. Since the mid- to late 1980s, shipwrecks in offshore areas have become highly vulnerable to interference by treasure hunters interested in profiting financially from the recovery of commercially valuable cargoes and other items. This is because advances in marine technology in the 1980s and 1990s have made it relatively straightforward for well-financed commercial organizations to do three things: (1) undertake systematic search operations over large areas of the continental shelf;[4] (2) locate targeted wrecks in the open oceans;[5] and (3) undertake recovery operations in deep water.[6] There is therefore a serious risk that many culturally significant shipwrecks never before subject to human interference will be exploited in an unregulated way and culturally valuable materials sold off, without record, on the open market.

Since the UNESCO initiative related to the marine environment, and was designed to regulate activities in that environment, its negotiation was far from a straightforward task. As well as being part of international cultural heritage law, the new treaty is also a constituent element of international maritime law and, in particular, international law of the sea. International law of the sea is a field renowned for being highly politically charged. In particular, it is subject to a long-running tussle between those States—the major maritime powers—that regard freedom of navigation as the primary imperative in oceans governance, and other States—far more numerous but with less maritime capability—that are motivated

[4] In 1998, an American company, Odyssey Marine Exploration, Inc, began successful search operations in the Mediterranean Sea for the wreck of the British warship, HMS *Sussex*. Over 400 square miles of seabed were searched, over four seasons, using side-scan sonar and bathymetric survey equipment. See further Sarah Dromgoole, 'Murky waters for government policy: The Case of a 17th Century British Warship and 10 Tonnes of Gold Coins' (2004) 28 Marine Policy 189–98.

[5] The discovery in August 2017 of USS *Indianapolis* lying at a depth of 5.5 km in the Philippine Sea illustrates state-of-the-art capabilities. See BBC News, 'Lost WW2 warship USS Indianapolis found after 72 years' (21 August 2017) <www.bbc.co.uk/news/world-us-canada-40991326> accessed 15 November 2017.

[6] In 1997, a British-based company, Blue Water Recoveries, recovered 179 tons of copper and tin ingots from the SS *Alpherat*, a wreck lying at a depth of 3,770 m. Blue Water Recoveries, 'Achievements' <www.bluewater.uk/com/achievements.htm> accessed 6 September 2018.

by an interest in exploiting their offshore areas and regulating activities therein. Crucially, those involved in negotiating the 2001 treaty needed to work within the framework of the 1982 United Nations Convention on the Law of the Sea (1982 Law of the Sea Convention, or UNCLOS),[7] the so-called 'Constitution for the Oceans', which governs activities in the marine environment. This famous treaty represents an intricate and finely poised balance between these two sets of interests. Among the many maritime-related matters that it deals with, it sets out a legal regime for each of the recognized maritime zones and makes some specific, though notoriously limited, provision for UCH.[8] The 1982 Law of the Sea Convention also—significantly—incorporates legal devices designed to ensure the durability over time of the jurisdictional compromise it enshrines.[9]

Although the initial purpose of the 2001 UCH Convention was to create a regulatory regime for activities directed at UCH that take place beyond the limits of national sovereignty, the 2001 UCH Convention is much more comprehensive in scope. Among other things, it makes provision for the regulation of activities in all maritime zones, including those under national sovereignty, and it incorporates detailed archaeological standards that must be applied to activities directed at UCH. These standards, which represent internationally accepted benchmarks for appropriate behavior, are set out in 'Rules'—enshrined in an Annex to the Convention—that have the same legal status as the main text of the treaty.[10] The focus is on activities 'directed at' UCH, defined as 'activities having underwater cultural heritage as their primary object and which may, directly or indirectly, physically disturb or otherwise damage underwater cultural heritage'.[11] The Convention also makes some provision for the regulation of activities that are not directed at UCH but may nonetheless 'incidentally affect' it, defined as 'activities which, despite not having underwater cultural heritage as their primary object or one of their objects, may physically disturb or otherwise damage underwater cultural heritage'.[12] Such activities include bottom-trawling by fishermen, the dredging out of navigation channels, and the laying of pipelines and cables.

In light of the political dynamics surrounding the Law of the Sea Convention, including disagreements over whether or not that treaty takes precedence over subsequent treaties in the maritime field, the regulatory regime that the 2001 UCH Convention establishes for sea areas beyond national sovereignty is complex. It

[7] United Nations Convention on the Law of the Sea (adopted 10 December 1982, entered into force 16 November 1994) 1833 UNTS 397 (1982 Law of the Sea Convention, or UNCLOS).

[8] See 1982 Law of the Sea Convention, arts 149 and 303.

[9] ibid. The treaty contains an explicit prohibition on incompatible *inter se* agreements (art 311(3)); does not permit reservations (art 309); provides for compulsory third party dispute settlement (pt XV, s 2); and includes requirements for formal amendment of the Convention that are notoriously tough (arts 312–14).

[10] 2001 UCH Convention, art 33, Annex (UCH Rules).

[11] ibid, art 1(6). See also Section I.B. below.

[12] 2001 UCH Convention, art 1(7).

relies heavily on a combination of States Parties making full use of pre-existing jurisdictional mechanisms and on a close degree of international cooperation and collaboration for its effectiveness.[13]

One of the most fundamental questions that drafters of the 2001 UCH Convention needed to determine was its material scope of application. How was UCH to be defined for the purposes of the Convention? It was generally accepted that the definition should be broad enough to encompass all types of UCH. An issue more open to question and of particular relevance to the shipwreck component of UCH was how to draw a distinction between material that should fall within the scope of the Convention and its heritage protection objectives, and material that more properly belonged within the realms of commercial maritime law.

The law of salvage, a central element of commercial maritime law that has no counterpart on land, is designed to encourage sea users to *rescue* 'maritime property'—traditionally ships and their cargoes—from peril at sea and to reunite such property with its owners. The incentive provided to the rescuer is a financial reward, assessed as a proportion of the commercial value of the property recovered. One core aim of many involved in the UNESCO initiative was to remove UCH from the salvage law regime, which is widely regarded as incompatible with heritage protection objectives. In light of this, the Convention's definition of UCH needed to clearly distinguish between material subject to the Convention's protective framework and that which would remain subject to commercial salvage law. Following the approach of some Scandinavian legislation, the drafters decided that a period of 100 years below water would be adopted as the dividing line. UCH is therefore defined in Article 1(1) of the Convention as meaning

> all traces of human existence having a cultural, historical or archaeological character which have been partially or totally under water, periodically or continuously, for at least 100 years.[14]

The following explicit, non-exhaustive illustrations are provided of traces of human existence that fall within the definition:

> sites, structures, buildings, artefacts and human remains, together with their archaeological and natural context; vessels, aircraft, other vehicles or any part thereof, their cargo or other contents, together with their archaeological and natural context; and objects of prehistoric character.[15]

[13] The extent to which the Convention creates *new* jurisdictional mechanisms is a moot point and one of the most controversial aspects of the Convention.

[14] 2001 UCH Convention, art 1(1)(a).

[15] ibid, art 1(1)(a)(i), (ii), and (iii). There are two explicit exclusions: pipelines and cables on the seabed, and other installations on the seabed that are still in use: art 1(1)(b) and (c).

During the treaty negotiations, some discussion centered on whether the new treaty should take a 'blanket' protective approach and apply to *all* material that has been underwater for a period of time, or instead take an approach based on protecting material of particular significance. Each approach is used in national legislation relating to UCH, though the former is more common. By specifying 'all' traces of human existence 'having a cultural, historical or archaeological character', Article 1(1) suggests a degree of ambivalence on the part of the negotiators as to which of these approaches they had opted to adopt. Is it the case that *all* traces of human existence underwater for at least 100 years fall within the Convention's protective framework, or is it possible that some material under water for that length of time may not be covered on the ground that it does not have 'a cultural, historical or archaeological character'? In light of the negotiating history of the Convention, and the fact that proposals to limit the scope of the treaty to material of significance were specifically rejected,[16] the general assumption appears to be that the wording 'having a cultural, historical or archaeological character' in Article 1(1) is, to all intents and purposes, superfluous since all material under water for at least 100 years could be regarded as having such character.[17]

In the marine environment, it is vital that an international regulatory regime is widely adopted in order to be effective. Without the support of the maritime powers, a treaty in the maritime sphere has little chance of fulfilling its objectives. In the case of the 2001 UCH Convention, the regulatory framework relies for its full effectiveness on the participation of the States whose flag vessels and nationals have the capability to undertake deep-water search and recovery operations. That capability lies almost exclusively in the hands of a small bloc of maritime States, including the United States, the Russian Federation, France, the United Kingdom, and Germany. After thirteen years of preparatory work and negotiations, many were enormously disappointed that all participating States did not agree to the final text of the Convention. Notably, despite considerable efforts to accommodate their interests, the majority of the crucially significant maritime States either abstained from the final vote or voted against the adoption of the treaty. Russia and Norway voted against the Convention; France, Germany, the Netherlands, and the United Kingdom abstained. The United States, which was not a member of UNESCO in 2001, expressed serious reservations about the final text. Notably, their concerns, at least as articulated, did not relate to the objectives of the Convention or its general principles, but rather to the wording of several key provisions impacting two specific issues: the extent of coastal State jurisdiction on the continental shelf and the status of sunken warships. In light of its traditional national approach to heritage

[16] Patrick O'Keefe, *Shipwrecked Heritage: A Commentary on the UNESCO Convention on Underwater Cultural Heritage* (2nd edn, IAL 2014) 34.

[17] ibid 34–35.

protection, the United Kingdom also objected to the lack of a significance criterion in the definition of UCH.

Despite initial disappointment at the failure to achieve a consensus, in the period since 2001 the Convention has garnered a promising level of support from the international community. At the time of writing, it has been ratified by sixty States.[18] The most significant ratification is that of France, which ratified the Convention in 2009, apparently after reaching the conclusion that the benefits the new treaty bestowed in terms of helping it to regulate commercial salvage of shipwrecks on its continental shelf outweighed any technical legal objections regarding the impact the treaty might have on coastal State jurisdiction and the status of its sunken warships. That one of the bloc of maritime States that had originally declined to support the Convention had come to the conclusion that ratification was in its overall national interest was seen by the treaty's proponents as a very encouraging sign, indicating—perhaps—that, after all, there was a prospect that other 'dissenting' maritime States might reach the same conclusion in the future.

The influence the 2001 UCH Convention has had internationally is already profound, even though many States that are significant in the UCH context presently remain outside the regime, including Greece and Turkey, and despite practical implementation of the treaty still being at a nascent stage. Any informed discussion of UCH protection anywhere in the world is now framed by the UCH Convention and undertaken with reference to its fundamental principles and standards for archaeological conduct.[19] The fact that these standards were incorporated in an Annex separate from the main text has been facilitative in this respect. It means that States (and individual heritage agencies and other organizations) have been able to make policy commitments to abide by the annexed Rules, or to ensure that activities under their control are conducted in accordance with those Rules, even when they are not subject to an international legal obligation to comply with the Convention itself. The UK government, for example, has adopted the Annex 'as best practice' in the management of UCH.[20] The Annex can also serve as a model.[21] The absence of any apparent objection to the Rules, and indeed widespread praise for them even on the part of the maritime powers, means that they are taking on the status of 'soft law'. They provide internationally accepted benchmarks against which all actions directed at UCH will now be judged.

[18] See UNESCO, Convention on the Protection of the Underwater Cultural Heritage: States Parties <www.unesco.org/eri/la/convention.asp?KO=13520&language=E&order=alpha> accessed 6 September 2018.

[19] See eg Ole Varmer, *Underwater Cultural Heritage Law Study*, US Department of the Interior, Bureau of Ocean Energy Management, OCS Study, BOEM 2014-005 (2014) esp 30.

[20] See HC Deb 24 January 2005, vol 668, col 46W and, most recently, HC Deb 31 October 2017, vol 630 [HCWS208].

[21] See Annex to the International Agreement Concerning the Shipwrecked Vessel RMS *Titanic* <www.gc.noaa.gov\\gcil_titanic-intl.html> accessed 6 September 2018.

B. Principles Relating to the Recovery and Disposition of Material from Shipwrecks

The general principles of the 2001 UCH Convention are set out in Article 2 and reiterated and elaborated upon in the Rules contained in the Annex. The core objective is the preservation of UCH for the benefit of humanity,[22] and the cardinal archaeological principle at the heart of the Convention is the principle of in situ preservation.

While the text does not say so in terms, the scheme of the Convention indicates that activities 'directed at' UCH must be authorized by a competent national authority.[23] While also not explicitly stated, there is a presumption that this will entail the use of a permit or licensing scheme. Activities 'directed at' UCH mean activities 'having [UCH] as their primary object' and 'which may, directly or indirectly, physically disturb or otherwise damage' UCH.[24] This has been interpreted as meaning activities undertaken with the deliberate intention of interfering with UCH,[25] including treasure hunting and archaeological work involving physical intervention. Authorization may be given for intrusive activities provided they are conducted 'for the purpose of making a significant contribution to protection or knowledge or enhancement of' UCH.[26] Anyone proposing such activities must submit to the competent national authority a 'project design' for approval.[27] Specific requisites laid down for the content of the design include: a statement of objectives for the project; the methodology and techniques to be used; anticipated funding; a conservation program for recovered artifacts 'in close cooperation with the competent authorities'; and 'deposition of archives, including underwater cultural heritage removed'.[28]

By virtue of Article 2(5) of the 2001 UCH Convention, preservation in situ must be considered 'as the first option' before any activities directed at UCH take place.[29] It has sometimes been argued that the preservation in situ principle, which derives from terrestrial archaeology, is not appropriate for application to shipwrecks given that their location on the seabed is a matter simply of misfortune and the seabed is not their natural location. However, this argument is founded on a misunderstanding of the purpose of the principle, which is not to preserve material in its natural and original context, but rather to ensure that a precautionary approach is adopted in decision-making concerning the future of a site. In other words, it should not be immediately assumed that excavation and recovery is *necessarily*

22 2001 UCH Convention, art 2(3).
23 ibid, art 22.
24 ibid, art 1(6).
25 O'Keefe (n 16) 36.
26 UCH Rules, r 1.
27 ibid, r 9.
28 ibid, r 10.
29 The principle is reiterated in r 1.

the best course of action. Depending on the circumstances, heritage assets may be safer left where they are, than recovered using inappropriate techniques, or recovered with inadequate provision being made for their conservation and eventual disposition. The 2001 UCH Convention does not say that preservation in situ is the *preferred* option;[30] however, it does say '[a]ctivities directed at underwater cultural heritage must use non-destructive techniques and survey methods *in preference* to recovery of objects' and excavation or recovery must be '*necessary* for the purpose of scientific studies or for the ultimate protection' of the UCH in question.[31]

The traditional commercial maritime sector was wary of the UNESCO initiative right from the start, and that wariness continued even after the text of the Convention was finalized.[32] The adoption of the principle of preservation in situ as a central tenet was a matter of concern.[33] This notion runs counter to the natural instincts of commercially minded individuals and organizations. Imbibed in the salvage law tradition, they tend to assume that the recovery of maritime property discovered on the seabed *is* the appropriate course of action, so that it can be reunited with its owner or, if there is no known owner, returned to the stream of commerce. Such action, certainly for any property that still retains commercial value, is regarded as economically logical. There is recognition within this community that material of historical and archaeological significance needs special treatment, but there is also a view that such provision could be catered for within the salvage law regime.[34] With equal, if not greater, conviction, many archaeologists and cultural heritage specialists regard salvage law, with the positive *incentivization* it gives to the recovery of material, as antithetical to the notion that archaeological material lying on, or embedded in, the seabed may well be more imperiled by recovery than by being left where it is. Depending on the precise circumstances, it may not be in any immediate danger at all; quite the contrary, it may be lying in a safe and preservative environment. Therefore, there may be no immediate necessity to effect a recovery.

Although many proponents of the UNESCO initiative aimed to ensure that UCH was removed altogether from the traditional salvage law regime, a potential legal obstacle was that one of the two articles in the Law of the Sea Convention that deals specifically with UCH, Article 303, includes an explicit saving for 'the law

[30] A point emphasized in guidelines to the Annex published by UNESCO: see Thijs Maarleveld, Ulrike Guérin, and Barbara Egger (eds), *UNESCO Manual for Activities Directed at Underwater Cultural Heritage: Guidelines to the Annex of the UNESCO 2001 Convention* (2013) 25 <www.unesco.org/culture/en/underwater/pdf/UCH-Manual.pdf> accessed 6 September 2018.

[31] UCH Rules, r 4 (emphasis added). See also 2001 UCH Convention, preambular cl 13.

[32] See Sarah Dromgoole, *Underwater Cultural Heritage and International Law* (CUP 2013) 53, 206–08.

[33] See 'Consideration of the UNESCO Convention on the Protection of Underwater Cultural Heritage: Report of the CMI Working Group' (2002) CMI YB 154–57; Archie Bishop, 'The Underwater Heritage Convention 2001' (2002) 3 Shipping and Transport Lawyer 18, 20.

[34] See Dromgoole (n 32) 207, which refers to an initiative to create a protocol to the 1989 Salvage Convention that would modify that treaty to take account of archaeological considerations.

of salvage or other rules of admiralty' with respect to 'objects of an archaeological and historical nature' that are 'found at sea'.[35] The term 'objects of an archaeological and historical nature', used in both Articles 303 and 149 of the Law of the Sea Convention, is interpreted broadly. The extent to which this provision in fact fettered the ability of the UNESCO negotiators to exclude salvage law altogether from application to UCH is debatable.[36] However, its existence may have influenced the eventual approach taken, which was to restrict the application of salvage law rather than to exclude it altogether.

Article 4 of the 2001 UCH Convention provides:

> Any activity relating to underwater cultural heritage to which this Convention applies shall not be subject to the law of salvage . . ., unless it:
> (a) is authorized by the competent authorities, and
> (b) is in full conformity with this Convention, and
> (c) ensures that any recovery of the underwater cultural heritage achieves its maximum protection.[37]

Taking account of the full scheme of the Convention, including its provision with respect to recovered UCH (discussed below), the impact of the three conditions for the application of salvage law imposed by this article is such that there would be little incentive for any Party discovering the site of a wreck falling within the scope of the Convention to pursue a salvage reward through the admiralty courts, at least insofar as those courts lie within the jurisdiction of a State Party to the treaty.[38]

In circumstances where the competent national authority concludes that recovery of UCH *is* 'necessary for scientific or protective purposes',[39] how, then, must the recovered material be treated under the terms of the Convention? Article 2 makes it clear not only that it must be preserved for the 'benefit of humanity' in conformity with the provisions of the Convention,[40] but also that it must be 'deposited, conserved and managed in a manner that ensures its long-term preservation'.[41] Rule 33 goes on to elaborate on this requirement, providing that the project archives, including any recovered material, 'shall, as far as possible, be kept together and intact as a collection in a manner that is available for professional and public access'.[42]

[35] See para 3 of art 303, Law of the Sea Convention, read with para 1. See also Dromgoole (n 32) 71–76.

[36] Dromgoole (n 32) 176–77.

[37] Article 4 also applies explicitly to the law of finds: for an explanation of the law of finds and its application to UCH, see ibid 171–72, 175.

[38] See ibid 202–04.

[39] 2001 UCH Convention, preambular cl 13.

[40] ibid, art 2(3).

[41] ibid, art 2(6).

[42] UCH Rules, r 33.

A central principle of the 2001 UCH Convention directly related to the question of the eventual disposition of recovered artifacts is that UCH 'shall not be commercially exploited'.[43] This principle, set out in bald terms in Article 2, is elaborated upon in Rule 2 of the Annex.

Rule 2, which is probably the most discussed provision in the entire Convention, is critically important in determining what can and cannot be done with recovered UCH. It provides:

> The commercial exploitation of underwater cultural heritage for trade or speculation or its irretrievable dispersal is fundamentally incompatible with the protection and proper management of underwater cultural heritage. Underwater cultural heritage shall not be traded, sold, bought or bartered as commercial goods.

This rule cannot be interpreted as preventing:

(a) the provision of professional archaeological services or necessary services incidental thereto whose nature and purpose are in full conformity with this Convention and are subject to the authorization of the competent authorities; or
(b) the deposition of underwater cultural heritage, recovered in the course of a research project in conformity with this Convention, provided such deposition does not prejudice the scientific or cultural interest or integrity of the recovered material or result in its irretrievable dispersal; is in accordance with the provisions of Rules 33 and 34; and is subject to the authorization of the competent authorities.[44]

The first paragraph of Rule 2 makes two things relatively clear. First, the prohibition in Article 2 on 'commercial exploitation' is not a ban on all forms of commercial exploitation. Rather, in essence it is a ban on the *sale* (or other exchange[45]) of UCH, certainly as 'commercial goods'.[46] Second, irretrievable dispersal of material is regarded as 'fundamentally incompatible' with the protection of UCH, indicating that irretrievable dispersal of items from an assemblage of material from the same site is impermissible under the terms of the Convention.

The second paragraph of Rule 2 contains two provisos to the statements set out in the first paragraph. Proviso (a) is comparatively straightforward: it makes

43 2001 UCH Convention, art 2(7).
44 Rules 33 and 34 make provision with respect to curation of the project archives.
45 See Dromgoole (n 32) 232.
46 The reference to the sale of UCH as 'commercial goods' is probably designed to make it clear that artifacts must not be treated like ordinary commercial items. Insofar as they are the subject of any exchange, their special nature must be taken into account. See Dromgoole (n 32) 234.

it clear that the provision of professional archaeological services by a commercial organization is permissible and not outlawed by the prohibition on commercial exploitation. In some jurisdictions, including the UK, it is common for professional archaeological services such as pre-development archaeological assessments and 'rescue' work to be undertaken by for-profit organizations. The meaning of proviso (b), by contrast, is quite opaque. The opacity derives in large part from the curious term 'deposition' that it employs. Its ordinary meaning is to deposit somewhere,[47] but in the context of proviso (b) that would not make much sense and therefore it might have an alternative meaning. The general view has been that it is intended as a synonym (or near equivalent) for the notion of 'deaccession'.[48] Deaccession is a practice within the museum sector wherein an accessioned museum object is removed from the museum collection and the concomitant care and status afforded it. This is the threshold step for disposal in certain circumstances of artifacts from museum collections. Proviso (b) indicates that processes akin to deaccession are permissible with respect to UCH project archives notwithstanding the fact they might involve the sale of UCH. However, among other things, they must not 'prejudice the scientific or cultural interest or integrity of the recovered material *or result in its irretrievable dispersal*'.[49]

It must be recalled that the original fundamental purpose of the UNESCO initiative was to counter the activities of commercial treasure hunters seeking to profit financially from the recovery of valuable cargoes and other objects from shipwrecks qualifying as UCH.[50] To profit financially, the sale of material (as opposed, say, to the commercial exhibition of material) is almost certainly required.[51] Unlike most of the other Rules in the Convention's Annex, the wording of Rule 2 was subject to political input at the UNESCO negotiations and it is for this reason that it is difficult to interpret. For the most part, the annexed Rules derived from the International Charter on the Protection and Management of Underwater Cultural Heritage, adopted by the International Council on Monuments and Sites (ICOMOS) in 1996, but a few amendments of a substantive nature were made for political reasons.[52] The wording of Rule 2 is deliberately ambiguous and designed as a compromise, providing a little wiggle room on the question of sale. There seems to be no such room on the question of irretrievable dispersal, however. The Convention appears to make it impermissible in any circumstances for items from

[47] Indeed, that is how it is intended to be interpreted when used elsewhere in the Convention, eg in r 10(o).

[48] See Dromgoole (n 32) 234. See also Maarleveld and others (n 30) 35. For a discussion of the status of this Manual, see Dromgoole (n 32) 361, n 96.

[49] Emphasis added.

[50] See 2001 UCH Convention, preambular cl 8.

[51] See Dromgoole (n 32) 213, referring to the commercial exploitation of artifacts from the *Titanic*.

[52] See Roberta Garabello, 'The Negotiating History of the Convention on the Protection of the Underwater Cultural Heritage' in Roberta Garabello and Tullio Scovazzi (eds), *The Protection of the Underwater Cultural Heritage: Before and After the 2001 UNESCO Convention* (Martinus Nijhoff 2003) 184–85.

an assemblage to be disposed of in such a way that they cannot later be reunited with the rest of the archive.

II. Difficulties in the Application of the 2001 UCH Convention's Recovery and Disposition Provisions to Shipwrecks and Shipwreck Assemblages

Under the terms of the 2001 UCH Convention, the recovery of objects is permissible but only if it is 'necessary for scientific *or protective* purposes'.[53] As far as shipwrecks are concerned, recovery of objects for protective purposes may be necessary for three main reasons. For located shipwrecks that contain or are reputed to contain substantial quantities of commercially valuable material, the current state of marine technology means that recovery operations of some kind may be the only practical way to protect the archaeological value of the site. At the least, items that are relatively accessible and therefore particularly vulnerable to clandestine looting may need to be recovered, otherwise those items and valuable contextual information may be lost. Second, a wreck may be located in a dynamic and unpredictable environment, rather than one that is stable and benign. Where this is the case, again recovery of material may be necessary in order that it is not damaged or destroyed by its environment, or simply washed away. Third, in many parts of the world, inshore—and, increasingly, offshore—marine areas are under intensive pressure from economic activities of all kinds that impact upon the seabed and therefore, potentially, upon material lying on or in the seabed. Therefore, a competent national authority may conclude that recovery of material from a particular wreck site is the best course of action for UCH protection.

Any project involving the recovery and bringing ashore of a significant quantity of material from a shipwreck will involve a substantial level of planning and advance provision for the temporary, and later permanent, conservation and disposition of the material. The material may well be bulky, such as components of the hull and fixtures and fittings of the vessel; if made of timber or other organic substance, it is likely to be waterlogged; and if made of ferrous metals, its condition may deteriorate when exposed to air. Special facilities may be required that are not widely available, such as conservation laboratories that can cater for large waterlogged structures. Conservation processes to stabilize and preserve material may well be time-consuming and costly. A permanent home for the project archive also needs to be found. Existing museums may lack the capacity, or indeed the interest, to accommodate marine archives.

53 2001 UCH Convention, preambular cl 13, which paraphrases part of the content of rr 1 and 4 (emphasis added).

The Rules in the Annex to the 2001 UCH Convention were drafted with full cognizance of these issues and are designed to ensure that they are addressed, where necessary, by those planning any activity 'directed at' UCH. However, there are two other issues that arise specifically in relation to shipwrecks that are less well catered for by the terms of the treaty, probably because they are likely to be most problematic in the context of relatively recent wrecks. The wrecks of the twentieth century are gradually falling within the scope of the Convention, but were not at the forefront of minds at the time the 2001 UCH Convention was adopted. One of the issues is the question of how to apply the provisions of the Convention to wrecks that were carrying bulk cargoes of a fungible nature (where each unit is identical, or nearly so) in circumstances where ownership of the cargo is readily identifiable; the second is the question of how to apply the provisions to wrecks that contain hazardous material.

The two types of wreck identified above are prevalent in the vast legacy of vessels that sank during the two World Wars. Many merchant vessels carrying bulk cargoes were sunk during these wars and many wartime marine casualties, both merchant and military, contain material that poses a hazard to humans and/or the environment, including munitions, heavy fuel oil and other noxious substances such as mercury and mustard gas. Given the way the 2001 UCH Convention defines its material scope of application, all wrecks from the First World War fall within the scope of the treaty and the difficulties discussed below will become even more acute as the centenary of the Second World War approaches. When the Convention was being prepared in the 1990s, however, the focus of those involved was on pre-twentieth-century heritage: the negotiators were, in a sense, looking backward, not forward. They were obviously aware that the 100-year 'cut-off' for material application meant that twentieth-century wrecks would shortly begin to fall within the scope of the new treaty; however, the centenary of the start of the First World War, 2014, still seemed quite a long way off. Time, however, passes all too quickly.

Before discussing the application of the Convention's provisions to the two types of wreck identified above, one further matter to be touched upon that, in the context of shipwrecks, gives rise to distinct issues and complexities, is the question of ownership.

A. Existence of Ownership Rights (and Responsibilities)

For a number of reasons, ownership rights may be more traceable in the case of sunken vessels and their cargoes than other forms of archaeological heritage asset. This is particularly the case with respect to more recent maritime casualties falling within the scope of the 2001 UNESCO Convention. Traditional maritime law principles, including salvage law and the law of wreck,[54] acknowledge the 'supremacy'

[54] At the heart of the traditional law of wreck is the notion that material brought ashore from shipwrecks should be reported to a 'Receiver of Wreck' so that it can be reunited with its owner.

of ownership rights over the rights of finders or others. From a legal perspective, the rights of owners can be, and often are, fettered to some extent to meet heritage objectives.[55] However, any circumscription of an owner's rights must not be arbitrary and must be proportionate to the 'common good' derived.[56] If restrictions amount to a 'taking', compensation may well be payable under national laws. The ownership of many of the wrecks that sank during the two World Wars is likely to be traceable and, quite often, may lie in State hands. In the case of sunken warships, as well as other State vessels engaged in non-commercial service at the time of sinking, express abandonment or other form of relinquishment or transfer of title is in all likelihood required before the State will lose its ownership rights.[57] In the case of many merchant wartime losses, the original owners are likely to have received compensation under war risks insurance schemes. Ownership rights will then fall to the insurer; in practice, often a State. The UK government alone, through its Department for Transport, exercises rights of title over nearly 5,000 merchant shipping casualties from the two World Wars as a result of paying out on war risk insurance claims.

Article 303 of the Law of the Sea Convention not only includes a saving for 'the law of salvage or other rules of admiralty' but also for 'the rights of identifiable owners'.[58] Again, although the implications of this saving may be relatively insignificant in practice,[59] its existence may nonetheless have had some impact on the approach taken in the 2001 UCH Convention toward ownership rights, which is that it simply ignores them. No reference is made to the concept of ownership, or any provision made for ownership rights. One must therefore assume that such rights still exist, but are fettered to some degree by the terms of the Convention. Equally, one must assume that the responsibilities concomitant with rights also still exist.

B. Wrecks Carrying Bulk Fungible Goods

Wrecks around the world sometimes contain bulk cargoes of fungible goods or bullion. The Convention would appear to bar commercial exploitation of these cargoes. However, as it would be highly impractical and surely scientifically unnecessary to store tons of such materials in museum-type housing, if the

[55] See Dromgoole (n 32) 111–12.

[56] ibid.

[57] The need for express relinquishment is not firmly established under customary international law, but see Article 4 of the Resolution on 'The Legal Regime of Wrecks of Warships and Other State-Owned Ships in International Law' adopted by the Institut de Droit International in 2015.

[58] 1982 Law of the Sea Convention, art 303(3).

[59] See discussion in Dromgoole (n 32) 114–15.

Convention prohibits disposal of these bulk resources it would appear to lead to absurd consequences.

In 2010, the UK's Department for Transport entered into a salvage contract with the American ocean exploration company, Odyssey Marine Exploration Inc., for the recovery of a consignment of silver from the wreck of SS *Gairsoppa*, a British merchant vessel sunk by a German U-boat in 1941. The silver was reported to be a combination of privately owned bullion (silver bars), insured by the UK government, as well as State-owned coins and ingots.[60] The wreck, lying in the Atlantic Ocean several hundred miles off the coast of Ireland, was discovered by Odyssey in 2011 lying at a depth of approximately 4,700 meters. According to a contemporary news report, it was 'settled upright on the seabed with its cargo holds open, [meaning that] remote-controlled robotic submarines should be able to retrieve the bullion'.[61]

In 2012, Odyssey recovered 48 tons of silver from the wreck,[62] reportedly worth approximately £24 million.[63] In 2013, a further 61 tons were recovered, in what Odyssey referred to as 'the largest and heaviest recovery of precious metal from a shipwreck in history'.[64]

During the search for the *Gairsoppa*, Odyssey also found the wreck of a British passenger steamer, SS *Mantola*, which was lying in 2,500 meters of water, approximately 100 miles from the *Gairsoppa*.[65] The *Mantola* had been sunk by a German torpedo in 1917 while carrying a shipment of silver, again covered by war risk insurance. The British Ministry of War Transport had, it seems, paid out £110,000 in compensation for the silver at the time of the vessel's loss.[66] In light of the discovery, a further salvage contract was entered into between Odyssey and the Department for Transport.

The UK government's overriding interest in these wrecks is financial. Each of them contains a sizeable quantity of bullion in which it has ownership rights. These, and in all likelihood a significant number of other, similar, wrecks hold out the prospect of a useful boost to the country's Exchequer.

If the United Kingdom were a Party to the 2001 UCH Convention, it would be under a duty to 'preserve underwater cultural heritage for the benefit of humanity in conformity with the provisions of [the] Convention'.[67] By virtue of the

[60] BBC News, 'Shipwreck of SS *Gairsoppa* reveals £150m silver haul' <www.bbc.co.uk\\news\\uk-15061868> accessed 23 November 2017.

[61] ibid.

[62] See Odyssey Marine Exploration's SS *Gairsoppa* Project Overview <www.shipwreck/net/ssgairsoppa.php> accessed 23 November 2017.

[63] '£24m Haul of Silver Recovered from Sunken Merchant Ship off Irish Coast' *Guardian* (18 July 2012) <https://www.theguardian.com/uk/2012/jul/18/treasure-haul-shipwreck-irish-sea> accessed 6 September 2018.

[64] Odyssey Marine Exploration's SS *Gairsoppa* Project Overview (n 62).

[65] See Odyssey Marine Exploration's SS *Mantola* Project Overview <www.shipwreck/net/ssgairsoppa.php> accessed 23 November 2017.

[66] See ibid.

[67] 2001 UCH Convention, art 2(3).

100-years under water criterion, the *Mantola* and the cargo on board now qualify as UCH under the Convention; it will be some time still before the same can be said for the *Gairsoppa*. Nonetheless, the historical and archaeological significance of these wrecks, and the shipments they were carrying, is likely to be the same: probably relatively small. However, the arbitrary time limit for determining the material scope of application of the Convention, along with its provisions on the recovery and disposition of material, mean that it would probably be impossible for the United Kingdom, if a State Party to the Convention, to 'liquidate' the financial value of its assets on board the *Mantola* in a way that was compliant with the Convention. While it could perhaps argue that the fact that the wreck had been discovered means that recovery of commercially valuable material on board, under a strictly regulated contract, may be warranted to avoid unauthorized plunder, compliance with the Rules relating to the disposition of material is likely to result in the financial value of the bullion being, in effect, permanently 'locked-up'. The question that needs to be asked is: is that outcome really justified for cultural reasons?

Some complex, and highly controversial, issues are presented by this illustration of the difficulties of applying the Convention to shipwrecks. There is a perilously fine line between allowing an *owner*—any owner, be it a State or private entity—to liquidate financial assets that have, at best, marginal historical or archaeological value and promoting the very sort of activities that the Convention was designed to deter. However, apart from the fact that a small number of States, the United Kingdom included, may be disinclined to ratify a Convention that has such an impact, the general point that underlies the illustration has wider ramifications. Is there any sense in requiring that *all* material recovered, including material that has no intrinsic cultural value, or large quantities of material that is fungible in character, be kept, if not in the project archive[68] then in a place and in circumstances which permit for reassembly of the entire collection? Surely, whatever the background situation, such a requirement simply stores up all sorts of practical problems for many marine archaeological projects?

Some comments and observations made by L'Hour, Director of the French Underwater Archaeology Research Department (DRASSM) related to First World War UCH[69] are worthy of note. L'Hour referred to three requests that DRASSM had received for permission, under French domestic legislation, to salvage cargoes

[68] Rule 33 of the UCH Rules provides that '[t]he project archives, including any underwater cultural heritage removed ... shall, *as far as possible*, be kept together and intact as a collection in a manner that is available for professional and public access'. This indicates that recovered material can be kept in a separate location, provided it remains possible to reassemble the collection.

[69] Michel L'Hour, 'Underwater Cultural Heritage from World War I: A Vast, Neglected and Threatened Heritage' in Ulrike Guérin, Arturo Rey da Silva, and Lucas Simonds (eds), *Underwater Cultural Heritage from World War I: Proceedings of the Scientific Conference on the Occasion of the Centenary of World War I, Bruges, Belgium, 26 and 27 June 2014* (UNESCO 2015) 97–104 <www.unesco.org/new/en/culture/themes/underwater-cultural-heritage/publications-resources/publications/> accessed 6 September 2018.

of raw materials from First World War wrecks. The cargoes comprised 1,370 tons of copper; 2,000 tons of nickel; and a shipment of tin. He then went on to comment:

> These cases are, plainly, very difficult for archaeologists, because it is never easy to argue that a 2,000-ton cargo of copper or nickel ore is of the utmost historical, artistic or archaeological interest. In most cases, a representative sample of the cargo, perhaps a few hundred ingots or a few hundred kilos of ore, would be sufficient to satisfy our scientific requirements. Especially since most of the companies which now apply for these permits have stopped using the grab and bucket in favour of methods that cause no damage to the wreck.[70]

It would be interesting to know whether the requests for authorization were made before or after France ratified the 2001 UCH Convention, and how DRASSM dealt with, or would now deal with, such license applications.

C. Hazardous Wrecks

There are many wartime wrecks around the world that contain oil and other noxious substances, including munitions, which pose a hazard to human life, the environment, and economic activity. Over time, as the wrecks deteriorate in condition, these hazards may increase. The owner is potentially liable for damage that results and may make an assessment—as in the case of the *Royal Oak*, discussed below—that intervention measures to prevent, or at least mitigate, damage need to be taken.[71] While the majority of hazardous wrecks date from the Second World War and, as yet, do not fall within the scope of the 2001 UCH Convention, there are known examples of First World War wrecks that contain hazardous material, including the liner *Lusitania*.[72] Nonetheless, the Convention does not make provision to accommodate the hazardous characteristics that such wrecks clearly possess.

One of Britain's most well-known twentieth-century wartime wrecks is HMS *Royal Oak*, a battleship famously sunk by a U-boat torpedo in 1939 with the loss of more than 800 lives, while at anchorage in Scapa Flow. Over recent years, the British Ministry of Defence has been attempting to deal with serious leakage of oil from the vessel's fuel tanks which is threatening the sensitive local marine

[70] ibid 101.

[71] This chapter focuses on the 2001 UCH Convention's provisions with respect to the recovery and disposition of material. However, some preventive or mitigatory action to deal with hazardous wrecks will give rise to other questions, eg where it is necessary to move a wreck that is a serious obstacle to navigation or to development activities.

[72] See further Sarah Dromgoole and Craig Forrest, 'The 2007 Nairobi Wreck Removal Convention and Hazardous Historic Shipwrecks' (2011) Lloyd's Maritime and Commercial L Q 92–122.

environment and the area's important fishing industry. The operations to remove the oil from the wreck are technically challenging and can only be undertaken in the summer months when the weather conditions are relatively benign. To offset the large costs of operations such as these, it appears to be common practice to sell off oil recovered by a process known as 'hot-tapping', which will still have commercial value.

Assuming the *Royal Oak* did fall within the scope of the 2001 UCH Convention and that the United Kingdom was a State Party, the first question that would need to be asked is whether the operations to remove the oil from the wreck would be compliant with the Convention? The oil itself would qualify as UCH under the terms of the treaty, even though it is likely to have negligible, if any, intrinsic historical or archaeological significance. The removal activities would constitute activities 'directed at' UCH and, as such, would have to be undertaken in accordance with the standards set out in the Convention's Annex. Rule 1 makes it clear that such activities may be authorized 'for the purpose of making a significant contribution to protection or knowledge or enhancement of underwater cultural heritage', and Rule 4 reinforces this by providing that excavation or recovery must be 'necessary for the purpose of scientific studies or for the ultimate protection of the underwater cultural heritage'. Removal purely for the purpose of protecting human life or the marine environment does not appear to be permissible and, therefore, removal of the oil would need to be necessary, at least in part, to protect UCH.[73] In some cases where the objective of activities is the removal of a hazard, this may be the case, but perhaps not always. If recovery to access the oil is permissible in principle, it is likely to be necessary to cut into the hull. Rule 1 requires that activities directed at UCH must be authorized 'in a manner consistent with the protection of that heritage'. While activities that might 'adversely affect' UCH or even be destructive of UCH are permissible in certain circumstances (bearing in mind that archaeological excavation is itself a destructive process), any adverse effect must not be 'more than is necessary for the objectives of the project'[74] and the 'methods and techniques used must . . . contribute to the preservation of the remains'.[75]

Assuming that the specific mode of recovery is permissible under the Rules, what then can be done with oil that is recovered? Would the common practice of selling off the tapped oil to recoup costs be permissible? One might argue, perhaps, that such sale was not an ordinary commercial sale and therefore was distinguishable from a sale 'as commercial goods'.[76] However, even if that argument was accepted, the sale undoubtedly would result in the irretrievable dispersal of material

[73] The Rules do make some reference to the protection of the marine environment in Rule 29, which stipulates that an environmental policy must be prepared 'to ensure that the seabed and marine life are not unduly disturbed' by activities authorized under the Rules.

[74] UCH Rules, r 3.

[75] ibid, r 4.

[76] See wording of r 2.

from the shipwreck assemblage. There seems no rational reason why one would want to keep bunker fuel oil of this kind in an archaeological project archive, or in circumstances where conceivably it could be reunited with the rest of the archive. There are also some very obvious reasons why one would not want to keep other types of material that might be recovered in similar circumstances, such as munitions and other material hazardous to human health.[77]

If the *Royal Oak* had been a casualty of the First World War rather than the Second, and the United Kingdom was a Party to the 2001 UCH Convention, as owner of the wreck it would be placed on the horns of a dilemma: recovery and irretrievable disposal of UCH could be a matter of practical, and perhaps legal, necessity (among other things to avoid breaching international law obligations to remove the hazard), but there would be question marks over the degree to which authorization of such action would breach the duty to 'preserve underwater cultural heritage for the benefit of humanity in conformity with the provisions of [the] Convention'.[78]

Conclusion

As previously noted, the 2001 UCH Convention is not only a part of international cultural heritage law but also of international maritime law. To date, there has been an uneasy relationship with the purely public law side of international maritime law, enshrined for the most part in the 1982 Law of the Sea Convention, and for this reason the 2001 UCH Convention is still regarded in many quarters as a politically controversial instrument. While the ratification by France indicates that the difficulties over compatibility with the 'Constitution for the Oceans' may be surmountable, these are not the only difficulties the Convention presents. The understandable desire to avoid loopholes that could be exploited by commercial treasure hunters has led to a regime for disposition of material that is remarkably rigid. In particular, the apparently inviolable principle that material from a shipwreck assemblage cannot be irretrievably dispersed under any circumstances throws up problems in the context of more modern wrecks that almost certainly were never properly thought through. A combination of disinterest, lack of understanding, and a degree of mutual suspicion meant that there was very little input from specialists in the commercial maritime industry during the UNESCO initiative. Consequently, issues were overlooked, as the text developed, that undoubtedly would have been flagged up by such specialists, not least the question of the

[77] Munitions are sometimes recovered after becoming entangled in fishing nets. Presumably, the same principles would apply. (Rule 13 of the Annex makes provision for 'chance discoveries', but its purpose is simply to allow for immediate conservation and stabilization measures to be taken with the authorization of a competent authority in the absence of a project design.)

[78] 2001 UCH Convention, art 2(3).

application of the Convention to hazardous wrecks.[79] While a great deal of attention was given to the compatibility of the new treaty with international law of the sea, relatively little attention was given to the way it would intersect with other areas of international maritime law, public and private, including the area commonly referred to as 'wreck removal'.[80]

One means of resolving at least some of the problems regarding deaccession would be to treat the 'character' criterion in the Convention's definition of UCH as having substantive meaning. One might argue, for example, that a bulk cargo of an unprocessed mineral ore such as tin, though underwater for at least 100 years, did not have 'a cultural, historical or archaeological character'. However, to take up such an argument would go against all expectations regarding the Convention and would seriously undermine its general scheme. One of the great strengths of the treaty is that a competent national authority with heritage expertise is the arbiter in determining how material falling within the broad scope of the Convention is treated (rather than, say, a finder or the judiciary). However, competent national authorities, such as the French DRASSM, need then to be trusted to make appropriate decisions, including on occasions determining that material judged to be of little or no archaeological significance, impractical to keep, or simply downright dangerous, can be irretrievably disposed of, even by its sale or destruction, provided that this 'does not prejudice the scientific or cultural interest or integrity of' the assemblage as a whole. Furthermore, where there is an identifiable owner, their interests—including both their rights and their potential liabilities—should be taken into account.[81]

It may be that the problems identified can only be properly addressed by amendment of the Convention. However, the technical hurdles that would need to be overcome to amend the treaty are substantial.[82] Furthermore, there is likely to be little, if any, appetite on the part of States Parties to institute amendment proceedings that would reopen the contentious question of commercial exploitation and the text of Rule 2. The United Kingdom—and possibly certain other States with a large wartime legacy[83]—may conclude that these questions, when set alongside

[79] At an early stage of the process, there appears to have been an assumption on the part of the International Maritime Organisation that the Convention would not apply to hazardous wrecks (or at least wrecks that posed a hazard to navigation); at the same stage, the International Maritime Committee (CMI) indicated it was not interested in the topic: see Dromgoole (n 32) 53.

[80] Even the intersection with the law of salvage is not as straightforward as the negotiators might have imagined: ibid 204–06. For a discussion of the Convention's interrelationship with the 2007 Wreck Removal Convention, see Dromgoole and Forrest (n 72). The expression 'wreck removal' is misleading. What is really meant is removal (or at least mitigation) of the hazard.

[81] For a discussion of the degree to which the owner's interests should be taken into account, see Dromgoole (n 32) 111-12. Obviously, a balance needs to be struck between the owner's private interests and the public interests of the international community as a whole.

[82] See 2001 UCH Convention, art 31. For a discussion, see Dromgoole (n 32) 363.

[83] For an interesting outline of the US position with respect to wartime wrecks, see James Delgado and Ole Varmer, 'The Public Importance of World War I Shipwrecks: Why a State Should Care and the Challenges of Protection' in Guérin (n 69) 105–15.

their other concerns, weigh the balance of their national interests on the side of non-accession, but whether that outcome is regarded as a price worth paying to avoid any reopening of the treaty text remains to be seen. In the meantime, at least until such time as Second World War wrecks start to fall within the scope of the Convention, competent national authorities appear to be left to deal with any difficulties that do arise on a case-by-case basis and with a pragmatic eye.

PART V

INTERSECTIONS OF INTERNATIONAL, NATIONAL, AND COMMUNITY INTERESTS IN CULTURAL HERITAGE

The final part of this volume considers various issues related to how international law responds to the unique character of cultural heritage, namely how it accommodates (or not) intersecting and sometimes-competing international, national, and community interests in cultural heritage. Such issues arise in a variety of contexts, some already explored elsewhere in this volume, but the chapters here focus on three distinct contexts: (1) the protection of cultural heritage within the 'right to participate in cultural life' set out in international human rights instruments; (2) developments in immunity from seizure for cultural objects loaned across territorial borders for exhibition or display; and (3) developments in international and regional regimes for controlling the import and export of cultural objects.

Beginning this part, Vanessa Tünsmeyer presents a functions-based framework for bridging international human rights and cultural heritage law.[1] She observes that UNESCO's activities in recent decades have contributed to the development of international cultural heritage law as its own area within public international law. By the very nature of cultural heritage law, namely its focus on cultural heritage and forms of cultural expression, she further notes that this field is closely linked to different human rights. Nonetheless, she argues that the link between cultural heritage law and international human rights law has been only recently, and incompletely, realized in recent instruments, even though States have obligations in both areas of international law. Tünsmeyer therefore examines the functions of cultural heritage and concludes that a functions-based approach presents a coherent way to

[1] Vanessa Tünsmeyer, 'Bridging the Gap Between International Human Rights and International Cultural Heritage Law Instruments: A Functions Approach' in Anne-Marie Carstens and Elizabeth Varner (eds), *Intersections in International Cultural Heritage Law* (OUP 2020) (Ch 13).

better bridge the gap—and therefore develop the intersection—between the two fields. In particular, she argues that this approach facilitates accommodation of State duties and rights under UNESCO instruments with individual and community rights under the respective human rights treaties.

Nout van Woudenberg then addresses several developments concerning immunity from seizure for cultural State property on loan, which support the recognition of an emerging rule of customary international law. According to van Woudenberg, a customary rule provides that cultural objects belonging to foreign States and on temporary loan for an exhibition are immune from seizure.[2] He surveys several developments in national immunity from seizure regimes, including those of the United States, Australia, and Poland, as well as a draft convention adopted by the International Law Association. These developments, while they support the existence of a customary rule, nonetheless show that the rule and its contours are not yet firmly established and remain subject to limitations. According to van Woudenberg, the customary rule remains underdeveloped or subject to other developments, particularly in the event of a serious breach of an obligation arising under a peremptory norm of general international law, or as applied to those cultural objects that are subject to return obligations under international or European law.

Finally, Robert Peters concludes this part by arguing that the protection of cultural heritage is an overarching international legal principle that provides common ground for further developments in public international law.[3] Within the debate of nationalism versus internationalism, he describes the development of international cultural heritage law, analyzes the notions and concepts used in this context, and highlights the existing shortcomings and loopholes in national and international legal frameworks in this field. He explores the concept of a World Heritage Trust and the designation of immovable cultural heritage as a World Heritage Site. He argues that the procedure used to designate World Heritage Sites has become a national contest between States to obtain as many designations as possible, rather than the international and non-partisan procedure it was intended to be. Peters then addresses the issue of trafficking in movable cultural heritage by arguing that an exclusive focus on patrimony and national export laws (nationalism) is unidimensional and insufficient to protect movable cultural heritage from trafficking. In contrast, the mutual recognition of export laws through export and import regulations is a much more comprehensive and truly international

[2] Nout van Woudenberg, 'Developments Concerning Immunity from Seizure for Cultural State Property on Loan' in Anne-Marie Carstens and Elizabeth Varner (eds), *Intersections in International Cultural Heritage Law* (OUP 2020) (Ch 14).

[3] Robert Peters, 'Nationalism versus Internationalism: New Perspectives Beyond State Sovereignty and Territoriality in the Protection of Cultural Heritage' in Anne-Marie Carstens and Elizabeth Varner (eds), *Intersections in International Cultural Heritage Law* (OUP 2020) (Ch 15).

approach (internationalism). In view of recent developments at the national level in Germany, as well as at EU level, Peters concludes that coordination between export and import regulations is necessary to protect cultural heritage against destruction and trafficking.

Anne-Marie Carstens and Elizabeth Varner

13

Bridging the Gap Between International Human Rights and International Cultural Heritage Law Instruments

A Functions Approach

Vanessa Tünsmeyer

Introduction

International cultural heritage law has concerned itself predominantly with the physical preservation of the object. This is not surprising since the field—if we accept international cultural heritage law to be its own subsection of public international law—has been birthed in the context of armed conflict and the law of war, a context which can be traced back centuries.[1] Concern for cultural heritage during armed conflict also gave birth to the first binding international treaty that focused exclusively on the protection of cultural heritage, the 1954 Hague Convention for the Protection of Cultural Property during Armed Conflict (1954 Hague Convention).[2] More recently, instruments developed under the auspices of the United Nations Educational, Scientific and Cultural Organisation (UNESCO) have gone beyond this State-centered focus to recognize the use of heritage to and within a given social entity other than the nation-state. It took time for the realization that heritage has important roles to play for individuals and communities to take hold in international law.[3] Yet, the majority of UNESCO treaties relating to cultural heritage emphasize the position of the sovereign State and its interests.[4] Given the prevalence of States within international law, this emphasis

[1] Lyndel Prott, 'The History and Development of Processes for the Recovery of Cultural Heritage' in Lyndel Prott (ed), *Witnesses to History: A Compendium of Documents and Writings on the Return of Cultural Objects* (UNESCO 2009) 2.

[2] Convention for the Protection of Cultural Property in the Event of Armed Conflict (adopted 14 May 1954, entered into force 7 August 1956) 249 UNTS 240 (1954 Hague Convention). See Craig Forrest, *International Law and the Protection of Cultural Heritage* (Routledge 2010) 56.

[3] Notably the Convention for the Safeguarding of the Intangible Cultural Heritage (adopted 17 October 2003, entered into force 20 April 2006) 2368 UNTS 3 (2003 ICH Convention).

[4] Anna Filipa Vrdoljak, 'Human Rights and Cultural Heritage in International Law' in Federico Lenzerini and Anna Filipa Vrdoljak (eds), *International Law for Common Goods* (Hart 2014).

Vanessa Tünsmeyer, Bridging the Gap Between International Human Rights and International Cultural Heritage Law Instruments In: *Intersections in International Cultural Heritage Law*. Edited by Anne-Marie Carstens and Elizabeth Varner. DOI: 10.1093/oso/9780198846291.003.0014

is not surprising. This State-focus in turn can threaten the human rights of non-dominant groups that possess a culture different from the State, notably minorities and indigenous peoples.[5]

If we accept, however, that cultural heritage also has a human rights dimension, due to the central position of cultural heritage in any given culture or social entity, the State-oriented focus of international cultural heritage law can become problematic.[6] State-driven readings and usages of cultural heritage can seek to strengthen a national cultural identity. For those members of the national community who—for whatever reason—do not fit within this narrative, access to, and use of, heritage becomes difficult. Examples are national monuments that are sacred sites where worship needs to be observed in secret, or the appropriation and mischaracterization of group heritage to further a national story. The human rights dimension of cultural heritage has largely been ignored in the adoption of binding instruments in international cultural heritage law, at least until the 2003 Convention for the Safeguarding of the Intangible Heritage (2003 ICH Convention).[7] International human rights law, in contrast to international cultural heritage law, by its very nature is focused not on the interests of the nation-state but rather on the individual, or the individual acting in community with others as a group.[8] This includes provisions that protect those individuals, or groups, who are at the margin or outside the dominant national-cultural community. States, in turn, have ratified treaties in both areas of public international law, international cultural heritage, and international human rights law.

Regardless of whether one accepts that cultural heritage has a human rights dimension or not, States are under binding human rights obligations—and this includes cultural rights. The link between the two fields has been affirmed by numerous international actors, inter alia the United Nations Committee on

[5] See eg IWGIA (International Work Group on Indigenous Affairs), Report: International Expert Workshop on the World Heritage Convention and Indigenous People (2013) 15–16, 28, 34–36 <http://issuu.com/iwgia/docs/international_workshop_-wh_and_ip_-report_web/3?e=0> accessed 1 November 2018 (conflict arising out of the Kenya Lake System as violation in connection with the implementation of the 1972 World Heritage Convention). See also Ellen Desmet, *Indigenous Rights Entwined with Nature Conservation* (Intersentia 2011) (analysis of regulatory interplay in relation to nature conservation).

[6] Cultural heritage is understood here in its broadest sense with the understanding that different cultures may value different forms of heritage (eg tangible over intangible), and this chapter employs the term 'cultural heritage' as it better encompasses the human rights dimension of cultural objects and traditions. The long-standing debate over choice of terminology in the field and the use of the two different terms in international cultural heritage law instruments, 'cultural property' and 'cultural heritage' has been covered expertly elsewhere. See eg Lyndel Prott and Patrick O'Keefe, 'Cultural Heritage' or 'Cultural Property' (1992) 1 ICJP 307.

[7] An alternative point would be earlier through the inclusion of the cultural landscapes category in the World Heritage Mechanism. See World Heritage Committee, Report, UNESCO Doc WHC-92/CONF.002/12 (14 December 1992). Vrdoljak speaks of 'long-standing cultural heritage instruments . . . being revisited and reinterpreted'. Vrdoljak (n 4) 169.

[8] William Barth, 'Cultural Rights: A Necessary Corrective to the Nation State' in Francesco Francioni and Martin Scheinin (eds), *Cultural Human Rights* (Martinus Nijhoff 2008) (developing the notion of cultural rights as a necessary counter-weight to the power of the nation-state).

Economic, Social and Cultural Rights, former UN Independent Expert and later Special Rapporteur in the Fields of Cultural Rights Shaheed, and Shaheed's successor, Special Rapporteur in the Field of Cultural Rights Bennoune.[9] Arguably, the wording of both Article 27 of the International Covenant on Civil and Political Rights (ICCPR) and the various cultural rights enshrined in Article 15 of the International Covenant on Economic, Social and Cultural Rights (ICESCR) already encompassed different forms of cultural heritage at the time of their adoption.[10] However, the formal recognition of this linkage between human rights and cultural heritage is fairly recent.[11] It has also received more attention in academic writings in recent years. Vrdoljak, for example, recognized this linkage between cultural heritage and human rights. She highlighted the role of cultural diversity as a bridge between cultural heritage and human rights. She developed the notion that culture and human rights dissolve 'boundaries in international law' by conceptualizing cultural diversity as a common good of unifying force.[12]

However, the acceptance of such a link between cultural heritage and human rights by international actors did not in itself clarify the precise scope of human rights obligations under international cultural heritage law. Neither does it specify how to connect the two in existing instruments that do not explicitly recognize the link, partially due to the time period in which they were drafted. Shaheed has observed that

> [a]lthough UNESCO instruments do not generally specify the rights of individuals and/or communities to cultural heritage, several entry points in the instruments themselves, or developed through practice, invite the adoption of a human rights-based approach.[13]

As examples for this widening of cultural heritage instruments, she cites the increasing role of communities in the 1972 Convention Concerning the Protection of the World Cultural and Natural Heritage (1972 World Heritage Convention)[14] by means of the updated guidelines and the role of communities in the 2003 ICH

[9] CESCR, General Comment No 21 on the right of everyone to take part in cultural life (2009) UN Doc E/C.12/GC/21 (21 December 2009); UNHRC 'Report of the independent expert in the field of cultural rights Farida Shaheed' (2011) UN Doc A/HRC/17/38 (21 March 2011); UNHRC 'Report of the Special Rapporteur in the field of cultural rights Karima Bennoune' (2016) UN Doc A/71/317 (9 August 2016) sec III.A.

[10] International Covenant on Civil and Political Rights (adopted 16 December 1966, entered into force 23 March 1976) 999 UNTS 171 (ICCPR); International Covenant on Economic, Social and Cultural Rights (adopted 16 December 1966, entered into force 3 January 1976) 999 UNTS 3 (ICESCR).

[11] In agreement, Vrdoljak (n 4) 140.

[12] Vrdoljak also draws attention to its inclusion in human rights instruments and in international cultural heritage law instruments which focus on the protection of ICH. ibid 139–41, 168–73.

[13] Shaheed (n 9) para 23.

[14] Convention Concerning the Protection of the World Cultural and Natural Heritage (open for signature 16 November 1972, entered into force 15 December 1975) 1037 UNTS 151 (1972 World Heritage Convention).

Convention.[15] While Shaheed did not specify what she considered to be 'entry points' or what the notion of entry points entails for the application of the respective fields, the former Special Rapporteur in the Field of Cultural Rights raised important questions: Namely, how do these different fields of international law intersect precisely? And what consequences could a joining of these fields in the areas that intersect entail for the respective fields, including the implementation of human rights?

This chapter aims to contribute to this discussion by proposing an approach by which affected human rights could be linked more expressly to the different treaties of international cultural heritage law: the functions approach.[16] It proposes that States protect cultural heritage because they identify or value certain uses of cultural heritage, referred to in this chapter as 'heritage functions'. It is argued that the intersection between the fields is through the functions which heritage has for individuals, a community, a people, or the nation-state. Section I develops this approach and propose the beginning of one possible categorization of cultural heritage functions in international cultural heritage law. Section II then proposes different functions to show that there is an overlap between the functions that are valued and (State obligations under) specific human rights. It will apply this model to link international cultural heritage law to one cultural right by a broad, teleological interpretation of the duty to protect or safeguard cultural heritage. Section III concludes this chapter by raising the implications of adapting this functions approach not only for States, but also for non-State actors.

I. The Functions of Heritage Approach

A. The Functions Approach Explained

Most binding instruments of international cultural heritage law include provisions that provide for or accommodate the protection of different forms of cultural heritage or cultural expressions.[17] This is done by explicitly enshrining protection of the selected heritage as the instrument's chosen objective, or providing for a State duty to protect it. Examples of such provisions include: Article1(a) and Article

[15] Shaheed (n 9) paras 24–25.

[16] cf Tolina Loulanski, 'Revising the Concept for Cultural Heritage: The Argument for a Functional Approach' (2006) 13 IJCP 207 (perceiving a similar shift in the understanding of heritage and using a comparable term but with a different focus). Loulanski traces the evolution of the heritage concept toward a 'newer functional direction' yet focuses on a plea for the reconceptualization of heritage as a concept.

[17] Both the terms 'protection' and 'safeguarding' are used in international instruments with a common, protective, core. Protection has different aspects depending on the form of cultural expression but can be understood to encompass preservation (from harm), maintenance, sheltering, or care-taking.

5(1) of the 2005 UNESCO Convention on the Protection and Promotion of the Diversity of Cultural Expressions (2005 Cultural Diversity Convention);[18] Article 1(a) of the 2003 ICH Convention; Article 4 of the 1972 World Heritage Convention; and Article 2(1) and the chapeau of Article 5 of the 1970 UNESCO Convention on the Means of Prohibiting and Preventing the Illicit Import, Export and Transfer of Ownership of Cultural Property (1970 UNESCO Convention).[19]

Protecting or safeguarding of cultural heritage can be interpreted to include not just the material dimension of heritage, but to protect those functions of cultural heritage that State governments identify within cultural heritage as relevant for themselves. These functions have led them to focus on physical preservation or protection of intangible cultural heritage in the first place. Values or functions that were or are reason for States adopting international cultural heritage law instruments are, in essence, those purposes or roles that heritage was or is seen to fulfill within a given nation-state or society. In this sense, heritage protection by States is essentially motivated by self-interest. State actions in the protection of cultural heritage are then motivated by either individual or a shared/common self-interest. This understanding of heritage protection as being motivated by State interest also aligns with the political nature of many international legal instruments.[20] Such a broad interpretation of protection or safeguarding would still be in line with the Vienna Convention on the Law of Treaties governing the interpretation of treaties by taking into account 'any relevant rules of international law applicable in the relations between parties'.[21] The starting point of this enquiry was increasing recognition of the relevancy of international cultural heritage law and human rights instruments to each other. Moreover, the ICCPR and the ICESCR are broadly ratified and will apply in most relations between Parties.

The question then arises of how far this express realization of the political nature of heritage protection by States in international cultural heritage law can affect, benefit, or threaten individual and community rights. The main potential benefit of going beyond a surface-level appreciation of cultural heritage rests in the congruence of heritage functions and a number of human rights. Thus, the chapter proposes that several functions can be identified that heritage fulfills in a society. Instruments of international cultural heritage law frequently specify the form of heritage worthy of protection, the dangers it should be protected

[18] Convention on the Protection and Promotion of the Diversity of Cultural Expressions (adopted 20 October 2005, entered into force 18 March 2007) 2440 UNTS 311 (2005 Cultural Diversity Convention) arts 1(a), 5(1).

[19] Convention on the Means of Prohibiting and Preventing the Illicit Import, Export and Transfer of Ownership of Cultural Property (adopted 14 November 1970, entered into force 24 April 1972) 823 UNTS 231.

[20] See eg Martti Koskenniemi, *The Politics of International Law* (Hart 2011); Steven Whitley, *The Democratic Legitimacy of International Law* (Hart 2010); Sir Hersch Lauterpacht, *The Function of Law in the International Society* (2nd edn, OUP 2011).

[21] Vienna Convention on the Law of Treaties (adopted 22 May 1969, entered into force 27 January 1980) 1155 UNTS 331, art 31(3)(c).

against, and the measures which can or should be taken to protect it. It is here that international cultural heritage law and human rights intersect. When heritage is selected as worthy of protection, we can ask: why do we protect it (namely, which functions do we value, and which do we ignore), who enjoys these functions (and who does not), and how? The functions, in effect, relate to dimensions of rights that are protected under existing human rights law treaties. When a State opts to protect certain forms of heritage through certain measures, it must still ensure respect for existing human rights obligations that arise out of a State's ratification of the ICESCR, the ICCPR, or both. The protection of heritage and its function is then only permissible if congruent with the functions that heritage fulfills under human rights law.

In the intersection between the two fields, heritage protection can then translate into protecting human rights rather than to use implementation of international cultural heritage law to circumvent existing human rights obligations. Moreover, by focusing on the function of heritage for the individual and/or communities in question, the protection of heritage as a means of human expression is in effect strengthened. This understanding is, however, premised on understanding cultural heritage not as a meta-level good whose physical protection would trump all other norms. Rather, it is both the outcome of and one of the means necessary for the enjoyment of different rights.[22]

The danger one might perceive in the functions approach rests in confusing a pragmatic acknowledgment of the political nature of international policy making in the area of cultural heritage, on the one hand, with a way for States to focus on their cultural (or rather identity) policies to the detriment of the protection of existing human rights, on the other. To put it simply, one advantage of treaties rests in their potential to remove a subject somewhat from political turbulence and disagreement by creating legal obligations and rights. Is the focus on the functions of heritage then not a re-admission of the political usages of heritage? One answer would be that the existing provisions in UNESCO instruments reserve large margins within which States can realize their cultural policies.[23] It is thus not really a question of inviting the political into heritage protection, but rather recognition of its (arguably very large) presence in the field.

By focusing on the human rights dimension of cultural heritage, the impact of such political usages of culture on human rights can be discussed more explicitly. The functions approach is then one way to articulate this human rights dimension. It cannot in itself remedy the dangers such politicization can carry for the

[22] Similar cultural heritage underlies the mandate of the Special Rapporteur in the Field of Cultural Rights. See Bennoune (n 9) para 13.

[23] Consider these two examples: (1) Textual: the State has the right to identify cultural heritage to be protected under 1970 UNESCO Convention, art 1; and (2) Procedural: the politicization of the World Heritage Procedure has been critically highlighted in different contexts. For an impression, see special issue on politics of heritage, Intl J of Heritage Studies 8(2) (2002).

enforcement of binding State obligations and legal rights, which exist by virtue of various human rights treaties. It may, however, aid heritage actors in streamlining their work with the human rights canon. It may even aid human rights actors in better evaluating the effect that arises out of instruments of international cultural heritage law on the enjoyment of human rights.

To be able to adopt an understanding of protection or safeguarding heritage that implies the protection of specific functions of heritage, however, we first need to identify which heritage functions are already recognized in international cultural heritage law instruments (see Section I.B.2. below), which human rights could relate with these functions (see Section II.A.). This investigation also must ultimately identify which aspects of a specific right require an action by the State as far as cultural heritage in its territory is concerned (see Section II.B for one example).

B. Heritage Functions Distilled from International Cultural Heritage Law Instruments

1. UNESCO and its influence on the focus of international cultural heritage law functions

A discussion of goals enshrined in instruments of international cultural heritage law must take into account the interests and goals of the dominant legislative body in the field, namely UNESCO. The UNESCO Constitution entrusts the organization with a number of tasks related to its central purpose, namely the contribution 'to peace and security' through a strengthening of international cooperation and the diffusion of knowledge.[24] The UNESCO Constitution identifies ignorance and a lack of mutual understanding as the central causes of war,[25] as these enable the denial of human dignity.[26] This ignorance is to be prevented by the distribution of knowledge, which explains the need for 'conservation and protection of the world's inheritance'.[27] Mutual understanding was perceived as the only means to ensure long-lasting peace, to which the organization must contribute. Francioni has highlighted that the UNESCO Constitution recognized cultural heritage as 'a distinct object of international protection', and that the organization's mandate led first to the development of the 1954 Hague Convention.[28]

[24] Constitution of the United Nations Educational, Scientific and Cultural Organization (adopted 16 November 1945, entered into force 4 November 1946), art I(1) (UNESCO Constitution).

[25] ibid, preamble, recital 2.

[26] ibid, preamble, recital 3.

[27] ibid, art I(2)(c). Forrest has argued that this in effect an expression of universalism. Craig Forrest, 'Cultural Heritage as the Common Heritage of Humankind: A Critical Re-Evaluation' (2007) 40 CILJSA 124, 129.

[28] Francesco Francioni, 'Cultural Heritage' in *Max Planck Encyclopedia of Public International Law* (OUP 2013) para 1..

To bridge the gap between culture and cultural heritage, it may be observed that the UNESCO Constitution accords heritage value as a vehicle of culture and knowledge. To conserve the object in question is to protect knowledge, which combats ignorance and ultimately prevents war. This transforms the protection of heritage into an existential need shared by all States.

This understanding of conservation and protection as the ultimate purpose of international cultural heritage law shines through in the 1970 UNESCO Convention (examined below) and is the pillar of the 1972 World Heritage Convention. The UNESCO Constitution explicitly recognizes culture as an instrument to strengthen respect for human rights and fundamental freedoms.[29] The interaction between culture and human rights has thus been recognized in UNESCO instruments since its beginning. It also appears in UNESCO soft law, for example in the 1976 Recommendation on the Participation of the People at Large in Cultural Life.[30] It did take time, however, for it to be recognized in a binding UNESCO treaty.[31]

2. Functions of heritage within international cultural heritage law instruments

In the majority of international cultural heritage law instruments, heritage functions are recognized implicitly, if at all, frequently in the preamble or the scope of the instruments. To discern which heritage functions have been recognized in international cultural heritage law instruments, the following references were considered: (1) any purpose or role ascribed to cultural heritage, either in the preamble or the body of an instrument (including any definition of heritage), and (2) any motivation given for protecting or conserving the heritage in question. Based on this analysis, this chapter describes the respective functions and then briefly discusses selected instruments that highlight these functions, rather than exploring all relevant instruments in the field[32] (chronologically). The sheer number of instruments by necessity limits this undertaking to listing the relevant functions.

[29] UNESCO Constitution, art I(1).

[30] UNESCO Recommendation on Participation by the People at Large in Cultural Life and their Contribution to It (adopted 26 November 1976) para 4(a), recommending that States adopt laws that 'guarantee as human rights those rights bearing on access to and participation in cultural life'.

[31] 2003 ICH Convention. See also n 7.

[32] Since its inception, UNESCO considers forty instruments as falling within its cultural mandate, twenty of which are of a soft law nature. This count includes six Conventions, fourteen Recommendations, and three Declarations that directly relate to cultural heritage, as well as others that relate to copyright law and other regulatory endeavors that are not at the core of the field. On top of this there is the 1995 UNIDROIT Convention to consider and, strictly speaking, any provisions in the law of war that deal with the protection of heritage, such as Article 27(1) of the regulations annexed to the 1907 Hague Convention governing land warfare. Convention (IV) Respecting the Laws and Customs of War on Land and its Annex: Regulations concerning the Laws and Customs of War on Land (adopted 18 October 1907, entered into force 26 January 1910) 187 CTS 227. On the latter, see Katja Lubina, 'Contested Cultural Property: The Return of Nazi Spoliated Art and Human Remains From Public Collections' (PhD thesis, Maastricht University 2009) 58.

In total, the analysis yielded seven functions:

(1) aesthetic,
(2) scientific,
(3) historic-educative,
(4) contributing to an individual's identity (formation),
(5) contributing to environmental protection or sustainable development,
(6) religious, and
(7) contributing to cultural exchange, thus strengthening peace or furthering human dignity.

This division and identification of functions merely represents one model set for identification; different approaches are possible. For example, the historic function (to be understood as heritage providing a witness to past events) is arguably closely linked to the identity formation function and also has educative and scientific components. Arguably other functions of heritage exist that are not necessarily recognized in the treaties, but which might have led to their adoption, such as economic benefits of recognizing a particular site as World Heritage. Despite different possibilities for grouping these functions, the adopted approach most closely resembled the emphasis in the instruments examined. Moreover, the identification of one possible model of functions is sufficient in order to support the claim of a functional interrelationship between cultural heritage and human rights law. In the following subsections, the seven functions will be explained briefly before connected human rights can be explored.

a. Aesthetic function of heritage

Cultural heritage clearly has an aesthetic function that renders it worthy of protection, if we accept that cultural material subsumed under the cultural heritage/cultural property concept in international cultural heritage law is at least partially congruent with what is commonly referred to as 'art'. One reference appears in the 1970 UNESCO Convention, which defines 'cultural property' as property that 'on religious or secular grounds, is specifically designated by each State as being of importance for archaeology, prehistory, history, literature, *art* or science' and that additionally belongs to certain enumerated categories.[33] Even more explicit is the 1972 World Heritage Convention, which in defining sites worthy of protection under the Convention speaks of

> works of man or the combined works of nature and man, and areas including archaeological sites which are of outstanding universal value from the historical, *aesthetic*, ethnological or anthropological point of vie'.[34]

[33] 1970 UNESCO Convention, art 1 (emphasis added).
[34] 1972 World Heritage Convention, art 1 (emphasis added).

b. Scientific function of heritage

The 1970 UNESCO Convention's general principles include the 'ambassadorial role of art' in 'spreading knowledge of other cultures'.[35] The Convention's preamble strikes a balance between the importance of heritage to a State and the heritage of humankind. This dual importance of cultural property[36] then justifies its preservation and protection. The preamble proclaims that to 'respect its own cultural heritage and that of all nations' is a 'moral obligation' on every State. The emphasis of the instrument clearly rests on the physical conservation of heritage. Moreover the words 'its true value can be appreciated only in relation to the *fullest possible information regarding* its origin, history and traditional setting' seem to highlight the (scientific) sourcing of heritage for knowledge.[37] Again, the definition of 'cultural property' set out in the 1970 UNESCO Convention highlights a number of different heritage functions, including the scientific one.[38] The importance of science is also highlighted in the 1972 World Heritage Convention, which defines world heritage in reference to its scientific importance ('outstanding universal value from the point of view of history, art, *or science*').[39]

c. The historic-educative function of heritage

The historic-educative function has two dimensions. On the one hand, an emphasis on the historic value of an object suggests the desire to preserve evidence of past mistakes and successes for future generations. Moreover, by teaching individuals to value the historic function of heritage, a contribution to the identity formation of the individual is made, especially where a specific heritage object or tradition is valued highly and has been embedded in a wider framework of narrating a community/nation/State identity. The historic function of heritage is highlighted, inter alia, in the 1972 World Heritage Convention and its definition of cultural heritage: for monuments, groups of buildings, and sites, their 'outstanding universal value from the point of view of history' can trigger the instrument's protective umbrella.[40]

d. Heritage as contributing to an individual's identity

Next to the role of history in identity formation, other conceivable links with heritage concern its role in being the source—or the space—for creative processes, communal or individual. While the 2003 UNESCO Declaration concerning the Intentional Destruction of Cultural Heritage clearly focuses on the physical

[35] 1970 UNESCO Convention, preamble and art 2. See also Patrick O'Keefe, *Commentary on the UNESCO 1970 Convention on Illicit Traffic* (IAL 2000) 33, 40.

[36] With the exception of the preamble, the 1970 UNESCO Convention uses the term 'cultural property' rather than 'cultural heritage'.

[37] 1970 UNESCO Convention, preamble (emphasis added). Compare O'Keefe (n 37) 33.

[38] 1970 UNESCO Convention, art 1.

[39] World Heritage Convention, art 1 (emphasis added).

[40] ibid.

preservation and protection of heritage,[41] the instrument's preamble recognizes the pivotal function of cultural heritage for identity construction for individuals, groups, and communities.[42]

e. *Heritage contributing to environmental protection and/or sustainable development*

Heritage protection can entail environmental protection and promotion of sustainable development. This environmental function is most obvious in the case of the World Heritage Convention, specifically the protection of natural heritage under Article 2 of the Convention. In this case, natural sites are valued for their scientific[43] or aesthetic[44] function, but conservation of nature in itself becomes an objective by giving certain natural features equal weight to constructed heritage. There are, in addition, a number of mixed sites[45] in which cultural and natural functions of a site intertwine. As highlighted at the beginning of this section, functions may closely interlink, and heritage can serve overlapping functions.

The second recital of the 2003 ICH Convention highlights the importance of intangible cultural heritage (ICH) for sustainable development. Sustainable development, understood as 'development that meets the needs of the present without compromising the ability of future generations to meet their own needs', reflects the desire to ensure development that does not destroy the environment to an irreparable degree.[46] Sustainable development has more dimensions, but generally its transgenerational conceptualization, the understanding of duties that must be fulfilled for the benefit of an unknown group of individuals, suits the similarly transgenerational aspect of heritage protection in international cultural heritage law. International cultural heritage law seeks to ensure the preservation of the past for the future and also encounters problems when contemporary usage threatens physical preservation. The two fields merely approach a similar struggle from opposite ends: development has for a long time been at the disproportionate cost of future generations, whereas heritage protection (due to its strict focus on material preservation for future generations) may disadvantage local communities who desire the usage of the protected heritage today.

41 UNESCO Declaration Concerning the Intentional Destruction of Cultural Heritage (adopted 17 October 2003) art 1 (2003 UNESCO Declaration Concerning Intentional Destruction).

42 2003 UNESCO Declaration Concerning Intentional Destruction, preamble, 5th recital.

43 1972 World Heritage Convention, art 2, second and third sentences.

44 ibid, second sentence.

45 At time of writing, thirty-five mixed sites are inscribed: <http://whc.unesco.org/en/list/&searchsites=&criteria_restrication=&type=mixed&region=&x=4&search=&order=&search_by_country=&y=9&media=&order=year> accessed 1 November 2018. This category was not featured in the original treaty but instead added through the Operational Guidelines promulgated by the World Heritage Committee. See World Heritage Committee, Operational Guidelines for the Implementation of the World Heritage Convention, UNESCO Doc WHC.17/01 (12 July 2017) s II.A, para 46.

46 World Commission on Environment and Development, 'Our Common Future', UN Doc A/42/427 [1987] Annex para 27.

f. Religious function of heritage

Protected heritage can serve a religious function in three ways. First, the protected heritage may constitute the space in which a ceremony is conducted, as in many of the mixed properties registered under the World Heritage Convention[47] or for churches, temples, and mosques entitled to protection under the 1954 Hague Convention.[48] Second, protected heritage objects may be (or may have previously been) used in religious ceremonies. Examples are objects that fall under one of the categories in the definition of 'cultural property' set out in the 1970 UNESCO Convention and that are classified on 'religious grounds'.[49] One example in this case would be a handwritten theological manuscript or a Bible under the 1970 UNESCO Convention.[50] Last, the protected heritage may also constitute a part of religious ceremonies or traditions. An example for this is the focus on traditional intangible forms of cultural heritage, such as rituals under the 2003 ICH Convention.[51]

g. The exchange of heritage as an exchange of cultures promoting peace and human dignity

This function is closely related to the UNESCO Constitution and reappears in a number of instruments, including the UNIDROIT Convention on Stolen or Illegally Exported Cultural Objects (1995 UNIDROIT Convention).[52] The second recital of the preamble of the 1995 UNIDROIT Convention echoes the UNESCO Constitution in that it highlights the need to protect heritage to ensure the 'dissemination of culture' in order to ensure mutual understanding.[53] This function is also featured in the 2001 Universal Declaration on Cultural Diversity, [54] which, rather than seeking the protection of a particular type of heritage, strives for the protection of a state of existence, namely the plurality of cultures. Heritage is thus protected due to its pivotal role within a given culture. The Declaration emphasizes the need to preserve cultural heritage 'as a record of human experience ... to foster creativity in all its diversity and to inspire genuine dialogue among cultures'.[55]

[47] See list of sites (n 47).
[48] 1954 Hague Convention, art 1(a).
[49] 1970 UNESCO Convention, art 1.
[50] Article 1(h).
[51] Article 2(c).
[52] Convention on Stolen or Illegally Exported Cultural Objects (adopted 24 June 1995, entered in force 1 July 1998) 34 ILM 1322 (1995 UNDROIT Convention).
[53] 1995 UNIDROIT Convention, 2nd recital: 'Convinced of the fundamental importance of the protection of cultural heritage and of cultural exchanges for promoting understanding between peoples, and the dissemination of culture for the wellbeing of humanity and the progress of civilisation.'
[54] UNESCO Universal Declaration on Cultural Diversity (adopted 2 November 2001).
[55] ibid, art 7.

This provision recognizes both the historic function of heritage and links the instrument to UNESCO's founding goal, striving for peace through mutual, cultural understanding.[56]

II. Heritage Functions and Their Application to Human Rights

A. Heritage Functions Related to Human Rights

Heritage functions under international cultural heritage law relate to a number of different human rights, in particular cultural rights,[57] for which heritage can play an important role. These rights most commonly attributed to the category of cultural rights[58] are, in order of their appearance in the ICESCR: the right to education;[59] the right to participate in cultural life;[60] the right to enjoy the benefits of scientific progress and its applications;[61] an author's right to benefit from his work;[62] and the freedom to undertake scientific research and creative activity.[63] Apart from these five component rights, cultural rights also include the freedom of members of a minority to enjoy their own culture,[64] as well as the freedom of religion.[65]

The following discussion focuses on one particular cultural right: the right to participate in the cultural life enshrined in Art 15(1)(a) ICESCR. It is an essential part of cultural rights and has been given further shape by the Committee on Economic, Social and Cultural Rights (CESCR) in its General Comment No 21 on the right of everyone to take part in cultural life.[66] Yet, to show that connections

[56] The need for cross-cultural communication is also emphasized in UNESCO Universal Declaration on Cultural Diversity, 7th recital preamble, art 2.

[57] On the difficulty of classifying cultural rights due to different understandings of the term culture, see Yvonne Donders, *Towards a Right to Cultural Identity?* (Intersentia 2002) 73–79.

[58] A different, well-known categorization of cultural rights can be found in the Fribourg Declaration on Cultural Rights [7 May 2007].

[59] ICESCR, art 13.

[60] ibid, art 15(1)(a).

[61] ibid, art 15(1)(b).

[62] ibid, art 15(1)(c). See CESCR General Comment No 17 on the right of everyone to benefit from the protection of the moral and material interests resulting from any scientific, literary, or artistic production of which he or she is the author (12 January 2006) UN Doc E/C.12/GC/17; Dominic McGoldrick, 'Culture, Cultures, and Cultural Rights' in Mashood Baderin and Robert McCorquodale (eds), *Economic, Social and Cultural Rights in Action* (OUP 2002).

[63] ICESCR, art 15(3). See Elissavet Stamatopoulou, 'Background Paper for the Day of General Discussion: Right to take part in cultural life (article 15(1)(a) of the Covenant)' (2008) UN Doc E/C.12/40/9 (9 May 2008) 3.

[64] ICESCR, art 27.

[65] ibid, art 18(1).

[66] CESCR, General Comment No 21. See Section II.B.1 below.

to other rights do exist, the table below indicatively links functions to a number of economic, social, and cultural rights, as well.

Function	Related Right(s)
Aesthetic	The right to participate in cultural life,[67] author's right to benefit from his work.[68]
Scientific	The right to enjoy the benefits of scientific progress and its applications,[69] right to education,[70] the right to an adequate standard of living as far as outcomes of scientific research have or could have an impact on this.[71]
Historic-educative	The right to education.[72] In making different types of cultural heritage accessible through eg tourism this function indirectly links to the right to work[73] as well.
Contributing to an individual's identity (formation)	Freedom of members of a minority to enjoy their own culture,[74] the right to participate in cultural life.[75]
Contributing to environmental protection or sustainable development	On a global scale arguably an individual's right to health,[76] where sustainable development in lesser developed countries is concerned also the right to food,[77] and the right to shelter.[78] Where natural areas are protected that fulfill a religious function, the freedom of religion[79] is also affected.
Religious	Freedom of religion, freedom of members of a minority to enjoy their own culture.[80]

[67] ICESCR, art 15(1)(a).
[68] ibid, art 15(1)(c).
[69] ibid, art 15(1)(b).
[70] ibid, art 13(1).
[71] ibid, art 11(1).
[72] ibid, art 13(1).
[73] ibid, art 6(1).
[74] ICCPR, art 27.
[75] ICESCR, art 15(1)(a).
[76] ibid, art 12(1).
[77] ibid, art 11(1).
[78] ibid, art 11(1).
[79] ICCPR, art 18(1).
[80] ibid, art 27.

Function	Related Right(s)
Contributing to cultural exchange thus strengthening peace and human dignity	The right to participate in cultural life,[81] human dignity as a core value inherent in all human rights.[82]

One commonly accepted method for deducing State obligations that arise under human rights treaties is the respect/protect/fulfill approach. This three-fold typology has been developed by a number of individuals, and was first applied by the CESCR,[83] which has emphasized its applicability to all human rights.[84] In 1997, the Maastricht Guidelines on Violations of Economic, Social and Cultural Rights emphasized that the tripartite typology (protect, respect, fulfill) applies to all human rights, and that 'the failure to perform any one of these three obligations constitutes a violation of such rights'.[85] Since then, the application of this typology to all human rights has been affirmed in numerous other instances, inter alia by Shaheed, the former Special Rapporteur in the Field of Cultural Rights.[86]

This method distills three types of State obligations: States have negative duties to refrain from violating a right themselves (duty to respect a right), as well as a duty to protect an individual from violations by others (duty to protect). The last type is arguably the broadest in scope. It imposes a positive obligation, namely the obligation to ensure that individuals enjoy the substance of a right (duty to fulfill).[87] While the specific content of each type of obligation differs depending on the (category of the) right in question, obligations exist under each dimension. With respect to the ICESCR, this means that a State must show 'measurable progress' with regard to the fulfill dimension, specifically evidence that it is taking active

[81] ICESCR, art 15(1)(a).

[82] ICCPR, ICESCR common preamble recital 1: 'Considering that … recognition of the inherent dignity and of the equal and inalienable rights of all members of the human family is the foundation of freedom, justice and peace in the world'.

[83] Initially in the context of a study on the right to food in 1989, see para 15, n 1 in CESCR, General Comment No 12 on substantive issues arising in the implementation of the International Covenant on Economic, Social and Cultural Rights (12 May 1999) UN Doc E/C.12/1999/5.

[84] ibid, para 15 ('The right to adequate food, *like any other human right*, imposes three types or levels of obligations on states parties' (emphasis added)); Donders (n 59) 87.

[85] Maastricht Guidelines on Violations of Economic, Social and Cultural Rights (Maastricht, 22–26 January 1997) s II.6 <http://www1.umn.edu/humanrts/instree/Maastrichtguidelines_.html> accessed 1 November 2018.

[86] Shaheed (n 9) para 65.

[87] CESCR, General Comment No 12 para 15.

steps[88] toward improving the protection of the right in question, under the concept of progressive realization.[89] The typology aids in identifying the respective obligations under existing rights. Once these obligations are identified it is possible to identify concrete links between cultural heritage and human rights by means of the functions approach that go beyond the mere recognition of the importance of cultural heritage to human rights. By concretizing State obligations through the respect/protect/fulfill typology and identifying the heritage functions which are protected by means of the functions approach, human rights obligations can be considered more explicitly in the protection of cultural heritage under international cultural heritage law.

B. Distilling State Obligations under the Right to Participate in Cultural Life

1. General Comment No 21 and the report of the independent expert on cultural rights on the access to cultural heritage

In its General Comment No 21, the monitoring body of the ICESCR gave its authoritative interpretation on the right of everyone to take part in cultural life.[90] It highlighted the connection between the right to cultural life[91] provided in the ICESCR and other cultural rights enshrined in the ICESCR, including the right to education.[92] CESCR identified education as the vehicle for a culture to transmit language and religion and highlighted its contribution to a better 'mutual understanding and respect for cultural values'.[93] The latter mirrors one of UNESCO's core concerns in international cultural heritage law—the presumption that heritage preservation will ultimate lead to better mutual understanding and thus peace. Unfortunately, the examined UNESCO instruments do not specify the precise connection between heritage protection and an increased mutual understanding. Possibly, the organization, like the committee, values the existence of heritage as an education source.[94]

[88] Affirmed in connection with art 15(1)(a) by General Comment No 21 para 45, on 'deliberate and concrete measures'.

[89] ICESCR art 2(1) ICESCR; CESCR, General Comment No 3 on the Nature of States Parties' Obligations (14 December 1990) UN Doc E/1991/23 (1991); Olivier de Schutte, *International Human Rights Law: Cases, Materials, Commentary* (CUP 2010) 500–12 (exploring implications of concept).

[90] CESCR, General Comment No 21.

[91] ICESCR, art 15(1)(a).

[92] CESCR, General Comment No 21 para 2.

[93] ibid.

[94] Thomas Nygren, 'UNESCO and Council of Europe Guidelines and History Education in Sweden 1960–2002' (2011) 2 Education Inquiry 37, 40–41. Nygren traces the focus on history teaching and its role for mutual understanding and peace in UNESCO materials. One of the three goals of history teachings asserted in these materials was the safeguarding of local cultural heritage, which was considered crucial to identification and unity formation. ibid.

The Committee clarified that the right to take part in cultural life is at its core a 'cultural choice' of the individual, the individual in association with others, or the individual within a community or group.[95] The right to take part in cultural life entails positive and negative State obligations. On the one hand, a State may not interfere 'with the exercise of cultural practices and with access to cultural goods and services'[96] unless the action can be classified as a permitted limitation. On the other hand, it must take steps to secure the necessary 'preconditions for participation, facilitation and promotion of cultural life' and 'access to and preservation of cultural goods'.[97] Facilitating or promoting access may mean supporting digitalization of heritage, or ensuring accessibility of cultural institutions (both physically and financially). Such positive obligations are of the utmost importance to international cultural heritage law and the work of UNESCO in the cultural sector because this is an area in which human rights obligations and heritage legislation and policies overlap.

The General Comment considers the position of cultural heritage in several instances. Moreover, it refers to a State's duty to take action that includes the preservation of 'cultural goods'.[98] The scope of protected 'cultural goods' is clarified by means of a non-exhaustive list and includes such diverse forms of cultural heritage as libraries, museums, sports stadiums, the arts 'in all forms', as well as 'the shared open spaces essential to cultural interaction' and various forms of intangible cultural heritage.[99] 'Preservation' is not specified further, but as the term 'cultural goods' appears predominantly in connection with the need to grant access to these resources,[100] and preservation only once (also in connection with 'access'[101]), one can deduce that the goal of preservation is the continued accessibility of diverse forms of heritage for present and presumably also future generations. Under this dimension, preservation and heritage protection become part of a State's duty to implement the ICESCR's provision on the right to cultural life.[102] The need to guarantee access has other implications as well, notably the need to ensure that museums and theaters are available to all[103] (which includes both economic accessibility, so that they remain affordable for all residents of a territory regardless of income differences, and physical accessibility for all residents)[104] and the obligation to preserve natural areas and maintain parks.

[95] CESCR, General Comment No 21 paras 7, 9.
[96] ibid, para 6.
[97] ibid.
[98] ibid, para 6.
[99] ibid, para 16(a).
[100] CESCR, General Comment No 21 para 6, para 15(b), para 49(b), para 70.
[101] ibid, para 6: 'ensuring preconditions for participation, facilitation and promotion of cultural life, and access to and preservation of cultural goods'.
[102] ICESCR, art 15(1).
[103] CESCR, General Comment No 21 para 16(a).
[104] ibid, para 16(b).

The General Comment issued by the committee in 2009 is complemented by the report of Shaheed on the right of access to and enjoyment of cultural heritage.[105] In the report, she remarks upon the shift in international cultural heritage law away from a pure protection approach toward 'the protection of cultural heritage as being of crucial value for individuals and communities in relation to their cultural identity'.[106] Shaheed evaluated and identified the 2003 ICH Convention as the instrument that allowed an increased recognition of the role of (intangible) cultural heritage for individual and communal identity.[107] Specifically, the increased attention to safeguarding cultural heritage important to the community has emphasized the link between cultural heritage and cultural identity in general.

However, recognition of the link between cultural identity and cultural heritage already existed in earlier international cultural heritage law instruments, albeit less explicitly and in a non-binding instrument: the 1976 Recommendation on Participation by the People at Large in Cultural Life and their Contribution to It.[108] The recommendation considers the position of cultural heritage in two situations. First, States are advised to adopt legislation or change it in order to 'reconcile the duty to protect and enhance everything connected with the cultural heritage, traditions and the past with the need to allow the endeavours of the present and the modem outlook to find expression'.[109] This suggests that a State must not encourage fossilization of culture through rigid preservation of past traditions but also allow contemporary, modern forms of cultural expressions. The second mention of cultural heritage is in the need to 'awaken [the] interest [of younger generations] in their cultural heritage'.[110] This statement attributes heritage to a segment of society, arguably seeking to strengthen the linkage between their identity and heritage. The 1976 UNESCO Recommendation was undoubtedly a promising step at the time. Apart from the above features, the Recommendation also includes several other provisions that connect to human rights.[111]

The linkage between human rights and cultural heritage has existed thus within international cultural heritage law for decades. The difficulty was a missing recognition of the linkage between the two fields in binding instruments of international law.[112] Authoritative human rights sources have recognized the connection

105 Compare Shaheed (n 9).

106 ibid, para 20.

107 ibid.

108 1976 UNESCO Recommendation (n 32).

109 ibid, para 4(p).

110 ibid, para 16.

111 See eg, ibid, para 4(b) ('provide effective safeguards for free access to national and world cultures by all members of society without distinction or discrimination based on race, colour, sex, language, religion, political convictions, national or social origin, financial situation or any other consideration and so to encourage free participation by all sections of the population in the process of creating cultural values').

112 The author is unsure whether Shaheed's statement 'the more recent the instrument, the stronger the link with rights of individuals and communities' (Shaheed (n 9) para 20) reflects the nature of State obligations imposed by the 2005 Convention on the Protection and Promotion of the Diversity of

explicitly and have begun to consider heritage in human rights terms. The functions approach could be one way to do the reverse within international cultural heritage law. As one example, to be able to read the objective of protecting heritage within the 1972 World Heritage Convention to mean to protect its educative function in a way to support State obligations under the right to education, we first need to have identified the respective State obligations under the relevant human rights treaties. To identify State obligations enshrined in cultural rights provision, the chapter adopts the respect/protect/fulfill typology, which is commonly accepted within international human rights law.

2. Obligations related to heritage under the respect/protect/fulfill typology

The right to participate or take part in cultural life, according to the CESCR, is characterized by three 'main components . . . (a) participation in, (b) access to, and (c) contribution to cultural life'.[113] Obligations under the respect/protect/fulfill typology exist for all three components. The first component mainly relates to the freedom of the individual to make cultural choices, such as to identify himself or herself as part of the community and to live accordingly.[114] For the State, this implies both negative and positive duties, also in relation to the treatment of cultural objects: Unless permitted under the limitation clauses contained in the ICESCR,[115] a State may not interfere with individual or communal cultural choices, even if they derogate from the desired 'national' culture. This corresponds to the duty to respect the right. Thus, if a community uses a particularly valuable cultural object, the State may only nominate the object to be of national importance and expropriate it if (a) a careful evaluation has deemed the preservation of cultural heritage to be a legitimate aim under national law, (b) the limitation is in line with the nature of the right, and (c) the expropriation is strictly necessary (specifically, there is no other less invasive measure available). This latter act of expropriation might even be necessary to protect the right to participate in cultural life of other individuals, depending on the importance of the object and the threat to its integrity through continued use. This is merely one example to show that steps to protect particular forms of heritage under national implementations of international cultural heritage law (which includes the preliminary step of identification) should only be taken after careful examination of *all* related obligations and rights affected.

The second component of the right, access to a culture, is an essential element of cultural rights.[116] It includes not only the right of an individual to have access to his

Cultural Expressions, which seems to be more an instrument designed to excuse State deviations from WTO law than a true reflection of individual rights in the area of cultural expressions. See also Vrdoljak (n 4) 149 on the nature of the 2005 Convention, 151 on the continued dominance of the State.

[113] CESCR, General Comment No 21 para 15.
[114] ibid, para 15(a).
[115] ICESCR, arts 4–5.
[116] Barth (n 8) 80.

or her own culture, but also to have access to the culture 'of others through education and information, and to receive quality education and training with due regard for cultural identity'.[117] This includes the right to 'benefit from the cultural heritage and the creation of other individuals and communities'.[118] With regard to minority or indigenous cultural heritage, the Committee has highlighted the need for States to respect the indigenous right to control and protect their cultural heritage (which amounts to a duty to respect as provided in the United Nations Declaration on the Rights of Indigenous Peoples.[119] If we apply the threefold typology, the obligation to respect individual access to cultural heritage may require a State to balance how granting access to particular forms of cultural heritage may affect access rights of others. Measures to ensure access to cultural heritage can, inter alia, include the obligation to take steps for the preservation of sacred sites,[120] budgetary support for specific programs that are aimed at increasing cultural programs in remote geographical areas or support for digital presentations of heritage to make it more accessible. The importance of access to cultural heritage was also emphasized in the report by the Special Rapporteur in the Field of Cultural Rights who observes that '[a]ccess to and enjoyment of cultural heritage are interdependent concepts—one implying the other'.[121]

Under the third component of the right, the individual has a right to (choose) to contribute to the cultural life of the community.[122] The threefold typology then implies that the State is prohibited from interfering with these spiritual/material/intellectual/emotional forms of expression. Moreover, the State has to protect the individual from undue outside interference with his or her rights. This obligation could, for example, include the adoption of guidelines for research where it affects minorities or indigenous peoples or their heritage. These obligations are complemented by the duty to provide the general conditions necessary for the individual to make cultural choices, that is to say to freely exercise her right to participate in the cultural entity of her choice.

As the analysis above has shown, cultural rights are multidimensional and require an adaptable implementation. This adaptability of human rights norms contrasts the dominance of State interests[123] and the one-sided focus of many international cultural heritage law instruments on the physical preservation/protection of (selected objects) and cultural expressions. This adaptability[124] can be

[117] CESCR, General Comment No 21 para 15(b).
[118] ibid.
[119] Annex to UNGA Res 61/295 (13 September 2007) art 31.
[120] Also, in relation to religion, S James Anaya, *Indigenous Peoples in International Law* (2nd edn, OUP 2004) 139.
[121] Shaheed (n 9) para 58.
[122] CESCR, General Comment No 21 para 15(c).
[123] Compare Vrdoljak (n 4) 144–47, 151.
[124] The committee develops these nuances through the terms acceptability, adaptability, and appropriateness, see General Comment No 21 para 16(c), (d), (e).

used to render international cultural heritage law more adaptable to contemporary challenges when we link the two areas more expressly.

C. Connecting the Protection of Cultural Heritage to the Right to Participate in Cultural Life

Having explored the functions of cultural heritage that are recognized within international cultural heritage law, and (some of) the obligations that States encounter within human rights law, one can apply the method to link the fields more explicitly. As one example, let us take the 1970 UNESCO Convention, an instrument adopted at a time when cultural rights were not a principal concern for many States that sought to combat the illicit traffic of heritage. The power to decide which heritage object is worthy of protection, and how, rests with the State.[125] The Convention makes clear that cultural heritage can be deemed worthy of protection for any number of reasons,[126] and these correspond to a number of functions, including the scientific and religious ones. The 1970 UNESCO Convention also lists a number of measures a State can take to protect heritage against illicit trade.[127]

This is in effect the case for most international cultural heritage law instruments. International cultural heritage law enables, empowers, or requires a State to take a number of different measures: measures to identify the heritage and, once the dangers that it faces are identified, measures to protect it. To be in line with international human rights law, the measures thus taken should be evaluated in light of their impact on the enjoyment of human rights. One way of doing so is to evaluate whether the heritage fulfills a specific function for an individual, a group, a community, or a people. The next step would be to consider if the heritage function is covered by an existing human right. Then the measure that the State is about to take under international cultural heritage law needs to align with its obligations to protect the human rights function of the heritage in question. The good thing is that international cultural heritage law instruments already recognize that heritage has different roles to play in everyday life. These instruments do thus already recognize some of the human rights functions that cultural heritage encompasses. The duty to protect heritage under international cultural heritage law can then be understood as the duty to protect the human rights functions of heritage.

There is an overlap between those functions of cultural heritage that are human rights functions and the duty under human rights treaties to fulfil a specific human right. This can, for example, be seen in the right to participate in cultural life. As was highlighted above, the right to participate in cultural life implies a cultural choice

125 1970 UNESCO Convention, arts 1, 2(1).
126 ibid, art 1.
127 ibid, art 5.

(by the individual or the community). Depending on the context, positive State action may be necessary to stimulate the continued existence of a culture in order to protect cultural choices of individuals who are members of a non-dominant culture. The protection of heritage in international cultural heritage law respectively can be motivated by a desire to increase the available resources for individuals to enjoy creative processes (inter alia through a plurality of available cultures which enrich each other). The protection of heritage then requires a State to ensure the framework necessary for the individual (non-dominant) culture to flourish. This connection is most apparent in the safeguarding of intangible cultural heritage under the 2003 UNESCO Convention. The steps taken to protect heritage as a cultural resource are measures which a State may take in order to fulfill the right to cultural life as provided in the ICESCR.[128]

Conclusion

The exploration of a functions approach to the protection of cultural heritage has centered on cultural rights and, more specifically, on the obligations arising out of the right to take part in the cultural heritage in connection with a State's duty to protect cultural heritage under international cultural heritage law. Further duties arise in connection with the duty to protect or safeguard cultural heritage under international cultural heritage law in connection with human rights, an issue beyond the scope of this chapter. The gap that was caused by the fragmented legislation of international cultural heritage law and the long-time treatment of the two areas as two distinct areas of international law (as far as binding instruments of international law) can be bridged. To do so, the remaining obligations arising out of other human rights that have already been examined in parts by various experts and different human rights bodies will need to be mapped out systematically. Moreover, a bridging of the two fields, and an interpretation of a State's duty to protect cultural heritage in light of its human rights obligations, would result in a growing influence of the interpretations and observations delivered by human rights monitoring bodies on international cultural heritage law—at least where the rights connect to cultural heritage through the heritage functions that are protected through the instrument. Considering cultural heritage in terms of human rights norms obligations is a trend which can already be detected in the reports adopted by human rights actors, notably both UN Special Rapporteurs in the Field of Cultural Rights.[129]

[128] ICESCR, art 15(1)(a).
[129] Shaheed (n 9); Bennoune (n 9); UNHRC 'Report of the Special Rapporteur in the field of cultural rights Karima Bennoune' (2017) UN Doc A/72/155, para 5.

Where international cultural heritage law has moved away from considering the preservation of the object in isolation toward an appreciation of the role of cultural heritage within a community, this shift has frequently been related to indigenous cultural heritage. This is due both to the centrality of cultural objects and traditional cultural expressions to the continued existence of indigenous peoples and the inclusion of indigenous rights in human rights discussions within the United Nations. Examples for this trend include the 1995 UNIDROIT Convention's consideration of the role of sacred or communally important objects[130] and the inclusion of communities through the World Heritage Committee's Five Cs initiative—focusing on Credibility, Conservation, Capacity-building, Communication, and Communities—into the strategic objectives of the UNESCO World Heritage program.[131] The importance of forms of intangible cultural heritage in many non-dominant cultures, notably indigenous cultures, has also resulted in the consideration of the role of heritage within a community under the 2003 ICH Convention.[132] Unfortunately, as a result of the dominance of States in the adoption of binding international instruments, international cultural heritage law has not taken further steps to account for the role of cultural heritage to both the individual and the community. These are, however, much needed. An example of the continued dominance of State interests over human rights can be seen in the 2005 Cultural Diversity Convention, especially if compared to the express inclusion of human rights in the corresponding soft law instrument.[133] By recognizing the human rights functions that heritage fulfills, a consistent heritage policy at the international and national, regional, and local level will need to consider these dimensions—which will then lead to a better protection of minority, as well as indigenous, access and participation rights.

Examining cultural heritage by means of the functions approach provides us with several insights. First, if we accept that cultural heritage fulfills a number of different, valued functions, that heritage also fulfills functions for the enjoyment of specific human rights, and only those functions that are in accordance with international human rights standards should be pursued in international cultural heritage law. Moreover, protection of heritage then must mean protection of heritage in a manner that is conducive to the protection of related human rights. This being said, rejecting the functions approach does not, of course, negate the continued existence of State obligations under cultural heritage law and international

[130] 1995 UNIDROIT Convention, arts 3(8), 5(3)(d), 7(2). Initial inclusion occurred due to efforts of representatives from Canada and Australia, see Lyndel Prott, *Commentary on the UNIDROIT Convention* (IAL 1997) 40.

[131] World Heritage Committee Decision 31 COM 13 B [2007]. The Five Cs refer to Credibility, Conservation, Capacity-building, Communication, and Communities.

[132] 2003 ICH Convention, art 1(1) 'the "intangible cultural heritage" means the practices . . . that communities, groups and, in some cases, individuals recognize as part of *their* cultural heritage' (emphasis added).

[133] UNESCO Universal Declaration on Cultural Diversity (n 56).

human rights law. Similarly, the proposed model does not create obligations where none exists under international law. Last, the proposition amounts to an interpretation method that is, in its nature, teleological. This means that it goes beyond a purely textual method of interpretation[134] and beyond the original intention of the drafters as identifiable by the preparatory works to a treaty. However, as has been laid out in this chapter, there are advantages in doing so, notably a protection of cultural heritage that is more consistent with other sectors of public international law. It is also more consistent with the reasons which underlie heritage protection, namely the functions that heritage is seen to fulfill.

If we accept the proposition that the functions or values that are appreciated in cultural heritage underlie its protection efforts, this proposition opens up another perspective for the evaluation of State reports on the implementation of human rights, as far as the protection of rights that relate to cultural heritage functions is concerned: if States do not protect connected human rights (or respect some elements but not the obligations arising out of the respective human right with regard to cultural heritage), then they must value certain heritage functions more than others—or else they act in a disorganized, inconsistent fashion. In this sense an examination of the human rights record of a State cannot only yield information on the depth to which cultural heritage is protected, but also in how far it pursues a policy of strengthening a national cultural identity by means of legislative, executive, and administrative action (possibly at the cost of minority or indigenous cultures). The evaluation of such information can aid in stimulating a debate amongst all actors on the national (or regional or local) level about the desired role of heritage within society.

Third, by interpreting the protective provisions of different international cultural heritage law instruments broadly, as proposed in Section II.B.1., it is possible to bridge the gap created by the different natures of international cultural heritage law and international human rights law. This interpretative method can have positive consequences not only for the human rights record of individual States, but it also allows international cultural heritage law to become more holistic in its approach by truly accepting the role of cultural heritage in different cultures and communities. This will entail, inter alia, a better protection of minority and indigenous rights in the implementation of international cultural heritage law instruments.

[134] *Territorial Dispute (Libyan Arab Jarnahiriyal v Chad)* (Judgment) [1994] ICJ Rep 6, para 41 ('Interpretation must be based above all upon the text of a treaty').

14

Developments Concerning Immunity from Seizure for Cultural State Property on Loan

Nout van Woudenberg

Introduction

A previous survey of developments in domestic regimes and in international law regarding protection for borrowed cultural objects led to the assertion that 'a relatively young rule of customary international law exists, to the extent that cultural objects belonging to foreign States and on temporary loan for an exhibition are immune from seizure'.[1] This conclusion nonetheless was subjected to the caveat that the rule is not yet firmly established or well defined in all its aspects, and that the rule is subject to various limitations.[2] The rule did not extend to those cultural objects that have been the subject of a serious breach of an obligation arising under a peremptory norm of general international law, or to those that were subject to return obligations under international or European law.[3] Six years later (at the time of writing), it is time to see how this has emerged further; has the rule of customary international law been strengthened since then, and if so, to what extent? Or have there been other developments of interest?

What is meant by immunity from seizure? For the purposes of this contribution, immunity from seizure means a legal guarantee that cultural objects on temporary loan from another State are protected against any form of seizure during the loan period.[4] The term is used in a comprehensive way, as in the 2004 UN Convention on Jurisdictional Immunities and Their Property (2004 UN Convention),[5] discussed more fully below, when using the term 'measures of constraint'.[6] The reason for providing cultural objects on loan with immunity from seizure is to ensure that

[1] Nout van Woudenberg, *State Immunity and Cultural Objects on Loan* (Brill 2012) 444.
[2] ibid.
[3] ibid.
[4] ibid 4. But there are other definitions of the same term. ibid 2–3.
[5] UNGA Res 59/38 (2 December 2004) UN Doc A/Res/59/38. See also van Woudenberg (n 1) 59–87.
[6] This includes every form of attachment, execution, sequestration, forfeiture, requisition, foreclosure, replevin, detinue, etc.

Nout van Woudenberg, Developments Concerning Immunity from Seizure for Cultural State Property on Loan In: *Intersections in International Cultural Heritage Law*. Edited by Anne-Marie Carstens and Elizabeth Varner. © Oxford University Press 2020. The several contributors DOI: 10.1093/oso/9780198846291.003.0015

cultural objects on loan will not be subject to seizure while in the borrower's jurisdiction and thereby to prevent cultural objects on loan from being used as 'hostages' in trade and/or ownership disputes.[7] This facilitates the lending of cultural objects for temporary exhibitions and overcomes the reluctance of lenders to send their cultural objects into a foreign jurisdiction.[8]

I. UN Convention on Jurisdictional Immunities of States and Their Property

In regard to codified rules on State immunity, the 2004 UN Convention on Jurisdictional Immunities of States and Their Property[9] can be considered as the most relevant global instrument. Yet, the 2004 UN Convention has not entered into force, although the number of States Parties is slowly but steadily growing and has reached twenty-two.[10] Thirty States Parties are needed for the 2004 UN Convention to enter into force.

It is important to recall that the Preamble expressly refers to State immunity as a principle of customary international law.[11] The 2004 UN Convention contains a provision which lists the categories of State property that shall not be considered as property specifically in use, or intended for use, by the State for other than government non-commercial purposes. Consequently, this type of property is immune from seizure, unless the State to which the property belongs (a) has explicitly consented to the taking of such measures or (b) has allocated or earmarked the property for the satisfaction of the claim that is the object of the proceeding.[12] One of these categories, set out in Article 21, concerns 'property forming part of an exhibition of objects of scientific, cultural or historical interest and not placed or intended to be placed on sale'.[13] As stated previously,[14] the International Law Commission agreed to adopt Article 21 relating to property forming part of an exhibition without much discussion, dispute, or counterpoise.

It may be interesting to investigate why the number of States Parties, although increasing steadily, is growing so slowly, and why primarily European States

[7] van Woudenberg (n 1) 7.

[8] ibid. For the general rules of State immunity, see ibid (ch 3).

[9] United Nations Convention on Jurisdictional Immunities and Their Property (adopted 2 December 2004, UNGA Res 59/38) UN Doc A/Res/59/38, Annex. See also Nout van Woudenberg, 'Enhancing the Mobility of Collections in the European Union' in Andrzej Jakubowski, Kristin Hausler, and Francesca Fiorentini (eds), *Cultural Heritage in the European Union* (Brill 2019) 226–27.

[10] Since the publication of *State Immunity and Cultural Objects on Loan* in 2012, when the Convention counted thirteen States Parties, the following new States Parties can be welcomed: Czech Republic, Equatorial Guinea, Finland, Iraq, Italy, Latvia, Liechtenstein, Mexico, and Slovakia.

[11] 2004 UN Convention, first preambular paragraph.

[12] 2004 UN Convention, art 21.

[13] ibid.

[14] van Woudenberg (n 1) 104.

recently have become States Parties to the 2004 UN Convention. A reason could be that, as an assumed codification of already existing customary international law, States would consider it of too limited benefit to become a Party, leaving aside that codification gives more clarity and less room for interpretation than unwritten rules.[15]

On the other hand, as new rules of international law emerge and other rules may be adapted, it may also be the case that some States consider the text in the meantime as partly outdated. In that regard, the declaration by Norway at the time of ratification, regarding Article 18 of the Convention,[16] is interesting to note. That article, regarding State immunity from pre-judgment measures of constraint, is quite absolute in its wording and provides that no pre-judgment measures of constraint against the property of a State may be taken in connection with a proceeding before the court of another State, unless and except to the extent that the State has expressly consented to the taking of such measures, or the State has allocated or earmarked the property for the satisfaction of the claim which is the object of that proceeding.[17]

Unlike in Article 19, concerning immunity from post-judgment measures of constraint, Article 18 makes no distinction between property in use or not in use for commercial purposes. Norway declared that:

> [I]n cases where it has been established that property of a State is specifically in use or intended for use by the State for other than government non-commercial purposes and is in the territory of the State of the forum, it is the understanding of Norway that Article 18 does not prevent pre-judgment measures of constraint from being taken against property that has a connection with the entity against which the proceeding was directed.[18]

This declaration does not, however, touch upon 'our' category of property. The UN Convention provides, by definition, that property forming part of an exhibition of objects of scientific, cultural, or historical interest and not placed or intended to be placed on sale is not to be considered as property specifically in use, or intended for use, by the State for other than government non-commercial purposes.[19]

[15] O'Keefe and Tams come up with different possibilities as to why States may be reluctant to become a party to the 2004 UN Convention. Five possible reasons are given, sometimes contradictory. For example: 'some States believe the finer points of the Convention neither to correspond to current or foreseeable custom nor to reflect sound policy' or 'some States, satisfied that the process of the Convention's drafting has identified or crystallized customary international rules on State immunity that accord sufficiently with the rules, legislative or otherwise, already applied by their courts, are content to proceed as presently'. Roger O'Keefe and Christian J Tams (eds), *The United Nations Convention on Jurisdictional Immunities of States and Their Property: A Commentary* (OUP 2013) xl–xli.

[16] Norway Declaration to the 2004 UN Convention (27 March 2006).

[17] 2004 UN Convention, art 18.

[18] Norway Declaration (n 16).

[19] State-owned exhibits for industrial or commercial purposes are not covered.

II. Declaration on Jurisdictional Immunities of State-Owned Cultural Property

In 2013, the authorities of Austria and the Czech Republic launched an initiative aimed at developing a declaration in support of the recognition of the customary nature of the abovementioned 2004 UN Convention, and specifically Article 21, in order to guarantee the immunity of State cultural property on loan.[20] The Austrian and Czech officials were prompted by the so-called *Diag Human* case,[21] whereby in May 2011 a Viennese District Court on request by Diag Human[22] ordered the seizure of three cultural objects owned by the Czech Republic lent to an exhibition in the Austrian National Gallery Belvedere in Vienna.[23]

Although the Viennese District Court ordered that the seizure had to be lifted on the basis of the generally acknowledged rules of international law,[24] as the contents of the 2004 UN Convention provided sufficient indications of State practice to assume that a rule of customary international law immunizing cultural State property on loan exists,[25] the Czech and Austrian authorities wanted to prevent similar cases in the future. The Netherlands was approached with the request to join this initiative, and it replied positively to that request.[26]

Originally, the initiative was launched in March 2013 by the Czech Republic, supported by Austria and the Netherlands, at the forty-fifth meeting of the Committee of Legal Advisers on Public International Law of the Council of Europe (CAHDI).[27] Later that same year, a declaration, the Declaration on Jurisdictional Immunities of State Owned Cultural Property, was presented at the forty-sixth meeting of the CAHDI.[28] It was recalled that the declaration 'had been elaborated

[20] Committee of Legal Advisers on Public International Law of the Council of Europe (CAHDI), News: Declaration on Jurisdictional Immunities of State Owned Cultural Property <https://www.coe.int/en/web/cahdi/news-cahdi/-/asset_publisher/FL6bNvghtkKV/content/declaration-on-jurisdictional-immunities-of-state-owned-cultural-property> accessed 17 September 2018; van Woudenberg (n 9) 227–29.

[21] *D H SE v Czech Republic*, LG Wien, 21.6.2011, 72 E 1855/11 z-20 (Regional Court of Vienna for Civil Matters, 21 June 2011) (summarizing court order of attachment dated 16 May 2011). See also van Woudenberg (n 1) 302–05.

[22] A Liechtenstein incorporated company trading in blood plasma.

[23] See *D H SE v Czech Republic* (n 21). The objects concerned were a painting by the Czech artist Emil Filla, *Two Women* (coming from the Moravian Gallery in Brno); a painting by fellow Czech national Vincenc Beneš, *The Dancer*; and a sculpture by the Czech artist Otto Gutfreund, called *The Embrace* (both coming from the National Gallery in Prague).

[24] ibid.

[25] The verdict is also to be found in the database of the Council of Europe (CAHDI). See Database of the CAHDI 'The Immunities of States and International Organisations'—Contribution of Austria—Jurisprudence of 25/10/2011 <http://www.cahdidatabases.coe.int/contribution/details/76> accessed 17 September 2018.

[26] The Legal Adviser of the Ministry of Foreign Affairs of the Czech Republic approached for this goal the Legal Adviser of the Ministry of Foreign Affairs of the Kingdom of the Netherlands.

[27] Strasbourg, 25–26 March 2013.

[28] (adopted 16–17 September 2013) <https://rm.coe.int/declaration-on-immunities-en/168071bb2d> accessed 17 September 2018.

as a legally non-binding document expressing a common understanding on *opinio juris* of the basic rule that certain kinds of State property (cultural property on exhibition) enjoyed jurisdictional immunity'.[29]

The substantive part of the Declaration on Jurisdictional Immunities of State Owned Cultural Property reads as follows:

> In accordance with customary international law as codified in the Convention property of a State forming part of its cultural heritage or its archives or forming part of an exhibition of objects of scientific, cultural or historical interest, and not placed or intended to be placed on sale cannot be subject to any measure of constraint, such as attachment, arrest or execution, in another State; and therefore, such measures of constraint can only be taken if immunity is expressly waived for a clearly specified property by the competent national authorities of the State owning the property or if the property has been allocated or earmarked by that State for the satisfaction of the claim which is the object of the proceeding concerned.[30]

So far, this declaration has been signed by Austria, the Czech Republic, and the Netherlands, as well as by Latvia, Slovakia, Georgia, Romania, Estonia, Albania, the French Republic, Armenia, Belgium, Belarus, Luxembourg, Ireland, the Russian Federation, Hungary, Finland, Portugal, and the Holy See.[31]

According to the preambular paragraphs, the signatories of the declaration expressed their desire to strengthen international cooperation in the field of culture, their recognition that the exchange of cultural property significantly contributes to the mutual understanding of nations. They also declared their resolve to promote the mobility of State-owned cultural property through temporary cross-border loans for public display.[32] The signatories felt the need to reaffirm the international legal framework applicable to State-owned cultural property on public display in another State on the basis of the customary international law on State immunity, as codified in the 2004 UN Convention.[33]

It is worth mentioning that CAHDI in 2006 had already set up a database on immunity of States and international organizations.[34] The database is completed by States and international organizations on their legal practice, thus jurisprudence,

[29] CAHDI, News: Declaration on Jurisdictional Immunities of State Owned Cultural Property (n 20).

[30] Declaration on Jurisdictional Immunities of State Owned Cultural Property (n 28).

[31] Listed in the order of signing.

[32] Declaration on Jurisdictional Immunities of State Owned Cultural Property (n 28) preamble, 2nd and 3rd recitals).

[33] ibid, 4th recital.

[34] Strasbourg, 23–24 March 2006, 31st Meeting; Database on the Immunities of States and International Organisations <https://www.coe.int/en/web/cahdi/database-immunities> accessed 17 September 2018.

legislation, and regulations. The starting point was a 'Pilot Project of the Council of Europe on state practice regarding state immunities', established in 2001, with a view to examining judicial practice on immunity of States and international organizations in the member and observer States of the Council of Europe.[35] So far, forty-five Member States of the Council of Europe have provided information. In addition, Canada, Israel, Japan, and Mexico have contributed to the database. As it is of importance to keep the database up to date,[36] the Netherlands is soon adding new information.[37]

III. ILA Initiative to Come to a Convention for all Cultural Property on Loan

In 2010, the International Law Association (ILA), a multinational, professional law organization, agreed to take up the topic of immunity from seizure for cultural objects on loan. The ILA was motivated by several reasons. First, it was at that time not very clear to what extent cultural objects on loan could benefit from immunity from seizure.[38] Second, no international codified instrument on immunity for cultural objects yet existed, as the 2004 UN Convention had not yet entered into force. Third, while the 2004 UN Convention regards only cultural State property, the ownership of more and more cultural objects is being transferred from State-owned to privately owned foundations. In its deliberations, the ILA noted that although it may well be the case that an emerging rule of customary international law can be identified, according to which cultural objects belonging to foreign States and on temporary loan for an exhibition are immune from seizure, this rule only applies to cultural State property, and only in regard to immunity from seizure. Therefore, a future global convention on immunity from seizure for all kinds of cultural property on loan, regardless whether it involves State property or private property, was considered by the ILA as the most appropriate way forward.[39] Also, a future convention should incorporate the issue of immunity from suit, next to immunity from seizure.[40] However,

[35] ibid, Background.

[36] ibid.

[37] Jurisprudence by the Court of Cassation, dated 1 December 2017, holding that as from 1 January 2018 there is an *ex officio* obligation of Dutch courts to investigate whether a State or international organization is entitled to immunity from suit.

[38] That was also one of my incentives to write *State Immunity and Cultural Objects on Loan*: 'it occurred to me that it was not clear whether States actually knew what the current state of affairs was with regard to immunity from seizure of cultural objects belonging to foreign States while on loan abroad', van Woudenberg (n 1) xiii (Foreword).

[39] Nout van Woudenberg and James AR Nafziger, 'The Draft Convention on Immunity from Suit and Seizure for Cultural Objects Temporarily Abroad for Cultural, Educational or Scientific Purpose' (2014) 21 IJCP 481, 483–84; van Woudenberg (n 9), 235–39.

[40] In the Draft Convention, seizure was defined as any legal process which temporarily or permanently prevents the return of the cultural object to the sending State. Immunity from seizure was defined

concerning the latter, the proposed convention foresees an 'opt out' clause in regard to immunity from suit, as the incorporation may be a bridge too far for potential States Parties. After all, and generally speaking, immunity from seizure is more accepted than immunity from suit. When a State lifts its immunity from suit, the immunity from seizure is not automatically lifted as well. Also, in several jurisdictions, the competence of civil courts can be based on the mere presence of property in the forum State.

Consequently, the Draft Convention on Immunity from Suit and Seizure for Cultural Objects Temporarily Abroad for Cultural, Educational or Scientific Purpose (2014 ILA Draft Convention),[41] as approved by the ILA at its 2014 Conference in Washington, provides for a general rule of immunity from suit and seizure of (all) cultural objects which are temporarily present in a receiving State for cultural, educational, or scientific purposes. An exception to this general rule of immunity exists where the cultural object is placed or intended to be placed on sale, or the cultural object is owned, possessed, or otherwise controlled by the receiving State or a physical or legal person resident in the receiving State.[42]

It is clear why the ILA attached importance to this kind of convention, as the text expresses the conviction that

> [I]mmunity from seizure can prevent cultural objects temporarily abroad for cultural, educational or scientific purposes from being subject to trade, ownership or other disputes, and that immunity from seizure facilitates the mobility of cultural objects and overcomes the reluctance of lenders to send their cultural objects into a foreign jurisdiction where they might be subject to some form of judicial seizures.[43]

It was considered important that the granting of immunity under the Draft Convention should not be a means of facilitating the cross-border movement of cultural objects that have been illegally exported, stolen, looted, or acquired illicitly. For that reason, the Draft Convention states that immunity from seizure or suit does not apply in cases where the receiving State is bound by conflicting obligations under international or regional law, including EU law.[44] This conclusion

as the legal guarantee that cultural objects which are temporarily present in the receiving State for cultural, educational, or scientific purposes will be protected against any form of seizure while present in that State. There was no definition in the Draft Convention of immunity from suit, but art 4, para 1 of the Draft Convention shows that immunity from suit meant that the temporary presence of the cultural objects in the receiving State for cultural, educational, or scientific purposes should not form the basis of any legal process in the receiving State.

[41] Draft Convention on Immunity from Suit and Seizure for Cultural Objects Temporarily Abroad for Cultural, Educational or Scientific Purpose, annexed to ILA Res 3/2014 (April 2014).

[42] ibid, art 1.

[43] ibid, preamble, 9th recital.

[44] ibid, art 5.

accords with the earlier assertion that 'a rule of customary international law does not extend to those cultural objects which are already subject to other return obligations under international or European law'.[45]

Unfortunately, so far, the work of the ILA in this regard has not been taken up by other relevant institutions. ILA-Resolution 3/2014 requests the Secretary-General of the ILA to forward a copy of the Final Report, including the Draft Convention, to the UN Secretary-General, the Director-General of the United Nations Educational, Scientific and Cultural Organization (UNESCO), the Hague Conference of Private International Law, Comité Juridique (COJUR/EU), CAHDI, the Council of Europe, and other appropriate international and regional organizations, such as, for instance, the International Council of Museums (ICOM).[46] It was hoped that especially UNESCO would take up the mantle, so that it would then follow the same path as the 2001 UNESCO Convention on the Protection of the Underwater Cultural Heritage (2001 UCH Convention).[47] After all, the ILA initially provided a first draft of that convention: the 1994 ILA Draft Convention on the Protection of Underwater Cultural Heritage.[48] The 2001 UCH Convention counts meanwhile fifty-eight States Parties.[49]

However, around the time of adoption by the ILA of the Draft Convention on Immunity from Suit and Seizure for Cultural Objects Temporarily Abroad for Cultural, Educational or Scientific Purposes, a high-ranking UNESCO officer privately indicated that the chances that UNESCO would take up the Draft Convention within due time would be very limited, giving two reasons.[50] The first reason was that UNESCO would like to focus more on the proper implementation of, and compliance with, already existing international instruments, instead of creating new ones. The other reason regarded the budget: as the financial resources of UNESCO were limited, and were even decreasing,[51] States that were keen on discussing specific topics should provide for extra budgetary funding.

[45] van Woudenberg (n 1) 444.

[46] ILA Res 3/2014 (April 2014).

[47] UNESCO Convention on the Protection of the Underwater Cultural Heritage (adopted 2 November 2001, entered into force 2 January 2009) 2562 UNTS 3 (2001 UCH Convention).

[48] Patrick J O'Keefe and James AR Nafziger, 'Report: The Draft Convention on the Protection of the Underwater Cultural Heritage' (1994) 25 ODIL 391, 391–418. See UNESCO, 'The History of the 2001 Convention on the Protection of the Underwater Cultural Heritage' UNESCO Doc CLT/CIH/MCO/2010/PI/167 (undated) <http://unesdoc.unesco.org/images/0018/001894/189450E.pdf> accessed 17 September 2018.

[49] <http://www.unesco.org/eri/la/convention.asp?KO=13520&language=E&order=alpha> accessed 17 September 2018.

[50] Telephone conversation between the author and a high-ranking UNESCO officer who asked to remain anonymous (April 2014).

[51] After UNESCO voted to admit Palestine as a full member in 2011, the United States and Israel refused to fulfill their budgetary obligations, which form 25 percent of UNESCO's total budget (22 and 3 percent, respectively).

IV. United States Foreign Cultural Exchange Jurisdictional Immunity Clarification Act

In order to properly understand this recently adopted Act, it might be appropriate to go back a little into history. As explained in *State Immunity and Cultural Objects on Loan*,[52] the US Congress adopted the Foreign Sovereign Immunities Act (FSIA)[53] on 21 October 1976. Under the FSIA, a foreign State is presumed to have immunity from jurisdiction of the state and federal courts in the United States, unless one of the exceptions applies.[54] The most common exceptions to the general grant of State immunity by the FSIA are the commercial exception[55] and the expropriation exception.[56] The FSIA is the exclusive basis of jurisdiction in state and federal courts in the United States in suits involving foreign States.[57]

In Sections 1609 to 1611 of the FSIA, the United States established a general rule of immunity from measures of constraint, but created limited exceptions to that immunity in specified circumstances for assets located in the United States.[58] Section 1609 reads as follows:

> [S]ubject to existing international agreements to which the United States is a party at the time of enactment of this Act the property in the United States of a foreign State shall be immune from attachment, arrest and execution except as provided in Sections 1610 and 1611 of this chapter.[59]

Section 1610(a) identifies the exceptions to immunity from attachment or execution that are applicable to the property of all foreign States, whereas Section 1610(b) identifies additional exceptions applicable to an agency or instrumentality of a foreign State engaged in commercial activity in the United States.[60] Section

[52] van Woudenberg (n 1) 110.

[53] 28 USC s 1330, 1332(a), 1391(f) and 1601–1611 (1976).

[54] van Woudenberg (n 1) 114.

[55] 28 USC s 1605(a)(2). On the basis of Section 1605(a)(2), a foreign State shall not be immune from the jurisdiction of the courts of the United States or of the States in any case in which the action is based upon a commercial activity carried on in the United States by the foreign state; or upon an act performed in the United States in connection with a commercial activity of the foreign state elsewhere; or upon an act outside the territory of the United States in connection with a commercial activity of the foreign state elsewhere and that act causes a direct effect in the United States.

[56] 28 USC s 1605(a)(3). Section 1605(a)(3) states that a foreign State shall not be immune from the jurisdiction of state or federal courts in the United States in any case in which rights in property taken in violation of international law are in issue and that property or any property exchanged for such property is present in the United States in connection with a commercial activity carried on in the United States by the foreign state; or that property or any property exchanged for such property is owned or operated by an agency or instrumentality of the foreign state … and that agency or instrumentality is engaged in a commercial activity in the United States.

[57] van Woudenberg (n 1) 111.

[58] ibid 139.

[59] 28 USC s 1609.

[60] 28 USC s 1610(a)–(b). See also van Woudenberg (n 1) 140. Subparagraph (b) is followed by subparagraphs (c) to (g).

1611 considers 'certain types of property which are immune from executions'. Unlike the 2004 UN Convention, cultural objects are not mentioned as a separate category.[61]

The United States has a second legislative regime applicable to immunity from seizure for cultural objects. Since 1965, the United States has recognized immunity from seizure protection for cultural objects through the federal Immunity from Seizure Act,[62] 'an act to render immune from seizure under judicial process certain objects of cultural significance imported into the United States for temporary display or exhibition, and for other purposes', as the subtitle says.[63] The United States was the first State worldwide to enact this kind of legislation.[64]

Based on this federal Immunity from Seizure Act, the US authorities may issue a notice stating that a certain object is of cultural significance and that the temporary exhibition or display thereof within the United States is in the national interest, based on which the object is exempt from seizure. It has happened a few times in practice, however, that claimants have (unsuccessfully) tried to seize the works of art despite the notice, as discussed further below, for instance in the *Romanov v The Florida International Museum Inc.* case,[65] the *Magness v Russian Federation* case,[66] the *Delocque-Fourcaud v Los Angeles County Museum of Art* case,[67] and the *Deutsch v Metropolitan Museum of Art* case.[68]

The federal Immunity from Seizure Act should be seen as a means to assure foreign lenders that their cultural objects will be safely and promptly returned to them.[69] Although strictly speaking the Act only foresees immunity from seizure, the aim of the US authorities was broader. The Act had not only been introduced to prevent seizure, but also with the aim of preventing the filing of ownership claims or any judicial process for the purpose of or having the effect of depriving an exhibiting institution of custody or control of a cultural object.[70]

To sum up the dilemma: the federal Immunity from Seizure Act provides for immunity from seizure under US federal law, whereby the FSIA could provide for an exception to the grant of immunity, for instance when property of a foreign State

[61] 28 USC s 1611. See also van Woudenberg (n 1) 144–45.

[62] 22 USC s 2459.

[63] van Woudenberg (n 1) 153.

[64] ibid 152.

[65] *Romanov v The Florida International Museum, No 95-000128-CI-008 (Cir Ct Pinellas County, Florida 1995).*

[66] *Magness v Russian Federation* 84 F Supp 2d 1357 (SD Ala 2000).

[67] *Delocque-Fourcaud v Los Angeles County Museum of Art* Case No CV-03-5027-R(CTx) (CD Cal 2003).

[68] *Deutsch v Metropolitan Museum of Art*, No 04 Civ. 8587 (SDNY 2004) slip op 55.

[69] van Woudenberg (n 1) 156.

[70] See HR Rep No 89-1070 (1965); S Rep No 89-747 (1965). See also van Woudenberg (n 1) 153–54, 159–60, 169, 172, 180–81, 198–99.

is used for a commercial activity in the United States.[71] The question is which Act prevails, in the case of both Acts interfering with each other.

In the *Magness v the Russian Federation* case, the court was of the opinion that it did not need to determine the applicability of the exceptions in the FSIA, as seizure was not permitted in this case due to the federal Immunity from Seizure Act, 'which specifically forbids the use of judicial process to seize another country's works of art or objects of cultural significance'.[72] However, several years later, in the *Malewicz v City of Amsterdam* case,[73] the court stated that the FSIA and the federal Immunity from Seizure Act did not interfere with each other and were not inconsistent.[74] The US Executive Branch was of the opinion that the court should not read a statute in a manner that would undermine the purpose of another statute, if other plausible constructions were available, and blamed the court for exactly doing that. It stated in an Amicus Curiae brief that it was

> [N]ot consistent with notions of fair play and substantial justice to assure a foreign sovereign that artwork is not subject to jurisdiction in the United States by providing protection under Section 2459 and then to assert in personam jurisdiction over the sovereign for a claim based on that artwork.[75]

The US authorities pointed out that in regard to the federal Immunity from Seizure Act, the explicit aim of Congress was to ensure that foreign lenders would not be subject to jurisdiction when they loaned immunized artwork for temporary exhibits in the United States that the Executive Branch determined to be culturally significant and in the national interest.[76]

One conclusion presented in *State Immunity and Cultural Objects on Loan* was that as a result of the rulings of the court in the *Malewicz* case, it might turn out to be necessary for the US Congress to amend the federal Immunity from Seizure Act, in order to reflect more appropriately the purpose of the US Government in issuing immunity from seizure declarations. After all, this purpose was to provide foreign institutions and museums with the full protection they desire, so that it covers not only seizure, but any proceedings for damages or for any ownership-related

[71] Moreover, in the *Malewicz* case, we have seen that the court was of the opinion that the City of Amsterdam, by lending cultural objects to two United States cultural institutions, had been engaged in a commercial activity, although the exhibition was of a non-profit nature. van Woudenberg (n 1) 155–56.

[72] *Magness* (n 66) 1359.

[73] 362 F Supp 2d 298 (DDC 2005). See also *Malewicz v City of Amsterdam* 517 F Supp 2d 322 (DDC 2007) (decision on renewed motion to dismiss).

[74] 362 F Supp 2d 298, 311-12 (DDC 2005). See also van Woudenberg (n 1) 178.

[75] Brief for the United States as Amicus Curiae in Support of Appellant, *Malewicz v City of Amsterdam* No 07-5247, 2008 WL 2223219 (DC Cir 14 May 2008).

[76] Conversation between the author and legal representatives of the US State Department, 6 and 7 December 2010; van Woudenberg (n 1) 200.

interest whatsoever.[77] This did not happen. Instead, the Foreign Cultural Exchange Jurisdictional Immunity Clarification Act[78] was introduced to amend the FSIA.[79]

The Foreign Cultural Exchange Jurisdictional Immunity Clarification Act resulted from a series of bills that percolated through the legislative process for more than two years. On 25 March 2014, a bill for the Foreign Cultural Exchange Jurisdictional Immunity Clarification Act was first introduced into the US House of Representatives.[80] A revised bill was later passed by both houses of the federal legislature, and the Foreign Cultural Exchange Jurisdictional Immunity Clarification Act was signed into law by then-President Obama on 16 December 2016.[81] The Act provides sovereign immunity for a foreign State for certain works of art that are imported into the United States from the foreign State for exhibition or display; its aim is to reinforce the shield protecting foreign art on temporary loan to American museums from judicial action.[82] The Act amends the FSIA so that an activity in the United States of a foreign State associated with a culturally significant artwork, imported by American museums for temporary exhibition, would not be characterized as a 'commercial activity'.[83] This clarification should make it easier for US cultural and educational institutions to temporarily borrow cultural objects from foreign States.[84]

[77] Conversation between the author and legal representatives of the US State Department, 6 and 7 December 2010.

[78] Pub L No 114-319, 130 Stat 1618 (2016) (codified at 28 USC 1605(h)).

[79] HR Rep No 114-141 (2015). The Report in the US House of Representatives stated, as the purpose of the bill for the Foreign Cultural Exchange Jurisdictional Immunity Clarification Act:

> Under current law, a provision in the Foreign Sovereign Immunities Act (FSIA) discourages foreign governments from lending government-owned artwork and objects of cultural significance to U.S. museums and educational institutions for temporary exhibition or display. Foreign governments are discouraged from such lending by the possibility that it will open them up to litigation in U.S. courts for which they would otherwise be immune. This legislation fixes this problem by making a narrowly tailored change to FSIA. This change will make it easier for U.S. museums and educational institutions to borrow works of art and other objects from abroad, increasing Americans' opportunities for cultural and educational development.

ibid 1–2.

[80] HR 4292, 113th Cong (2014).

[81] Pub L No 114-319, 130 Stat 1618 (2016) (stating that '[t]his Act may be cited as the "Foreign Cultural Exchange Jurisdictional Immunity Clarification Act"' and amends the FSIA by adding in section 1605 new subsection (h) on 'Jurisdictional Immunity for Certain Art Exhibition Activities'). Earlier that year an interesting overview was published of the issue of immunity from seizure for loaned art in the United States: Colleen Murphy, 'Immunity of Loaned Art from Seizure in the United States and the Necessity of Legislative Reform to Ensure the Continuation of International Lending' (2016) 36 Rev of Litigation 105.

[82] Statement by the [White House] Press Secretary (16 December 2016) <https://obamawhitehouse.archives.gov/the-press-office/2016/12/16/statement-press-secretary-hr-710-hr-875-hr-960-hr-1150-hr-2726-hr-3218> (accessed 17 September 2018). See also Rick St Hilaire, 'Bipartisan Cultural Property Immunity Bill Passes the House Again' (updated 16 December 2016) <http://culturalheritagelawyer.blogspot.nl/2016/12/bipartisan-cultural-property-immunity.html> accessed 17 September 2018.

[83] Steve Chabot (House Bill Sponsor), 'Press Release: House Approves Chabot Legislation to Facilitate Art and Cultural Exchange' (9 June 2015).

[84] HR Rep No 114-141 (2015) 2.

The new Act amended part of the FSIA by the insertion of a new subsection, titled 'Jurisdictional Immunity for Certain Art Exhibition Activities'.[85] It excludes as a 'commercial activity' any activity in the USA of a foreign State, or of any carrier, associated with a temporary exhibition or display if

> an object of cultural significance is imported into the United States from any foreign State pursuant to an agreement for its temporary exhibition or display between a foreign State that is its owner or custodian and the United States or cultural or educational institutions within it; and
>
> the President, or the President's designee, has determined, with notice in the Federal Register, that such work is culturally significant and its temporary exhibition or display is in the national interest.[86]

However, there are some exceptions to the general rule above, whereby as a consequence no immunity is provided. In the discussions leading to the Act, for example, the US Congress paid special attention to victims of Nazi crimes: 'in recognition of the unprecedented scale of art theft by Nazi Germany and in light of the longstanding policy interest in ensuring that victims of Nazi crimes have an opportunity to pursue justice, the legislation also contains an exception for Nazi-era claims.'[87] The Foreign Cultural Exchange Jurisdictional Immunity Clarification Act further provides a second, more generic exception to the general rule of immunity from seizure, under the heading of 'Other Culturally Significant Works', and again for cases asserting jurisdiction under the FSIA's expropriation exception, for certain works that were confiscated or misappropriated after 1900.[88] For both the 'Nazi-era claims' and the 'Other Culturally Significant Works', the Act provides that a court must determine 'that the activity associated with the exhibition or display is commercial activity', as defined in the FSIA.[89]

Thus, Section 1605 of the FSIA was amended accordingly, so that no immunity is provided under the headings of 'Nazi-Era Claims' and 'Other Culturally Significant Works' in cases concerning rights in property taken in violation of international law in which the action is based upon a claim that the work was taken

> between 30 January 1933 and 8 May 1945 by the government of Germany or any government in Europe occupied by, assisted by, or allied with the German government; or

[85] 28 USC s 1605(h).
[86] ibid.
[87] HR Rep No 114-141 (2015) 2.
[88] 28 USC s 1605(h)(2)(B).
[89] 28 USC s 1605(h)(2)(A)(iii) and (B)(iv).

> after 1900 in connection with the acts of a foreign government as part of a systematic campaign of coercive confiscation or misappropriation of works from members of a targeted and vulnerable group.[90]

It is interesting, but also logical to see, that the abovementioned exception in regard to Holocaust confiscated cultural objects is in conformity with the conclusions stated in *State Immunity and Cultural Objects on Loan* and that (a rule of customary international law in regard to) immunity from seizure would not apply to Holocaust confiscated cultural objects.[91] With regard to cultural objects illicitly acquired during armed conflict,[92] the prevailing sentiment is indeed that such objects should not deserve protection.[93] Although not legally, but certainly morally, binding, many States have subscribed to the Washington Conference Principles,[94] the Vilnius Declaration,[95] or the Terezin Declaration.[96] These are (legally) non-binding principles aiming to assist in resolving issues in relation to Nazi-confiscated art. The principles aim to come up with moral and fair solutions in cases where the legal path can no longer be followed, for example because of the statute of limitations. Moreover, several States such as the Netherlands, Germany, Austria, France, as well as some other States, established Restitution or Spoliation Committees in order to restitute cultural objects to heirs of Second World War victims.[97]

Several States have also declared that Holocaust confiscated art would not be eligible for immunity. For instance, since 2012, the explanatory letter to the Guarantor's Declaration of the Netherlands contains the following text:

> The plunder of cultural objects during armed conflict is to be considered as a serious breach of an obligation arising under a peremptory norm of general international law. Under international law, States are obliged to refrain from recognizing such a situation as lawful and should not assist in the maintenance of that situation or its consequences. The provision of immunity for such illicitly acquired objects would be at odds with this obligation. The guarantor's

[90] HR 6477, 114th Cong (2014). See alsoHR Rep No 114-141 (2015): 'in recognition of the unprecedented scale of art theft by Nazi Germany and in light of the longstanding policy interest in ensuring that victims of Nazi crimes have an opportunity to pursue justice, the legislation also contains an exception for Nazi-era claims'.

[91] van Woudenberg (n 1) 435–42.

[92] When I refer to armed conflict, I refer to armed conflicts of the twentieth and twenty-first centuries, as the first international legally binding agreement in this regard originates from 1899.

[93] van Woudenberg (n 1) 439.

[94] Washington Conference Principles on Nazi-Confiscated Art, Washington (3 December 1998).

[95] Vilnius Forum Declaration, Vilnius (5 October 2000).

[96] Terezin Declaration of the Holocaust Era Assets Conference, Terezin (30 June 2009).

[97] See also Tabitha Oost, *In an Effort to do Justice? Restitution Policies and the Washington Principles* (Centre of Art, Law and Policy, University of Amsterdam 2012); Evelien Campfens (ed), *Fair and Just Solutions?* (Eleven International 2014).

declaration does, therefore, not apply to such cultural objects (including Judaica).[98]

V. Newly Developed Legislation in Regard to Immunity from Seizure for Cultural Objects on Loan

During the last years, only a few States have developed legislation in regard to immunity from seizure for cultural objects on loan.

A. Hungary

In 2012, Hungary adopted legislation on the special protection for cultural objects on loan.[99] The aim of the law is to ensure the widest possible cultural access. The Explanatory Note to the Act states in its general part that, although the current legal environment does not hinder the organization of temporary cultural exhibitions, it is becoming increasingly important for lenders from all around the world that a specific immunity rule is established. The law applies to cultural objects loaned for a temporary cultural, scientific, entertainment, or educational exhibition that does not exceed a period of twelve months.[100] It regards both foreign cultural State property, as well as foreign privately owned cultural objects. The Explanatory Note to the Act underlines that the protection offered is not limited to fine art, but that it covers a whole range of cultural goods, such as archaeological finds. This law does not protect cultural objects that are subject to a return or restitution procedure because of their illegal acquisition or transfer of ownership or their illicit import or export.[101] The law does not provide immunity from suit; it solely prevents the

[98] See also van Woudenberg (n 1) 279.

[99] Act No 95 of 2012 on the Special Protection of Borrowed Cultural Goods, adopted by the Hungarian Parliament on 26 June 2012. See English translation: <www.unesco.org/culture/natlaws/media/pdf/hungary/hu_act_protborrowedcltprop_12_entof> accessed 17 September 2018. The original language version can be found at: <http://njt.hu/cgi_bin/njt_doc.cgi?docid=151216.232571> accessed 17 September 2018. See also van Woudenberg (n 1) 331–32. Many thanks to Dr Henriett Galambos, Head of the legal department, Szépművészeti Múzeum, Budapest, Hungary. Also, many thanks to Boglárka Borbély for the translation of the Explanatory Note to the Act. See van Woudenberg (n 9) 233–34.

[100] There is one exception to that period: in the event that damage occurred during the time of exhibition, it can be extended by the period of time necessary for its restoration, with a maximum of four months.

[101] In this context, the Explanatory Note refers to Act No 80 of 2001 on the Return of Cultural Objects Unlawfully Removed, established in order to harmonize with Council Directive 93/7/EEC of 15 March 1993 on the return of cultural objects unlawfully removed from the territory of a Member State [1993] OJ L74/74; to Act No 28 of 2001 by which the 1995 UNIDROIT Convention on Stolen or Illegally Exported Cultural Objects had been promulgated; and to Decree-Law No 2 of 1979 on the Promulgation of the 1970 UNESCO Convention on the Means of Prohibiting and Preventing the Illicit Import, Export and Transfer of Ownership of Cultural Property.

imposition of coercive measures. The special protection is not provided automatically; an advance procedure needs to be followed where relevant information needs to be handed over, after which the National Office of Culture Heritage can issue a certificate (State guarantee) declaring the period of special protection.

Hungary has never explicitly stated that cultural State property on loan is immune from seizure under customary international law. It is not clear, therefore, whether the legislation in the Hungarian view should be seen as a codification of an existing rule of customary international law, or whether the legislation was enacted because of the assumed absence of such a rule. The apparent incentive for this legislation was 'the towering insurance costs connected to the Cézanne exhibition of the Szépművészeti Múzeum',[102] although not everyone in Hungary subscribes to that opinion.[103] Nevertheless, as the law also covers privately owned cultural property, it in any case provides an added value in regard to the protection of cultural objects, as privately owned objects in any case would not fall under a rule of customary international law. The exception to the immunity under Hungarian law, namely that there is no protection for cultural objects that are subject to a return or restitution procedure because of their illegal acquisition or transfer of ownership or their illicit import or export, is in conformity with my conclusion in regard to the exceptions to a rule of customary international law.[104]

B. Australia

Australia would not like to count on a rule of customary international law to provide immunity for cultural objects on loan.[105] The Foreign States Immunities Act entered into force in April 1986.[106] The application of foreign State immunity under the Act to cultural objects on loan is not clear and depends on the circumstances in each particular case, especially whether a cultural object is involved in a commercial transaction. Where the cultural objects belonging to a foreign State are involved in a commercial transaction and court proceedings arise, the objects will be immune from execution of a judgment, unless they constitute commercial property.[107] This only applies to cultural State property on loan, not to cultural property owned by other entities.

Until recently, Australia did not have a specific immunity from seizure regulation with regard to cultural objects loaned from abroad. The Protection of Movable

[102] Péter Inkei and Veronka Vaspál, Compendium: Cultural Policies and Trends in Europe. Country Profile: Hungary (December 2014) .

[103] Personal expressions by Hungarian art professionals to me.

[104] van Woudenberg (n 1) 444.

[105] ibid 419.

[106] Act of 16 December 1985, No 196 of 1985. Acts of the Parliament of the Commonwealth of Australia passed during the year 1985 (1996) vol II, 2696, 25 ILM 715.

[107] van Woudenberg (n 1) 357.

Cultural Heritage Act,[108] adopted in 2005, provided for a certain level of protection: if someone intended to import an Australian protected object (as defined by the Act) for a temporary exhibition and subsequently wanted to export the said object again, one could apply to the Australian authorities for a certificate of exemption authorizing the exportation of the object.[109] That is not, however, the same as immunity from seizure.

In 2013, Australia adopted the Protection of Cultural Objects on Loan Act[110] (Australian Act).[111] Over the years, more and more States worldwide adopted immunity from seizure legislation, and therefore Australian cultural institutions found that it became more difficult to procure art loans without an immunity statute.[112] It was not so much because of concrete seizures, or the threat thereof that urged Australia to enact this piece of legislation. Australia wanted to stay a safe haven and an interesting and trustful host for international exhibitions,[113]

[108] (Cth) Act No 11 of 1986 as amended by Act No 8 of 2005. Through this Act, Australia gives effect to the 1970 UNESCO Convention on the Means of Prohibiting and Preventing the Illicit Import, Export and Transfer of Ownership of Cultural Property.

[109] van Woudenberg (n 1) 357–58.

[110] 2013 (Cth) Act No 12 of 2013 (Australian Act). On the basis of the Protection of Cultural Objects on Loan Act, the implementing Protection of Cultural Objects on Loan Regulation 2014 has been promulgated on 2 October 2014. Select Legislative Instrument No 142, 2014. See also Department of Communications and the Arts (Australia), 'Protection of Cultural Objects on Loan Scheme' <https://www.arts.gov.au/funding-and-support/protection-cultural-objects-loan-scheme> accessed 17 September 2018.

[111] For a more extensive overview, see Craig Forrest, 'Immunity from Seizure and Suit in Australia: The Protection of Cultural Objects on Loan Act 2013' (2014) 21 IJCP 143–72. The late Professor Norman Palmer served as an important adviser to the Australian Government in regard to this Act. See 'RIP Norman Palmer' (*Elginism* (blog), 6 October 2016) <http://www.elginism.com/elgin-marbles/rip-professor-norman-palmer/20161006/8165/> accessed 17 September 2018. Thereafter, the Government of New Zealand approached Professor Palmer for assistance. Up to now, however, New Zealand has not enacted immunity from seizure legislation, although it investigated the possibility in the years 2012–13. See Manatū Taona/Ministry for Culture and Heritage (New Zealand), Discussion Paper: 'Immunity from Seizure for Cultural Objects on Loan' (July 2012) <https://mch.govt.nz/files/Immunity%20discussion%20paper%20(D-0432238).PDF> accessed 31 January 2020; Manatū Taona/Ministry for Culture and Heritage (New Zealand), Press Release: 'Immunity from Seizure for Cultural Objects on Loan Discussion Document Released' <https://mch.govt.nz/immunity-seizure-cultural-objects-loan-discussion-document-released> accessed 31 January 2020; Manatū Taona/Ministry for Culture and Heritage (New Zealand), 'Immunity from Seizure for Cultural Objects on Loan Submissions' (July 2013) <https://mch.govt.nz/mi/immunity-seizure-cultural-objects-loan-submissions-july-2013> accessed 31 January 2020.

[112] See Forrest (n 111) 145.

[113] Commonwealth of Australia, *Parliamentary Debates Second Reading Speech* House of Representatives 28 November 2012, 13646 (Mr Crean). Mr Crean, Australian Minister for the Arts, stated:

> Although the risk of legal claims being made on cultural objects while they are on loan in Australia is low, foreign lenders are increasingly reluctant to loan to Australia's major cultural institutions in the absence of national legislation. As a result, loan negotiations between Australian cultural institutions and foreign lenders have become protracted and in some cases loans have been denied.... It will reassure foreign lenders that Australia is a secure destination for loans and enable our great cultural institutions to successfully compete for world-class exhibitions.

ibid.

also with the thought that this would enrich the cultural experience for Australian audiences, would draw visitors from abroad, and would deliver significant economic benefits.[114] The main objective of this Act is 'to encourage lenders to lend objects for temporary public exhibition in Australia under arrangements involving certain institutions'.[115] The Australian Act only regards objects that are normally in a foreign State but are imported into Australia on loan for temporary public exhibition under temporary loan arrangements made between the foreign lender[116] and a borrowing institution[117] that have been pre-approved (on application) by the Minister for the Arts.[118] Protection lasts for a maximum of twenty-four months, starting on the date at which the object has been imported into Australia.[119] The import should not contravene a law of the Commonwealth prescribed by regulation that gives effect to an international agreement,[120] such as the 1970 UNESCO Convention on the Means of Prohibiting and Preventing the Illicit Import, Export and Transfer of Ownership of Cultural Property.[121] Thus, it is clear that the protection under this Act does not apply when this would contravene Australia's international obligations, such as those in regard to illicit import and export, as well as international return obligations.[122]

The Australian Act provides for both immunity from seizure and immunity from suit; proceedings for an action *in rem* relating to the cultural object cannot be started, nor can proceedings for an action *in personam* relating to the object against a protected person[123] for the object.[124] In addition, the Act provides for protection

[114] ibid.

[115] Australian Act, s 3, para 1.

[116] A covered 'lender' could also be a natural person not ordinarily residing in Australia. ibid, s 5 (Definitions).

[117] A 'borrowing institution' means an organization (whether a person or not) that collects and publicly exhibits in Australia objects that are of interest for archaeological, artistic, ethnological, historical, literary, scientific, or technological reasons. It should be established by a law of the Commonwealth, a State, or a Territory, or prescribed by regulation as a borrowing institution. ibid.

[118] This approved borrowing institution should be either an exhibiting institution for the object (which means the borrowing institution that has made arrangements for the temporary public exhibition of the object in Australia), the parent of such an institution, or an exhibition facilitator for the object that has an arrangement with either an exhibiting institution for the object or the parent of such an institution. ibid. The approval lasts for up to five years.

[119] Under certain conditions prescribed in the Act, an extension is possible. ibid.

[120] Forrest (n 111) 153.

[121] Convention on the Means of Prohibiting and Preventing the Illicit Import, Export and Transfer of Ownership of Cultural Property (adopted 14 November 1970, entered into force 24 April 1972) 823 UNTS 231 (1970 UNESCO Convention).

[122] Another important exception is stated in s 8(1)(f) of the Australian Act: the protection does not apply if the object is a Class A object as defined in the Protection of Movable Cultural Heritage Act 1986 when the object is imported, referring to significant Australian cultural heritage. Class A objects are those Australian protected objects whose export is prohibited, and include important Aboriginal and Torres Strait Islander heritage, as well as iconic objects such as Ned Kelly's armor and specific Victoria Crosses. ibid.

[123] The term 'protected person' is defined in s 5 of the Australian Act, and is considerable extensive. It could be, amongst others, the lender of the object or a person engaged by the lender.

[124] Australian Act, s 9. There are some narrowly described exceptions to the rule.

from enforcement of judgments and orders.[125] In principle, nothing can be done in relation to the object to enforce a judgment or order of a federal court or a court of a state, territory, or foreign country that (a) is a judgment or order *in personam* against a protected person for the object; or (b) is a judgment or order *in rem* relating to the object. Moreover, the cultural object cannot be seized or forfeited under a law of the commonwealth, a state, or a territory.[126] There are some exceptions, merely referring to Australia's obligations under international law, whereby specifically the international legal obligations in regard to proceeds of crime are mentioned, referring to parts of the implementing Proceeds of Crime Act 2002.[127] Finally, Section 14 of the Act is of interest, regarding the relationship with other laws and stating that the Act has effect despite any other law of the Commonwealth and despite any rule of common law or equity (including, for example, a rule of private international law).[128] One can consider this section as a kind of 'safety net' section, in order to rule out any possible immunity gap that may still exist.

C. Poland

After attempts a few years earlier,[129] Poland enacted immunity from seizure legislation in 2015, described by commentators 'as a response to recurrent difficulties in receiving exhibits for displays organized by Polish museums'.[130] The legal protection against seizure for cultural objects on loan was established by an amendment to the 1996 Museum Law (Polish Amendment).[131] The immunity is not provided automatically, as a formal application procedure needs to be followed and

[125] Australian Act, s 10. This section also describes some exceptions to this rule, merely but not exclusively related to other obligations under international law.

[126] Australian Act, ss 11–12.

[127] (Cth) Act No 85, 2002. See Australian Act, ss 9(4)(a), 10(4)(a), 11(2)(b), 12(2)(b). One can think of a situation where an object is used in relation to money laundering or (other) transnational organized crimes.

[128] With the exception, of course, of the Acts mentioned in this Act itself, such as the Proceeds of Crime Act 2002.

[129] van Woudenberg (n 1) 332; van Woudenberg (n 9) 235.

[130] Paulina Gwoździewicz-Matan and Andrzej Jakubowski, 'Enhancing the Mobility of Collections and Access to Cultural Heritage: Immunity of Cultural Objects from Seizure in Poland' (1 February 2017) Intl J Cultural Policy (online). <www.tandfonline.com/doi/full/10.1080/10286632.2017.1284827?scroll=top&needAccess=true> accessed 17 September 2018. The authors gave some examples of these recurrent difficulties. In 2009, the National Museum in Warsaw could not obtain certain masterpieces from Russian museums for the exhibition titled 'Le siècle français: 18th Century French Paintings and Drawings', due to the Russian position not to lend exhibits to States that did not adopt anti-seizure regulations. In 2012, the Czech Republic denied the loan of works of art for another exhibition by the Museum and the Royal Castle in Warsaw, 'Europe Jagiellonica Art and Culture in Central Europe under the Reign of the Jagiellonian Dynasty (1386–1572)'. This was a direct consequence of the *Diag Human* case.

[131] Law on the Alteration of the Acts Regulating the Access to Some Professions (5 August 2015) (Polish Amendment). See s 4 on 'the legal protection of movable property of artistic, historical or scientific value lent from abroad for a temporary exhibition organized on the territory of the Republic of Poland.'

an application needs to be filed with the Polish Ministry of Culture and National Heritage.[132] In the event of an import contrary to Polish law, or if the object concerned was exported illegally, the conditions for immunity will not be met. The legislation does not extend to immunity from suit,[133] but only regards immunity from seizure. It provides for protection lasting up to twelve months. The Polish legislation is not limited to cultural State property, as its protection applies to natural and legal foreign non-State lenders as well.

Consistently, Poland was of the opinion that based on customary international law, cultural State property was immune from seizure.[134] However, it also made clear that Polish cultural property taken out of Poland as war trophies during the Second World War could never be considered as foreign cultural property and consequently immune from seizure.[135] That also makes it clear why the Polish law states that cultural objects exported illegally are not entitled to immunity.

Conclusion

Since the publication of *State Immunity and Cultural Objects on Loan* in 2012, there have been a few new developments. Only a few more States became Party to the 2004 UN Convention on Jurisdictional Immunities of States and Their Property, and these were mostly European States. As this global instrument on State immunity still has not entered into force, the Czech Republic and Austria, joined by the Netherlands, elaborated in the Committee of Legal Advisers on Public International Law of the Council of Europe a declaration expressing a common understanding on *opinio juris* of the basic rule that cultural State property on exhibition enjoys immunity. Meanwhile, the International Law Association developed a Draft Convention on immunity from suit and seizure of (all) cultural objects that are temporarily present in a receiving State for cultural, educational, or scientific purposes. In the United States of America, more protection was provided to cultural State property on loan by means of the Foreign Cultural Exchange Jurisdictional Immunity Clarification Act. As far as is known, solely three additional States developed immunity from seizure legislation for cultural objects on

[132] ibid. A decision is published in the Official Bulletin; within thirty days after the date of publication, one can lodge an objection to the decision.

[133] It prevents neither claims related to foreign property on loan (actions *in rem*) nor actions against a foreign lender (actions *in personam*).

[134] This has been stated, among other moments, by the Polish Ministry of Cultural and Natural Heritage on the occasion of a questionnaire by the Immunity from Seizure subgroup of the Expert Working Group Mobility of Collections of the European Union in the spring of 2009.

[135] This has been stated, among other moments, by the Polish Ministry of Cultural and Natural Heritage on the occasion of a questionnaire by the Immunity from Seizure subgroup of the Expert Working Group Mobility of Collections of the European Union in the spring of 2009. van Woudenberg (n 1) 219, 413.

loan: Hungary, Australia, and Poland, adding important State practice to the identified emerged rule of customary international law.

Although the developments above strengthen the existence of the rule of customary international law on immunity from seizure for cultural State property on loan, they also confirm the exceptions to that rule as identified previously:

> [T]he rule of customary international law stating that cultural objects belonging to foreign States are immune from seizure while on temporary loan for an exhibition does not extend to those cultural objects which have been the subject of a serious breach of an obligation arising under a peremptory norm of general international law,[136] or which are already subject to return obligations under international or European law.[137]

136 This includes Holocaust confiscated art in my view.
137 van Woudenberg (n 1) 444.

15

Nationalism Versus Internationalism

New Perspectives Beyond State Sovereignty and Territoriality in the Protection of Cultural Heritage

*Robert Peters**

Introduction

Tangible cultural heritage is the materialized concept of peoples' identity, cultural background, and religion. Therefore, cultural heritage has always been linked to a certain people or community, as well as to a certain geographic territory. Despite attempts to protect cultural heritage from ancient times,[1] notions such as nation-state and national cultural patrimony have not emerged until the era of nation-building. In international law, the fundamental principles of State sovereignty and territoriality grant States the right to designate their 'national cultural heritage'. At the same time, international cultural heritage law has developed new principles through international treaty law, such as the 1970 UNESCO Convention on the Means of Prohibiting and Preventing the Illicit Import, Export and Transfer of Ownership of Cultural Property (1970 UNESCO Convention)[2] and the 1972 UNESCO Convention Concerning the Protection of the World Cultural and Natural Heritage (1972 World Heritage Convention).[3] These Conventions establish State obligations to cooperate in protecting cultural heritage and combatting its trafficking.

Within the context of the developments in international cultural heritage law, different notions such as 'cultural heritage of all mankind',[4] 'world heritage of mankind',[5] or 'cultural heritage of humanity'[6] have been employed within international

* This chapter expresses the author's personal views.

[1] Patty Gerstenblith, 'The Disposition of Movable Cultural Heritage' (Ch 1) in this volume.

[2] Convention on the Means of Prohibiting and Preventing the Illicit Import, Export and Transfer of Ownership of Cultural Property (adopted 14 November 1970, entered into force 24 April 1972) 823 UNTS 231 (1970 UNESCO Convention).

[3] UNESCO Convention Concerning the Protection of the World Cultural and Natural Heritage (adopted 16 November 1972, entered into force 17 December 1975) 1037 UNTS 151 (1972 World Heritage Convention).

[4] Convention for the Protection of Cultural Property in the Event of Armed Conflict (adopted 14 May 1954, entered into force 7 August 1956) 249 UNTS 240, Preamble (1954 Hague Convention).

[5] 1972 World Heritage Convention, Preamble.

[6] UNESCO Convention on the Protection of the Underwater Cultural Heritage (adopted 2 November 2001, entered into force 2 January 2009) 2562 UNTS 3, Preamble (2001 UCH Convention).

Robert Peters, Nationalism Versus Internationalism In: *Intersections in International Cultural Heritage Law.* Edited by Anne-Marie Carstens and Elizabeth Varner.
DOI: 10.1093/oso/9780198846291.003.0016

treaty law in order to describe the universal value of tangible and intangible cultural heritage. Despite the manifestation of the universal value of cultural heritage in international treaty law, however, these same instruments vest in each individual State the duty and authority not only to determine what constitutes its national cultural patrimony, but also to nominate its cultural or natural sites for recognition in international registries to facilitate the protection of cultural heritage on an international level. Thus, these international treaties allow States Parties to nominate qualifying cultural or natural sites in their respective territories for inclusion in the World Heritage List, established by the 1972 World Heritage Convention,[7] in the International Register of Cultural Property under Special Protection, established by the Convention for the Protection of Cultural Property in the Event of Armed Conflicts (1954 Hague Convention),[8] and the List of Cultural Property under Enhanced Protection, established by the 1999 Second Protocol to the 1954 Hague Convention.[9] Similar to the 1972 World Heritage Convention, the 2003 Convention for the Safeguarding of the Intangible Cultural Heritage (2003 ICH Convention)[10] establishes a Representative List of the Intangible Cultural Heritage of Humanity[11] in order to ensure better visibility of the intangible cultural heritage and awareness of its significance, and to encourage dialogue which respects cultural diversity.[12] Similar to the World Heritage List, the Representative List is based on nominations from States Parties to the Convention, not the communities or groups whose intangible cultural heritage is represented and that the 2003 ICH Convention aims at safeguarding. Even though these Conventions focus on the concept of cultural internationalism and the universal value of cultural heritage, all three continue to conform to the traditional pattern of State power; in terms of public international law, this means that they fundamentally rely on the principle of State sovereignty.[13]

This chapter starts by discussing the principle of State sovereignty in light of international cultural heritage law. Both immovable cultural heritage (sites) and movable cultural heritage (objects) are firmly linked to a State's territory and

[7] The List has a total of 1,121 properties: 869 cultural, 213 natural, and 39 mixed sites in 167 States. World Heritage List <http://whc.unesco.org/en/list/> accessed 2 February 20202 February 2020 .

[8] 1954 Hague Convention, arts 8 and 9; International Register of Cultural Property under Special Protection, UNESCO Doc CLT/HER/CHP (23 July 2015).

[9] Second Protocol to The Hague Convention for the Protection of Cultural Property in the Event of Armed Conflict (adopted 26 March 1999, entered into force 9 March 2004) 2253 UNTS 172, art 10; UNESCO, 'List of Cultural Property under Enhanced Protection' (December 2017). List of Cultural Property under Enhanced Protection <http://www.unesco.org/new/en/culture/themes/armed-conflict-and-heritage/protection/enhanced-protection/> accessed 2 February 2020 .

[10] UNESCO Convention for the Safeguarding of the Intangible Cultural Heritage (adopted 17 October 2003, entered into force 20 April 2006) 2368 UNTS 1 (2003 ICH Convention).

[11] The Representative List of the Intangible Cultural Heritage of Humanity has 463 inscriptions corresponding to 127 States Parties, see <https://ich.unesco.org/en/lists> accessed 2 February 2020 .

[12] 2003 ICH Convention, art 16(1).

[13] See Charter of the United Nations (adopted 26 June 1945, entered into force 24 October 1945) 59 Stat 1031, art 2, s 1 ("principle of the sovereign equality of states")1 UNTS XVI (UN Charter).

depend on the State's power to protect (or neglect) it. This raises the question of how 'national' the international cultural heritage law regime really is. It also requires a reexamination of the relevancy of Merryman's dichotomy of nationalism versus internationalism[14] and a discussion of whether this conceptualization has been surpassed by new developments within this field.

This includes an analysis of the procedure used to designate World Heritage Sites and explores the options available to a World Heritage Trust to shift the current paradigm, in which States compete to obtain the largest number of designations. Second, the chapter examines the effects of export regulation based on national sovereignty concerns on movable cultural heritage. Despite the fact that the 1970 UNESCO Convention requires States Parties to protect cultural property against illicit import *and* export,[15] only a few States, such as Canada and Germany, have done so in a comprehensive manner, as will be shown later; the majority of States have only enacted export laws designed to protect their own cultural heritage. However, these latter laws fail to restrict the influx of protected cultural objects belonging to other States' cultural heritage. At first glance, national export laws appear to be limited to a national dimension. However, as this chapter demonstrates, such laws can have a large international impact if they are mutually recognized by States.

Against this background and in light of the United Nations Security Council (UNSC) Resolution 2347 (2017),[16] which calls upon States to adopt 'adequate and effective regulations on export *and* import of cultural property', the chapter explores recent legal developments—first, at a national level in regard to the 2016 German law reform,[17] and second, at the level of the European Union (EU) in regard to the most recent 2019 EU Import Regulation.[18] An analysis of these developments demonstrates that export and import regulations must develop hand in hand in order to protect cultural heritage against destruction, looting, and trafficking, and that only the mutual recognition of export laws is truly international.

I. The Principle of State Sovereignty and the Universal Value of Cultural Heritage

Despite all efforts in international cultural heritage law, one of the fundamental legal principles remains the principle of State sovereignty. Sovereignty can be

[14] John Henry Merryman, 'Two Ways of Thinking About Cultural Property' (1986) 80 AJIL 831–53.

[15] 1970 UNESCO Convention, arts 3, 5.

[16] UNSC Res 2347 (24 March 2017), UN Doc S/RES/2347 (2017) para 17(b) (hereafter UNSC Res 2347).

[17] Act on the Protection of Cultural Property (Cultural Property Protection Act—KGSG, German CPA) of 31 July 2016, Federal Law Gazette 2016, BGBl Part I, 2016, p 1914 (Germany).

[18] Regulation (EU) 2019/880 of the European Parliament and of the Council of 17 April 2019 on the introduction and the import of cultural goods [2019] OJ L151/1 (EU Import Regulation).

defined as the supreme and independent power over a certain territory and those within it; this authority extends to all activities associated with self-governance, such as making, executing, and applying laws, imposing and collecting taxes, making war and peace, and forming treaties or engaging in commerce with other States.[19] With regard to cultural heritage law, it is this principle that establishes the link between a State's territory, its people, and the cultural heritage located within its territory. Consequently, a general assumption exists under international law that (tangible) cultural heritage is a resource that States have a right to control—similarly to any natural resource found on or in the State's soil.[20]

In this vein, the 1970 UNESCO Convention[21]—with its emphasis on preventing the trafficking in movable cultural heritage—views cultural heritage predominantly in terms of national cultural property, first and foremost, reinforcing the concept of cultural nationalism. It defines cultural property as 'property, which, on religious or secular grounds, is *specifically designated by each state* as being of importance for archaeology, prehistory, history, literature, art or science'[22] and which falls within any of eleven enumerated categories. As a consequence, cultural property is inextricably linked to the concept of territoriality, through the designation of a 'country of origin'.[23] On this basis, an export of cultural property is considered illicit if the object was stolen or illicitly exported in breach of the State's national export regulations. Similarly to the 1970 UNESCO Convention, the 1995 UNIDROIT Convention on Stolen or Illegally Exported Cultural Objects (1995 UNIDROIT Convention)[24] is based on the principles of State sovereignty and territoriality.

Although intangible cultural heritage is not a material 'resource', cultural traditions, practices, or expressions establishing intangible cultural heritage can be fostered by a State as being part of a certain national identity or—in turn—exploited and/or suppressed if not being in line with the desired national identity. The latter is especially true in cases where the cultural tradition belongs to an ethnic or religious minority. The principle of State sovereignty therefore gives States almost exclusive rights over cultural heritage situated in their territory. This control by States over designating minority cultural traditions, however, raises the question of how 'national' the international cultural heritage law regime really is.

19 Jeffrey Lehman and Shirelle Ph, *West's Encyclopedia of American Law* (2nd edn, vol IX, West 2005).

20 Janna Thompson, 'Cultural Property, Restitution and Value' (2003) 20 J of Applied Philosophy 252.

21 See 1970 UNESCO Convention, which has 140 States Parties at the time of publication <http://www.unesco.org/eri/la/convention.asp?KO=13039&language=E> accessed 2 February 2020 .See also Patty Gerstenblith, 'The Disposition of Movable Cultural Heritage' (Ch 1) in this volume.

22 1970 UNESCO Convention, art 1 (emphasis added).

23 ibid, art 2(1).

24 UNIDROIT Convention on Stolen or Illegally Exported Cultural Objects (adopted 24 June 1995, entered into force 1 July 1998) 34 ILM 1322 (1995 UNIDROIT Convention).

II. Nationalism Versus Internationalism: What is Truly International?

Generally, internationalism can be defined as a political principle of transnational or global cooperation based on common interests.[25] As a result, it stands in opposition to nationalism and advocates a greater political, cultural, and economic cooperation among nations and people. Within the cultural heritage context, Merryman has established 'two ways of thinking' about nationalism versus internationalism: on the one hand, 'nationalism' refers to national constraints on the trade in cultural property and to the protection of the integrity of national patrimony; on the other hand, the opposing concept of 'internationalism' refers to a preference for free trade in cultural property and against national export restrictions.[26] The first 'way of thinking', as he argues, is national or even nationalistic, as it conceives cultural property as belonging to the country of origin. The second 'way of thinking' is international and/or cosmopolitan, as it views cultural property as heritage of humanity and therefore supports the broadest possible access, free trade, and circulation to facilitate cultural exchange and understanding.[27]

This distinction, however, has been criticized by Nafziger, among others, as a contrived dichotomy[28] and as unidimensional, since it primarily justifies a free-trade approach. According to Nafziger, the internationalists are interested in promoting a general free trade in cultural property, unfettered by mutual cooperation among States.[29] Along these lines, Merryman's approach has also been challenged as a 'black and white representation' being too narrow because cultural heritage is much more complex'.[30] Cultural objects can be seen in various ways: as, on the one hand, moveable artifacts subject to individual (property) rights that may be economically advantageous and culturally useful to exchange in international commerce; and, on the other hand, as being part of a unique cultural heritage that may be protected by public (national) patrimony laws.[31]

In turn, the assumption of a 'country of origin' can also be challenged, based primarily on two considerations. First, the fact that modern State borders were mainly

[25] N D Arora, *Political Science* (Tata McGraw-Hill 2011) 2.

[26] Merryman, 'Two Ways of Thinking' (n 14) 831.

[27] ibid 834.

[28] James R Nafziger, 'The Present State of Research' in Académie de Droit International de la Haye (ed), *Le Patrimoine Culturel de L'humanité* (Martinus Nijhoff 2007) 244.

[29] ibid 246.

[30] Francesco Francioni, 'The Evolving Framework for the Protection of Cultural Heritage in International Law' in Silvia Borelli and Federico Lenzerini (eds), *Cultural Heritage, Cultural Rights, Cultural Diversity* (Martinus Nijhoff 2012) 3.

[31] ibid.

drawn in the nineteenth or early twentieth centuries and often do not correspond to the boundaries of the ancient civilizations undermines the supposition that all such cultural objects inherently belong to a current State's territory. State borders, in the Middle East or Africa particularly, were drawn on the basis of the haphazardly colonial apportionment in previous centuries. Second, within the context of trafficking in cultural property and its question of return, it might be argued that affiliation may weaken over time. This is because cultural identities and cultural symbols may change as time elapses, because the idea of a nation as a primeval community with an essence that remains constant through time is inconsistent with current understandings of political identity.[32] In this vein, Merryman also criticizes the use of the term 'heritage', because it implies a right to return or 're-patriation' to a *patria*, a country of origin or homeland. Given his internationalist perspective, Merryman balks at the idea that cultural objects belong to and in a specific nation, particularly because these notions stem from a form of 'romantic nationalism'.[33]

Nonetheless, the principle of territoriality is widely recognized in international law and thus forms the basis of most legal instruments in international law, including the field of international cultural heritage law. Based on the principle of territoriality, many States have adopted cultural heritage laws (State ownership laws) that vest ownership of archaeological and cultural resources in that State.[34] States claim that both their ownership laws and their national export laws serve to protect cultural heritage sites from destruction. They also claim that keeping cultural property within their national borders assists in the preservation of these objects in their original cultural context.[35] Within the context of this argument, it is fundamental for States to define, within their State sovereignty, their national cultural heritage and to control its export. The importance of such border and customs controls is particularly evident in times of war and political unrest, when the weakening or absence of these controls is frequently correlated with enormous increases in the trafficking in cultural property, as is the case in Yemen, Syria, and Iraq.[36] As will be shown later, States also confirm the concept of national cultural heritage by reciprocally enforcing other States' national export laws through import restrictions, as for example, though bilateral agreements, or national laws implementing the 1970 UNESCO Convention.

[32] Thompson, 'Cultural Property' (n 20) 257.

[33] John Henry Merryman, 'Protection of the Cultural Heritage?' (1990) 38 American J of Comparative L (Supp) 521.

[34] See (nn 68–70) and accompanying text.

[35] Alexander A Bauer, 'New Ways of Thinking About Cultural Property: A Critical Appraisal of the Antiquities Trade Debates' (2008) 31 Fordham Intl L J 700.

[36] See Patty Gerstenblith, 'The Disposition of Movable Cultural Heritage' (Ch 1) in this volume.

III. The Concepts of 'National Cultural Heritage' and 'Cultural Heritage of Humanity'

As demonstrated, the concept of national cultural heritage is based on the principles of State sovereignty and State territoriality. It is widely used by States to justify national export regulations within the context of the 1970 UNESCO Convention or, for example, EU law.[37] In turn, the concept of the cultural heritage of humanity is much more recent. It did not develop in opposition to national cultural heritage—as one might think in terms of nationalism versus internationalism—but because of it. While cultural objects may constitute the tangible and intangible cultural heritage of a particular group, community, nation, or State, many of these cultural objects have also been regarded as a testimonial to the common history of humankind. The universal importance of the history and development of humanity is self-evident: archaeological and skeletal remains of the earliest traces of humankind, and the knowledge derived from their examination, are not only important to the State in which they are found, but to all peoples.[38] The same is true for unique and outstanding examples of human civilization, such as the pyramids of Egypt or the Maya temples.

The term 'cultural heritage'—like 'cultural property'—was first established in the 1954 Hague Convention, which defines cultural property as 'movable or immovable property of great importance to the cultural heritage of every people'.[39] However, it was only with the 1972 World Heritage Convention that the recognition of cultural heritage developed as a broader legal concept based on the general premise that 'parts of the cultural and natural heritage are of outstanding interest and therefore need to be preserved as part of the world heritage of mankind as a whole'.[40] This premise is complemented by the premise that the destruction or deterioration of cultural heritage constitutes a harmful impoverishment of the heritage of all nations.[41] In a similar vein, the 2001 UNESCO Convention on the Protection of the Underwater Cultural Heritage (2001 UCH Convention)[42] refers to underwater cultural heritage as 'an integral part of the cultural heritage of humanity'.[43] Consequently, the broader concept of cultural heritage of humanity

[37] Council Directive (EU) 2014/60 of the European Parliament and of the Council of 15 May 2014 on the return of cultural objects unlawfully removed from the territory of a Member State and amending Regulation (EU) 1024/2012 [2014] OJ L159/1; specifically on EU law: Robert Peters 'The Protection of Cultural Property: Recent Developments in Germany in the Context of New EU Law and the 1970 UNESCO Convention' (2016) 2 Santander Art and Culture L Rev 85–102.

[38] Craig Forrest, *International Law and the Protection of Cultural Heritage* (Routledge 2010) 11.

[39] 1954 Hague Convention, art 1.

[40] World Heritage Convention, sixth recital.

[41] ibid, second recital.

[42] 2001 UCH Convention.

[43] ibid. See first recital.

encompasses a common interest in safeguarding, irrespective of location and ownership rights.[44]

IV. Immovable Cultural Heritage

A. The 1972 World Heritage Convention: A National Contest?

Based on a common interest, the 1972 World Heritage Convention[45] attempts to promote a legal framework to preserve outstanding cultural and natural sites.[46] Since its entry into force in 1975, 193 States have become Party to the Convention,[47] which has, in turn, gained the broadest international acceptance possible under international law. One could argue that the Convention with its World Heritage List has become the figurehead of UNESCO because of its universal recognition and its generally positive perception. The Convention operates through the World Heritage Committee,[48] which sets the criteria for establishing the 'outstanding universal value' of sites to be designated (Operational Guidelines).[49] Each site inscribed as world heritage remains under the control of the State on whose territory it is located.

B. Current Obstacles and the Concept of a World Heritage Trust

Early attempts in 1965 and 1971 to establish a World Heritage Trust (Trust), which would have exercised extraterritorial control over the designated sites under international custody, were rejected by the majority of States based on the fact that such proposals impinged on territorial sovereignty.[50] Although the Convention does not limit the sovereignty of the State, it clearly expresses the position that it is in the interest of the international community to preserve each site for future generations of humanity.[51] In other words, the protection and preservation of world heritage

[44] Francesco Francioni, 'Culture, Heritage and Human Rights: An Introduction' in Francesco Francioni and Martin Scheinin (eds), *Cultural Human Rights* (Brill 2008) 7.

[45] 1972 World Heritage Convention.

[46] ibid. See Preamble.

[47] List of States Parties to the 1972 World Heritage Convention, <https://whc.unesco.org/en/statesparties/> accessed 2 February 2020.

[48] The Committee is composed of twenty-one States Parties elected by the UNESCO General Conference.

[49] World Heritage Committee, Operational Guidelines for the Implementation of the World Heritage Convention, UNESCO Doc WHC.17/01 (12 July 2017) s I.E.

[50] Preliminary Study on the Legal and Technical Aspects of a Possible International Instrument for the Protection of Monuments and Sites of Universal Value, UNESCO Doc 16C/19 (31 July 1970) Annex, para 50.

[51] Florian Pfeifle, 'UNESCO-Weltkulturerbe' (2010) 4 *Schriften zum Öffentlichen Immobilienrecht und Infrastrukturrecht* 21.

sites are a concern of all States Parties and thus a duty of the international community as a whole.[52]

At the time of its creation, the 1972 World Heritage Convention did not contain provisions for the establishment of an autonomous authority. However, it might be time to reconsider the proposal of a Trust, funded by the States Parties to the Convention, as it could manage the designated sites, independently from the State's sovereignty. This would not only improve the management of sites and reduce violations against protection requirements, but also slow down the inflation of inscriptions: despite the World Heritage Committee's efforts to reduce the number of inscriptions, each year around twenty-five sites are added to the World Heritage List (currently consisting of 1,121 properties).[53] Consequently, the inscription of sites would become less of a national contest—as it sometimes seems to be the case—at the annual meetings of the World Heritage Committee because States Parties would have to yield competency, and therefore State sovereignty, with regard to the management of and the authority over the sites inscribed. While States might oppose such a system with regard to certain types of site, such a scheme might be appealing with regard to other sites, such as, for example, the Central Amazon,[54] as one of the planet's richest regions in terms of biodiversity, or for certain politically charged cultural World Heritage Sites, such as the old city of Jerusalem.[55] Moreover, such a Trust might be a viable solution to sites which, though being located within one State, have a much broader importance to humanity as, for example, the Nazi concentration camp of Auschwitz;[56] a place that serves as a memorial, a reminder, and 'a sign of warning of the many threats and tragic consequences of extreme ideologies and denial of human dignity'.[57] In the examples given, an autonomous international agency composed of international experts, potentially under the auspices of the International Council on Monuments and Sites (ICOMOS), which already offers advice to UNESCO on World Heritage Sites, rather than a committee composed of States, like the World Heritage Committee, could foster the easing of political tensions over certain sites, improve the professional management of sites despite national capacities, and thereby preserve them best as part of the cultural heritage of humanity.

[52] 1972 World Heritage Convention art 6.

[53] See recently inscribed properties: 29 sites (2019), 20 sites (2018), 21 sites (2017), 21 sites (2016); 27 sites (2015) <http://whc.unesco.org/en/newproperties/> accessed 2 February 2020.

[54] Brazil, Central Amazon Conservation Complex, inscribed in 2000 <http://whc.unesco.org/en/list/998> accessed 2 February 2020.

[55] Old City of Jerusalem and its Walls (site proposed by Jordan) inscribed to the World Heritage List in1981; inscribed in 1982 on the List of World Heritage in Danger <http://whc.unesco.org/en/list/148> accessed 2 February 2020.

[56] Poland, Auschwitz Birkenau—German Nazi Concentration and Extermination Camp (1940–1945) inscribed in 1979 <http://whc.unesco.org/en/list/31> accessed 2 February 2020.

[57] ibid. See last para of the 'Statement of Significance' for the inscription <http://whc.unesco.org/en/list/31> accessed 2 February 2020.

V. Movable Cultural Heritage

A. The 1970 UNESCO Convention: Endorsing National Export Provisions

Whereas the 1972 World Heritage Convention focuses on the protection of immovable cultural heritage through the inscription of sites, the 1970 UNESCO Convention, in turn, focuses on movable cultural heritage and endorses the bond to the 'country of origin'. Since—for reasons of practicability—there is no list of World Movable Cultural Property, the basic principle of the 1970 UNESCO Convention is that States Parties must protect their national cultural property through national legislation in order to prevent 'the impoverishment of the cultural heritage of the countries of origin'.[58] In terms of nationalism versus internationalism, this clearly falls on the side of nationalism. Interestingly, the Convention also indicates that 'international co-operation constitutes one of the most efficient means of protecting each country's cultural property'.[59] However, the 1970 UNESCO Convention does not prohibit the export of cultural property in itself, nor does it harmonize national export provisions; these vary from State to State. Only some States have established a specific date that acts as a threshold for the limits on exportation: cultural objects created prior to this date are not allowed to be exported without a valid export certificate. Examples include Israel (before 1700 BC), [60] Cyprus (before 1850),[61] and Brunei (before 1894).[62] The majority of States has established a so-called moving date based on the age of the cultural object; examples include Kuwait (for objects more than 40 years old),[63] Indonesia (for objects more than 50 years old),[64] Belize (for objects more than 150 years old),[65] and Yemen (for objects more than 200 years old).[66]

In addition to national export regulations adopted by most European States, the EU has established uniform export regulations,[67] which are binding on all

[58] 1970 UNESCO Convention, art 2.

[59] ibid.

[60] Antiquities Law (Israel) 5738 (1978) art 1 <http://www.unesco.org/culture/natlaws/media/pdf/israel/isr_antiquitieslaw_engorof.pdf> accessed 2 February 2020.

[61] Antiquities Law (Cyprus), (ch 31), art 2(1) <http://www.mcw.gov.cy/mcw/da/da.nsf/DMLlaw_en/DMLlaw_en?OpenDocument> accessed 2 February 2020.

[62] Laws of Brunei (2002), (ch 31), art 2(1) <http://www.unesco.org/culture/natlaws/media/pdf/brunei/brunei_lawant_02_enorof> accessed 2 February 2020.

[63] Princely Decree no 11 (1960) Law of Antiquities (Kuwait), art 3 <http://www.unesco.org/culture/natlaws/media/pdf/kuwait/kuw_decree_11_law_antiquities_engtof.pdf> accessed 2 February 2020.

[64] (1a) law No 5 Indonesia (1992) art 1 <http://www.unesco.org/culture/natlaws/media/pdf/indonesie/indonesia_compilation_of_law_2003_engl_orof.pdf> accessed 2 February 2020.

[65] Ancient Monuments and Antiquities Act of Belize, ch 259 (1972) art 2 <http://www.unesco.org/culture/natlaws/media/pdf/belize/belize_monuments_antiquities_ordinance_engorof.pdf> accessed 2 February 2020.

[66] Antiquities law Yemen No 21 (1994) art 3 <http://www.unesco.org/culture/natlaws/media/pdf/yemen/yemen_lawantiquities1997_engtof.pdf> accessed 2 February 2020.

[67] Council Regulation (EC) 116/2009 of 18 December 2008 on the export of cultural goods [2008] OJ L39/1 (EU Export Regulation).

EU Member States, in order to control the export of cultural property outside the Single European Market. The EU export provisions depend on certain categories of cultural objects based on age and financial thresholds (for example, archaeological objects more than 100 years old, with no financial threshold; mosaics, drawings, and photographs more than 50 years old and valued above €15,000; and paintings more than 50 years old and above €150,000). In addition to export laws, several States have established national ownership laws. These laws generally aim to protect cultural sites, limit archeological excavations, and designate that all archeological items are State property upon discovery. Early examples of such laws include Greece (1834),[68] the Ottoman Empire (1874),[69] and Italy (1907).[70]

The connection between a State and a specific cultural object is, however, not sufficiently defined by the 1970 UNESCO Convention. In line with the overall national approach of the Convention, this is left to the determination of each State's national regulation without a right of review by either another State or an international body. Thus, it remains completely within a State's discretion to designate what constitutes its national cultural heritage. The only requirement the Convention sets out is that the cultural object has been found in, created in, or has legitimately entered the State beforehand.[71] There is, however, no time limit for cultural property to have remained in a State's territory before that State may legitimately claim it as national cultural heritage. Most importantly, however, States have to implement the 1970 UNESCO Convention into their national law in order to enforce the obligations under the Convention, especially with regard to returning illegally exported cultural property, and to give effect to foreign export regulations. While several States have failed to implement the 1970 UNESCO Convention (including UNESCO headquarters host country France),[72] other States lack proper implementation with regard to recognizing other States' export laws. As this chapter will demonstrate, most States protect

[68] Law No 3028 of 2002 (Greece) art 21.

[69] For the text of the law, published on 24 March 1874, see Asar-i Atika Nizamnamesi, Düstur (vol III, Matbaa-i Amire 1876) 426–31; Grégoire Aristarchi Bey (ed), *Règlement sur les antiquités, Législation ottoman* (vol III, Nicolaïdès, 1874) 162–67; for more information, see: Zainab Bahrani, Zeynep Celik, and Edhem Eldem (ed), *Scramble for the Past: A Story of Archaeology in the Ottoman Empire 1753–1914* (Salt Galata 2012).

[70] Legge 386 Tutela della conservazione dei monumenti e degli oggetti d'antichità e d'arte (1907) <http://www.unesco.org/culture/natlaws/media/pdf/italy/italia_loi27_06_1907_ita_orof.pdf> accessed 2 February 2020 . The law of 1907 was amended in 1939 and in 2004. See Law No 1089 (1939) replaced by the Italian Code of the Cultural and Landscape Heritage (Codice dei beni culturali e del paesaggio), Decree No 42 (2004) <http://www.unesco.org/culture/natlaws/media/pdf/italy/it_cult_landscapeheritge2004_engtof.pdf.> accessed 2 February 2020 .

[71] 1970 UNESCO Convention, art 4(a–e).

[72] See *Federal Republic of Nigeria v Alain de Montbrison*, Paris Appeal Ct, 5 April 2004, No 2002/09897. Nigeria based its claim on the 1970 UNESCO Convention but the claim was rejected because the Convention, ratified by France in 1997, was not directly applicable and no legislation implementing the provisions of the Convention had been enacted.

their own national cultural heritage but do not provide for the mutual recognition of foreign export laws.

B. The 1995 UNIDROIT Convention: General Interests Beyond National Export Provisions

The 1995 UNIDROIT Convention[73] was established in order to fill some gaps of the 1970 UNESCO Convention.[74] In contrast to the 1970 UNESCO Convention, it does not rely on the recognition of foreign export laws; instead, it requires that the State requesting the return of a cultural object establish that it has been 'illegally exported' under its national law.[75] As a result, States that lack national import regulations, but ratified the 1995 UNIDROIT Convention, can no longer refuse to return cultural objects by simply arguing that they cannot enforce foreign national export laws.[76] Instead of limiting the 1970 UNESCO Convention's broad definition of cultural property,[77] the 1995 UNIDROIT Convention includes additional criteria with regard to the requirements for the return of illegally exported cultural objects. For example, the State requesting the return must prove that the removal of the object from its territory 'significantly impairs' specific interests, namely, the physical preservation of the object and/or its context, its integrity, its traditional or ritual use by a tribe or indigenous community, and the 'significant cultural importance for the requesting state'.[78] The approach taken by the Convention is thus quite remarkable, since it expands the interests beyond the territorial interest of States (principle of territoriality) to other non-territorial interests associated with the cultural object itself. Furthermore, it includes the recognition of the cultural importance of the object in question for groups and/or peoples within the territory of the requesting State. By including the latter criteria, the Convention emphasizes that the cultural affiliation of the object is of equivalent importance in determining whether or not an object should be returned to the requesting State.[79]

Unlike the 1970 UNESCO Convention, the 1995 UNIDROIT Convention is self-executing. As a result, it does not require national implementation by its States Parties. That said, both the rather small number of States Parties to the 1995 UNIDROIT Convention (forty-eight States)[80] and the absence of cases resolved

[73] 1995 UNIDROIT Convention.

[74] 1970 UNESCO Convention.

[75] Beat Schönenberger, *Restitution von Kulturgut* (Stämpfli Verlag Bern 2009) 89 (Schönenberger).

[76] Kurt Siehr, 'Vereinheitlichung des Rechts der Kulturgüter in Europa?' in Jürgen Basedow, Ulrich Drobnig, Reinhard Ellger, Klaus Hopt, Hein Kötz, Rainer Kulms, and Ernst-Joachim Mestmäcker (eds), *Aufbruch nach Europa, 75 Jahre Max-Planck-Institut für Privatrecht* (Mohr Siebeck 2001) 89.

[77] 1970 UNESCO Convention, art 1.

[78] 1995 UNIDROIT Convention, art 5(3).

[79] Schönenberger (n 75) 89.

[80] List of States Parties, <http://www.unidroit.org/status-cp> accessed 2 February 2020.

under its provisions demonstrate the reluctance of States to commit to self-executing treaties in general and to this Convention in particular. Nevertheless, by introducing general interests as additional conditions for the return of illegally exported cultural objects, the Convention explicitly presumes the existence of universal values associated with cultural heritage.[81] Although these criteria do not limit the sovereign right of States to designate their national cultural heritage, they certainly underline the concept of universal values, particularly as they do not derive from a national perspective, but support an international approach to cultural heritage.

C. Specific Regulations on Import, Export, and Trade in Cultural Property

In a broader context, the principle of State sovereignty is not only relevant to national cultural heritage but also because it establishes the fundamental right of States to control both the import and export of all kinds of goods—not just cultural property. This control is usually accomplished through national border and customs controls. In times of war or political unrest, however, such controls cease to exist and trafficking flourishes. Therefore, in reaction to the looting in the aftermath of the Iraq war, the United Nations Security Council adopted Resolution 1483[82] in 2003, which obligates States 'to take appropriate steps to facilitate the safe return' of Iraqi cultural property illegally removed, including 'the prohibition on trade in or transfer of such items.' Similarly, the UN Security Council adopted Resolution 2139[83] in 2014 with regard to Syria. In response to both Resolutions the European Union as well as some individual States adopted sanctions on Iraqi and Syrian cultural property; in 2003, the EU adopted specific regulations on Iraq,[84] which prohibit the import, export, and trade in Iraqi cultural property. In 2014, the EU adopted similar measures for Syria.[85] Both EU regulations are directly applicable to all EU Member States. As a result, the import and export of and the trade in Iraqi and Syrian cultural property are banned throughout the European Union. In the same vein, the United States enacted provisions for Iraq (2004) [86] and Syria (2016).[87]

[81] See Merryman's discussion about 'the injection of object-oriented values into the UNIDROIT Convention' in: John Henry Merryman, 'The Nation and the Object' (1994) 3 IJCP 61, 71.

[82] UNSC Res 1483 (2003) (adopted 22 May 2003) UN Doc S/RES/1483 (2003).

[83] UNSC Res 2139 (2014) (adopted 22 February 2014) UN Doc S/RES/2139 (2014).

[84] See Article 3 of Council Regulation (EC) 1210/2003 of 7 July 2003 concerning certain specific restrictions on economic and financial relations with Iraq and repealing Regulation (EC) 2465/96 [2003] OJ L 169/6.

[85] Council Regulation (EU) 1332/2013 of 13 December 2013 amending Regulation (EU) 36/2012 concerning restrictive measures in view of the situation in Syria [2013] OJ L335/3.

[86] Emergency Protection for Iraqi Cultural Antiquities Act of 2004, Pub L 108-429, 118 Stat 2434 (2014).

[87] Protect and Preserve International Cultural Property Act, PubL 114-151, 130 Stat 369 (2016).

D. What is Lacking: General Import Regulations

Despite the specific restrictions on Iraqi and Syrian cultural property, general import regulations are absent. In March 2017, however, the UN Security Council adopted Resolution 2347 (2017), calling upon States to consider adopting 'adequate and effective regulations on export and import, including certification of provenance'.[88] This resolution was not limited to a specific State (as with Iraq and Syria), and as such is even more important in terms of *general* import regulations. Since general import regulations are still missing in international cultural heritage law, the 2017 UNSC Resolution, despite its weak wording ('calling upon' instead of 'requesting' States),[89] nevertheless can be deemed an important step that could accelerate future developments in public international law.

Like the 1970 UNESCO Convention, the 1995 UNIDROIT Convention mentions the terms 'export' and 'illegally exported' several times; the term 'import', which is used in the 1970 UNESCO Convention, however, is not mentioned in the text of the 1995 UNIDROIT Convention. This may be due to the fact that the 1995 UNIDROIT Convention specifically focuses on restitution of stolen and return of illegally exported cultural objects. Yet, import and export are two sides of the same coin—especially in terms of fighting illicit trafficking. Thus, true internationalism should be based on one simple rule: illegally exported cultural property from one State should be considered as illegally imported into another State. Although the 1970 UNESCO Convention requires States to protect cultural property against illicit import and export[90] and 'to prohibit the import of stolen cultural property',[91] most of the 140 States Parties to the Convention have enacted only national export laws, which apply to their *own* cultural heritage; they have failed to create import provisions that would protect other States' cultural heritage. Only a few States have enacted import regulations following their ratification of the 1970 UNESCO Convention, namely the United States,[92] Switzerland,[93] Canada,[94] and Germany.[95]

As observed by Gerstenblith,[96] the reactive approach to implementation of the 1970 UNESCO Convention in the United States[97] and Switzerland[98] does not

[88] ibid, para 17(b).

[89] See Patty Gerstenblith, 'The Disposition of Movable Cultural Heritage' (Ch 1) of this volume; Kristin Hausler, 'The UN Security Council, the Human Rights Council, and the Protection of Cultural Heritage: A Matter of Peace and Security, Human Rights, or Both?' (Ch 8).

[90] 1970 UNESCO Convention, arts 3, 5.

[91] ibid, art 7.

[92] The United States of America joined the 1970 UNESCO Convention on 2 September 1983 (acceptance).

[93] Switzerland joined the 1970 UNESCO Convention on 3 October 2003 (acceptance).

[94] Canada joined the 1970 UNESCO Convention on 28 March 1978 (acceptance).

[95] Germany joined the 1970 UNESCO Convention on 30 November 2007 (ratification).

[96] Patty Gerstenblith, 'The Disposition of Movable Cultural Heritage' (Ch 1) of this volume.

[97] Convention on Cultural Property Implementation Act (CPIA) 19 USC 2601 (1983).

[98] Federal Act on the International Transfer of Cultural Property 2003 (Cultural Property Transfer Act) 444.1, 20 June 2003, <https://www.bak.admin.ch/bak/en/home/cultural-heritage/transfer-of-cultural-property/legal-basis.html> accessed 2 February 2020.

recognize foreign export laws per se but rather requires supplemental bilateral agreements. In practice, the number of bilateral agreements has been quite limited, both in the United States[99] and Switzerland.[100] If all current 140 States Parties to the 1970 UNESCO Convention were to follow this approach, a total number of more than 9,700 bilateral agreements would have to be drawn up;[101] a tremendously costly and ineffective approach. Moreover, it is not clear why international treaty law, whose primary purpose is to regulate an issue among all its States Parties, should be implemented into national law by drawing up the requirement of additional bilateral agreements only with some selected States Parties, with the consequence that other States Parties are not able to evoke the provisions of the 1970 UNESCO Convention.

Whereas the United States and Switzerland require bilateral agreements in order to enforce import restrictions for specific categories of cultural property set out in these bilateral agreements, both Canada (since 1985) and Germany (since 2016) provide general import regulations on cultural property protected by all other States Parties to the 1970 UNESCO Convention. Canada's Cultural Property Export and Import Act[102] states that 'after the coming into force of a cultural property agreement in Canada and a reciprocating state, it is illegal to import into Canada any foreign cultural property that has been illegally exported from the reciprocating state'.[103] This is the case even if the cultural property arrives in Canada via a third State. Unlike in US and Swiss law, a 'cultural property agreement' does not exclusively refer to bilateral agreements but includes the 1970 UNESCO Convention; thus, cultural property illegally exported from other States Parties to the Convention may not be imported into Canada.[104] Cultural property imported into Canada may be detained by the Canadian border controls if it does not have proper paperwork. The importer must ensure (1) that the object has been legally exported from the foreign State, and (2) that it has all the necessary documents, such as export permits.

Along these lines, Germany enacted similar import regulations in 2016,[105] and did so within a general cultural property law reform. While Canada only has one

[99] Bilateral agreements have been concluded with 18 out of the 140 States Parties to the 1970 UNESCO Convention <https://eca.state.gov/cultural-heritage-center/cultural-property-advisory-committee/current-import-restrictions> accessed 2 February 2020.

[100] Bilateral agreements have been concluded with 8 out of the 140 States Parties to the 1970 UNESCO Convention <https://www.bak.admin.ch/bak/en/home/cultural-heritage/transfer-of-cultural-property/bilateral-agreements.html> accessed 2 February 2020.

[101] The 140 States Parties to the 1970 UNESCO Convention would have to conclude bilateral agreements with respectively 139 other States Parties to the Convention (140 x 139) divided by 2 = 9,730).

[102] Cultural Property Export and Import Act, RSC, 1985, c C-51, s 37 (Canada). <http://laws-lois.justice.gc.ca/eng/acts/C-51/> accessed 2 February 2020.

[103] ibid, s 37(2).

[104] See Memorandum on Export and Import of Cultural Property (D19-4-1, 6 June 2016) <http://www.cbsa-asfc.gc.ca/publications/dm-md/d19/d19-4-1-eng.pdf> accessed 2 February 2020.

[105] German CPA (n 17).

border, Germany is geographically positioned in the heart of Europe, which makes import control much more difficult. In addition, Germany is an EU Member State within the Single European Market without inner border control. This, and strong criticism by the art and antiquities market, have made the 2016 German law reform a difficult political endeavor. At the same time, it makes it an interesting case study that might have an impact on future legal developments.

E. Combining Import and Export Regulations: The 2016 Law Reform in Germany

Germany ratified and implemented the 1970 UNESCO Convention in 2007[106]—which was quite late in comparison with Canada (1978) and the United States (1983). This 2007 law, however, did not last long. The major problems in the application of the law were outlined in a government evaluation report, presented to parliament in 2013;[107] among these were the lack of proper export and import regulations, as well as ineffective return provisions. These difficulties led to the 2016 reforms.[108]

The 2007 law was a political compromise, aimed at achieving an implementation law that was 'neither too lax and hence damaging to Germany's reputation nor too strict and thus no longer practicable'.[109] Being aware of this difficulty, parliament therefore requested with the adoption of the 2007 law that the government conduct an evaluation and submit an evaluation report on the law's impact. The German government concluded in the 2013 evaluation report that, first, the excessive burden on the German art and antiques market, feared in 2007, had failed to materialize. Second, the report noted that despite several requests for return submitted by foreign States, there was not a single case where the 2007 law had actually led to the return of cultural property. This was the result of the law's relatively stringent requirements for a return, which States seeking return found very difficult to meet, namely, the requirement that cultural objects must be cataloged individually in a list of cultural property protected by States Parties to the 1970 UNESCO Convention. Whereas it was within German legal tradition to list protected cultural objects, most foreign States do not keep lists of protected cultural objects since the majority of States protect cultural property by types/categories, not by cataloging individual objects. Third, existing difficulties associated with the

[106] German Act of 18 May 2007 (Federal Law Gazette 2007, Part I, 757).

[107] Federal Government report on the protection of cultural property, 2013 (BT-Drs. 17/13378) <https://www.bundesregierung.de/ContentArchiv/DE/Archiv17/Artikel/2013/04/2013-04-24-kulturgutschutz.html> accessed 2 February 2020 .

[108] German CPA (n 17).

[109] See explanatory memorandum to the Act on the Return of Cultural Property, BT-Drs 16/1371, 12.

application of the law could not be remedied through jurisprudence due to the law's restrictive provisions.

In sum, while the report was a rather staggering denunciation of the law, it provided a frank assessment of the problems and suggested practical solutions. The report concluded with specific suggestions for amending Germany's cultural property laws. These suggestions later formed the four pillars of the 2016 reform: (1) import and export provisions; (2) provisions for the return of cultural property; (3) due diligence provisions in dealing with cultural property; and (4) penal sanctions. Although publicly criticized by the German art and antiquities market as being onerous and too restrictive,[110] the 2016 law sets out new standards in protecting cultural property.

First, the 2016 law provides for harmonized import and export regulations. Whereas the import regulations of the 2007 law required the establishment of inventories of cultural objects protected by foreign States, the new law relies on the simple rule that cultural property illegally exported from one State is considered as illegally imported into Germany. Thus, similar to Canada's legislation, the new German law is based on mutual recognition and enforces foreign export rules for cultural property in line with the 1970 UNESCO Convention. With regard to cultural property in Germany, the new law requires, in turn, an export license not only for the export from Germany outside the EU (based on the EU export regulation),[111] but also—in line with general EU law[112]—for the export outside Germany but within the EU. Whereas the vast majority of EU Member States has already adopted national export provisions like those Germany now has, only the Netherlands (as well as parts of Belgium) do not require such an export license within the EU. In order to mitigate the burden the 2016 law reform might have on the German art and antiquities market, the financial thresholds for an export license within the EU have been doubled with regard to the categories of cultural property established under EU law.[113]

Second, the conditions for the return of illegal exported cultural property are streamlined with international standards: The 2016 law grants a right of return for all cultural objects illegally exported from another State Party to the 1970 UNESCO Convention after the date of both the requesting State's and Germany's ratification of the 1970 UNESCO Convention (26 April 2007). With regard to EU Member States, the 2016 law transposes the provisions for the return of cultural

[110] See for example: Alexander Forbes and Isaac Kaplan, 'Germany's Onerous New Art Export Law, Explained', *Artsy* (11 July 2016) <https://www.artsy.net/article/artsy-editorial-what-germany-s-strict-new-regulations-mean-for-the-international-art-market> accessed 2 February 2020.

[111] EU Export Regulation (n 67).

[112] Treaty on the Functioning of the European Union, OJ C 326 (26 October 2012) art 36.

[113] EU Export Regulation (n 67).

property as set out by Directive 2014/60/EU,[114] providing for the return of illegally exported cultural property within the EU.

Third, the new law establishes due diligence provisions not only for the professional art and antiquities market, but also for everyone selling cultural property, including private individuals in online auction platforms. These new due diligence provisions require the seller to make sure that cultural objects have not been stolen, illegally imported, or illegally excavated. This due diligence also includes 'verifying relevant information that can be obtained *with reasonable effort* or carrying out any other examination that a reasonable person would carry out'.[115] Such provisions are also in line with modern standards of consumer protection: a buyer of cultural property should be assured of the legality of his or her financial investment and not face the risk of being confronted with a claim for return made by a foreign State or private entity. Moreover, the law makes reference to the Red Lists published by the International Council of Museums (ICOM),[116] which classify endangered categories of cultural property in the most vulnerable areas of the world in order to prevent them from being sold or illegally exported. The law also includes special due diligence requirements with regard to Nazi-looted art, 'if it has been proven or is assumed that the cultural property was taken from its original owner between 30 January 1933 and 8 May 1945 due to National Socialist persecution'.[117]

Fourth, the new law establishes stronger penal sanctions (up to five years of imprisonment) and administrative offenses in case of violation of the import and export as well as the due diligence requirements. Although the new law will not solve all problems, it is a major step forward in combatting the trafficking in cultural property. Penal sanctions are part of such a robust system.

F. Recent Developments: Import and Export in the Context of EU Law

Despite specific import restrictions on Iraqi and Syrian cultural property, a key element in international cultural heritage law is still missing: namely, the broad-scale adoption of general import provisions. Whereas import regulations are commonplace for other goods (such as medicine, chemicals, and foodstuffs), this is not yet the case for cultural property. As has been shown, only a few States, such as Canada and Germany, provide for general import regulations; most States do not

[114] Council Directive (EU) 2014/60/EU of the European Parliament and of the Council of 15 May 2014 on the return of cultural objects unlawfully removed from the territory of a Member State and amending Regulation (EU) 1024/2012 [2014] OJ L 159/1.

[115] German CPA (n 17), s 41 (emphasis added).

[116] International Council of Museums (ICOM) Red Lists of Cultural Objects at Risk <http://icom.museum/resources/red-lists-database/> accessed 2 February 2020.

[117] German CPA (n 17), s 44.

provide for import regulations, or do so only in a selective manner through bilateral agreements, such as the United States or Switzerland.

Although the 2016 German law provides for import and export regulations, the practical effect of national import regulations is limited within the Single European Market, which has eliminated national customs border controls among its EU Member States. Without a uniform EU import regulation, EU law allows legal loopholes, whereby unlawfully removed cultural property from outside the EU (ie States Parties to the 1970 UNESCO Convention) can enter the EU without any import controls. Once these objects are within EU borders, smugglers benefit from the free movement of goods within the EU. In other words, trafficking in cultural property is not suppressed, but rather encouraged. This, however, is not only a matter for the EU to remedy but—as affirmed by UNSC Resolution 2347— is relevant to the entire international community.

With regard to the current import restrictions, the small number of cultural objects from Iraq and Syria that have been seized in the EU demonstrates that there are several obstacles in the practical application of both EU regulations.[118] Most notably, these regulations can be circumvented if the importer of a cultural object claims that it originates from another State in that region (for example Jordan or the UAE). Accurate identification of the origin of cultural property is extremely difficult, costly, and time consuming. Therefore, the problem of proof of origin means that the restrictive measures in the case of Iraq and Syria seem to have little effect in practice. With a general EU import regulation, however, such controls would also be in force for all States Parties to the 1970 UNESCO Convention outside the EU. In practical terms: claiming that the object is not from Iraq or Syria, but rather from a neighboring State, would not circumvent the EU regulations (currently limited to Iraqi and Syrian cultural objects), because the legal export from any third State must be proven upon import into the Single European Market.

In addition, a general EU import regulation is important because most EU Member States cannot meet their legal obligation 'to prohibit the import of stolen cultural property' as established by the 1970 UNESCO Convention.[119] Currently, only two EU Member States have not yet ratified the 1970 UNESCO Convention: Ireland and Malta (Latvia ratified in early 2019).[120] One solution to this problem would be EU-level ratification of the 1970 UNESCO Convention. The

[118] France: one case in 2016 (two bas-reliefs from Syria); United Kingdom: one case in 2015 (antique coins from Syria); Germany: two cases in 2013 and 2016 (Sumerian clay cuneiform tablet and thirteen ancient artifacts, returned to Iraq). See Deloitte, 'Final Report on "Fighting illicit trafficking in cultural goods: analysis of customs issues in the EU"' (June 2017) <https://ec.europa.eu/taxation_customs/sites/taxation/files/annex_08_dg_taxud_study_fighting_illicit_trafficking_in_cultural_goods_en.pdf> accessed 2 February 2020.

[119] 1970 UNESCO Convention, art. 7.

[120] List of States Parties to the 1970 UNESCO Convention, <http://www.unesco.org/eri/la/convention.asp?KO=13039&language=E> accessed 2 February 2020.

EU took this approach to the 2005 UNESCO Convention on Cultural Diversity[121] in 2006. However, this more recent Convention provides for accession by a 'regional economic integration organization'.[122] Similar provisions are absent from the 1970 UNESCO Convention and the 1995 UNIDROIT Convention, both of which only allow States to join the respective Conventions.

Since EU ratification of the 1970 UNESCO Convention is not permitted—unless the Convention is amended—the only option is to adopt EU import regulations. Such an instrument would also improve the implementation of the 1970 UNESCO Convention in the EU Member States already Party to the Convention. An important first step was taken in the realization of an EU import regulation through the proposal's inclusion in the Work Plan for Culture (2015–18), adopted in 2014.[123] In addition, the culture ministers of France, Germany, and Italy addressed the importance of an EU import regulation in a joint statement in 2015.[124] In July 2017, the EU Commission presented its proposal for an EU import regulation[125] and couched it within the framework of the 2016 EU Action Plan to fight against the financing of terrorism.[126]

While there was no doubt that the creation of common import standards at EU level are essential, the approach taken by the EU Commission (Directorate-General for Taxation and Customs Union) is surprising for several reasons: first, the proposal limited its scope to certain categories of cultural property 'older than 250 years', despite the fact that EU law[127] as well as international treaty law[128] do not contain such a high age limit. Second, the proposal introduced the notion of 'export country' [129] to complement the notion of 'source country'.[130] The EU Commission's proposal employed these two notions in order to differentiate between States Parties and non-States Parties to the 1970 UNESCO Convention. While the

[121] Convention on the Protection and Promotion of the Diversity of Cultural Expressions (adopted 20 October 2005, entered into force 18 March 2007) 2440 UNTS 311.

[122] ibid, art 29.

[123] Work Plan for Culture (2015–2018) Doc 14491/14 <http://data.consilium.europa.eu/doc/document/ST-16094-2014-INIT/en/pdf> accessed 2 February 2020.

[124] See press release, <https://www.bundesregierung.de/Content/DE/Pressemitteilungen/BPA/2015/12/2015-12-08-bkm-illegaler-handel.html?nn=811064> accessed 2 February 2020.

[125] European Commission, 'Proposal for a Regulation of the European Parliament and of the Council on the import of cultural goods' EC Doc COM (2017) 375 final (13 July 2017) <https://ec.europa.eu/info/law/better-regulation/initiatives/com-2017-375_en> accessed 2 February 2020.

[126] Action Plan for strengthening the fight against terrorist financing [COM (2016) 50 final].

[127] See EU Export Regulation (n 67) providing in its Annex several age limits of 50, 75, 100, and 200 years depending on the category of cultural object (eg archaeological objects: 100 years).

[128] The 1970 UNESCO Convention does not provide age limits except with regard to archaeological objects: 100 years.

[129] European Commission's proposal for an Import Regulation (n 129), art 2(1c) defines 'export country' as 'the last country in which the cultural goods were permanently held in accordance with that country's laws and regulations before their dispatch to the Union'; in this context, art 2(1d) defines 'permanently' as 'a period of time of at least one month and for purposes other than temporary use, transit, export or dispatch'.

[130] ibid, art 2(1b) defines 'source country' as 'the country in the current territory of which the cultural goods were created or discovered'.

majority of States (140 States Parties to the 1970 UNESCO Convention) should operate on the principle of the 'export country', only non-States Parties should have had the benefit of being classified as 'source country'. The EU Commission's approach was presumably intended to minimize administrative burdens since the requirements to be met upon import vary between these two categories of States. However, neither the differentiation nor the notion of 'export country' are used by the 1970 UNESCO Convention, the 1995 UNIDROIT Convention, nor any other international treaty in international cultural heritage law. Both Conventions are exclusively based on the fundamental principle of the 'country of origin'. Thus, according to the EU Commission's proposal it was only relevant for the legality of an import whether the cultural object was legally exported from this 'export country' (country of last location) and regardless of whether the object was legally exported from its 'country of origin'.

Consequently, the EU Commission's approach taken would have had two effects: first, it would have promoted 'forum shopping' by encouraging the import of cultural objects into the EU via States Parties to the 1970 UNESCO Convention with the weakest control system. This approach would therefore not have been in line with the aim of fighting the trafficking in cultural property and not in line with existing international law, namely the 1970 UNESCO Convention and the UNSC Resolution 2347 . Second, since many States Parties do not limit the export of cultural objects that do not originate from their territory, the effect of the EU Commission's proposal would have been a stricter protection of cultural objects of States not having yet ratified the 1970 UNESCO Convention—a rather absurd result. In other words, that which was intended as a privilege for States Parties to the 1970 UNESCO Convention would have been in fact a disadvantage.

As a result, the EU Commission's proposal was entirely redrafted until final negotiations between the EU Commission, the Council, and the European Parliament—the so called formal trilogue meetings—took place in late 2018 and early 2019. The legislative process was concluded by the vote of the European Parliament in March 2019[131] and by the formal approval of the Council in April 2019.[132]

The 2019 EU Import Regulation unifies and strengthens the protection of non-EU cultural property from being trafficked into the Single European Market. At the same time, the Regulation intends to make organized crime more difficult, in particular 'where such illicit trade could contribute to terrorist financing'.[133]

[131] European Parliament legislative resolution of 12 March 2019 on the proposal for a regulation of the European Parliament and of the Council on the import of cultural goods (COM(2017)0375 – C8-0227/2017 – 2017/0158(COD)) <http://www.europarl.europa.eu/doceo/document/TA-8-2019-0154_EN.html> accessed 2 February 2020.

[132] Regulation (EU) 2019/880 of the European Parliament and of the Council of 17 April 2019 on the introduction and the import of cultural goods [2019] OJ L151/1 (EU Import Regulation).

[133] ibid, art 1(1).

The EU Import Regulation entered into force on 28 June 2019 and is binding to all EU Member States. It only applies to cultural property originating from States outside the EU;[134] thus, it does not apply to the (re-)import of cultural property created or discovered within the EU. Hence, a cultural object illegally excavated in an EU Member State and subsequently illegally exported (eg from Italy into the United States) will not be covered by the EU Import Regulation upon its (re-)import into the Single European Market.

The 2019 EU Import Regulation provides a system of import license and importer statement for certain categories of cultural goods listed in the Annex of the Regulation.[135] An import license is required for cultural objects most at risk, namely archaeological finds (regular and clandestine) and items removed from monuments and sites, being more than 250 years old and without financial threshold (Annex, Part B).[136] Other cultural objects (Annex, Part C) require an importer statement if they exceed 200 years in age with a minimum financial threshold of €18,000.[137] The application for an import license 'shall be accompanied by any supporting documents and information providing evidence that the cultural goods in question have been exported from the country where they were created or discovered in accordance with the laws and regulations of that country or providing evidence of the absence of such laws and regulations at the time they were taken out of its territory'.[138] In the case of an importer statement, the statement has to consist of a signed declaration 'stating that the cultural goods have been exported from the country where they were created or discovered in accordance with the laws and regulations of that country at the time they were taken out of its territory'.[139]

As a general deadline, the 2019 EU Import Regulation establishes a new cut-off date, 24 April 1972.[140] This is when the 1970 UNESCO Convention, adopted on 14 November 1970, entered into force.[141] If, however, the country where the cultural object was created or discovered cannot be reliably determined, or the export, creation, or discovery of the object pre-dated the 1972 cut-off date, it is sufficient for the importer to provide evidence (in case of an import license)[142] or to declare (in case of an importer statement)[143] that the cultural object in question has been exported in accordance with the laws and regulations of *the last country* where it was located for a period of more than five years and for purposes

[134] ibid, art 1(2).
[135] ibid, arts 4–5.
[136] ibid, art 4.
[137] ibid, art 5.
[138] ibid, art 4(4).
[139] ibid, art 5(2)a.
[140] ibid, arts 4(4)b, 5(2).
[141] 1970 UNESCO Convention, art 21.
[142] EU Import Regulation, art 4.
[143] ibid, art 5.

other than temporary use, transit, re-export, or transshipment. Whereas this provision is comprehensible from a practical point of view, it bears the risk of a significant loophole in the effectiveness of the Regulation,[144] especially because trafficked cultural property is often stored for years or even decades until it resurfaces on the market. For that very reason, the Regulation's provision of the country of last location[145] should have foreseen a period of at least thirty years (instead of five). Moreover, the minimum age threshold should uniformly have been 100 years (instead of 250 and 200 years, as in Annex Part B and C), in order to be in line with other EU treaties and international treaty law. In order to minimize administrative burden for both the importer and the EU Member States' national authorities, the Regulation foresees a centralized electronic system,[146] to be established by the EU Commission within six years (thus at the latest in 2025),[147] for the storage and the exchange of information between the authorities of the EU Member States, in particular regarding import licenses and importer statements.

Most importantly, however, the 2019 EU Import Regulation follows—like Canada's 1985 law and Germany's 2016 law—the simple rule that cultural property illegally exported is considered as being illegally imported. Based on this principle, the EU import regulation reads: 'The introduction of cultural goods … which were removed from the territory of the country where they were created or discovered in breach of the laws and regulations of that country shall be prohibited'.[148]

The coming years will show how effective the 2019 EU Import Regulation will be and how it will work in practice. Moreover, it will be interesting to see whether Brexit will turn the United Kingdom into a hub for trafficking in cultural objects offshore the EU customs territory since the United Kingdom, as one of the largest art marketplaces worldwide, will not be bound by EU legislation and thus not by the 2019 EU Import Regulation.

Conclusions

Whereas national export laws appear to be limited to the national dimension at first glance, they turn out to be international in a broader framework, but only if they are mutually recognized by States. Import and export are two sides of the same coin. Although the 1970 UNESCO Convention aims at fostering mutual recognition of national export laws, it fails to provide sufficient provisions to support this aim, because most States Parties exclusively protect their own cultural

[144] See also Patty Gerstenblith, 'The Disposition of Movable Cultural Heritage' (Ch 1) in this volume.
[145] EU Import Regulation, arts 4(4), 5(2).
[146] ibid, art 8.
[147] ibid, arts 8(1) and 16(2)b.
[148] ibid, art 3(1).

heritage. These laws, however, vary from State to State and are far from being standardized, even though the 1995 UNIDROIT Convention offers common standards for identifying general interests: namely, preservation, integrity, and affiliation.[149] In this context, Merryman rightly identifies 'the injection of object-oriented values into the 1995 UNIDROIT Convention'.[150]

The international cultural heritage law regime has, however, not yet fully embraced such general interests; too often it persists in its one-dimensional conceptualization of national cultural heritage. Even the 1972 World Heritage Convention with its List has experienced an inflationary trend that seems to represent more a national contest, rather than a solid basis for establishing effective measures to guarantee the protection and safeguarding of all World Heritage Sites and thus of the cultural heritage of humanity.

While Merryman's approach is based on internationalism, it is really nothing more than a substantiation of the free-trade approach, which—at its core—exclusively fosters the interests of a few States and private collectors. Based on the fundamental principle of State sovereignty under international law, it is, however, the right of States to define their national cultural heritage. Consequently, the argument frequently presented by the art and antiquities market that certain States protect 'too much' of their cultural heritage is therefore without merit in international law. As such, mutual cooperation in cultural heritage matters would be, as a matter of fact, truly international. In turn, the rationale for cultural internationalism turns out not to be international, but rather simply commercial in nature.[151] Although the general principles of international law, such as State sovereignty and territoriality, persist, they are not without limits. The deliberate destruction of cultural heritage is not within the national right of States, since it belongs to the cultural heritage of humanity.[152] International law has recognized that the threats to cultural heritage occur not only during war and armed conflict, but also during times of peace, and include clandestine excavations, trafficking, mass tourism, environmental pollution, or underwater expeditions—all of which have an international dimension.[153] Therefore, the protection of cultural heritage is no longer considered as exclusively a matter of State sovereignty, but rather as a common concern of the entire international community.[154] The UNSC Resolution 2347 that calls upon

[149] See Robert Peters, 'Beyond Restitution: Resolving International Cultural Heritage Disputes' (PhD thesis, European University Institute 2011) 177 <http://cadmus.eui.eu/handle/1814/20054> accessed 2 February 2020.

[150] Merryman, 'The Nation and the Object' (n 81) 71.

[151] Nafziger (n 28).

[152] See the UNESCO Declaration Concerning the Intentional Destruction of Cultural Heritage (2003), UNESCO Doc 32 C/Res 33, Annex (in response to the deliberate destruction of the Buddhas of Bamiyan, Afghanistan, in 2001).

[153] Sabine von Schorlemer, *Internationaler Kulturgüterschutz* (Duncker and Humblot 1992) 101.

[154] Kerstin Odendahl, *Kulturgüterschutz* (Mohr Siebeck 2005) 130.

States to consider adopting adequate and effective import and export regulations as well as the 2019 EU Import Regulation head in the right direction. It is, however, similarly important that States evaluate and, if needed, amend their national cultural property laws, as Germany did in 2016, based on the simple rule: illegally exported cultural property from one State should be considered as illegally imported into another State.

Index

Note: *For the benefit of digital users, indexed terms that span two pages (e.g., 52–53) may, on occasion, appear on only one of those pages.*

The manufacturer's authorised representative in the EU for product safety is Oxford University Press España S.A. of el Parque Empresarial San Fernando de Henares, Avenida de Castilla, 2 – 28830 Madrid (www.oup.es/en or product.safety@oup.com). OUP España S.A. also acts as importer into Spain of products made by the manufacturer.

www.ingramcontent.com/pod-product-compliance
Lightning Source LLC
LaVergne TN
LVHW011904200926
848484LV00002B/522

9780198846291